INFORMATION SYSTEMS SECURITY & ASSURANCE SERIES

# Legal and Privacy Issues in Information Security

THIRD EDITION

Joanna Lyn Grama

JONES & BARTLETT
LEARNING

*World Headquarters*
Jones & Bartlett Learning
5 Wall Street
Burlington, MA 01803
978-443-5000
info@jblearning.com
www.jblearning.com

Jones & Bartlett Learning books and products are available through most bookstores and online booksellers. To contact Jones & Bartlett Learning directly, call 800-832-0034, fax 978-443-8000, or visit our website, www.jblearning.com.

Substantial discounts on bulk quantities of Jones & Bartlett Learning publications are available to corporations, professional associations, and other qualified organizations. For details and specific discount information, contact the special sales department at Jones & Bartlett Learning via the above contact information or send an email to specialsales@jblearning.com.



**Production Credits**
Director of Product Management: Laura Pagluica
Product Manager: Edward Hinman
Content Strategist: Melissa Duffy
Content Coordinator: Paula-Yuan Gregory
Manager, Project Management: Jessica deMartin
Project Specialist: Roberta Sherman
Digital Project Specialist: Rachel DiMaggio
Marketing Manager: Michael Sullivan
Product Fulfillment Manager: Wendy Kilborn
Composition: S4Carlisle Publishing Services
Project Management: S4Carlisle Publishing Services
Cover Design: Kristin E. Parker
Media Development Editor: Faith Brosnan
Rights Specialist: James Fortney
Cover Image: © mirjanajovic/DigitalVision Vectors/Getty Images
Printing and Binding: LSC Communications

**Library of Congress Cataloging-in-Publication Data**
Names: Grama, Joanna Lyn, author.
Title: Legal and privacy issues in information security / Joanna Lyn Grama.
Other titles: Legal issues in information security
Description: Third edition. | Burlington, Massachusetts : Jones & Bartlett Learning, [2022] | Includes bibliographical references and index.
Identifiers: LCCN 2020028528 | ISBN 9781284207804 (paperback)
Subjects: LCSH: Information storage and retrieval systems--Law and legislation--United States. | Data protection--Law and legislation--United States. | Information storage and retrieval systems--Security measures--Law and legislation--United States.
Classification: LCC KF1263.C65 G73 2022 | DDC 342.7308/58--dc23
LC record available at https://lccn.loc.gov/2020028528

6048

Printed in the United States of America

25 24 23 22 21  10 9 8 7 6 5 4 3 2

# Contents

Preface xix

Acknowledgments xxi

About the Author xxiii

PART I **Fundamental Concepts** 1

CHAPTER 1 **Information Security Overview** 3

**Why Is Information Security an Issue?** 4

**What Is Information Security?** 5

What Is Confidentiality? 6
What Is Integrity? 7
What Is Availability? 8

**Basic Information Security Concepts** 10

Vulnerabilities 10
Threats 12
Risks 14
Safeguards 15
Choosing Safeguards 18

**What Are Common Information Security Concerns?** 18

Shoulder Surfing 18
Social Engineering 19
Phishing and Targeted Phishing Scams 19
Malware 20
Spyware and Keystroke Loggers 21
Logic Bombs 21
Backdoors 22
Denial of Service Attacks 22

**What Are the Mechanisms That Ensure Information Security?** 23

Laws and Legal Duties 23
Contracts 23
Organizational Governance 24
*Data Protection Models* 24

**U.S. National Security Information** **25**

Voluntary Organizations 26

**Do Special Kinds of Data Require Special Kinds of Protection?** **26**

**CHAPTER SUMMARY** **27**

**KEY CONCEPTS AND TERMS** **28**

**CHAPTER 1 ASSESSMENT** **28**

**ENDNOTES** **29**

CHAPTER 2 **Privacy Overview** **31**

**Why Is Privacy an Issue?** **32**

**What Is Privacy?** **33**

Types of Personal Information 34

**How Is Privacy Different from Information Security?** **35**

**What Are the Sources of Privacy Law?** **36**

Constitutional Law 36

Federal Law 38

*Freedom of Information Act (1966)* *38*

*Privacy Act (1974)* *39*

*E-Government Act (2002)* *39*

*Electronic Communications Privacy Act (1986)* *39*

*The Wiretap Act (1968, amended)* *39*

*Census Confidentiality (1952)* *39*

*Mail Privacy Statute (1971)* *40*

*Cable Communications Policy Act (1984)* *40*

*Driver's Privacy Protection Act (1994)* *40*

State Laws 40

Common Law 41

*Intrusion Into Seclusion* *41*

*Portrayal in a False Light* *42*

*Appropriation of Likeness or Identity* *42*

*Public Disclosure of Private Facts* *42*

Voluntary Agreements 43

**What Are Threats to Personal Data Privacy in the Information Age?** **44**

Technology-Based Privacy Concerns 44

*Spyware* *44*

*Cookies, Web Beacons, and Clickstreams* *45*

*Wireless Technologies* *47*

*GPS Technology* *48*

*Security Breaches* *48*

People-Based Privacy Concerns 49

*Social Networking Sites* *50*

*Online Data Gathering* *51*

**What Is Workplace Privacy? 51**

Telephone, Voicemail, and Email Monitoring 52

*Telephone and Voicemail Monitoring 52*

*Email Monitoring 53*

Computer Use Monitoring 54

*Off-Duty Computer Monitoring 55*

Video Surveillance Monitoring 55

*Special Rules for Public Employees 56*

**What Are General Principles for Privacy Protection in Information Systems? 57**

Privacy Policies 58

International Privacy Laws 59

**CHAPTER SUMMARY 59**

**KEY CONCEPTS AND TERMS 60**

**CHAPTER 2 ASSESSMENT 60**

**ENDNOTES 61**

CHAPTER 3 **The American Legal System 63**

The American Legal System 64

Federal Government 64

*Legislative Branch 65*

*Executive Branch 67*

*Judicial Branch 67*

State Government 70

**Sources of American Law 73**

Common Law 73

Code Law 74

Constitutional Law 74

How Does It All Fit Together? 74

**Types of Law 75**

Civil 75

Criminal 76

Administrative 77

**The Role of Precedent 78**

**Regulatory Authorities 79**

**What Is the Difference Between Compliance and Audit? 80**

**How Do Security, Privacy, and Compliance Fit Together? 81**

**CHAPTER SUMMARY 82**

**KEY CONCEPTS AND TERMS 82**

**CHAPTER 3 ASSESSMENT 83**

**ENDNOTES 84**

PART II **Laws Influencing Information Security** 85

CHAPTER 4 **Security and Privacy of Consumer Financial Information** 87

**Business Challenges Facing Financial Institutions** 88

**The Different Types of Financial Institutions** 89

**Consumer Financial Information** 90

**Who Regulates Financial Institutions?** 90

The Federal Reserve System 91
Federal Deposit Insurance Corporation 92
National Credit Union Administration 93
Office of the Comptroller of the Currency 94
Special Role of the Federal Financial Institutions Examination Council 95
Special Roles of the Consumer Financial Protection Bureau and the Federal Trade Commission 96
*Consumer Financial Protection Bureau* 96
*Federal Trade Commission* 96

**The Gramm-Leach-Bliley Act** 97

Purpose, Scope, and Main Requirements 97
The Privacy Rule 98
The Safeguards Rule 99
The Pretexting Rule 102
Oversight 103

**Federal Trade Commission Red Flags Rule** 103

Purpose 103
Scope 103
Main Requirements 104
Oversight 105

**Payment Card Industry Standards** 106

Purpose 107
Scope 107
Main Requirements 108
Oversight 108

**Case Studies and Examples** 109

FTC Privacy and Safeguards Rule Enforcement 109
Credit Card Security Example 110

**CHAPTER SUMMARY** 111

**KEY CONCEPTS AND TERMS** 111

**CHAPTER 4 ASSESSMENT** 111

**ENDNOTES** 112

CHAPTER 5


**Security and Privacy of Information Belonging to Children and in Educational Records 115**

**Challenges in Protecting Children on the Internet 116**

Identification of Children 117
First Amendment and Censorship 118
Defining Obscenity 118

**Children's Online Privacy Protection Act 119**

Purpose of COPPA 119
Scope of the Regulation 120
Main Requirements 121
*Privacy Policy 121*
*Privacy Policy Content 121*
*Gaining Parental Consent 122*
Oversight 124

**Children's Internet Protection Act 124**

Purpose 124
Scope of the Regulation 125
Main Requirements 125
*Content Filtering 125*
*Internet Safety Policy 127*
*Exceptions 127*
Oversight 128

**Family Educational Rights and Privacy Act (FERPA) 128**

Scope 128
Main Requirements 129
*Annual Notification 130*
*Access to Education Records 130*
*Amendment of Education Records 131*
*Disclosure of Education Records 131*
Disclosure Exceptions Under FERPA 132
Security of Student Records Under FERPA 133
Oversight 133
State Laws Protecting Student Data 134

**Case Studies and Examples 134**

Children's Privacy 135
Release of Disciplinary Records 135

**CHAPTER SUMMARY 136**

**KEY CONCEPTS AND TERMS 136**

**CHAPTER 5 ASSESSMENT 137**

**ENDNOTES 138**

CHAPTER 6 **Security and Privacy of Health Information** **139**

**Business Challenges Facing the Healthcare Industry** **140**

**Why Is Healthcare Information So Sensitive?** **141**

**The Health Insurance Portability and Accountability Act** **143**

Purpose 143
Scope 145
Main Requirements of the Privacy Rule 147
*Required Disclosures* *148*
*Permitted Uses and Disclosures* *149*
*Uses and Disclosures That Require Authorization* *154*
*Minimum Necessary Rule* *155*
*Other Individual Rights Under the Privacy Rule* *155*
*Privacy Notices* *157*
*Administrative Requirements* *159*
*Breach Notification Provisions* *160*
Main Requirements of the Security Rule 161
*Safeguards and Implementation Specifications* *162*
Oversight 168

**The Role of State Laws Protecting Medical Records** **169**

**Case Studies and Examples** **169**

OCR Enforcement Information 169
HIPAA and Federal Trade Communications Act 169

**CHAPTER SUMMARY** **171**

**KEY CONCEPTS AND TERMS** **171**

**CHAPTER 6 ASSESSMENT** **171**

**ENDNOTES** **172**

CHAPTER 7 **Corporate Information Security and Privacy Regulation** **175**

**The Enron Scandal and Securities-Law Reform** **176**

Corporate Fraud at Enron 176

**Why Is Accurate Financial Reporting Important?** **179**

**The Sarbanes-Oxley Act of 2002** **181**

Purpose and Scope 182
Main Requirements 183
*Public Company Accounting Oversight Board* *183*
*Document Retention* *185*
*Certification* *187*
Oversight 191

**Compliance and Security Controls** **192**

COBIT 192
GAIT 192
ISO/IEC Standards 193

NIST Computer Security Guidance 194
**SOX Influence in Other Types of Companies 194**
**Corporate Privacy Issues 195**
**Case Studies and Examples 196**
**CHAPTER SUMMARY 197**
**KEY CONCEPTS AND TERMS 197**
**CHAPTER 7 ASSESSMENT 197**
**ENDNOTES 198**

**CHAPTER 8** **Federal Government Information Security and Privacy Regulations 201**

**Information Security Challenges Facing the Federal Government 202**
**The Federal Information Security Modernization Act 204**
Purpose and Scope 204
Main Requirements 204
*Agency Information Security Programs 204*
*The Role of NIST 207*
*Central Incident Response Center 211*
*National Security Systems 212*
Oversight 213
**Protecting Privacy in Federal Information Systems 214**
The Privacy Act of 1974 214
The E-Government Act of 2002 215
OMB Breach Notification Policy 217
Import and Export Control Laws 218
**Case Studies and Examples 219**
**CHAPTER SUMMARY 220**
**KEY CONCEPTS AND TERMS 221**
**CHAPTER 8 ASSESSMENT 221**
**ENDNOTES 222**

**CHAPTER 9** **State Laws Protecting Citizen Information and Breach Notification Laws 225**

**History of State Actions to Protect Personal Information 226**
ChoicePoint Data Breach 226
**Breach Notification Regulations 227**
California Breach Notification Act 228
Other Breach Notification Laws 230
*Activities That Constitute a Breach 230*
*Time for Notification 230*

*Contents of Notification* *231*
*Encryption Requirements* *232*
*Penalties for Failure to Notify* *232*
*Private Cause of Action* *233*

**Data-Specific Security and Privacy Regulations** **234**

Minnesota and Nevada: Requiring Businesses to Comply With Payment Card Industry Standards 234
Indiana: Limiting SSN Use and Disclosure 236
California: Protecting Consumer Privacy 238

**Encryption Regulations** **239**

Massachusetts: Protecting Personal Information 239
Nevada Law: Standards-Based Encryption 241

**Data Disposal Regulations** **242**

Washington: Everyone Has an Obligation 242
New York: Any Physical Record 243

**Case Studies and Examples** **244**

**CHAPTER SUMMARY** **245**

**KEY CONCEPTS AND TERMS** **245**

**CHAPTER 9 ASSESSMENT** **246**

**ENDNOTES** **247**

**CHAPTER 10** **Intellectual Property Law** **249**

**The Digital Wild West and the Importance of Intellectual Property Law** **250**

**Legal Ownership and the Importance of Protecting Intellectual Property** **250**

**Patents** **252**

Patent Basics 253
*Patent Requirements* *253*
The Patent Application Process 256
Infringement and Remedies 257
What Is the Difference Between Patents and Trade Secrets? 258

**Trademarks** **259**

Trademark Basics 261
*Use in Commerce* *262*
*Distinctive* *262*
Trademark Registration 263
Infringement and Remedies 265
Relationship of Trademarks on Domain Names 266

**Copyright** **268**

Copyright Basics 268
Copyright Registration 270
Infringement and Remedies 271
*Fair Use* *272*

**Protecting Copyrights Online—The Digital Millennium Copyright Act (DMCA) 274**

DMCA Basics 274

*Technology Protection Measures 274*

*Online Copyright Infringement 276*

*Computer Maintenance 277*

DMCA Unintended Consequences 277

*Title 1 Concerns 278*

*Title II Concerns 278*

**Case Studies and Examples 278**

Trade Secrets 278

Service Provider Liability for Copyright Infringement 279

Digital Collections 280

**CHAPTER SUMMARY 280**

**KEY CONCEPTS AND TERMS 281**

**CHAPTER 10 ASSESSMENT 281**

**ENDNOTES 282**

**CHAPTER 11**

**The Role of Contracts 285**

**General Contracting Principles 286**

Contract Form 286

Capacity to Contract 287

Contract Legality 288

Form of Offer 288

Form of Acceptance 289

Meeting of the Minds 291

Consideration 291

Performance and Breach of Contract 292

Contract Repudiation 294

**Contracting Online 295**

Legal Capacity Online 297

Form of Offer and Acceptance 297

*Email Communications 298*

*Text and Instant Messages 298*

*Twitter and Other Social Networking Sites 299*

Existence and Enforcement 300

Authenticity and Nonrepudiation 300

**Special Types of Contracts in Cyberspace 301**

Shrinkwrap Contracts 303

Clickwrap Contracts 303

Browsewrap Contracts 305

**How Do These Contracts Regulate Behavior? 306**

**Emerging Contract Law Issues 307**

Cloud Computing 308
Information Security Terms in Contracts 309
*Data Definition and Use 310*
*General Data Protection Terms 310*
*Compliance With Legal and Regulatory Requirements 311*
**Case Studies and Examples 312**
Contract Formation via Email 312
**CHAPTER SUMMARY 313**
**KEY CONCEPTS AND TERMS 313**
**CHAPTER 11 ASSESSMENT 314**
**ENDNOTES 315**

**CHAPTER 12** **Criminal Law and Tort Law Issues in Cyberspace 317**

**General Criminal Law Concepts 318**
Main Principles of Criminal Law 319
*Type of Wrongful Conduct 319*
*Elements of a Crime 319*
*Jurisdiction 321*
Criminal Procedure 323
**Common Criminal Laws Used in Cyberspace 326**
The Computer Fraud and Abuse Act (1984) 326
Computer Trespass or Intrusion 329
Theft of Information 329
Interception of Communications Laws 330
Spam and Phishing Laws 330
Cybersquatting 332
Malicious Acts 332
Well-Known Cybercrimes 333
**General Tort Law Concepts 334**
Strict Liability Torts 334
Negligence Torts 335
Intentional Torts 337
Civil Procedure 338
**Common Tort Law Actions in Cyberspace 341**
Defamation 341
Intentional Infliction of Emotional Distress 343
Trespass Torts 344
Privacy Violations 345
**Case Studies and Examples 346**
CAN-SPAM Act 346
Defamation on College Campuses 346
**CHAPTER SUMMARY 347**
**KEY CONCEPTS AND TERMS 347**

**CHAPTER 12 ASSESSMENT** 348
**ENDNOTES** 349

**PART III** **Security and Privacy in Organizations** 351

**CHAPTER 13** **Information Security Governance** 353

**What Is Information Security Governance?** 354
Information Security Governance Planning 355
Common Information Security Governance Roles 356
Information Security Governance and Management 357
Information Security Governance in the Federal Government 358
**Information Security Governance Documents** 359
Policies 360
Standards 361
Procedures 361
Guidelines 362
Creating Information Security Policies 363
*Policy Development Process* *363*
**Recommended Information Security Policies** 367
Acceptable Use Policies 368
*AUP Terms* *370*
*Enforcement* *371*
Anti-Harassment Policies 372
Workplace Privacy and Monitoring Policies 373
Data Retention and Destruction Policies 374
*Data Retention Policies* *375*
*Data Destruction Policies* *376*
Intellectual Property Policies 377
Authentication and Password Policies 377
Security Awareness and Training 379
**Case Studies and Examples** 380
Acceptable Use Case Study 380
**CHAPTER SUMMARY** 382
**KEY CONCEPTS AND TERMS** 382
**CHAPTER 13 ASSESSMENT** 383
**ENDNOTES** 384

**CHAPTER 14** **Risk Analysis, Incident Response, and Contingency Planning** 387

**Contingency Planning** 388
**Risk Management** 389
Risk Assessment Process 390

*Risk Assessment Team* *391*
*Identifying Assets, Vulnerabilities, and Threats* *392*
*Likelihood and Potential Loss* *394*
*Document Needed Controls* *398*
Risk Response 400
Training Employees 401
Continuous Monitoring 401

**Three Types of Contingency Planning 401**

Incident Response Planning 402
*Incident Response Team* *403*
*IR Plan Process* *404*
Disaster Recovery and Business Continuity Planning 407
*DR/BC Team* *408*
*DR/BC Plan Development* *409*
Testing the Plan 412

**Special Considerations 414**

Addressing Compliance Requirements 414
When to Call the Police 415
Public Relations 415

**CHAPTER SUMMARY 416**

**KEY CONCEPTS AND TERMS 416**

**CHAPTER 14 ASSESSMENT 417**

**ENDNOTES 418**

**CHAPTER 15** **Computer Forensics and Investigations 419**

**What Is Computer Forensics? 420**

**What Is the Role of a Computer Forensic Examiner? 423**

**Collecting, Handling, and Using Digital Evidence 425**

The Investigative Process 426
*Identification* *426*
*Preservation* *426*
*Collection* *427*
*Examination* *429*
*Presentation* *430*
Ethical Principles for Forensic Examination 431

**Legal Issues Involving Digital Evidence 432**

Authority to Collect Evidence 432
*The Fourth Amendment and Search Warrants* *432*
*Federal Laws Regarding Electronic Data Collection* *435*
Admissibility of Evidence 439
*The Hearsay Rule* *441*
*The Best Evidence Rule* *442*

CHAPTER SUMMARY 442
KEY CONCEPTS AND TERMS 442
CHAPTER 15 ASSESSMENT 443
ENDNOTES 444

APPENDIX A Answer Key 447

APPENDIX B Standard Acronyms 451

APPENDIX C Law and Case Citations 455

APPENDIX D The Constitution of the United States of America 465

Glossary of Key Terms 483

References 495

Index 513

*To my son, A.J., and my husband, Ananth*

# Preface

## Purpose of This Book

This book is part of the Information Systems Security & Assurance Series from Jones & Bartlett Learning (www.jblearning.com). Designed for courses and curriculums in Information Technology (IT) Security, Cybersecurity, Information Assurance, and Information Systems Security, this series features a comprehensive, consistent treatment of the most current thinking and trends in this critical subject area. These titles deliver fundamental information-security principles packed with real-world applications and examples. Authored by Certified Information Systems Security Professionals (CISSPs), they deliver comprehensive information on all aspects of information security. Reviewed word for word by leading technical experts in the field, these books are not just current, but forward-thinking—putting you in the position to solve the cybersecurity challenges not just of today, but of tomorrow as well.

This book discusses information security, privacy, and the law. Information security is the practice of protecting information to ensure the goals of confidentiality, integrity, and availability. Information security makes sure that accurate information is available to authorized individuals when it is needed. Governments, private organizations, and individuals all use information security to protect information. Sometimes these organizations do a very good job of protecting information. Sometimes they do not.

When governments, private organizations, and individuals do a poor job of protecting the information entrusted to them, legislatures respond with new laws that require a more structured approach to information security. The U.S. federal government has enacted several laws that focus on protecting different types of information. This third edition takes into account the changing legal and regulatory landscape, and growth in privacy concerns, since this book was first published. Finding out which law applies to a particular situation, or type of data, or how best to think about privacy issues related to specific situations or data, is often confusing.

This book tries to help eliminate that confusion. Part One of the book discusses common concepts in information security, privacy, and the law. These concepts are used throughout the book. Part Two discusses the federal and state laws and legal concepts that affect how governments and organizations think about information security. This part uses laws and case studies to help explain these concepts. A quick-reference list of the federal laws and cases that are discussed in the book is included at the end of the book. Finally, Part Three focuses on how to create an information security program that addresses the laws and compliance requirements discussed throughout the book.

## Learning Features

The writing style of this book is practical and conversational. Step-by-step examples of information security concepts and procedures are presented throughout the text. Each chapter begins with a statement of learning objectives. Illustrations are used both to clarify the material and to vary the presentation. The text is sprinkled with Notes, Tips, FYIs, Warnings, and Sidebars to alert the reader to additional and helpful information related to the subject under discussion. Chapter Assessments appear at the end of each chapter, with solutions provided in the back of the book.

Chapter summaries are included in the text to provide a rapid review or preview of the material and to help students understand the relative importance of the concepts presented.

## Audience

The material is suitable for undergraduate or graduate computer science majors or information science majors, students at a 2-year technical college or community college who have a basic technical background, or readers who have a basic understanding of IT security and want to expand their knowledge.

## New to This Edition

The text has been updated to address major legal developments since 2015 impacting the practice of information security and privacy, including revised case examples and references to illustrate concepts explained in the text. It has also updated endnotes and references for students who wish to learn more about concepts explained in the book.

## Theory Labs

This text is accompanied by Cybersecurity Theory Labs. These hands-on labs provide guided exercises and case studies where students can learn and practice foundational cybersecurity skills as an extension of the lessons in this textbook. For more information or to purchase the labs, visit go.jblearning.com/grama3e.

# Acknowledgments

The third time is the charm, as they say! Many talented people worked long hours to make the third edition of this book a reality, and they all have my sincere appreciation. I wish to thank Jones & Bartlett Learning for inviting me back to work on this edition. The competence of the Jones & Bartlett team makes revision work so much easier. Carole Jelen, my literary agent, continues to earn my gratitude for answering my endless questions with grace and good humor.

I am fortunate to have the support of friends and family members in all that I do. I would especially like to thank my friends and colleagues at Vantage Technology Consulting Group for encouraging me when the "writing times" were tough. In addition, the cheer, advice, subject matter review, and emergency cookie packages from friends Cathy Bates, Faith Graham, Pam Hermes, Amy Keene, Kim Lindros, Kim Milford, Matt Morton, Tim O'Brien, Patricia Rosen, David Seidl, Valerie Vogel, and Jon Young were invaluable. You all are the best and I am grateful for your friendship.

Finally, my husband, Ananth, and son, A.J., deserve special thanks for their tireless support. I am a very lucky person. My love, always, to you both.

# About the Author

**Joanna Lyn Grama** (JD, CISSP, CIPT, CRISC) is an associate vice president at Vantage Technology Consulting Group. She has more than 20 years of experience in higher education with a strong focus on law, IT security policy, compliance, governance, and data privacy issues.

Grama is a former member of the U.S. Department of Homeland Security's Data Privacy and Integrity Advisory Committee (appointed to the Committee by Secretary Janet Napolitano) and served as the chairperson of its technology subcommittee. Grama is also vice president of the board of directors for the central Indiana Information Systems Audit and Control Association (ISACA) chapter; and a member of the International Association for Privacy Professionals (IAPP); the American Bar Association, Section of Science and Technology Law, Information Security Committee; and the Indiana State Bar Association. She is a frequent speaker on a variety of IT security topics, including identity theft, personal information security, and university security and privacy compliance issues.

# PART I

# Fundamental Concepts


CHAPTER 1 Information Security Overview 3

CHAPTER 2 Privacy Overview 31

CHAPTER 3 The American Legal System 63

CHAPTER 1

# Information Security Overview

ENSURING THAT INFORMATION is secure is not solely the responsibility of technicians in computer data centers. It also concerns governments, corporations, and private individuals. The digital revolution greatly changed how people communicate and do business. Because information exchanges now take place instantly, and because almost everyone shares data of some kind, you should question how all organizations use and protect data.

This text is about information security and the law. Information security seeks to protect government, corporate, and individual information and is a good business practice. Many organizations today want a reputation for properly protecting their own and their customers' data, because a good reputation can make a company stand out from its competitors, increase sales, or make a government agency seem more trustworthy.

Laws also protect information, especially private personal information. They require that data be protected in certain ways. Laws are not optional; if a law applies to an organization, then the organization must follow the law. Laws make information security more than just a good business practice. They make it a business requirement.

## Chapter 1 Topics

This chapter covers the following topics and concepts:

- Why information security is an issue
- What information security is
- What the basic information security concepts are
- What common information security concerns are
- How different types of information require different types of protection
- Which mechanisms protect information security
- How special kinds of data require special kinds of protection

### Chapter 1 Goals

When you complete this chapter, you will be able to:

- Describe the key concepts and terms associated with information security
- Describe information security goals and give examples of each
- Describe common information security concerns
- Describe mechanisms used to protect information security

## Why Is Information Security an Issue?

Every day the news media reports stories such as these:

- Someone attacks a university computer and gains access to the records of over 30,000 students and staff members. These records include names, photographs, and Social Security numbers (SSNs).
- A hospital experiences a cyberattack that prevents hospital staff from accessing computer systems and patient records. Therefore, the hospital must turn away patients until its computer systems and access are restored.
- A bank loses a backup tape, potentially exposing more than 1 million customer records. The tape is never found.
- A company that processes credit cards stores unencrypted account information on its servers. Attackers gain access to the servers, exposing over 40 million accounts.
- An email scam targets an organization by asking employees to verify their account settings. When employees respond, they provide their computer usernames and passwords. Attackers then use those credentials to access and compromise the organization's computer systems.

Organizations use and store a lot of data to conduct their business operations. For many, **information** is one of their most important assets. Organizations use large and complex databases to keep track of customer product preferences, as well as manage the products and services that they offer customers. They also transfer information to other businesses so that both companies can benefit.

Organizations collect data for many reasons. Much of the data they collect is *personal information*, which can be used to identify a person. Personally identifiable information includes the following:

- SSNs
- Driver's license numbers
- Financial account data, such as account numbers or personal identification numbers (PINs)

- Health data and biometric data
- Authentication credentials, such as logon or usernames and passwords

Based on media reports, security breaches appear to be growing both in number and in the severity of damage they cause to organizations. These breaches result in data that is lost, stolen, disclosed without permission, or rendered unusable. A security breach can damage an organization's reputation, which may prompt customers take their business elsewhere. Following a breach, the organization may also have to pay fines and/or defend itself in court. If a security breach is particularly bad, an organization's leaders can face criminal charges.

As noted, an organization that fails to protect its information risks damaging its reputation—or worse. *Information security* is the term that generally describes the types of steps an organization should take to protect its information.

## What Is Information Security?

**Information security** is the study and practice of protecting information. Its main goal is to protect the **confidentiality**, **integrity**, and **availability** of information. Professionals usually refer to this as the *C-I-A triad*, or sometimes the *A-I-C triad*. (A *triad* is a group of three things considered to be a single unit.)

The C-I-A triad appears in **FIGURE 1-1**.

The need to protect information is not a new concept. For instance, Julius Caesar used a simple letter-substitution code to share secrets with his military commanders. Caesar used this type of code, called a *Caesar cipher*, to ensure that his enemies could not read his messages. **Cryptography** is the practice of hiding information so that unauthorized persons cannot

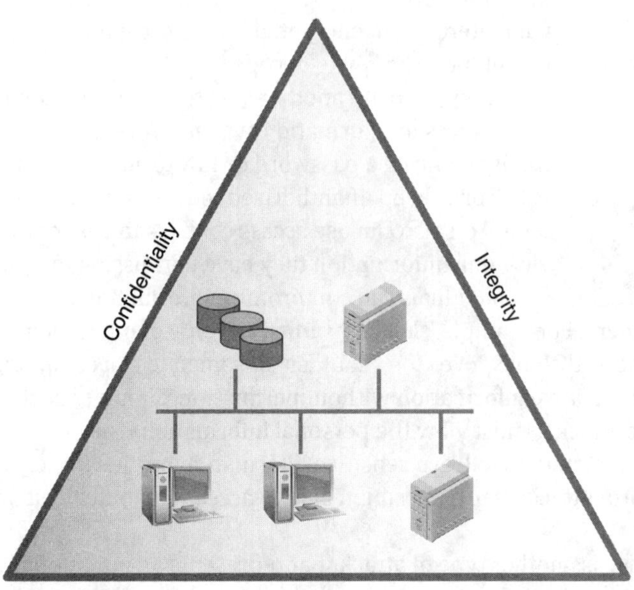


**FIGURE 1-1**
The C-I-A triad.

**NOTE**

You might think that information security refers only to data stored on a computer. However, it refers to information in both paper and electronic form.

read it. Using cryptography preserves confidentiality, because only those with the secret key are able to read an encoded note.

Secret decoder badges were popular during the golden days of radio (about 1920–1950). Business sponsors often paid for decoders to market their products, and radio program fan clubs gave them to their members to promote specific radio shows. These secret decoder badges often used a Caesar cipher.

In some ways, however, information security is a relatively new area of study. Modern computing systems have existed only since the 1960s, and the internet did not exist in its current form until almost 1983. The first well-known computer security incident was discovered in 1986, and President Obama created the first "cybersecurity czar" in the federal government in 2009.

The range of information security topics may seem overwhelming. However, it is important to keep in mind that the main goal of information security is to protect the confidentiality, integrity, and availability of data.

## What Is Confidentiality?

Confidentiality means that only people with the right permission can access and use information. It also means protecting information from unauthorized access at all stages of its life cycle. You must create, use, store, transmit, and destroy information in ways that protect its confidentiality.

**NOTE**

Cliff Stoll described the first well-known computer security incident in his book *The Cuckoo's Egg: Tracking a Spy Through the Maze of Computer Espionage.* Stoll noticed an error in the records of systems connected to the internet's predecessor—the Advanced Research Projects Agency Network (ARPANET). During the investigation, he exposed an international plot to steal information from U.S. computer systems.

Encryption is one way to make sure that information remains confidential while it is stored and transmitted. The encryption process converts information into code that is unreadable. Only people authorized to view the information can decode and use it, thereby protecting the information's confidentiality. Attackers who intercept an encrypted message cannot read it because they do not have the key to decode it.

Access controls, another way to ensure confidentiality, grant or deny access to information systems. An example of an access control is requiring a password or PIN to access a computer system. Passwords keep unauthorized individuals out of information systems. You also can use access controls to ensure that individuals view only information they have permission to see.

Individuals can compromise information confidentiality on purpose or by accident. For example, **shoulder surfing** is a type of intentional attack. It occurs when an attacker secretly looks "over the shoulder" of someone at a computer and tries to discover his or her sensitive information without permission. Shoulder surfing is a visual attack, because the attacker must view the personal information. This term also describes attacks in which a person tries to learn sensitive information by viewing keystrokes on a monitor or keyboard. Attackers use the stolen data to access computer systems and commit identity theft.

**Social engineering** is another type of attack that represents an intentional threat to confidentiality. These attacks rely heavily on human interaction. They take advantage of how people normally talk with one another and interact. It is not a technical attack, but rather involves tricking other people to break security rules and share sensitive information. Social engineering attackers take advantage of human nature, such as kindness, helpfulness, and trust. Because the attackers are so charming, their victims want to help them by providing information. The attacker then uses the information obtained from the victim to try to learn additional sensitive information. The attacker's ultimate goal is to obtain enough information to access computer systems or gain access to protected areas.

**FYI**

The classic film *The Sting* is a great example of a social engineering scam. In the movie, two con artists, played by Paul Newman and Robert Redford, set up an elaborate plan to con a man out of his money. Their scam, which takes advantage of human nature, relies heavily on manipulating the victim and those around him.

Kevin Mitnick is perhaps one of the best-known computer hackers of all time. In his book *The Art of Deception*, he writes that he gained much of the information he used to compromise computer systems through social engineering. Mitnick said that it was very easy to get information from people if he asked questions in the right way.

Confidentiality compromises also take place by accident. For example, an employee of the U.S. Transportation Security Administration (TSA) posted a redacted copy of a TSA manual on a federal website in December 2009. This manual described how TSA agents should screen airline passengers and luggage. It also contained the technical details of how airport screening machines work. The manual contained pictures of identification cards for average Americans, Central Intelligence Agency employees, and U.S. legislators.

The TSA posted the manual by mistake, and for several months the public had access to the manual online. Although TSA employees had redacted some portions of the manual, the TSA improperly performed technical aspects of the redaction. Therefore, some people were able to uncover the original information with common software tools. Those people then reposted the manual on several other nongovernmental websites. Some of these websites posted the document with all of the original text available.

The manual also highlighted the increase in airport security requirements after the September 11, 2001 terrorist attacks. Once posted, the unredacted material could have been used by attackers to exploit new airport security measures. The TSA argued that posting the manual did not compromise the safety of U.S. air travel. Nonetheless, lawmakers immediately questioned the TSA about the incident and asked how the TSA would mitigate the disclosure. Lawmakers wanted to know how the government could prevent other websites from reposting the unredacted manual. They also asked what the TSA would do to prevent similar mistakes in the future.

## What Is Integrity?

Integrity means that information systems and their data are accurate. It ensures that changes cannot be made to data without appropriate permission. If a system has integrity, it means that the data in the system is moved and processed in predictable ways and does not change when it is processed.

Controls that ensure the correct entry of information protect the data's integrity. In a computer system, this means that if a field contains a number, the system checks the values that a user enters to make sure that the user actually entered numbers. Making sure that only authorized users have the ability to move or delete files on information systems also protects integrity. Antivirus software is another example of a control that protects integrity. This type of software checks to make sure that there are no viruses in the system that could harm it or change the data in it.

Information system integrity can be compromised in several ways, either accidentally or intentionally. For example, an employee may accidentally mistype a name or address during data entry. Integrity is compromised if the system does not prevent or check for this type of error. Another common type of accidental compromise of integrity is an employee deleting a file by mistake.

Integrity compromises also can take place intentionally. Employees or external attackers are potential threats. For example, suppose an employee deletes files that are critical to an organization's business. The employee might do this on purpose because of some grievance against the organization. Employees or others affiliated with an organization are sometimes called *insider threats* when they purposefully harm an organization's information systems. **External attackers** also are a concern. They can infect information systems with computer viruses or vandalize a webpage. External attackers who access systems without permission and deliberately change them harm confidentiality and integrity.

In 2007, three Florida A&M University students installed secret keystroke loggers on computers in the university registrar's office. A *keystroke logger* is a device or program that records keystrokes made on a keyboard or mouse, which the students used to obtain the usernames and passwords of registrar employees. For a fee, the hackers modified 650 grades in the computer system for other students, changing many failing scores to an "A." The student hackers also changed the residency status of other students from "out-of-state" to "in-state," which resulted in the out-of-state students paying less tuition.

The university discovered the keystroke loggers during a routine audit. It then found the modified data. Although the university fixed the incorrect data, the student hackers accessed the system and changed the data again. However, the university discovered the hackers' identities through additional security measures such as logging and audit review.

Prosecutors charged the student hackers with breaking federal laws. The court sentenced two of them to 22 months in prison each. In September 2009, it sentenced the third student hacker to 7 years in prison.

The Florida A&M case illustrates how safeguards can be implemented to protect the integrity of computer systems. Routine security audits can detect unauthorized or harmful software on a system.

## What Is Availability?

Availability, the security goal of making sure information systems operate reliably, ensures that data is accessible when it needs to be. It also helps to ensure that individuals with proper permission can use systems and retrieve data in a dependable and timely manner.

Organizations need to have information available to conduct their business. When systems work properly, an organization can function as intended. Ensuring availability means that systems and information are available during peak hours when customer demand is high. System maintenance should be scheduled for off hours when customer demand is low.

Availability can be protected in several ways. Information systems must recover quickly from disturbances or failures. Organizations create plans that describe how to repair or recover systems after an incident. These plans specify how long systems may be offline before an organization starts to lose money or fails to meet its business goals. In the worst case, an organization might go out of business if it cannot repair its information systems quickly.

Organizations also can protect system availability by designing systems to have no single points of failure. A **single point of failure** is a piece of hardware or application that is key to the functioning of the entire system. If that single item fails, a critical portion of the system could fail. Single points of failure also can cause the whole system to fail.

An easy example of a single point of failure is a modem, which connects an organization to the internet. If the modem fails, the organization cannot connect to the internet. Thus, if the organization does most of its business online, the modem failure can really hurt its business.

Organizations also can protect availability by using redundant equipment that has extra functional elements designed into it. In the event of a failure, the extra elements make sure that the piece of equipment is still able to operate for a certain period. Backing up systems also ensures their availability.

Attackers target availability in order to harm an organization's business. As an example, a **denial of service (DoS) attack** disrupts information systems so they are no longer available to users. These attacks also can disable internet-based services by consuming large amounts of bandwidth or processing power, as well as disable an organization's website. These services are critical for businesses that sell web-based products and services or provide information via the internet.

Not all DoS attacks directly target information systems and their data. Attackers also target physical infrastructures. For example, an organization can experience a loss of availability if an attacker cuts a network or power cable. The result is the same as a technical DoS attack: Customers and other audiences cannot reach the needed services.

Unplanned outages can also negatively impact availability. An *outage* is an interruption of service. For example, natural disasters may create outages, such as a power outage after an earthquake. Outages also take place if a technician accidentally cuts a service cable.

A website experiencing an increase in use can result in a loss of availability. When Michael Jackson died in 2009, for example, the internet experienced a massive increase in search queries from people trying to find out what had happened to him. The rapid rise in search traffic caused Google to believe it was under a DoS attack. In response to this perceived attack, Google slowed down the processing of "Michael Jackson" queries. Users entering those queries received error messages until Google determined its services were not under attack.

**NOTE**

Domain Name Service (DNS) providers translate internet domain names into Internet Protocol (IP) addresses. In 2016 the Mirai malware was used to attack a major DNS provider named Dyn. The Dyn attack was one of the largest DoS attacks to date, affecting websites for large companies such as Netflix, Amazon, and the *New York Times*.

The Michael Jackson/Google example shows that organizations can take actions to make sure their information systems are available to their customers. These actions can alert organizations to an issue, prompting them to take steps to correct it.

## Basic Information Security Concepts

Several different concepts are helpful in understanding information security and the laws that affect it. Laws that regulate information security often use risk management, the process of understanding the risks that an organization faces and then taking steps to address or mitigate them, to justify them. You will briefly learn about basic risk management concepts and terms here.

### Vulnerabilities

A **vulnerability** is a weakness or flaw in an information system. They may be construction or design mistakes, as well as flaws in how an internal safeguard is used or not used. Not using antivirus software on a computer, for instance, is a vulnerability. Vulnerabilities can be *exploited* (used in an unjust way) to harm information security.

There are many different types of vulnerabilities. You can classify them into the following broad categories:

- People
- Process
- Facility
- Technology

People can cause several vulnerabilities. For example, one employee could know too much about a critical function in an organization. This is a violation of the **separation of duties** principle. This rule requires that two or more employees must split critical task functions so that no one employee knows all of the steps of the critical task. When only one employee knows all of the steps of a critical task, that employee can use the information to harm the organization. The harm may go unnoticed if other employees cannot access the same information or perform the same function.

> **NOTE**
>
> A common example of the separation of duties principle is a rule requiring two people to sign organization checks. This is so one person cannot steal from the organization by writing and signing checks made out to himself or herself. Requiring two signatures thus protects the organization.

Process-based vulnerabilities are flaws or weaknesses in an organization's procedures that an attacker can exploit to harm security. Process-based vulnerabilities include missing steps in a checklist, as well as not having a checklist in the first place. Another process vulnerability is the failure to apply hardware and software vendor patches in a timely manner. A **patch** is a piece of software or code that updates a program to address security or other operational problems. Patches are available for many types of software, including operating systems. Software and information systems may be open to attack if patches are not properly applied.

Facility-based vulnerabilities are weaknesses in physical security. Buildings, equipment, and other property are resources an organization must protect. An example of poor physical security is an organization that does not have a fence around its property. Another is an open server room that any employee can access.

Vulnerabilities also can be technology based. Improperly designed information systems fall into this category. Some design flaws allow people to access information systems without permission. After gaining entry, the person may enter unauthorized code or commands that disrupt the system. Unpatched and outdated applications are technology vulnerabilities. So are improperly configured equipment, such as firewalls or routers.

Customers do not like flaws in the products that they buy. Therefore, they expect vendors to inform them quickly about product flaws. *Vulnerability management* programs make sure that vendors find any flaws in their products and quickly correct them. They also ensure that customers are made aware of problems so they can take protective action. The Microsoft Corporation, for example, issues a monthly security bulletin for customers that lists known vulnerabilities in the company's products. The bulletin also explains how to address them. This bulletin is part of Microsoft's vulnerability management program.

**Exploits** are successful attacks against a vulnerability. They take place in a period known as the **window of vulnerability**, as shown in **FIGURE 1-2**. This window opens when someone discovers a vulnerability and closes when a vendor reduces or eliminates it. Exploits take place while the window is open.

The window of vulnerability is a notable concept. In some ways, this window is shrinking fast because more people are interested in information security. Many people have developed the skills to find new vulnerabilities. Often they report them to the company that provides the product or service so the company can fix the vulnerability. Not all people act with good intentions, however: There are also people with the skills needed to find and exploit vulnerabilities who do so for financial gain.

The number of vulnerabilities appears to be growing. The National Vulnerability Database (NVD) recorded almost 52 new vulnerabilities per day in December 2019.[1] One reason for this could be that information systems are becoming larger and more complex. Another possibility is that as more people work together to create new systems, the likelihood of introducing flaws increases. Poor programming practices may be another reason. Vulnerabilities also may be increasing because of a lack of quality controls to make sure that systems are secure and work as intended.

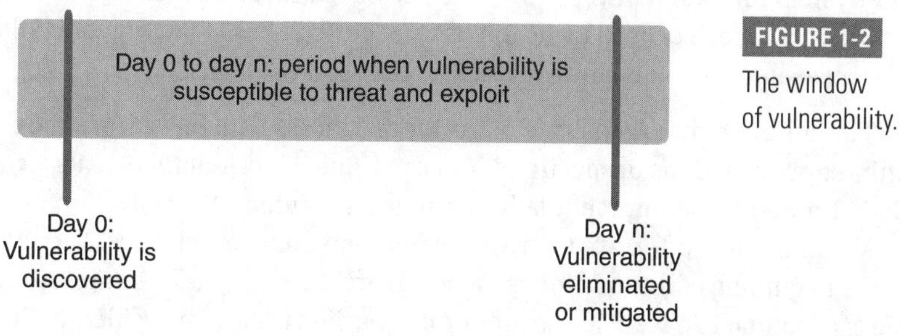


**FIGURE 1-2** The window of vulnerability.

> **NOTE**
>
> Some vulnerabilities are exploited almost as soon as they are discovered. The term for this is a **zero-day vulnerability**. It is unique because the vulnerability is exploited before a vendor provides a patch or some other fix.

The number of known vulnerabilities also may be increasing because some developers use well-known programming codes and components to design systems. They also use well-known software in the systems they design. Using familiar components makes it easier for many people to work together on the same project. There are dangers, however. The better known the code, hardware, or software, the greater the chance that an attacker also has the necessary skills to find vulnerabilities in the final product.

## Threats

**Threats** are anything that can harm an information system. They are successful exploits against vulnerabilities. A threat source—which is a person or a circumstance—carries out a threat or causes it to take place.

It is worth taking some time to understand how vulnerabilities and threats are related. For example, an organization may have few controls to prevent an employee from deleting critical computer files. This lack of controls is the vulnerability. A well-meaning employee could delete files by mistake. In this case, the employee is the threat source. The threat is the action of deleting the critical files. If the employee deletes the files, a successful exploit of the vulnerability has taken place. If the files are not recoverable, or recoverable only at great expense, the incident harms the organization and its security. In this example, availability and integrity are compromised.

Threats fall into broad categories:

- **Human**—Threats carried out by people. Common examples are internal and external attackers. Even the loss of key personnel in some instances is a type of human threat. People threats include both good actors and bad actors. Good actors include well-meaning employees; bad actors are attackers who intend to harm an organization.
- **Natural**—Uncontrollable events such as earthquakes, tornadoes, fires, and floods. These types of threats are not predictable, and organizations cannot control these types of threats.
- **Technological and operational**—Threats that operate inside information systems to harm information security goals. Malicious code is an example of these threats. Hardware and software failures are technology threats. Improperly running processes are also threats.
- **Physical and environmental**—Facility-based threats. These types of threats can include a facility breach caused by lax physical security. Loss of heating or cooling within a facility is an example of an environmental threat.

Threats are either deliberate or accidental. *Accidental threats* are the results of either unintentional actions or inactions. You can think of accidental threats as mistakes or "acts of God." Unintended equipment failure also is an accidental threat.

Mistakes most often are the result of well-meaning employees. The file deletion example at the beginning of this section is an accidental threat. The TSA employee improperly posting the manual to a website, as mentioned earlier, is also an accidental threat. Organizational policy and security training and awareness can help mitigate such mistakes.

An act of God that disrupts services or compromises information security is an accidental threat. Earthquakes, tornadoes, floods, and wildfires caused by lightning or other natural events, are all examples of acts of God. It is hard for organizations to plan for these types of threats, although they can take basic precautions against some types of natural disasters by building redundant systems. An organization also may choose not to build facilities in areas prone to environmental instability.

**NOTE**

The U.S. government maintains the NVD, a searchable database of known security flaws and weaknesses. It also includes listings of known system problems. The National Cyber Security Division of the U.S. Department of Homeland Security sponsors the NVD. You can find it at http://nvd.nist.gov/home.cfm.

All organizations must plan for equipment failure. Sometimes equipment breaks through no fault of its operators. Sometimes it reaches the end of its life and simply stops working. Unfortunately, it is hard for organizations to plan for such failures. This is especially true if the equipment that fails is particularly specialized or expensive. Organizations can mitigate this type of threat by building redundant systems and keeping spare parts on hand.

*Deliberate threats* are intentional actions taken by attackers. Both internal and external attackers are deliberate threats. **Internal attackers** have current relationships with the organization that they are targeting. They can cause a lot of damage in computer systems because they have special knowledge about those systems. Internal attackers are often called malicious insider threats because they use their legitimate access to knowingly harm an organization. Upset employees are often the cause of internal attacks. They might wish to harm the organization by causing a loss of productivity. They also may wish to embarrass the organization or hurt its reputation. These attackers may purposefully delete files or disclose information without permission. They also may intentionally disrupt the availability of information systems.

Internal attackers also can take advantage of lax physical security. They might do this to steal resources such as confidential information. Theft of resources is a problem for many organizations.

In 2007, a former Coca-Cola employee was sentenced to 8 years in prison for stealing Coca-Cola trade secrets. She also was ordered to pay $40,000 in restitution.[2] This employee stole Coca-Cola secrets and tried to sell them to rival Pepsi. Surveillance video showed the employee putting company documents into bags and leaving the building. She did the same thing with a container of a Coca-Cola product sample. All of these actions were violations of Coca-Cola company policies. The theft was discovered when Pepsi informed Coca-Cola.

**NOTE**

*Act of God* is a legal term that describes a natural event or disaster for which no person is responsible.

External attackers are another concern. They usually have no current relationship with the organization they are targeting. Some are former employees with special knowledge about the organization. External hackers include spies, saboteurs, and terrorists. Many seek financial gain. Others want to embarrass an organization, make a political statement, or exploit systems for a challenge.

**NOTE**

It is not possible to identify every security vulnerability, to plan for every threat, or to identify all risks. Even when you identify risks, you cannot limit all risk of harm.

Organizations must take steps to avoid threats. When an employee leaves an organization, the organization should promptly remove his or her access to information systems and to physical property. Good information security practices also help reduce threats posed by external attackers. These include patching known vulnerabilities in hardware and software. They also include monitoring access to systems and engaging in logging and audit review.

## Risks

A **risk** is the likelihood that a threat will exploit a vulnerability and cause harm to the organization. These impacts from threats vary but can generally be sorted into six categories:

- **Financial**—Risks that affect financial resources or financial operations
- **System/Service**—Risks that impact how an organization provides information technology (IT) systems and services
- **Operational**—Risks that affect the normal operation of information systems and services
- **Reputational**—Risks that negatively affect an organization's reputation or brand
- **Compliance**—Risks that relate to a possible violation of a law, regulation, or organizational policy
- **Strategic**—Risks that may have a lasting impact on an organization's long-term viability

You can measure impact in terms of money costs or by perceived harm to the organization.

Not all risks receive or require the same level of attention from an organization. Organizations engage in complex risk analysis and risk management programs to classify and respond to risks. A brief overview of some risk analysis and management terms is included here.

*Risk analysis* is the process of reviewing known vulnerabilities and threats. Organizations generally classify the probability that a threat will exploit a vulnerability as low, medium, or high. They then attempt to assess the impact of a successful exploit. An organization should address risks that have large impacts on the organization and its information security.

All organizations must assess risk, as well as respond to it. Organizations have several options for responding to risk. Common responses include:

- Risk avoidance
- Risk mitigation
- Risk transfer
- Risk acceptance

Organizations apply safeguards to respond to vulnerabilities, threats, and, ultimately, risk. A safeguard is any protective action that reduces exposure to vulnerabilities or threats. A risk response strategy determines how safeguards should be applied.

Organizations can try to get rid of risk by applying safeguards to fix vulnerabilities and control threats. **Risk avoidance** is the process of applying safeguards to avoid a negative impact. A risk avoidance strategy seeks to eliminate all risk. This is often very difficult or expensive.

Organizations also can mitigate risk to reduce, but not eliminate, a negative impact. This response strategy is called **risk mitigation**. Using this strategy, organizations apply safeguards to vulnerabilities and threats to lower risk to an acceptable level. The amount of risk left over after applying safeguards is called **residual risk**.

Organizations also transfer risk. In a strategy of **risk transfer**, an organization passes its risk to another entity, at which point the risk impact is borne by the other entity. An organization might choose this type of strategy when the cost of mitigating risk is more expensive than transferring it. For example, organizations could purchase cyber liability insurance in response to a potential risk. By purchasing these policies, which have grown popular in the last several years, the organization transfers its risk to the insurance company, which bears the cost of any risk impact. While the terms of these insurance policies vary, they can cover losses caused by unauthorized access to information systems, system interruption, and crime.

An organization also can decide to deliberately take no action against an identified risk, which is called **risk acceptance**. This type of strategy means that avoiding, mitigating, or transferring risk is not part of the organization's risk response plan. Organizations do not take decisions to accept risk lightly, but may choose to accept the risk if the cost of the risk itself is less than the cost to avoid, mitigate, or transfer the risk.

## Safeguards

A **safeguard** reduces the harm posed by information security vulnerabilities or threats and may eliminate or reduce the risk of harm. They are **controls** or countermeasures, terms that can be used interchangeably.

**FYI**

A passphrase is a long password that is made of a sequence of words or text. Unlike passwords, which are usually shorter, passphrases are usually 20 characters or more. The best passphrases are easy to remember. However, they should be hard to guess—for example, they should not be famous quotes from popular books.

Safeguards belong to different classifications according to how they work. These classification levels are:

- Administrative
- Technical
- Physical

**Administrative safeguards** are rules implemented to protect information and information systems. These safeguards usually take the form of organizational policies, which state the rules of the workplace. Laws and regulations may influence these safeguards. One common administrative safeguard is the workplace rule of **need to know**.

By applying need to know, an employer gives employees access only to the data they need to do their jobs. An employee does not receive access to any other data even if he or she has appropriate clearance. Using need-to-know principles makes it harder for unauthorized access to occur and protects confidentiality. There eventually should be technical enforcement of these principles. However, the first step is specifying that a workplace will follow them.

**Technical safeguards**, also called *logical safeguards*, are the rules that state how systems will operate and are applied in the hardware and software of information systems. Technical safeguards include automated logging and access-control mechanisms, firewalls, and antivirus programs. Using automated methods to enforce password strength is a technical control.

One technical safeguard that companies use to protect information security is the access control rule of **least privilege**. This rule, which is very similar to the need-to-know rule, means that systems should always run with the least amount of permissions needed to complete tasks. For example, some operating systems allow administrators to set up different privilege levels for system users. This helps enforce least privilege concepts. Users with administrative privileges can access all system functions, and therefore can fully manipulate and modify the system and its resources.

*Local users*, in contrast, have fewer privileges. They are able to use only some programs or applications. They cannot add, modify, delete, or manipulate the computer system. *Power users* have more privileges than local users but fewer privileges than administrators do. Power users may use and access many functions of the computer system. However, they may not modify critical functions of the operating system.

**Physical safeguards** are actions that an organization takes to protect its actual, tangible resources. These safeguards keep unauthorized individuals out of controlled areas and people away from sensitive equipment. Common physical safeguards are:

- Key-card access to buildings
- Fences
- Doors
- Locks
- Security lighting
- Video surveillance systems
- Security guards
- Guard dogs

A more sophisticated example of a physical security control is a **mantrap**, as shown in **FIGURE 1-3**. A mantrap is a method of controlled entry into a facility that provides access to secure areas such as a research lab or data center. This method of entry has two sets of doors on either end of a small room. When a person enters a mantrap through one set of doors, the first set must close before the second set can open. This process effectively "traps" a person in the small room.

**FIGURE 1-3**

An example of a mantrap.

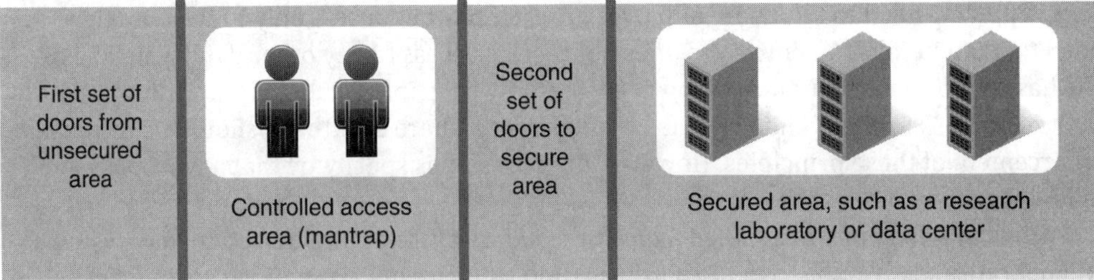

Often a person must provide different credentials at each set of mantrap doors. For example, the first set of doors might allow access to the mantrap via a card reader, in which an employee scans an identification badge to gain entry. The second set of doors then may require a different method to open, such as entering a PIN on a keypad. Technicians often configure mantraps so that both sets of doors lock if a person cannot provide the appropriate credentials at the second set of doors. When locked in a mantrap, the person must await "rescue" by a security guard or another official.

Mantraps are not just for highly sensitive data centers or labs. Some apartment buildings apply a modified mantrap concept to building entry. In these buildings, any individual can access the lobby area of the apartment building. However, only people with keys or access cards may pass through a locked security door and enter the building's interior. Usually, only residents have the proper credentials to enter the interior. Guests to the building need to use an intercom or telephone system to contact the resident they want to visit. The apartment resident can then "buzz" guests through the locked door to allow access to the building's interior.

You also can classify safeguards based on how they act. These classification levels are:

- Preventive
- Detective
- Corrective

*Preventive controls* are safeguards used to prevent security incidents. These controls keep an incident from happening. For example, door locks are a preventive safeguard, because they help keep intruders out of the locked area. Fencing around a building is a similar preventive control. Teaching employees how to avoid information security threats is another preventive control.

*Detective controls* are safeguards put in place in order to detect, and sometimes report, a security incident while it is in progress. Examples of detective controls include logging system activity and reviewing the logs. Log review can look for unauthorized access or other security anomalies that require attention. An *anomaly* is something strange or unusual—activity that is not normal.

*Corrective safeguards* are automated or manual controls put in place in order to limit the damage caused by a security incident. Some types of databases allow an administrator to "roll back" to the last known good copy of the database in the event of an incident. Corrective controls also can be quite simple: locking doors inadvertently left unlocked, for example.

**TABLE 1-1** summarizes the safeguards described in this section.

**TABLE 1-1 A Safeguards Matrix**

| SAFEGUARD TYPE | PREVENTIVE | DETECTIVE | CORRECTIVE |
|---|---|---|---|
| Administrative | Organization hiring policy | Organization periodic background checks policy | Discipline policy |
| Technical (Logical) | Least privilege principle | Antivirus software | Updating firewall rules to block an attack |
| Physical | Locks on doors to critical areas | Burglar alarms | Locking a door that was inadvertently left unlocked |

### Choosing Safeguards

Organizations may have difficulty choosing safeguards, so they use reference guides to help with this task. Two of the most common guides are the "ISO/IEC 27002:2013, Information Technology—Security Techniques—Code of Practice for Information Security Controls" (2013) and "NIST Special Publication 800-53 (Rev. 4), Security and Privacy Controls for Federal Information Systems and Organizations" (2013).

The International Organization for Standardization (ISO) and the International Electrotechnical Commission (IEC) first published ISO/IEC 27002 in December 2000. These two groups work together to create standards for electronic technologies. ISO/IEC 27002 has 14 major sections. Each discusses a different category of information security safeguards or controls. They explain why organizations should use the listed controls and how to use them. Security practitioners often use ISO/IEC 27002 as a practical guide for developing security standards and best practices.

"NIST Special Publication 800-53 (Rev. 4), Security and Privacy Controls for Federal Information Systems and Organizations" was published in 2013 (and updated in 2015) by the National Institute of Standards and Technology (NIST). This document states the minimum safeguards required in order to create an effective information security program. NIST developed this guidance specifically for federal agency use on federal information systems. Many nongovernmental organizations also use the document to help guide their own information security programs. Revision 5 of this guidance, currently titled "Security and Privacy Controls for Information Systems and Organizations," was published in 2017. This draft was still undergoing the review process at the time this chapter was written.

## What Are Common Information Security Concerns?

Information security practitioners have their hands full. This section describes some of the concerns that practitioners deal with daily.

### Shoulder Surfing

As mentioned previously in this chapter, shoulder surfing occurs when an attacker looks over the shoulder of another person at a computer to discover sensitive information that the attacker has no right to see. This is not a technical exploit. The attacker could be attempting to learn usernames and passwords or discover sensitive information by viewing keystrokes on a monitor or keyboard. Shoulder surfing is a concern at public places such as automated teller machines (ATMs) or self-service credit card terminals at grocery stores.

Shoulder surfing can also can be a concern at airports, coffee shops, and other places with wireless access. Computer users may attempt to access email accounts, bank accounts, and other sensitive information while in these public places. Usually the computer user is focusing on their computing device and not paying attention to the people around them. While the user's guard is down, they may not notice that the coffee drinker at the next table is shoulder surfing and recording the computer user's sensitive information.

## Social Engineering

Social engineering describes an attack that relies heavily on human interaction. It is not a technical attack. This type of attack involves tricking other people and taking advantage of their human nature to break normal security procedures and gain sensitive information.

These attacks are sometimes simple to carry out. For instance, an attacker telephones a large organization and identifies himself as a member of that same organization's technology group. He has a conversation with the person who answered the phone.

**Technical TIP**

You can guard against shoulder surfing attacks by shielding keypads with your hands. You also can hide an ATM screen by blocking it with your body so that attackers cannot view the screen. Laptop privacy guards and privacy shields also work well. These shields, which are placed over a monitor when computing in public places, restrict viewing angles so a person can only see the information on a monitor or screen when directly in front of it. Organizations may wish to purchase these types of privacy guards for workers who frequently travel. That way the person can work on business data in public places, such as an airport, while not worrying about shoulder surfing attacks.

The attacker might ask about that person's internet connectivity or computing equipment. The person answering the call, who is inclined to be helpful and participate in the conversation, trusts the attacker because he said that they both work for the same organization.

The attacker may ask for the person's username, identification number, or logon name at the end of the call, claiming that this is for verification purposes. The person answering the call might provide that information because it seems to be a reasonable request. Without much effort, the attacker has gained information that could be used to access organizational resources. This is a social engineering attack.

## Phishing and Targeted Phishing Scams

Phishing is a form of internet fraud that takes place in electronic communications where attackers attempt to steal valuable information from their victims. These attacks can take place via email, instant messages, or internet chat rooms. These attackers are *phishing* for confidential information, including:

- Credit card numbers
- SSNs
- User logon credentials
- Passwords

A phishing attack may look similar to a legitimate message from a known organization that is familiar to the intended victim. It may also attempt to look similar to a message from well-known organizations such as banks or large corporations, or even the company that the intended victim works for.

Phishing messages usually request that the recipients click on a uniform resource locator (URL) to verify their account details. When the victim clicks on the URL, a website opens that looks similar to a legitimate site and prompts the victim to enter personal information to verify his or her identity. In reality, the site that the victim navigated to is a fake website, often a copy of a trusted site, designed only to capture the victim's personal information.

*Spear phishing* is a targeted phishing scam in which attackers may target a particular organization. This is a more sophisticated form of attack where a message might look as if it is from a highly trusted and authentic source. Attackers often research the targeted organization to make their messages look authentic. This background research is easy because of the wealth of information on the internet. Spear phishing messages may use an organization's logo or terms specific to it in their attempt to obtain information about the targeted organization, such as logons and passwords to the organization's information systems.

*Whaling* is a type of targeted phishing scam in which attackers target corporate executives. The federal judiciary circulated an alert in 2008 that warned that some corporate executives had received a scam email that claimed to be a grand jury subpoena. However, the email was not a real subpoena. Executives unintentionally downloaded malware onto their computer systems when they clicked on a link in the "subpoena" email.

Business email compromise (BEC) attacks are sophisticated phishing scams that target recipients who are responsible for processing payments at organizations. The goal of these types of attacks is to conduct unauthorized money transfers. The U.S. Federal Bureau of Investigation reported that BEC attacks led to the loss of over $12.5 billion across the world from October 2013 to May 2018.[3]

**FYI**

The Morris worm was one of the first internet computer worms. Robert Morris Jr., a student at Cornell University in 1988, created the worm. His experimental piece of code spread very quickly and infected some computers multiple times. Ultimately, over 6,000 computers were infected. It also overwhelmed government and university networked systems. Morris was charged with violating the 1986 Computer Fraud and Abuse Act. He was convicted and sentenced to a $10,000 fine, 400 hours of community service, and 3 years' probation.

## Malware

**Malware** is a general term that refers to any type of software that performs some sort of harmful, unauthorized, or unknown activity. The term *malware* is a combination of the words *malicious* and *software*. Malware is usually a computer virus or worm, or a combination of one or more viruses or worms.

Computer viruses are programs that spread by infecting applications on a computer. These types of programs are called viruses because they resemble biological viruses. They copy themselves in order to infect a computer. Viruses can spread over a computer network or the internet. They also can spread from computer to computer on infected disks, CDs, DVDs, or universal serial bus (USB) thumb drives. When the infected virus code is executed, it tries to place itself into uninfected software.

A computer worm is similar to a virus. Unlike a virus, however, a computer worm is a self-contained program that does not require external assistance to propagate. Some well-known internet worms include the Morris worm, SQL Slammer, and Blackworm.

A Trojan horse is a subset of malware that pretends to be a legitimate and desirable software file that a user wants. In reality, it is malicious. A Trojan horse spreads when a user downloads the seemingly legitimate file. While the user believes a legitimate file is downloading, the Trojan horse is actually loading. This type of malware is especially prevalent on social networking sites. Accepting virtual "gifts" on these sites can often expose users to nasty surprises.

Ransomware is a subset of malware that prevents organizations and users from accessing data or information systems until they pay a ransom. The ransomware may encrypt data to make it inaccessible, or it may lock information systems, until an organization pays the attacker to decrypt the data or unlock the system. Ransomware is not new, but its use across all industries has been growing.

## Spyware and Keystroke Loggers

Spyware and keystroke loggers are also forms of malware. Spyware is any technology that secretly gathers information about a person or organization. Many users inadvertently download spyware with other programs from the internet. Spyware hides on a system, where it collects information about individuals and their internet browsing habits. Cookies set by websites can allow spyware to track the sites that a person visits. This is especially dangerous because some cookies can contain website logon and password information. Spyware can slow computer systems, hog resources, and use network bandwidth. Some spyware programs install other programs on a computer system, which can make a computer system open to other attacks.

A keystroke logger is a device or program that records keystrokes made on a keyboard or mouse. Attackers secretly install keystroke loggers and then are able to recover computer keyboard entries and sometimes even mouse clicks from them. They can review the data retrieved from a keystroke logger to find sensitive information such as usernames, passwords, and other confidential user information. The student hackers in the Florida A&M example discussed earlier in this chapter used a keystroke logger, which allowed them to obtain computer access credentials from data the logger collected. Keystroke loggers can be software-based or they can be a physical device that plugs into a computer or is hidden in a keyboard.

## Logic Bombs

A logic bomb is harmful code intentionally left on a computer system that lies dormant for a certain period. When specific conditions are met, it "explodes" and carries out its malicious function. Programmers can create logic bombs that explode on a certain day or when a specific event occurs. Attackers also program logic bombs to explode in response to no action; for example, a logic bomb may explode when its creator does not log onto the target computer system for a predetermined number of days.

Upset employees sometimes use logic bombs. In October 2008, for example, Fannie Mae fired an employee from his Unix engineer position but failed to disable his computer access to Fannie Mae systems until nearly 4 hours after his firing. The engineer allegedly tried to hide a logic bomb in the computer system during that time. This logic bomb was set to activate the morning of January 31, 2009, and designed to delete 4,000 Fannie Mae servers when activated.

Fannie Mae IT professionals accidentally found the logic bomb 5 days after the former employee planted the "explosive." The employee was indicted in January 2009 for unauthorized computer access. In October 2010 he was convicted in U.S. federal court of computer sabotage and sentenced to 3 years in prison.

## Backdoors

A backdoor, also called a *trapdoor*, is a way to access a computer program or system that bypasses normal mechanisms. Programmers sometimes install a backdoor to access a program quickly during the development process to troubleshoot problems. This is especially helpful when developing large and complex programs. Programmers usually remove backdoors when the programming process is over. However, they can easily forget about the backdoors if they do not follow good development practices.

A backdoor is a security vulnerability regardless of its initial purpose. Attackers search for system backdoors to exploit them. Sometimes attackers install backdoors on systems they want to visit again. Attackers can have virtually unhindered access to a system through a backdoor.

**NOTE**

The computer worm MyDoom, first discovered in January 2004, installed backdoors on infected Microsoft Windows computers. Attackers could then send spam email from the infected machines, which helped to spread the worm. Some versions of the MyDoom worm also blocked access to popular antivirus software vendor websites. This made it very hard to remove the worm.

## Denial of Service Attacks

You learned about DoS attacks that disrupt information systems earlier in the chapter. Attackers do this so that the systems are not available for legitimate users. These attacks can disable an organization's web page or internet-based services.

A **distributed denial of service (DDoS) attack** is another form of DoS attack that occurs when attackers use multiple systems to attack a targeted system. These attacks really challenge the targeted system, because it often cannot ward off an attack coming from hundreds or thousands of different computers. A DDoS attack sends so many requests for services to a targeted system that the system or website is overwhelmed and cannot respond.

In a DDoS attack, the attacker takes control of multiple systems to coordinate the attack. They call this type of attack "distributed" because it involves multiple systems to launch the attack. Usually the attacker exploits security vulnerabilities in many machines. The attacker then directs the compromised machines to attack the target. Another term for these compromised machines is *zombies*. Major websites are often DDoS attack victims. These systems handle a lot of traffic by design and pose an attractive target for DDoS attackers seeking to compromise a system's availability.

**NOTE**

In 2013, Google Ideas and Arbor Networks created a live data visualization of DDoS attacks around the world. In January 2020 the United States was one of the most popular destination countries for these types of attacks. To see the map, visit www.digitalattackmap.com.

Information security deals with these types of issues every day. Organizations can implement safeguards to help decrease the impact of such attacks.

# What Are the Mechanisms That Ensure Information Security?

Protecting information is not easy. It is often expensive and time consuming to do well. The security of a system relates to the time taken to implement safeguards and their cost. Highly secure information systems take significant time and expense to create. Alternatively, if an organization wants to implement secure systems quickly, it must be prepared to spend money. If it wants to keep time and money costs low, it must be prepared for lower security.

## Laws and Legal Duties

Most organizations are subject to several laws. Although this text focuses on laws that affect information security, these are not the only types of laws organizations must follow. For example, they may have to follow workplace safety laws and fair labor standards. Other laws may include those dealing with equal employment opportunity, hazardous materials disposal, and transportation. An organization must make sure that it follows all of the laws that apply to it.

*Industry sector* is a term that describes a group of organizations that share a similar industry type. They often do business in the same area of the economy. In the United States, Congress enacts laws by industry sector. These laws address the protection of data used by organizations in a particular industry, such as finance or health care. Even the federal government has laws that it must follow to secure certain types of information. Some of these laws have very specific requirements.

Organizations also must follow general legal duties. For example, executives must act reasonably and in the best interest of the organization. This means they must use good judgment when making decisions for the organization.

## Contracts

The action of paying someone to do work on your behalf is called outsourcing. Many organizations outsource IT functions to save money. Outsourced functions can include data center hosting, email facilities, and data storage.

For example, it is very expensive for organizations to build their own data center. It is often cheaper for some of them to rent equipment space in another organization's data center.

An organization cannot avoid its legal duties by outsourcing functions. It must enter into a contract with the company to which it is outsourcing. A *contract* is a legal agreement between two or more parties that sets the ground rules for their relationship. The parties use a contract to define their relationship and state their

 **NOTE**

Data centers are not inexpensive. In January 2010, Facebook, a social networking application and website, announced plans to build its first data center. In 2018 the company reported that it had 15 data centers, with more planned. The company estimates that it has 2.45 billion active monthly users around the world, requiring sizable server and data storage needs.

obligations. Organizations must include specific security clauses and safeguards in outsourcing contacts to make sure they meet their legal obligations.

## Organizational Governance

An organization's governance documents form the basis for its information security program. These documents include:

- Policies
- Standards
- Procedures
- Guidelines

> **NOTE**
> As discussed earlier in the chapter, a policy is an administrative safeguard.

They show the organization's vow to protect its own information and that which is entrusted to it. Policies are the top level of governance documents. A *policy* tells an organization how it must act and the consequences for failing to act properly. It is important for an organization's management team to support its policies, because policies often fail without that top-level support.

Standards state the activities and actions needed to meet policy goals. They state the safeguards necessary to reduce risks and meet policy requirements. Standards do not refer to particular technologies, operating systems, or types of hardware or software.

Procedures are step-by-step checklists that explain how to meet security goals. Procedures are the lowest level of governance documents. They often are tailored to a certain type of technology. They also can be limited to the activities of specific departments, or even specific users in departments. Procedures are revised often as technology changes.

Guidelines, which are recommended actions and guides for employees, tell users about information security concerns and suggest ways to deal with them. Guidelines should be flexible for use in many situations.

### *Data Protection Models*

One way that organizations put their governance documents into practice is by creating data protection models. In addition to following relevant laws for certain types of data, an organization might also protect data based upon its sensitivity to the organization. Not all information has the same level of sensitivity. An organization must weigh the sensitivity of information against the way in which it wants to use that information. To do this easily, an organization might choose to create data protection models to classify the different types of information it uses.

To create a data protection model, an organization first creates data classification levels. These levels serve as the basis for specifying certain types of safeguards for different categories of data. Information that would not harm the organization with its disclosure might be labeled *public* information. This would be the lowest classification of data and would typically have no special rules for its use.

Information that would harm the organization, its reputation, or its **competitive edge** if publicly disclosed might be called *confidential*. Another term that is often used for this type of information is *restricted*.

**NOTE**

Because businesses compete for customers and money, they must distinguish themselves from their competitors. A competitive edge is the designs, blueprints, or features that make one organization's products or services unique. Protecting competitive edge is one of the functions of information security.

Organizations take many steps to protect this type of information. For example, they create rules that prevent unauthorized access to it. Other rules might address the sharing and storage of this information and its disposal.

An organization must carefully review its data and put it in the proper classification level. For example, if an organization has advertising materials that it freely gives to its customers, it would probably assign these materials to the "public" category. The organization has no special rules for how employees should protect this information, so employees are able to freely use, copy, and share this type of information. The organization also might have design blueprints for its products. These documents contain the secrets that make the organization's products special. This type of material is labeled "restricted." Employees are limited in how they can use, copy, or share this information.

Data classification is a common way to think about protecting data. The general rule for protecting information is that the more sensitive or confidential the information, the fewer people that should have access to it. Very sensitive information should have more safeguards, whereas information that is not as sensitive does not need such extensive protection.

Another part of protecting information involves reviewing security goals in the C-I-A triad. All organizations must decide which goals are most important to them. For some organizations, making sure their data is available and accurate is the most important goal. These organizations use controls that ensure that correct data is always available to their customers.

Military or government organizations may place a higher value on confidentiality and integrity goals because they value secrecy and accuracy. It is usually very important to them that sensitive data not fall into the wrong hands. It is equally important that their data be correct, because key personnel rely on it when making decisions. These organizations use controls that ensure that data is accurate and protected from unauthorized access.

## U.S. National Security Information

The U.S. government also classifies its data and specifies rules for using classified information. President Barack Obama signed *Executive Order 13526* in December 2009, which describes a system for classifying national security information. The Order establishes three classification levels—confidential, secret, and top secret. The difference between the levels is the amount of harm that could be caused to U.S. security if the data were disclosed to an unauthorized person.

- *Confidential* describes information that could cause damage to U.S. security if disclosed to an unauthorized person. This is the lowest data classification level.
- *Secret* describes information that could cause serious damage to U.S. security if disclosed to an unauthorized person.
- *Top secret* is the highest classification level. This type of information could cause exceptionally grave damage to U.S. security if disclosed to an unauthorized person.

The Order also sets forth the rules to follow when using national security information. Among other rules, it states how the information must be marked and identified. It also gives instructions on how long it must remain classified. In addition, the Order specifies when to release such information to the public.

### Voluntary Organizations

Individuals and organizations may belong to voluntary membership groups that seek to promote information security. Group members often have rules that they agree to follow. These rules usually set forth behavior expectations and are usually ethical in nature. They sometimes are called a code of practice or code of ethics.

Whole organizations also participate in voluntary membership groups and agree to follow the terms of codes of conduct. For example, the Internet Commerce Association (ICA) adopted a code of conduct for its member organizations in 2007 to provide for fair practice in the domain name industry. Its rules require protection of intellectual property rights, as well as for members to abide by internet fraud laws, including laws to stop the spread of phishing scams. You can learn more about the code at www.internetcommerce.org/about-us/code-of-conduct/.

## Do Special Kinds of Data Require Special Kinds of Protection?

The United States does not have one comprehensive data protection law. Therefore, many laws focus on different types of data found in different industries. They also focus on how that data is used. Several federal agencies regulate compliance with these types of laws.

The Health Insurance Portability and Accountability Act (HIPAA) regulates some kinds of health information. The Department of Health and Human Services (HHS) and Office of Civil Rights (OCR) oversee HIPAA compliance. The Gramm-Leach-Bliley Act (GLBA) protects some types of consumer financial information. The Federal Trade Commission (FTC) ensures compliance. **TABLE 1-2** lists several important laws, the information they regulate, and the agency that enforces them. Many of these laws will be further explored in this book.

TABLE 1-2 Laws That Influence Information Security

| NAME OF LAW | INFORMATION REGULATED | REGULATING AGENCY |
| --- | --- | --- |
| Gramm-Leach-Bliley Act | Consumer financial information | Federal Trade Commission |
| Red Flags Rule | Consumer financial information | Federal Trade Commission |
| Payment Card Industry Standards* | Credit card information | Credit card issuers via contract provisions |
| Health Insurance Portability and Accountability Act | Protected health information | Department of Health and Human Services |
| Children's Online Privacy Protection Act | Information from children under the age of 13 | Federal Trade Commission |
| Children's Internet Protection Act | Internet access in certain schools and libraries | Federal Communications Commission |
| Family Educational Rights and Privacy Act | Student educational records | U.S. Department of Education |
| Sarbanes-Oxley Act | Corporate financial information | Securities and Exchange Commission |
| Federal Information Systems Management Act | Federal information systems | Office of Management and Budget, and Department of Homeland Security |
| State breach notification acts | State information systems containing protected health information | Varies among states |

*The Payment Card Industry (PCI) Standards are not a law. Organizations that wish to accept credit cards for payment of goods and services must follow these standards.

## CHAPTER SUMMARY

Information security is the study and practice of protecting information, which is important because information is valuable. Organizations need data to conduct business. Governments need information to protect their citizens. Individuals need information to interact with businesses and government agencies, as well as stay in touch with friends and family over the web. Information is a critical resource that must be protected.

The main goal of information security is to protect the confidentiality, integrity, and availability of information. Basic information security concepts include vulnerabilities, threats, risks, and safeguards.

## KEY CONCEPTS AND TERMS

Administrative safeguard
Availability
Competitive edge
Confidentiality
Control
Cryptography
Denial of service (DoS) attack
Distributed denial of service (DDoS) attack
Exploit
External attacker
Information
Information security
Integrity
Internal attacker
Least privilege
Malware
Mantrap
Need to know
Patch
Physical safeguard
Residual risk
Risk
Risk acceptance
Risk avoidance
Risk mitigation
Risk transfer
Safeguard
Separation of duties
Shoulder surfing
Single point of failure
Social engineering
Technical safeguard
Threat
Vulnerability
Window of vulnerability
Zero-day vulnerability

## CHAPTER 1 ASSESSMENT

1. What are the goals of an information security program?
   A. Authorization, integrity, and confidentiality
   B. Availability, authorization, and integrity
   C. Availability, integrity, and confidentiality
   D. Availability, integrity, and safeguards
   E. Access control, confidentiality, and safeguards
2. An employee can add other employees to the payroll database. The same person also can change all employee salaries and print payroll checks for all employees. What safeguard should you implement to make sure that this employee does not engage in wrongdoing?
   A. Need to know
   B. Access control lists
   C. Technical safeguards
   D. Mandatory vacation
   E. Separation of duties
3. An organization obtains an insurance policy against cybercrime. What type of risk response is this?
   A. Risk mitigation
   B. Residual risk
   C. Risk elimination
   D. Risk transfer
   E. Risk management
4. Which of the following is an accidental threat?
   A. A backdoor into a computer system
   B. A hacker
   C. A well-meaning employee who inadvertently deletes a file
   D. An improperly redacted document
   E. A poorly written policy
5. What is the window of vulnerability?
   A. The period between the discovery of a vulnerability and mitigation of the vulnerability
   B. The period between the discovery of a vulnerability and exploiting the vulnerability
   C. The period between exploiting a vulnerability and mitigating the vulnerability
   D. The period between exploiting a vulnerability and eliminating the vulnerability
   E. A broken window
6. A technical safeguard is also known as a ______.

**7.** Which of the following is not a threat classification?

A. Human
B. Natural
C. Process
D. Technology and operational
E. Physical and environmental

**8.** What information security goal does a DoS attack harm?

A. Confidentiality
B. Integrity
C. Authentication
D. Availability
E. Privacy

**9.** Which of the following is an example of a model for implementing safeguards?

A. ISO/IEC 27002
B. NIST SP 80-553
C. NIST SP 800-3
D. ISO/IEC 20072
E. ISO/IEC 70022

**10.** Which of the following is not a type of security safeguard?

A. Corrective
B. Preventive
C. Detective
D. Physical
E. Defective

**11.** It is hard to safeguard against which of the following types of vulnerabilities?

A. Information leakage
B. Flooding
C. Buffer overflow
D. Zero-day
E. Hardware failure

**12.** What are the classification levels for the U.S. national security information?

A. Public, sensitive, restricted
B. Confidential, secret, top secret
C. Confidential, restricted, top secret
D. Public, secret, top secret
E. Public, sensitive, secret

**13.** Which safeguard is most likely violated if a system administrator logs into an administrator user account in order to surf the internet and download music files?

A. Need to know
B. Access control
C. Least privilege principle
D. Using best available path
E. Separation of duties

**14.** Which of the following are vulnerability classifications?

A. People
B. Process
C. Technology
D. Facility
E. All of these are correct.

**15.** What is a mantrap?

A. A method to control access to a secure area
B. A removable cover that allows access to underground utilities
C. A logical access control mechanism
D. An administrative safeguard
E. None of these is correct.

## ENDNOTES


1. National Vulnerability Database, *NVD Dashboard.* https://nvd.nist.gov/general/nvd-dashboard (accessed January 19, 2020).
2. CNBC, "Ex-Coca-Cola Worker Sentenced to 8 Years in Trade Secrets Case," May 2007. https://www.cnbc.com/id/18824080 (accessed January 19, 2020).
3. Federal Bureau of Investigation, "Business E-Mail Compromise: The 12 Billion Dollar Scam," July 2018. https://www.ic3.gov/media/2018/180712.aspx (accessed January 20, 2020).

CHAPTER 2

# Privacy Overview

PRIVACY IS AN area of growing importance for people and organizations. This growth roughly corresponds with the growth of the internet, which has made it possible for people to share all types of information very quickly. Organizations collect and use information to conduct business, governments collect and use information to provide services and security for their citizens, and individuals share information to get goods and services. People also share information to network while looking for jobs and to catch up with old friends. However, this increased collection of information comes with questions about proper information use.

This chapter provides an overview of privacy issues. Because privacy is a very large field, it is impossible to discuss all of the unique and interesting issues in the field of privacy. For the most part, this chapter is limited to the areas where information technology and privacy meet. This chapter also will address general privacy concepts.

## Chapter 2 Topics

This chapter covers the following topics and concepts:

- Why privacy is an issue
- What privacy is
- How privacy is different from information security
- What the sources of privacy law are
- What threats to privacy there are in the Information Age
- What workplace privacy is
- What general principles for privacy protection exist in information systems

## Chapter 2 Goals

When you complete this chapter, you will be able to:

- Describe basic privacy principles
- Explain the difference between information security and privacy

- Describe threats to privacy
- Explain the important issues regarding workplace privacy
- Describe the general principles for privacy protection in information systems

## Why Is Privacy an Issue?

Advances in technology are forcing people to think about how their personal data is used and shared. To give some examples:

- A chef enters her email address on a website to buy a new blender. She then begins to receive junk email from many different appliance companies.
- A school district fires an elementary school teacher after parents complain to the school principal about unprofessional pictures on the teacher's personal web page.
- A professor gives students a homework assignment. The students must use the internet to collect as much publicly available data as possible about a particular government official.
- An organization tracks how many users visit its website each day. It records the number of times users click on links on the homepage and tracks each user's computer Internet Protocol (IP) address. It also tracks the web page that each user was on immediately before visiting the organization's web page.
- A person buys an MP3 player at a thrift shop. The person later discovers that the MP3 player contains files on U.S. military personnel, including their Social Security numbers (SSNs).

Advances in technology change how people live. For example, the discovery of electricity led to huge societal advances. Today, electrical service is a utility that many take for granted. The creation of the telephone allowed people to communicate over greater distances. Today, it seems unusual to find an adult who does not carry a smartphone that provides both voice and data services.

The rise in internet use also has the potential to change how people live. According to U.S. Census Bureau data, it is estimated that over 88 percent of U.S. households had internet access in 2018.[1] You can expect that number to continue to grow.

People use the internet for almost everything: learning, entertainment, and work. You can search the internet for almost any type of data. (In fact, almost every endnote in this book contains a reference to a website.) The internet is also used as a forum for sharing all types of information nearly instantaneously. The internet allows media companies to report on world events immediately. Anyone can publish anything to the world with just the click of a mouse.

However, the rise of the internet has led to some privacy concerns:

- Increased access to information
- Increased amount of information
- Electronic tracking and monitoring

This increased access to information has some complications. For example, anyone in the world can view information published on the internet. Therefore, even enemies of the government can view government information posted online. People can copy and use articles posted to the internet without the author's permission. Blogs and pictures that appear on personal web pages for family and friends to view are sometimes available to anyone, anywhere.

The amount of information on the internet is also a concern. Larger and more complex information systems allow businesses and governments to collect more and more individual data, which has led to the concept of *Big Data*. Big Data refers to large and complex data collections. Sophisticated applications review and analyze data collected from many sources. The owners of these systems can accumulate large amounts of data about people, which they can use for their own purposes. For example, they can create highly detailed individual profiles by combining their data with that of other systems. They also can sell the data they collect to third parties. Privacy issues are challenged by Big Data collections because the collections contain vast amounts of information from many different sources.

**NOTE**

A **search engine** is a program that retrieves files and data from a computer network. You use a search engine to search the internet for information. Google, the most used internet search engine, has become so popular that "to google"—meaning to search the internet for information—was added to the Oxford English Dictionary in June 2006.[2]

People leave electronic footprints in many places on the internet. *Internet service providers* (*ISPs*) maintain logs that track performance information. Websites track the actions of visitors to the site, and organizations may track and record the internet and email activities of employees. Service providers of all types back up their logs and data for disaster recovery purposes. These backups contain personal information. Many people do not know that their activities are recorded, stored, and monitored in so many different ways.

Electronic tracking and monitoring also create privacy concerns. Many people believe that they are anonymous on the internet and that when they surf the internet or post information their actions are private. They are not.

**NOTE**

A **blog** is a personal, online journal. The word "blog" comes from the words *web* and *log*. A blog author uses this online journal to publish comments and personal observations.

Most people want certain types of data kept secret. They believe that if they must share their data, they should at least be able to control how the data is subsequently used. These beliefs form part of the basis of the concept of privacy.

## What Is Privacy?

**Privacy** is a simple term that describes many different but related concepts. Writers spend a lot of time trying to define different types of privacy concepts, which is hard because privacy issues often overlap. There are two very general ways of thinking about privacy concepts:

- Freedom from government observation and intrusion
- Freedom to control one's own personal information

The rise of technology and the internet further complicates these simple definitions and our understanding of privacy issues.

At its core in the technology realm, privacy means that a person has control of his or her personal data. *Control* means that a person can specify whether he or she wants to share information and the purposes for which he or she wants to share that information. And, if the person decides to share information, control means that he or she should also have a say in how that data is collected, used, and shared. Control means that a person has a choice about when he or she is tracked and monitored.

Privacy rights are individual rights that exist independent of any type of technology. Privacy is a large area of study. In particular, this chapter discusses personal data privacy concerns created or heightened because of an increase in electronic information gathering, storage, monitoring, and transmission.

**FYI**

A core privacy right for most Americans is the concept that the government's power to interfere in the privacy of its citizens is limited. This means that people and their information must be free from unreasonable government intrusion. The government must not investigate a person or his or her personal information without a good reason. Courts spend a lot of time defining when governments are allowed to investigate their citizens.

## Types of Personal Information

The types of information that a person considers private are usually very personal. However, what is very private information for one person may not be as private for others. Information that most people generally consider private includes the following:

- **SSN or other identification numbers**—This includes an individual's driver's license and passport numbers.
- **Financial information**—This includes bank and credit card account numbers. This also includes investment and retirement account information. Most people also consider the amount of money in these accounts private information.
- **Health information**—This includes diagnoses and prescription drug information. Most people consider information regarding mental illness to be highly sensitive and private.
- **Biometric data**—This type of data includes fingerprints, DNA analysis, and iris scanning. It also includes data about a person's physical or behavioral traits. Security professionals and security equipment use biometric data to identify a particular person. **Biometric data** is special because it is unique to an individual and cannot easily be changed.
- **Criminal history data**—This includes criminal charges, the outcome of a criminal case, and any punishment that a person may have received.

### Public Records and Privacy

Some types of information that people may consider private is actually publicly available information. **Public records** are records that the law states must be available to the public. Government entities create or file these types of records, most of which are available to the public free or for a small fee. Today most government agencies make these records available to the public via the internet, which makes it easier for the government to meet its legal requirements to make them available to the public. It also makes it easier for almost anyone to access the records. However, people often have little control over the content of public records and how others use the data.

Laws determine whether a record is public or not. The law designates some records as public because there is a compelling interest in making them public, such as notifying people about government actions. Items that are often public records include the minutes of meetings of government agencies, real estate filings, and court records, including most types of criminal records. Sex offender registration lists are also public records in most communities, as are professional license records.

Another type of public record is the court docket. A **docket** is the official schedule of a court and the events in the cases that are pending before a court. Many federal, state, and local court systems publish dockets online. Electronic dockets may even include the actual documents filed in a court case, which are called pleadings. **Pleadings** can contain data about civil lawsuits and criminal actions, as well as personal information.



- **Family data**—This includes information about family members and relationships.
- **Other**—This includes any other information that a person wants to keep secret. Often this type of information may embarrass a person if released to the public.

## How Is Privacy Different from Information Security?

**NOTE**

The U.S. Freedom of Information Act (FOIA) governs access to public records of the U.S. federal government. Most states have similar laws for the public records of state government and agencies. These types of laws often are called "sunshine" laws because they shine light onto the inner workings of government agencies.

Information security and privacy are closely related. However, they are not the same. Privacy is defined here as an individual's right to control the use and disclosure of his or her own personal information. This means individuals have the opportunity to assess a situation and determine how their data is used. Information security, in contrast, is the process used to keep data private.

Just because information is secure does not mean it is private. Likewise, just because information was collected in a privacy-protective way does not mean it is secure. Privacy with respect to information systems means that people have control over and can make choices about how their information is collected, used, stored, and shared. Information security concepts and controls are used to carry out those choices. Privacy cannot exist in information systems without security.

We are still learning about how privacy and information security concepts work together as our technology and regulatory environment becomes more complex. Today information security and privacy practitioners need to have a fundamental understanding of both topics to be effective.

## What Are the Sources of Privacy Law?

Most people consider the right to privacy to be a fundamental human right. Several different sources define the scope of this right to privacy. In the United States these sources include:

- Constitutional law
- Federal law
- State law
- Common law
- Voluntary agreements

### Constitutional Law

The U.S. Constitution, the source of legal authority for the U.S. government, states the relationship between the federal government and the states. It also provides some authority for certain individual rights retained by all U.S. citizens. For example, constitutional rights are basic individual rights recognized in the U.S. Constitution.

Most people consider privacy to be a basic constitutional right. Yet, the U.S. Constitution does not use the word *privacy* anywhere. However, you can piece together the constitutional right to privacy from several different provisions. U.S. Supreme Court cases have interpreted the scope of this right. When we talk about a constitutional right to privacy, we are most often referring to the right to be free from government observation and intrusion.

The following amendments to the U.S. Constitution contribute to the right to privacy:

- First Amendment, which reads, "Congress shall make no law respecting an establishment of religion, or prohibiting the free exercise thereof; or abridging the freedom of speech, or of the press; or the right of the people peaceably to assemble, and to petition the government for a redress of grievances." U.S. Constitution, amend. 1.

  This amendment sets forth the right to freedom of religion, speech, the press, and assembly. Within these rights is the implicit right of freedom of thought, which has a privacy component.
- Third Amendment, which reads, "No soldier shall, in time of peace be quartered in any house, without the consent of the owner, nor in time of war, but in a manner to be prescribed by law." U.S. Constitution, amend. 3.

  This amendment means that the government cannot force people to house government soldiers in their homes. This gives people a limited right to privacy in their homes.
- Fourth Amendment, which reads, "The right of the people to be secure in their persons, houses, papers, and effects, against unreasonable searches and seizures, shall not be violated, and no warrants shall issue, but upon probable cause. . . ." U.S. Constitution, amend. 4.

  This amendment truly forms the basis for many of the privacy rights that Americans enjoy today. This amendment protects against unreasonable government searches and seizures.

**NOTE**

The Constitutional Convention adopted the U.S. Constitution in 1787, which applies to all the states in the country. It is both the oldest written constitution still in use by any nation today as well as the shortest constitution.

- Fifth Amendment, which reads, "No person shall be . . . compelled in any criminal case to be a witness against himself. . . ." U.S. Constitution, amend. 5.

  This amendment provides several protections. Many people know it for its "right to remain silent." One interpretation is that it protects the privacy of one's thoughts.

Each of these amendments sets forth general elements that are part of an overall right to privacy. The U.S. Supreme Court first acknowledged that a person has an interest in being "let alone" in 1834 in a case called *Wheaten v. Peters* (1834). In 1890, Samuel Warren and Louis Brandeis more fully explained this right to privacy in their article "The Right to Privacy." This article referred to a right they called "the right to be let alone." Legal cases today still refer to the phrase "the right to be let alone," which now includes the idea that people have the right to be free from intrusions by the government.

The first U.S. Supreme Court decision to state a constitutional right to privacy was *Griswold v. Connecticut* (1965). In this case, the Supreme Court found that the right to privacy was a fundamental right that was present in the Constitution. Subsequent Supreme Court cases have further defined the scope of this right.

In *Katz v. United States* (1967), the U.S. Supreme Court held that the Fourth Amendment of the U.S. Constitution protects a person's right to privacy. The holding meant that the right of privacy belongs to the individual and not just locations (such as a person's home). In this case, Charles Katz was convicted of illegal gambling. He had used a public payphone to place his bets, and the government listened to his telephone conversations through a listening device attached to the phone booth, even though the government did not have a warrant to listen to the conversations. The conversations were later used as evidence to convict Katz. The U.S. Supreme Court held that Katz's right to privacy was not diminished just because he used a public payphone booth. Justice Harlan, in his concurring opinion in this case, used the famous term "a reasonable expectation of privacy."

**NOTE**

The first 10 amendments to the constitution, called the Bill of Rights, outline specific limits on government power. You can learn more about the U.S. Constitution and view a high-resolution copy at https://www.archives.gov/founding-docs/constitution.

**FYI**

In U.S. Supreme Court cases, the Court writes a "majority opinion" that explains the decision of the court. It also explains how the justices arrived at their decision. A "concurring opinion" is one that agrees with the court's majority decision. The justice or justices writing the concurring opinion may have a different explanation for how they reached the same decision that the majority decided. A "dissenting opinion" disagrees with the majority opinion. The justice or justices writing the dissenting opinion explain why they disagree with the majority.

"A reasonable expectation of privacy" is a belief regarding private places that society recognizes as valid. Courts use the idea of a reasonable expectation of privacy to determine whether an ordinary person would believe he or she was in a private place. If a person believes that he or she is in a private place, then there are limits on the government's ability to observe or interfere with the person while he or she is in that space. For instance, people have a reasonable expectation of privacy in their homes. This is why government agencies usually must have a search warrant before searching a person's home. However, people do not have a reasonable expectation of privacy when they are out on a public street.

In *Whalen v. Roe* (1977), the U.S. Supreme Court specifically recognized a right of "informational privacy." This right focuses on the ability to control information. This case reviewed a New York law that created a state database of the names and addresses of patients who were prescribed narcotic drugs, based on mandatory information provided by doctors. The New York law was challenged on the basis that it unconstitutionally infringed on a right to privacy.

The Supreme Court upheld the validity of the New York law, noting that the law included procedures that properly protected the privacy of information included in the database. However, the Court did not reject the possibility that some types of government data collection would be improper. The Court wrote, "We are not unaware of the threat to privacy implicit in the accumulation of vast amounts of personal information in computerized data banks or other massive government files." As early as 1977 the Court recognized the future privacy concerns inherent in Big Data collections.

Other Supreme Court cases have continued to define the scope of the constitutional right to privacy. *United States v. White* (1971) found that there is no right of privacy in information voluntarily shared with another person. In *Smith v. Maryland* (1979), the Court found that there is no right to privacy in electronic communications' routing information. In *NASA v. Nelson* (2011), the Court found that performing background checks on contract NASA employees does not violate any constitutional right to information privacy. And in *Carpenter v. United States* (2018), the Court ruled that the government must get a warrant before accessing a person's cell phone location data.

**NOTE**

Case law refers to the decisions courts make in the cases they decide. Most high-level courts, such as the U.S. Supreme Court and the highest-level state courts, publish their opinions on cases. These opinions contribute to the body of case law, which is a part of common law.

## Federal Law

Federal laws are the laws that a country's federal government creates. No comprehensive data privacy law exists in the United States. Similar to the laws that regulate information security, U.S. federal laws that address information privacy are also industry-based. These laws put limits on the use of personal information based on the nature of the underlying data. Congress has enacted laws to protect various types of data, some of which are described in this section.

**NOTE**

The U.S. Code, the official record of U.S. laws, outlines the laws of the United States and is published every 6 years. The U.S. Code is available online at https://www.govinfo.gov/app/collection/uscode.

### *Freedom of Information Act (1966)*[3]

This Act establishes the public's right to request information from federal agencies, including paper documents and electronic records. The law applies to federal executive branch agencies and offices, which must comply with the law and provide requested information. There are nine FOIA exemptions; data in these categories do not have to be provided to the requester. Agencies are required to provide information to the public about how to make a FOIA request. Anyone can file a FOIA request. For more information on FOIA, see http://www.foia.gov.

### Privacy Act (1974)[4]

This Act applies to records created and used by federal agencies. It states the rules for the collection, use, and transfer of **personally identifiable information (PII)** and requires federal agencies to tell people why they are collecting personal information. Federal agencies also must provide an annual public notice, which must describe their record-keeping systems and the data in them. The Act also requires federal agencies to have appropriate administrative, technical, and physical safeguards to protect the security of the systems and records they maintain.



### E-Government Act (2002)[5]

This Act requires the federal government to use information technologies that protect privacy. The Act requires federal agencies to conduct Privacy Impact Assessments (PIAs), which are done when an agency develops information technology systems to collect and process individually identifiable information. A PIA makes sure that systems are evaluated for privacy risks. The law also requires privacy protection measures to secure the data in the systems. Federal agencies also must post their privacy policies to their websites.

### Electronic Communications Privacy Act (1986)[6]

This Act sets out the provisions for access, use, disclosure, and interception of electronic communications, including telephone, cell phones, computers, email, faxes, and texting. The government cannot access these types of communications without a search warrant. This Act is an amendment to the original Wiretap Act and expands that act's privacy protections. The Act includes three parts:

- The Wiretap Act
- The Stored Communications Act
- The Pen Register Act

The Act was extensively updated by the 2001 Uniting and Strengthening America by Providing Appropriate Tools Required to Intercept and Obstruct Terrorism Act (USA PATRIOT Act).

### The Wiretap Act (1968, amended)[7]

These statutes forbid the use of eavesdropping technologies without a court order. The law protects all email, radio communications, data transmission, and telephone calls. Amendments to the original Wiretap Act include protection for electronic communications.

### Census Confidentiality (1952)[8]

This law requires the U.S. Census Bureau to keep census responses confidential. The statute also forbids the Bureau from disclosing any data allowing a person to be individually identified. The law states that census responses can be used only for statistical purposes that do not show individual or household personal data. A "census" is a count of the population of a country.

In the United States, people are required by law to respond to the census. People were allowed to respond to the 2020 U.S. census online, marking the first time that an online response option was offered for a decennial census. The 2020 U.S. Census is also unique

**NOTE**

The mailbox restriction rule, adopted in 1934,[10] allows only the U.S. Postal Service to put postal mail in a person's physical mailbox at his or her home. This rule is the reason why other commercial delivery services cannot deliver parcels to mailboxes.

because many of the deadlines for responding to the census were extended because of the COVID-19 nationwide public health emergency.

### *Mail Privacy Statute (1971)*[9]

This law protects U.S. postal mail from being opened by another without the recipient's consent. Domestic mail can be opened without consent only if there is a valid search warrant for that mail. This law only applies to postal mail.

### *Cable Communications Policy Act (1984)*[11]

This Act is not specifically about privacy, but it does contain privacy provisions. It states that cable companies must provide a yearly written privacy notice to each customer that informs the customers about the cable company's data collection and disclosure practices. Cable providers also must ask their customers for permission before using the cable system to collect personal information. In addition, the Act requires cable providers to get customer consent before they disclose customer data. However, consent is not required if the disclosure is required by a court order.

### *Driver's Privacy Protection Act (1994)*[12]

This Act requires states to protect the privacy of personal information contained in motor vehicle records. Protected information includes any personal data in the record, such as the driver's name, address, phone number, SSN, driver's license identification number, photograph, height, weight, sex, and date of birth.

The U.S. Congress passed the Driver's Privacy Protection Act, introduced by Senator Barbara Boxer of California, in 1994. One of Senator Boxer's reasons for introducing the Act was the 1989 murder of a California actor. A stalker obtained the actor's address from the California Department of Motor Vehicles, then later went to the actor's home and killed her.

## State Laws

State constitutions are the documents that form the individual state governments and are the highest form of law for state governments. They apply to the people who live in a particular state.

Eleven state constitutions recognize a right to privacy: Alaska, Arizona, California, Florida, Hawaii, Illinois, Louisiana, Montana, New Hampshire, South Carolina, and Washington.[13] These state constitutions provide clear privacy guarantees. The Montana state constitution reads, "The right of individual privacy is essential to the well-being of a free society and shall not be infringed without the showing of a compelling state interest."[14]

The California state constitution notes, "All people are by nature free and independent and have inalienable rights. Among these are enjoying and defending life and liberty, acquiring, possessing, and protecting property, and pursuing and obtaining safety, happiness, and privacy."[15] In general, California has been a leader among states in enacting laws that recognize and protect the privacy rights of its citizens.

The State of New York was the first state to add a right of privacy into its statutes after Warren and Brandeis published their article "The Right to Privacy."[16] Many states have since written a right of privacy into their laws.

Other states have recognized a right of privacy through their case law. In 1905, for example, the Georgia Supreme Court recognized a right to privacy,[17] making it the first state to recognize, through case law, a right to privacy implicit in its own Constitution.

State governments also create laws to protect data. For example, all 50 states, the District of Columbia, Guam, Puerto Rico, and the Virgin Islands have enacted breach notification laws.[18] These laws require an organization to notify state residents if it experiences a security breach that involves the personal information of the residents.

States also have industry-specific laws that protect certain types of data, such as financial, health, and motor vehicle information. For example, as of this writing, 26 states have enacted laws to prevent employers from asking employees for their social media passwords.[19]



## Common Law

The U.S. Supreme Court did not specifically recognize a constitutional right to privacy until 1965. However, U.S. common law recognized certain privacy torts as early as 1902. A **tort** is some sort of wrongful act or harm that hurts a person. Tort law governs disputes between individuals. In a tort case, the injured party may sue the wrongdoer for damages.

**Common law** is a body of law developed through legal tradition and court cases. For the most part, the U.S. common law is a body of law and legal principles inherited from England. Common law changes very slowly. It develops as judges decide court cases.

Four privacy torts still exist today, and most states give either common law or statutory recognition to these torts. Statutory recognition means that the state has included the tort in the written laws of the state. The four privacy torts are:

- Intrusion into seclusion
- Portrayal in a false light
- Appropriation of likeness or identity
- Public disclosure of private facts

### *Intrusion Into Seclusion*

The *intrusion into seclusion* privacy tort is the act of invading a person's private space. The intrusion into private space takes several forms: It can be a physical intrusion, but it can also be an intrusion through electronic means, such as using an eavesdropping device. The intrusion must be highly offensive to a reasonable person. In this tort, the legal wrong occurs as soon as the private space is invaded. Understanding what constitutes a private space is important for this tort.

In 2009, the Supreme Court of Ohio found that people have a reasonable expectation of privacy in their cell phones.[20] This is because cell phones can hold large amounts of personal data. Other courts have held that people have a reasonable expectation

**NOTE**

The California Office of Privacy Protection, created in 2000, protects the privacy rights of state residents. California was the first state to create this type of agency, which has an extensive website that includes privacy tips and consumer information. In 2013 the office disbanded and its privacy-protective functions moved to the California Department of Justice.

of privacy in the data stored on their personal computers. This is especially true if they take steps to protect the data, including encrypting the data or using a password to protect the computer.

### *Portrayal in a False Light*

The *portrayal in a false light* privacy tort involves publishing highly offensive private information about an individual to create a bad impression. The information published is true, but it is published in an offensive way. This tort often is confused with **defamation**, which is another type of tort that involves maliciously saying false things about another person.

The portrayal in a false light privacy tort occurs when a person's photograph or image is used to create a bad impression. For example, taking a picture for a magazine of a person standing outside of a bar might create the impression that the person is a customer, which might be offensive if the person holds a position of high respect in the community. In this case, the person photographed could sue for invasion of privacy based on portrayal in a false light.

In 1993, the Alabama Supreme Court reviewed a false light case.[21] In that case, a greyhound racetrack took a picture of a group of men sitting together, which was later used in advertising materials. The men sued for false light. The Alabama court held that the men did not state a claim for false light because they were in a public place. The court said there was nothing offensive about sitting at the track. It also said that the men consented to the taking of the photograph because they did not move or object when the photographer appeared and began taking pictures. These types of torts are very dependent on the facts and circumstances of each case.

### *Appropriation of Likeness or Identity*

The *appropriation of likeness or identity* privacy tort, the oldest privacy tort, involves appropriating, or taking, an individual's name or likeness without that person's consent for financial gain. This tort often occurs with public figures if their likeness is used without their permission to sell a product or service. Court cases have held that likeness includes identifiable characteristics of a person, including his or her voice or mannerisms.

In 1992, a Samsung advertisement featured a robot dressed in a blond wig and evening gown hosting a futuristic version of a popular game show. Vanna White, a game show host, sued Samsung for appropriating her identity for commercial gain.[22] She successfully argued that being a game show host on a popular game show was her identity. She won the case.

**NOTE**

The **reasonable person standard** is a legal concept used to describe an ordinary person. This fictitious ordinary person represents how an average person would think and act. Courts use this standard to determine if the conduct that is complained about in a lawsuit is offensive to an ordinary person. Conduct is wrongful if a reasonable person finds it offensive.

### *Public Disclosure of Private Facts*

The *public disclosure of private facts* privacy tort involves the publication of embarrassing private facts. The facts publicized must be so embarrassing that a reasonable person would be offended by their publication. The disclosures must be true. Also, they must be truly private. Facts published as part of the public record are not private. Many courts have applied a "newsworthy" defense to this tort, which allows the media to report on newsworthy incidents without fearing a lawsuit for public disclosure of private facts.

The Maryland Court of Appeals has held that the publication of a criminal "mug" shot is not a privacy violation based on the public disclosure of private facts privacy tort.[23] This is because the mug shot is originally published as part of the public record.

**NOTE**

All of the privacy torts can be waived by consent. A person may not bring a tort action against an alleged wrongdoer if he or she permits the privacy invasion. Those who give permission for use of their likeness, intrusion into their private spacc, or publication of facts about them cannot later claim that they were harmed.



## Voluntary Agreements

Protecting personal data privacy grows harder as technology advances. People must understand their privacy choices in order to protect their data. Governments and organizations must understand the information that they need to provide. Organizations use **fair information practice principles** to help specify how they collect and use data. However, organizations are not legally required to follow these principles; instead, they use them to make sure they are properly informing people about their data collection practices.

The U.S. Department of Health, Education, and Welfare developed the "Code of Fair Information Practice Principles" in 1973 because there was no federal law that protected personal data. These principles stated that there should be no secret recordkeeping systems. The principles also required that individuals have a way to find out if information is collected about them, because individuals must have a way to correct inaccurate data. These practices eventually formed the basis for the 1974 federal Privacy Act.

In 1980, the Organization for Economic Cooperation and Development (OECD) adopted the "OECD Guidelines on the Protection of Privacy and Transborder Flows of Personal Data" to protect personal data. They are an extension of the 1973 U.S. fair information practices. The United States was actively involved in creating the OECD guidelines, which help guide privacy legislation for OECD members. These guidelines were revised in 2013. The OECD continues to provide recommendations on how to implement the guidelines in today's complex technology environment.

**NOTE**

The OECD was established in 1961 to promote a market economy. There are 36 members. The United States has been a member since 1961.

The OECD guidelines contain eight privacy principles:

- **The Collection Limitation Principle**—Individuals must know about and consent to the collection of their data. This is sometimes known as the data minimization principle.
- **The Data Quality Principle**—Any data collected must be correct.
- **The Purpose Specification Principle**—The purpose for data collection should be stated to individuals before their data is collected.
- **The Use Limitation Principle**—Data should be used only for the purposes stated when it was collected.
- **The Security Safeguards Principle**—The collected data must be protected from unauthorized access.

- **The Openness Principle**—People can contact the entity collecting their data to discover where their personal data is collected and stored. This is sometimes known as the data transparency principle.
- **The Individual Participation Principle**—People must know if data about them has been collected. People also must have access to their collected information.
- **The Accountability Principle**—The entity collecting data must be held accountable for following the privacy principles.

Compliance with fair information practice principles is encouraged through voluntary membership in self-regulating organizations. Organizations often choose to regulate themselves to keep governments from making laws that would limit their behavior. Organizations can participate in a **seal program** to show their compliance with fair information practice principles.

A seal program, run by a trusted third-party organization, verifies that an organization meets industry-recognized privacy practices. If the organization meets the required standards, then it is allowed to display a privacy seal on its website. The seal, an image that customers recognize, is used to signify a trustworthy organization. Common seal programs in the United States are WebTrust, TRUSTe, and the Better Business Bureau.

**NOTE**

You can read the Better Business Bureau accreditation standards here: https://www.bbb.org/bbb-accreditation-standards. How do these voluntary standards help protect consumer privacy? What makes up the fair information practice principles evidenced in the BBBOnline standards?

## What Are Threats to Personal Data Privacy in the Information Age?

Privacy concerns existed before technology became an issue. It seems, however, that privacy concerns are more urgent now because of advances in technology. This is because people often have very little control over how their data is collected, used, and shared electronically. People are concerned about how much information is collected about them and how their data will be used later. The rise in electronic communications makes people wonder how private their lives truly are. This section discusses some of today's privacy concerns.

### Technology-Based Privacy Concerns

Technology-based privacy concerns are caused by advances in technology. These concerns arise because of the types of data that can be collected with various technologies.

#### *Spyware*

Spyware, a type of malware, is any unwanted software that secretly gathers information about a person or system and shares it with an unknown third party. Spyware poses a threat to personal data privacy because of the nature of the information and the secret manner in which it collects that data. Spyware can easily record very personal information such as account numbers, usernames, and passwords. These programs also can record internet search queries and other personal data.

FYI

Spyware, keystroke loggers, and adware raise privacy concerns because they are secretly downloaded onto a user's computer. People have no control over the software or data it collects. Some users unknowingly agree to download this type of software onto their computers when the programs are part of a legitimate software application that a user wants to download. When users agree to End-User License Agreements (EULAs), they may also agree to install the spyware as well.



Twenty states have laws that specifically address spyware.[24] Utah was the first state to enact an anti-spyware law, which was quickly challenged by an advertising company that argued the law unconstitutionally limited its right to advertise. A court granted an *injunction*, a formal order for someone to stop doing something, in the case. In this case, Utah was prohibited from enforcing its new anti-spyware law.

Utah legislators then worked to revise the state anti-spyware law. Current Utah law prohibits pop-up advertising that uses spyware to target the ads that users see on their computers. The law authorizes the Utah attorney general to prosecute violations.[25]

**Adware** is software that displays advertising to a user. It can display banner advertisements, redirect a person to other websites, or display **pop-up advertisements** on a person's computer that open a new web browser window to display ads. Some types of adware are also spyware. This adware displays targeted advertisements based on secretly collected user information.

 **NOTE**

A keylogger is a hardware device or program that records all keystrokes made on a keyboard or mouse.

### *Cookies, Web Beacons, and Clickstreams*

A **cookie** is a small string of text that a website stores on a user's computer. Cookies contain text—you cannot execute them the way you do a program file. Cookies are not considered spyware because they are not executable. A cookie by itself is not dangerous or a privacy threat. However, other individuals and companies can use cookies in ways that invade your privacy.

There are two kinds of cookies:

- **First-party cookies**—Exchanged between a user's browser and the website the user is visiting.
- **Third-party cookies**—Set by one website but readable by another site. Third-party cookies are set when the web page a user visits has content on it that is hosted by another server.

Cookies are used for many things that most computer users consider beneficial. For example, they can be used by a website to remember information about visitors to the site. They also can save your settings if you "personalize" a web application that you regularly use.

However, advertising companies that sell content and advertising to companies with a web presence often use third-party cookies. Advertisers can track their cookies over several websites and use the tracked information to create a profile of each user's browsing habits. They then direct targeted advertisements to the users. This is a privacy concern.

A **web beacon** is a small, invisible electronic file that is placed on a web page or in an email message that counts users who visit a web page. A web beacon, also called a web bug, can tell if a user opened an email message and took some action with it. It can also monitor user behavior. A clear GIF (Graphics Interchange Format) is a type of image format that is often used as a web beacon because clear GIFs are invisible and very small.

Web beacons recognize several different types of data. When you retrieve a web beacon, it recognizes your computer's IP address, your browser, and the time you retrieved the beacon. Web beacons usually track users by a random identification number that contains no personally identifiable data.

Spammers sometimes use web beacons to verify whether an email address is valid. If a recipient opens a spam message with a web beacon, information is returned to the spammer, which shows that the message was opened. An opened email message generally indicates a valid email address, which is valuable to a spammer. That way, they can send the email address even more junk mail.

Web beacons cause privacy concerns because they secretly monitor user behavior as well as internet browsing patterns. Web beacons let website operators know which pages a user looks at. They also disclose the order in which the pages are viewed. Information tracked by web beacons and cookies, when combined, can potentially identify a computer user, which is a privacy concern.

A **clickstream** is the data trail that an internet user leaves while browsing. Movements are recorded as a user moves through a website and clicks on links to request information. A clickstream is essentially a set of digital footprints that track an internet user's steps.

Clickstream data, which can be recorded by websites and ISPs, helps webmasters learn how computer users are using their sites. For example, clickstream data can be used to determine the order in which users click on web pages or links on web pages. Clickstream data can be collected and stored. It can act as the basis for modifying websites for better user experience. Clickstream data also can make online advertising more effective.

Many of the technologies described so far are used to create an online profile for a user. **Online profiling** is the practice of tracking a user's actions on the internet to create a profile that contains information about the user's online habits and preferences. It can be used to direct targeted advertising toward a specific user. **Targeted advertising** is advertising that is designed to appeal to a consumer's specific interests.

A profile can contain very detailed information about the user's online habits. One concern with online profiles is that they might contain PII. Many people believe their online actions should be private. Data for online profiles is often gathered without the user's knowledge or consent, which is a privacy concern.

> **TIP**
>
> Most modern internet browsers have privacy settings that allow you to choose whether to accept cookies from the websites you visit. You also can configure browsers to warn you before a cookie is accepted, and to block third-party cookies automatically. You should always use the most privacy-protective settings that your internet browser will allow, provided that you can still get your work done.

> **TIP**
>
> You can try to avoid web beacons in email messages by not downloading messages that contain images. That is why many email programs prevent pictures from downloading automatically. The email program lets you decide whether to download images.

### Wireless Technologies

We use several different wireless communication systems every day. In fact, many adults carry smartphones that incorporate two or more wireless technologies. The term *wireless* is used generally to refer to several different technologies that allow devices to connect to one another without wires. These technologies include:

- Radio Frequency Identification
- Bluetooth
- Near Field Communications



**Radio Frequency Identification (RFID)** is a technology that uses radio waves to transmit data to a receiver. It is a way to identify unique items using radio waves. The main purpose of RFID technology is to allow "tagged" items to be identified and tracked. Sometimes you will hear devices that use this technology called a RFID tag or chip.

You can incorporate RFID tags for many different uses:

- **To track pets**—A veterinarian inserts a small tag under the skin of a household pet. You can then identify and track the pet if it becomes lost.
- **To track inventory**—The anti-theft tags attached to clothing in department stores are RFID tags that can be used to catch and deter shoplifters. A librarian can place RFID tags in books to ensure that they do not leave the library without proper checkout.
- **To track people or their trips**—Some proximity card readers use RFID tags to "unlock" doors to allow the person carrying the card to enter secure areas. E-ZPasses used by many states to collect tolls on roads and bridges use this technology.

Most RFID tags do not contain a battery. Instead, the tags are activated when a receiver is within range and sending out radio waves. The receiver initiates communication with the tag, which responds with self-identifying data. It is possible for unauthorized persons to read the information that the tag sends if transmission between the receiver and tag is not secured or protected.

Individuals have very little control over the information contained on an RFID tag. RFID technology poses privacy concerns in that it can track a person's movements and daily habits. You do not need an RFID tag inserted under your skin to be tracked by RFID technology. Cell phones, purses and briefcases, and driver's licenses or credit cards can be equipped with RFID tags as well. This tracking can be completely secret if you do not know that the items you are carrying contain an RFID tag.

Information exposure is also a concern. Information contained on an RFID tag can be exposed to unauthorized individuals if the communication channel between the tag and receiver is not secure. Individuals usually have no control over these channels and are unable to take steps to secure them.

**Bluetooth**, a short-range wireless communication, was designed to replace data cables that connect devices to one another. Bluetooth connectivity can be found in many different devices such as

 **NOTE**

The U.S. federal government has been issuing the U.S. Electronic Passport, also known as E-Passport, since 2007. This passport is the same as a regular U.S. passport, but it has an RFID tag placed in the back cover that stores the passport holder's personal information and a digital photograph. It also contains a digital signature to protect the chip from being altered. The government has taken several steps to help protect the personal information on the E-passport. You can read about those steps at https://www.dhs.gov/e-passports.

laptop computers, cell phones, speakers, fitness trackers, and headphones. As long as devices are Bluetooth compatible, they can "pair" or connect to one another. They do not need Wi-Fi or cellular data networks to connect. However, Bluetooth devices must be near one another to connect. Once devices are connected, they can share data quickly with one another.

Similar to RFID, information tracking and exposure is a concern with Bluetooth use. In addition, Bluetooth connections are often visible to other Bluetooth users in the vicinity. This can make Bluetooth devices easily identifiable targets for hackers.

**Near Field Communication (NFC)** is a short-range wireless technology that works only when two electronic devices are about 5 centimeters apart. Similar to Bluetooth, NFC does not need to use Wi-Fi or a cellular network. Because devices have to be very close together for NFC to work, concerns about information exposure are somewhat mitigated. NFC is used for tasks such as making mobile payments from a mobile device.

### *GPS Technology*

A **global positioning system (GPS)** uses satellites above the Earth to compute the location of a GPS receiver. GPS receivers can be incorporated into many devices and use several different satellites to calculate time and location. For example, they are used in automobile navigation units. Runners use GPS receivers built into heart rate monitors to help measure the distances that they have run. GPS units are built into many cell phones to help locate cell phone users in an emergency. Cell phone applications also use GPS technology to track other users and family members.

GPS technology raises many of the same issues as RFID technology. GPS technology precisely tracks a receiver's every step. Thus, a person with GPS technology enabled on a cell phone can be tracked every minute of every day. GPS units also are placed in cars. Individuals may not know that their cars or cell phones have GPS units that track their every move. People have very little control over the location information that a GPS unit can track and provide.

In 2012, the U.S. Supreme Court held that installing a GPS unit on a car is considered a search under the Fourth Amendment to the U.S. Constitution.[26] In *U.S. v. Jones* (2012), the government initially got a search warrant to install the GPS device on the defendant's car. However, government agents did not follow the terms of that search warrant when they installed the device. The Court held that, for the installation of the GPS unit to be valid, police officers must get a search warrant and execute it properly.

> **NOTE**
>
> The Federal Communications Commission (FCC) Enhanced 911 (E911) initiative requires cell phone carriers to be able to pinpoint their customers' locations within 100 meters. This allows emergency responders to reach cell phone users more quickly in a crisis. GPS is one of the technologies used to help pinpoint customer location.

### *Security Breaches*

The Privacy Rights Clearinghouse maintains a list of U.S. security breaches that involve records that contain personal information. The clearinghouse began collecting this data in January 2005. As of October 2019, the site reported that over 10 billion records have been involved in security breaches. The list is available at https://privacyrights.org/data-breaches.

A **security breach** is a compromise of any security system that results in the loss of PII. After a breach, unauthorized individuals potentially can access data in the system.

Any organization can experience a security breach. Security breaches can be caused by direct external attacks, poor internal safeguards, or both. Breaches can occur within computer systems, as well as when physical security systems, such as a perimeter gate or fence, are compromised.

Security breaches are a large privacy concern. Organizations store vast amounts of personal information. One security breach has the potential to expose the personal information of a large number of people. This data can be used to commit identity theft and other types of fraud. Most people are upset when organizations entrusted with their personal information experience a security breach. Every U.S. state has a breach notification law that requires organizations to notify customers in the event of a breach. Customers can then monitor their financial accounts and personal data to protect them from misuse.

 **NOTE**

*Security breach fatigue* is the idea that consumers receive too many data breach notifications and no longer take action to protect themselves when they receive a breach notification.



## People-Based Privacy Concerns

People-based privacy concerns are caused by people's actions. These concerns are raised when people compromise others' privacy. They also are caused when people take actions that compromise their own data privacy. Many information security attacks can also result in privacy violations. They include:

- **Phishing**—Phishing is a form of internet fraud in which attackers attempt to steal valuable information, usually via email. Phishing scams are a privacy concern for both individuals and organizations. For the individual, a successful phishing attack can result in the loss of personal information. For organizations, if an employee responds to a scam with username and password information, the organization can experience a large data breach. That breach can involve customers' personal information.
- **Social engineering**—Social engineering attacks rely on human interaction. They involve tricking people to gain sensitive information.
- **Shoulder surfing**—Shoulder surfing occurs when an attacker looks over the shoulder of another person to discover sensitive information.

In each of these types of attacks, attackers are trying to get data they do not have permission to have, often in an attempt to get PII to exploit. Chapter 1 discusses these information security attacks further.

**Dumpster diving**, another threat to data privacy, involves sifting through trash to discover personal information. It is an issue because individuals and organizations dispose of personal information in unsecure ways. Thieves then steal PII to commit identity theft. Shredding documents before placing them in the trash is a safe disposal method.

In May 2009, a New York law firm was preparing to move. The firm hired a document destruction company to help it dispose of old client files, many of which contained PII on clients. The personal information included medical records, SSNs, and other personal data. Six dumpsters full of intact client files ended up on the street. Media outlets reported that several people were noticed rummaging through the bins and looking at documents.

### Social Networking Sites

Personal data privacy is not compromised just by the actions of third parties. People can harm their own privacy by participating in online social networks, which have the potential to expose a lot of personal information. **Social networking sites** are website applications that allow users to post information about themselves. These sites promote interaction between people.

Some social networking sites are employment-based and promote professional networking. They allow users to post their work history and information and connect with other users in the same industry or across industries. Other social networking sites are purely social. They allow users to share snapshots of their lives with family and friends. Users often share large amounts of highly personal data on social networking sites. Some social networking sites are hobby-based and allow users with similar interests to share information. Common social networking sites include Facebook, Twitter, LinkedIn, Instagram, and Pinterest.

Social networking has two main privacy concerns:

- Information (over) sharing
- Security

**Information (Over) Sharing.** On social networking sites, users share lots of information about themselves in a virtually unlimited forum, such as details about their daily schedules, finances, and family members. Some social networking sites, particularly those that are hobby-based, allow for very detailed sharing about specific topics. For instance, genealogy platforms often contain a social networking function that can allow users to share ancestry and even genetic data. Oversharing can put people and their safety at risk. Thieves can use this information to stalk them, steal from a person's home, or target them for identity theft.

Most social networking sites allow users to control some privacy settings. However, users may not be knowledgeable about all of the settings. Sometimes the privacy settings on social networking sites are difficult to understand. If they are hard to understand, users may not use them. People often do not realize how much information is available on the internet through social media sites and that other users have access to that information.

A fugitive from New York State was caught in Terre Haute, Indiana, in February 2010. Police tracked him down because he posted his workplace on his social networking profiles. Police arrested him at his job, then posted this message on his Facebook account: "It was due to your diligence in keeping us informed that now you are under arrest."

**Security.** Another privacy concern about social networking sites is their security. Many sites allow users to add applications (called "apps") and other third-party software to their profiles. These applications enhance the social networking experience through providing games and ways to connect with other users of the same social network. If these applications do not use proper security practices, personal information can be exposed. A compromise in an application can disclose data stored on a user's profile. Social networking users often have little control over information used or shared by these types of applications.

> **NOTE**
>
> Creeping means to track someone on social media through viewing all of a person's social media sites to understand what is going on in his or her life. Some people consider creeping to be as intrusive as stalking, which is a crime. Others consider it to be less intrusive and similar to snooping.

In 2018, the Cambridge Analytica scandal showed that the relationship between social media users, social media platforms, and applications on social media platforms can be particularly complex. In the scandal, data-analysis firm Cambridge Analytica was accused of improperly acquiring and using the data of 50 million Facebook users without the users' consent. Cambridge Analytica got the Facebook user data in 2014 through an app called *thisisyourdigitallife*. The terms of service for the app said that personal information was not collected, but that was a lie. The collected data was then later used by Cambridge Analytica to provide voter profiling and targeted advertising services during the 2016 U.S. presidential election. Cambridge Analytica was able to access the data by taking advantage of the access permissions that Facebook granted to applications.

Because of the scandal and its fallout, Cambridge Analytica went bankrupt. In addition, the U.S. Federal Trade Commission (FTC) investigated Facebook. In 2019 the FTC imposed a $5 billion penalty on Facebook for violating consumer privacy.[27] The FTC also filed a complaint against Cambridge Analytica. You can read more about the scandal in the FTC's December 2019 opinion, located at https://www.ftc.gov/enforcement/cases-proceedings/182-3107/cambridge-analytica-llc-matter.



### *Online Data Gathering*

The internet has made it much easier to learn personal details about people. People can search the internet for data on their neighbors, coworkers, family members, prospective dates, and public figures. Almost every person has some sort of digital presence. Social networking sites, personal web pages, media websites, and government public records databases can be easily reviewed for personal information. Although there are legitimate uses for viewing online personal data, it also can be used to harass and threaten victims.

Many of the privacy concerns discussed in this section existed before the internet. They just did not exist on the same level as they do now. Today it is trivial to discover personal information about other people. **Identity theft** is one of the fastest-growing crimes, because it is becoming easy to find and misuse others' personal information. Identity theft occurs when a person's PII is used without permission to commit other crimes.

**NOTE**

Up to 10 million Americans are victims of identity theft each year, according to the FTC. You can learn more about identity theft at https://www.ftc.gov/news-events/media-resources/identity-theft.

## What Is Workplace Privacy?

**Workplace privacy** is a term that describes privacy issues in the workplace. Privacy can be implicated in several ways in the workplace. For example, hiring, firing, and performance reviews all have potential privacy concerns, and how employers interact with employees in these matters can have privacy implications.

As a rule, most U.S. employees have very little expectation of privacy in their workplaces. Very few states have enacted laws about workplace privacy issues, although some states may have laws relating to general issues, such as telephone wiretapping. Not all states have considered the impact of those laws in the workplace.

Employers can use technology, such as electronic communications, to make workers more productive. Employers provide employees with equipment to use at work. This equipment includes desktop and laptop computers, cell phones, telephones, voicemail, email, and internet access. These technologies allow employers a greater opportunity to monitor how their employees are working each day. This is called workplace monitoring.

This section will discuss the following types of monitoring:

- Telephone and voicemail monitoring
- Video surveillance monitoring
- Computer use monitoring (including internet access)
- Email monitoring

For the most part, workplace monitoring is permissible in the United States. Courts are just beginning to address the limits of an employer's ability to monitor employees. Employers usually are permitted to monitor their employees so long as the employer has a legitimate business reason to do so. However, employers have great discretion in determining legitimate business reasons for monitoring.

Workplace monitoring is legitimate when used to measure employee productivity and workplace safety. It is also legitimate when used to protect employer assets and prevent theft. Workplace monitoring can also properly be used to:

- Ensure that employees are properly using the organization's sensitive data
- Verify that employees are not violating other policies (such as acceptable use policies)
- Protect the company from liability for bad acts committed by employees

## Telephone, Voicemail, and Email Monitoring

Some organizations monitor employee telephone, voicemail, and email conversations as a part of routine activities. One reason to do this is to make sure the employees are providing good customer service. Employees have few protections from this type of monitoring.

### *Telephone and Voicemail Monitoring*

An employer's right to monitor telephone conversations must be reviewed under federal and state law. Federal protection for electronic communications is found in the Electronic Communication Privacy Act (ECPA). It also protects telephone calls. Under this law, generally the use of eavesdropping technologies to record a telephone conversation requires a court order.

**NOTE**

Gartner estimates that almost 80 percent of companies will be monitoring their employees in some way in 2020.[28]

However, telephone conversation monitoring in the ordinary course of business may be allowed without a court order. To use this ECPA exception, an employer must state a legitimate business interest in monitoring telephone calls. Employers also must show that the monitoring occurred on equipment provided by a communications service provider.

Courts tend to give employers deference when reviewing their legitimate business reason for monitoring. In most cases, the reason is met if the monitoring is even slightly related to business matters. Employee telephone calls with customers about services or products that the employer provides clearly relate to business matters and can be monitored. Monitoring telephone calls for quality control purposes also is a legitimate business purpose.

For monitoring to stand up in court, an employer must show that the monitoring took place on equipment supplied by its phone system service provider. The equipment used to monitor calls must be more than a simple tape recorder. In *Deal v. Spears* (1992), the Eighth Circuit Court of Appeals found that a recorder purchased at a consumer electronics store did not qualify as ordinary telephone equipment.[29] The court held that even though the employer's reason for monitoring was legitimate (the prevention of theft), the exception was not met. The monitoring was a violation of federal law.

Federal law allows monitoring only when the conversation clearly relates to the employer's business. Employers must immediately stop monitoring a call once they determine that it is personal. Personal calls are outside of the ordinary course of business.

However, employers may always monitor employee telephone calls when the employee gives consent. In this case, an employer must provide notice of the monitoring. It also must show that its employees consented to the monitoring. Employers can prove that they gave notice by putting their monitoring policy in the employee handbook. They can show that an employee consented to monitoring by having employees sign an acknowledgment form. There is no violation of the ECPA if an employee gives the employer permission to monitor the employee's call.

Most state laws have wiretap statutes that are based on federal law. There may be subtle differences from state to state. In Delaware, for example, employers must provide written notice before monitoring calls.[30] In Connecticut, all parties to the conversation must give consent before a call can be monitored.[31]

There is far less regulation with employer monitoring of stored voicemail messages. Under federal law, employers that provide electronic communication services may access messages once they are stored in their computer or telephone systems, which they can do without notifying employees. If an employer owns the telephone system, then it may legally access stored voicemails.



### *Email Monitoring*

Email monitoring is very similar to telephone conversation monitoring. The federal wiretap laws in place for monitoring telephone conversations also apply to intercepting email conversations. Similar to telephone conversations, real-time email monitoring may be permitted in some instances. An employer may intercept employee email using equipment furnished by the provider of electronic communication services. However, an employer must have a legitimate business purpose for intercepting email.

Email monitoring does raise some questions that are different from telephone conversation monitoring. For instance, email is different because it can be stored indefinitely on the employer's equipment. Under federal law, stored electronic communications can be accessed by the organization that provides the electronic communications service. This "stored communication" exception is very broad. If the employer provides the email service, then it may properly access stored emails from that service.

Under federal law, employee consent always permits an employer to monitor an employee's email. State laws generally permit email monitoring in a manner that is similar to telephone monitoring. There may be occasional variations among the states. In Delaware, for example, employers must provide written notice before monitoring email communications.

Court cases generally have found that employers are free to read email messages when the employer provides the email account. These courts sometimes, but not always, consider whether the email was intercepted for a legitimate business reason or if it was viewed from its storage location.

Sometimes employees access their private, web-based email accounts from employer-provided equipment. This is a different issue from employers' monitoring of work-provided email. Employers who access private email accounts may run into problems with the federal law, even if the employee has accessed that private account from a work-provided computer, because the ECPA prohibits employers from accessing an employee's personal email account. Courts have found that employers act inappropriately if they use computer-monitoring equipment to obtain usernames and passwords to employee personal accounts. If the employer then accesses those private email accounts without permission, it is considered an ECPA violation.

## Computer Use Monitoring

Employers may monitor employee computer and internet use for many reasons. In addition to the business reasons already mentioned, employers may monitor computer and internet use to discourage inappropriate online conduct at work. This could include discouraging online shopping during work hours or viewing adults-only websites.

Employees generally do not have any reasonable expectation of privacy in their use of employer-provided resources. An employer generally is allowed to monitor an employee's use of work-provided computers and internet access. This monitoring includes reviewing files and software on the computer. It also includes tracking internet use and the web pages that an employee visits.

An employer can monitor computer or internet use in many ways:

- Employing keystroke loggers to monitor keystrokes made in a certain period, or the number of websites visited
- Tracking how much time employees spend in software applications provided for work purposes to measure productivity
- Using software programs to measure employee time spent on the internet. Employers can also block employee access to some web pages to limit the types of sites that employees can access from work.

There is no federal prohibition against employer computer or internet-use monitoring when the employer provides the equipment to the employee. Computer and internet monitoring is permitted in most states. Connecticut[32] and Delaware[33] are notable exceptions. These states require employers to give notice before monitoring computer use.

Many questions are unanswered concerning the limits of employer computer use and internet monitoring. Court opinions provide little guidance. Employees that challenge employer computer monitoring claim that the monitoring infringed upon their reasonable expectation of privacy in the use of the work computer. Different courts in different areas have come to different conclusions.

Some courts have ruled that an employee never has any privacy in employer-provided computers. Other courts have decided that an employee may have a reasonable expectation of privacy in employer-provided computers. These cases are very fact-dependent. For

### Monitoring an Employee's Personal Computer

A potential question also arises when employers allow employees to use their own personal equipment at work. In *United States v. Barrows* (2007), an employee brought his personally owned laptop computer to work, which he connected to his employer's network. He used the computer at work in an open workspace area and did not password-protect his computer. While he was away from his desk, another employee accessed his computer and found illegal materials.

The Tenth Circuit Court of Appeals held that the employee did not have a reasonable expectation of privacy in his personal computer.[34] There was no expectation of privacy because he had connected the computer to his employer's computer network. The court also said the employee had no expectation of privacy in the machine because he used it in an open area, left it on when he was not using it, and took no steps to password-protect the machine.



instance, if an employee keeps the computer in his or her locked office and uses a password to protect the machine, he or she might have a reasonable expectation of privacy in the work computer. Courts also look at whether the employer had a written policy that gave employees notice of monitoring.

### *Off-Duty Computer Monitoring*

Computer use and internet monitoring create individual privacy concerns. For example, internet monitoring can be invasive. People use the internet to research many things, and sometimes very sensitive things. An employer who monitors internet use might inadvertently learn very personal things about an employee.

Another privacy concern is the monitoring of an employee's off-duty internet activity. Employers can easily search the internet for information related to potential and current employees. They can view employee postings on blogs, web pages, or email lists, as well as comments made in response to media articles.

Many large employers have fired employees for online comments made on their own time when those comments are related to the employer's business. Often the employer is most worried about social media posts that could harm the employer's reputation. For example, in 2004 Delta Airlines fired a flight attendant for pictures that she posted on her personal website. The flight attendant was wearing her Delta Airlines uniform in the posted pictures. She later sued Delta for firing her. The case was ultimately settled, but the terms are confidential.

**NOTE**

A majority of states limit the ability of an employer to fire an employee for off-duty activity. Most of these laws deal with activities such as alcohol or cigarette use. These laws state that an employer cannot fire an employee for use that was both off-duty and away from the employer's premises.

## Video Surveillance Monitoring

Employers may want to use video surveillance to monitor their employees. They can use video surveillance to protect against workplace theft, as well as protect workplace safety and monitor productivity.

Workplace video surveillance monitoring generally is allowed if employees are given notice. Employers must have a legitimate business reason for the surveillance. Employers must not use video surveillance to monitor places where employees have a reasonable expectation of privacy. Areas considered private include restrooms, employee lounges, or private offices. Employers must be careful when using hidden video surveillance, because it can be a privacy violation if the person under hidden surveillance has a reasonable expectation of privacy in the area under surveillance.

Some states have laws that set limits on what employers may videotape, and employers can run into complications with federal and state wiretapping laws if video surveillance also includes audio recording. Audio recording can trigger the wiretap acts.

### *Special Rules for Public Employees*

Some special rules exist for workplace monitoring of public employees. **Public employees** are employees that work for the federal, state, or local government. Individuals in public

#### Workplace Monitoring and Employee Privacy

In *City of Ontario v. Quon* (2010), the U.S. Supreme Court overturned a federal appeals court holding that an employee's privacy rights are violated if his employer reads personal text messages sent on an employer-provided device.

In the case, a California police officer was provided with an employer-issued pager. The police department had a general computer, internet, and email use policy that stated the use of the equipment was limited to city business. The police department did not have a formal policy about text messaging. Officers were told that text messages sent on the pager would not be reviewed so long as the officers reimbursed the department for charges that went above the service contract amount.

The police officer, in this case, was a heavy user of the pager. He always paid the police department for the excess use amounts. Eventually, the police department decided to audit pager use to determine whether the basic service contract amount needed to be increased.

The police department requested transcripts of the text messages sent from the pagers, which the pager service provider gave the police department. The department reviewed the transcripts of the police officer's text messages. The police officer sued, stating that reading the messages violated various federal laws and his right to privacy.

The Ninth Circuit Court of Appeals said that the police officer had a reasonable expectation of privacy in the text messages sent from his pager. The court based its decision on the fact that the department said there would be no review of pager text messages. The police department appealed that ruling.

In June 2010, the U.S. Supreme Court ruled that reviewing the police officer's text messages did not violate federal law or the police officer's privacy rights. The Court held that the police department's audit of pager use was not intrusive and was for a legitimate purpose. The Court also found that the police officer did not have a reasonable expectation of privacy in the text messages.

Although this case deals with a public employee, it does help provide clarity for all employers on the acceptable limits of electronic communications monitoring. One thing that the case does help highlight is that all employers must have very clear policies on the use of electronic communication devices. You can read the Supreme Court's decision in this case at http://www.supremecourt.gov/opinions/09pdf/08-1332.pdf.

employment have some extra privacy protections because their employer is the government. The federal constitution protects individuals from interference by the government. State employees have similar extra protections because of rights provided in state constitutions.

The Fourth Amendment protects federal employees from unreasonable government search and seizure. Therefore, the federal government must provide employees with notice if it intends to monitor the electronic communications of its employees. Even though the government might have to take additional steps to make sure that employee monitoring is legal, courts have recognized the government's right to engage in workplace surveillance for legitimate business reasons.

Workplace monitoring continues to be a sensitive issue for both employers and employees. Employers typically win legal challenges against workplace monitoring practices, especially if the monitoring is for a legitimate business purpose. To protect their own personal privacy, employees must assume that equipment provided by their employers is for work activities only. Employees should not engage in personal computer and internet activities on an employer's computer if they wish to protect their privacy.



## What Are General Principles for Privacy Protection in Information Systems?

Designing information systems in ways that protect data privacy is very important. Customers will be loyal to organizations that protect privacy. Organizations must understand how their customers feel about data privacy. Even though people are sharing more information than ever before, some feel that their privacy is under attack. Organizations must keep in mind that people want to control their personal data.

Organizations can use the fair information practice principles discussed earlier in this chapter to help define the best way to approach privacy. Many information system activities impact personal data privacy. Data collection, storage, use, retention, and destruction practices must be reviewed to make sure that privacy is ensured at each stage in the data life cycle. The steps in the data life cycle (shown in **FIGURE 2-1**) are:

- Data collection
- Data use
- Data storage
- Data retention
- Data destruction

In the data collection phase, organizations must clearly state the types of data that they need to collect. They also must determine how they are going to collect data from their customers. *Active data collection* practices that are obvious to the customer should be used. Customers are aware of active data collection practices. The use of web-based forms clearly indicates to a customer that data collection activities are taking place. Customers understand what data is being collected because they are providing the information.

FIGURE 2-1

The data life cycle.

Organizations should avoid passive collection methods. *Passive data collection* happens secretly when an organization uses devices such as cookies and web beacons. Customers may not know that data collection is occurring with these collection methods.

Organizations must make sure that they use the data that they collect in ways that the customer has approved. They should use the data for no purpose other than what was specified when the data was collected. Information systems will need configuration so that the collected data is available only for its approved use. Organizations also must make sure that only authorized individuals have access to the data. Data must not be disclosed to employees who have no business need for the data.

Organizations also must ensure that they know how the collected data is used within the system. Data must not change when processed in the system. Organizations also will want to include system checks that verify that the personal data collected remains accurate.

Systems sometimes allow customers to create "accounts" that hold their personal data. The organization must ensure that it uses appropriate access control measures for those accounts. These measures protect accounts from unauthorized access. Organizations should also verify that records are updated accurately.

Finally, organizations must keep track of where collected personal data is stored in their systems. Appropriate safeguards are needed to protect the stored data. Organizations may choose to encrypt the collected personal data to protect it from disclosures or security breaches. Employers also should use safeguards to make sure that employees do not store the data on removable media. Personal data must be stored securely to protect it from disclosure.

Organizations should retain personal data only as long as it is needed. Laws and organizational policies specify the appropriate retention periods. An organization must dispose of the data when the retention period expires, using a method that destroys old data in both primary and backup storage systems.

## Privacy Policies

Organizations that collect personal data from customers should develop a privacy policy. This policy clearly explains all the protections the organization uses at each stage in the data life cycle, informs customers about personal data collection practices, and explains how the organization uses the data that it collects. The policy manages the privacy expectations of customers and the security obligations of the organization.

## International Privacy Laws

**NOTE**

The United Nations has a webpage that shows worldwide data protection and privacy legislation: https://unctad.org/en/Pages/DTL/STI_and_ICTs/ICT4D-Legislation/eCom-Data-Protection-Laws.aspx

The United States does not have a comprehensive data privacy law, although many other nations that conduct business with the United States do have such laws. This difference can make business transactions hard at times.

European nations recognize privacy as a basic human right. The European Union's (E.U.) General Data Protection Regulation (GDPR) is a revolutionary and comprehensive data privacy law.[35] The GDPR, which was approved in 2016 and came into force in May 2018, sets limits on the collection and use of personal data belonging to an E.U. data subject. The law also grants significant rights to E.U. data subjects. One of the most famous rights is the *right to be forgotten*. Under this provision, data subjects can request that organizations permanently delete the data subject's personal information.

**NOTE**

Under the E.U. GDPR, a data subject is any identified or identifiable natural person. The data subject does not have to be an E.U. citizen. They just have to be physically present in the E.U.

The GDPR is revolutionary because it attempts to regulate organizations outside of the E.U. that collect the data of E.U. data subjects. Organizations located in the E.U. must comply with the GDPR. In addition, organizations that offer goods or services to people in the E.U. or that collect data on people located in the E.U. also must follow the law, even if the organization is not located in the E.U. The GDPR has a very broad scope because it applies to organizations both inside and outside the E.U. Organizations that fail to follow the GDPR are subject to very large fines.

## CHAPTER SUMMARY

Privacy is a right that people no longer are taking for granted. People want to have control over their personal information. They want to be able to choose how third parties collect, use, and store their information. The growth in electronic communication and data transfer has changed how individuals view privacy and how organizations must protect it. Organizations must use information security principles to make sure they respect a person's individual privacy choices.

## KEY CONCEPTS AND TERMS

Adware
Biometric data
Blog
Bluetooth
Clickstream
Common law
Cookie
Defamation
Docket
Dumpster diving
Fair information practice principles
Global positioning system (GPS)
Identity theft
Near Field Communication (NFC)
Online profiling
Personally identifiable information (PII)
Pleadings
Pop-up advertisements
Privacy
Public employees
Public records
Radio Frequency Identification (RFID)
Reasonable person standard
Seal program
Search engine
Security breach
Social networking sites
Targeted advertising
Tort
Web beacon
Workplace privacy

## CHAPTER 2 ASSESSMENT

1. What does a seal program verify?
   A. That an organization meets recognized privacy principles
   B. That an organization meets recognized legal principles
   C. That a third party is trusted
   D. That a website does not use cookies
   E. None of these is correct.
2. What techniques are used to create a list of the web pages that a computer user visits?
   A. Adware, malware, and phishing
   B. Malware, cookies, and web beacons
   C. Web beacons, clickstreams, and spyware
   D. Malware, spyware, and cookies
   E. Clickstreams, cookies, and web beacons
3. Which amendment protects against unreasonable searches and seizures?
   A. First
   B. Third
   C. Fourth
   D. Fifth
   E. Seventh
4. Privacy refers to a person's right to control personal data.
   A. True
   B. False
5. What is the source of legal authority for the U.S. government?
   A. The United States Code
   B. The common law
   C. Supreme Court decisions
   D. The U.S. Constitution
   E. The Declaration of Independence
6. Which of the following is *not* a privacy tort?
   A. Intrusion into seclusion
   B. Portrayal in a false light
   C. Appropriation of likeness or identity
   D. Defamation
   E. Public disclosure of private facts
7. The OECD privacy protection guidelines contain _______ privacy principles.

**8.** Which principle means that an individual should be told the reason for data collection before the data is collected?

A. The collection limitation principle
B. The purpose specification principle
C. The use limitation principle
D. The openness principle
E. The accountability principle

**9.** What are the two types of cookies?

A. First-party and third-party cookies
B. Active and passive cookies
C. First-party and second-party cookies
D. Rational and irrational cookies

**10.** What is a web beacon?

A. Text stored on a computer user's hard drive
B. A small, invisible electronic file
C. A pop-up advertisement
D. Executable code
E. A data trail left by a computer user

**11.** Employer monitoring of employees in the workplace is generally allowed.

A. True
B. False

**12.** To monitor telephone conversations, an employer must use equipment provided by a phone system service provider and have ______.

**13.** Why is biometric data unique?

A. It can be used to identify a person.
B. It is data about a person's physical traits.
C. It can be used to commit identity theft.
D. It cannot easily be changed.
E. None of these is correct.

**14.** Which of the following is *not* a people-based privacy threat?

A. Social engineering
B. Web beacons
C. Shoulder surfing
D. Dumpster diving
E. Social networks

**15.** What is used to ensure privacy?

A. Biometric data
B. Encryption
C. Information security
D. Monitoring
E. Online profiling



## ENDNOTES


1. U.S. Census, "American Community Survey, Presence and Types of Internet Subscriptions in Household Table B28002," 2018. https://data.census.gov/cedsci/ (accessed April 28, 2020).
2. Oxford English Dictionary, "New Words List June 2006," June 2006. https://public.oed.com/updates/new-words-list-june-2006/ (accessed April 28, 2020).
3. U.S. Code Vol. 5, sec. 552.
4. U.S. Code Vol. 5, sec. 552a.
5. U.S. Code Vol. 44, various sections.
6. U.S. Code Vol. 18, sec. 2701.
7. U.S. Code Vol. 18, sec. 2510.
8. U.S. Code Vol. 13, sec. 9.
9. U.S. Code Vol. 39, sec. 3623.
10. U.S. Code Vol. 18, sec. 1725.
11. U.S. Code Vol. 4, sec. 551.
12. U.S. Code Vol. 18, sec. 2721.
13. National Conference of State Legislatures, "Privacy Protections in State Constitutions," November 7, 2018. https://www.ncsl.org/research/telecommunications-and-information-technology/privacy-protections-in-state-constitutions.aspx (accessed April 28, 2020).
14. Montana Constitution, art. II, sec. 10.
15. California Constitution, art. 1, sec. 1.
16. New York Civil Rights Law, art. 5. sec. 50–52 (1903).
17. *Pavesich v. New England Life Ins. Co.*, 50 S.E. 68 (Ga. 1905).
18. National Conference of State Legislatures, "Security Breach Notification Laws," March 8, 2020. https://www.ncsl.org/research/telecommunications-and-information-technology/security-breach-notification-laws.aspx (accessed April 27, 2020).

19. National Conference of State Legislatures, "State Social Media Privacy Laws," May 22, 2019. https://www.ncsl.org/research/telecommunications-and-information-technology/state-laws-prohibiting-access-to-social-media-usernames-and-passwords.aspx (accessed April 27, 2020).
20. *State v. Smith*, Slip Opinion No. 2009-Ohio-6426 (Oh. 2009).
21. *Schifano v. Greene County Greyhound Park, Inc.*, 624 So.2d 178 (Ala. 1993).
22. *White v. Samsung Electronics of America, Inc.*, 989 F.2d 1512 (9th Cir. 1992). Did you know that the famous wheel in the Wheel of Fortune gameshow weighs 2,400 pounds?
23. *Pemberton v. Bethlehem Steel Corp.*, 502 A.2d 1101 (Md. App.), cert. denied, 508 A.2d 488 (Md.), cert. denied, 107 S.Ct. 571 (1986).
24. National Conference of State Legislatures, "State Social Media Privacy Laws," October 30, 2018. https://www.ncsl.org/research/telecommunications-and-information-technology/state-spyware-laws.aspx (accessed April 27, 2020).
25. Spyware Control Act, Utah Code, title 13, ch. 40 sec. 13-40-101 to 401 (2004); repealed and reenacted in 2010 as the Utah E-Commerce Integrity Act.
26. *United States v. Jones*, 132 S.Ct. 945 (2012).
27. U.S. Federal Trade Commission, "In the Matter of Facebook, Inc.," April 28, 2020. https://www.ftc.gov/enforcement/cases-proceedings/092-3184/facebook-inc (accessed April 28, 2020).
28. Gartner, "The Future of Employee Monitoring," May 3, 2019. https://www.gartner.com/smarterwithgartner/the-future-of-employee-monitoring/ (accessed April 28, 2020).
29. *Deal v. Spears*, 980 F.2d 1153 (8th Cir. 1992).
30. Delaware Code Title 19, ch. 7, sec. 705.
31. Connecticut General Statutes Title 52, sec. 570d.
32. Connecticut General Statutes Title 31, sec. 48d.
33. Delaware Code Title 19, ch. 7, sec. 705.
34. *United States v. Barrows*, 481 F.3d 1246 (10th Cir. 2007).
35. European Union, "Regulation on the Protection of Natural Persons With Regard to the Processing of Personal Data and on the Free Movement of Such Data, and Repealing Directive 95/46/EC (Data Protection Directive), 2016/679." April 14, 2016.

CHAPTER 3

# The American Legal System

FOR OVER TWO DECADES, the shows in the *Law and Order* franchise have been popular with television viewers. Each episode transports viewers into the world of American criminal law and process. A crime, investigation, and judicial process are neatly wrapped in a 1-hour episode, from the dramatic opening theme song with its scene-changing "clang" sound, to the final scene when justice is served. *Law and Order* episodes focus on criminal law, which is one aspect of the American legal system.

This chapter provides a high-level overview of the legal system in the United States. It is important for Americans to have a general understanding of this system because it affects us every day. We are bound by a system of laws that regulate our behavior and contribute to an ordered society. Laws reflect our values, and they evolve over time.

The American legal system, its history, and its processes are a fascinating area of study. Many talented judges, attorneys, and law scholars have written excellent books about it. This chapter provides only an overview, but will outline a framework that can enable you to do further reading and research on this topic.

## Chapter 3 Topics

This chapter covers the following topics and concepts:

- How the American legal system is organized
- What the sources of American law are
- What the types of law are
- What the role of precedent is
- What regulatory authorities are
- What the difference is between compliance and audit
- How security, privacy, and compliance fit together

## Chapter 3 Goals

When you complete this chapter, you will be able to:

- Describe the American legal system
- Explain sources of law
- Distinguish between different types of law
- Explain the role of precedent
- Describe the role of regulatory authorities
- Explain the difference between compliance and audit
- Describe how security, privacy, and compliance fit together

# The American Legal System

The American legal system is composed of many distinct parts: federal and state governments, laws, and courts. Federal law exclusively governs some areas of the U.S. legal system; other areas depend on the subtle nuances of state law. Some parts of the legal system are based on written laws, called *statutes* or *codes*, which are developed by governments. Other areas of the law depend on principles developed from years of legal tradition and court decisions. There are two main types of laws. Civil law provides for the resolution of disputes between private individuals, organizations, or governments. Criminal law governs the prosecution of those charged with serious offenses against public order, such as murder.

The basis for the American system of government, and the American legal system, is the U.S. Constitution.

## Federal Government

The U.S. Constitution was ratified in 1789 and sets forth the structure of the U.S. federal government. Representatives from almost all of the states in existence at the time worked together to draft the Constitution. The state representatives realized that there were some areas in which a strong federal government was needed in order to keep the states united. However, the state representatives did not want a federal government that was too strong, nor did they want any one portion of the federal government to have too much power. These considerations help explain the current structure of the federal government.

The U.S. Constitution calls itself "the supreme Law of the Land."[1] It is the fundamental authority for the American federal system of government. The Constitution defines three co-equal roles in the federal government:

- Legislative
- Executive
- Judicial

**Eligibility Requirements for the President and Members of Congress**

The Constitution provides eligibility requirements for the president and members of Congress. The president must be a natural-born U.S. citizen and must be at least 35 years old. The president must have been a resident of the United States for at least 14 years at the time of election.[2]

Senators must be at least 30 years old. They must have been citizens of the United States for at least 9 years. They must also be residents of the state from which they are elected.[3]

House members must be at least 25 years old. They must have been citizens of the United States for at least 7 years. They must also be residents of the congressional district from which they are elected.[4]

The legislative branch makes the laws, the executive branch enforces the laws, and the judicial branch reviews the laws to make sure they are constitutional. This is the "checks and balances" system that describes the relationship among the three branches of the federal government. Each branch of government has a separate sphere of authority (balances). The actions of each branch of government are subject to review by the other branches (checks).



The U.S. Constitution also defines the relationship between the federal government and the states. At the time that the Constitution was drafted and ratified, people debated the appropriate relationship between the federal and state governments. The previous legal document that established the federal government, the Articles of Confederation, was too weak to keep the states joined together. However, an overly strong federal government was seen as an obstacle that would prevent states and individuals from controlling their own affairs. The states wanted to make sure that they retained the authority to control their own affairs. The Constitution contains specific provisions to reflect this divided authority.

The Constitution also provides some of the fundamental rights of individuals. Individual rights are located primarily in the Bill of Rights, which was ratified in 1791. The term *Bill of Rights* refers collectively to the first 10 amendments to the Constitution. These amendments are the basis for the personal rights that Americans hold most dear:

- Freedom of speech (First Amendment)
- Freedom of religion (First Amendment)
- Freedom from unreasonable search and seizure (Fourth Amendment)
- The right against self-incrimination (Fifth Amendment)

 **NOTE**

Rhode Island was the only original state that did not send representatives to the Constitutional Convention.

 **NOTE**

*Federalism* is a term that describes the relationship between the states and the U.S. federal government.

### *Legislative Branch*

The lawmaking authority of the legislative branch of the federal government is outlined in Article I, section 8 of the Constitution. Collectively, the legislative branch is called Congress. The federal government actually has limited lawmaking power. Congress cannot make any laws outside the scope that the Constitution specifically delegates to it.

The U.S. Congress consists of two chambers: the U.S. Senate and the U.S. House of Representatives. The Senate has 100 members, two senators from each state. In this way, the

Senate represents all states equally. The House of Representatives has 435 members. The House represents the population, as each Representative represents a congressional district. Congressional districts all have roughly the same number of people. The current number of people in each congressional district is 711,000. The congressional districts are redrawn after each decennial census and will next be redrawn after the 2020 census. Each state gets at least one representative no matter its total population size.

Article I, section 8 of the Constitution lists the powers delegated to Congress, which are very broad. Congress has the power to:

- Declare war
- Establish the post office
- Maintain armed forces
- Coin (or print) money
- Regulate commerce
- Make other laws necessary for carrying out its constitutional duties

The Commerce Clause grants Congress the power to regulate commerce between the states.[5] Congress uses this provision as justification to regulate trade, or any other commercial activity, between the states. Many Supreme Court cases have reviewed the limits of this power. In general, if an activity has the potential to affect the trade relations between the states, then Congress is able to legislate it.

Congress also has the power to enact laws that are "necessary and proper" for carrying out its duties.[6] Congress can use the power implied in this section to legislate in several different areas.

The Constitution specifies the basic lawmaking process. A *bill* is the initial draft of a potential law. Both chambers of Congress must approve the same bill, and the president must sign it before it becomes a law.[7]

The procedural documents of both chambers describe the process for moving bills through each chamber. Once a bill is introduced, it is generally assigned to a specialty committee. The bill is revised during the committee process, which usually includes hearings to determine why a law is needed in the first place. After the hearings, the committee votes on whether the bill should be sent to the full chamber for consideration. When a bill passes one chamber, it is forwarded to the other chamber for consideration.

> **NOTE**
>
> **Preemption** refers to the legal concept that means that a higher-ranking law will exclude or preempt a lower-ranking law on the same subject. This rule especially holds in the federal legislative context with respect to the Commerce Clause. States are preempted from making laws that may affect the trade relations between the states.

Once a bill passes both chambers, it goes to a *conference committee* made up of both senators and representatives. This committee reviews both the Senate and House of Representatives' versions of the bill. This committee cannot substantially change the bills being compared, but tries to reach a compromise on both versions of the bill. When the committee reaches a resolution on the bill, they report back to their respective chambers. Each chamber votes on the bill again. If the original conference committee cannot reach an agreement, the bill may be assigned to a new conference committee or go back into committees of each chamber for additional revisions.

The speaker of the House of Representatives and the president of the Senate sign all bills that pass in Congress before delivering them to the president. The president has 10 days to sign the bill. If the president does not sign it within 10 days, then it becomes law just as if the president had signed it.

### Executive Branch

Article II establishes the power of the executive branch of government. The president of the United States, a nationally elected official, leads the executive branch of government. The president is also the commander-in-chief of the U.S. armed forces and is often considered the "face" of the United States.

The president has the power to enforce the laws of the United States and the responsibility for maintaining the day-to-day operations of the U.S. government. The president also has the power to sign or veto any legislation that Congress passes. (Congress can then override a presidential veto with a two-thirds vote of both the House and the Senate.) Once the president signs the legislation, it becomes an *Act of Congress*, a federal law passed by the Congress and signed by the president.

The president also appoints federal judicial, executive, and administrative officials. The Senate must approve some of the president's appointees, such as Cabinet members or federal judicial appointees. The president also has the power to negotiate and enter into treaties with other countries. However, the U.S. Senate must ratify those treaties.

> **NOTE**
>
> Federal laws are published in the United States Code, which is published by the federal government every 6 years. The current version was published in 2018. You can find online versions of the code at https://uscode.house.gov/.

The role of the U.S. Cabinet is to advise the president. The Cabinet includes the U.S. vice president and the heads of 15 executive departments. President George Washington established the first Cabinet. Although the Constitution recognizes that the president should have advisers in executive departments, it does not specify the type or number of executive departments. Congress creates the executive departments.



### Judicial Branch

Article III of the Constitution establishes the judicial branch of the federal government. This Article vests the judicial power of the United States in one supreme court. The U.S. Supreme Court is the highest court in the country.

The U.S. Supreme Court is the only court specifically required by the U.S. Constitution. Congress has the authority to determine the actual number of Supreme Court justices; currently, there are nine. The president nominates the justices when there is a vacancy on the Court. The Senate must confirm the nomination. Supreme Court nominees are usually highly respected state or federal judges or highly respected attorneys.

Supreme Court justices, similar to all federal judges, are appointed for life. They serve until their retirement, death, or removal. Supreme Court justices can be removed only if they are impeached and convicted by Congress. The Constitution requires that all federal court judges be appointed for life for a simple reason: to help promote an independent judiciary. The drafters of the Constitution did not want the review of law to be dependent upon popular political ideas. Instead, they wanted federal judges appointed for life, so that they could not be fired if their decisions were unpopular or not favorable to a

**TABLE 3-1** Members of the U.S. Supreme Court as of January 2020.

| NAME | POSITION | APPOINTING PRESIDENT | DATE TERM BEGAN |
|---|---|---|---|
| John G. Roberts | Chief Justice | George W. Bush | September 2005 |
| Clarence Thomas | Associate Justice | George H. W. Bush | October 1991 |
| Ruth Bader Ginsburg | Associate Justice | Bill Clinton | August 1993 |
| Stephen Breyer | Associate Justice | Bill Clinton | August 1994 |
| Samuel Alito | Associate Justice | George W. Bush | January 2006 |
| Sonia Sotomayor | Associate Justice | Barack Obama | August 2009 |
| Elena Kagan | Associate Justice | Barack Obama | August 2010 |
| Neil Gorsuch | Associate Justice | Donald Trump | April 2017 |
| Brett Kavanaugh | Associate Justice | Donald Trump | October 2018 |

particular political party. **TABLE 3-1** lists the members of the U.S. Supreme Court as of January 2020.

**Structure of the Federal Judiciary.** It is important to understand how the different courts in the federal system relate to one another. Once this structure is understood, it can be applied generally to state judicial systems.

Courts have the ability to hear only *cases*, or disputes, that are within their jurisdiction. **Jurisdiction** describes the types of cases that a court has the authority to hear. There are three main types of jurisdiction used to describe the function of a court:

- **Original jurisdiction**—The power of a court to hear the initial dispute between parties. These courts conduct trials. Usually trial courts have **original jurisdiction**.
- **Concurrent jurisdiction**—Jurisdiction that is shared by several different courts.
- **Appellate jurisdiction**—The power of a court to review a decision made by a lower court.

In the federal court system, federal courts have *limited jurisdiction*. That means that they can hear only certain types of cases that fall within a limited subject matter. The jurisdiction of the federal courts is determined by the Constitution and laws made by Congress. Federal courts can hear only the following kinds of cases:

- Disputes regarding federal laws or constitutional issues
- Disputes between residents of different states where the amount of money in controversy is greater than $75,000[8]

A court cannot hear cases that fall outside its functional or subject matter jurisdiction.

In addition to establishing the Supreme Court, Article III of the Constitution also gives Congress the power to make as many lower-level federal courts as needed. Under this power, Congress has established district courts, appellate courts, and some specialized courts.

District courts are the lowest level of courts in the federal court system. There are 94 judicial districts in the United States, with each state having at least one judicial district. Some states may be divided into many judicial districts, and each district may have more than one judge. The number of judges in a district is determined by the number of cases, or caseload, in the district. Usually only one judge hears a case at the trial court level.

The district courts are the workhorses of the federal judicial system and serve as courts of original jurisdiction. They might hear disputes between parties or conduct criminal trials for violations of federal law. Each federal district court also has its own bankruptcy court. The Constitution gives the federal government the sole power over bankruptcy law.

The next level of courts is the intermediate appellate courts. In the federal system, these courts are called the U.S. Courts of Appeals. There are 13 Courts of Appeals. The 94 district courts are grouped into 12 geographical circuits. There is also one circuit, called the Federal Circuit, which hears cases from specialized courts. The Courts of Appeals hear appeals from the district courts in their circuit. For example, the Seventh Circuit Court of Appeals hears cases from Illinois, Indiana, and Wisconsin. The home for the Seventh Circuit is in Chicago, Illinois. The number of judges in each circuit is determined by Congress. These courts usually hear cases in three-judge panels.

**NOTE**

**Federal question jurisdiction** refers to the power of federal courts to hear only disputes about federal laws or constitutional issues. **Diversity of citizenship jurisdiction** refers to the power of federal courts to hear only disputes between citizens of different states that are above a certain dollar amount.



The Court of Appeals is a court of **appellate jurisdiction**. Courts of Appeals do not review the facts of a case, nor do they accept any additional evidence for the case. Instead, they review the record of the trial court only for mistakes of law.

The highest level of court in any judicial system, state or federal, is often called a "court of last resort." The highest court in the U.S. federal system is the U.S. Supreme Court, a court of appellate jurisdiction. For the most part, the Supreme Court decides cases on appeal from the U.S. Court of Appeals.

The Supreme Court reviews the decision of the lower court to make sure that it complies with the law. The Supreme Court is under no obligation to review a decision from the U.S. Court of Appeals. A party has to ask the Supreme Court to review the case by using a petition called a *writ of certiorari*, which the Supreme Court justices review. The Court usually approves the petition if four of the nine justices decide that the Court should look at the case. The Court might decide to hear a case if it presents a question of whether a federal law is unconstitutional. It also might decide to hear a case if two or more of the federal appellate courts have ruled differently on the same question of federal or U.S. Constitutional law.

The Supreme Court has exclusive original jurisdiction to decide cases about disputes between state governments. It exercises **concurrent jurisdiction** with federal district courts in some cases, and exercises this original jurisdiction very rarely. Most of the cases heard before the Supreme Court are appeals cases.

The Supreme Court has the power to decide cases that involve questions about the federal Constitution and other federal laws. It can review both state and federal laws to make sure that those laws do not conflict with the U.S. Constitution. The authority to review

FIGURE 3-1
Structure of the U.S. federal court system.

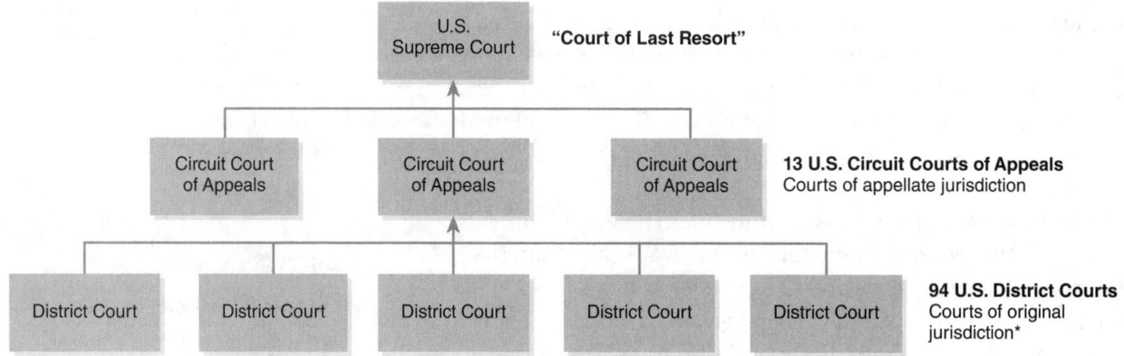


*This figure does not include the structure for special courts of limited jurisdiction.

> **NOTE**
>
> In the law, an *appeal* is a formal request for a higher authority to review the decision of a lower court. Any party who is unhappy with the judgment received in a district court can appeal to the Court of Appeals for that district. The unhappy party must be able to show that the trial court made a legal error that affected the *holding*, or decision, in the case.

laws in this way is called **judicial review**. The Supreme Court is the final authority on cases heard in the federal court system; as such, the decisions of the U.S. Supreme Court cannot be appealed. **FIGURE 3-1** shows the structure of the U.S. federal court system.

## State Government

In negotiating and drafting the U.S. Constitution, state governments gave up some of their own power in order to create the federal government. They did this because the first system of government after the American Revolution that was organized under the Articles of Confederation did not work. That document did not create a national government that could require unity on subjects of common interest. The U.S. Constitution changed that relationship.

Under the Constitution, powers that are not specifically granted to the federal government in the Constitution remain with the states. The Tenth Amendment to the Constitution formalized this relationship. The Tenth Amendment says, "The powers not delegated to the United States by the Constitution, nor prohibited by it to the States, are reserved to the States respectively, or to the people."[9]

State governments existed before the federal government as we know it today. Similar to the federal government, most states are organized under a constitution, which may vary widely from the U.S. Constitution. Although the federal Constitution primarily describes the relationship between the federal government and the states, state constitutions primarily describe the relationship between a state and its citizens. For this reason, state constitutions often list many more individual rights than are listed in the federal Constitution. State constitutions also tend to be longer than the federal Constitution. Finally, state constitutions are generally easier to change than the federal Constitution.

There are typically three branches to most state governments, roughly aligned in the same manner as the federal government. Most state legislatures resemble the legislative branch of the federal government and have two different legislative chambers. A governor leads the state executive branch.

State governments have the general authority to govern and make laws for the state and its citizens. However, this power is not absolute. The federal Supremacy Clause limits this broad power to make laws.[10]

The Supremacy Clause sets forth the rule that the federal Constitution, treaties, and federal law outrank any conflicting state laws. This clause means that the U.S. Constitution and federal laws are the highest laws in the land and states must follow the federal laws. The clause permits states to make their own laws only so long as those laws do not conflict with the U.S. Constitution or other federal laws. Because the U.S. Constitution limits the federal government in the types of laws that it can enact, there are still plenty of areas for state governments to legislate.

**NOTE**

The State of Alabama is widely recognized as having the longest state constitution. It has 799 amendments. The current constitution, adopted in 1901, is the state's sixth constitution.

Most states have a judicial system that looks similar to the federal system, with a system of trial courts, appellate courts, and courts of last resort. The trial courts, the original jurisdiction courts for a state, are organized by geographical location, with county-level courts being the typical entry-level courts for hearing most disputes. Trial courts have the general authority to hear all sorts of cases, but they are usually limited to hearing disputes between citizens of the state.

**NOTE**

Only the state of Nebraska has a *unicameral legislature*, meaning it has only one legislative chamber. All other states have a *bicameral legislature*, meaning they have two chambers. The U.S. Congress is a bicameral legislature.

States usually have two appellate courts: a state intermediate appellate court and a state supreme court. States usually only have one type of each court. The intermediate appellate courts hear appeals from the trial courts, whereas the state supreme court hears appeals from the appellate court. It is important to remember that not all states have the exact same structure, even though you can draw parallels when discussing structure in general. These courts may go by different names in different states. For example, the highest court in New York is called the New York Court of Appeals. In many states, the *court of appeals* is the intermediate appellate court. **FIGURE 3-2** shows the general structure of a state court system.

The relationship between the state and federal court systems is very interesting. The U.S. Supreme Court has complete authority over courts in the federal system. It also has complete authority over interpretations of federal law and the U.S. Constitution. However, the Supreme Court has no authority over the organization or procedures used by state courts. The Supreme Court may not interpret issues that rely solely on state law or issues arising under state constitutions. Only the highest court in a state is allowed to make interpretations about that state's law.

Federal and state courts do not exist in separate spheres. State courts do have the power and authority to review cases that concern issues of constitutional or federal law.

FIGURE 3-2

General structure of the U.S. state court system.

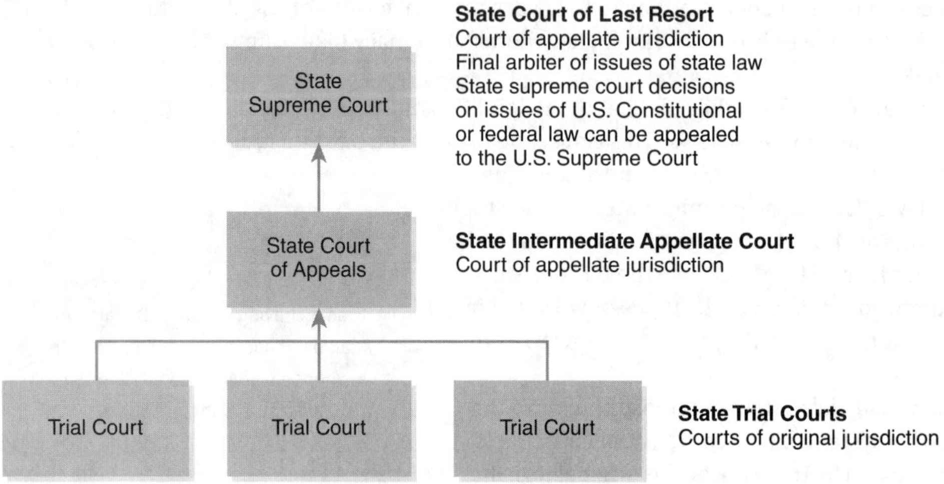


**TABLE 3-2** A Comparison of the Federal and State Judicial Systems

| | STATE JUDICIAL SYSTEM | FEDERAL JUDICIAL SYSTEM |
|---|---|---|
| **Courts of Original Jurisdiction** | Trial courts | U.S. District Courts |
| **Courts of Appellate Jurisdiction** | Intermediate appellate courts | Circuit Courts of Appeal |
| **Courts of Last Resort** | State supreme court | U.S. Supreme Court |
| **Scope of Authority** | General authority to hear all disputes; authority is limited to disputes involving state citizens | Cases must involve a federal question or involve disputes between citizens of different states and be over $75,000 |
| **Authority of Court of Last Resort** | Final, unless the case involves a federal question; if so, case can be appealed to U.S. Supreme Court | Final |

However, the state courts must yield to the superiority and previous decisions of the Supreme Court when doing so. The U.S. Supreme Court can review a state court case in the event that the case concerns a question of federal law or a federal constitutional issue. **TABLE 3-2** compares the federal judicial system with a generic state judicial system.

## Sources of American Law

The law is not secret, but it is complex. Many of the processes and procedures in the law have evolved over time. They are a combination of the will of the federal and state governments, longstanding traditions about right and wrong, and society's values. It is no wonder that finding out what law applies to a particular situation is sometimes puzzling.

This chapter has already discussed several sources of law:

- U.S. Constitutional law
- U.S. federal law
- State constitutional law
- State laws

Now it is time to put these sources in context for the American legal system. This next section discusses the general sources of law and how they relate to one another.

### Common Law

The common law is a body of law that is developed through legal tradition and court cases. The U.S. common law is a body of law and legal principles inherited from England that changes very slowly—it develops as judges decide court cases. Therefore, it is sometimes also known as *case law* or *judge-made law*.

In the common law, courts decide cases by referring to established legal principles and the customs and values of society. They also look at decisions made in earlier cases to see if the cases are similar. If the cases are similar, a new case should reach a similar result. Finally, formal principles of logic and reason are used to help reach a decision when the result is unclear.

Parties arguing a common law case use a similar approach. Attorneys may argue that the customs and values of society have changed such that a new result is appropriate. Attorneys also may attempt to distinguish the facts of the current case from the facts of earlier cases. In all instances, attorneys must use logic and reason to form the basis for their arguments.

The American legal system generally follows the common law tradition. Many countries colonized by the English have adopted similar systems. After the Revolutionary War, common law grew in America and was heavily influenced by "new" American social and economic values. The common law has continued to evolve, and judicial decisions continue to influence it. The development of the common law continues so long as its decisions and conclusions are not in conflict with other laws, such as constitutional documents or state and federal statutes.

Common law principles are often included within the code law of the federal or state government. An example of this is privacy torts. There are four privacy torts that came to be recognized as torts through the evolution of common law. Courts gradually heard cases regarding issues related to the subject matter area of these torts. As they heard the cases, some courts would recognize the tort and allow the cause of action. Some would not. Gradually, many states adopted the four privacy torts and some states have even written the torts into their statutes.

In the United States, the common law continues to be very influential in civil law areas such as torts, contract law, and property law.

## Code Law

**Code law** is law that is enacted by legislatures. It is also sometimes called *statutory law*. This is the written law that is adopted by governments. In its truest form, code law attempts to state the complete system of law for a state or federal government. Citizens and members of the legal profession are all bound by the terms of the written law.

In the United States, the common law and code law work together in most states to form the laws that society must follow. There has been a strong movement within the law to codify the common law. This is to help make sure that citizens understand the law. Many states have codified their common law criminal principles into written law. Some states also have codified parts of their civil (noncriminal) laws. Once a code or statute provision is made that addresses the common law, it supersedes the common law in that area. The principles and traditions of common law are transformed into a code of laws.

**NOTE**

No discussion of the law would be complete without a Latin phrase or two. Code law is called *lex scripta*, meaning law that is written down. Common law is called *lex non scripta*, meaning law that is not written down.

## Constitutional Law

The U.S. Constitution is the final source of authority for issues involving U.S. federal laws. When federal laws are disputed, they are subject to scrutiny to determine whether the law is constitutional. If the law is not constitutional, it is invalid. If the law is constitutional, then it is the source of authority for its particular subject matter.

Similarly, state constitutions are the final source of authority for issues involving state law. So long as the state constitutional provision itself is not in conflict with the U.S. Constitution or federal law, then it will be the final decision on state laws. If a state law is constitutional (under both the state and, if challenged, U.S. Constitution), then it is the source of state authority for its particular subject.

**NOTE**

Louisiana is the only state that does not base its law on common law principles. Instead, the laws of the state are based upon the Napoleonic Code, which is the French civil code.

## How Does It All Fit Together?

The American legal system contains many different levels of written (codified) and unwritten (uncodified) laws. This is why it is sometimes hard to figure out what the "law" is with respect to a new situation. When an attorney or judge has to analyze the law that applies to a certain situation, he or she applies the rules of statutory construction for looking at an issue. The rules of statutory construction generally mean that the laws of the legislature (code law) are given greater deference than the laws of the courts (common law). If codes are in conflict with the common law, then the text of the code should control the outcome of the case. The problem in analysis occurs when a code has ambiguous terms.

When reviewing a legal issue, an attorney or court might start by first reviewing whether the issue involves a question that can be answered by the U.S. Constitution or a state constitution. If the legal issue involves a question of federal law, the U.S. Constitution is the first authority that should be consulted. The same principle applies for questions of state law.

If the legal issue cannot be resolved by looking at constitutional laws, the next step is to look at the code law. For federal issues, federal statutes would be reviewed. For state issues, state statutes would be reviewed. The attorney or court will look to see that the issue fits clearly within the scope of the code law. If the issue is clearly resolved by looking at code, then the analysis is complete.

When the issue cannot be resolved by looking at the code, attorneys and lawyers turn to the common law to find the guidance needed to resolve the case. For federal issues, federal common law doctrine and federal court cases need to be reviewed. For state issues, state common law doctrines and court cases need to be reviewed. Key in the review of common law is the influential role of precedent, which is discussed later in this chapter.

**NOTE**

Legal issues are rarely resolved simply by looking at statutes. If they were, there would be little need for attorneys or courts. Often a statute is poorly written. For example, its terms and provisions could be ambiguous or open to interpretation. Sometimes statute writers simply do not anticipate the legal issue that is being considered. Attorneys and courts are needed to resolve ambiguities and new legal issues.

## Types of Law

The legal system usually distinguishes between **procedural law** and **substantive law**. Substantive law is also known as subject matter law. Subject matter areas of law are areas in which an attorney might specialize. For instance, contract law, tort law, elder law, and intellectual property law are just some of the many different subject matter areas within the study of law. Attorneys often choose to specialize in a particular area of law simply because there are so many areas of study within the law.

This section discusses the different types of procedural law. Procedural law deals with the processes that courts use to decide cases. Procedural areas of the law are designated to ensure **due process**, which means that all parties in a case are entitled to a fair and consistent process within the courts. There are three types of procedural law:

- Criminal
- Civil
- Administrative



### Civil

**Civil procedure** deals with the procedures and processes that courts use to conduct civil trials. Civil trials concern claims between individuals. Substantive areas of law such as contract law and property law are civil law areas. The parties in these types of cases must follow civil procedure rules when bringing disputes to court.

In the federal courts, a case begins when a complaint is filed with the court. A *complaint* is a court document that sets forth the names of the parties and the facts and legal claims. This is how a lawsuit begins.

In the federal system, the rules outlining the civil trial process are found in the Federal Rules of Civil Procedure. These rules are made by the Supreme Court and approved by Congress. State courts also have rules for how civil trials are conducted. Often state rules are based upon the Federal Rules of Civil Procedure. These rules were last updated in 2018.

**NOTE**

The rules for civil procedure can be complicated. The Federal Rules of Civil Procedure has 86 regular rules (not including special rules for admiralty or maritime claims).

Most civil trial cases must be proven by a **preponderance of the evidence**. This is the lowest level of proof in a civil case. Preponderance of the evidence means that it is more probable than not that an action (or wrong) took place. Although it is simplistic to express this standard as a percentage, preponderance of the evidence means the probability of an action taking place is greater than 50 percent. Some civil cases, such as actions to terminate parental rights, use the "clear and convincing evidence" standard. To meet this standard, a party must convince a court that it is more likely than not that an action (or wrong) took place.

## Criminal

**Criminal procedure** deals with the rules that courts follow in criminal law cases. It also includes the processes for investigating and punishing crimes. The federal and state governments have criminal codes. These codes specify the actions that constitute a *crime*.

Crimes are wrongs against society and are prosecuted by the government against an alleged wrongdoer. The federal or state official with the power to pursue criminal cases is called a *prosecutor*.

In the federal system, the rules outlining the criminal trial process are called the Federal Rules of Criminal Procedure. State courts also have rules for how criminal trials are conducted. Most states have rules that are modeled after the federal rules. Most criminal law cases are tried in front of a jury, which decides questions of fact. The judge's role is to watch over the proceedings and decide questions of law.

The standard of proof for most criminal cases is **beyond a reasonable doubt**. This is the highest level of persuasion that a prosecutor must meet. This burden is met when a prosecutor proves to a jury that there can be no reasonable doubt in the mind of a reasonable person that a defendant is guilty. The reasonable doubt standard does not mean that the reasonable juror is 100 percent convinced that a defendant is guilty. It does mean, however, that a juror must be fully satisfied that reasonable doubt has been eliminated.

### Burdens of Proof in the O.J. Simpson Trials

The different burdens of proof for different types of cases can be confusing. The O.J. Simpson criminal and civil trials best illustrate the basic difference between criminal and civil law.

In June 1994, Nicole Brown Simpson and Ronald Goldman were murdered. Five days later O.J. Simpson was arrested for those murders. Simpson pleaded "not guilty" to the charges in late July 1994. In October 1995, a criminal jury announced that it found O.J. Simpson "not guilty" of the murders.

In May 1995, the Goldman family and Nicole Brown Simpson's estate filed civil wrongful death actions against O.J. Simpson. In February 1997, the civil jury found Simpson liable for the deaths of Ronald Goldman and Nicole Brown Simpson. Finding a defendant liable in a civil case is the rough equivalent of a guilty finding in a criminal case. It means that the defendant is held responsible for the action that is complained about.

O.J. Simpson was found "not guilty" of murder in the criminal case, but he was found liable in the civil case. The reason for the apparently inconsistent results is that the murder case was tried in the criminal system and the wrongful death case was a civil action. There are different burdens of proof in each system.

A government has such a high burden of proof to meet in criminal cases because a criminal penalty usually includes jail time, financial penalties, or even a death sentence. These penalties infringe on fundamental rights to liberty, property, and life. Therefore, a government may impose these penalties only with very strong proof that a person has committed the crime.

## Administrative

**Administrative procedure** sets forth the process under which administrative agencies make and enforce rules. The federal government and most states delegate some regulatory and enforcement functions to administrative agencies. Governments delegate some of these functions in very detailed ways and for very specific reasons. When governments delegate power in this way, it is possible to have an agency that creates rules (a legislative function), enforces rules (an executive function), and reviews rules (a judicial power). Agency power is a combination of the power of all three branches of government.

The actions of these agencies are the focus of administrative procedure. Because these agencies are carrying out a function of the government, there must be processes put in place to ensure that all persons appearing before agencies are dealt with in a fair and consistent manner. At the federal government level, the Administrative Procedure Act (1946) helps define the federal administrative process. This act states the procedures for agency rulemaking, enforcement, and review.

The Administrative Procedure Act also allows U.S. federal courts to review agency decisions. There is a different burden of proof for administrative cases. In these cases, an administrative decision is valid so long as it is not "arbitrary and capricious" or an abuse of the law. An arbitrary and capricious decision is one made without a reasonable connection between the facts of the case and the administrative outcome.

**FIGURE 3-3** shows the burden-of-proof hierarchy in administrative, civil, and criminal cases.



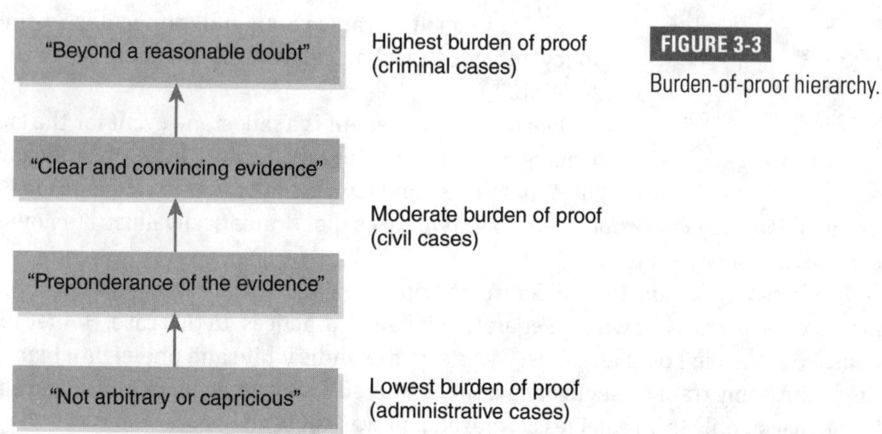


**FIGURE 3-3**
Burden-of-proof hierarchy.

## The Role of Precedent

The doctrine of **precedent** is one of the most important traditions in the American legal system. This doctrine means that courts will look at the decisions made in prior cases to determine the appropriate resolution for new cases.

For example, the U.S. Supreme Court has the power to decide cases that involve questions about the federal Constitution and other federal laws. The Supreme Court is the final authority on cases heard in the federal court system. If other, lower courts in the federal system have a new case that concerns an issue that the Supreme Court has already addressed, those lower courts are required to follow the law as it was interpreted by the Supreme Court. State courts also must follow the decisions of the U.S. Supreme Court to the extent that the state court is reviewing issues that include U.S. constitutional or federal law.

> **NOTE**
>
> A *case of first impression* is a case for which there is no precedent. These cases raise a legal issue that has never before been decided.

The doctrine of precedent also is referred to as the doctrine of *stare decisis*, which means "to stand by things decided" in Latin. *Stare decisis* means that lower courts must follow the decisions of the court above it so long as those decisions are relevant to the case that the lower court is deciding.

Without precedent and its related concepts, there can be no predictability in the law. Precedent makes the law stable. The U.S. Supreme Court has recognized the value of precedent numerous times. In 1932, Justice Louis Brandeis stressed the importance of precedent when he wrote, "*Stare decisis* is usually the wise policy, because in most matters it is more important that the applicable rule of law be settled than that it be settled right."[11] Precedent is used to ensure that laws are fairly and consistently applied.

The doctrine of precedent is not absolute. Precedent can change when it is apparent that society's values on a particular issue have changed. Precedent also can change when a high court finds that the application of precedent is unreasonable. In *Payne v. Tennessee* (1991), Chief Justice William Rehnquist wrote, "Adhering to precedent is usually the wise policy, because, in most matters, it is more important that the applicable rule of law be settled than it be settled right. Nevertheless, when governing decisions are unworkable or are badly reasoned, this Court has never felt constrained to follow precedent. *Stare decisis* is not an inexorable command; rather, it is a principle of policy and not a mechanical formula of adherence to the latest decision."[12]

> **NOTE**
>
> A *landmark court decision* is a decision that establishes new precedent. Landmark cases can significantly change how the legal system views and interprets the law. Many of the cases discussed in this book are landmark cases.

Overturning precedent is a milestone event for the law because it changes established legal principles. In essence, it changes the rules that judges and lawyers follow. *Plessy v. Ferguson* (1896) and *Brown v. Board of Education* (1954) are two cases that dramatically illustrate how precedent changes as society evolves.

In *Plessy v. Ferguson*, the U.S. Supreme Court legalized racial segregation practices. These practices also were known as "separate but equal" practices. In this case, Homer Plessy boarded a train in Louisiana. Plessy was seven-eighths white and one-eighth black. He sat in the whites-only train car. Louisiana law considered Plessy to be black and required him to sit in the blacks-only train car. Plessy refused and was subsequently arrested.

In *Plessy*, the plaintiff argued that these separate but equal practices violated the Fourteenth Amendment of the U.S. Constitution. The Fourteenth Amendment requires that all citizens be provided equal protection under law. In its decision, the Court held that separate but equal practices, such as having train cars segregated based upon race, were not inherently unequal. The Court stated that these practices did not violate the U.S. Constitution. For almost 60 years, "separate but equal" was the law. The court's ruling was used to justify several discriminatory "Jim Crow" segregation laws used throughout the United States that segregated blacks and whites in schools, restaurants, restrooms, and public transportation. These laws were challenged again in the 1954 case, *Brown v. Board of Education*.

The *Brown* case was a consolidation of five different cases from four different states that all addressed the same issue: racial segregation in public schools. In *Brown*, the plaintiffs argued that "separate but equal" practices were inherently unfair. They argued that in reality these practices perpetuated the inferior treatment of blacks and had a negative impact on black Americans. Plaintiffs, represented by the National Association for the Advancement of Colored People (NAACP), challenged the Court to overrule the precedent set in *Plessy v. Ferguson*.

In *Brown*, a unanimous U.S. Supreme Court reversed its holding in *Plessy*. In *Brown*, Chief Justice Warren wrote, "We conclude that, in the field of public education, the doctrine of 'separate but equal' has no place. Separate educational facilities are inherently unequal. Therefore, we hold that the plaintiffs and others similarly situated for whom the actions have been brought are, by reason of the segregation complained of, deprived of the equal protection of the laws guaranteed by the Fourteenth Amendment."[13]

The *Brown* decision was remarkable because the Court departed from the precedent set in *Plessy*. In fact, the Court specifically rejected the reasoning that it had used to support its decision in *Plessy*. *Brown* established new legal precedent, that separate but equal laws are unconstitutional.



## Regulatory Authorities

As discussed in the administrative procedure section, the federal government delegates some regulatory and enforcement functions to administrative agencies, typically subject matter expert agencies. These delegations are made because it would be impossible for Congress to make timely laws in some of the many different areas that are regulated by the federal government.

According to the federal Administrative Procedure Act, an *agency* is any government authority besides Congress and the courts. Federal agencies fall under the executive branch of the government and are used to help carry out the day-to-day activities of the government. Agencies may have many different functions. For example, many of the laws in the United States are actually administered by regulatory agencies. These agencies create rules, enforce compliance, and hand out sanctions within their specified area.

The president usually has the responsibility for overseeing the federal agencies. Federal agencies also can be created under other federal agencies. For instance, the U.S. Department of Agriculture oversees several different federal agencies.

**NOTE**

The oldest federal law enforcement agency is typically recognized as the U.S. Marshals Service, which was formed in 1789.

Congress also can create independent agencies that report directly to it. One such independent federal agency is the Federal Trade Commission (FTC). Its mission is to promote consumer protection and eliminate practices that are harmful to competitive business in many areas of the economy. The FTC, created in 1914 under the Federal Trade Commission Act, is one of the most important regulatory authorities for consumer and some business practices issues, including online business practices.

The FTC reports to Congress on its actions. The FTC is led by five commissioners, who each serve a 7-year term. The commissioners are nominated by the president and confirmed by the Senate. The president also chooses one commissioner to act as chairman. To maintain the independence of the Commission, no more than three commissioners can belong to the same political party. The FTC has seven regional offices across the United States.

Most federal agencies have the ability to make rules. The rulemaking authority of the FTC is described in the Federal Trade Commission Act, which states that the FTC can make "rules which define with specificity acts or practices which are unfair or deceptive acts or practices in or affecting commerce."[14] The Act states the process for how the rules are made. After the FTC makes a rule, anyone who violates the rule can be sanctioned by the FTC.

Regulatory authorities provide another type of law that must be considered when thinking about the American legal system. These administrative agencies have the power to create and enforce regulations that are considered equal to the law passed by the federal government. Individuals and organizations can be subject to penalties for violating agency rules.

## What Is the Difference Between Compliance and Audit?

People often get *compliance* and *audit* confused, so it is helpful to understand these terms because you will encounter them often. Audit and compliance are often associated with legal activities, which is why they are included in this chapter.

In the legal system, **compliance** is the action of following applicable laws and rules and regulations. Generally speaking, for an organization compliance involves not only following laws and regulations, but also following the organization's own policies and procedures. Compliance must be documented. With respect to law, it is not enough to *say* that an organization is compliant. The organization must *prove* that it is compliant.

Processes that might be used to demonstrate compliance include:

- Creating policies or other organizational governance documents to comply with legal or regulatory requirements
- Comparing compliance requirements against an organization's daily practices, and modifying those practices as needed
- Developing and implementing monitoring systems in computer systems to alert the organization if security measures required by law or regulation are compromised
- Creating training and awareness activities that educate employees about compliance requirements

Compliance not only includes the actual state of being compliant, but it also includes the steps and processes taken to become compliant. Compliance usually asks the questions:

"What are the rules?" and "How must the rules be followed?" Compliance is demonstrated daily through processes and procedures.

Audit is separate from compliance. An **audit** is an evaluation and verification that certain objectives are met. An audit can review laws, rules, regulations, policies, and procedures to ensure that an organization is complying with stated requirements. Audit looks at the processes that are put in place to meet compliance objectives and makes sure that those processes are accurate and are actually followed.

Audits may occasionally be performed by independent organizations. An organization also can have an internal audit function that ensures that organizations are following its internal policies and procedures.

An audit is an inspection at a fixed point in time. In the truest sense of the word, audits do not take place daily. An audit usually asks the questions: "Are the rules being followed?" and "How are the rules being followed?"

Sometimes it is helpful to consider an example. Under the FTC's Red Flags Rule,[15] for instance, a covered organization is required to have a written identity theft prevention program. The program that is developed must provide for the identification, detection, and response to activities that could indicate identity theft.

The compliance functions that must be met include:

- Identify activities that could indicate identity theft.
- Determine how the organization will detect such activities.
- Determine how the organization will respond to such activities.
- Create a written identity theft prevention program.
- Educate employees about their responsibilities in the identity theft prevention program.

The questions that would be verified in an audit include:

- Did the organization properly identify activities that could indicate identity theft?
- Did the organization properly determine how it will detect such activities?
- Are the organization's responses to activities appropriate to prevent identity theft?
- Did the organization create a written identity theft program?
- Was the identity theft program approved by management?
- Are employees meeting their responsibilities under the identity theft prevention program?

Compliance is demonstrated by the processes and procedures that an organization uses to meet the law. Audit verifies that those processes and procedures actually do satisfy the legal requirements.

## How Do Security, Privacy, and Compliance Fit Together?

Security, privacy, and compliance issues form a complicated web. Information security is the practice of protecting information to ensure the goals of confidentiality, integrity, and availability. Information security makes sure that accurate information is available to authorized individuals when it is needed.

**NOTE**

Compliance requirements are often understood as the minimum level of action that a person or organization must take to meet legal or regulatory requirements. However, nothing prevents a person or organization from creating good information security or privacy practices that exceed legal minimum requirements. In fact, having good practices that exceed the minimum requirements set in applicable law or regulations is often seen as a competitive advantage.

In contrast, privacy encompasses people's right to have control of their personal data. Privacy means that a person has the right to specify how his or her data is collected, used, and shared. Information security practices can be used to make sure that a person's privacy decisions are respected.

Organizations do not always do a good job of either information security or protecting privacy. For that reason, laws are enacted that force organizations to take a more structured approach to information security and privacy. To date, there have been no laws enacted in the United States that comprehensively address information security or data privacy. Instead, laws are made to protect certain types of information on an industry basis, such as laws regulating health data for the healthcare industry. Organizations that hold or process those types of information must follow the relevant laws. This text discusses some of these laws in the following chapters.

When laws addressing information security or data privacy are enacted, organizations impacted by these laws must take actions to meet them. If an organization fails to meet its obligations, it can be subject to sanctions. Compliance is the action of following the applicable laws and rules and regulations. Compliance efforts are supported by documenting organizational controls and enhancing the capabilities of information systems to ensure information security.

## CHAPTER SUMMARY

The American legal system, its history, and its processes regulate our behavior and contribute to an ordered society. Laws evolve over time. The American legal system is a reflection of the laws imposed by federal and state governments, longstanding traditions about right and wrong, and society's values.

Individuals and organizations must follow laws, rules, and regulations. Regulatory compliance is influencing security and privacy practices. Organizations must take a more structured approach to addressing information security and privacy issues in order to meet their compliance requirements.

## KEY CONCEPTS AND TERMS

Administrative procedure
Appellate jurisdiction
Audit
Beyond a reasonable doubt
Civil procedure
Code law
Compliance
Concurrent jurisdiction
Criminal procedure
Diversity of citizenship jurisdiction
Due process
Federal question jurisdiction
Judicial review
Jurisdiction
Original jurisdiction
Precedent
Preemption
Preponderance of the evidence
Procedural law
Substantive law

## CHAPTER 3 ASSESSMENT

1. What is the U.S. federal court of last resort?
   A. The U.S. Supremacy Court
   B. The U.S. District Court
   C. The Ninth Circuit Court of Appeals
   D. The Federal Court of Appeals
   E. The U.S. Supreme Court

2. What is judicial review?
   A. The power of courts to review the decisions of other courts
   B. The power of courts to review laws
   C. The power of the president to review the decisions of the courts
   D. The power of Congress to review the decisions of the courts
   E. A variety show featuring people in wigs and black robes

3. What is appellate jurisdiction?
   A. The power of some courts to review the decisions of others
   B. The power of courts to resolve disputes between individuals
   C. The process by which courts conduct civil trials
   D. The process by which courts conduct criminal trials
   E. The power of courts to declare a law unconstitutional

4. What article of the U.S. Constitution sets forth the powers of the president?
   A. Article V
   B. Article IV
   C. Article III
   D. Article II
   E. Article I

5. What is a case of first impression?
   A. The first case that court hears when it is in session
   B. A case that changes established precedent
   C. A case for which there is no established precedent
   D. A case that is appealed
   E. None of these is correct.

6. The Federal Trade Commission is which type of federal agency?
   A. Independent
   B. Subordinate
   C. Coordinate
   D. Executive
   E. Congressional

7. The doctrine of precedent is also known as ______.

8. What is procedural law?
   A. Branches of law that deal with property cases
   B. Branches of law that set forth the structure of the judiciary system
   C. Branches of law that deal with following precedent
   D. Branches of law that deal with processes that courts use to decide cases
   E. None of these is correct.

9. What is common law?
   A. A system of law inherited from England
   B. A system of law inherited from France
   C. A system of law that relies upon established legal principles and traditions
   D. A system of law inherited from France and a system of law that relies upon established legal principles and traditions
   E. A system of law inherited from England and a system of law that relies upon established legal principles and traditions

10. Compliance is ______, audit is ______.
    A. Following the rules, verifying that the rules were followed
    B. Verifying that the rules were followed, following the rules
    C. Making the rules, enforcing the rules
    D. Enforcing the rules, making the rules
    E. None of these is correct.

11. A federal agency is granted its authority by ______.

**12.** Which U.S. Constitution clause describes Congress' authority to regulate trade between states?

A. The Supremacy Clause
B. The Necessary and Proper Clause
C. The Limitation of Powers Clause
D. The Commerce Clause
E. The Impeachment Clause

**13.** The U.S. Supreme Court has ______ justices.

**14.** How many representatives are in the U.S. House of Representatives?

A. 100
B. 1,000
C. 435
D. 400
E. 50

**15.** There are ______ federal district courts.

## ENDNOTES

1. U.S. Constitution, article VI.
2. U.S. Constitution, article II, sec. 1.
3. U.S. Constitution, article I, sec. 3.
4. U.S. Constitution, article I, sec. 2.
5. U.S. Constitution, article I, sec. 8, cl. 3.
6. U.S. Constitution, article I, sec. 8, cl. 18.
7. An entire generation of Americans learned about the lawmaking process from *Schoolhouse Rock!*, which was a series of animated educational videos about basic topics. You can watch the "I'm Just a Bill" video on YouTube at: https://youtu.be/FFroMQlKiag.
8. U.S. Code Vol. 28, sec. 1332.
9. U.S. Constitution, amendment X.
10. U.S. Constitution, article VI, sec. 2.
11. *Burnet v. Coronado Oil & Gas Co.*, 285 U.S. 393, 406 (1932) (Justice Louis Brandeis dissenting).
12. *Payne v. Tennessee,* 501 U.S. 808, 809 (1991) (internal citations and punctuation omitted).
13. *Brown v. Board of Education,* 347 U.S. 483, 495 (1954).
14. Federal Trade Commission Act (1914), U.S. Code Vol. 15, sec. 57a (2006).
15. *Identity Theft Red Flags Rule,* Code of Federal Regulations, Title 16, sec. 681.2.

# PART II

# Laws Influencing Information Security

CHAPTER 4 Security and Privacy of Consumer Financial Information 87

CHAPTER 5 Security and Privacy of Information Belonging to Children and in Educational Records 115

CHAPTER 6 Security and Privacy of Health Information 139

CHAPTER 7 Corporate Information Security and Privacy Regulation 175

CHAPTER 8 Federal Government Information Security and Privacy Regulations 201

CHAPTER 9 State Laws Protecting Citizen Information and Breach Notification Laws 225

CHAPTER 10 Intellectual Property Laws 249

CHAPTER 11 The Role of Contracts 285

CHAPTER 12 Criminal Law and Tort Law Issues in Cyberspace 317

CHAPTER 4

# Security and Privacy of Consumer Financial Information

IDENTITY THEFT IS a rapidly growing crime. Consumer financial information is a gold mine for an identity thief, who can use this information to establish a new identity. Identity theft victims spend time and money repairing damage caused by identity thieves to restore their good name and their credit. Identity theft is a crime that can have a large impact on a person's financial situation.

Banks and other financial institutions use consumer financial information when they conduct business with their customers. This information is valuable and must be protected. The 2019 Verizon Data Breach Investigation Report stated 71 percent of the data breaches that it analyzed were motivated by financial gain. The financial industry is one of the top industries targeted.[1] This chapter focuses on the laws and regulations that financial institutions must follow to protect the security and privacy of consumer financial information.

## Chapter 4 Topics

This chapter covers the following topics and concepts:

- What the business challenges facing financial institutions are
- What the different types of financial institutions are and who regulates them
- What consumer financial information is
- What the Gramm-Leach-Bliley Act is
- What the Federal Trade Commission Red Flags Rule is
- What the Payment Card Industry Standards are
- What some case studies and examples are

## Chapter 4 Goals

When you complete this chapter, you will be able to:

- Describe the business challenges facing financial institutions
- Define a financial institution and consumer financial information

- Explain the main information security and privacy protections of the Gramm-Leach-Bliley Act
- Describe the Federal Trade Commission Red Flags Rule
- Describe the Payment Card Industry Standards

## Business Challenges Facing Financial Institutions

Media reports about financial institutions experiencing a data breach are not unusual:

- In 2019, Capital One reported a data breach involving sensitive information from over 100 million people. The hacker was a former employee at a cloud computing company used by Capital One.
- Equifax, a national credit reporting agency, reported a data breach in 2017. Hackers stole Social Security numbers (SSNs) and other personal information of 143 million Americans.
- In 2013, U.S. authorities arrested seven people who were part of a hacking network that targeted financial institutions around the world. The thieves used the data that they stole to withdraw over $45 million in cash from ATMs around the world.
- Heartland Payment Systems reported that hackers accessed its computer systems in late 2008. This company processed 100 million payroll and credit card payments per month for more than 250,000 businesses. The hackers might have had access to the system for a couple of weeks. The company reported over $170 million in losses from the breach.[2]
- A Wyoming bank employee accidentally sent an electronic file to an incorrect email address in 2009. The file contained the personal information of 1,300 bank customers.

**NOTE**

Although definitions may vary slightly, a *mega-breach* is a data breach affecting more than 10 million people.

Financial institutions collect and use sensitive consumer financial information and face many challenges in protecting this data. These challenges come from external threats such as hackers, as well as from insiders, and include malicious and nonmalicious actions. Scams that target financial institution customers include:

- Phishing scams designed to steal banking account credentials
- Identity theft schemes that borrow money or pass counterfeit checks in the victim's name
- Mortgage foreclosure scams designed to defraud customers of money
- Investment scams with high-pressure sales tactics
- Tax scams from attackers demanding money for overdue taxes

Consumers demand that financial institutions protect their data and their money. They also want financial institutions to protect them from financial harm if this data is disclosed or stolen.

Consumers are not the only victims of identity theft. Financial institutions become identity theft victims when thieves use a consumer's financial information to do business with the institution. Identity thieves can open bank accounts in the victim's name and write bad checks, create counterfeit checks to use on a victim's account, or take out loans in the victim's name. Many bank rules and regulations force financial institutions to bear the cost of many of these actions. A recent study estimated that the global banking industry had over $18 million in cybercrime-related costs in 2018.[3]

The financial industry is highly regulated. These institutions must follow regulations designed to protect the security and privacy of data that they collect and use, which place a compliance burden on financial institutions.

## The Different Types of Financial Institutions

The National Bank Act of 1864 established the national banking system in the United States.[4] The Act still governs U.S. national banks even though Congress has updated it many times since 1864. Understanding the types of organizations that are considered financial institutions is important to understanding how the national banking system works. Most people know that financial institutions include banks and credit unions. Other organizations that provide financial services to customers include:

- Savings and loan associations
- Finance companies
- Insurance companies
- Investment companies

Several laws also define the types of organizations that are considered financial institutions. For example, the Fair Credit Reporting Act of 1970 (FCRA) defines financial institutions as banks, savings associations, and credit unions.[5] It also includes any organization that holds a transaction account on behalf of a customer as a financial institution. This law has a very specific definition.

Not all laws are that precise. The Bank Secrecy Act of 1970 has a long list of organizations that are financial institutions for the purposes of that law. The list includes banks, securities brokers, insurance companies, and pawnbrokers.[6]

The Bank Secrecy Act of 1970 also is known as the Currency and Foreign Transactions Reporting Act.[7] Congress created this law to fight drug trafficking, money laundering, and other crimes. The Act keeps banks and other financial institutions from being used by criminals to hide or transfer money and tries to keep criminals from profiting from illegal acts. The definition of a financial institution is broad for this reason.

The Gramm-Leach Bliley Act (GLBA) defines a financial institution as an institution that conducts financial activities.[8] This law, which is discussed later in this chapter, then points to the Bank Holding Company Act of 1956 for a list of actions that are considered financial activities. These include lending, exchanging, or investing money. They also include insurance and other financial advising services.[9]

You must read laws carefully since different laws may define the same term in different ways. It is always important to make sure that you understand how terms are used in each law.

## Consumer Financial Information

A consumer is a person who buys goods or services. Consumer information is the personally identifiable information that a person provides to get a good or service. In the financial industry, customers provide their information to get services from banks or other financial institutions. People use it to get home or car loans, apply for credit cards, or open checking accounts.

Items that a person buys for personal, family, or household use are called **consumer goods.** Services that a person buys for personal, family, or household use are called **consumer services.** These terms are not used to refer to goods or services purchased by a business.

Consumer financial information includes many items other than a person's name. It can include:

- SSNs
- Driver's license numbers
- Address and telephone numbers (current and former)
- Employment history (current and former)
- Income information

Consumer financial information also can include a spouse's employment and income history. It is all information that a consumer provides to a financial institution to get a product or service.

**FYI**

Many people access their banking accounts through online bank websites. A 2019 survey from the American Bankers Association showed 70 percent of consumers use their mobile devices to manage their bank accounts.[10] Some people also have multiple accounts at multiple banks. To protect your financial information, use different strong passwords for each online account. Always enable multifactor authentication if that option is available to you.

## Who Regulates Financial Institutions?

Several different federal agencies regulate the different kinds of financial institutions. This section focuses briefly on those agencies. These agencies enforce the consumer protection laws discussed later in this chapter. State governments may also regulate financial institutions. However, this chapter does not discuss that type of regulation.

There are four federal regulatory agencies for U.S. financial institutions. These agencies make sure that U.S. financial institutions are *sound*, which means they are financially healthy and safe. These agencies also make sure that their institutions follow federal law. The federal bank regulatory agencies are:

- The Federal Reserve System
- The Federal Deposit Insurance Corporation

- The National Credit Union Administration
- The Office of the Comptroller of the Currency

**TABLE 4-1** summarizes the agencies and the financial institutions that they regulate.

## The Federal Reserve System

Congress created the Federal Reserve System in 1913. The Federal Reserve Act of 1913 was passed to address financial uncertainty.[11] Bank and business failures were having a tremendous impact on the U.S. economy. The Federal Reserve Act was intended to provide the nation with a more stable economy.

The Federal Reserve System is the central bank of the United States.[13] Essentially, it is a bank for other banks, as well as a bank for the federal government. The Fed, an independent federal agency that reports directly to Congress, is responsible for directing the nation's monetary policy and maintaining the stability of the U.S. financial system.

In addition to serving as the bank for the U.S. government, the Fed is the main regulatory authority for:

- State-chartered banks that choose to become members of the Federal Reserve System
- Bank holding companies. The Fed also supervises companies that control banks (called bank holding companies)
- Foreign banks that operate in the United States
- Foreign branches of U.S. member banks.

**NOTE**

The U.S. Gross Domestic Product (GDP) fell by 4.8 percent during the first quarter of 2020. This was a result of the 2020 COVID-19 nationwide public health emergency.[12]

**NOTE**

The Federal Reserve System is also known as "the Fed."

**TABLE 4-1** Federal Banking Regulatory Agencies

| AGENCY NAME | PRIMARY REGULATORY RESPONSIBILITY |
|---|---|
| Federal Reserve System (The Fed) | State-chartered member banks<br>Bank holding companies<br>Foreign banks that operate in the United States<br>Foreign branches of U.S. member banks |
| Federal Deposit Insurance Corporation (FDIC) | Federally insured depository institutions<br>State-chartered banks that are not members of the Fed |
| National Credit Union Administration (NCUA) | Federally chartered credit unions<br>Federally insured credit unions |
| Office of the Comptroller of the Currency (OCC) | Nationally chartered banks<br>Federal savings associations<br>U.S. federal branches of foreign banks |

**FIGURE 4-1**

The structure of the U.S. Federal Reserve System.

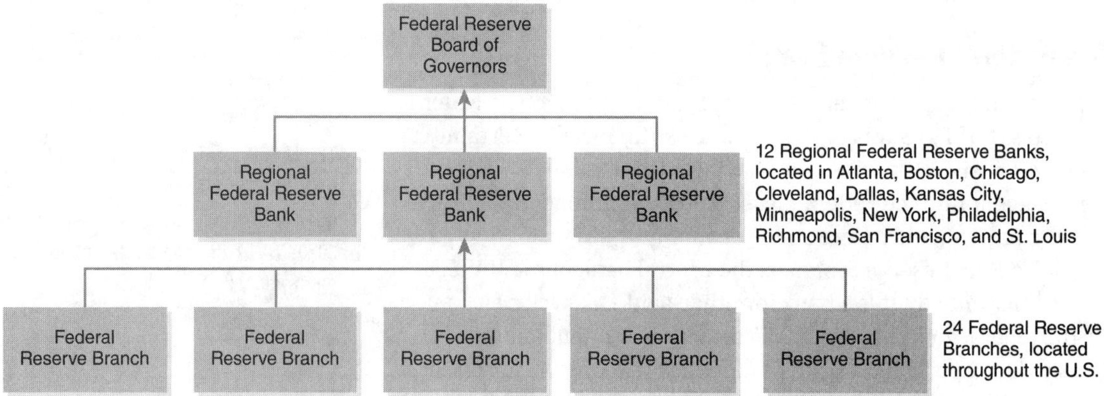


State-chartered banks are not required to become Fed members. State-chartered banks that are not Fed members are regulated by the Federal Deposit Insurance Corporation (FDIC). National banks are required to be members of the Federal Reserve System, but they are not regulated by the Fed. The Fed supervises and examines the financial institutions that it regulates to make sure that those institutions are complying with the law. Because many different agencies regulate banks, the Fed's enforcement authority extends to state member banks of the Fed and some foreign banks that operate in the United States.

The structure of the Fed includes a Board of Governors, located in Washington, DC, and 12 regional Federal Reserve banks. The Board consists of seven members who are nominated by the president and must be confirmed by the Senate. Each member serves for a single 14-year term. The terms of each member are staggered so that only one term expires at a time. The chair and vice-chair of the Board of Governors are also nominated by the president and confirmed by the Senate. These positions are filled by current members of the Board of Governors, who serve in these positions for a 4-year term.

There are 12 regional Federal Reserve banks located throughout the United States that serve different geographic districts. These Reserve Banks have 24 branches that carry out a variety of banking functions. The main customers of the Reserve Banks are other banks; the Reserve Banks hold the cash reserves of other institutions and distribute U.S. currency and coin within their region. They also supervise and review member banks to make sure that they are sound. **FIGURE 4-1** illustrates the structure of the Federal Reserve System.

**NOTE**

A *depositor* is a person who has deposited money into an account at a bank. Deposit accounts allow money to be added and withdrawn by the account owner. A savings or checking account is a type of deposit account, whereas an investment account is not a deposit account.

## Federal Deposit Insurance Corporation

The FDIC was formed in 1933 to provide deposit insurance to banks. Congress formed the FDIC originally as a temporary government corporation under the Banking Act of 1933.[14] The FDIC was formed in response to bank failures during the Great Depression.

 **NOTE**

From 1929 to 1933, bank failures resulted in about $1.3 billion in losses to depositors.

No depositor has lost any money on insured funds because of a bank failure since FDIC insurance began on January 1, 1934.[15] Congress made the FDIC a permanent federal agency in 1935 under the Banking Act of 1935.

The FDIC insures deposits made in banks and savings associations. The FDIC ensures deposit accounts only. It does not insure securities or mutual funds. When the FDIC was formed in 1933, the original deposit insurance limit was $2,500. In 2020, the deposit insurance limit was 100 times that amount, or $250,000.

 **NOTE**

To help protect the U.S. economy during the recession in 2008 to 2009, Congress raised the FDIC insurance amount to $250,000 per depositor.

The FDIC insures deposit accounts in almost every bank in the United States for protection in the event of a bank failure. If a bank fails, the FDIC returns the money that a customer put in the bank, up to the deposit insurance limit. However, the FDIC works to prevent bank failures by monitoring the economy. It also enforces regulations that require banks to act in a sound manner. All national banks are required by law to be insured by the FDIC.

The FDIC, the primary federal regulator for state-chartered banks that do not join the Federal Reserve System, examines and supervises over 3,000 banks. The FDIC reviews the banks that it regulates to make sure that those institutions are complying with the law.

The FDIC has a five-member board of directors. Three of the directors are appointed by the president and confirmed by the Senate. These members each serve 6-year terms. The other two members of the board are the government officials who serve as the comptroller of the currency and the director of the Consumer Financial Protection Bureau (CFPB). No more than three of the members of the FDIC board may be from the same political party. The chair and vice-chair of the board of directors are also nominated by the president and confirmed by the Senate. These positions are filled by current members of the board and have 5-year terms. The FDIC has eight regional offices.



## National Credit Union Administration

Congress enacted the Federal Credit Union Act in 1934.[16] That law allowed federally chartered credit unions to form. The National Credit Union Administration (NCUA) is an independent federal agency formed in 1970.[17] Its role is to charter and supervise federal credit unions.

A *credit union* is a cooperative financial organization that can have federal, state, or corporate affiliations. Members of a credit union share the same affiliation. They might live in the same city or work for the same employer. A credit union is a nonprofit institution that is run by its members, who pool their money together at a credit union to save and make loans to one another.

**NOTE**

Federal credit unions often use the word *federal* in their name. They may also use the initials F.C.U., or "federal credit union."

The NCUA operates the National Credit Union Share Insurance Fund (NCUSIF), created by Congress in 1970. All federal credit unions must be insured by the NCUSIF. This fund also insures deposits in state-chartered credit unions that qualify for the fund. The NCUSIF operates similar to the deposit insurance provided by the FDIC. It protects almost 95 million federal credit union account holders. It also insures a majority of state-chartered credit unions.

**NOTE**

No credit union member has lost any money on deposit accounts because of the failure of credit unions insured by the NCUSIF.

The NCUA supervises all federal credit unions and NCUSIF-insured state credit unions. It also issues guidance and enforces the provisions of the Federal Credit Union Act. The NCUA is the regulatory enforcement authority for federal credit unions, and it shares enforcement authority for some laws with other federal agencies. The NCUA enforces the GLBA consumer privacy provisions for federal credit unions. The FTC enforces those provisions for federally insured, state-chartered credit unions.

The NCUA has a three-member board of directors. The president nominates board members, who then must be confirmed by the Senate. Board members serve 6-year terms. Their terms are staggered so that only one term expires at a time. No more than two board members can be from the same political party. The NCUA has five regional offices across the United States that charter and supervise federal credit unions in their regions.

## Office of the Comptroller of the Currency

The Office of the Comptroller of the Currency (OCC) was originally established in 1863.[18] The National Bank Act of 1864 is the law that authorizes the OCC today. The OCC, which is a part of the U.S. Department of the Treasury, charters and supervises national banks and federal savings associations. Federal savings associations, also called thrifts, are organizations that accept savings account deposits and then invest the proceeds of those deposits in home mortgages. National banks and federal savings associations are members of the Federal Reserve System and are required to be insured by the FDIC.

**NOTE**

In July 2011, the Office of Thrift Supervision became part of the OCC. Before becoming part of the OCC, the Office of Thrift Supervision was the entity responsible for regulating federal savings associations.

The OCC is led by a comptroller who is appointed by the president, confirmed by the Senate, and serves a 5-year term. The comptroller also serves as a member of the board of directors of the FDIC. The OCC supervises and regulates about 1,400 national banks and federal savings associations. It has the authority to enforce laws and regulations against national banks and federal savings associations.

**NOTE**

National banks often use the word *national* or the phrase *national association* in their name. They also may use the initials "N.A."

**FYI**

Federal savings banks and savings and loan associations often use the words *federal*, *federal association*, *federal savings bank*, or *federal savings and loan association* in their name. They also may include initials for those terms, such as "F.A.," "F.S.B.," or "F.S.L.A."

## Special Role of the Federal Financial Institutions Examination Council

Congress established the Federal Financial Institutions Examination Council (FFIEC) in 1979. It was created by the Financial Institutions Regulatory and Interest Rate Control Act of 1978 (FIRA).[19] The FFIEC promotes uniform practices among the federal financial institutions and their regulators. Its purpose is to:

- Establish principles and standards for the examination of federal financial institutions.
- Develop a uniform reporting system for federal financial institutions.
- Conduct training for federal bank examiners.
- Make recommendations regarding bank supervision matters.
- Encourage the adoption of uniform principles and standards by federal and state banks.[20]

The council has six members. They are:

- The chair of the FDIC
- The chair of the NCUA
- The comptroller from the OCC
- The director of the CFPB
- A member of the Board of Governors of the Fed
- The chair of the FFIEC State Liaison Committee

**NOTE**

An examination is the periodic evaluation of a bank, which includes a review of the health of the bank and its compliance with banking regulations. An examination might include a review of management and operations, as well as the bank's policies. A bank examiner is the person who conducts this review.

The chair of the FFIEC serves for 2 years. The chair position rotates among members of the council. The member agencies fund the FFIEC.

The FFIEC has six task forces. Representatives from each agency serve on each task force, which includes at least one senior official from each of the member agencies:[21]

- **Consumer compliance**—This task force promotes a uniform approach to consumer protection laws and regulations. It develops proposed policies and procedures for the agencies to use in their regulatory activities.
- **Examiner education**—This task force oversees the FFIEC's intra-agency examiner education programs. The task force also develops specific programs in response to requests from the FFIEC or its members.
- **Information sharing**—This task force promotes sharing electronic information among FFIEC members to help them meet their regulatory responsibilities.
- **Reports**—This task force establishes uniform financial reports for FFIEC members.
- **Supervision**—This task force establishes supervision and examination procedures for FFIEC members. Its purpose is to help reduce regulatory burden by promoting effective supervision and examination practices.
- **Surveillance systems**—This task force develops systems to monitor the financial condition and performance of financial institutions.

The FFIEC is required to submit an annual report to Congress on its activities. The FFIEC does not regulate financial institutions because it has no authority to do so. The federal agencies carry out their own enforcement actions against banks in their jurisdiction.

## Special Roles of the Consumer Financial Protection Bureau and the Federal Trade Commission

The CFPB and the Federal Trade Commission (FTC) are two entities that have consumer protection functions.

### Consumer Financial Protection Bureau

The CFPB was created in 2010,[22] and its purpose was to protect consumers in the financial industry. Unlike the Fed, FDIC, NCUA, and OCC, which regulate financial institutions directly, the CFPB focuses solely on consumers. The CFPB is an independent agency that ensures that all consumers have access to financial products and services. It also ensures that financial products and services are offered in ways that are fair and competitive. The CFPB has the authority to examine financial institutions to ensure that the institutions are complying with federal consumer financial laws.

The CFPB is led by a director who is nominated by the president and confirmed by the Senate. The CFPB has six primary divisions and several advisory committees, including:

- Consumer advisory board
- Community bank advisory council
- Credit union advisory council
- Academic research council

### Federal Trade Commission

The FTC is an independent federal agency created by Congress in 1914 under the Federal Trade Commission Act.[23] Similar to the CFPB, the FTC is an important regulatory authority for consumer protection issues. The mission of the FTC is to protect consumers and make sure that business is competitive. It tries to eliminate practices that are harmful to business. The FTC has responsibilities under 46 different federal laws. Most of these laws include consumer protection elements.

Under the Federal Trade Commission Act, the FTC can investigate "the organization, business, conduct, practices, and management of any person, partnership, or corporation engaged in or whose business affects commerce."[24] It also can stop unfair and deceptive acts or trade practices.[25] Most of the FTC's authority comes from this law. The FTC makes and enforces rules for some parts of the financial industry. However, the FTC cannot regulate banks, thrifts, or federal credit unions—the other federal banking regulatory agencies already regulate them. The FTC does enforce laws at nonbanking institutions such as consumer finance companies, debt counseling companies, and credit bureaus.

The FTC is led by five commissioners. Each commissioner serves a 7-year term. They are nominated by the president and confirmed by the Senate. The president also chooses one commissioner to act as the chair. To maintain the independence of the FTC, no more than three commissioners can belong to the same political party.[26] The FTC has seven regional offices across the United States.

> **NOTE**
>
> **Unfair trade practices** are business practices that a consumer cannot avoid and that cause injury. **Deceptive trade practices** are any business practices that include false or misleading claims.

In 2012 the CFPB and the FTC signed an agreement to coordinate their efforts to protect consumers.[27] The agreement also helped to avoid duplication of effort between the two agencies. As part of the agreement, the agencies agreed to meet regularly and to coordinate their rulemaking efforts. They also agreed to share consumer complaints. Both agencies work closely with federal banking regulatory agencies when enacting rules to protect consumer financial information.

## The Gramm-Leach-Bliley Act

Congress passed the Gramm-Leach-Bliley Act (GLBA), also known as the Financial Services Modernization Act of 1999, in 1999.[28] It is the primary law governing the protection of consumer financial information. The law made great changes in the banking industry, allowing banks, securities, and insurance companies to merge, which was not allowed before the law. The financial industry urged Congress to pass the law so that customers could use one company for all their financial needs.

GLBA allowed large companies to merge. In doing so, these new, larger corporations would have access to sizable amounts of consumer financial information. Therefore, people feared that their privacy would suffer. This fear was not unreasonable, because financial institutions often sold customer banking information to other companies. To help alleviate this fear, Congress included privacy protections in the GLBA.

### Purpose, Scope, and Main Requirements

GLBA applies to financial institutions. It defines a financial institution as any institution that engages in financial activities. The definition of financial activities is very broad. It includes borrowing, lending, providing credit counseling, debt collection, and other activities.[29]

The law requires financial institutions to protect a customer's nonpublic financial information. It states that "each financial institution has an affirmative and continuing obligation to respect the privacy of its customers."[30] This means institutions must provide privacy and security protections to its customers and the customers' **nonpublic personal information (NPI).**

Nonpublic personal information is personally identifiable financial information that a consumer gives to a financial institution.[31] NPI also includes private information that an institution gets from other sources. It also includes lists or descriptions of consumers that are prepared by using this kind of information. NPI can be in paper or electronic form and includes:

- SSN
- Financial account numbers
- Credit card numbers
- Date of birth
- Name, address, and phone numbers when collected with financial data
- Details of any transactions or the fact that an individual is a customer of a financial institution

NPI does not include publicly available information about a consumer. Publicly available personal information is available to the general public. It can be made public through state or federal

 **NOTE**

A person's address in a phone book is publicly available.

records or disclosures that are required by law. Information can be made public in different ways, such as records filed in a county recorder's office. Financial institutions cannot assume that certain types of personally identifiable information are publicly available. They must take reasonable steps to make sure that information is actually publicly available if they want to claim that it is publicly available.

GLBA requires financial institutions to follow three main rules to protect consumer financial information:

- Privacy Rule
- Safeguards Rule
- Pretexting Rule

GLBA applies to consumer financial transactions. These are transactions made for personal, family, or household services. GLBA does not apply to business transactions.

## The Privacy Rule

Under the GLBA Privacy Rule,[32] a financial institution may not share NPI with non-affiliated third parties unless the institution gives notice to the consumer. The notice must tell consumers about the types of data that the institution collects and how it uses that information. This is called a notice of privacy practices. GLBA also requires that consumers have a chance to opt-out of some data sharing. The GLBA Privacy Rule went into effect on July 1, 2001.

**FYI**

Congress originally gave the federal bank regulatory agencies, the Securities and Exchange Commission (SEC), and the FTC the authority to create rules to enforce the GLBA privacy provisions. All of the agencies created and issued similar regulations that are tailored for their respective oversight areas. In 2010, the Dodd-Frank Act[33] transferred the rulemaking authority to the CFPB. The CFPB then restated the implementing regulations in a document known as Regulation P.[34]

GLBA distinguishes between customers and consumers for its notice requirements:[35]

- A *customer* is a consumer who has a continuing relationship with a financial institution. An institution must give a customer written notice of its privacy practices as soon as the customer relationship begins.
- A *consumer* is any individual who obtains a consumer financial product or service from a financial institution. A financial institution does not have to give consumers notice of its privacy practices if it does not share its consumers' NPI with nonaffiliated parties.

A person is a customer of a financial institution if he or she has an ongoing relationship with the institution. For example, a person with a checking or savings account at a bank has an ongoing relationship with that bank. An example of a consumer without a customer relationship is a person who withdraws cash from an ATM machine that does not belong to his or her personal bank.

GLBA requires that certain information be included in the privacy notice.[36] For example, the financial institution must describe the types of NPI that it collects. It must disclose how it shares NPI with affiliated and nonaffiliated third parties. Finally, it must state how it protects a customer's NPI. Customers must receive a copy of the privacy notice annually for as long as the customer relationship continues.

The privacy notice also must provide a customer with an opportunity to stop a financial institution from sharing the customer's NPI with nonaffiliated third parties.[37] This is called an "opt-out" provision. The privacy notice must tell customers how to opt-out. If a customer does not opt-out, then the financial institution can share NPI in the ways described by its privacy notice.

GLBA does not give customers the right to opt-out of situations where a financial institution shares NPI with its affiliates. There are also some instances where customers cannot opt-out at all. For example, customers cannot opt-out of a disclosure that is required by law.

GLBA did not specify how a financial institution should write its notice of privacy practices. Many of the first-created notices were hard to read because they contained legal and complex language. That made it difficult for people to understand their rights. It was also very hard to compare the privacy policies of different financial institutions.

After customers complained about the hard-to-read notices, Congress responded quickly. The Financial Services Regulatory Relief Act of 2006 amended the GLBA Privacy Rule so that it required the agencies responsible for enforcing the Privacy Rule to propose a model form for privacy notices. Congress directed that this model form should be easy to read and understand.

On November 17, 2009, the federal bank regulatory agencies, the SEC, and the FTC announced that they had completed the model form.[39] All of the agencies amended their privacy regulations to include use of it. The agencies made an online form builder available in April 2010. The Model Privacy Notice Form is shown in **FIGURE 4-2**.

 **NOTE**

A nonaffiliated party is an entity that is not legally related to a financial institution. Affiliated parties, in contrast, have a legal relationship of some kind. An affiliated party is an entity that controls, is controlled by, or is under the common control of another entity. Affiliates are businesses that are within the same corporate family.

 **NOTE**

The FCRA also allows customers to opt-out of some types of information sharing. Under that law, customers can stop financial institutions from sharing their credit report or credit applications with affiliates. GLBA privacy notices must include this disclosure.

 **NOTE**

In 2001, the Privacy Rights Clearinghouse studied the privacy notices of 60 financial institutions. The study found that most notices were written at a third- or fourth-year college reading level.[38]



## The Safeguards Rule

GLBA requires the federal bank regulatory agencies, the SEC, and the FTC to issue security standards for the institutions that they regulate.[40] This is commonly referred to as the Safeguards Rule. The law requires that each agency establish standards that:

- Protect the security and confidentiality of customer information.
- Protect against threats to the security or integrity of customer information.
- Protect against unauthorized access to or use of customer information that could result in harm to a customer.

**FIGURE 4-2A**

The Model Privacy Notice Form.

Federal Trade Commission (see https://www.ftc.gov/sites/default/files/attachments/press-releases/federal-regulators-issue-final-model-privacy-notice-form/privacymodelform.pdf).

Rev. [insert date]

| **FACTS** | **WHAT DOES [NAME OF FINANCIAL INSTITUTION] DO WITH YOUR PERSONAL INFORMATION?** |
|---|---|
| **Why?** | Financial companies choose how they share your personal information. Federal law gives consumers the right to limit some but not all sharing. Federal law also requires us to tell you how we collect, share, and protect your personal information. Please read this notice carefully to understand what we do. |
| **What?** | The types of personal information we collect and share depend on the product or service you have with us. This information can include:<br>■ Social Security number and [income]<br>■ [account balances] and [payment history]<br>■ [credit history] and [credit scores] |
| **How?** | All financial companies need to share customers' personal information to run their everyday business. In the section below, we list the reasons financial companies can share their customers' personal information; the reasons [name of financial institution] chooses to share; and whether you can limit this sharing. |

| Reasons we can share your personal information | Does [name of financial institution] share? | Can you limit this sharing? |
|---|---|---|
| **For our everyday business purposes—** such as to process your transactions, maintain your account(s), respond to court orders and legal investigations, or report to credit bureaus | | |
| **For our marketing purposes—** to offer our products and services to you | | |
| **For joint marketing with other financial companies** | | |
| **For our affiliates' everyday business purposes—** information about your transactions and experiences | | |
| **For our affiliates' everyday business purposes—** information about your creditworthiness | | |
| **For our affiliates to market to you** | | |
| **For nonaffiliates to market to you** | | |

| **To limit our sharing** | ■ Call **[phone number]**—our menu will prompt you through your choice(s)<br>■ Visit us online: **[website] or**<br>■ Mail the **form** below<br>**Please note:**<br>If you are a *new* customer, we can begin sharing your information [30] days from the date we sent this notice. When you are *no longer* our customer, we continue to share your information as described in this notice.<br>However, you can contact us at any time to limit our sharing. |
|---|---|
| **Questions?** | Call [phone number] or go to [website] |

✂ - - - - - - - - - - - - - - - - - - - - - - - - - - - - - - - - - -

**Mail-in Form**

| **Leave Blank OR** [If you have a joint account, your choice(s) will apply to everyone on your account unless you mark below.<br>❑ Apply my choices only to me] | Mark any/all you want to limit:<br>❑ Do not share information about my creditworthiness with your affiliates for their everyday business purposes.<br>❑ Do not allow your affiliates to use my personal information to market to me.<br>❑ Do not share my personal information with nonaffiliates to market their products and services to me. | |
|---|---|---|
| | Name<br>Address<br><br>City, State, Zip<br>[Account #] | **Mail to:**<br>[Name of Financial Institution]<br>[Address1]<br>[Address2]<br>[City], [ST] [ZIP] |

Page 2

| Who we are | |
|---|---|
| **Who is providing this notice?** | [insert] |
| **What we do** | |
| **How does [name of financial institution] protect my personal information?** | To protect your personal information from unauthorized access and use, we use security measures that comply with federal law. These measures include computer safeguards and secured files and buildings.<br><br>[insert] |
| **How does [name of financial institution] collect my personal information?** | We collect your personal information, for example, when you<br>▪ [open an account] or [deposit money]<br>▪ [pay your bills] or [apply for a loan]<br>▪ [use your credit or debit card]<br><br>[We also collect your personal information from other companies.]<br>**OR**<br>[We also collect your personal information from others, such as credit bureaus, affiliates, or other companies.] |
| **Why can't I limit all sharing?** | Federal law gives you the right to limit only<br>▪ sharing for affiliates' everyday business purposes—information about your creditworthiness<br>▪ affiliates from using your information to market to you<br>▪ sharing for nonaffiliates to market to you<br><br>State laws and individual companies may give you additional rights to limit sharing. [See below for more on your rights under state law.] |
| **What happens when I limit sharing for an account I hold jointly with someone else?** | [Your choices will apply to everyone on your account.]<br>**OR**<br>[Your choices will apply to everyone on your account—unless you tell us otherwise.] |
| **Definitions** | |
| **Affiliates** | Companies related by common ownership or control. They can be financial and nonfinancial companies.<br>▪ *[affiliate information]* |
| **Nonaffiliates** | Companies not related by common ownership or control. They can be financial and nonfinancial companies.<br>▪ *[nonaffiliate information]* |
| **Joint marketing** | A formal agreement between nonaffiliated financial companies that together market financial products or services to you.<br>▪ *[joint marketing information]* |
| **Other important information** | |
| [insert other important information] | |

FIGURE 4-2B

The Model Privacy Notice Form, page 2.

Federal Trade Commission, https://www.ftc.gov/sites/default/files/attachments/press-releases/federal-regulators-issue-final-model-privacy-notice-form/privacymodelform.pdf

Congress did not require the regulatory agencies to work together to create these standards, as it did for the Privacy Rule.[41] Therefore, the SEC issued its standards in June 2000. The federal bank regulatory agencies worked through the FFIEC to create joint guidelines that were issued in 2001. The FTC issued its Safeguards Rule in May 2002. Financial institutions regulated by the FTC had to comply with its rule by May 2003. This section will refer to the FTC Safeguards Rule.

The FTC Safeguards Rule[42] requires financial institutions to create a written *information security program* that must state how the institution collects and uses customer information. It must also describe the administrative, technical, or physical controls used to protect that information. The program must protect information in paper and electronic form.

The FTC rule requires that a financial institution's information security program be a good fit for its size and complexity. The program also must be suitable for the sensitivity of the customer information that the institution uses. As part of its program, an institution must:

- Assign an employee to coordinate the program.
- Conduct a risk assessment to identify risks to the security, confidentiality, and integrity of customer information and assess current safeguards to make sure that they are effective.
- Design and implement safeguards to control the identified risks.
- Select service providers and make sure that any contract includes terms to protect customer information.
- Review the information security program on an ongoing basis to account for changes in the business.

The Safeguards Rule allows financial institutions to pick the controls that best protect their customer information. It specifies three areas that institutions must review:

- Employee management and training
- Information systems design
- Detecting and responding to attacks and system failures

Institutions must be sure to address these areas when conducting their risk assessments. They also must make sure that these areas are included in their information security program.

A financial institution also must make sure that its service providers protect customer information. A *service provider* is an entity that provides services to a financial institution. A business that handles outsourced tasks is a service provider. These providers may access customer information when they provide services to an institution. Institutions must require their affiliates and service providers to protect customer information.

**FYI**

The FTC announced in March 2019 that it was seeking comments on proposed changes to the Safeguards Rule, which were due in August 2019. As of this writing, the FTC has not made any updates to the Safeguards Rule. You can track the progress of any updates to the rule at https://www.regulations.gov/docket?D=FTC-2019-0019.

## The Pretexting Rule

GLBA's final consumer protection is the Pretexting Rule.[43] **Pretexting**, also known as social engineering, is trying to gain access to customer information without proper authority to do so.

Under the law, it is illegal to make false, fictitious, or fraudulent statements to a financial institution or its customers to get customer information. It is also illegal to use forged, counterfeit, lost, or stolen documents to do the same thing. These rules try to stop identity theft before a crime is committed. Courts can impose criminal penalties if these rules are violated.

Most financial institutions address pretexting in their information security programs. It is covered as part of security awareness and training activities. Employees are trained to recognize and report pretexting.

### Oversight

GLBA compliance oversight falls to different federal agencies. Oversight is based on the type of financial institution under review. The federal bank regulatory agencies (the Fed, FDIC, OCC, and NCUA) enforce GLBA for the institutions that they regulate. For example, the SEC oversees GLBA for securities brokers and dealers. Each agency can bring an action against the institutions that they regulate for not complying with GLBA.

The FTC enforces GLBA for any financial institution that is not regulated by one of the other agencies. Similar to the other agencies, the FTC may bring an action against any financial institution that does not comply with GLBA. The FTC has been quite active in pursuing GLBA enforcement actions.

## Federal Trade Commission Red Flags Rule

Congress passed the Fair and Accurate Credit Transaction Act of 2003 (FACTA) in response to the growth in identity theft crimes.[44] FACTA made it harder for consumer financial information to be used to commit these crimes through changes to the FCRA.

Congress recognized that the financial industry has a role in protecting customers from identity theft. Therefore, FACTA required the federal bank regulatory agencies and the FTC to work together to create rules that would identify and respond to possible instances of identity theft. These agencies issued a joint rule, known as the Identity Theft Red Flags Rule,[45] on November 9, 2007.

### Purpose

The purpose of the Red Flags Rule is to fight identity theft. The rule requires covered financial institutions to be on the lookout for certain warning signs that might indicate identity theft is taking place in consumer financial transactions.

> **NOTE**
>
> A **Red Flag** is any "pattern, practice, or specific activity that indicates the possible existence of identity theft."[47]

The Red Flags Rule is not a data security rule. It does not require institutions to protect data in a certain way. Instead, it requires them to be flexible and responsive to different business situations where identity theft could be possible.[46]

### Scope

The Red Flags Rule applies to financial institutions and creditors that have covered accounts. Financial institutions are state and federal banks, credit unions, and savings and loan associations that are regulated by the Fed, FDIC, OCC, and NCUA.

Under the Red Flags Rule, a *creditor* is any person or organization that regularly extends, renews, or continues customer credit; and who also:

- Receives or uses consumer reports in connection with a credit transaction
- Gives information to consumer reporting agencies in connection with a credit transaction
- Loans a person money[48]

The definition of *covered account* is also broad. There are two types of covered accounts. The first type is an account that is used "primarily for personal, family, or household purposes, that involves or is designed to permit multiple payments or transactions."[49] Examples of this type of account include:

- Credit card accounts
- Car loan accounts
- Utility accounts
- Cell phone carrier accounts

**NOTE**

Payment in arrears refers to payments that are made after a business provides goods or services. Many businesses bill in arrears. They include utility companies, medical providers, and cell phone service providers.

The second type of covered account is an account for which identity theft is a reasonably foreseeable risk because of the use of the account. The risk includes harm to a customer. It also could be harmful to the soundness of the financial institution or creditor. These types of accounts are considered covered accounts if the potential for identity theft is "reasonably foreseeable."

Organizations fall within the scope of the Red Flags Rule because of their actions. They may not rely on just the definitions of "financial institution," "creditor," or "covered account" to determine if they must comply with the Rule. Organizations must comply with the Red Flags Rule if they act similar to financial institutions or creditors and use accounts that resemble covered accounts.

**FYI**

The Red Flag Program Clarification Act of 2010 tightened the definition of creditor and exempted service providers such as doctors and healthcare professionals, lawyers, and accountants from the application of the Red Flags Rule.[50] Associations that represented these professions filed numerous lawsuits to stop the FTC from enforcing the Red Flags Rule against these professions. They claimed that Congress did not intend that service providers who were paid in arrears be considered creditors under the Red Flags Rule. Congress agreed with those arguments when it passed the Red Flags Clarification Act.

## Main Requirements

Under the Red Flags Rule, covered entities must develop a written *Identity Theft Prevention Program*. This program must detect, prevent, and mitigate identity theft in covered accounts. The written program must address both new and existing covered accounts.

Organizations can take the size and complexity of their operations into account when preparing their program. Larger companies that handle more accounts may need a more detailed plan, whereas smaller companies with fewer accounts may not need a very detailed plan. The written program must be appropriate for the organization.

An organization's board of directors must approve the program. If an organization does not have a board of directors, then a senior official must approve the program. The Rule requires organizations to train their employees about their written programs. Organizations also must review their relationships with third-party service providers. Organizations must make sure that those activities do not raise any Red Flags.

A written program must have the following components:

- Identify Red Flags that apply to the organization.
- Determine how the Red Flags will be detected during business processes.
- Determine how to respond to Red Flags that are detected.
- Review the written program periodically.

The agencies that worked together to create the Red Flags Rule realized that it may be difficult for organizations to determine activities that might raise a Red Flag. They created five different Red Flag categories:

1. Alerts or notifications received from consumer reporting agencies or service providers
2. Suspicious documents
3. Suspicious personal identifying information
4. Unusual or suspicious activity of a covered account
5. Notice from customers, law enforcement authorities, or other persons regarding possible identity theft in connection with covered accounts

The agencies also provided 26 examples of activity that might be considered a Red Flag.[51] The categories of Red Flags and some of the examples that fall in each category are provided in **TABLE 4-2**.

Once an organization identifies an action that might raise a Red Flag, it must take steps to detect that activity in its normal business practices. For example, an organization decides that forged or altered documents are a potential Red Flag. It must then detect when documents are forged or altered. Other ways to detect Red Flags could include asking customers to provide additional identification.

The proper response to a Red Flag depends on the situation. An organization could contact the customer or monitor accounts as a potential response. An organization also can investigate a potential Red Flag and determine that a response is not needed, depending upon the circumstances.

## Oversight

Each agency that worked together to create the Red Flags Rule enforces it within their authority. The Federal Reserve System, FDIC, OCC, and NCUA regulate most financial institutions. Because financial institutions are highly regulated, it makes sense for Red Flags Rule enforcement to stem from one of these regulatory agencies. Note that in 2010, the Dodd-Frank Act transferred rulemaking and enforcement of the Red Flags Rule to the SEC for the institutions that it regulates. The FTC enforces the rule for all other organizations.

**TABLE 4-2** Red Flag Categories and Examples

| RED FLAG CATEGORY | RED FLAG EXAMPLES |
|---|---|
| Alerts, Notifications, and Warnings From a Credit Reporting Company | A fraud alert placed on a consumer report<br>A credit freeze placed on a consumer report<br>A consumer report indicating a pattern of activity that does not match the customer's historical activity |
| Suspicious Documents | Identification documents that look altered or forged<br>A signature on a document does not match the signature in the customer's file<br>A photograph on an identification document that does not resemble the person presenting the identification document |
| Suspicious Personal Identifying Information | Personal information provided that does not match external information sources, for example, an address that does not match the customer's consumer report<br>Incomplete personal information provided when opening an account<br>Personal information provided that does not match the information in the customer's file |
| Unusual or Suspicious Activity on a Covered Account | A covered account used in a manner that does not match the customer's historical activity<br>An unpaid account with no history of nonpayment on that account<br>Frequent new use of a covered account that was unused for a long period |
| Notice From Customers or Others About Identity Theft | Customer notification to the covered organization about suspected identity theft<br>Law enforcement notification to the financial institution or creditor about fraudulent activity |

Federal civil fines are possible for violations of the Red Flags Rule. Only the government can impose sanctions for violating the Red Flags Rule. The Red Flags Rule does not permit a *private right of action*. This means that individuals cannot sue financial institutions or creditors if they violate the Red Flags Rule.

## Payment Card Industry Standards

Americans have over 375 million open credit card accounts.[52] Credit cards essentially allow you to borrow money to buy things. You borrow the money from the bank that issues the credit card in exchange for a promise to pay the loan back within a certain period. If you fail to pay the loan by the due date, you are charged interest on the loan. Your credit card number is sensitive consumer financial information. If your credit card information is stolen, unauthorized users could impersonate you and make large purchases in your name. Credit card companies work hard to ensure that your credit card information is kept secure during transactions. They accomplish this work through the Payment Card Industry Security Standards Council (PCI Council).

The PCI Council is made up of representatives of the major credit card companies.[53] The major credit card companies, also called credit card brands, are:

- MasterCard
- Visa
- American Express
- JCB International
- Discover

The PCI Council is not a government agency; rather, it is a private industry organization. The PCI Council, formed in 2006, creates safeguards designed to protect credit card data. Any merchant or service provider who accepts credit cards must follow the safeguards. This list of security measures is called the Payment Card Industry (PCI) Data Security Standard (DSS). The most recent version of the DSS, version 3.2.1, was released in May 2018.[54] A new version of PCI DSS is expected to be released in late 2020. This chapter addresses version 3.2.1 of the standard.

## Purpose

Before the PCI Council was formed, each credit card company made up its own security requirements that applied to the credit cards that it issued. Merchants who accepted credit cards for payment had to follow these standards. Most merchants wanted to accept more than one type of credit card, and it was hard for them to follow so many different standards. The first DSS combined the standards of the founding credit card companies into one standard.

**NOTE**

Cardholder data is the data available from a credit card. It includes cardholder name, expiration date, account number, and verification numbers. The data is printed on the card and can be contained in the magnetic stripe on the back of the card.

The DSS offers a single approach to safeguarding sensitive cardholder data for all credit card issuers. It identifies 12 basic categories of security requirements that must be followed to protect credit card data.

## Scope

All merchants who accept credit cards must comply with the PCI DSS. PCI has different compliance requirements for different merchants that are based upon the size of the merchant's credit card operations. There are four basic merchant levels:

- **Level 1** – Over 6 million transactions annually
- **Level 2** – Between 1 and 6 million transactions annually
- **Level 3** – Between 20,000 and 1 million transactions annually
- **Level 4** – Less than 20,000 transactions annually

These basic levels are subject to adjustment because each of the credit card brands sets its merchant levels individually. For example, Visa merchant Level 1 includes merchants that process over 6 million Visa transactions per year.[55] MasterCard Level 1 includes any merchant that processes 6 million MasterCard transactions per year or meets Visa's Level 1 criteria.[56] MasterCard Level 1 also includes merchants that:

- Have suffered a data breach that compromised account data, or
- Any merchant that MasterCard feels should be a Level 1 merchant to minimize risk

Any merchant that accepts credit cards must comply with the DSS. This means that they must implement and follow the DSS rules. The credit card brands enforce DSS compliance. Most of the credit card brands also require merchants to validate their compliance with the rules. This means that it is not enough for the merchant to *say* that it is compliant with the rules; instead, the merchant must *prove* that it is compliant with the rules.

**NOTE**

A *merchant* is a businessperson who sells goods or services to earn a profit. A merchant can be a large, well-known store or small corner grocery store. For the PCI DSS, a merchant is any entity that accepts credit cards for payment.

Different merchant levels have different validation requirements set by the credit card brands. Visa requires its Level 1 merchants to have an independent evaluation each year.[57] They also must have a quarterly network scan by an approved vendor. A Level 3 merchant, which is a smaller merchant than a Level 1 merchant, has different requirements. Under the Visa validation requirements, a Level 3 merchant must only complete an annual self-assessment form and have a quarterly network scan.

### Main Requirements

**NOTE**

The complete list of PCI DSS requirements is available at https://www.pcisecuritystandards.org/.

The DSS applies only to the systems that process, store, or transmit credit card data.[58] The DSS has specific requirements that each merchant must follow to protect cardholder data. These are the minimum set of requirements for protecting cardholder data. The DSS requirements use preventative, detective, and corrective controls to secure credit card data. The DSS has six high-level categories and 12 major rules. The main categories of controls and rules are listed in **TABLE 4-3**.

Each DSS rule has several subrequirements that explain how the rule should be met. Merchants must understand how their information systems work to implement the DSS requirements and subrequirements. Merchants also must understand their business processes and be aware of how credit card data is used within their systems. They must consider data security as part of their everyday business operations.

### Oversight

The PCI Security Standards Council does not manage compliance programs. It also does not levy penalties for noncompliance. The Council only creates the DSS and provides merchants with resources to comply with those standards. Each of the individual credit card companies enforces the DSS for its own cards and the merchants who use those cards. Most credit card companies use the threat of financial penalties to compel DSS compliance. Compliance is contractually based. It is required through contracts between credit card companies, banks that issue the cards, banks that process credit card transactions, and the merchant.

Penalties for DSS noncompliance tend to be tied to events that expose cardholder data. For example, Visa requires its merchants to notify it immediately if they experience a breach involving credit card data.[59] Visa may impose a penalty of up to $100,000 per event if it is not notified immediately. Fines can be increased if it is determined that a merchant was not

**TABLE 4-3** PCI DSS v.3.2.1 Categories of Controls and Rules

| DSS CONTROL CATEGORY | MAIN RULES |
|---|---|
| Build and Maintain a Secure Network and Systems | Merchants must install and maintain firewall and router configurations to protect cardholder data.<br>Merchants may not use vendor-supplied defaults for passwords and other security measures. |
| Protect Cardholder Data | Merchants must take action to protect stored cardholder data.<br>Merchants must encrypt cardholder data while it is transmitted across public networks. |
| Maintain a Vulnerability Management Program | Merchants must use antivirus software that is updated regularly.<br>Merchants must develop and use secure systems and applications. |
| Implement Strong Access Control Measures | Merchants must use need-to-know principles to restrict access to credit card data.<br>Merchants must control access to system components.<br>Merchants must restrict physical access to cardholder data. |
| Regularly Monitor and Test Networks | Merchants must monitor access to network resources and cardholder data.<br>Merchants must test their security systems and processes regularly. |
| Maintain an Information Security Policy | Merchants must create an information security policy. |

DSS compliant at the time of the breach. Similarly, fines may be reduced if the merchant can show that it was compliant with the DSS at the time of the breach.



## Case Studies and Examples

The following case studies show how the laws discussed in this chapter are used. These case studies are real-world examples of how regulatory agencies apply laws and rules to protect consumer information.

### FTC Privacy and Safeguards Rule Enforcement

The FTC enforces the GLBA Privacy and Safeguards Rule against some types of financial institutions. The FTC can begin an investigation on its own or in response to a consumer complaint.

In July 2019, the FTC filed a complaint against Equifax, Inc., a credit-reporting agency. Equifax reported a data breach in 2017 in which hackers stole SSNs and other personal information on 143 million Americans. In its complaint, the FTC alleged that Equifax failed to secure customer personal information stored on its network. This is a violation of the GLBA Safeguards Rule.

The FTC argued that Equifax had a series of basic security failures that led to the breach. These failures happened over several months and included:

- Failure to patch critical vulnerabilities in Equifax information systems
- Failure to maintain a technology asset inventory, which meant that Equifax did not properly scan all its assets for vulnerabilities
- Failure to segment its computer network
- Failure to encrypt highly confidential information, such as SSNs, stored on its information systems
- Failure to detect intrusions into legacy information systems
- Failure to update expired security certificates on its information systems

**NOTE**

The FTC documents related to the Equifax breach are available at https://www.ftc.gov/enforcement/cases-proceedings/172-3203/equifax-inc.

The CFPB and 50 U.S. states and territories also filed complaints against Equifax. Their complaints alleged violations of different laws. Only the FTC had jurisdiction over Equifax for violations of the GLBA Safeguards Rule. The FTC, CFPB, and the states all worked together to solve their complaints against Equifax.

In late July 2020, Equifax agreed to pay at least $575 million to settle all claims with the CFPB, FTC, and the states. That settlement agreement amount could be increased by $125 million if the original settlement amount fails to compensate consumers for their losses related to the breach.

With respect to the GLBA Safeguards Rule, Equifax also agreed to:

**NOTE**

Consumers can learn more about their rights related to the Equifax settlement at www.ftc.gov/equifax.

- Comply with the GLBA Safeguards Rule and establish a comprehensive information security program that contains the requirements specified in the order.
- Provide yearly reports on the status of its information security program to its board of directors.
- Obtain an independent assessment of its information security program every 2 years. The assessor selected must be approved by the FTC in advance.
- Report yearly to the FTC that it is following the FTC's settlement agreement.
- Notify the FTC within 10 days if it experiences an information security incident.

The FTC's settlement agreement with Equifax ends in July 2039. Equifax must follow the terms in the settlement agreement until the agreement expires.

## Credit Card Security Example

Target is a popular department store in the United States and Canada. On December 19, 2013, Target reported that the credit and debit card data of over 40 million customers was compromised in a security breach.[60] It reported that the compromise took place throughout the United States during the busy Thanksgiving-to-Christmas shopping season. Credit cardholders who shopped in Target stores from November 27 to December 15, 2013, were affected by the breach.

Target reported that it found malware on its cash registers on December 15. Company officials said that they immediately deleted the malware. They then began to notify their customers about the incident. On December 27, 2013, Target reported that encrypted personal identification number, or PIN, information was also compromised in the breach. PINs are passwords used in debit card transactions.

On January 17, 2014, Target reported that the attack it suffered during the height of the holiday shopping season may have affected an additional 70 million customers.[61] Their personal information—names, addresses, and phone numbers—was stolen. The massive data breach was further reported to have extended beyond the 2013 holiday shopping season to people who had not shopped at Target for years.

Target's costs associated with the breach were extensive. Visa, Mastercard, American Express, and Discover all made claims against Target for the data breach. Target paid $86 million to Visa and Mastercard to settle claims associated with the breach. In its 2016 annual report, Target reported that it had experienced $292 million in expenses related to the breach.

## CHAPTER SUMMARY

Consumer financial information is valuable. In the wrong hands, it can be used to commit identity theft. The U.S. federal government regulates how this information can be used. The financial industry also takes steps to guard this information. These laws and standards work together to protect consumers from identity theft.

## KEY CONCEPTS AND TERMS

Consumer goods
Consumer services
Deceptive trade practices
Nonpublic personal information (NPI)
Pretexting
Red Flag
Unfair trade practices



## CHAPTER 4 ASSESSMENT

**1.** What are consumer goods?

A. Items purchased for personal use
B. Items purchased for family use
C. Items purchased for household use
D. All of these are correct.
E. None of these are correct.

**2.** Which rule is not a GLBA consumer protection provision?

A. The Safeguards Rule
B. The Red Flags Rule
C. The Privacy Rule
D. The Pretexting Rule
E. None of these is correct.

**3.** Which federal agency regulates national banks?

A. The Office of the Comptroller of the Currency
B. The Federal Reserve System
C. The Federal Deposit Insurance Corporation
D. The Consumer Financial Protection Bureau
E. The Federal Trade Commission

**4.** What is the organization that promotes uniform reports among federal banking institutions?

A. The Fed
B. The FFIEC
C. The FTC
D. The NCUA
E. The SEC

5. What is a Red Flag?
   A. A crime
   B. An activity that prevents identity theft
   C. An activity that might indicate identity theft
   D. An activity that mitigates identity theft
   E. None of these is correct.

6. Pretexting is also called ______.

7. Which of the following is nonpublic personal information?
   A. Personally identifiable financial information provided by a customer to a financial institution
   B. Personally identifiable financial information provided by a financial institution to a customer
   C. Personally identifiable financial information provided by a financial institution to an affiliate
   D. Personally identifiable financial information provided by an affiliate to a financial institution
   E. Personally identifiable financial information provided by an affiliate to a customer

8. A written information security program under the Safeguards Rule must include:
   A. Technical safeguards.
   B. Physical safeguards.
   C. Administrative safeguards.
   D. A designated employee to run the program.
   E. All of these are correct.

9. The ______ established the national banking system in the United States.

10. What is the central bank of the United States?
    A. The FDIC
    B. The Fed
    C. The NCUA
    D. The OCC
    E. The CFPB

11. Which of the following is *not* a federal bank regulatory agency?
    A. The FDIC
    B. The NCUA
    C. The FTC
    D. The OCC
    E. The Fed

12. What customer option must be included in a privacy practices notice?
    A. Disclosure
    B. Opt-out
    C. Opt-in
    D. Notice
    E. None of these is correct.

13. The Payment Card Industry Standard includes ______ categories of security requirements.

14. The Payment Card Industry Standards are enforced by the Federal Trade Commission.
    A. True
    B. False

15. What is a customer?
    A. A consumer with a past relationship with a financial institution
    B. A consumer with no relationship with a financial institution
    C. A consumer with a continuing relationship with a financial institution
    D. A consumer who wants to enter into a relationship with a financial institution
    E. None of these is correct.

## ENDNOTES

1. Verizon, "2019 Data Breach Investigations Report," 2019. https://enterprise.verizon.com/resources/reports/dbir/ (accessed April 29, 2020).
2. Secureworks, "A Famous Data Security Breach & PCI Case Study: Four Years Later," October 25, 2012. https://www.secureworks.com/blog/general-pci-compliance-data-security-case-study-heartland (accessed April 29, 2020).
3. Ponemon Institute, "The Cost of Cybercrime," 2019. https://www.accenture.com/_acnmedia/pdf-96/accenture-2019-cost-of-cybercrime-study-final.pdf#zoom=50 (accessed April 29, 2020).

4. National Bank Act (1864), 13 Stat. 99 (1864), current version at U.S. Code Vol. 12.
5. Fair Credit Reporting Act (1970), U.S. Code Vol. 15, sec. 1681, *et seq*.
6. U.S. Code Vol. 31, sec. 5312.
7. Bank Secrecy Act (1970), Pub. L. No. 91-508, 84 Stat. 1114 to 1124, codified as amended in scattered sections throughout U.S. Code Vols. 12, 15, and 31.
8. Gramm-Leach-Bliley Act (1999), Title V of the Financial Services Modernization Act of 1999, Pub. L. No. 106-102, 113 Stat. 1338, codified at U.S. Code Vol. 15, sec. 6801, *et seq*.
9. U.S. Code Vol. 12, sec. 1843(k)(4).
10. American Bankers Association, "Digital Banking Infographic," November 12, 2019. https://www.aba.com/news-research/research-analysis/digital-banking (accessed April 29, 2020).
11. Federal Reserve Act (1913), Pub. L. No 63-43, 38 Stat. 251, codified as amended throughout U.S. Code Vol. 12.
12. CNN, "America's Economy Just Had Its Worst Quarter Since 2008," April 29, 2020. https://www.cnn.com/2020/04/29/economy/us-economy-downturn-coronavirus/index.html (accessed April 29, 2020).
13. Board of Governors of the Federal Reserve System, "Structure of the Federal Reserve System," March 3, 2017. https://www.federalreserve.gov/aboutthefed/structure-federal-reserve-system.htm (accessed April 29, 2020).
14. Banking Act of 1933 (also called the Glass-Stegall Act), Pub. L. No. 73-66, 48 Stat. 162, codified as amended throughout U.S. Code Vol. 12.
15. Federal Deposit Insurance Corporation, "Who Is the FDIC?" May 3, 2017. https://www.fdic.gov/about/learn/symbol/index.html (accessed April 29, 2020).
16. Federal Credit Union Act (1934), U.S. Code Vol. 12, sec. 1751, *et seq*.
17. National Credit Union Association, "About NCUA," Undated. https://www.ncua.gov/about-ncua (accessed April 29, 2020).
18. Office of the Comptroller of the Currency, "Who We Are," Undated. https://www.occ.treas.gov/about/who-we-are/index-who-we-are.html (accessed April 29, 2020).
19. Financial Institutions Regulatory and Interest Rate Control Act (1978), Pub. L. No. 95-630, 92 Stat. 3641, codified as amended in scattered sections of U.S. Code.
20. U.S. Code Vol. 12, sec. 3305.
21. Federal Financial Institutions Examination Council, "Annual Report 2019," March 30, 2020. https://www.ffiec.gov/PDF/annrpt19.pdf (accessed April 29, 2020).
22. Consumer Financial Protection Bureau, "Creating the Consumer Bureau," Undated. https://www.consumerfinance.gov/about-us/the-bureau/creatingthebureau/ (accessed April 29, 2020).
23. Federal Trade Commission Act (1914), U.S. Code Vol. 15, sec. 41–58.
24. U.S. Code Vol. 15, sec. 46(a).
25. U.S. Code Vol. 15, sec. 45(a)(1).
26. Federal Trade Commission, "About the FTC," Undated. https://www.ftc.gov/about-ftc (accessed April 29, 2020).
27. Federal Trade Commission, "Federal Trade Commission, Consumer Financial Protection Bureau Pledge to Work Together to Protect Consumers," January 23, 2012. https://www.ftc.gov/news-events/press-releases/2012/01/federal-trade-commission-consumer-financial-protection-bureau (accessed April 29, 2020).
28. Gramm-Leach-Bliley Act (1999), Title V of the Financial Services Modernization Act of 1999, Pub. L. No. 106-102, 113 Stat. 1338, codified at U.S. Code Vol. 15, sec. 6801, *et seq*.
29. U.S. Code Vol. 12, sec. 1843(k)(4).
30. U.S. Code Vol. 15, sec. 6801(a).
31. U.S. Code Vol. 15, sec. 6809.
32. U.S. Code Vol. 15, sec. 6801–6803.
33. Dodd-Frank Wall Street Reform and Consumer Protection Act (2010), Pub. L. No. 111–203, 124 Stat. 1376–2223, codified as amended in scattered sections throughout U.S. Code Vols. 12 and 15.
34. Code of Federal Regulations, Title 12, sec. 1016.
35. U.S. Code Vol. 15, sec. 6809.
36. U.S. Code Vol. 15, sec. 6803.
37. U.S. Code Vol. 15, sec. 6802.
38. Privacy Rights Clearinghouse, "Oversight Hearing on Financial Privacy and the Gramm-Leach-Bliley Financial Services Modernization Act: Testimony for U.S. Senate Committee on Banking, Housing and Urban Affairs," September 20, 2002. https://privacyrights.org/resources/oversight-hearing-financial-privacy-and-gramm-leach-bliley-financial-services (accessed April 29, 2020).
39. Code of Federal Regulations, Title 16, sec. 313.
40. U.S. Code Vol. 15, sec. 6801(b).

41. U.S. Code Vol. 15, sec. 6805(b)(2).
42. Standards for Insuring the Security Confidentiality, Integrity and Protection of Customer Records and Information ("Safeguards Rule"), Code of Federal Regulations, Title 16, sec. 314.
43. U.S. Code Vol. 15, sec. 6821.
44. Fair and Accurate Credit Transaction Act of 2003 (FACTA), Pub L. No. 108-159, 117 Stat. 1952, made amendments to the Fair Credit Reporting Act of 1970.
45. Code of Federal Regulations, Title 16, sec. 681.1, Appendix A.
46. Federal Register 72, No. 217 at 63,719, background information.
47. Code of Federal Regulations, Title 16, sec. 681.1(b)(9).
48. U.S. Code Vol. 15, sec. 1681a(r)(5).
49. Code of Federal Regulations, Title 16, sec. 681.1(b)(3)(i).
50. Red Flag Program Clarification Act of 2010, 15 U.S.C. 1681m(e)(4), Pub. L. No. 111-319, 124 Stat. 3457 (Dec. 18, 2010).
51. Code of Federal Regulations, Title 16, sec. 681.1, Appendix A.
52. American Bankers Association, "Credit Card Monitor," February 2020. https://www.aba.com/-/media/documents/reports-and-surveys/2019-q3-credit-card-monitor.pdf?rev=9c1664304c9149a8a08e6d146791126f (accessed April 29, 2020).
53. PCI Security Standards Council, "About Us," Undated. https://www.pcisecuritystandards.org/about_us/ (accessed April 29, 2020).
54. PCI Security Standards Council, "PCI Data Security Standard, v 3.2.1," May 2018. https://www.pcisecuritystandards.org/document_library (accessed April 29, 2020).
55. VISA, "PCI Compliance Helps Keep You and Your Customers Safe," Undated. https://usa.visa.com/support/small-business/security-compliance.html (accessed April 29, 2020).
56. Mastercard, "What Merchants Need to Know About Securing Transactions," Undated. https://www.mastercard.ca/en-ca/merchants/safety-security/security-recommendations/merchants-need-to-know.html (accessed April 29, 2020).
57. VISA, "Information Security," Undated. https://cw.visa.com/run-your-business/small-business/information-security/compliance-validation.html (accessed April 29, 2020).
58. PCI Security Standards Council, "PCI Data Security Standard, v 3.2.1," May 2018. https://www.pcisecuritystandards.org/document_library (accessed April 29, 2020).
59. VISA, "What to Do if Compromised," October 1, 2019. https://usa.visa.com/dam/VCOM/download/merchants/cisp-what-to-do-if-compromised.pdf (accessed April 29, 2020).
60. Target Corporation, "Target Confirms Unauthorized Access to Payment Card Data in U.S. Stores," December 19, 2013. https://corporate.target.com/press/releases/2013/12/target-confirms-unauthorized-access-to-payment-car (accessed April 29, 2020).
61. Target Corporation, "Target Provides Update on Data Breach and Financial Performance," January 10, 2014. https://corporate.target.com/press/releases/2014/01/target-provides-update-on-data-breach-and-financia (accessed April 29, 2020).

# Security and Privacy of Information Belonging to Children and in Educational Records

CHAPTER 5

SEVERAL LAWS ARE in place in the United States to protect children when they are online. The Children's Online Privacy Protection Act (COPPA) governs how information from children is to be collected and used. If you host a website that collects information from children, COPPA applies to you. The Children's Internet Protection Act (CIPA) protects minors from obscene or objectionable material on school or library computers. These computers must implement technology to filter objectionable content. The Family Educational Rights and Privacy Act (FERPA) protects the privacy rights of students and their educational records. Students and parents have the right to review these records. Additionally, schools cannot release records without the written consent of a student or parent.

This chapter begins with a discussion of children and the internet, and the unique challenges website operators face in protecting children. The chapter then provides details about COPPA, CIPA, and FERPA.

## Chapter 5 Topics

This chapter covers the following topics and concepts:

- What challenges exist in protecting children on the internet
- What the Children's Online Privacy Protection Act (COPPA) is
- What the Children's Internet Protection Act (CIPA) is
- What the Family Educational Rights and Privacy Act (FERPA) is

## Chapter 5 Goals

When you complete this chapter, you will be able to:

- List some of the challenges with protecting children on the internet
- Identify the purpose and scope of COPPA, and describe its main requirements and oversight responsibilities

- Identify the purpose and scope of CIPA, and describe its main requirements and oversight responsibilities
- Identify the purpose and scope of FERPA, and describe its main requirements and oversight responsibilities

## Challenges in Protecting Children on the Internet

U.S. children ages 8 to 18 spend over 7 hours a day using electronic media. This includes television, music, computer use, and video game use.[1] This also means that children may be exposed to age-inappropriate content, online marketing, online harassment and bullying, and inappropriate data collection activities. Parents, schools, and website providers all have different roles to play in protecting children when they are online. It is not unusual to hear about cases where website operators run afoul of the laws that attempt to protect children:

- In 2019, a social media company paid $170 million to settle charges with the Federal Trade Commission (FTC) and New York attorney general. The FTC alleged that the company violated the Children's Online Privacy Protection Act (COPPA). The company collected persistent identifiers known as cookies from children before getting parental permission. The penalty was the largest ever imposed in a COPPA case.[2]
- In 2018, the FTC alleged that a company that provided internet-connected toys violated COPPA. It was the first time the FTC took action in a case involving privacy and internet-connected toys. The FTC said that the toy company collected the personal information of hundreds of thousands of children through a mobile application without notifying parents or obtaining their consent. The company also failed to use reasonable and appropriate data security measures to protect personal information it collected. Both activities violated COPPA.
- A student sued a local school board alleging that the school had violated the student's First Amendment rights. The lawsuit alleged that the school's internet filtering software blocked too much legitimate content. In this case, computers in the school library blocked access to websites that promoted gay rights, but allowed access to websites that opposed gay rights. The student did not challenge that federal law required the school to use filtering software to block obscene material. In 2012, a federal court judge found that the school's blocking software configuration was unconstitutional. It ordered the school to reconfigure its software to make sure that it did not discriminate against different viewpoints.[3]

Although most people agree that children should be protected when they are online, they do not always agree on how that should be accomplished. For example, some people suggest that a parent should monitor a child's internet access and decide if the child's internet activities are acceptable. Others suggest that laws should be in place to protect the child even if a parent is not monitoring the child's internet use. As you will see in this chapter, several laws have been enacted to protect children. Most of these laws are directed at the website operators who provide online content to children.

However, even when enacting laws, challenges still exist. These include:

- **Identification of children**—How can website operators distinguish between adults and children online?
- **First Amendment and censorship**—When does censoring certain types of content violate the First Amendment?
- **Defining objectionable content**—Where is the dividing line between material that is merely inappropriate for children and that which is truly objectionable?

## Identification of Children

In 1993, the *New Yorker* published the now-famous cartoon by Peter Steiner with the caption, "On the Internet, nobody knows you're a dog." It is just as hard to separate children from adults on the internet. To protect children, you must be able to identify them. Although you can require identification from restaurant customers to ensure they are old enough to purchase alcohol, it is not easy to require identification when users access a website. Most users can easily remain anonymous when they are online. This creates a problem for website operators. Most of the laws that aim to protect children while they are online require website operators to be able to distinguish children from adults.

Website operators can use several methods to distinguish children from adults. These include:

- **Requiring user input**—A website can require users to identify if they are children or adults. For example, users can select a check box indicating they are over a certain age. They can be required to enter an age or a birth date. This is not a foolproof method, however, because people can simply lie about their age. If a child accesses an age-restricted website under false pretenses, the website operator can still be liable for providing objectionable content to a child.
- **Requiring payment**—If a website has material that should be restricted from children, it can require a payment to access the site. Payment can be made using a credit card, a PayPal account, or another method that a child is unlikely to be able to use. The payment may be a nominal fee, such as 99 cents. It could also be a larger fee designed to generate revenue. A payment requirement can be effective because children generally do not have access to means of payment.
- **Using parental controls**—Some operating systems include parental controls. So do many applications. **Parental controls** allow a parent to restrict their children's access to objectionable material based on different ratings.
- **Requiring parental consent**—If a child wishes to access a particular website, that site can block the child's access until a parent provides permission. This means that the website operator implements controls to verify that a parent is providing consent to access the website.

**NOTE**

The Entertainment Software Rating Board (ESRB) is a self-regulating nonprofit that assigns independent ratings to computer and video game content in the United States. This includes games available online. The ratings help parents select appropriate games and other content for their children. Website operators can voluntarily rate their websites according to ESRB so that parental controls work properly. Visit http://www.esrb.org to learn more.

## First Amendment and Censorship

The First Amendment, which is a part of the Bill of Rights, grants certain rights related to freedom of speech. It also protects freedom of the press and the free exercise of religion. First Amendment issues come into play on the internet in many different ways:

- Individuals online have a First Amendment right to view lawful content, including content that others might find troubling.
- Website operators and other content creators have a First Amendment right to post lawful content, including content that others might find troubling.

The U.S. Supreme Court has said that the right to freedom of speech applies to the internet.[4] This means that the government cannot restrict an adult's access to content on the internet. However, the government can restrict a child's access to harmful online materials if the government has a compelling reason to do so.

When the government restricts a child's access to objectionable online materials, other issues are raised. Does it violate a website operator's rights to force it to censor material because a child might view it? If individuals are required to identify themselves before they can use a website, such as proving that they are not children, does that restrict their free speech? Does it restrict free speech if individuals are required to identify themselves by name in comments on a website? If libraries are required to use filters on computers to keep children from viewing objectionable content, does it restrict the free speech rights of adults who also use those same computers?

Many of these issues continue to evolve within the context of the laws discussed in this chapter.

## Defining Obscenity

The laws discussed in this chapter protect the privacy of children. They also protect children from harmful content. For the most part, this harmful content is content that would be considered obscene. Most people agree that children should not see obscene material. However, it is difficult to legally define what obscene material is.

### I Know It When I See It

A 1964 U.S. Supreme Court case shows the difficulty of defining obscenity.[5] In *Jacobellis v. Ohio*, a movie theater manager was convicted under state law of illegally possessing and exhibiting an obscene film. The state supreme court upheld the conviction. However, the U.S. Supreme Court later reversed that decision.

In this case, the Court agreed that the First Amendment does not protect pornography or obscenity. It disagreed about whether the motion picture was obscene. In the Court's decision, Justice Potter Stewart expressed the difficulty of defining what is obscenity and pornography. He wrote, "But I know it when I see it, and the motion picture involved with this case is not that."

This case was decided over 50 years ago. Yet the challenge of identifying obscenity still exists today.

The U.S. Supreme Court addressed this in 1973. In *Miller v. California* the Court said that for material to be identified as "obscene," it must meet three conditions. The conditions are based on the average person applying contemporary community standards to a review of the material. The three conditions are that the material:

- Appeals predominantly to prurient interests—*prurient* indicates a morbid, degrading, and unhealthy interest in sex
- Depicts or describes sexual conduct in a patently offensive way
- Lacks serious literary, artistic, political, or scientific value[6]

It is not always easy to apply this definition. What one person considers obscene, another person may consider healthy. Material that one person finds informative may be deemed tasteless by another. Material that is offensive to one person may be viewed as valuable by another. How a person views material is often influenced by societal, family, community, and religious values.

## Children's Online Privacy Protection Act

The COPPA[7] passed in November 1998 and first went into effect in April 2000. COPPA governs how websites collect information from children under the age of 13. The FTC oversees COPPA compliance and has the power to make rules for COPPA compliance. The FTC rule governing COPPA, called the *COPPA Rule*, was first drafted in 1999 and most recently revised in 2013. In 2019 the FTC began the process of revising the COPPA Rule because of the fast pace of technology change. However, it may take years before an updated rule is finalized and released.

> **NOTE**
> The three conditions for defining obscenity are known as the *Miller test*.

Websites must follow specific rules under COPPA to collect and use information from children. There are several important definitions in the COPPA Rule:

- **Child**—Any person under the age of 13
- **Parent**—The legal guardian of a child
- **Operator**—A website operator, or operator of an online service, who collects or maintains personal information about users

### Purpose of COPPA

The primary purpose of COPPA is to protect children's privacy on the internet, as well as protect them from age-inappropriate content and online marketing. Websites must follow specific rules if they collect or use a child's personal information. For example, they must obtain a parent's consent before doing so. They must also post a privacy policy explaining their practices.

Personal information includes:

- A child's first and last name
- A child's email address or other online contact information such as an Instant Messaging username or voice over Internet Protocol (VOIP) identifier

- A child's screen name or username
- A child's physical address, such as his or her home address
- A child's telephone number
- A child's Social Security number (SSN)
- Photographs, video, or audio files that contain a child's image or voice
- Geolocation data that identifies a physical address
- Any persistent identifier, such as an internet cookie or Internet Protocol (IP) address, that is used to recognize a user over time and across different websites
- Any other information concerning a child or the child's parents that a website operator collects from a child and combines with any other data about a child[8]

Any personal information that is collected must be protected. This means that the website operator must protect the confidentiality, security, and integrity of this data. Website operators must ensure the information is not made publicly available to others. This includes making sure it is not displayed on a home page of a website, on a message board, or in a chatroom. The law allows website operators to share this kind of data only for specific reasons. However, when website operators share this information, they must share it only with third parties who can properly protect it.[9]

**NOTE**

COPPA is not the same as the Child Online Protection Act (COPA). COPA was enacted in 1998 to protect minors from access to harmful material on the internet. However, courts ruled that COPA violated free speech and the law never went into effect. The Children's Internet Protection Act (CIPA) is similar to what COPA attempted to accomplish and is discussed later in this chapter.

## Scope of the Regulation

COPPA applies to anyone operating online services that collect or use information about children under the age of 13. This includes situations where the website operator directly collects the information, as well as situations where the website operator lets third parties collect the information. Even general-audience websites might have to follow the COPPA Rule. If operators of general-audience sites know they are collecting data from children, then they must comply with COPPA. For example, an operator might know that its site is collecting data from children if it asks users to share their birth date. An operator that collects demographic data such as school attendance and grade completion might also know that children are using its website. Website operators are also required to protect the security of any information that they do properly collect from children.

The definition of website or online service is broad. In addition to websites, it also includes:

- Mobile apps
- Internet gaming platforms
- Advertising networks
- Connected toys and other internet-connected devices
- Internet-enabled location services[10]

## Main Requirements

COPPA has two main rules that websites must follow in order to comply with the rule. Operators must:

- Post a privacy policy
- Get verifiable parental consent before collecting information from children

### Privacy Policy

Under COPPA, websites must post a privacy policy.[11] The privacy policy states the kind of information the site collects about children. It also states how the site will use the information. The COPPA Rule tells operators the terms that must be included in the privacy policy.

COPPA requires that a website privacy policy should be easily visible and accessible. The rule requires that a link to the privacy policy should be included on the home page of the website. The rule also requires that the link should be posted on every area of the website where a child's personal information is collected.[12] A COPPA-compliant privacy policy must be accessible from a clear and prominent link. This means the link needs to stand out and be noticeable to users of the website. A website designer can achieve this in a variety of ways. For example, the designer can use different type sizes, fonts, colors, or contrasting backgrounds to highlight the link. In addition, the privacy policy must be clearly labeled to indicate it is a privacy policy. The most common label is "Privacy Policy." Other examples of clear labels are "Privacy Statement" and "Information Practices Statement."

 **NOTE**

COPPA does not specifically use the phrase "privacy policy." It requires website operators to provide a notice on their websites that identifies the collected information. However, the FTC's COPPA Rule calls this notice a "privacy policy."

### Privacy Policy Content

The privacy policy needs to contain specific information to be COPPA-compliant. For example, it must be clearly written and easy to read. The format is not as important as the content. At a minimum, the policy must contain:

- **Operator contact information**—This includes the name, mailing address, telephone number, and email address of all operators collecting or using the information collected on the website. If several operators are collecting information, the policy can list the contact details for only one operator under two conditions. First, the names of all operators must be listed in the privacy policy or in a link accessible from that policy. Second, the listed operator must respond to all questions about the policy. It also must answer questions about how data is collected and used on the site.
- **Notice of what information is collected**—The policy must be specific. A generic term such as "contact information" is not acceptable. Instead, the policy should specify the child's name, address, telephone number, gender, age, and email address.
- **Notice of how information is collected**—A website can collect information actively or passively. A user entering information into a form is active collection. In contrast, a web cookie that collects personal information is passive collection. The privacy policy must clearly state how information is collected.

- **Notice of how the information will be used**—Websites must state how the information will be used. It must be specific. For example, a website could collect email addresses for newsletter subscriptions. It could collect mailing addresses for prizes. It could also collect the information for sales and marketing purposes. Each use must be clearly stated.
- **Notice of whether the information is disclosed to third parties**—The website must also state whether collected information is shared with a third party. These are any entities that are not the operator of the website. Third parties also include entities that do not provide internal support for the website. Parents may refuse to share the collected data with third parties.
- **Assurance that participation is not conditioned on data collection**—That is, a website cannot require children to submit contact details in order to be allowed to use the site. Websites are not allowed to collect more information than necessary for a child to participate in an activity. This prevents the website from collecting too much information about a child. For example, a website may collect an email address for an online newsletter subscription. Collecting a physical mailing address for an online newsletter is not reasonable. The privacy policy should clearly state that a website will not condition participation on information collection.
- **Parental rights**—The policy must state that a parent can review information collected on his or her child. Parents can also tell the website to delete any data it has collected, as well as refuse further data collection. They can also refuse to allow the website to share collected information with third parties.

### *Gaining Parental Consent*

COPPA has specific rules about getting parental consent. This consent is required if a website wants to use and collect data from a child. Website operators must take reasonable steps to make sure that a parent receives direct notice of the operator's data collection practices. This notice must include:

- That the operator has collected the parent's online contact information from the child in order to obtain parental consent
- That the parent's consent is required to collect, use, or disclose the child's information. The notice must state that the operator will not collect, use, or disclose the child's information without parental consent
- The specific items of data that the website operator wants to collect from the child
- A link to the website privacy policy
- How the parent can give verifiable consent to the collection, use, and disclosure of the child's information
- That if the parent does not provide consent within a reasonable time, the operator will delete the parent's online contact information from its records[13]

Under COPPA, parental consent must be verifiable. Only a parent can give consent. A website operator must verify the identity of the parents that it contacts. This becomes especially important if the parent requests to see the information held about his or her child. Website operators must have measures in place to prevent the information from being released to the wrong party.[14]

Parents have other rights under the COPPA Rule. The website must re-notify parents whenever it changes its data collection and use procedures. Parents must be allowed to review information collected from their children. They also must be allowed to revoke their consent. If a parent revokes his or her consent, website operators must stop collecting, using, or disclosing that data immediately. Parents also can request that a website operator delete data held on their children. Website operators must make parents aware of how to exercise these additional rights.

 **NOTE**

There are many websites directed toward children. Next time you visit one of them, see if you can find the website's privacy policy. Is it easy to find? Does it contain the terms discussed in this section?

Consent is not required at all in some instances. Websites do not need parental consent if they are collecting an email address to respond to a one-time request from a child. Nor do they need consent to provide the initial notice to the parent. Consent is also not required to collect a child's name and online contact information to protect the security of the website.

In some instances, upfront consent is not required. In these special circumstances, the website must still later tell parents that it collected data. For example, a website can collect a child's name, parent's name, and online contact information in order to protect a child's safety. If a website collects this information, it must later tell parents that it collected the information and it must not use this information for any other purpose.[15]

### Verifying Parental Consent

A website operator can use one of several methods to verify a person is a parent of a child and get consent for data collection. These include:

- **Sending signed printed forms**—These may be sent via mail, fax, or email. An electronic scan of a signed consent form is permissible.
- **Provide government-issued identification**—Parents can provide copies of government-issued ID that can then be checked against a database. In this situation, website operators must delete the identification record once the verification process is completed.
- **Using credit cards or other online payment forms**—The credit card or online payment mechanism can verify details about the parent.
- **Using toll-free numbers**—Parents can call and provide details to verify their identities.
- **Using video conference**—Parents can connect via video conference to trained personnel in order to provide details to verify their identities.
- **Answering knowledge-based questions**—Parents can answer a series of challenge questions that would be difficult for a child to answer.

Some operators suggest that these methods are too costly to be practical. Therefore, many websites try to avoid the law. They do not collect information on children, and their privacy statement reflects this. Users are required to indicate they are at least 13 years old before information is collected. They might do this by entering their age on a website form or checking a box indicating they are at least 13 years old. However, it is possible for children to easily overcome these types of controls.

## Oversight

> **NOTE**
> The FTC summarizes the COPPA Rule at http://www.business.ftc.gov/privacy-and-security/childrens-privacy.

The FTC provides oversight for COPPA. The FTC investigates complaints of websites that violate COPPA. It can also bring enforcement actions and impose civil penalties for COPPA violations. The FTC provides many tools to help website operators comply with the law.

# Children's Internet Protection Act

The CIPA,[16] which was passed in 2000, requires schools and libraries that receive funding from the U.S. government for internet access to filter offensive and sexually explicit online content. The goal of the program is to limit children's access to offensive and age-inappropriate content on the internet. Under CIPA, a minor is anyone under the age of 17.[17] These schools and libraries had until July 1, 2004, to first comply with CIPA.

> **NOTE**
> Note the differences in ages between CIPA and COPPA. COPPA defines a child as anyone under the age of 13. CIPA defines a minor as anyone under the age of 17.

> **NOTE**
> A *visual depiction* is any picture, image, or graphic image.

CIPA was quickly challenged. The American Library Association and the American Civil Liberties Union sued the U.S. government, claiming CIPA violated the free speech rights of adults. They also claimed the law was so broad that it could prevent minors from getting information about topics such as breast cancer. In 2002, the U.S. District Court for the Eastern District of Pennsylvania agreed that CIPA violated First Amendment rights and that the government could not enforce CIPA. The U.S. government appealed that decision.[18]

The suit went to the U.S. Supreme Court. In *United States et al. v. American Library Association, Inc. et al.* in 2003, the U.S. Supreme Court overturned the District Court ruling and upheld the law. The Supreme Court said that the law was constitutional because it was conditional. That is, only schools and libraries that chose to receive federal funding to subsidize their internet access costs were required to follow the law. If it wanted to, a school or library could choose not to accept the funding. If that happened, then it did not have to comply with CIPA.

## Purpose

The primary purpose of CIPA is to protect minors from accessing offensive content on the internet. Offensive content includes visual depictions of material that is any of the following:

- Obscene
- Child pornography
- Harmful to minors

Under CIPA, *obscene* and *child pornography* are defined by referring to other laws. CIPA does specifically define the phrase *harmful to minors*. It includes any visual content that:

- Taken as a whole and with respect to minors, appeals to a prurient interest in nudity, sex, or excretion

FYI

E-Rate funding provides discounts to schools and libraries for internet access and telecommunications services. This funding is collected as part of the universal services fee paid by consumers to use telecommunications services. The goal of this funding is to help all schools and libraries have affordable internet access. Discounts range from 20 to 90 percent of the service costs depending on the need of the school or library. Part of the E-Rate application requires schools and libraries to state affirmatively that they are complying with CIPA. The E-Rate program provided $4.15 billion in funding in 2019. Learn more at https://www.fcc.gov/consumers/guides/universal-service-program-schools-and-libraries-e-rate.

- Depicts, describes, or represents, in a patently offensive way with respect to what is suitable for minors, an actual or simulated sexual act or sexual contact, actual or simulated normal or perverted sexual acts, or a lewd exhibition of the genitals
- Taken as a whole, lacks serious literary, artistic, political, or scientific value as to minors[19]

## Scope of the Regulation

The E-Rate program provides discounts to most schools and libraries for internet access. Any school or library that receives federal funding from the E-Rate program must comply with CIPA. However, schools and libraries do not have to accept these funds. They can either pay for the internet access with other funds, or choose not to use the internet.

## Main Requirements

CIPA has two main requirements. The first is that schools and libraries that accept E-Rate funding must implement technologies that filter offensive visual content so that minors do not access it. The second requirement is that schools implement an internet safety policy.

### *Content Filtering*

The primary requirements of CIPA mandate the filtering of offensive content so that minors do not see it. Although this may seem difficult, there are tools to make the job easier. CIPA's term for such a tool is **technology protection measure (TPM)**. A TPM is any technology that can block or filter the objectionable content.[20] Remember that under CIPA, a TPM must filter visual content.

Consider **FIGURE 5-1**. This figure shows a proxy server used to filter content. A **proxy server** accepts internet requests from clients, retrieves the pages, and serves them to the client. Content filters filter out objectionable content. As shown, you would configure the internal clients to access the internet through a proxy server.

The proxy server has a content filter that blocks all content marked as unacceptable. Some filters can also block content to email and instant messaging programs. Similarly, the filter allows all content marked as acceptable based on filter lists.

Third-party companies sell subscriptions to filter lists. These companies constantly search the internet, identify restricted materials, and add it to the filter lists. When a

FIGURE 5-1

Proxy server used for content filtering.

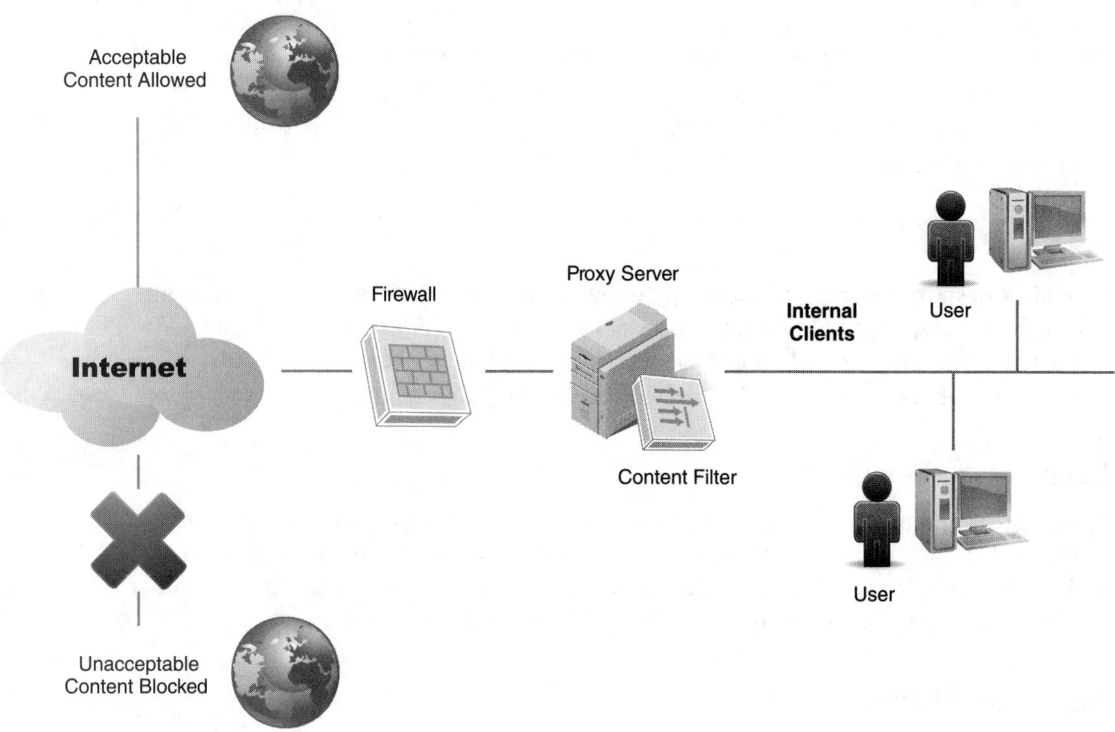


network administrator adds the filter to an organization's proxy server, the server blocks the prohibited material.

In addition to filtering with lists such as the previously described ones, TPMs can also include monitoring technologies that track a child's online activities. They can also limit the amount of time that a child can spend on the internet. In addition, TPMs include age-verification systems that restrict online access to adults.

The Federal Communications Commission (FCC) recognizes that a TPM cannot be 100 percent effective.[21] However, neither CIPA nor the FCC defines what level is acceptable. A third-party company may claim its filter is CIPA compliant. However, there is no certification process to verify that a filter is CIPA compliant. The FCC has stated that local authorities should determine which measures are most effective for their community. The FCC rules specifically state that the U.S. federal government may not establish the criteria for making this determination and that it must be handled at the local level.[22]

Although a proxy server is a common method of filtering, CIPA does not specify where to filter the content. An internet service provider (ISP) may be able to filter it, or you may be able to purchase software to install on individual computers for filtering purposes. CIPA states *what* must be filtered but not *how* to filter it.

### Proxy Servers in Any Company

Many companies use proxy servers. Their use is not restricted to CIPA compliance. Many companies choose to restrict employees' access to different internet websites. For example, a company may want to prevent employees from accessing gambling sites. To do so, it can purchase a subscription to lists of gambling sites from one of the third-party sites that provide filter lists. The company can then install this filter on its proxy server.

When the user tries to access the prohibited site, the proxy server can instead show a different page. For example, the server could redirect the user to a web page that states, "Access is restricted." This page also could show the company's acceptable usage policy. Additionally, many proxy servers log all activities. Administrators are able to view the logs to determine which employees are trying to access restricted sites.

### *Internet Safety Policy*

To comply with CIPA, schools and libraries must adopt and enforce an internet safety policy that must be made available to all users of the facility. The policy must address the following items:

- Access by minors to inappropriate matter on the internet
- The safety and security of minors when using electronic mail, chatrooms, and other forms of direct electronic communication
- Unauthorized access, such as "hacking," and other unlawful activities
- Unauthorized disclosure, use, and dissemination of a minor's personal information
- The measures designed to restrict minors' access to harmful materials

An internet safety policy must educate minors about appropriate online behavior. This includes how to use social networking websites and chatrooms safely. The policy must include information on how to recognize cyberbullying, as well as how minors should respond to it.[23]

### *Exceptions*

One of the main criticisms of CIPA is that schools and libraries are not implementing it properly. CIPA requires schools and libraries to filter visual depictions that may be harmful to minors. This means that images must be censored. However, sometimes access to text and entire websites are inadvertently blocked. In addition, sometimes the TPMs used by libraries may not work correctly and may actually allow minors access to obscene materials. Finally, often TPMs deny access by both adults and children to constitutionally protected content.

According to CIPA, a school or library must be able to disable the TPM for any adult who has a need to view content for a research or other lawful purpose. An adult is anyone over the age of 17. If a school or library refuses to disable a TPM for an adult that requests it, then the school or library is potentially infringing on the First Amendment rights of that adult. This is because they are censoring adult access to protected content. Under CIPA, an adult does not have to state why he or she wants the TPM disabled.

The *United States et al. v. American Library Association, Inc. et al.* Supreme Court ruling in 2003 explicitly mentioned this point. One of the reasons that the Supreme Court held that the law was constitutional is because a TPM could be disabled for any adult that requests it.

Libraries can use any method to disable the TPM that works best for their location. For example, library personnel could label some computers as "adult only." Librarians would then have to monitor and prevent minors from using these computers. Librarians also could log onto a program designed to disable the TPM. Only personnel with the proper credentials could disable the TPM. Another method is to require an administrator to disable the TPM. Upon request by a patron, the librarian could contact an administrator to disable the TPM.

### Oversight

The FCC has oversight for CIPA. However, little oversight action is required. When a public school or library requests E-Rate funding, it must certify that they will comply with CIPA. This certification is usually all that is required.

If a TPM fails, the school or library is expected to take steps to resolve the failure. Patrons may complain to the library for specific instances such as a TPM blocking too much content or not enough content. If the library does not resolve patron complaints, then the patron can file a complaint with the FCC, which may investigate those complaints. Any school or library that fails to comply with CIPA must refund any E-Rate funds or discounts that it received. Depending on the situation, other criminal laws such as laws against providing false statements to the government could apply to CIPA violations.

## Family Educational Rights and Privacy Act (FERPA)

FERPA was passed in 1974.[24] The primary goal of FERPA is to protect the privacy of student educational records. An *educational record* includes any personal and education data on a student maintained by an educational agency or institution. Under FERPA, parents have the right to inspect and review a student's educational records. However, these rights do not belong to a parent forever. When the student reaches age 18, these rights pass to the student.

### Scope

FERPA applies to any education agencies or institutions that receive funding from the U.S. Department of Education (ED). Educational agencies or institutions include:

- Primary and secondary schools
- Vocational colleges
- Colleges and universities
- Community colleges
- State and local educational agencies
- Schools or agencies offering preschool programs

For readability, the phrase "educational agency or institution" will often be shortened to "school" in this section.

The type of funding that these institutions receive from the federal government can be direct or indirect. Schools may receive funding outright from the ED. This is direct funding. If a college student receives a federal grant or federal aid and uses this as payment to a university, then the university is receiving federal funding. This is indirect funding and the

### FERPA and Peer-Grading

Many professors use peer-grading techniques. Students may be required to work on a project together and grade each other at the completion of the project. Additionally, students may be required to exchange assignments or tests and grade each other. Some professors require students to call out other students' grades in class. This is acceptable under FERPA.

Under FERPA, a school cannot publish students' grades, not even on a bulletin board outside of a classroom. This prohibition does not extend to peer grading. The U.S. Supreme Court decided this in 2002. In *Owasso Independent School District No. I-011 v. Falvo*, the court decided that peer grades are not maintained as education records. Therefore, FERPA does not protect them from disclosure.

university must comply with FERPA. Because federal funding is so valuable, and comes from so many different sources, almost all schools comply with FERPA.

If any educational agency or institution chooses not to comply with FERPA, it cannot receive any federal funds. Sometimes private schools and universities do not receive federal funds. In these cases, these institutions do not have to comply with FERPA.

**NOTE**

FERPA formally defines personally identifiable information (PII). Several other laws and regulations also define PII. PII can be a name, a SSN, biometric data, or any data used to identify a person. Several laws and regulations specify different types of PII that must be protected.

## Main Requirements

FERPA has four main requirements: annual notification, access to education records, amendment of education records, and disclosure of education records.

To carry out these requirements, FERPA has several important definitions.[25] These include:

- **Student**—Any individual that has ever been in attendance at an educational institution and for whom the institution maintains education records.
- **Attendance**—A student's physical attendance at an educational institution. It includes any virtual attendance such as video conference or correspondence course. Attendance via the internet, by satellite, or through other methods used by the school is also included.
- **Education records**—Any records related to a student maintained by an educational agency or institution. These include written documents, computer media, video, film, or photographs. Records maintained by any outside party acting for the agency or institution are also included.

FERPA also defines PII and places limits on how this data can be used and disclosed. Under FERPA, PII includes:

- A student's name
- The name of the student's parent or other family members
- The address of the student or student's family

- A personal identifier, such as the student's SSN, student number, or biometric record
- Other identifiers, such as the student's date of birth, place of birth, and mother's maiden name
- Other information that is connected to a specific student that would allow a reasonable person in the school community to identify the student
- Information requested by a person who the school reasonably believes knows the identity of the student to whom the education record relates

It is important to know what might be included in a student's education record. The rules can be complex. Demographic information such as race and gender cannot be given out if it is directly connected with a student name. FERPA protects grades or transcripts of grades. Disciplinary records are considered a part of the student educational record. Behavioral notes on the student are also protected if the notes are kept in the student record. Under FERPA, the private notes of faculty and staff are not usually considered educational records. If the faculty or staff notes are kept in a student record then they are considered part of the educational record.

It is possible for a student record to contain additional information outside the scope of FERPA. FERPA does not require schools to reveal this data when access to an educational record is requested. For example, a school does not have to reveal parental financial records, confidential letters of recommendation, or statements of recommendation.

### Annual Notification

FERPA requires schools to provide an annual notification to students and parents. This notice lets parents and eligible students know what their FERPA rights are. The annual notification also must state how to file a complaint with the Department of Education if the school violates any of FERPA's provisions.[26]

The annual notification must identify school officials that have access to educational records without consent. FERPA allows any school official that has legitimate educational interest in the record to view it without specific consent. These officials must be identified in the annual notification. The school has great freedom in identifying these officials. They could be teachers, instructors, professors, administrative personnel such as principals or provosts, or local board of education personnel.

Finally, FERPA requires that the school provide the annual notice "by any means that are reasonably likely to inform the parents or eligible students of their rights."[27] This means that the school might have to translate the notice into different languages. It also must consider whether it should provide the notice in alternative formats to disabled students or parents.

### Access to Education Records

The most fundamental right under FERPA is student and parental access to the student's educational records. The parent or eligible student has the right to inspect and review any educational records maintained by the school.[28] Under FERPA, schools must respond within 45 days to a request to inspect and review educational records.

In most instances, the school does not have to make copies of the records. It only needs to make them available for review and inspection. If the parent or student requests copies, the school may charge a small copying fee.

There are special access rules for colleges and universities. These rules apply to situations where an educational record for the student may also contain confidential information about the student's parents. This happens often in situations where parents provide their own financial information to help a student receive federal financial aid. In these situations, colleges and universities do not have to give a student access to the financial records of his or her parents.[29]

**NOTE**

Eligible students are students over the age of 18 or those who are attending a postsecondary institution. FERPA parental rights transfer to the student when the student becomes an eligible student.

**FYI**

Schools are required to make and provide copies of the educational records in special circumstances. If a parent does not live within commuting distance to the school and cannot come to the school to inspect the records, then the school must provide the parent with copies.

Finally, a school is not required to create an educational record where none exists. Sometimes students or parents might request a report or record that is not already part of the educational record. In these cases, the school does not have to create that report just because a parent asked for it.

### *Amendment of Education Records*

FERPA allows parents and students the right to request amendment of student educational records. A parent may ask that a school amend information in the record that is incorrect or misleading. The school's annual notification must specify the procedure for how to request this correction.[30]

**NOTE**

Schools are required to hold hearings on amendment disputes within a reasonable time after it receives a request for a hearing. The school must give the parent or eligible student notice of the time, date, and location of the hearing.

Schools are not required to honor the request for correction if the school does not believe that the student's record is incorrect. The school must notify the parent or student of this decision. If a school does not amend a student educational record, then the parent or eligible student has the right to a hearing on that decision.[31] The purpose of the hearing is to determine if the school's decision was appropriate. The school and the parents will present their cases to the hearing officer. If the hearing officer decides that the school's decision was appropriate, then the parent or eligible student must be allowed an opportunity to provide a written statement that is added to the student's educational record. The written statement can comment on the information under dispute in the record. It can also state why the parent or student disagrees with the decision of the school not to amend the record.

### *Disclosure of Education Records*

In general, educational agencies or institutions must have permission from either a student or the student's parents in order to disclose educational records and student PII. The school

**NOTE**

It is important to remember that the parent has these rights until the student reaches the age of 18 or is attending a postsecondary institution. After that point, the parent no longer has the rights. Only the child has the rights. In other words, a parent may be paying for a 20-year-old son or daughter's college education, but the parent does not have the right to inspect his or her child's educational records.

must obtain written consent to release this data. Most schools have forms for this purpose. The procedure for using these forms is usually included in the school's annual notification.

To disclose student educational records, written consent must include:

- Which records will be disclosed
- The purpose of the disclosure
- Who will receive the record
- The date the consent is granted
- Signature of the student or parent
- Signature of the school official releasing the data[32]

Parents and students can refuse to give consent to have their data released. However, the school can still release data to certain entities under FERPA exceptions. The next section explains these exceptions.

## Disclosure Exceptions Under FERPA

A school can release student records without prior consent in some cases. As mentioned earlier in this section, school officials, such as principals or teachers, can view student educational records. These officials must have a legitimate educational interest to view the record. School officials cannot view a student record merely if they are curious about a student's performance.

*Directory information* can also be released without student or parental consent. Directory information includes a student's name, address, telephone number, date and place of birth, awards, and dates of attendance. Under no circumstances should the directory information include PII information such as a student's SSN or student identification number.

Schools must identify which student data is specifically defined as directory information. Schools also must tell parents and eligible students how to request that the school not share this information. All of this information must be included in the school's annual notice.[33] The release of directory information is the primary FERPA disclosure exception. Schools frequently rely on this exception.

FERPA allows a school to disclose student PII in several other ways that do not require prior written consent:

- Schools can transfer a student's educational record to a new school if a student is moving from one school to another.
- Schools can provide student PII to an accrediting organization to prove that the school is performing to specific standards.
- Schools can provide student PII in some financial aid situations.
- Schools may disclose student educational records in response to a court order or lawful subpoena.
- School may disclose student PII if it will aid personnel in an emergency situation.
- Postsecondary schools can disclose the PII of a student over age 18 to that student's parents if the student is considered a dependent for U.S. federal tax purposes.

The emergency situation exception became important in early 2020 during the coronavirus disease 2019 (COVID-19) outbreak. During the outbreak, the Department of Education reminded all schools that health records maintained by the school could be disclosed, without consent, if the school believed that the COVID-19 virus posed a serious risk to the health or safety of an individual student at the school. The emergency situation exception is limited in time to the period of the emergency and generally does not allow for a blanket release of PII from student education records.[34]

Schools must maintain records of all of the requests and disclosures of student educational records.[35] These records must include the parties who received the student PII and the reason for the disclosure. This record of disclosures must be maintained for as long as the school maintains the underlying educational record.

## Security of Student Records Under FERPA

FERPA has no specific information security requirements that schools must use to protect student educational records. For example, FERPA does not contain a requirement that schools notify parents and students if an unauthorized person accesses student records. Instead, schools just have to record the unauthorized disclosure in the student record.

Even though it is not required under FERPA, the U.S. Department of Education does encourage educational institutions to take steps to protect student information. The department suggests that schools consider the following factors to implement security measures:

- The type of information to be protected
- The size and complexity of the educational institution
- The resources available to the institution
- Security safeguards used by other institutions in similar circumstances[36]

Although FERPA does not have specific information security requirements, the Department of Education often uses other laws to encourage colleges and universities, in particular, to protect student data. For example, the U.S. Department of Education Office of Federal Student Aid (FSA) administers student financial aid awards. Colleges and universities that administer federal student financial aid have agreed to comply with the Gramm-Leach-Bliley Act (GLBA) as part of their agreement with FSA. This means that those colleges and universities must show that all federal student aid applicant information is protected from unauthorized access.[37]

## Oversight

The Family Policy Compliance Office (FPCO) in the U.S. Department of Education provides oversight for FERPA and investigates FERPA complaints. Only parents and students over the age of 18 may make complaints against schools for FERPA violations. Complaints must be submitted to the FPCO within 180 days of the date that the FERPA violation is alleged to have occurred.[38] The FPCO resolves FERPA complaints and enforces its decisions by withholding federal funding to the schools that have violated the law.

### How to Respond to Requests

A school may receive many different kinds of requests for information. Any personnel that have access to records should have training on how to respond. Put yourself in the situation of the person answering the phone. How would you respond to these questions if you were an employee at a college or university?

An employer calls and asks about a student who graduated last year. Specifically, the employer asks if the student graduated. Does FERPA restrict the release of this information? How do you respond?

- FERPA covers this information. You may need to explain this to the employer.
- You can give the information to the employer if the student signs a consent form.

A student needs a copy of his transcript. He asks a friend to pick it up for him. What should you tell the friend when he shows up?

- FERPA restricts the school from giving the friend this information.
- You may check the student's record to see if it has a signed consent form for this friend. If not, the transcript should not be given out.
- The student must sign a consent form.

A mother calls about her 17-year-old son. She wants to know if her son will be graduating with his class. Does the parent have rights to this information? What do you tell her?

- FERPA rights transferred to the son when he started attending classes at the university. The parent does not have rights to this information. You may want to explain the FERPA requirements to the mother.
- Encourage the mother to talk with her son. In other words, ask her son if he will be graduating. You can provide information on how someone can reenroll in classes.

The mayor recently made a speech and mentioned a student at your school. The mayor talked about how the student had earned a specific degree and was now working on a higher-level degree. You know that the student never completed any degree at your school. What should you do?

- FERPA protects this information. You should not take any action.
- If the mayor or the mayor's office requests the information, you cannot release it without a consent form.

### State Laws Protecting Student Data

In addition to the protections afforded by FERPA, many states also have state laws designed to protect student privacy. For example, 40 states passed 125 laws related to student privacy from 2013 to 2018.[39] Many of these laws were put into place because of the rise in online learning activities. States were worried that vendors would have access to student information and would use or share student data improperly. Often these laws try to extend FERPA protections and have even more restrictions about what student data a school can share with others.

## Case Studies and Examples

The following case studies provide some real-world background on COPPA and FERPA. These examples provide insight into how the laws are challenged and viewed.

## Children's Privacy

Website operators have an obligation to follow COPPA if they know that they are collecting information from children.

In 2019, the FTC charged operators of the Musical.ly video social networking app with violating COPPA. Musical.ly is now known as TikTok. The FTC alleged that Musical.ly knew many children were using the app. It also alleged that Musical.ly failed to seek parental consent before collecting personal information from users under the age of 13. Even though Musical.ly was a general use website, the FTC said that Musical.ly had received thousands of complaints from parents upset that their children under age 13 had created Musical.ly accounts. Because it had received so many complaints, Musical.ly could not argue that it had no knowledge that children were using the app.

As part of its settlement agreement with the FTC, Musical.ly agreed to pay $5.7 million to settle the FTC's claims. Musical.ly also had to agree to comply with COPPA by:

- Notifying parents about the app's collection and use of children's personal information
- Getting parental consent before collecting and using data from children
- Deleting personal information when parents request it
- Removing all videos made by children under the age of 13

The FTC documents related to the Musical.ly case are available at https://www.ftc.gov/enforcement/cases-proceedings/172-3004/musically-inc

## Release of Disciplinary Records

Disciplinary records are a part of student records. Because FERPA protects student records, it thereby protects disciplinary records. A student's consent is required before releasing any of these records.

A U.S. district court in the Southern District of Ohio decided this in 2000. The U.S. Court of Appeals affirmed the decision in 2002. However, the case actually started in 1995 and has a colorful history.

In 1995, the Miami University (located in Ohio) student newspaper asked Miami University to provide disciplinary records on students. This was to track crime trends on campus. The university refused to release the records. The paper then made a request using the Ohio Public Records Act. Miami University released the records but removed all personally identifiable information. They also removed information such as the date, time, and location of the incidents.

Editors of the paper thought that the university removed too much information from the records, so they went to the Ohio Supreme Court seeking full disclosure of the records. In a divided decision, the Ohio Supreme Court agreed and ruled that FERPA does not cover the disciplinary records. Miami University tried to take the case to the U.S. Supreme Court, but the Court chose not to hear the case in 1997.

Miami University notified the U.S. Department of Education (ED) that it did not think it was able to comply with FERPA based on the decision. The university also adopted a policy of releasing disciplinary records to any third-party requestor. Ohio State University also released similar records and notified ED that it planned to honor future requests. ED disagreed and thought that the Ohio Supreme Court made a mistake.

ED filed a motion to stop both universities from releasing these records. The U.S. district in the Southern District of Ohio heard the case. The universities did not dispute the facts and were willing to allow the court to rule. However, the school newspaper filed a motion to intervene. Although the newspaper was not named in the suit, it wanted its voice heard.

The newspaper claimed that ED did not have authority in the case. Instead, ED could take action only after the release of records, not before. However, the circuit court disagreed. It determined that ED did have authority. Additionally, the circuit court determined that disciplinary records are education records and covered by FERPA. The court ordered the universities not to release the information.

The newspaper appealed this decision to the U.S. Court of Appeals, arguing that FERPA violates the First Amendment and the district court did not recognize this violation. However, the U.S. Court of Appeals upheld the district court's decision in 2002. Even today, schools must not release student disciplinary records without student consent.

ED documents related to the Miami University case are available at http://www2.ed.gov/policy/gen/guid/fpco/ferpa/library/unofmiami.html and http://www2.ed.gov/policy/gen/guid/fpco/courtcases/miami.html.

## CHAPTER SUMMARY

This chapter covered several laws designed to protect the rights of children and students. The COPPA protects the information of children. It prohibits websites from collecting information about children without a parent's consent. COPPA defines a child as anyone under the age of 13.

The CIPA requires schools and libraries to filter website traffic. CIPA ensures that children do not view objectionable material from these publicly funded locations. CIPA defines a child as anyone under the age of 17.

The FERPA requires schools to protect educational records. Schools need written consent before releasing educational records. The student or parent has the right to review these records. FERPA grants these rights to the parent until the child reaches the age of 18. At that point, the right passes to the student.

## KEY CONCEPTS AND TERMS

Parental controls

Proxy server

Technology protection measure (TPM)

## CHAPTER 5 ASSESSMENT

1. Obscenity is easy to define.
   A. True
   B. False
2. Website operators who attempt to restrict access for children may be accused of violating basic rights. What amendment concerns these rights?
   A. First Amendment
   B. Fifth Amendment
   C. Ninth Amendment
   D. Tenth Amendment
3. Which law is designed to protect children's personal information while they are using online resources?
   A. CIPA
   B. COPPA
   C. FERPA
   D. Bill of Rights
   E. All of these are correct.
4. COPPA defines "child" as anyone under the age of ______.
5. How can a website operator verify parental consent to comply with COPPA?
   A. Using signed, printed forms
   B. Using toll-free numbers
   C. Using email
   D. Using signed, printed forms and toll-free numbers
   E. None of these is correct.
6. A website is collecting information on children. What must be included on the website to comply with COPPA?
   A. Parental consent forms
   B. Privacy policy
   C. Definition of children
   D. a Contact Us page
   E. All of these are correct.
7. Libraries and schools that accept E-Rate funds must comply with ______.
8. Libraries and schools that accept E-Rate funds must implement a ______ to filter objectionable content.
9. CIPA requires certain content to be restricted for minors. How old is a minor?
   A. Anyone under the age of 13
   B. Anyone under the age of 16
   C. Anyone under the age of 17
   D. Anyone under the age of 18
   E. Anyone under the age of 21
10. CIPA requires a library to be able to disable the TPM for some situations.
    A. True
    B. False
11. What law governs the release of student educational information?
    A. CIPA
    B. COPPA
    C. FERPA
    D. Department of Education
    E. All of these are correct.
12. Under FERPA, what type of information can a school release about a student without the student's consent?
    A. Directory information
    B. Personally identifiable information (PII)
    C. Name and student ID number
    D. All of these are correct.
    E. None of these is correct.
13. A parent believes a school is not following FERPA requirements. After trying to resolve it with the school, where can they file a formal complaint?
    A. FERPA compliance office
    B. Family Policy Compliance Office
    C. Federal Communications Commission
    D. Federal Trade Commission
    E. Office of Federal Student Aid
14. What must a school obtain before releasing information about a student to a third party?
    A. Verbal consent
    B. Written consent
    C. Signed affidavit
    D. Notarized consent
    E. Nothing
15. Disciplinary records are a part of educational records.
    A. True
    B. False

## ENDNOTES


1. Rideout, V., and Robb, M. B. (2019). The Common Sense census: Media use by tweens and teens, 2019. San Francisco, CA: Common Sense Media, https://www.commonsensemedia.org/research/the-common-sense-census-media-use-by-tweens-and-teens-2019 (accessed March 24, 2020).
2. Federal Trade Commission, "Google and YouTube Will Pay Record $170 Million for Alleged Violations of Children's Privacy Law," September 4, 2019. https://www.ftc.gov/news-events/press-releases/2019/09/google-youtube-will-pay-record-170-million-alleged-violations (accessed March 24, 2020).
3. American Civil Liberties Union, "Court Orders Missouri School District to Stop Censoring LGBT Websites," February 15, 2012. https://www.aclu.org/press-releases/court-orders-missouri-school-district-stop-censoring-lgbt-websites (accessed March 24, 2020).
4. Reno v. American Civil Liberties Union, 521 U.S. 844 (1997).
5. Jacobellis v. Ohio, 378 U.S. 184 (1964).
6. Miller v. California, 413 U.S. 15 (1973).
7. United States Code, Title 15, sec. 6501–6506.
8. Code of Federal Regulations, Title 16, sec. 312.2.
9. Code of Federal Regulations, Title 16, sec. 312.8.
10. Federal Trade Commission, "Children's Online Privacy Protection Rule: A Six-Step Compliance Plan for Your Business," June 2017. https://www.ftc.gov/tips-advice/business-center/guidance/childrens-online-privacy-protection-rule-six-step-compliance (accessed March 24, 2020).
11. Code of Federal Regulations, Title 26, sec. 312.3.
12. Code of Federal Regulations, Title 26, sec. 312.4.
13. Code of Federal Regulations, Title 26, sec. 312.4.
14. Code of Federal Regulations, Title 26, sec. 312.5.
15. Code of Federal Regulations, Title 26, sec. 312.5.
16. Pub. L. No. 106-554, 114 Stat. 2763A-335, codified in scattered sections of U.S. Code.
17. Code of Federal Regulations, Title 47, sec. 54.520.
18. United States v. American Library Association, 201 F.Supp.2d 401 (E.D. Pa. 2002), reversed 539 U.S. 194 (2003).
19. Code of Federal Regulations, Title 47, sec. 54.520.
20. Code of Federal Regulations, Title 47, sec. 54.520.
21. U.S. Department of Commerce, National Telecommunications and Information Administration, Report to Congress, "Children's Internet Protection Act Study of Technology Protection Measures in Section 1703," August 2003. https://www.ntia.doc.gov/files/ntia/publications/ciparepor t08142003.pdf (accessed March 24, 2020).
22. Code of Federal Regulations, Title 47, sec. 54.520.
23. Code of Federal Regulations, Title 47, sec. 54.520.
24. United States Code, Title 20, sec. 1232g.
25. Code of Federal Regulations, Title 34, sec. 99.3.
26. Code of Federal Regulations, Title 34, sec. 99.7.
27. Code of Federal Regulations, Title 34, sec. 99.7.
28. Code of Federal Regulations, Title 34, sec. 99.10.
29. Code of Federal Regulations, Title 34, sec. 99.12.
30. Code of Federal Regulations, Title 34, sec. 99.7.
31. Code of Federal Regulations, Title 34, sec. 99.20.
32. Code of Federal Regulations, Title 34, sec. 99.30.
33. Code of Federal Regulations, Title 34, sec. 99.31.
34. U.S. Department of Education, "FERPA and the Coronavirus Disease 2019 (COVID-19)," March 2020. https://studentprivacy.ed.gov/resources/ferpa-and-coronavirus-disease-2019-covid-19 (accessed March 24, 2020).
35. Code of Federal Regulations, Title 34, sec. 99.32.
36. Federal Register 73, No. 237 at 74,843–74,844, background information (2008).
37. U.S. Department of Education, "Dear Colleague Letter GEN -16-12," July 1, 2016. https://ifap.ed.gov/dear-colleague-letters/07-01-2016-gen-16-12-subject-protecting-student-information (accessed March 24, 2020).
38. Code of Federal Regulations, Title 34, sec. 99.64.
39. FERPA SHERPA, "State Student Privacy Laws," Last updated 2019. https://ferpasherpa.org/state-laws/ (accessed March 24, 2020).

CHAPTER 6

# Security and Privacy of Health Information

HEALTH INFORMATION CAN be used in several different ways. For example, doctors and other healthcare professionals use and share it to provide medical care. Insurance companies and employers share it for insurance coverage and payment. However, many people worry that this type of information could be used improperly. For example, insurance companies could use it to deny healthcare coverage. Employers could use it to decide not to hire someone. Thieves could steal medical information and use it to commit medical identity theft.

Healthcare providers no longer store health information only in paper files. Many providers use computer systems to create and store electronic health records (EHRs). When information is stored electronically, data may be combined from several different sources. It is possible to create comprehensive medical records that contain a lot of data about a person; therefore, the healthcare industry must take steps to secure these types of records.

This chapter focuses on laws that protect the privacy and security of health information. For the most part, this chapter focuses on the unique challenges presented by growing amounts of electronic health information. This chapter also discusses how federal and state laws work together to protect this information.

## Chapter 6 Topics

This chapter covers the following topics and concepts:

- What the business challenges facing the healthcare industry are
- Why healthcare information is sensitive
- What the Health Insurance Portability and Accountability Act (HIPAA) is
- What the role of state law in protecting medical records is
- What some case studies and examples are

## Chapter 6 Goals

When you complete this chapter, you will be able to:

- Describe the business challenges facing the healthcare industry
- Explain why healthcare information is sensitive
- Explain the main parts of the Health Insurance Portability and Accountability Act (HIPAA)
- Describe the role of state law in protecting the confidentiality of medical records

# Business Challenges Facing the Healthcare Industry

The healthcare industry faces many of the same privacy and security challenges as other industries. The difference is the type of data that is used. The healthcare industry collects consumer financial and personal health information. Healthcare providers collect consumer financial information to make sure that consumers pay for medical goods and services. They collect health information to provide these goods and services. Many people consider health information to be very sensitive.

The healthcare industry often collects data from several sources and stores this data in electronic form. For example, hospital computer systems contain notes from hospital employees and primary care physicians. These systems may also record data from equipment and medication tracking systems that can be linked to individual patients. Health insurance companies collect and combine patient data from different providers. It is important for organizations to maintain the security of computer systems that hold health data. Patients demand that this data be protected. Unfortunately, health information often is compromised in data breaches, which can cause problems for healthcare consumers.

**NOTE**

In November 2018, Anthem, Inc. agreed to pay $16 million to settle allegations that it violated federal laws that protected patient records. Anthem is one of the largest health benefit companies in the United States. The health information of 79 million people was exposed in a series of cyber attacks that targeted Anthem in 2014 and 2015.[1]

Health information can be exploited and used improperly. One such crime is **medical identity theft**, a specialized type of identity theft in which thieves steal a person's name and other parts of his or her medical identity. They then use this information to get medical services or goods. When the thief gets health care, providers may add treatment notes about the thief on the victim's medical record. The thief can use personal information

**FYI**

A 2015 study by the Ponemon Institute estimated that victims of medical identity theft pay, on average, almost $13,500 in costs linked to the theft.[2]

obtained from health records to steal health insurance information and make a false claim for healthcare services. Unpaid medical charges could end up on the victim's credit report.

Medical identity thieves are not exclusively computer hackers or members of organized crime rings. Healthcare providers, such as doctors, dentists, and hospital employees, also can be identity thieves. In 2003, for example, an employee at a cancer center stole the identity of a center patient. The identity thief was sentenced to 16 months in prison and ordered to pay restitution.[3]

In 2019, a medical clinic office worker was arrested on charges of identity theft and wire fraud. The office worker's job gave her access to patient medical information, which she stole and sold. She was caught when she tried to sell the stolen patient information to a law enforcement officer. A search of her home and vehicle when she was arrested turned up stolen information on 113 patients. The office worker pleaded guilty to the charges in January 2020 and was sentenced to 4 years in federal prison.[4]

Medical identity theft is very serious, as it can damage a victim's finances with false insurance claims for services. Similar to regular identity theft, victims must spend time and money resolving payment disputes and credit issues. It also can affect payment for a victim's future medical care. If a thief's medical information becomes a part of the victim's medical record, the victim may not qualify for some medical insurance benefits.

Medical identity theft also can harm a person's physical safety. In this crime, healthcare providers enter diagnoses and treatment notes about the identity thief onto a victim's medical record. If doctors rely on those false notes later, they could give a victim an erroneous diagnosis. If false health information concerns life-threatening conditions, a victim could even be killed by an incorrect course of treatment.

Medical identity theft is a problem because it can be hard to correct false information in a medical record. Because health information is shared electronically for several purposes such as treatment and payment, it can be hard to determine all of the places where false information must be corrected.

## Why Is Healthcare Information So Sensitive?

Most people consider their medical information to be among the most sensitive types of personal information because it can be full of private details that people do not want to share. However, people must share these details with healthcare providers to receive treatment. Providers include this information in medical records. These records contain information on diagnoses, lab results, and treatment options. They also contain information about chronic conditions or mental health counseling, as well as private details about a person's lifestyle.

Doctor/patient confidentiality is a long-held tradition. The Hippocratic Oath, a pledge that many medical school students recite upon their graduation which dates back to the fourth century B.C.E., recognizes this belief. The traditional version of the oath states: "Whatever I see or hear in the lives of my patients, whether in connection with my professional practice or not, which ought not to be spoken of outside, I will keep secret, as considering all such things to be private."[5] The statement means that a doctor will keep the patient's health secrets.

 **NOTE**

When a judge orders defendants to pay restitution, it is paid to victims to compensate them for damages related to a crime.

Health records often contain intimate details about a person. People fear that they will be embarrassed if their health information is not kept secret. Some people may even fear for their lives if particularly intimate facts, such as reasons for health counseling, are disclosed. Another fear among people is that others may discriminate against them. They fear that insurance companies or employers could reject them because of information in their health records. For instance, people who have been treated for anxiety or high blood pressure in the past might fear that their application for private life insurance will be denied. People with a known genetic predisposition for certain types of diseases might fear that they will be denied health insurance.

The U.S. government recognizes the special sensitivity of some medical records. For example, the Drug Abuse Prevention, Treatment, and Rehabilitation Act of 1980[6] protects patient information about alcohol or drug abuse. This law applies to any federally assisted alcohol or drug abuse treatment program. It states that these programs may not disclose patient information without consent. There are very few exceptions to this rule. Patient information can be disclosed without consent only in limited situations. For example, a treatment program may disclose patient information in a medical emergency or to report child abuse.

People often feel as if they have little control over where their health information is shared, which is a privacy concern. Providers share health information for treatment purposes. It is also shared with government agencies if payment is made through government programs such as Medicaid or Medicare. It is also shared with insurance companies. Insurance companies sometimes ask for health insurance records to make decisions about whether a person is a suitable risk for life or health insurance. These records are shared in court cases, particularly if a plaintiff claims an injury in a lawsuit. They are used to prove that a defendant caused the plaintiff's injury and is liable for that injury.

**FYI**

The MIB Group, Inc. is an industry group of U.S. and Canadian insurance companies that helps protect against fraud in the insurance industry. Group members share information about life, health, and long-term care insurance applicants to make sure that applicants do not conceal or hide certain types of health information. Insurance companies need some of this information to determine whether a person is insurable. This helps avoid fraudulent insurance applications and claims. MIB members share this information in a coded format to protect privacy.

The MIB is subject to several U.S. security and privacy laws. These include the Gramm-Leach-Bliley Act (GLBA), the Health Insurance Portability and Accountability Act (HIPAA), and Canadian privacy legislation. To learn more about the MIB, visit http://www.mib.com.

People can do very little to mitigate an improper disclosure of their health information. Although they may feel a social stigma if certain facts are shared indiscriminately or exposed in a data breach, there are few ways to correct that stigma. For instance, people recovering from substance abuse might not want other people to know. They may be concerned that society will judge them unfairly for their past substance abuse. They also may be concerned about being denied employment or other opportunities. They may worry that they could be prosecuted for using illegal substances. No amount of money or fines assessed against a provider who improperly discloses this information can compensate a patient for such embarrassment or fear. People cannot be instructed to "forget" this type of information once they hear it.

The federal government recognizes that health information is highly sensitive. The HIPAA is the best-known U.S. law protecting the security and privacy of health information.

## The Health Insurance Portability and Accountability Act

Congress passed the HIPAA in 1996 to help make health insurance portable. HIPAA is used to fight health insurance fraud and eliminate waste. It also simplifies how health insurance is administered.

HIPAA was amended in 2009 by the Health Information Technology for Economic and Clinical Health Act (HITECH Act),[7] which was part of the American Recovery and Reinvestment Act (ARRA) of 2009. The HITECH Act included the most sweeping changes to HIPAA since the law was first created.

### Purpose

HIPAA is best known for its rules that protect the privacy and security of personally identifiable health information. These terms are part of the law's "Administrative Simplification" requirements. Although these rules are the focus of this chapter, it is important that you know that HIPAA has other provisions as well. They were enacted so that health insurance could be *portable*, or carried from one employer to another. Before HIPAA, some workers felt that they were stuck in a job because they feared they would lose their health insurance if they changed jobs.

HIPAA protects healthcare coverage when workers change jobs. In this way, it protects both workers and their families. It forbids a new employer's health plan from denying coverage for some reasons, and prohibits employers from discriminating against workers based on certain conditions, such as pregnancy. It also limits employer-provided health plans from using preexisting conditions as reasons for excluding workers from the plan.

> **NOTE**
>
> *Job lock* refers to situations where workers feel locked into their jobs. They are afraid they will lose their employer-provided benefits if they leave.

A *preexisting condition* is a health condition that existed before a person applies for a medical or other insurance policy. Insurance companies have different ways of dealing with these types of conditions. Some may provide only partial coverage for them. Others may not cover them at all. Still other companies may cover the condition only after a certain period of time has passed.

HIPAA protects workers in group health plans. Employers that offer health insurance coverage typically offer these types of plans. HIPAA does not require that employers offer health coverage. If they do, however, HIPAA applies. Most of HIPAA's rules apply to situations when workers change jobs or move from one group health plan to another. This is the "portability" portion of the law. HIPAA does not apply to situations where a worker had no health coverage at all and then gets a job with healthcare coverage.

HIPAA's preexisting condition rules are very important, because they help prevent job lock. They also promote mobility. HIPAA limits preexisting condition exclusions in two ways.

### The 2009 HITECH Act

In February 2009, Congress passed the HITECH Act, which was part of the ARRA of 2009. ARRA was a $787 billion stimulus package President Obama signed into law on February 17, 2009. ARRA contained incentives to encourage the adoption of healthcare information technologies; and as such anticipated an increase in the use and exchange of electronic protected health information (EPHI). Because of this, the HITECH Act was included to strengthen HIPAA privacy and security protections for protected health information (PHI).

The Department of Health and Human Services (HHS) rules implementing the HITECH Act were published in January 2013 and took a long time to create. The HITECH Regulations became effective March 26, 2013, and compliance was required by September 23, 2013. The HITECH Act and HHS regulations made major changes to the steps that healthcare providers must take to protect the privacy and security of health information. The HITECH Act also created a federal breach notification law for healthcare information. This means that healthcare providers must notify people if their health information is involved in a security breach.

Sometimes the HITECH Act's provisions will be highlighted in the text of this chapter because it represented such a large change to the original HIPAA legislation.

### The Difference Between COBRA and HIPAA

Often the words *COBRA* and *HIPAA* are used when discussing continuing health benefits following job loss or resignation. Although both laws work together to help protect employees and their health benefits, they have different functions.

COBRA, the Consolidated Omnibus Budget Reconciliation Act of 1986,[8] allows some types of employees (and their families) to continue their health coverage when they change or lose a job. COBRA is usually more expensive than health coverage under the employer's plan. However, it is usually less expensive than individual coverage through a private health insurance company.

COBRA covers employer-provided health plans that have 20 or more employees. It also applies to health coverage offered by federal, state, and local governments. Former employees qualify for COBRA if they leave a job voluntarily. They also are eligible for COBRA if they are terminated for any reason other than gross misconduct. To be eligible for COBRA, a former employee must have been enrolled in an employer's health plan at the time of separation from the job.

When employees leave their job, they must receive a notice from their employer about COBRA eligibility. Former employees who qualify are entitled to health coverage that is the same as they had while they were employed. Under COBRA, former employees must pay their own health insurance premiums. This includes any amount a former employer might have previously paid on the employees' behalf. COBRA benefits usually last for a maximum of 18 months.

COBRA lets employees continue to get health coverage that they had through an employer for a certain period of time. HIPAA, in contrast, makes sure that an employee is not discriminated against in new health coverage because of health history and preexisting conditions.

First, it allows employer-provided health plans to look back only 6 months for preexisting conditions. A condition counts as preexisting only if a worker received treatment for it sometime over the 6 months before enrolling in a health plan. If a worker did not receive treatment for the condition in those 6 months, then the condition is not preexisting.

The second limitation applies to conditions that are determined to be preexisting. HIPAA limits the amount of time that employer-provided health plans can force a worker to "sit out" of coverage because of these conditions. Before HIPAA, health plans could force workers with preexisting conditions to do without coverage for those conditions for a very long time. In most instances, HIPAA limits this waiting period to 12 months. However, that period can be shortened in many situations.

HIPAA also provides some protection against discrimination based upon genetic testing results. HIPAA states that the results of these types of tests alone cannot be considered a preexisting condition. There must be an illness diagnosis to trigger a preexisting condition. This rule is very important as more people become aware of their genetic histories. Genetic testing is used to determine if a person is more likely to have some illnesses or diseases. This information is very sensitive. Under HIPAA, a woman who has been genetically tested and has the breast cancer gene cannot be denied coverage in an employer-provided health plan if she has not been diagnosed with breast cancer. Just having the gene cannot be considered a preexisting condition.

More than 30 million people have taken consumer genetic information tests offered by companies such as Ancestry and 23andMe.[9] These consumer tests give people access to their genetic information without involvement from a healthcare provider.

Other HIPAA provisions were aimed at improving U.S. health care. These provisions, called the "Administrative Simplification" provisions as previously noted, were designed to encourage "the development of a health information system through the establishment of standards and requirements for the electronic transmission of certain health information."[10] As part of these provisions, HIPAA required the HHS to make rules regarding the privacy of individually identifiable health information. HHS was also required to create security standards to protect this information. This chapter addresses the Privacy and Security Rules.

**FYI**

The Genetic Information Nondiscrimination Act (GINA) of 2008[11] protects against some types of genetic testing discrimination. It states that health insurance companies cannot use genetic testing results to make eligibility decisions about a healthy person. They also cannot use that information to determine the cost of premiums. In addition, the law states that employers cannot use genetic information when making hiring, firing, or other job decisions, and bars employers or health insurance plans from requiring genetic testing. The future of GINA remains uncertain as genetic testing continues to explode and become more common. In addition, challenges to the Affordable Care Act, pending in late 2019 and 2020, may weaken some of GINA's protections.

## Scope

HIPAA's Privacy and Security Rules tell covered entities how they may use **protected health information (PHI)**, which refers to any individually identifiable information about the health of a person. PHI includes past, present, or future information regarding mental and physical health data.[12] It also includes information about paying for health care. PHI is commonly considered to be all information that is put in a person's medical record and can take any form.[13] The one exception to PHI is that it does not include information about individuals who have been dead for more than 50 years.

**NOTE**

PHI includes notes that your doctor puts in your medical record. It also includes any conversations your doctor has with anyone else about your health care. Billing information for healthcare goods and services provided to you is considered PHI. Information that your health insurance company has about your health care may also be PHI.

HIPAA requires covered entities to handle PHI in certain ways. The law defines covered entities to include health plans, healthcare clearinghouses, and any healthcare provider that transmits certain types of health information in electronic form.[14]

A *health plan* is an individual or group plan that pays for medical care. It includes group health plans of more than 50 people, a health insurance issuer, and health maintenance organizations (HMOs). The government's Medicare and Medicaid programs are examples of health plans, as are military healthcare programs. All health plans must follow HIPAA.

Many workers receive health insurance plans through their employers that help provide medical care for workers and their families through insurance or reimbursement. These are also group plans, with the workers and their families as the "group" that is being insured.

A *healthcare clearinghouse* is an organization that processes health information that is in a nonstandard format. For example, HIPAA requires that some healthcare transactions be conducted in electronic format, as specified by HHS. However, some healthcare providers may not have the ability to conduct these transactions electronically. If they do not, they might enter into contracts with other organizations called clearinghouses, which handle the electronic transactions on the provider's behalf. Clearinghouses include billing services or repricing companies, as well as companies that facilitate business operations between healthcare providers and insurers. A clearinghouse is covered by HIPAA because it conducts electronic healthcare transactions.

A *healthcare provider* is a covered entity under HIPAA. As previously noted, a **covered entity** is any health plan, healthcare clearinghouse, or healthcare provider that transmits certain types of health information in electronic form. The HIPAA Security and Privacy Rules "cover" them. An entity is covered if it provides health care and if it shares certain types of information electronically. This is a two-part test. A healthcare provider is a person or organization that provides healthcare services, including preventive and diagnostic physical care. It also includes mental health counseling and services. In short, a provider performs all activities traditionally associated with health care. Providers include doctors and clinics, dental practices, and pharmacies.

**FYI**

The HHS provides tools to help entities determine whether they are covered by HIPAA. Those tools are available at https://www.hhs.gov/hipaa/for-professionals/covered-entities/index.html.

Even if an entity provides health care, it may not be a covered entity. A healthcare provider is only a covered entity under HIPAA if it shares certain types of information electronically. HHS calls the information that is shared a *standard transaction*. A standard transaction is an electronic exchange of information for healthcare activities that falls within defined categories. If a healthcare provider electronically shares information that falls within a category, then it must share it in a particular way.

HHS has defined some standard transactions. It also determines the format requirements for each standard. These formats provide efficiency in processing healthcare data. Some HHS standard transactions include information related to:

- Billing and claims payment
- Health plan eligibility
- Enrollment and disenrollment in a health plan
- Health plan premium payments

HIPAA also applies to the **business associates** of covered entities. A business associate is an organization that performs a healthcare activity for a covered entity. Covered entities may outsource some healthcare functions to other organizations. If these functions include using PHI, then they are business associate functions. Common business associate functions include claims and billing processing. They also can include quality assurance review if it involves the use of PHI. Legal services can even be business associate activities when those services require the use of PHI.

Business associates that did not strictly meet the definition of covered entity did not have to follow HIPAA when the law was first passed. This was problematic for covered entities since their business associates often handled PHI and the covered entity was responsible for ensuring that the PHI was protected properly. As a result, covered entities and business associates entered into complicated agreements that described how the business associates needed to protect PHI. However, this changed when Congress passed the HITECH Act of 2009. Under the HITECH Act, business associates must specifically follow the HIPAA Privacy and Security Rules.[15] HHS may now directly require business associates to comply with HIPAA. It can also audit business associates to make sure that they are complying with the law and can directly impose penalties on noncompliant business associates. Today, business associates are held to the same standard as covered entities.

Covered entities and business associates (together called "covered entities" in this text for simplicity) that use PHI must follow the HIPAA Privacy and Security Rules. The Privacy Rule dictates how covered entities must protect the privacy of PHI. The Security Rule, in contrast, states how they must protect the confidentiality, integrity, and availability of electronic PHI.

## Main Requirements of the Privacy Rule

HHS published the final Privacy Rule in December 2000; it was first modified in August 2002. In January 2013, HHS published regulations implementing the HITECH Act that made changes to many portions of the Privacy Rule. Initial compliance with the Privacy Rule was required in April 2003. The Privacy Rule is the first time the U.S. government has specified federal privacy protections for PHI. The HHS said that the Privacy Rule had three main purposes:

- To allow consumers to control the use of their health information. This includes providing consumers with a way to access their health information
- To improve health care in the United States by restoring consumer trust in the healthcare system
- To create a national framework for health privacy protection[16]

Under the Privacy Rule, covered entities may not use or disclose people's PHI without their permission. However, the Rule also specifies situations where use or disclosure is allowed without permission. The term **use** refers to how a covered entity shares or handles PHI within its organization. Use refers to how employees of a covered entity might handle PHI to provide health care. **Disclosure** refers to how a covered entity shares PHI with other organizations that may not be affiliated with it. A person must specifically consent to a use or disclosure that is not permitted by the Privacy Rule.

The Rule also requires covered entities to put safeguards in place to protect a person's PHI. Covered entities must limit how their employees use and access PHI. They also must create training programs for their employees on how to protect PHI.

### *Required Disclosures*

Under the Privacy Rule, there are only two situations in which a covered entity must disclose PHI:

1. When a person requests access to his or her PHI
2. When HHS is investigating the covered entity

A covered entity must disclose PHI when a person requests access to his or her PHI. Under the Privacy Rule, people have the right to access, review, and get a copy of their PHI. They also have the right to request that their PHI be sent directly to a third party. This right extends to almost all records held by a covered entity that are used to make decisions about that person. It includes PHI held in medical records, billing information, and insurance claim information.

The Privacy Rule recognizes that people may not be able to request their own PHI for some reason. The Rule allows people who are legally authorized to act for another to request PHI on that person's behalf. For instance, parents can request the PHI of their minor children. A *minor* child is one who is under the age of legal adulthood, which is determined on a state-by-state basis. For most situations in the United States, a minor is a person under the age of 18.

Covered entities must respond to a person's request to access PHI within a specific period. The Rule requires covered entities to respond in 30 days. This period can be extended to another 30 days with written notice to the requestor.[17] Additional extensions of time are also allowed in some instances.

A covered entity may charge a reasonable fee for copying the records and sending them to the requestor. If the records are maintained in an electronic format, then requestors have the right to receive their records in that electronic format.

**NOTE**

A covered entity may not charge people requesting access to their PHI a storage retrieval fee, as that is specifically disallowed by the Privacy Rule. However, a covered entity may charge for labor and supplies needed to copy the records. It also may charge for postage and any electronic media needed to provide the records.

There are some types of PHI that a covered entity does not have to provide, even if a person specifically requests it. However, if a covered entity chooses to deny access to PHI, then it must specify in writing why it is denying access. It should explain the reason for the denial and how to appeal the denial.

Some types of PHI access denials are not appealable. For example, people cannot challenge a covered entity's decision to deny access to PHI in some of the following situations:

- Information that is compiled in anticipation of a lawsuit
- Psychotherapy notes
- Any information release that would be denied under the Privacy Act of 1974
- Any information that prisons compile on inmates.

The covered entity must conduct a risk assessment about the risks of providing access before issuing a denial.

A covered entity may choose to deny a person access to his or her PHI if it believes that the PHI requested is reasonably likely to endanger the life or physical safety of the person making the request. The covered entity may also deny access if it believes that the access could cause substantial harm to another person. A person may appeal this decision. If that happens, a licensed healthcare professional who did not participate in the original decision to deny access will review the appeal.[18]

The second type of situation where a covered entity must disclose PHI is when HHS is investigating the covered entity.[19] This typically happens to ensure the entities are following the Privacy Rule. A person may file a complaint with HHS if he or she believes that a covered entity is not properly handling PHI. HHS is then allowed to access PHI if it is necessary to review compliance with the Privacy Rule.

**FYI**

HHS provides a Health Information Privacy Complaint for consumer use. The complaint is available at https://www.hhs.gov/hipaa/filing-a-complaint/index.html.

### *Permitted Uses and Disclosures*

A covered entity is permitted to use and disclose a person's PHI without written consent in several situations. A use or disclosure that does not fall within the situations described by the Rule is not permitted unless a person specifically allows it.[20] HHS allows the following uses and disclosures of PHI without consent:

- Made to a person about his or her own PHI
- Made for treatment, payment, and healthcare operations
- Made after giving a person an opportunity to opt out of the use
- Made for public health and safety activities
- Limited data sets of PHI used or disclosed for specified activities

**Uses and Disclosures Made to a Person About His or Her Own PHI.** A covered entity may always disclose a person's PHI to him or her without written consent. This makes sense because healthcare providers must communicate with people about their own care. It would not facilitate efficient health care if people had to specifically authorize covered entities to discuss their health care with them. Providing a person's PHI to him or her when requested also is a required disclosure under the Privacy Rule.

**Treatment, Payment, and Healthcare Operations.** A covered entity may use a person's PHI for its own treatment, payment, or healthcare operations.[21] These are the most common covered entity activities. The Privacy Rule defines each of these terms. A covered entity is engaging in *treatment activities* when it is giving health care or services to a person.[22] These activities include managing a patient's health care among several providers, as well as referring a patient to another provider. A covered entity also can disclose PHI for the treatment activities of another covered entity. For example, a dentist can send a copy of a patient's dental records to an orthodontist who needs that information to treat the patient.

*Payment activities* are actions to get payment for healthcare goods and services.[23] A covered entity may disclose PHI without consent for these activities, which include billing and collection functions. They also include submitting claims for services to health insurance companies. Covered entities also may disclose PHI to another covered entity for the payment activities of the other entity. For instance, a doctor can share a person's health insurance coverage with a laboratory that it uses to process patient blood work because the lab needs the information in order to bill the patient for the services that it provides to the doctor.

*Healthcare operations* are actions that support the covered entity's business.[24] A covered entity may use a person's PHI for these activities without consent. These activities, which are the administrative and financial functions needed to run the business, include review processes to make sure that a covered entity is compliant with the laws that it must follow. Healthcare operations include quality assessment and improvement actions. A covered entity may not usually share any PHI used for these purposes with another covered entity. The only time it is allowed is when both entities have a relationship with the person.

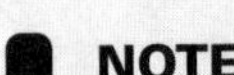
**NOTE**

Covered entities may disclose PHI to other healthcare providers for treatment and payment purposes. These providers do not have to be covered by the Privacy Rule.

Covered entities may choose to get a person's consent to use PHI for treatment, payment, and healthcare operations. However, it is not required under the Privacy Rule.[25] Even when a covered entity gets consent to share PHI for these purposes, it should always make sure that it uses and discloses PHI in a way that is consistent with its notice of privacy practices. These notices are discussed in this chapter.

**Uses and Disclosures Made After an Opportunity to Opt-Out.** There are some situations where a covered entity may use or disclose a person's PHI only after the person has had an opportunity to opt-out of the use or disclosure.[26] An *opt-out* is a more informal type of consent that only applies in limited situations. A written consent is not needed so long as a person was advised of the right to opt-out. These situations include publishing a patient's name and condition in a facility directory and sharing PHI with a person's family and friends.

Some covered entities, such as hospitals, maintain a directory of patient information. Nursing homes do this too, using this directory to list the person's name, facility room number, and general condition. However, the directory contains a limited amount of PHI. A common example of a facility directory is a list of people who are patients at a hospital. The covered entity must ask patients if they want their data included in the directory. Many covered entities ask patients this question when they enter the facility for treatment as part of a pre-admission checklist.

Covered entities also may disclose a person's PHI to his or her family, friends, and caregivers without written consent. The person must be given an opportunity to opt-out of the disclosure. However, so long as a person does not object, a covered entity can share the person's PHI with friends, family, and caregivers. Covered entities also can share information with friends, family, and caregivers for treatment or payment purposes.

However, this does not mean that a covered entity may share all PHI with every friend, family member, or caregiver. A person may place limits on these types of disclosures. For example, the person may specify that some, but not all, family members can receive PHI from a covered entity. For instance, a doctor may not discuss a patient's health information with his or her mother if the patient says not to.

In addition, a covered entity must use professional judgment in sharing PHI in this manner if a patient is not present or is unable to object to a disclosure. For example, a patient cannot object to a disclosure if unconscious. In these cases, the covered entity must decide that sharing the PHI is in the patient's best interest. For instance, an emergency department doctor may share information about a person's condition with his or her family and friends if the person is in surgery.

Just because a covered entity is allowed to share PHI under the Rule does not mean that it has to do so. For example, the covered entity is not required to share PHI if the patient is not present or is unable to object to the disclosure. Instead, it can choose not to disclose any PHI until someone can talk to the patient.

**FYI**

HHS has created guidance for patients to help them understand when healthcare providers may share their PHI. That guidance is available at https://www.hhs.gov/hipaa/for-individuals/guidance-materials-for-consumers/index.html.

**Uses and Disclosures Made for Public Health and Safety Activities.** HHS recognized that there are some situations where a covered entity should disclose a person's PHI. For example, sometimes it is necessary for the good of society.[27] A covered entity does not need a person's consent to disclose PHI in these situations. It also does not need to give a person a chance to object. Generally, these situations involve public safety and welfare. HHS felt that requiring a person's consent to disclose PHI in these situations could negatively affect society. In general, a covered entity may disclose PHI to certain government entities without consent for the following purposes:

- To provide vital statistics
- To control communicable diseases
- To report abuse and neglect
- When required by other laws
- For law enforcement purposes

***Vital Statistics and Communicable Diseases.*** A covered entity may disclose a person's PHI without consent to report births, deaths, and other vital statistics. Often these types of reports are required by state law; therefore, a covered entity must report these events to public health authorities. It may also disclose PHI to these authorities to prevent or control disease, injury, or disability. These types of disclosures of PHI do not require consent. For instance, New York healthcare providers must report certain diseases to their local health departments; for example, they must report highly contagious diseases and diseases that might indicate bioterrorism. Diseases that must be reported immediately include smallpox, anthrax, botulism, and typhoid. These diseases are serious public health threats.

The HITECH Act added regulations that allow covered entities to provide proof of immunization to schools if required for admittance. This is because schools play an important role in making sure children are vaccinated. In these cases, covered entities have to document that an individual agreed to the disclosure of the records.[28]

**NOTE**

Public health is the branch of medicine that is concerned with the health of a community of people. A public health authority is a state or federal agency that is responsible for public health matters. For example, a state or local health department is a public health authority, as is the federal Centers for Disease Control and Prevention (CDC).

***Abuse and Neglect.*** A covered entity may disclose PHI about victims of child abuse or neglect without consent.[29] However, the covered entity may disclose the PHI only to government agencies that have the legal authority to receive these reports. Child welfare and social services agencies are allowed by state law to receive reports about child abuse and neglect. Law enforcement agencies also are allowed to receive these types of reports.

All U.S. states have laws that require healthcare providers to report evidence of child abuse and neglect. Other professionals that work with children, such as teachers, have similar requirements. They must report information either to state social services agencies or to local law enforcement. States make these laws because it is important to the public welfare to protect children.

The Privacy Rule contains slightly different provisions for adult victims of abuse, neglect, or domestic violence.[30] A covered entity may disclose PHI about adult victims of these crimes if the disclosure is required by law and if the patient allows it. The covered entity may still disclose PHI if a patient does not allow the disclosure, or cannot agree to the disclosure. In that case, the covered entity must use its professional judgment to determine that the disclosure is necessary; for example, if it must be made to prevent serious harm to the person.

A covered entity must promptly notify a person or his or her personal representative if it makes a disclosure of PHI in these cases. However, there are some exceptions to this general rule. The covered entity does not have to notify an adult victim if it believes that informing him or her would place the victim at risk of harm. The covered entity also does not have to notify the individual's personal representative if it believes that the representative is responsible for the victim's injuries.

**FYI**

Attorneys are allowed to issue subpoenas for information as part of lawsuits, often as part of the discovery process. **Discovery** is the legal process used to gather evidence in a lawsuit. A discovery request is a request for information from one party in a lawsuit to the other party. These requests also can be made to witnesses. Subpoenas issued by attorneys as part of the discovery process do not require court approval. When a subpoena issued as part of discovery requests PHI, the individual involved must be notified.

***Required by Law and Law Enforcement.*** A covered entity may use or disclose PHI to the extent that it is required by law.[31] In these situations, the covered entity is usually disclosing the PHI to some sort of governmental legal entity. For example, it may disclose PHI in response to a court order or court-ordered warrant. It may also disclose PHI in response to a subpoena issued by a grand jury. If the covered entity is providing PHI in response to a discovery request generated as part of a lawsuit, then it must notify the person who is the subject of the PHI. That person must have a chance to object to the discovery request.

Covered entities may also disclose PHI without consent for some law enforcement activities. For example, they may provide some types of PHI to help identify or locate a suspect, witness, or missing person. Information that a covered entity can provide in these situations is limited to identifying information, such as name and address. It also includes distinguishing physical characteristics that could be used to identify the person that the police are looking for.

Covered entities may also provide PHI without consent if it is requested by law enforcement and it is about a victim of crime. They can also disclose PHI as needed to identify or apprehend a violent criminal. Covered entities may alert law enforcement about a person's death if they believe that the death was caused by criminal activity. They also may disclose PHI to law enforcement or government officials if they believe there is a serious threat to health or safety.

**Limited Data Sets Used or Disclosed for Specified Activities.** A *limited data set* is PHI that does not contain any data that identifies a person because it is stripped of certain identifiers. These identifiers must be redacted from the PHI. Redaction means protected information is removed or obscured in a document before sharing that document with other individuals or groups.

A covered entity may share limited data sets for research, healthcare operations, and public health activities. It does not need a person's permission to share them. Identifiers that must be removed from PHI in order to create a limited data set are:[32]

- Name
- Street address (except that some geographical information may remain if certain conditions are met)
- Telephone and fax numbers
- Email addresses
- Social Security numbers
- Medical record numbers
- Health plan beneficiary numbers
- Account numbers
- Certificate/license numbers
- Vehicle identifiers and serial numbers, including license plate numbers
- Device identifiers and serial numbers
- Web Universal Resource Locators (URLs)
- Internet Protocol (IP) address numbers
- Biometric identifiers, including finger and voice prints
- Full face photographic images and any similar images
- Any other unique identifying number, characteristic, or code that identifies a person or his or her PHI

A limited data set is still PHI; therefore, a covered entity must enter into a data use agreement with the organization that receives it.[33] The data use agreement specifies how the PHI in the limited data set will be protected.

### *Uses and Disclosures That Require Authorization*

A covered entity must get people's written consent in order to use or disclose their PHI in ways that are not expressly allowed under the Privacy Rule.[34] Under the Rule, written consent is called an **authorization**. These are very specific documents that allow PHI to be shared. A written authorization is required for many purposes, such as to disclose psychotherapy notes and to use PHI in marketing materials.

A covered entity must get an authorization before it discloses PHI if a permitted use or disclosure does not apply. This comes into play in many ways. A covered entity needs an authorization to share a person's PHI with an employer for employment purposes. Even if a person asks the covered entity to provide this information to an employer, he or she must sign an authorization. A parent will need to sign an authorization on behalf of his or her minor child to have the covered entity disclose PHI to the child's school. This might be required to allow children to participate in some school activities such as sporting events.

**NOTE**

*De-identified data* is data that has been stripped of all information that could identify an individual. De-identified data is not PHI. The HHS has issued guidance about how to de-identify data.

**FYI**

HIPAA uses the term *authorization* to distinguish between consent to use or disclose PHI and other types of consent that are used in the healthcare industry. For example, *informed consent*, written consent from a patient to undergo a medical treatment, is a basic rule in health care. This type of consent explains the risks and benefits of treatment. When patients sign informed consent documents, they are agreeing to undergo the treatments specified. These forms are very different from a Privacy Rule authorization that allows PHI to be shared. When people consent to sharing their PHI, they show their consent by signing an authorization. This eliminates confusion among different types of documents used in the healthcare industry.

The Privacy Rule forbids a covered entity from requiring a person to sign an authorization in order to receive healthcare treatment. The covered entity cannot condition benefit eligibility on signing an authorization. This is so that covered entities cannot force people to sign authorizations under pressure by withholding needed care.

The Privacy Rule requires authorizations to contain specific terms. It also states situations in which an authorization is defective. A defective authorization is not valid. Authorizations are defective if the expiration date stated in the authorization has passed. They are also invalid if they are not filled out completely, or if a person has revoked them.

An authorization must be in plain language. This means that it should not contain any legal terms or other terms that are hard for a person to understand. A valid authorization must contain the following elements:[35]

- A specific and meaningful description of the PHI that will be used or disclosed
- Identification of the people who are allowed to make the requested use or disclosure

- Identification of the people who will receive the use or disclosure
- A clear description of the reason for the requested use or disclosure
- The date that the authorization will expire
- The signature of the person and the date

The Privacy Rule requires that covered entities provide people with a copy of any authorizations that they sign.

### *Minimum Necessary Rule*

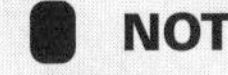

**NOTE**

The Privacy Rule minimum necessary rule is similar to the general information security principle of need to know. Only the information needed to carry out a function or activity should be disclosed.

A covered entity is permitted to use and disclose some types of PHI without an authorization. These situations were described earlier in this chapter. However, this does not mean that it should always disclose the entire allowable amount of PHI available to it. Any time a covered entity discloses PHI, it must follow the **minimum necessary rule.**[36] In other words, it may disclose only the amount of PHI absolutely necessary. The amount disclosed must be able to satisfy the reason why the information is being used or disclosed, but no more. Covered entities must create internal processes and procedures to make sure that employees access only the amount of PHI needed to do their jobs.

A covered entity must use professional judgment and make reasonable efforts to limit its use or disclosure of PHI. For instance, a healthcare provider should not disclose a person's entire medical record if only a portion of it is needed to be responsive to a request.

There are some exceptions to this rule.[37] Uses or disclosures of PHI made by a healthcare provider for treatment purposes are not subject to the minimum necessary rule. It also does not apply to disclosures made to people about their own PHI, or to uses or disclosures made when a person specifically authorizes the use or disclosure. It also does not apply to uses or disclosures required by law or made to HHS for its complaint investigation function.

### *Other Individual Rights Under the Privacy Rule*

The Privacy Rule gives people additional rights regarding their PHI. These rights help people make sure that their PHI is used properly.

**Amendments of PHI.** A person has the right to ask that a covered entity amend the person's PHI.[38] However, a covered entity does not have to correct data in the record. Instead, it can include the amendment in the record. That way the integrity of the record is maintained. Other entities that might rely on the unamended PHI to the person's detriment must be notified of the amendment. The covered entity that makes this amendment also must notify the other entities, as well as anyone else the individual specifies.

A covered entity must respond to a request to amend PHI within 60 days.[39] That time can be extended for 30 more days if the covered entity notifies the requestor in writing. A covered entity may choose not to amend PHI for some reason. For example, a covered entity does not have to amend PHI if it did not create the PHI that is in question. It also does not have to amend PHI if it determines that the PHI in the record is accurate and complete.

If an entity chooses to deny a request to amend PHI, then it must issue a written denial notice to the person who requested the amendment.[40] The denial notice must contain the basis for the denial, as well as a statement of the person's right to disagree with the denial. A person may submit a statement of disagreement to the covered entity, which may prepare a rebuttal to the person's statement of disagreement. If a request for amendment is denied, the covered entity must include the following in the person's record:

- Identification of the PHI that is under dispute
- A copy of the person's request to amend the PHI
- A copy of the covered entity's denial of the request
- A copy of the person's statement of disagreement
- A copy of the covered entity's rebuttal statement

All of this information must be included in future uses or disclosures of the PHI that is under dispute.

**Accounting of Disclosures.** Covered entities must keep records of how they disclose a person's PHI. Under the Privacy Rule, a person has the right to receive an accounting of how the covered entity has used or disclosed the person's PHI.[41] People have the right to get an accounting of disclosures of PHI made in the 6 years before the date of their request. They also can request accountings for shorter periods.

A covered entity does not have to account for every PHI disclosure that it makes. The Privacy Rule states that some kinds of disclosures do not have to be included in an accounting. However, any disclosure not specifically excluded must be included and tracked. **TABLE 6-1** compares different types of disclosures.

A covered entity must provide a person a first accounting in a 12-month period at no charge.[42] If he or she requests more than one accounting in that period, then the covered entity can charge a reasonable fee for each subsequent request. However, the covered entity must inform the person that it intends to charge a fee for an extra accounting and give the person a chance to withdraw or change the request in order to avoid the fee.

A covered entity must respond to a request for an accounting in writing within 60 days.[43] This period can be extended 30 days with notice to the person who has requested the accounting. When it responds, the covered entity must include the following information:

- Date of disclosure
- Name of recipient
- Description of the PHI disclosed
- Reason for the disclosure, or a copy of the request for the disclosure

The HITECH Act made changes to the accounting of disclosures requirement for EPHI. These changes apply to cases where a covered entity maintains an EHR for a person. An EHR is an electronic record or healthcare information created by a covered entity. If a covered entity keeps an EHR, then it must provide a person with an accounting of the treatment, payment, and healthcare operation disclosures made from that EHR.[44] This expanded requirement applies only to disclosures from an EHR. In cases involving an EHR, a person has a right to get an accounting only for the 3 years before the date of the request. In 2011 HHS proposed additional regulations that address how disclosures from an EHR should be accounted for. The proposed regulations were withdrawn in 2018. At the time of this writing, new regulations had not been proposed.

**TABLE 6-1** Different Types of Disclosures

| DISCLOSURES THAT ARE NOT TRACKED | DISCLOSURES THAT MUST BE TRACKED |
|---|---|
| Disclosures made to carry out treatment, payment, and healthcare activities* | Disclosures to HHS for its compliance functions |
| Disclosures to individuals | Disclosures required by law |
| Disclosures made after an authorization is received | Disclosures required for public health activities |
| Incidental disclosures | Disclosures made to report abuse |
| Disclosures where the person had the opportunity to opt-out | Disclosures for judicial and administrative proceedings (in response to subpoenas and court orders) |
| Disclosures for national security or intelligence purposes | Disclosures for law enforcement purposes |
| Disclosures to correctional institutions or to law enforcement officials having custody of an inmate | Disclosures for research purposes (unless authorized or made via a limited data set) |
| Disclosures that are part of a limited data set | Disclosures to the public health agencies |
| Disclosures made more than 6 years before the date of the person's request for an accounting | Disclosures to avert a threat of serious injury<br>Disclosures made by mistake (inadvertent disclosures)<br>Any other disclosures not specifically excluded by the Privacy Rule |

*The HITECH Act has different tracking requirements for disclosures made from an EHR.

### *Privacy Notices*

Covered entities must inform people about their privacy practices.[45] The Privacy Rule requires covered entities to let people know how they use and disclose their PHI. It does this in a privacy policy. A covered entity must use and disclose PHI only in the ways described by its privacy policy.

A covered entity must use plain language to draft its notice, so that an average person is able to understand the notice. The Privacy Rule requires the notice to include specific parts:

- A title that reads: "THIS NOTICE DESCRIBES HOW MEDICAL INFORMATION ABOUT YOU MAY BE USED AND DISCLOSED AND HOW YOU CAN GET ACCESS TO THIS INFORMATION. PLEASE REVIEW IT CAREFULLY." The covered entity must display this header in prominent type.
- A description of how the covered entity may use and disclose a person's PHI. It should include examples of disclosures that the entity makes for treatment, payment, and healthcare operations. This description should state when the covered entity is allowed to use or disclose PHI without a person's consent, and when the covered entity must have consent.

### Incidental and Inadvertent Disclosures

The difference between incidental and inadvertent disclosures of PHI is important to understand. Even though they sound similar, they are very different.

*Incidental disclosures* are permitted disclosures under the Privacy Rule. Covered entities do not have to track these types of disclosures. An incidental disclosure can result from any use or disclosure that is allowed under the Privacy Rule. They are allowed so long as a covered entity implements safeguards to limit the amount of PHI exposed though an incidental disclosure.

Examples of incidental disclosures include:

- A customer at a pharmacy hears the pharmacist quietly discussing a medication with another customer. This is an incidental disclosure because it occurs during an activity that is allowed under the Privacy Rule. The permitted activity is the covered entity's treatment activities.
- A patient going to a hospital to pay a bill briefly views another patient's payment information on the billing clerk's computer monitor. The first patient can see this information only briefly before the clerk accesses the patient's own record. This is an incidental disclosure because it is a result of the covered entity's permitted payment activities.

Covered entities must take steps to limit incidental disclosures. This includes speaking quietly when discussing conditions with patients and their families. It also includes shielding monitors from public view as much as possible.

Inadvertent disclosures are different. *Inadvertent disclosures* are disclosures that are not allowed under the Privacy Rule. Covered entities must track inadvertent disclosures. They also must provide an accounting of these types of disclosures if a person requests it. These disclosures happen by mistake. An example would be if a covered entity discloses PHI without a valid authorization when one was needed. Under the HITECH Act, some types of inadvertent disclosures could even be considered an impermissible data breach that requires further action.

- A description of the person's rights with respect to his or her PHI. This section should also include information on how a person can exercise these rights. The covered entity must include information about its complaint processes, as well as information about the person's right to complain to HHS.
- A statement that the covered entity is required by law to maintain the privacy of PHI. This statement must include the entity's legal duties with respect to PHI.
- The contact information of a person the individual can contact to ask additional questions about the covered entity's privacy notice.

A covered entity's privacy policy must contain an effective date. The covered entity must revise and redistribute its notice any time it makes a material change to the notice. Covered entities must make the notice available to anyone who asks for it. It also must make the notice available on any website that it maintains.

**NOTE**

Many of the elements that are required in the Notice of Privacy Practices contain portions of the fair information practice principles.

Different types of covered entities have additional rules to follow when giving their privacy notices to individuals.[46] For example, health plans must distribute their privacy notices to people when they enroll in the health plan. They also must make sure that plan participants receive a copy of the notice at least once every 3 years.

In some cases, the Privacy Rule does not require healthcare clearinghouses to develop a notice of privacy practices; for example, if the only PHI that they create or receive is as a business associate of another covered entity.

**NOTE**

A *material change* is a change in an organization's operating practices that is significant. Material changes can affect how people understand their rights or interact with an organization.

Healthcare providers have additional rules to follow for distributing their notices to individuals. Providers must give the notice to a person no later than when they first provide services to that person. They also must make a good-faith effort to get the person's written acknowledgment of receipt of the notice. A provider must document a person's receipt of the notice if it cannot gain a receipt from the person. In emergencies, the healthcare provider must provide its notice of privacy practices to a patient as soon as it is reasonable. A healthcare provider must also post its notice in a clear and prominent location where patients can read the notice. Covered entities must retain copies of privacy notices that they distribute. They must also retain written acknowledgments.

### *Administrative Requirements*

A covered entity has administrative duties under the Privacy Rule.[47] For example, it must designate a privacy official who is responsible for developing the covered entity's privacy policies and procedures. HHS allows a covered entity to scope its privacy policies and programs to its size and structure. This allows covered entities some discretion when they create their programs. Covered entities that are large with complex structures must develop policies appropriate for that structure. Smaller entities are not held to the same standard, and therefore must develop their own policies.

The covered entity must also designate a person to receive consumer privacy complaints. This person handles complaints about the entity's own privacy policies, as well as consumer complaints about the Privacy Rule. This person also answers questions about the entity's privacy notice. The privacy official often serves as this contact person.

Covered entities must create policies and procedures to protect the privacy of all PHI.[48] These policies include destroying PHI properly. They can also include requirements that paper medical charts be secured in locked file cabinets. This requirement is similar to the HIPAA Security Rule. However, the Security Rule applies only to EPHI.

Covered entities must train all their employees—even part-time employees, volunteers, and interns—on the Privacy Rule and its privacy policies and procedures. A covered entity also must have a discipline policy for workers who violate the Privacy Rule. This is called a sanctions policy.

**FYI**

HHS relies on National Institute of Standards and Technology (NIST) guidelines to specify how PHI should be secured during storage and transmission. PHI is considered secured if a covered entity encrypts it according to these guidelines. The HHS guidance can be found at https://www.hhs.gov/hipaa/for-professionals/breach-notification/guidance/index.html.

### Breach Notification Provisions

The Privacy Rule requires covered entities, including business associates, to mitigate an unauthorized use or disclosure of PHI.[49] Before the HITECH Act, a covered entity did not have to notify individuals that their PHI was used or disclosed in an unauthorized manner. However, the HITECH Act now requires them to do so. It creates notification requirements that covered entities must follow in the event of a breach of unsecured PHI.[50] Both covered entities and business associates must follow these rules.

A *breach* is any impermissible use or disclosure of unsecured PHI that compromises the security or privacy of the PHI. Any unauthorized use or disclosure is presumed to be a breach under the law. In some cases, a covered entity might be able to show that there is a low probability that PHI was compromised. If it can do that, then the breach notification requirements do not apply.

To show that there is a low probability that PHI has been compromised, a covered entity must engage in a risk assessment. To conduct the risk assessment, a covered entity must review:

- **The PHI that was involved in the breach**—Is the PHI involved very sensitive? Is it more likely to lead to identify theft?
- **Who used or received the PHI**—Does the entity know who used the PHI? Was it an impermissible use or disclosure?
- **Was the PHI actually acquired?**—Was the PHI involved actually viewed? Was is downloaded by the unauthorized individual?
- **Have risks been mitigated?**—If the entity knows who used the PHI, can it get assurances that they will not disclose or use the data further? Can the entity ensure that PHI has been destroyed?

The covered entity must weigh all these factors. It also must conduct this risk assessment in good faith. As noted earlier, if the risk assessment demonstrates that there is a low probability that the PHI has been compromised, then the breach notification requirements do not apply.[51]

The HITECH breach notification provisions apply to unsecured PHI, which refers to PHI that is not protected by a technology that renders it unusable or unreadable. Unsecured PHI is PHI that is not encrypted or properly destroyed. PHI must be encrypted through a process that is approved by HHS to be considered secure. In April 2009, HHS issued guidance on what technologies were acceptable to encrypt PHI. It will update this guidance yearly.

Unsecured PHI includes PHI that is not disposed of properly. PHI is considered unsecured during destruction if it is still readable or recoverable after disposal. PHI that is shredded or completely destroyed is disposed of properly.

**NOTE**

Neither HIPAA nor the HITECH Act provides a **private cause of action**. This means that neither law gives people a right to sue a covered entity that wrongfully uses their PHI. An individual would have to use a different legal theory, such as negligence, to sue a covered entity that wrongfully uses his or her PHI.

Covered entities must provide notice to people who are affected by a breach of unsecured PHI.[52] These are the people whose PHI was disclosed, or potentially disclosed, because of the breach. The covered entity must notify them no later than 60 days after it discovers the breach.[53] A breach is *discovered* on the first day that the covered entity knows about the breach. Individuals must be notified about the situation without "unreasonable delay." This means that a covered entity must notify individuals as soon as it can reasonably do so. A covered entity may delay notification if a law enforcement official requests it.

Any notice to an individual must include:

- A complete description of what happened
- A description of the PHI involved
- A description of what the covered entity is doing to mitigate the breach
- Steps the person should take to protect himself or herself from harm such as identity theft
- Contact information for the covered entity[54]

The HITECH Act also specifies the method for notifying people of a breach of their unsecured PHI. The default way to provide notice is via first-class mail. However, there are other ways to provide notice in some circumstances. For example, a covered entity can provide notice via email if the individual has agreed to receive communications by email. If the breach involves more than 500 people, then the covered entity must also immediately notify HHS about the breach,[55] as well as local media so news outlets can help inform people. All covered entities must submit annual reports to the HHS about breaches involving fewer than 500 people.

## Main Requirements of the Security Rule

HHS published the Security Rule in February 2003. This information security rule requires covered entities to use security safeguards that protect the confidentiality, integrity, and availability of **electronic protected health information (EPHI)**. EPHI is patient health information that is computer based. Covered entities were required to comply with the Rule by April 20, 2005.

Similar to the Privacy Rule, the Security Rule was the first time the U.S. government stated federal protections for EPHI. Under the Rule, covered entities must protect all EPHI that they create, receive, maintain, or transmit from reasonably anticipated threats.[56] They also must guard against uses or disclosures of EPHI that are not allowed by the Privacy Rule.

### Electronic Health Records and Personal Health Records

In January 2005, President Bush called for the creation of a nationwide network of EHRs within 10 years. An *EHR* refers to government-endorsed technologies that allow healthcare providers to store, retrieve, and share medical information. The goal of an EHR is to make paper medical records obsolete.

The HITECH Act allocates $19.2 billon to promote the adoption of EHRs. Beginning in 2011, healthcare professionals who used approved EHR technologies were eligible for some types of incentives to help cover the cost of adopting EHR technologies. Healthcare providers that moved too slowly to adopt EHR did not receive the incentives.

An EHR is different from a *personal health record (PHR)*. PHRs are health records that are compiled and maintained by a person or other non-medical provider third party, whereas EHRs are compiled and maintained by healthcare providers. A PHR typically refers to individual-compiled health records in an electronic format. People can compile and store this information on their computers. They also can use applications and tools offered by third parties. Many health insurance companies give their members access to tools that allow them to compile PHRs. These tools and PHRs are specific to the health insurance plan.

**NOTE**

The Security Rule contains document retention requirements. Covered entities must maintain their Security Rule documentation for 6 years after it is created. They also must maintain old documents for 6 years after they are retired. The 6-year time limit starts to run on whichever date (creation or retirement) is later.

Covered entities must create policies and procedures to comply with the Security Rule.[57] They must review their documents on a regular basis and update them as needed, as well as provide training to their employees. They also must make security program documents available to employees in printed manuals or on websites. A covered entity also must have a sanctions policy to discipline workers who violate the Security Rule.

The Security Rule allows covered entities flexibility in creating their overall security program. The Rule does not require covered entities to use specific types of technology. In creating their program, covered entities may think about:

- The size and complexity of the entity
- Its technical infrastructure, hardware, and software security resources
- The costs of security measures
- The potential risks to EPHI[58]

### *Safeguards and Implementation Specifications*

The Security Rule requires covered entities to use information security principles to protect EPHI through the use of administrative, physical, and technical safeguards. The Rule contains instructions on each safeguard, as well as standards that must be implemented for each safeguard. These standards include a list of items, called *implementation specifications*, that a covered entity must put into practice.

There are some implementation specifications that a covered entity must implement, which are called *required* specifications. Other specifications are *addressable*. Covered entities have more discretion when considering addressable specifications. For these specifications, it must assess whether that control is reasonable and appropriate in its environment.[59] If it is, then the covered entity must use it.

If an addressable specification is not reasonable and appropriate, the covered entity does not have to use it. However, it must document why the specification was not appropriate. It also must implement an equivalent control, which should accomplish the goal of the addressable specification.

**Administrative Safeguards.** Half of the safeguards required by the Security Rule are administrative in nature. These safeguards are actions, policies, and procedures that a covered entity must implement in order to follow the Security Rule.[60] There are nine different administrative requirements. A covered entity must implement the following standards:

- Security management process
- Assigned security responsibility
- Workforce security
- Information access management
- Security awareness and training
- Security incident procedures
- Contingency plan

- Evaluation
- Business associate contracts[61]

The *security management process* standard guides a covered entity in creating its security program. It has four required implementation specifications. To comply with this standard, a covered entity must conduct a risk analysis and engage in risk management. It must also create a sanction policy and review information system activity.

Risk analysis is used to assess the vulnerabilities, threats, and risks that could harm EPHI. Risk management is the process of implementing controls to reduce risk. Information system activity review is the process of reviewing system logs and records. Covered entities must review them to make sure that EPHI is being used properly.

**NOTE**

Risk analysis and risk management are standard information security concepts. HHS has issued guidance on risk analysis and assessment under the Security Rule. You can learn more at https://www.hhs.gov/hipaa/for-professionals/security/guidance/guidance-risk-analysis/.

Covered entities are required to name an official responsible for Security Rule compliance because of the *assigned security responsibility* standard. This standard is similar to the Privacy Rule provision that requires covered entities to designate a privacy official. The privacy and security officials do not have to be the same person.

Under the *workforce security* standard, covered entities must implement need-to-know policies for EPHI access and ensure that all employees have appropriate access to EPHI. They also must ensure that employees without proper authority are not able to access EPHI. There are three addressable specifications in this standard. To the extent that it is appropriate for its operations, the covered entity must implement authorization and supervision procedures. It must also implement workforce clearance and termination procedures.

Each of these specifications helps to ensure proper access to EPHI. The authorization and supervision procedures are used to make sure that an individual user has the authority to use EPHI in certain ways. Under the workforce clearance specification, a covered entity must create procedures to confirm that an employee's access to EPHI is correct. The termination procedures specification requires covered components to terminate employee access to EPHI when an employee leaves a covered entity.

The *information access management* standard is closely related to the workforce security standard. It requires covered entities to create policies to access EPHI that must be consistent with the Privacy Rule. The standard has one required and two addressable implementation specifications.

The *security awareness and training* standard requires covered entities to create training and awareness programs for all members of its workforce. This standard has four addressable specifications. Where appropriate, the covered entity must implement password management procedures. It must also create logon monitoring procedures. Other procedures must protect against malicious software. The entity also should provide security updates to its workforce.

Under the *security incident procedures* standard, covered entities must implement policies to respond to security incidents. This standard has one required implementation specification. The covered entity must identify security incidents and respond to them. It also must attempt to mitigate the harm caused by security incidents, as well as document security incidents and their outcomes. In some cases, a security incident under the Security Rule leads to unauthorized use or disclosure of PHI under the Privacy Rule. In these cases, the Privacy Rule might require covered entities to notify the individuals affected by the breach.

The *contingency plan* standard requires covered entities to develop policies to recover access to EPHI in the event of an outage or disaster. This standard contains three required and two addressable specifications. It also requires covered entities to prepare data backup, disaster recovery, and emergency operation plans. Together, the plans state how an organization backs up and restores its EPHI. The emergency operations plan requires covered entities to protect EPHI when it is operating in emergency mode. Where reasonable, the covered entity must also create procedures to test and review its contingency plans.

**NOTE**

Under the Security Rule, a security incident is unauthorized access or use of information. It can be successful unauthorized access or just attempted unauthorized access. Incidents also include interference with the operation of information systems.[62]

**TIP**

Remember that under the Security Rule, a covered entity must apply an addressable and appropriate implementation specification if it is reasonable. A covered entity must document why it does not implement one of these types of specifications. It must then implement an equivalent control if possible.

The *evaluation* standard requires the covered entity to review its security safeguards program. It must regularly review changes to its information systems and practices and make sure that its safeguards still protect EPHI. The covered entity can perform this evaluation on its own. It also can hire external organizations to conduct this review.

The *business associate contracts* standard requires covered entities to make sure that their business associates protect EPHI. Covered entities must enter into written contracts with any organizations that use EPHI on their behalf. These are called business associates agreements. Business associates agreements are required under both the Privacy and Security Rules. A covered entity must identify all of its business associates, as well as make sure that it has contracts will all of them.

**TABLE 6-2** summarizes the administrative safeguards required by the Security Rule. It also includes a summary of required and addressable implementation specifications.

**Physical Safeguards.** Physical safeguards are controls put in place to protect a covered entity's physical resources.[63] These measures protect information systems, equipment, and buildings from environmental threats. The Security Rule contains four physical security standards that a covered entity must put into practice:[64]

- Facility access controls
- Workstation use
- Workstation security
- Device and media controls

Under the *facility access controls* standard, covered entities must implement policies that limit physical access to their computer systems, as well as access to the buildings where these systems are located. Only authorized individuals should be allowed to access these systems and facilities. This standard has four addressable implementation specifications.

Where appropriate, the covered entity must create access contingency plans. These plans allow access to facilities and systems during emergencies. A covered entity also must create a facility security plan, which is designed to protect systems and buildings from

**TABLE 6-2** Administrative Safeguards

| SAFEGUARD | REQUIRED SPECIFICATIONS | ADDRESSABLE SPECIFICATIONS |
|---|---|---|
| Security Management Process | Risk Analysis<br>Risk Management<br>Sanction Policy<br>Information System Activity Review | |
| Assigned Security Responsibility | Required | |
| Workforce Security | | Authorization and/or Supervision<br>Workforce Clearance Procedure<br>Termination Procedures |
| Information Access Management | Isolating Healthcare Clearing-house Function | Access Authorization<br>Access Establishment and Modification |
| Security Awareness and Training | | Security Reminders<br>Protection From Malicious Software<br>Logon Monitoring<br>Password Management |
| Security Incident Procedures | Response and Reporting | |
| Contingency Plan | Data Backup Plan<br>Disaster Recovery Plan<br>Emergency Mode Operation Plan | Testing and Revision Procedure<br>Applications and Data Criticality Analysis |
| Evaluation | Required | |
| Business Associate Contracts and Other Arrangements | Required | |

unauthorized access, tampering, and theft. When it seems appropriate, covered entities must create access control and validation procedures, as well as measures to manage visitor access. They also should document repairs and modifications to a facility.

The Security Rule contains two required standards related to workstation security. Neither standard has implementation specifications. In the *workstation use* standard, a covered entity must make sure that employees use workstations properly. This means that it should review the applications used on workstations, as well as whether those applications introduce security risks that could harm EPHI. For example, a covered entity might decide that it is too risky to allow workstations used to access EPHI to connect to the internet. The covered entity must look at workstation use for both on-site and off-site locations.

According to the *workstation security standard*, covered entities must implement physical safeguards for workstations that access

**NOTE**

Under the Security Rule, a workstation is a computing device as well as any electronic media used by or around the device. Examples include a laptop or desktop computer or any similar device.[65]

EPHI to ensure that access to the workstation is restricted to authorized users. For example, a covered entity might protect workstations by keeping them in areas that only authorized employees are allowed to access.

Under the *device and media controls* standard, a covered entity must track information systems containing EPHI in and out of a facility. They also must track system movement within a facility. This standard has two required and two addressable implementation specifications.

Under this standard, a covered entity is required to create media disposal and media reuse policies. Covered entities must make sure that EPHI is destroyed or made unusable before the covered entity disposes of electronic media. The process for accomplishing this is described in a media disposal policy. A covered entity must also create media reuse policies, which state that EPHI must be removed from electronic media that is going to be made available for reuse. These policies must take into account media reuse within a covered entity. They also should address media reuse outside of a covered entity.

**TABLE 6-3** summarizes the physical safeguards required by the Security Rule. It also includes a summary of required and addressable implementation specifications.

**Technical Safeguards.** Technical safeguards are applied in the hardware and software of an information system.[66] The Security Rule contains five technical security standards.[67] It does not require that any specific type of technology be used to follow the Rule. A covered entity must implement the following standards:

- Access controls
- Audit controls
- Integrity controls
- Person or entity authentication
- Transmission security

The *access control* standard requires covered entities to use access control rules to limit authorized access to systems that store EPHI. The implementation specifications require covered entities to assign unique usernames to anyone who uses its systems. They also must create procedures to access EPHI in an emergency. Addressable specifications include using

**TABLE 6-3** Physical Safeguards

| SAFEGUARD | REQUIRED SPECIFICATIONS | ADDRESSABLE SPECIFICATIONS |
|---|---|---|
| Facility Access Controls | | Contingency Operations<br>Facility Security Plan<br>Access Control and Validation Procedures<br>Maintenance Records |
| Workstation Use | Required | |
| Workstation Security | Required | |
| Device and Media Controls | Disposal<br>Media Reuse | Accountability<br>Data Backup and Storage |

automatic logoff processes that end an electronic session after a period of inactivity. A covered entity also should encrypt EPHI. Together, these controls limit access to EPHI.

The *audit controls* standard requires covered entities to review activity in information systems that store or use EPHI. The entity must decide what audit controls it needs to implement to protect its EPHI. Audit controls are then used to look for unauthorized access.

The *integrity controls* standard requires covered entities to create policies to protect EPHI from improper modification or destruction. This is an important control to protect EPHI. Healthcare providers rely on EPHI to treat patients, and EPHI that has been improperly modified can put a patient in danger. This standard has one addressable specification. When it is appropriate, covered entities must authenticate EPHI. These electronic mechanisms are used to make sure that EPHI has not been improperly changed or destroyed.

Covered entities are required to create procedures to verify that a person or entity trying to access EPHI is who he or she claims to be. This is the *person or entity authentication* standard. Authentication credentials are used to ensure that a person is who he or she claims to be. These credentials include passwords, tokens, smart cards, and biometric credentials.

The *transmission security* standard requires covered entities to guard against unauthorized access to EPHI during transmission. A covered entity must review how it transmits EPHI and determine if there is a risk of unauthorized access. This standard includes two addressable specifications. Where appropriate, the covered entity must implement security measures that protect EPHI from being modified during transmission. It also must encrypt EPHI during transmission if appropriate.

**TABLE 6-4** summarizes the technical safeguards required by the Security Rule. It also includes a summary of required and addressable implementation specifications.

The Security Rule and safeguards requirements are designed to protect all sorts of EPHI. HHS recognizes that sometimes covered entities might need more guidance as technology quickly evolves. For example, HHS has issued guidance to help covered entities secure mobile devices. It has also issued guidance to help covered entities securely access remote EPHI.

**TABLE 6-4** Technical Safeguards

| SAFEGUARD | REQUIRED SPECIFICATIONS | ADDRESSABLE SPECIFICATIONS |
|---|---|---|
| Access Control | Unique User Identification<br>Emergency Access Procedure | Automatic Logoff<br>Encryption and Decryption |
| Audit Controls | Required | |
| Integrity | | Mechanism to Authenticate Electronic Protected Health Information |
| Person or Entity Authentication | Required | |
| Transmission Security | | Integrity Controls<br>Encryption |

**FYI**

Covered entities have great incentive to encrypt EPHI. This incentive exists even though many Security Rule implementation specifications do not require encryption. The incentive exists because the breach notification requirement of the Privacy Rule does not apply to the unauthorized use or disclosure of encrypted EPHI. A covered entity thus saves itself from this requirement if it encrypts its EPHI.

## Oversight

HHS oversees compliance with the HIPAA Privacy and Security Rules. It delegates this function to the Office for Civil Rights (OCR), which enforces both rules. It is also responsible for protecting people from discrimination in social services programs.

The OCR has enforced the Privacy Rule since the 2003 compliance date. It began enforcing the Security Rule in July 2009. Before that, the Centers for Medicare and Medicaid Services (CMS) enforced the Security Rule. CMS is also a part of HHS.

The HITECH Act changed many of the oversight and enforcement functions for HIPAA and required HHS to improve how it enforced the Privacy and Security Rules. To do this, the HHS secretary delegated Security Rule enforcement to the OCR. This change eliminated duplicate rule enforcement. HHS hopes to be more efficient by having one office enforce both rules.

The OCR can fine covered entities that do not comply with the Privacy and Security Rules. The maximum fine for a Security or Privacy Rule violation is $1.5 million per year, which is annually adjusted for inflation.[69] Minimum fines range from $100 to $50,000 per violation. The penalty amount is determined by reviewing the nature of the violation. The OCR also will weigh how the covered entity responded to the violation when it determines a fine.

A person may be subject to criminal liability if he or she obtains or discloses PHI in violation of HIPAA. The HITECH Act clarifies that any person who wrongfully obtains or discloses PHI can be held criminally responsible. This includes a covered entity, its employees, or any other person. A person must know that his or her conduct is wrongful under HIPAA. The U.S. Department of Justice handles HIPAA criminal violations.

The HITECH Act allows states to enforce HIPAA compliance. States did not have this authority before. State attorneys general can stop covered entities from engaging in practices that harm state residents and compromise their PHI. They also can recover damages on behalf of state residents who are harmed by a covered entity's conduct. The first state to use this new enforcement power was Connecticut.

**NOTE**

HHS must bring an enforcement action against a noncompliant covered entity within 6 years of the date of the violation.[70]

**FYI**

In 2018 HHS investigated 32,770 cases related to the HIPAA Security and Privacy Rules.[68] A flowchart of the OCR complaint process is available at http://www.hhs.gov/ocr/privacy/hipaa/enforcement/process.

## The Role of State Laws Protecting Medical Records

HIPAA sets the floor for PHI security and privacy protections. This means that states are free to create laws and rules that provide more protections than HIPAA. Covered entities have to comply with both laws. Generally speaking, the controlling law is whichever law is stricter, or provides greater patient rights.

Any state law that is contrary to HIPAA is not allowed. A state law is contrary if it is impossible for the covered entity to comply with both the state law and HIPAA. In these situations, the state laws are preempted by HIPAA.

States enact many laws that may affect PHI. These laws can provide more rights than allowed by HIPAA. For instance, in 2008 California enacted some of the strictest patient privacy protections in the country. California's laws specify harsh penalties for providers caught snooping in patient medical records. California healthcare providers must report privacy breaches more quickly than is specified in HIPAA. The California law requires healthcare providers to notify people within 15 days of a breach of a patient's medical information.[71]

It is important to review both state law and federal law when reviewing questions about the security and privacy of PHI. You must review both types of laws to make sure that covered entities are appropriately protecting this information.

## Case Studies and Examples

The following case studies show how the laws discussed in this chapter are used. These case studies are real-world examples of how regulatory agencies apply laws and rules to protect PHI.

### OCR Enforcement Information

The OCR posts HIPAA Privacy and Security Rule enforcement news on its webpage, as well as summaries of enforcement activities. It also posts monthly statistics about its activities, as well as case examples and resolution agreements for HIPAA violations.

The OCR enforcement activities webpage can be found at https://www.hhs.gov/hipaa/for-professionals/compliance-enforcement/index.html.

### HIPAA and Federal Trade Communications Act

Sometimes an act can touch several compliance laws. In 2006, an Indianapolis, Indiana, television news station conducted an investigative report on prescription privacy. As part of its report, the news station looked at the contents of pharmacy dumpsters to see if pharmacies properly disposed of patient information. It checked the contents of unsecured, unlocked dumpsters. There was nothing stopping the public from sifting through these dumpsters.

The news station reported that CVS pharmacies were throwing sensitive personal information in the trash. CVS, one of the largest pharmacy retailers in the United States, has more than 6,000 stores. The investigation found that CVS was throwing away unredacted pill bottles that included patient names, addresses, physician names, and the names of medication.

CVS also threw away medication instruction sheets containing personal information, as well as pharmacy receipts with credit card and health insurance account numbers. All of this information was unredacted PHI. Other media outlets reported that CVS stores across the United States also were improperly disposing of PHI.

Information about the "Prescription Privacy" investigative report can be found at https://www.wthr.com/article/news/investigations/13-investigates/part-one-prescription-privacy/531-811d33f4-344c-4614-922d-a9e75a5fa1b4.

At the time, CVS's privacy policy stated: "CVS/pharmacy wants you to know that nothing is more central to our operations than maintaining the privacy of your health information ('Protected Health Information' or 'PHI'). PHI is information about you, including basic information that may identify you and relates to your past, present, or future health or condition and the dispensing of pharmaceutical products to you. We take this responsibility very seriously."

CVS disposal practices were investigated by the HHS and the Federal Trade Commission (FTC). It was the first time that HHS and the FTC worked together on an investigation. HHS, through the OCR, investigated CVS for violations of the HIPAA Privacy Rule and found that CVS violated the Privacy Rule in several ways. Its review indicated that CVS did not properly safeguard PHI during the media disposal process. It also found that CVS did not properly train its employees on how to dispose of PHI, or have a sanctions policy.

The FTC investigated CVS for violations of the FTC Act. It alleged that CVS made false and deceptive statements about its privacy policies, promised customers that it would protect unauthorized access to personal information, and did not actually do this. These misleading types of statements are illegal under the FTC Act.

CVS responded that there was no verification of the media reports. However, it settled charges with the FTC and HHS to resolve the cases. The FTC consent agreement required CVS to create a comprehensive information security program to protect the personal information that CVS collects from consumers and employees. The order also required CVS to get an independent audit of its security program every 2 years until 2029. In addition, CVS may not make any misrepresentations about the company's security practices.

The FTC complaint and consent agreement can be found at http://www.ftc.gov/enforcement/cases-and-proceedings/cases/2009/06/matter-cvs-caremark-corporation-corporation. (Look for the February 18, 2009, entries.)

**NOTE**

An HHS resolution agreement is similar to an FTC consent order. Both are settlement agreements.

Under the HHS resolution agreement, CVS agreed to pay \$2.25 million to settle all claims. It also agreed to follow a corrective action plan that required it to create policies to comply with the HIPAA Privacy Rule. To do so, it must create policies and procedures to safeguard PHI during disposal and establish an employee training program. CVS also must create an employee sanctions policy to discipline employees who fail to follow the Privacy Rule. The HHS resolution agreement also requires independent review of CVS compliance. CVS must be reviewed each year. The agreement requires 3 years of monitoring. The HHS resolution agreement and corrective action plan can be found at http://www.hhs.gov/ocr/privacy/hipaa/enforcement/examples/cvsresolutionagreement.html.

## CHAPTER SUMMARY

Personal health information is one of the most sensitive types of confidential information. Personal health information is no longer limited to paper files; today, this type of information is often stored in electronic form. However, no matter what its form, this information must be protected. Healthcare providers must take steps to ensure its privacy and security.

They are required to do so by both federal and state laws, and face fines and other penalties for failing to protect this information.

## KEY CONCEPTS AND TERMS

Authorization
Business associates
Covered entity
Disclosure
Discovery
Electronic protected health information (EPHI)
Medical identity theft
Minimum necessary rule
Private cause of action
Protected health information (PHI)
Use

## CHAPTER 6 ASSESSMENT

1. An addressable implementation specification must be used if it is _____.

2. What is the maximum fine for a single violation of the HIPAA Privacy or Security Rule?

   A. $100
   B. $1,500
   C. $1 million
   D. $1.5 million
   E. It is unlimited.

3. Covered entities must notify affected individuals of a breach within ______ days.

4. HIPAA limits the preexisting condition waiting period to ______ months.

5. What conditions must be met to be considered a healthcare provider under HIPAA?

   A. Provide healthcare services to a person.
   B. Conduct standard transactions electronically.
   C. Handle electronic transactions on a clearinghouse's behalf.
   D. Provide healthcare services to a person and conduct standard transactions electronically.
   E. None of these is correct.

6. A business associate is _____.

7. What term refers to how a covered entity shares PHI within the organization?

   A. Disclosure
   B. Discuss
   C. Use
   D. Handle
   E. None of these is correct.

8. A covered entity must disclose PHI to a person's family and friends in an emergency.

   A. True
   B. False

9. A covered entity must respond to a person's request to access PHI within ______ days.

10. Which uses and disclosures of PHI are allowed without a person's consent?
    A. Made for a person about his or her own PHI
    B. Made for treatment, payment, and healthcare operations
    C. Made for public safety and health activities
    D. All of these are correct.
    E. None of these is correct.

11. What term refers to how a covered entity shares PHI with other organizations?
    A. Disclosure
    B. Discuss
    C. Use
    D. Handle
    E. None of these is correct.

12. What is the legal process used to gather evidence in a lawsuit?
    A. Disclosure
    B. Discovery
    C. Forensics
    D. Trial
    E. None of these is correct.

13. Which entity enforces the HIPAA Privacy Rule?
    A. FDIC
    B. FTC
    C. OCR
    D. CDC
    E. None of these is correct.

14. Which rule is similar to the information security concept of need to know?
    A. Use rule
    B. Clearinghouse rule
    C. Operations rule
    D. Absolute rule
    E. Minimum necessary rule

15. A HIPAA breach is a breach of ______ PHI.

## ENDNOTES

1. U.S. Department of Health and Human Services, "Anthem Pays OCR $16 Million in Record HIPAA Settlement Following Largest U.S. Health Data Breach in History." October 15, 2018. https://www.hhs.gov/about/news/2018/10/15/anthem-pays-ocr-16-million-record-hipaa-settlement-following-largest-health-data-breach-history.html (accessed July 5, 2020).
2. Ponemon Institute, "Fifth Annual Study on Medical Identity Theft." February 2015. https://static.nationwide.com/static/2014_Medical_ID_Theft_Study.pdf?r=65 (accessed July 5, 2020).
3. CBS News, "Cancer Patient Catches ID Thief," November 6, 2004. https://www.cbsnews.com/news/cancer-patient-catches-id-thief/ (accessed March 1, 2020).
4. U.S. Department of Justice, "Leesburg Woman Sentenced To 48 Months In Prison For Aggravated Identity Theft And Wire Fraud," May 19, 2020. https://www.justice.gov/usao-mdfl/pr/leesburg-woman-sentenced-48-months-prison-aggravated-identity-theft-and-wire-fraud (accessed July 5, 2020).
5. National Library of Medicine, "Greek Medicine: The Hippocratic Oath," Translated by Michael North, 2002. http://www.nlm.nih.gov/hmd/greek/greek_oath.html (accessed March 1, 2020).
6. Drug Abuse Prevention, Treatment, and Rehabilitation Act (1980), U.S. Code Vol. 42, sec. 290dd-2 (2020).
7. Health Information Technology for Economic and Clinical Health Act of 2009 (HITECH Act), Pub. L. No. 111-5, 123 Stat. 226, codified at U.S. Code Vol. 42, sec. 300jj *et seq.*, and sec. 17901 *et seq.* (2018).
8. Consolidated Omnibus Budget Reconciliation Act (1986), Pub. L. No. 99-272, 100 Stat. 82 (1986).
9. CNBC, "Consumer DNA Testing Has Hit a Lull—Here's How It Could Capture the Next Wave of Users," August 25, 2019. https://www.cnbc.com/2019/08/25

/dna-tests-from-companies-like-23andme-ancestry-see-sales-slowdown.html (accessed March 1, 2020).
10. Health Insurance Portability and Accountability Act (1996), Pub. L. No. 104-191, sec. 261.
11. Genetic Information Nondiscrimination Act of 2008 (GINA), Pub. L. No. 110-233, 122 Stat. 881 (2008).
12. Code of Federal Regulations, Title 45, sec. 160.103.
13. Code of Federal Regulations, Title 45, sec. 160.103.
14. U.S. Code Vol. 42, sec. 1320d.
15. Code of Federal Regulations, Title 45, sec. 164.104(b).
16. Federal Register 65, No. 250 at 82463 (background information).
17. Code of Federal Regulations, Title 45, sec. 164.524(b).
18. Code of Federal Regulations, Title 45, sec. 164.524(d).
19. Code of Federal Regulations, Title 45, sec. 164.502(a)(2).
20. Code of Federal Regulations, Title 45, sec.164.502.
21. Code of Federal Regulations, Title 45, sec. 164.506(c).
22. Code of Federal Regulations, Title 45, sec. 164.501.
23. Code of Federal Regulations, Title 45, sec. 164.501.
24. Code of Federal Regulations, Title 45, sec. 164.501.
25. Code of Federal Regulations, Title 45, sec. 164.506(b).
26. Code of Federal Regulations, Title 45, sec. 164.510.
27. Code of Federal Regulations, Title 45, sec. 164.512.
28. Code of Federal Regulations, Title 45, sec. 164.512(b).
29. Code of Federal Regulations, Title 45, sec. 164.512(b).
30. Code of Federal Regulations, Title 45, sec. 164.512(c).
31. Code of Federal Regulations, Title 45, sec. 164.512(a).
32. Code of Federal Regulations, Title 45, sec. 164.514(e)(2).
33. Code of Federal Regulations, Title 45, sec. 164.514(e)(4).
34. Code of Federal Regulations, Title 45, sec. 164.508.
35. Code of Federal Regulations, Title 45, sec. 164.508(c)(1).
36. Code of Federal Regulations, Title 45, sec. 165-502(b).
37. Code of Federal Regulations, Title 45, sec. 165-502(b)(2).
38. Code of Federal Regulations, Title 45, sec. 164.526.
39. Code of Federal Regulations, Title 45, sec. 164.526(b)(2).
40. Code of Federal Regulations, Title 45, sec. 164.526(d).
41. Code of Federal Regulations, Title 45, sec. 164.528.
42. Code of Federal Regulations, Title 45, sec. 164.528(c)(2).
43. Code of Federal Regulations, Title 45, sec. 164.528(d).
44. HITECH Act, sec. 13405(c).
45. Code of Federal Regulations, Title 45, sec. 164.520.
46. Code of Federal Regulations, Title 45, sec. 164.520(c).
47. Code of Federal Regulations, Title 45, sec. 164.530.
48. Code of Federal Regulations, Title 45, sec. 164.530.
49. Code of Federal Regulations, Title 45, sec. 164.530(f).
50. HITECH Act, sec. 13402.
51. Fed. Register No. 78, 5642-43 (January 25, 2013).
52. Code of Federal Regulations, Title 45, sec. 164.404.
53. Code of Federal Regulations, Title 45, sec. 164.404.
54. Code of Federal Regulations, Title 45, sec. 164.404.
55. Code of Federal Regulations, Title 45, sec. 164.408.
56. Code of Federal Regulations, Title 45, sec. 164.306.
57. Code of Federal Regulations, Title 45, sec. 164.316(b).
58. Code of Federal Regulations, Title 45, sec. 164.306.

59. Code of Federal Regulations, Title 45, sec. 164.306(d).
60. Code of Federal Regulations, Title 45, sec. 164.304.
61. Code of Federal Regulations, Title 45, sec. 164.308.
62. Code of Federal Regulations, Title 45, sec. 164.304.
63. Code of Federal Regulations, Title 45, sec. 164.304.
64. Code of Federal Regulations, Title 45, sec. 164.310.
65. Code of Federal Regulations, Title 45, sec. 164.304.
66. Code of Federal Regulations, Title 45, sec. 164.304.
67. Code of Federal Regulations, Title 45, sec. 164.312.
68. U.S. Department of Health & Human Services, "Enforcement Results by Year," April 3, 2019. https://www.hhs.gov/hipaa/for-professionals/compliance-enforcement/data/enforcement-results-by-year/index.html (accessed March 1, 2020).
69. Federal Civil Penalties Inflation Adjustment Act Improvements Act of 2015, enacted as part of the Bipartisan Budget Act of 2015, Public Law 114-74, section 701, 129 Stat. 599 (Nov. 2, 2015).
70. Code of Federal Regulations, Title 45, sec. 160.414.
71. Health Facilities Data Breach, California Health and Safety Code sec. 1280.15.

CHAPTER 7

# Corporate Information Security and Privacy Regulation

THIS CHAPTER FOCUSES on special security issues faced by publicly traded companies. Public companies must comply with a law that tries to improve corporate responsibility and stop fraudulent financial reporting. Rules and regulations created in response to the law impact information systems that process financial data. The rules require that these systems be reviewed to make sure that they appropriately control information security risks and threats to financial data.

This chapter reviews why Congress created this law. It also reviews how the law influences information security practices. Finally, it discusses how this law affects other kinds of organizations.

## Chapter 7 Topics

This chapter covers the following topics and concepts:

- How the Enron scandal led to securities-law reform
- Why accurate financial reporting is important
- What the Sarbanes-Oxley Act (SOX) is
- What compliance and security controls are
- How SOX influences other types of companies
- What some corporate privacy issues are
- What some case studies and examples are

## Chapter 7 Goals

When you complete this chapter, you will be able to:

- Describe the difference between public and private companies
- Explain the history behind the Sarbanes-Oxley Act
- Discuss the main requirements of the Sarbanes-Oxley Act

- Explain the role of the Public Company Accounting Oversight Board
- Describe how Section 404 internal control requirements impact information security
- Discuss frameworks used to guide Sarbanes-Oxley internal control requirements

## The Enron Scandal and Securities-Law Reform

Enron. WorldCom. Tyco. Adelphia. These companies have come to represent a wave of corporate scandal that plagued America in the early 2000s. Each company engaged in varying levels of mismanagement, questionable financial deals, and accounting fraud. The activities at these companies shook investor confidence in U.S. corporations. They also tarnished the reputations of financial services professionals such as analysts, accountants, and auditors. Consider the following:

- Once called the "Most Innovative Company in America," energy company Enron filed for bankruptcy in December 2001. It used several different fraudulent accounting methods to hide billions of dollars of debt from its investors and lenders.
- Cable company Adelphia filed for bankruptcy in June 2002. In 2004, a federal jury convicted Adelphia's founder of bank and securities fraud. He was sentenced to 15 years in prison.
- Telecommunications company WorldCom filed for bankruptcy in July 2002. At the time, it was the largest bankruptcy in U.S. history. In July 2005, a federal court sentenced the chief executive officer (CEO) of WorldCom to 25 years in prison for corporate fraud.
- In June 2005, a jury convicted a former Tyco CEO of theft, conspiracy, securities fraud, and falsifying business records. A court in New York sentenced him to between 8 and 25 years in prison. He was ordered to pay restitution and fines of more than $200 million.

The financial mismanagement at these companies contributed to the largest reform in U.S. securities laws since the Great Depression. The Enron bankruptcy is the case that spurred Congress to act. It is important to understand the Enron scandal to appreciate how significant the reform was.

### Corporate Fraud at Enron

The Enron case has become a part of American pop culture, as its name is now synonymous with corporate greed and scandal. Nearly 20 years after the scandal, it continues to hold our attention.

Enron, which was based in Houston, Texas, formed in 1985 through the merger of two natural gas companies. Kenneth Lay was the CEO of the company. By the mid-1990s, Enron was the leading U.S. natural gas company.

## Public Versus Private Companies

A **public company** is also called a publicly traded company. Many investors own a public company, in which investors own a portion of the company in the form of stock. A stock represents a share of a corporation's profits or assets. A person's percentage of ownership in the corporation depends on how many shares of stock he or she owns.

Shareholders are entitled to portions of a public company's profits. Their share, called a **dividend**, represents each shareholder's portion of the company's earnings. People who own more shares of stock receive larger dividends.

Public corporations are allowed to sell stocks and bonds. A bond represents a loan to the corporation for a specified period. The corporation must pay bondholders back the full value of the bond, plus interest. However, a person who owns a corporate bond does not have any ownership in a corporation. Only stocks represent an ownership interest. Stocks and bonds together are called **securities**.

In the United States, the stock of a public company is traded on a stock exchange. The two most popular U.S. stock exchanges are the New York Stock Exchange (NYSE) and the NASDAQ Stock Market. National securities exchanges are registered with the U.S. Securities and Exchange Commission (SEC). You can learn more at https://www.sec.gov/fast-answers/divisionsmarketregmrexchangesshtml.html.

Almost all securities sold in the United States must be registered with the SEC. To register its securities, a company must file documents about its financial condition with the SEC on a regular basis. Investors review these documents to make informed investment decisions.

A public company is different from a **privately held company**, in which a small group of private investors owns a privately held company. In some cases, the investors all might be members of the same family. A private company does not have to answer to shareholders in the same way that a public company does. A private company distributes its profits to its owners.

Private companies do not have to register with the SEC. They also do not have to file documents with the SEC that show their financial position. The largest private companies in the United States include Cargill, Koch Industries, and Albertsons.[1]



Enron grew quickly because it took advantage of energy market deregulation in the late 1980s. It bought and sold gas and electricity through futures contracts. These investments were initially very successful. As it grew, Enron expanded into other markets. It purchased steel mills, water utilities, and even tried to enter the internet broadband market. It also expanded internationally, pursuing opportunities in England, Mexico, and India.

From 1997 to 2001, *Fortune* magazine put Enron on its "Most Innovative Companies in America" list.[2] In 2000, it named Enron to its "World's Most Admired Companies" list.[3] Enron grew from 7,500 employees in 1996 to more than 20,000 employees in 2001. Its stock was valuable. Enron encouraged its employees to include Enron stock in their retirement portfolios.

To the outside world, Enron was a very successful company. Its required filings with the U.S. SEC showed that it was making money. It appeared to be able to translate its success in the energy markets to other markets. Financial analysts continued to recommend Enron stock. Investors continued to buy it.

In reality, Enron was struggling. It lost billions of dollars on its international investments. Enron also started to face increased competition in the energy business. It began to lose its market share in energy futures contracts because other energy companies started to use Enron's own strategies to become profitable.

By the late 1990s, Enron was in financial trouble and needed to raise money to meet its operating expenses. However, it did not want to do this in a way that would alarm its investors or alert them to potential trouble, which could cause its stock price to fall. Maintaining a high stock price was important to bring in new investors. It also was critical to being able to maintain credit lines with banks.

**FYI**

A *futures contract* is a contract for the sale of a good. One party agrees to sell the other party an asset at some point in the future. The two parties agree on the future quantity and price for the asset at the time the contract is made. Companies use futures contracts as an investment tool rather than as an actual contract to supply goods.

Enron executives engaged in several complicated financial transactions to hide its losses. Its chief financial officer (CFO), Andrew Fastow, created several affiliated companies, then hid Enron's losses in the financial records of these companies. The Enron CFO and other employees who worked with him owned many of these affiliated companies and profited from the transactions between Enron and the affiliated companies.

These transactions were very complex and complicated to understand because Enron often changed the names of its different divisions. It also moved assets back and forth between divisions. Many of these transactions violated traditional accounting principles, which are called generally accepted accounting principles (GAAP). They are the rules for the accounting process. Accountants prepare financial statements according to these rules, which are designed to promote accurate accounting records.

Enron also mislabeled loans that it received from banks to hide the transactions on its own financial statements so that its investors would not know about them. By some reports, Enron borrowed about $8.6 billion from 1992 to 2001.[4] However, it hid these loans from its investors. During this time, Enron filed earnings statements with the SEC that misstated its financial position. The SEC filings were hard to understand. They also showed that Enron appeared to be making money.

In February 2001, CEO Kenneth Lay retired. The new CEO, Jeffrey Skilling, had been instrumental in taking Enron into new trading markets in the 1990s. He and CFO Andrew Fastow oversaw most of Enron's business practices.

In April 2001, many financial analysts began to question Enron's complicated financial statements.[5] Enron, however, continued to portray the image of a successful company. Jeffrey Skilling unexpectedly resigned from the CEO post in August 2001, at which time the board of directors asked Kenneth Lay to return to Enron as its CEO, which he did.

In October 2001, Enron announced its first ever loss. The SEC noticed this announcement and began to review Enron's financial statements. Enron also began its own investigation. In late October, the Enron board of directors established a special committee, led by Director

William C. Powers, to investigate the affiliated companies created by Fastow. The report that the committee issued is known as the "Powers Report."[6]

In November 2001, Enron announced that it was amending its 1997–2001 financial statements because of accounting errors. This announcement shook investor confidence in Enron, and its stock price began to drop. Banks would no longer issue it credit to meet its operating expenses. At the end of November 2001, Enron stock was worth less than a dollar per share.[7]

**FYI**

The Powers Report, released in February 2002, noted that Enron's executive officers mismanaged many aspects of the company's business. It also placed blame on Enron's Board of Directors for failing in its corporate oversight duties. It blamed Enron's accounting advisor, Arthur Andersen, for failing to provide objective accounting advice. You can read a copy of the report at http://i.cnn.net/cnn/2002/LAW/02/02/enron.report/powers.report.pdf.

On December 2, 2001, Enron filed for bankruptcy. At the time, it was the largest bankruptcy ever. In January 2002, Enron removed its stock from the New York Stock Exchange (NYSE).[8]

The fallout from the Enron case was enormous. Employees who had invested their retirement savings in Enron stock lost $1.3 billion.[9] The accounting firm Arthur Andersen, Enron's auditor, closed down. The U.S. government prosecuted many of Enron's top executives for their involvement in its business dealings. Some of these prosecutions were difficult because it was hard to determine which executives were involved in the fraud, and which executives were not. The complexity of Enron's financial dealings contributed to this difficulty.

CFO Andrew Fastow entered into a plea agreement with the U.S. government. He agreed to testify against Jeffrey Skilling and Kenneth Lay in exchange for a sentence of no more than 10 years in prison. In September 2006, a federal court sentenced him to 6 years in prison. He also paid more than $30 million in restitution. Fastow was released from prison in December 2011.

Enron founder and CEO Kenneth Lay was convicted in May 2006 for fraud and conspiracy. He died of a heart attack in July 2006. The court vacated his conviction after his death because he died before he could appeal.

Former CEO Jeffrey Skilling was convicted in 2006 on federal fraud charges. A federal court sentenced him to 24 years in prison. He appealed his conviction to the U.S. Supreme Court, which heard oral arguments in March 2010. On June 24, 2010, the U.S. Supreme Court ruled that the government had improperly applied a law used to convict Skilling and sent the case back to a lower court. In June 2013, Skilling was sentenced to 14 years in prison. He was released from jail in 2019.[10]

## Why Is Accurate Financial Reporting Important?

Enron was one of many large corporate scandals in the early 2000s that shook investor confidence in the U.S. economy. Because of the scope of the fraud and the damage to Enron investors, the U.S. Congress held numerous hearings and committee meetings related to the aftermath of the scandal.[11] Enron significantly misstated its financial condition in the financial statements that it filed with the SEC, leading its investors to lose money because of these fraudulent financial statements.

The Enron scandal showed why accurate financial information is important. Enron was able to sustain itself for at least 5 years because of inaccurate financial reporting. During this period, financial analysts continued to recommend its stock as a good investment. The public and Enron employees invested in it. However, these people had significant losses when Enron's troubles became public and the company finally declared bankruptcy. Enron duped its investors. By the time everyone knew the truth, it was too late to recover investment losses. Investors thus lost confidence in large public companies.

The financial statements that a company files with the SEC are among the main sources of information that investors use to research that company. These documents help investors determine the true financial condition of a company. After the Enron scandal, the SEC required more information to be reported on these forms. It also required that the accuracy of these forms be certified in several different ways.

Public companies are required to file several financial disclosure statements with the SEC. These forms help investors understand the financial stability of a company. The most commonly filed forms are:

- Form 10-K—Annual report
- Form 10-Q—Quarterly report
- Form 8-K—Current report

A company uses **Form 10-K** to file its annual report. Federal law requires that publicly traded companies submit these reports each year. Depending on their size, companies must file this report within 60 to 90 days after the end of their fiscal year. The larger a company is, the faster it has to file its report.

Form 10-K is a very detailed disclosure of a company's financial condition. A company must fully describe its business in its 10-K disclosure, explain how it is organized and how it operates, and provide its financial statements. These statements include balance sheets, statements of income and cash flows, and statements of shareholder equity. An independent auditor must audit the company's financial statements, and the auditor's report must be included in the Form 10-K filing. In addition, the CEO and CFO of a company, as well as the majority of the company's board of directors, must sign the company's Form 10-K.

**Form 10-Q** is a company's quarterly report, which is required by federal law. Companies must file these reports after the end of each of their first three quarters in a fiscal year. These reports are usually less detailed than the end-of-the year 10-K filing. Depending on their size, companies must file this report within 40 to 45 days after the end of each fiscal quarter.

Companies must file **Form 8-K** if they experience a major event that could affect their financial condition, because shareholders and investors should know about these events. Companies must file a Form 8-K with the SEC within 4 days of a major event.[12] This period is shortened in some instances. For example, a company must file Form 8-K with the SEC immediately if it becomes aware of insider trading activities.

FYI

A company's two main financial documents are its *balance sheet* and *profit and loss statement*. The balance sheet provides a summary of the company's financial condition at a certain period. This is commonly prepared on a monthly basis. A profit and loss statement is used to determine whether a company made a profit during a certain period.



General events that trigger a Form 8-K disclosure requirement include:

- Filing for bankruptcy
- Selling off significant assets
- Acquiring another company
- Getting a loan
- Board member resignation
- Board member elections
- Any changes to board governance documents

People need accurate financial information so that they can invest wisely and make money. Therefore, the SEC recommends that potential investors carefully review a company's prospectus and financial reports. You can read the SEC's list of information that investors should review before investing at http://www.investor.gov. The benefit of reviewing information from several different sources is that an investor can get a better picture of a company's financial condition.

It can be very hard for investors to detect fraud, as was the case in the Enron scandal. Therefore, the SEC recommends that investors look for potential red flags as they review a company's financial condition. Red flags include companies that have high-value assets, but low revenues. It also includes odd items listed in the footnotes of the company's financial statements. Both of these red flags were present in the Enron scandal.

## The Sarbanes-Oxley Act of 2002

Congress passed the Public Company Accounting Reform and Investor Protection Act in 2002.[13] More commonly known as the Sarbanes-Oxley Act of 2002, it is called SOX or Sarbox in many resources. The Act was named after its sponsors, Senator Paul Sarbanes of Maryland and Representative Michael Oxley of Ohio. It was passed in response to corporate scandals such as Enron, WorldCom, and Adelphia. SOX proposed extensive changes to the Securities Act of 1933 and the Securities Exchange Act of 1934.

SOX moved through both the U.S. House of Representatives and Senate at a quick pace. It was originally introduced in the U.S. House of Representatives in February 2002, just months after the Enron scandal became public. On July 25, 2002, both the House and Senate voted on the final version of SOX. President George W. Bush then signed SOX into law on July 30, 2002. As he signed it, he called SOX "the most far-reaching reforms of American business practices since the time of Franklin Delano Roosevelt."[14]

 **NOTE**

A company uses a *prospectus* to describe the securities that it offers for sale. The prospectus describes the company's business plan.

## Purpose and Scope

Congress hoped that SOX reforms would prevent another Enron scandal. The main goal of SOX was to protect shareholders and investors from financial fraud. SOX increased corporate disclosure requirements and created strict penalties for violations of its provisions. SOX has 11 different titles. They are:

- **Public Company Accounting Oversight Board (Title I)**—Establishes the Public Company Accounting Oversight Board (PCAOB). The PCAOB oversees the firms that audit public companies.
- **Auditor Independence (Title II)**—Forbids auditors from providing some types of non-audit services to their clients.
- **Corporate Responsibility (Title III)**—Requires corporations to create audit committees on their board of directors. The audit committee is responsible for hiring the corporation's outside auditors.
- **Enhanced Financial Disclosures (Title IV)—**Enhances the amount of information that public companies must provide on their SEC filings. This section requires companies to report on internal controls that affect their financial reports.
- **Analyst Conflicts of Interest (Title V)—**Establishes rules to make sure that securities analysts can give independent opinions about a public company's stock risk.
- **Commission Resources and Authority (Title VI)**—Gives the SEC authority to discipline investment firms for unprofessional conduct. This section also gives the SEC additional funding to support its programs.
- **Studies and Reports (Title VII)**—Requires the SEC to review public accounting firms. The SEC must do this at least every 3 years. This section also requires the SEC to issue reports about how the securities market operates.
- **Corporate and Criminal Fraud Accountability (Title VIII)—**Imposes document retention requirements on companies and auditors. It protects whistleblowers, and also bans retaliation against employees who participate in fraud investigations. This section also imposes criminal penalties for violating SOX.
- **White-Collar Crime Penalty Enhancements (Title IX)—**Requires CEOs and CFOs to certify that the company's financial reports fairly represent its financial condition. It creates criminal penalties for signing fraudulent statements.
- **Corporate Tax Returns (Title X)—**Is a statement from Congress that strongly suggests that a CEO sign the federal income tax return of a corporation.
- **Corporate Fraud and Accountability (Title XI)—**Establishes criminal liability for certain types of fraud committed by corporate officers. It also increases penalties for some types of corporate crime.

 **NOTE**

A small public company is a company with less than $75 million of public stock.

SOX supplements current federal securities laws. It applies to publicly traded companies that must register with the SEC. This includes international companies that trade stock on U.S. stock exchanges. However, SOX does not apply to privately held companies.

## Main Requirements

SOX is a very detailed act with many provisions. This chapter focuses on the parts of the act that have had the most impact on information technology (IT) functions. When SOX was first enacted, many companies assumed that it did not have any IT components. Congress did not mention IT anywhere within the act.

This opinion changed as companies began to review their SOX compliance requirements. Many SOX provisions require companies to verify the accuracy of their financial information. Because IT systems hold many types of financial information, companies and auditors quickly realized that these systems were in scope for SOX compliance. That meant that how those systems are used and the controls used to safeguard those systems had to be reviewed.

The relationship between IT and SOX compliance continues to evolve. This section reviews the SOX provisions that have an IT impact. First, this section reviews the PCAOB, which creates standards that auditors must follow when reviewing the activities of public companies. These standards help auditors determine the IT controls that they must review. The creation of the PCAOB is one of the most notable SOX reforms.

Second, this section reviews SOX provisions that impact records management functions. These provisions have an impact on IT operations because of the vast amount of data that is stored electronically. These provisions are important because they affect how IT systems are configured.

Finally, SOX requires the executive management of a company to certify that there are controls in place to protect the accuracy of company information. This is the area where SOX compliance has caused the biggest challenge for companies and IT professionals.

### *Public Company Accounting Oversight Board*

Before the creation of SOX, auditors and accountants belonged to a self-regulating profession. A profession is self-regulating when it creates and enforces its own rules of conduct. Federal and state laws place few oversight requirements on members of self-regulating professions.

An attorney is a common example of a member of a self-regulating profession. Attorneys must meet minimum state law requirements to become licensed. After that, their professional behavior is largely judged by commissions made up of other attorneys who enforce rules of professional conduct. The profession itself determines what these rules of professional conduct should be.

**FYI**

Information security professionals belong to a largely self-regulating profession. This is especially true when information security professionals obtain certifications that require the certificate holders to follow a code of conduct.

The Enron scandal proved that self-regulation does have some drawbacks. Enron's accounting firm, Arthur Andersen, provided it with accounting, auditing, and consulting services. Enron was a large Andersen client that paid Andersen $52 million for auditing and consulting services in 2001.[15] Even the Powers Report noted that there was a lack of critical advice from its auditors at Arthur Andersen in reviewing Enron's publicly filed financial statements.[16] This may have been because Arthur Andersen was reluctant to challenge such an important client.

Congress created the PCAOB to provide a layer of government oversight on auditing activities. The PCAOB, which oversees the audit of public companies, was created in order to ensure that audit reports for public companies are fair and independent. Under SOX, the PCAOB has several duties.[17] It must:

- Register accounting firms that prepare audit reports for public companies.
- Establish standards for the preparation of audit reports.
- Conduct inspections of registered public accounting firms.
- Conduct investigations and disciplinary proceedings against registered public accounting firms.
- Perform other duties or functions necessary to carry out SOX.
- Enforce SOX compliance.
- Set a budget for the PCAOB, and manage its operations.

> **NOTE**
>
> You can learn more about the role of the PCAOB by visiting its webpage at http://pcaobus.org.

The PCAOB has five members. The SEC selects these members and appoints them to staggered terms. The SEC can remove PCAOB members if needed. PCAOB members are to be "individuals of integrity and reputation who have a demonstrated commitment to the interests of investors and the public."[18] They must be financially literate. This means that they must be able to understand financial statements. Only two members of the PCAOB are allowed to be certified public accountants (CPAs); the remaining three members cannot. Furthermore, members of the PCAOB are not allowed to have any financial interest in an accounting firm. **FIGURE 7-1** shows the structure of the PCAOB.

**FIGURE 7-1**

PCAOB structure.

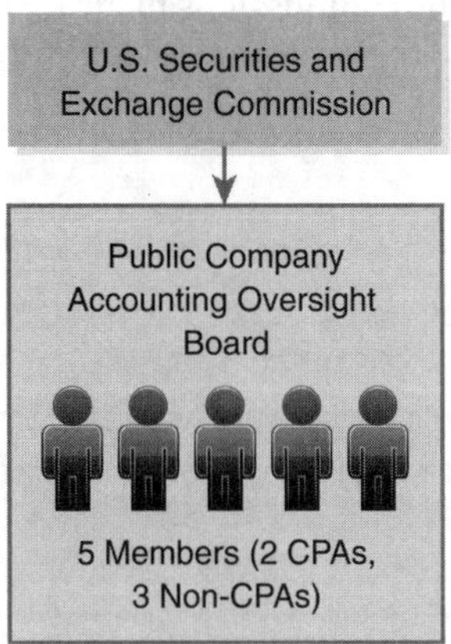

**FYI**

The SEC believes that a single set of globally accepted accounting principles will benefit U.S. companies. Therefore, it is evaluating whether it should adopt the International Financial Reporting Standards (IFRS), created by the International Accounting Standards Board. You can learn about IFRS at http://www.ifrs.com/ifrs_faqs.html. The SEC has studied the IFRS extensively and compared them with U.S. accounting principles. Although the SEC has not approved IFRS for use by U.S. public companies, interest in a global framework for financial reporting remains.[19]



One of the main functions of the PCAOB is to set standards for how auditors review public companies. It has created standards related to auditing, ethics and independence, quality control, and attestation, which must be approved by the SEC. The PCAOB bases many of its standards on GAAP, the principles established by the Financial Accounting Standards Board (FASB). The SEC has recognized GAAP as authoritative and requires financial statements to be prepared in accordance with GAAP.

The PCAOB's Auditing Standard 2201 provides guidance on how an auditor performs an audit of a company's internal controls over financial reporting (ICFR). This standard addresses how to audit controls applied to a company's IT systems and processes where those systems and processes impact the production of the company's financial reports. The standard specifies a top-down approach that might limit the scope of review of IT systems. The standard also recommends that auditors focus their review on areas of the highest risk. In 2019, the PCAOB reported that auditors need to be aware of cybersecurity incidents at the companies that they audit. This is because the integrity of the data generated by the company's IT systems could be compromised by a cybersecurity incident. If the data generated or processed by the IT systems is not accurate, then the company's financial statements could contain errors.[20]

**NOTE**

At the end of 2019 there were over 7,000 U.S. public companies. The market value of their stock was over $45 trillion.[21]

### *Document Retention*

SOX contains some records retention provisions. It is important to know about them because companies store many of their records electronically; in fact, some studies estimate that 93 percent of all business documents are created and stored electronically.[22] Companies must understand how their IT systems work in order to meet SOX retention requirements.

SOX requires auditors and public companies to maintain audit papers for 7 years.[23] Audit papers are documents used in an audit that support the conclusions made in an audit report. SOX takes a very broad view of the type of records that must be saved. This includes work papers, memoranda, and correspondence. It also includes any other records created, sent, or received in connection with the audit. SOX also includes electronic records.

SOX also requires that a public company retain the records and documentation that it uses to assess its ICFR. These controls are discussed in the next section. Guidance issued by the SEC recognizes that this documentation takes several different forms, as well as electronic data. Companies must permanently retain this information.

### Is the PCAOB Constitutional?

The constitutionality of SOX was challenged soon after it was enacted into law in a case called *Free Enterprise Fund and Beckstead and Watts v. Public Company Accounting Oversight Board.*

The Free Enterprise Fund and Beckstead and Watts LLP filed the case in 2006. The Free Enterprise Fund is a public interest organization, whereas Beckstead and Watts LLP was an accounting firm. The plaintiffs argued that SOX is unconstitutional. In particular, they argued that the PCAOB is unconstitutional because its creation and operation violate the constitutional separation of powers doctrine.

The plaintiffs argued that separation of powers is violated because the PCAOB is an executive branch agency that the president has virtually no control over. Under SOX, the SEC alone has the power to appoint PCAOB members. In addition, PCAOB members can be fired only for cause, and only by the SEC. The president, and even the SEC, has little authority to control PCAOB members once they are appointed.

The plaintiffs argued that it violates the section of the Constitution that gives the president the power to appoint and remove officers of the executive branch. They also argued that under the Constitution, Congress is not permitted to set up a structure that bypasses the president's authority.

The case was filed in the U.S. District Court for the District of Columbia. The District Court granted summary judgment for the PCAOB and upheld the constitutionality of SOX. In August 2008, the Circuit Court for the D.C. Circuit affirmed the decision of the lower court. The U.S. Supreme Court heard arguments in the case on December 7, 2009, and issued its decision in June 2010.

In its decision, the Court found that the way that the PCAOB is created does indeed violate the separation of powers doctrine. Even though the portion of SOX that creates the PCAOB is unconstitutional, however, the Court said that SOX is still good law. It also said that the PCAOB could continue to function. The Court's decision means that the SEC can now fire PCAOB members at will (or for any reason at all), instead of just for good cause.

You can view the Supreme Court's decision on the *Free Enterprise* case at https://www.supremecourt.gov/opinions/09pdf/08-861.pdf.

In 2010, the Dodd-Frank Wall Street Reform and Consumer Protection Act expanded the role of the PCAOB. The Act gave the PCAOB additional oversight of the audits of brokers and dealers. It also gave the PCAOB the power to conduct inspections, bring enforcement action, and set standards.[24]

**FYI**

Many federal and state laws contain records retention requirements. SOX is another law to add to that list. Organizations should develop document retention policies to help them track their different obligations.

The penalties for failing to retain records for the right amount of time can be severe. SOX makes it a crime for a person or company to knowingly and willfully violate its records retention provisions. A person who violates this provision can face fines and serve up to 10 years in prison.

SOX also makes it a crime for any person to tamper with or destroy any record in an attempt to interfere with a federal investigation.[25] Unlike other parts of SOX, this provision applies to any organization. Private companies also must follow it. People who violate this section can face fines of up to $10 million, as well as up to 20 years in prison.

Companies must make sure that electronic records are stored properly so that they can satisfy SOX retention requirements. They must store the records for the right amount of time. They also must make sure that those records are destroyed properly when the retention period expires.



### *Certification*

SOX requires companies to report accurate financial data to protect their investors from harm. To encourage a company to report accurate data, SOX requires its CEO and CFO to certify the company's SEC filings. SOX certification provisions require executives to establish, maintain, and review certain types of internal controls for their company.

**Disclosure Controls.** SOX Section 302 requires CEOs and CFOs to certify a company's SEC reports. The purpose of the certifications is to put executive management on notice of the company's financial condition. The SEC can hold a CEO or CFO liable for submitting inaccurate financial reports. It makes sense that both the CEO and CFO would have to make these certifications as they are the officers who are most knowledgeable about the company's finances and overall condition.

A certification attests to the truth of certain facts. The SEC requires a certification to be included on several different forms, such as a company's Form 10-Q and Form 10-K reports. (These certifications do not need to be included on Form 8-K.) Under the law,[26] a CEO and CFO each must certify that:[27]

- They have reviewed the report.
- The report does not contain untrue or misleading statements about the company.
- The financial statements fairly represent the company's financial condition.
- The executive is responsible for creating disclosure controls and procedures that are designed to bring material information about the company to the executive's attention, and the controls are reviewed 90 days before filing the report.
- The executive has disclosed all significant deficiencies in its internal controls to their auditor.
- Whether any significant changes in the internal controls have occurred since they were last evaluated.

The controls required under Section 302, called **disclosure controls**, are very broad. They are the processes and procedures that a company puts in place to make sure that it makes timely disclosures to the SEC. They are how management stays informed about the company's operations. These controls must address any change in information that affects company resources. They bring events to the executive's attention so that they can be reported to the SEC.

Disclosure controls are different from SOX **internal controls**. Internal controls are the processes and procedures that a company uses to provide reasonable assurance that its financial reports are reliable. The next section reviews these controls. Internal controls address only processes that protect the reliability of financial reports, whereas disclosure controls are broader. They include internal controls.[28] **FIGURE 7-2** shows the relationship between disclosure controls and internal controls.

FIGURE 7-2

Relationship between disclosure controls and internal controls.

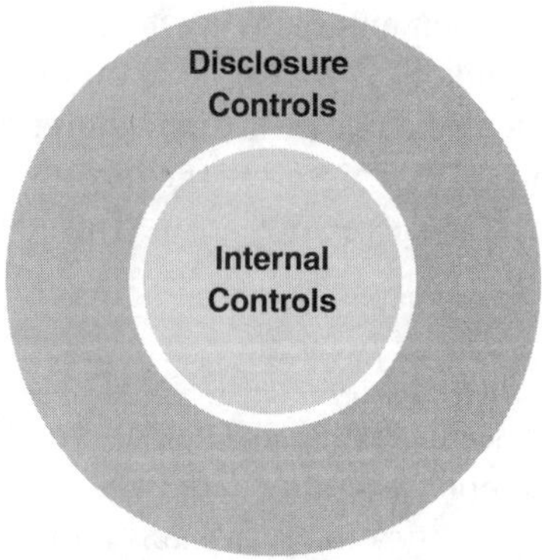


SOX Section 906 imposes criminal liability for fraudulent certifications. Under this section, CEOs and CFOs who knowingly certify fraudulent reports may be fined up to $1 million. They also could be imprisoned for up to 10 years. An officer who willfully makes a fraudulent certification may be fined up to $5 million and could be imprisoned up to 20 years.[29]

**Internal Controls.** SOX Section 404 requires a company's executive management to report on the effectiveness of the company's ICFR.[30] They must make this report each year on their Form 10-K filing. Under this section, management must create, document, and test ICFR. After management makes its yearly report on its ICFR, outside auditors must review the report and verify that the ICFR work. This section has caused compliance headaches for IT professionals.

Under SEC rules, ICFR are processes that provide reasonable assurance that financial reports are reliable.[31] ICFR provide management with reasonable assurance that:

- Financial reports, records, and data are accurately maintained.
- Transactions are prepared according to GAAP rules and are properly recorded.
- Unauthorized acquisition or use of data or assets that could affect financial statements will be prevented or detected in a timely manner.

SOX does not define reasonable assurance. The SEC and PCAOB recognize that reasonable assurance does not mean absolute assurance.[32] However, it is a high level of assurance that satisfies management that ICFR are effective. Management must be confident that these controls protect financial reporting mechanisms.

The SEC requires that management use evaluation criteria established by recognized experts to review the company's ICFR and help ensure that they are effective. The SEC has recognized only one specific framework that meets its requirements: the COSO Framework. The Committee of Sponsoring Organizations (COSO) of the Treadway Commission first created its "Internal Control—Integrated Framework" in 1992. The framework,

**NOTE**

SOX has no specific requirements that cybersecurity risks and incidents must be disclosed. However, the SEC has issued guidance that an organization may need to disclose any cybersecurity risks and incidents in order to ensure that its other required disclosures are not misleading.[34] For example, it must disclose its cybersecurity risks if those risks would make investment in the organization risky.

### What Is COSO?

COSO was established in 1985 to identify factors that contributed to fraudulent financial reporting. Five U.S. financial organizations sponsored COSO: the American Accounting Association, the American Institute of Certified Public Accountants (AICPA), Financial Executives International, the Institute of Internal Auditors (IIA), and the Institute of Management Accountants. COSO is a nonprofit organization.

Since 1987, COSO has recognized the need for the creation of ICFR. It released its first guidance on internal controls, called the "COSO Internal Control—Integrated Framework," in 1992. The COSO framework says that internal controls are effective when they give the management of a company reasonable assurance that:

- It understands how the entity's operational objectives are being achieved.
- Its published financial statements are being prepared reliably.
- It is complying with applicable laws and regulations.

The COSO Framework was updated in 2013 because the business environment has grown more complex since the framework was initially issued. One of the primary contributors to this complexity is the use of IT in business.

The COSO Framework has five components that organizations can use to review their IT profile. They are:

- **Control environment**—This is the organization's culture. Control environment factors include management philosophy and the competence of the organization's people. The control environment sets the foundation for the other components of the framework. With reference to IT, the organization should understand how technology is used within the business.
- **Risk assessment**—This refers to the identification and review of risks that are internal and external to the organization. Does the organization understand the risks to its technology environment?
- **Control activities**—This refers to how policies and procedures are followed throughout the organization. Has the organization implemented information security controls to mitigate the risks to its technology environment?
- **Information and communication**—This addresses how an organization communicates information internally to its employees, how an organization communicates to external parties, and how information systems store and generate data. Does the organization have mechanisms for communicating about risks and potential information security events that impact the organization's systems?
- **Monitoring**—This refers to how the organization monitors its internal control systems. Does the organization monitor its information security controls and update them when needed?

You can learn more about COSO's "Internal Control—Integrated Framework" by visiting its website: https://www.coso.org/Pages/default.aspx.



commonly called the "COSO Framework," was revised in 2013. Many U.S. businesses use this framework to assess their internal control systems.[33]

SOX Section 404 compliance is not easy. It is very general about the types of ICFR that companies must implement. It does not give a good definition for ICFR generally, and it does not address IT controls at all. In 2007, the SEC issued additional guidance to help companies assess ICFR during their Section 404 review in response to many complaints about the large scope of a Section 404 review. Many of these complaints focused on how to address IT controls.

The SEC stated two broad principles in its guidance:

- Management should assess how its internal controls prevent or detect significant deficiencies in financial statements.
- Management should perform a risk-based review of the effectiveness of these controls.

The SEC also said that management must exercise its professional judgment to limit the scope of a Section 404 review. It reminded companies that SOX applies to internal controls, including IT controls, that affect financial reporting only.[35]

Management must review general IT controls to make sure that IT systems operate properly and consistently. The controls must provide management with reasonable assurance that IT systems operate properly to protect financial reporting. **TABLE 7-1** shows how the goals of ICFR match up with information security goals.

It is clear today that management's review of an organization's ICFR must include a review of IT controls as well. Although the COSO Framework does not specifically address the types of IT controls that an organization should implement, it issues guidance on how to address IT risk. Organizations use many approaches to evaluate their IT controls. Some organizations follow the Guide to Assessment of IT Risk (GAIT) framework. Others use "Control Objectives for Information and Related Technology" (COBIT). Both of these frameworks appear to meet the SEC's requirements for a suitable evaluation framework.

**NOTE**

SOX does not specify the IT controls that companies need to implement. Instead, companies must determine the best controls for their own systems.

Some companies outsource their IT functions; however, a company cannot escape SOX Section 404 liability by outsourcing financial functions. SOX requires companies to monitor ICFR for outsourced operations as well. Many companies do this by asking their outsourcing companies to provide them with a System and Organization Controls (SOC) report.

Created by the AICPA, SOC audits review a service organization's control activities related to the services that it provides to its customers. These audits review the IT controls on the outsourced service. A SOC audit helps a service organization show that it has proper safeguards in place to protect its customer's data.

There are three levels of SOC reports:

- **SOC 1**—Report on Controls at a Service Organization Relevant to User Entities' Internal Control Over Financial Reporting. These reports are used by auditors to assess the ICFR at one entity that does business with another entity. There are two types of SOC 1 reports that

**TABLE 7-1** Internal Controls and Information Security Goals

| STEPS TAKEN TO MEET INTERNAL CONTROLS | INFORMATION SECURITY GOALS |
|---|---|
| Financial reports, records, and data are accurately maintained. | Integrity |
| Transactions are prepared according to GAAP rules and properly recorded. | Integrity, availability |
| Unauthorized acquisition or use of data or assets that could affect financial statements will be prevented or detected in a timely manner. | Confidentiality, integrity, availability |

can be created. These reports are generally only shared between the organizations that are doing business with one another.

- **SOC 2**— Report on Controls at a Service Organization Relevant to Security, Availability, Processing Integrity, Confidentiality, or Privacy. These reports are used by an entity to demonstrate to potential customers that it has good information security practices. These reports specifically address security, availability, processing integrity, confidentiality, and privacy. They also address corporate governance and risk management processes. There are two types of SOC 2 reports that can be created. These reports may be shared with potential customers, usually under a confidentiality agreement so the information in the report is kept private.
- **SOC 3**—Trust Services Report for Service Organizations. These reports are similar to SOC 2 reports. However, they do not contain the same level of detail regarding information system operations. These reports only contain the auditor's assessment of whether or not the outsourced functions meet certain control objectives. They do not contain details about those functions. These reports may be widely shared with potential customers.[36]

**NOTE**

In 2017, the AICPA created the SOC for Cybersecurity. This framework helps an organization assess its own cybersecurity risk management program and helps the organization report on the effectiveness of its controls for information security.

Many companies may ask a service provider to share its SOC 2 or SOC 3 report before entering into an outsourcing relationship. Many service organizations have these reports prepared in advance so that they can respond quickly to a customer request.

## Oversight

The SEC oversees most SOX provisions. The mission of the SEC, which was created under the Securities and Exchange Act of 1934, is to protect investors and maintain the integrity of the securities industry.

The SEC has five commissioners, all appointed by the U.S. president, who each serve for 5-year terms. No more than three of the commissioners may belong to the same political party. The SEC has 11 regional offices in the United States.[37]

SOX gives the SEC specific duties. For example, the SEC is required to designate the members of the PCAOB. It is also required to review various operations of public companies to make sure that they are following SOX.

SOX requires the SEC to review a public company's Form 10-K and Form 10-Q reports at least once every 3 years.[38] It must do this to try to detect fraud and inaccurate financial statements that could harm the investing public. The SEC has discretion in deciding how often to review companies. SOX states the factors that the SEC should consider when deciding to conduct a review. Under SOX, the SEC must consider:

- Whether a company has amended its financial reports
- Whether a company's stock price fluctuates significantly when compared with other companies
- How much stock the company has issued
- The difference between a company's stock price and its earnings
- Whether a company is large and affects a particular sector of the economy
- Any other factor that the SEC considers relevant

The SEC also enforces SOX compliance. It has the power to investigate and sanction public companies that do not comply with SOX.

## Compliance and Security Controls

Assessing ICFR in IT systems can be difficult. IT professionals have several different frameworks that they can use for reviewing IT controls, some of which you are already familiar with. Many of these frameworks help companies decide which controls to implement.

### COBIT

In 1996, the Information Systems Audit and Control Association (ISACA) released the first version of "Control Objectives for Information and Related Technology" (COBIT). Several versions of COBIT have been released. Even though ISACA has moved away from use of the term *control objective* in its framework, it has kept the popular term *COBIT* for the name of the framework. The most recent version of COBIT was released in 2019.[39]

The COBIT 2019 framework aims to help organizations create value from their IT assets.[40] COBIT also provides a framework for the governance and management of those assets. It has six key principles:

- Providing stakeholder value
- Adopting a holistic approach
- Understanding that governance is dynamic
- Separating governance from management
- Tailoring governance to the organization's needs
- Covering the whole organization

COBIT 2019 does not state specific actions that an organization must take to build an IT governance framework. Instead, it provides a list of processes and practices that an organization should review. It has 40 governance and management objectives. This list provides organizations with a method for making their own decisions about technology governance and management. It is technology neutral, and also general enough that any type of organization, profit or nonprofit, can use the framework.

Similar to earlier versions, COBIT 2019 refers to the COSO Framework. You can learn more about COBIT at http://www.isaca.org.

### GAIT

The IIA created the GAIT series in January 2007. The IIA first created the GAIT methodology to help auditors and companies comply with SOX Section 404, as well as help identify controls where a failure might cause an error in a financial statement. GAIT was most recently updated in 2009.

The GAIT methodology helps auditors and companies scope Section 404 reviews of IT controls. It realizes that companies must implement ICFR in IT systems. Similar to the SEC and PCAOB, GAIT advocates a top-down, risk-based approach to review IT controls. GAIT has four main principles:

- A top-down approach should be used to review risks and IT controls.
- The review of risks and IT controls should be limited to financially significant systems, applications, or data.
- IT controls and risks exist at various layers in an IT system (application, database, operating system, and network infrastructure).
- IT processes should be mitigated by IT control objectives, not individual controls.



FYI

The words *framework* and *methodology* are often used interchangeably. However, they are actually different things. A framework is a loose structure that guides an organization toward a particular goal. A framework is intended to be flexible. A methodology, by contrast, is a set of defined principles and practices that lead toward a particular goal. A methodology is intended to be inclusive of all tasks needed to accomplish a goal. A framework is flexible and can actually embed multiple practices and methodologies.

Similar to COBIT, GAIT does not recommend individual controls. Instead, it specifies a series of control objectives. Companies are free to choose the individual controls that meet the control objectives. Information security objectives are included in the GAIT guidance to the extent that they scope to systems that impact a company's financial reports. The IIA has also issued several practice guides that address current topics in IT and information security.

You can learn more about GAIT at https://na.theiia.org/standards-guidance/recommended-guidance/practice-guides/Pages/GAIT-Methodology.aspx.

## ISO/IEC Standards

The International Organization for Standardization (ISO) and International Electrotechnical Commission (IEC) have created two standards that companies can use to implement information security controls. The two standards work together: One guides information security governance, whereas the other reviews how to implement security controls. The standards are:

- ISO/IEC 27001:2013, "Information Technology—Security Techniques—Information Security Management Systems—Requirements"
- ISO/IEC 27002:2013, "Information Technology—Security Techniques—Code of Practice for Information Security Controls"

ISO/IEC 27001 provides a framework for creating an information security management system. It uses a risk-based approach to review how information security is managed within an organization, and reviews the processes that management teams must consider to operate, monitor, review, and maintain IT systems.

ISO/IEC 27002 lists information security safeguards. Unlike COBIT and GAIT, ISO/IEC 27002 does describe specific controls. It has 14 major sections, with each section reviewing a different category of information security controls. The standard explains why organizations should use the listed controls. It also explains how to use the controls. The 14 sections are:

- Information security policy
- Information security organization
- Human resources security
- Asset management
- Asset control
- Cryptography
- Physical and environmental security
- Operations security
- Communications security
- Information system acquisition, development, and maintenance
- Supplier relationships
- Information security incident management
- Information security business continuity management
- Compliance

The ISO/IEC standards are specific to information security. Companies can use these standards to make sure that their information security practices provide reasonable assurance that ICFR are effective. See Table 7-1 for the relationship between SOX internal controls and information security goals.

**NOTE**

NIST is currently updating SP 800-53 (Rev. 4). As of the writing of this chapter, the final public draft of SP 800-53 (Rev. 5) had been released for final public comment. The update integrates both information security and privacy controls. It is intended to provide a comprehensive approach for safeguarding new technologies.

### NIST Computer Security Guidance

Finally, some organizations turn to the National Institute of Standards and Technology (NIST) for information security control guidance. NIST creates information security guidance for federal agencies. These agencies must comply with Federal Information Security Modernization Act (FISMA).

Many nongovernmental organizations also use NIST publications to guide their own information security programs. "NIST Special Publication 800-53 (Rev. 4), Security and Privacy Controls for Federal Information Systems and Organizations" states the minimum security controls that organizations should use to create an effective information security program.

You can learn more about NIST computer security resources at http://csrc.nist.gov/. SOX does not provide public companies with specific advice on how to use IT controls. Many organizations use the frameworks reviewed in this chapter to guide their SOX Section 404 compliance activities.

## SOX Influence in Other Types of Companies

With few exceptions, SOX applies only to public companies. However, many different types of organizations have been affected by SOX. This is because SOX promotes good corporate governance practices. Many of these principles make sense for other organizations as well.

In addition to the certification provisions discussed earlier, SOX governance provisions include:

- **Independent directors**—SOX requires a public company to create an independent board of directors. Directors are independent when they do not have financial ties to the company. In some cases, the independence rules extend to members of the director's immediate family.
- **Audit committee**—SOX requires public companies to have an audit committee on their board of directors. This committee works with outside auditors to make sure that financial reports are accurate.
- **Conflicts of interest**—SOX requires executives to disclose certain types of conflicts of interest



A private company might implement SOX controls because it hopes to become a public company someday. Following SOX principles will make the transition from private to public easier. If a private company follows SOX principles, it might be in a better position to attract investors, as it will have processes in place that allow investors to review the company's financial condition. Investors will be more likely to invest in companies that show financial transparency.

Nonprofit organizations also have an incentive to follow SOX. Good governance in a nonprofit organization is very important. Nonprofits depend on grants from other entities to support their operations. They also depend on individual donations. People will not contribute to nonprofits that are not managed well. Nonprofits that adopt SOX governance principles can prove that they have controls in place to properly manage the organization and its finances. A reputation for good governance also will encourage more donations.

In some ways, SOX compliance has become synonymous with good governance. Companies that follow SOX practices prove that they have controls in place to prevent and detect wrongdoing. This can be important if a company is involved in litigation about bad governance practices. A plaintiff's lawyer will surely point out if a board did not follow SOX good governance practices. It will not matter whether the company was required by law to follow SOX or not. Because SOX is a best practice that many companies follow, the implication that a company did not follow SOX can be damaging.

## Corporate Privacy Issues

Corporate information privacy covers several issues. Because companies have a number of different kinds of records, they must approach privacy from many angles. The three major corporate privacy concerns are:

- Privacy of employee data
- Privacy of customer data
- Privacy of corporate data

In general, employees have no expectation of privacy in their workplaces. In most cases, this means that employers can monitor an employee's work activities, as well as telephone and email conversations. Employers can also monitor employee internet access and computer use. In most cases, it is best if employers give their employees notice that they are monitoring employees in this way.

**NOTE**

A nonprofit organization does not distribute its profits to owners or shareholders. Instead, it puts its profits back into the organization to help pursue its goals. Many charities are nonprofit organizations.

Employers also can monitor employee workspaces and offices. They can use closed circuit television (CCTV) or other video tools to do this. Similar to other types of monitoring, it is best if the employer gives notice about the monitoring. Although the ability to monitor is broad, employers usually cannot monitor locations such as bathrooms, locker rooms, and employee lounges. Some courts have held that employees do have a reasonable expectation of privacy in these areas.

Companies must protect certain types of information belonging to their employees. For example, if a company provides an employee health plan, it must keep some information private. The Health Insurance Portability and Accountability Act (HIPAA) requires companies to protect some information about employee health plans. A company with an on-site health clinic must protect employee medical records under HIPAA and state laws.

Companies also must protect customer data. Some companies must protect consumer information in special ways. For example, the Gramm-Leach-Bliley Act (GLBA) requires companies to protect consumer financial information. Some states also have laws that require companies to protect the personally identifiable information (PII) of their customers. If the company suffers a security breach that compromises PII, then it must inform its customers about the breach. The purpose of these laws, called data breach notification laws, is to help protect people from identity theft.

Finally, companies have their own internal records to protect. These records may contain data about the company's organization, finances, human resources, and legal matters. In general, a company's directors and officers always have the ability to see all company records. In a small company, the owner has this right. They also can enter employee offices to review records. They have the ability to do this in the regular course of business because they are responsible for the business and its successful operation.

In corporations, the directors of a company have an absolute right to be able to inspect the company's records. Shareholders also have a right to inspect corporate records. However, the shareholder's inspection right is not as broad as a director's right. In most states, shareholders have a right to inspect some records during regular business hours. They must make a written request to inspect corporate records that must include the shareholders' reason for wanting to review the records.

Companies also have records regarding their products and services that they must protect. Some of these records might be trade secrets, information about company products or services that helps one company compete against another company. Trade secrets are a form of intellectual property; therefore, a company must protect its trade secret information. If a company properly protects this kind of information, it is entitled to legal protection.

## Case Studies and Examples

Investors can learn about a company's financial information from many different places. One place to learn information is from the SEC's Electronic Data Gathering and Retrieval (EDGAR) database. All public companies that are required to register with the SEC file their required reports through EDGAR.

You can search for a public company's filings on EDGAR. The URL is https://www.sec.gov/edgar/search-and-access. Pick a public company and try to search for it on EDGAR. Good companies to search include Microsoft Corp., Apple Inc., Starbucks Corp., Zoom Video Communications, and the Walt Disney Company. Look at the company's most recent Form 10-K report. Item 9A is the SOX Section 404 report on internal controls. What do these sections tell you? What can you learn about the company that you have searched? You can learn more about how to read these forms at https://www.sec.gov/fast-answers/answersreada10khtm.html.



## CHAPTER SUMMARY

Congress created the Sarbanes-Oxley Act in response to scandal. It passed SOX to help improve investor confidence in publicly traded companies. SOX places rules on public companies and other organizations that promote trustworthy financial reports. The scope of SOX extends to any public company functions or processes that impact financial reporting. The scope of SOX within a company is very broad. SOX requires that companies review many IT processes to make sure that they are trustworthy.

The scope of SOX is broad. Its influence extends even to organizations that are not required to follow it. For example, private companies and nonprofit organizations may choose to follow SOX to show their commitment to good governance.

## KEY CONCEPTS AND TERMS

Disclosure controls
Dividend
Form 8-K
Form 10-K
Form 10-Q
Internal controls
Privately held company
Public company
Securities

## CHAPTER 7 ASSESSMENT

1. What types of companies must follow all Sarbanes-Oxley Act provisions?
   A. Public
   B. Private
   C. Nonprofit
   D. Governmental
   E. None of these is correct.
2. A dividend is a shareholder's earnings in a company.
   A. True
   B. False
3. What is the main goal of the Sarbanes-Oxley Act?
4. How many days after a major event must a company file Form 8-K?
   A. Two
   B. Three
   C. Four
   D. Five
   E. None of these is correct.

5. Which corporate scandals led to the creation of the Sarbanes-Oxley Act?
   A. Enron
   B. WorldCom
   C. Adelphia
   D. Tyco
   E. All of these are correct.
6. What are internal controls over financial reporting (ICFR)?
7. How many members of the Public Company Accounting Oversight Board may be certified public accountants?
   A. Five
   B. Four
   C. Three
   D. Two
   E. None of these is correct.
8. Sarbanes-Oxley Act Section 404 tells organizations the types of controls that they must implement in their IT systems to protect financial reporting.
   A. True
   B. False
9. Which framework has the U.S. Securities and Exchange Commission official approved as suitable evaluation criteria for internal controls?
   A. COBIT
   B. COSO
   C. GAIT
   D. ISO/IEC
   E. None of these is correct.
10. Which Sarbanes-Oxley Act provision causes the most concern for information technology professionals?
   A. Section 302
   B. Section 309
   C. Section 404
   D. Section 906
   E. None of these is correct.
11. A company's chief information security officer and chief financial officer must sign a Section 302 certification.
   A. True
   B. False
12. How often must the U.S. Securities and Exchange Commission review a public company's Form 10-K and Form 10-Q reports?
   A. Twice a year
   B. Every year
   C. Every other year
   D. Every 3 years
   E. Every 5 years
13. What does an ICFR do?
14. Under the Sarbanes-Oxley Act, how many years must public companies keep audit papers?
   A. Five
   B. Six
   C. Seven
   D. Eight
   E. None of these is correct.
15. A public company must file a Form 10-K at the end of each quarter.
   A. True
   B. False

## ENDNOTES

1. Forbes, "America's Largest Private Companies," December 2019. https://www.forbes.com/largest-private-companies/list/#tab:rank (accessed April 11, 2020).
2. CNN, "The Guiltiest Guys in the Room," July 5, 2006. http://money.cnn.com/2006/05/29/news/enron_guiltyest/index.htm (accessed April 11, 2020).
3. Fortune, "The World's Most Admired Companies," October 2, 2000. http://money.cnn.com/magazines/fortune/fortune_archive/2000/10/02/288448/index.htm (accessed April 11, 2020).
4. Kroger, John, "Enron, Fraud, and Securities Reform," Colorado Law Review, Vol. 76, Issue 1 (2005): 57.

5. Houston Chronicle, "Jury Hears Ex-Enron CEO Curse in Wall Street Call," February 2, 2006. https://www.chron.com/business/enron/article/Jury-hears-ex-Enron-CEO-curse-in-Wall-Street-call-1637608.php (accessed April 11, 2020).
6. Powers, William C., "Special Investigative Committee of the Board of Directors of Enron Corp.," February 1, 2002. http://i.cnn.net/cnn/2002/LAW/02/02/enron.report/powers.report.pdf (accessed April 11, 2020).
7. The New York Times, "An Implosion on Wall Street," November 29, 2001. http://www.nytimes.com/2001/11/29/opinion/an-implosion-on-wall-street.html (accessed April 11, 2020).
8. Houston Business Journal, "Enron Delists Stock as Financial Woes Continue," January 18, 2002. http://www.bizjournals.com/houston/stories/2002/01/21/story3.html (accessed April 11, 2020).
9. CNN, "401(k) Investors Sue Enron," November 26, 2001. http://money.cnn.com/2001/11/26/401k/q_retire_enron_re/ (accessed April 11, 2020).
10. New York Times, "Jeffrey Skilling, Former Enron Chief, Released After 12 Years in Prison," February 22, 2019. https://www.nytimes.com/2019/02/22/business/enron-ceo-skilling-scandal.html (accessed April 11, 2020).
11. Congressional Research Service, "Enron: A Select Chronology of Congressional, Corporate, and Government Activities," March 2003. http://www.policyarchive.org/handle/10207/1392 (accessed April 11, 2020).
12. U.S. Securities and Exchange Commission, "Form 8-K." https://www.sec.gov/fast-answers/answersform8khtm.html (accessed April 11, 2020).
13. Sarbanes-Oxley Act of 2002, Pub. L. No. 107-204, 116 Stat. 745 (codified as amended in scattered sections of U.S. Code Vol. 15).
14. The New York Times, "Bush Signs Bill Aimed at Fraud in Corporations," July 30, 2002. https://www.nytimes.com/2002/07/31/business/corporate-conduct-the-president-bush-signs-bill-aimed-at-fraud-in-corporations.html (accessed April 11, 2020).
15. Time, "Enron: Who's Accountable?" January 13, 2002. http://content.time.com/time/magazine/article/0,9171,1001636,00.html (accessed April 11, 2020).
16. Powers Report, see note 6, at pp. 24–25.
17. U.S. Code Vol. 15, sec. 7211.
18. U.S. Code Vol. 15, sec. 7211.
19. U.S. Securities and Exchange Commission, "Work Plan for the Consideration of Incorporating International Financial Reporting Standards Into the Financial Reporting System for U.S. Issuers, Final Report," July 13, 2012. http://webapp01.ey.com.pl/EYP/WEB/eycom_download.nsf/resources/ZRG_Emerging_Trends_Survay.pdf/$FILE/ZRG_Emerging_Trends_Survey.pdf (accessed April 18, 2020). See also CFA Institute, "IFRS: International Financial Reporting Standards," Undated. https://www.cfainstitute.org/en/advocacy/issues/international-finance-reporting-stds (accessed April 18, 2020).
20. Public Company Accounting Oversight Board, Staff Preview of 2018 Inspection Observations, May 6, 2019. https://pcaobus.org/Inspections/Documents/Staff-Preview-2018-Inspection-Observations.pdf (accessed April 18, 2020).
21. Public Company Accounting Oversight Board, "2019 PCAOB Annual Report," March 24, 2020. https://pcaobus.org/About/Administration/Documents/Annual%20Reports/2019-PCAOB-Annual-Report.pdf (accessed April 18, 2020).
22. Dlabay, L., Burrow, J. L., Business Finance. 2007, Cengage Learning, p. 339.
23. U.S. Code Vol. 17, sec. 210.2-06.
24. Dodd-Frank Wall Street Reform and Consumer Protection Act of 2010, Pub. Law. No. 111-203; 124 Stat. 1376-2223, codified as amended in scattered sections of U.S. Code Vol. 15 (2012).
25. U.S. Code Vol. 18, sec. 1519.
26. U.S. Code Vol. 15, sec. 7241.
27. U.S. Code Vol. 18, sec. 1519.
28. U.S. Securities and Exchange Commission, "Final Rule: Management's Report on Internal Control Over Financial Reporting and Certification of Disclosure in Exchange Act Periodic Reports," June 5, 2003. http://www.sec.gov/rules/final/33-8238.htm#iib3a (accessed April 26, 2020).
29. U.S. Code Vol. 18, sec. 1350.
30. U.S. Code Vol. 15, sec. 7262.
31. U.S. Securities and Exchange Commission, "Final Rule: Management's Report on Internal Control Over Financial Reporting and Certification of

Disclosure in Exchange Act Periodic Reports," June 5, 2003. http://www.sec.gov/rules/final/33-8238.htm#iib3a (accessed April 26, 2020).

32. U.S. Securities and Exchange Commission, "Staff Statement on Management's Report on Internal Control Over Financial Reporting," May 16, 2005. http://www.sec.gov/info/accountants/stafficreporting.htm (accessed April 26, 2020). See also Public Company Accounting Oversight Board, "AU Section 230: Due Professional Care in the Performance of Work," June 12, 2007 amendments. http://pcaobus.org/Standards/Auditing/Pages/AU230.aspx#ps-pcaob_8b4d2389-b14e-4358-a4b2-93e6360eb378 (accessed April 26, 2020).
33. Committee of Sponsoring Organizations of the Treadway Commission, "Guidance on Internal Control," No date. http://www.coso.org/IC.htm (accessed on April 26, 2020).
34. U.S. Securities and Exchange Commission, "CF Disclosure Guidance: Topic No. 2, Cybersecurity," October 13, 2011. https://www.sec.gov/divisions/corpfin/guidance/cfguidance-topic2.htm (accessed April 26, 2020).
35. U.S. Securities and Exchange Commission, "Commission Guidance Regarding Management's Report on Internal Controls Over Financial Reporting," Code of Federal Regulations, Title 17, sec. 241. Available at: https://www.sec.gov/rules/interp/2007/33-8810.pdf (accessed April 26, 2020).
36. American Institute of Certified Public Accountants, "System and Organization Controls: SOC Suite of Services," No date. https://www.aicpa.org/interestareas/frc/assuranceadvisoryservices/sorhome.html (accessed April 26, 2020).
37. U.S. Securities and Exchange Commission, "About the SEC," November 22, 2016. https://www.sec.gov/about.shtml (accessed April 26, 2020).
38. U.S. Code Vol. 15, sec. 7266.
39. ISACA, "COBIT 5: A Business Framework for the Governance and Management of Enterprise IT," 2012. http://www.isaca.org/COBIT/Pages/COBIT-5-Framework-product-page.aspx (accessed December 30, 2013).
40. ISACA, "COBIT 2019: Introduction and Methodology," 2018. Available at: https://www.isaca.org/resources.

CHAPTER 8

# Federal Government Information Security and Privacy Regulations

IN A 2009 SPEECH, then U.S. President Barack Obama said that America's digital infrastructure is a "strategic national asset."[1] He urged a broad plan to protect the security and privacy of federal information systems, stating that the nation's digital infrastructure must be better protected. Both the federal government and private organizations have a role to play.

This chapter reviews how the federal government protects its information systems. These systems hold personal data about U.S. residents, conduct the business of running the country, hold sensitive security data, and are used for the nation's defense. This chapter reviews the security and privacy laws that protect these systems.

## Chapter 8 Topics

This chapter covers the following topics and concepts:

- What the information security challenges facing the federal government are
- What the Federal Information Security Modernization Act (FISMA) does
- How the federal government protects privacy in information systems
- What import and export control laws are
- What some case studies and examples are

## Chapter 8 Goals

When you complete this chapter, you will be able to:

- Describe the federal government's information security challenges
- Explain the main requirements under the Federal Information Security Modernization Act
- Describe the role of the National Institute of Standards and Technology (NIST) in creating information security standards
- Discuss approaches to protecting national security systems (NSSs)

- Describe how the U.S. federal government protects privacy in information systems
- Review import and export control laws

## Information Security Challenges Facing the Federal Government

In 2010, Vivek Kundra, then federal chief information officer (CIO), said that the government's computers are attacked millions of times each day.[2] In 2018, federal agencies reported over 31,000 information security incidents involving federal information technology (IT) systems.[3] That government IT systems are frequently attacked and suffer information security incidents is not surprising. Government computer systems hold data that is critical for government operations. They hold data on people living in the United States, including employment, tax, and citizenship data. They also hold data on businesses operating in the United States, as well as data that are used to protect the United States from threats.

**NOTE**

You can view analytics for U.S. government websites at https://analytics.usa.gov/. At 7:00 a.m. ET on May 16, 2020, there were over 140,000 people on government webpages. The most popular websites were for the U.S. Postal Service and Internal Revenue Service.

The government faces many of the same information security challenges that private entities face. Federal IT systems and the data in them are attractive targets for criminals:

- Hackers stole the background investigation records from the Office of Personnel Management (OPM). The sensitive personnel files on over 21.5 million current, former, and prospective federal employees and contractors were stolen, including almost 5.6 million records with fingerprints. The incident led to a congressional investigation and the resignation of some OPM leaders.
- Thieves stole a laptop from a researcher's car that belonged to the National Institutes of Health (NIH). The laptop held the personal information of 2,500 people involved in an NIH study.
- Attackers illegally accessed the USAJOBS database and stole account and contact information. USAJOBS is the federal government's employment website. The government said that the thieves did not access sensitive personal information.
- The U.S. State Department warned 400 people about a computer security breach. The attackers stole passport application information, including Social Security numbers (SSNs). The thieves used the data to open credit card accounts.
- Spies broke into the Pentagon's computer systems. They stole data on the Department of Defense's Joint Strike Fighter aircraft.

Since 1987, the U.S. government has worked to protect federal IT systems. The first law to address federal computer security was the Computer Security Act (CSA).[4] Under the CSA, every federal agency had to inventory its IT systems. Agencies also had to create security plans for those systems and review their plans every year.

In 2002, Congress created the Federal Information Security Modernization Act (FISMA).[5] It created FISMA, in part, because of the September 11, 2001, terrorist attacks in New York City and Washington, DC, which highlighted the need for better information security. FISMA recognizes that information security is crucial. It superseded most of the CSA.

Today, the Federal Information Security Modernization Act of 2014 (FISMA 2014) is the main law addressing federal government computer security protection.[6] FISMA 2014 largely superseded the 2002 act. In this book, FISMA refers both to FISMA 2014 and to those provisions of FISMA 2002 that were either incorporated into FISMA 2014 or were not changed.

### What Is Cyberwar?

On October 11, 2012, then U.S. Secretary of Defense Leon Panetta stated that attacks on the nation's critical infrastructure could be "a cyber Pearl Harbor; an attack that would cause physical destruction and the loss of life."[7] Many people worry about "cyberwar" or "information warfare." However, cyberwar does not take place on a physical battlefield, or on the sea or in the air. Instead, it is a conflict that takes place in or purposefully affects information systems.

The term *cyberwar* refers to conflicts between nations and their militaries. Cyberwar attacks are carried out at the direction of a particular nation. This is the main distinction between cyberwar and other types of information system attacks that are reported in the news media. Cyberwar could affect military information systems, nongovernment information systems, and private industry information systems. It includes not only threats to national security, but also threats to industry, commerce, and intellectual property. It could even include larger threats to how governments function generally. Consider these examples:

- It is believed that Russia used many different tactics, including spreading propaganda on social media, to interfere in the 2016 U.S. national elections.[8]
- The 2015 attacks on the Ukrainian power grid are largely thought to be acts of cyberwar committed by Russia.[9]
- The 2014 cyberattack against U.S.-based Sony Pictures Entertainment is believed to have been ordered by the North Korean government.[10]

Military, government, and private information systems are connected and difficult to protect. This makes defining true acts of cyberwar very difficult. The prospect of a cyberwar between nations is every bit as concerning as a conventional war. As of the writing of this book, there are no cyberwar treaties in place. Some have been introduced between various countries, and at the United Nations, but none have been adopted or ratified.

Secretary of Defense Leon E. Panetta, "Remarks by Secretary Panetta on Cybersecurity to the Business Executives for National Security, New York City" (New York, NY: Oct. 11, 2012). Available at: http://www.gao.gov/assets/660/652170.pdf (accessed February 4, 2014); BBC News, "Ukraine power cut was cyber attack." January 11, 2017, https://www.bbc.com/news/technology-38573074 (accessed May 16, 2020); The New York Times, "The World Once Laughed at North Korean Cyberpower. No More." October 15, 2017, https://www.nytimes.com/2017/10/15/world/asia/north-korea-hacking-cyber-sony.html (accessed May 16, 2020)

This chapter focuses on how the federal government protects its IT systems and discusses many of FISMA's provisions. You should be aware that this area of law is complex and changes often.

# The Federal Information Security Modernization Act

The Federal Information Security Modernization Act of 2014 recognized the complex nature of the federal computing environment.[11] It also sought to improve oversight of federal information security activities and provide a framework for making sure that information security controls are effective. This is important because the U.S. government anticipates spending over $18 billion on cybersecurity in the fiscal year 2021.[12]

## Purpose and Scope

FISMA defines *information security* as protecting IT systems to provide confidentiality, integrity, and availability.[13] IT systems must be protected from unauthorized use, access, disruption, modification, and destruction.

FISMA has six main provisions. The law:

- Sets forth agency information security responsibilities
- Requires a yearly independent review of agency information security programs
- Authorizes the National Institute of Standards and Technology (NIST) to develop information security standards for IT systems that do not contain unclassified information
- Gives the Office of Management and Budget (OMB) and Department of Homeland Security (DHS) specific oversight responsibilities
- Clarifies that national security systems (NSSs) must be secured using a risk-based approach
- Provides for a central federal security incident response (IR) center

FISMA applies to federal agencies. These agencies fall under the executive branch of the U.S. government and report to the president. Examples of federal agencies include the Federal Aviation Administration, the Social Security Administration, and the Department of Education.

FISMA also applies to contractors who perform services on behalf of a federal agency. For example, researchers at universities who work with federal agencies may have to follow FISMA requirements on their own IT systems because those systems could store federal data.

## Main Requirements

FISMA has many requirements. This section will review many of them. First, this section reviews what federal agencies must do to comply with FISMA. Second, it reviews how the NIST helps agencies shape their information security programs. Third, it reviews the federal central IR center. Finally, it reviews how FISMA applies to **national security systems (NSSs)**. NSSs are IT systems that hold military, defense, and intelligence information.

### *Agency Information Security Programs*

FISMA requires each federal agency to create an agency-wide information security program.[14] Even agencies with NSSs must create these programs. An agency's information security program must include:

- **Risk assessments**—Agencies must perform risk assessments. They must measure the harm that could result from unauthorized access to or use of agency IT systems. Agencies must base their information security programs on the results of these risk assessments.
- **Policies and procedures**—Agencies must create policies and procedures to reduce risk to an acceptable level. The policies must protect IT systems throughout their life cycle. Agencies also must create configuration management policies.
- **Subordinate plans**—Agencies must make sure that they have plans for securing networks, facilities, and systems or groups of IT systems. These plans are for technologies or system components that are a part of the larger information security program.
- **Security awareness training**—Agencies must give training to employees and any other users of their IT systems. This includes contractors. This training must make people aware of potential risks to the agency's IT systems. It also must make people aware of their duties to protect these systems.
- **Testing and evaluation**—Agencies must test their security controls at least once a year. They must test management, operational, and technical controls for each IT system.
- **Remedial actions**—Agencies must have a plan to fix weaknesses in their information security program.
- **Incident response**—Agencies must have an IR procedure. They must state how the agency detects and mitigates incidents. The procedure must include reporting incidents to the DHS United States Computer Emergency Readiness Team (US-CERT) as needed.
- **Continuity of operations**—Agencies must have business continuity plans as part of their information security programs.

An agency's information security program applies to any other organization that uses the agency's IT systems or data. An agency must protect the IT systems that support the agency's operations, even if another agency or contractor provides the systems. This can broaden the scope of FISMA, especially because IT systems and functions are often outsourced.

One of the most important parts of a FISMA information security program is that agencies test and evaluate it. FISMA requires each agency to perform "periodic testing and evaluation of the effectiveness of information security policies, procedures, and practices."[15] Agencies must test every IT system at least once a year, and test those with greater risk more often.

Agencies must also review their security controls. Some kinds of security controls are required under FISMA. The NIST has the authority to create these minimum requirements.[16] Agencies must follow the standards that NIST creates. An agency must make sure that it implements these controls properly. It must also make sure that the controls work. The yearly testing requirement recognizes that security is an ongoing process. Agencies must always monitor their information security risk. They must monitor the controls put in place to mitigate that risk as well. The head of the agency is responsible for determining the right level of risk for the agency.

Agencies must also follow NIST guidance in performing their annual reviews. If an agency uses a different model to perform its review, that model must include the same elements that NIST does. The important role of NIST is discussed later in this chapter.

**NOTE**

CISOs must be information security professionals and must have the "professional qualifications, including training and experience, required to administer" FISMA requirements.[19]

**NOTE**

CyberScope, which was created by the DHS, allows a real-time data feed that helps agencies and the OMB quickly assess the agency's information security posture.

Under FISMA, agencies must name a senior official to be in charge of information security.[17] In most agencies, this is the chief information security officer (CISO), who is responsible for FISMA compliance. The CISO's main job duties must focus on information security. Under FISMA, a CISO must have the resources necessary to make sure that the agency can comply with FISMA.

Agencies have several different reporting requirements under FISMA. For example, agencies must submit monthly electronic data feeds to the DHS through a program known as CyberScope. The purpose of these data feeds is to continuously monitor the security posture of the federal agency's information systems.

Each agency must report yearly to the OMB on its FISMA compliance activities. An agency also must send a copy of its yearly report to the following:

- House of Representatives Committee on Oversight and Government Reform
- House of Representatives Committee on Homeland Security
- House of Representatives Committee on Science and Technology
- Senate Committee on Homeland Security and Governmental Affairs
- Senate Committee on Commerce, Science, and Transportation
- U.S. Government Accountability Office (GAO)
- The agency's congressional authorization and appropriations committee[18]

An agency's FISMA report is shared widely and must be in unclassified form.[22] An agency's yearly report must review its information security program. Items reviewed must include:

- The adequacy of the program
- A description of each major information security incident experienced by the agency
- The total number of information security incidents experienced by the agency
- A description of any information security incident experienced by the agency that compromised personally identifiable information (PII).

It also must assess the agency's progress on correcting any weaknesses in the program or security controls. The agency must also respond to a set of questions about its security practices, which are asked in CyberScope. Each year the DHS publishes the questions that will be asked in the following year.

In addition to reporting on their information security activities, agencies must also report on their privacy activities. For example, they have to share information on their privacy training programs and their breach notification policy. They also must give a progress report on their efforts to eliminate the unnecessary use of SSNs and other PII.[23]

The yearly report also must include the results of an independent evaluation of the agency's information security program. Some agencies have an **inspector general (IG)**. If an agency has an IG, then the IG may carry out this evaluation. Some agencies do not have an IG. If they do not, the head of the agency must hire an external auditor to perform the evaluation.[25]

### What Is an Inspector General?

An inspector general (IG) is an official who reviews the actions of a federal agency. An IG examines the agency's activities to make sure that it is operating efficiently and following good governance practices. IGs are independent officials by law. The agency that an IG reports to cannot prevent the IG from performing an audit or investigation. The Inspector General Act of 1978 defined an IG's role.[20] An IG is responsible for:

- Conducting independent and objective audits, investigations, and inspections
- Preventing and detecting waste, fraud, and abuse
- Promoting economy, effectiveness, and efficiency
- Reviewing pending legislation and regulations
- Keeping the agency head and Congress informed about agency activities[21]

IGs are appointed to their positions based on their experience in accounting, auditing, law, and investigations. They are not political officials. Some agency heads may appoint and remove their own IGs.

The president nominates IGs for major federal agencies, and the Senate approves them. Only the president can remove these IGs. The president nominates IGs in the Department of Commerce, Department of Justice, and OMB, as well as in some other agencies.



### *The Role of NIST*

FISMA requires the Department of Commerce to create information security standards and guidelines. The Commerce Department delegated this responsibility to NIST, an agency of the Department of Commerce. Under FISMA, NIST must create:

- Standards that all federal agencies use to categorize their data and IT systems
- Guidelines recommending the types of data and IT systems to be included in each category
- Minimum information security controls for IT systems

**NOTE**

Before CyberScope, the FISMA reporting process was time- and paper-intensive. For example, in 6 years, the Department of State produced 95,000 pages of paper to meet its FISMA reporting requirements. It spent $133 million to create these reports.[24]

The OMB has stated that agencies must follow NIST standards and guidelines for non-NSSs. These standards and guidelines help agencies meet their FISMA obligations. NIST creates two different types of documents: Federal Information Processing Standards (FIPS) and Special Publications (SPs). FIPS are standards, whereas SPs are guidelines.

**NOTE**

In general, a standard states mandatory actions that an organization must take to protect its IT systems. A guideline states recommended actions that an organization should follow.

Federal agencies must follow FIPS. They must comply with new FIPS within 1 year of their publication date. FIPS do not apply to NSSs.

NIST creates FIPS when there is a compelling reason to do so. It creates a FIPS if there is no acceptable industry standard or solution for the underlying information security issue.

As of this writing, there are 11 FIPS for information security. You can view them at https://csrc.nist.gov/publications/fips.

NIST uses procedures described in the Administrative Procedures Act (APA) to create FIPS. The APA states formal procedures for creating rules and regulations. This formal process ensures due process and makes sure that all interested agencies have a chance to comment on draft FIPS. NIST publishes a proposed FIPS in the Federal Register, which is available for public review for 30 to 90 days. The Department of Commerce must approve FIPS before they can be finalized.[26]

### What Is FedRAMP?

In 2011, the United States adopted a "Cloud First" strategy as part of the Federal Government IT Modernization Act. That strategy advocated that federal agencies evaluate using cloud computing solutions for IT operations. In 2018, the U.S. federal government released its "Cloud Smart" strategy. Cloud Smart provides guidance surrounding the information security and workforce skills needed to adopt cloud computing models.[27]

The Federal Risk and Authorization Management Program (FedRAMP) is a government-wide program developed by NIST, the U.S. General Services Administration, DHS, and the Department of Defense.[28] NIST also advises the FedRAMP program on FISMA compliance.

Any cloud computing services that store federal data must be FedRAMP approved. The FedRAMP program has a list of cloud computing providers that hold a FedRAMP designation. Federal agencies can purchase cloud computing services more quickly from vendors that have those designations.

FedRAMP outlines a standard approach to assess the security of cloud products and services. The FedRAMP security assessment framework is based on the NIST risk management framework (RMF). FedRAMP defines the minimum information security controls needed to safeguard cloud computing systems storing, accessing, and using federal data. Those controls are based on NIST SP 800-53, as revised.

To learn more about FedRAMP, visit https://www.fedramp.gov/.

U.S. Office of Management and Budget, "Federal Cloud Computing Strategy." Undated, https://cloud.cio.gov/strategy/ (accessed May 16, 2020); Federal Risk and Authorization Management Program, "FedRAMP Security Assessment Framework." November 15, 2017, https://www.fedramp.gov/assets/resources/documents/FedRAMP_Security_Assessment_Framework.pdf (accessed May 16, 2020).

SPs are computer security guidelines that are more general than FIPS. NIST creates SPs in collaboration with industry, government, and academic information security experts. NIST does not use the very formal FIPS drafting process to create these documents.

Federal agencies have some flexibility in using the SPs for guidance. They help guide federal agencies in strengthening their IT systems. The OMB understands that this may lead to different results among federal agencies. It acknowledges that different results are expected. Agencies have no flexibility in implementing FIPS, as they are mandatory.

NIST uses a RMF approach to FISMA compliance. This framework is outlined in "SP 800-37, Revision 2, Risk Management Framework for Information Systems and Organizations."[29] This approach helps protect IT systems during their whole life cycle. Federal agencies must use the RMF provided by NIST to assess the information security and privacy risks to their IT systems.

The NIST RMF outlines six steps to protect federal IT systems. They are:

1. Categorize IT systems.
2. Select minimum security controls.
3. Implement security controls in IT systems.
4. Assess security controls for effectiveness.
5. Authorize the IT system for processing.
6. Continuously monitor security controls.

**NOTE**

You can view the information security SPs at https://csrc.nist.gov/publications/sp800.

NIST's RMF recommends a continuous process of categorization, assessment, and monitoring. **FIGURE 8-1** shows this process.

NIST guides agencies at each RMF step. "FIPS 199, Standards for Security Categorization of Federal Information and Information Systems," helps them categorize their IT systems.[30] It serves as the starting point for an agency's information security program and helps them separate their IT systems into categories based on risk. Agencies then apply security controls to their IT system based upon their category.

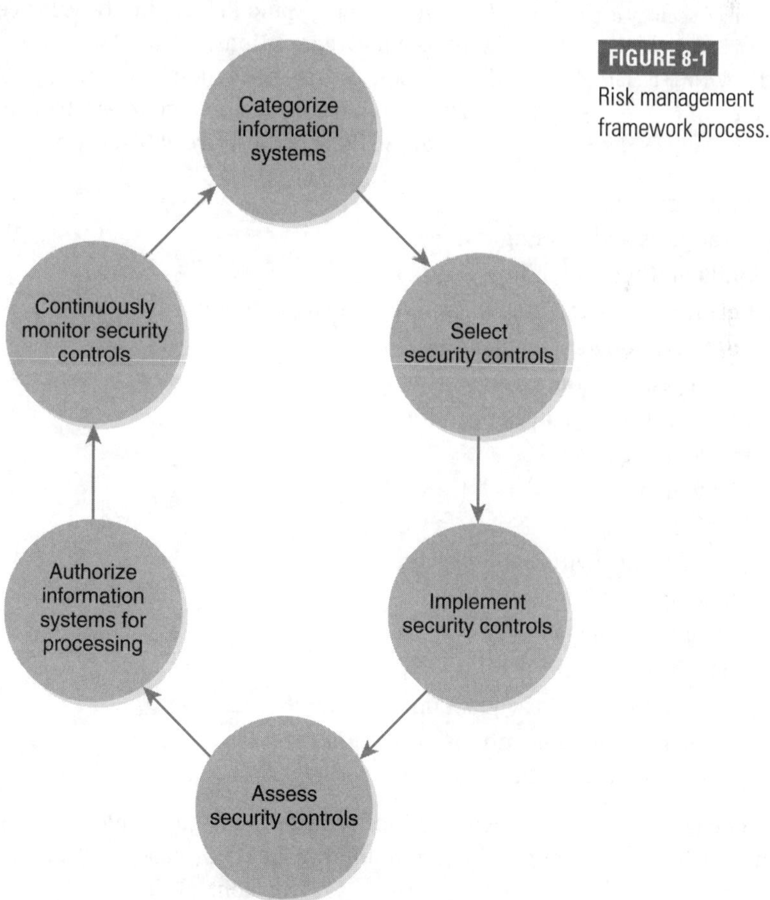


**FIGURE 8-1**
Risk management framework process.

Under FIPS 199, agencies must first assess the impact on IT systems because of a loss of confidentiality, integrity, or availability. The *security category* expresses that impact. FIPS defines three security categories. They are:

- **Low**—The loss of confidentiality, integrity, or availability has a limited adverse effect on the agency, its information assets, or people. A low impact event results in minor damage to assets.
- **Moderate**—The loss of confidentiality, integrity, or availability has a serious adverse effect on the agency, its information assets, or people. A moderate impact event results in significant damage to assets.
- **High**—The loss of confidentiality, integrity, or availability has a severe or catastrophic adverse effect on the agency, its information assets, or people. A high impact event results in major damage to assets.

**NOTE**

At the time of this writing, NIST had released a final public draft of NIST SP 800-53, Revision 5. This revision includes major enhancements to information security and privacy controls. It is anticipated that the final version of SP 800-53, Rev. 5 will be released in late 2020 or early 2021.

After the agency determines the security category, it must decide which controls to use. NIST created two documents to help with this task. They are "FIPS 200, Minimum Security Requirements for Federal Information and Information Systems"[31] and "SP 800-53, Revision 4, Security and Privacy Controls for Federal Information Systems and Organizations."[32] The OMB requires that agencies use these documents to make their security control decisions.

These documents require agencies to specify controls in 17 areas. FIPS 200 lists these areas. They are:

- Access control
- Awareness and training
- Audit and accountability
- Certification, accreditation, and security assessments
- Configuration management
- Contingency planning
- Identification and authentication
- Incident response
- Maintenance
- Media protection
- Physical and environmental protection
- Planning
- Personnel security
- Risk assessment
- System and services acquisition
- System and communications protection
- System and information integrity

Agencies must apply the right security controls. They must tailor controls to the level of impact. SP 800-53 defines the minimum thresholds, or baselines, for each category. For example, agencies must use low-impact security controls in IT systems where an adverse event has a low impact. It must follow a similar practice for moderate and high impacts.

**TABLE 8-1** SP 800-53 Access Control Baselines for Wireless Access

| SECURITY CONTROL AREA (FIPS 200) | LOW-IMPACT SYSTEM CONTROLS (SP 800-53) | MODERATE-IMPACT CONTROLS (SP 800-53) | HIGH-IMPACT SYSTEM CONTROLS (SP 800-53) |
|---|---|---|---|
| **Access control (wireless access controls)** | Federal agencies must:<br>• Establish use restrictions for wireless access, configuration requirements, and implementation guidance<br>• Authorize wireless access to an information system before allowing access | In addition to implementing low-impact controls, the agency must also:<br>• Protect wireless access to the system using authentication and encryption | In addition to implementing low- and moderate-impact controls, the agency must also:<br>• Identify users allowed to configure wireless networking capabilities<br>• Limit wireless communications to organization-controlled boundaries |



**TABLE 8-1** shows an example of how FIPS 200 and SP 800-53 work together. The example shows the different baselines for wireless access in the access control area.

Agencies can use other NIST guidelines to help them improve their security controls. For example, NIST has created an SP for protecting the confidentiality of PII.[33] An agency could use this SP to strengthen its access control baseline for employees that access PII. Once a federal agency has implemented security controls, it must test them.

The OMB requires federal agencies to test their security controls. "NIST SP 800-53A, Revision 4, Assessing Security and Privacy Controls in Federal Information Systems and Organizations: Building Effective Assessment Plans" walks agencies through security control assessments.[34] These assessments are performed throughout the RMF stages.

NIST's RMF requires agencies to authorize their IT system for processing. This means that an agency must test its systems and approve its operation. This process is based on a review of the risk of operating the system. An agency must specifically accept the risks of operation before allowing an IT system to operate.

Finally, agencies must continuously monitor their security controls and make sure that they are effective. They also must document any changes to their IT systems and assess them for new risks.

### *Central Incident Response Center*

Under FISMA, the government must have a federal IR center, which must:

- Give technical support to agencies about handling information security incidents.
- Compile and analyze data about information security incidents.
- Inform agencies about current and potential threats and vulnerabilities.
- Inform agencies about threats, vulnerabilities, and incidents to be considered as part of the agencies' risk assessment process.
- Consult with NIST and agencies with NSSs about information security incidents.[35]

**NOTE**

In 2018, 31 percent of the incidents reported to NCCIC/US-CERT involved employee violations of a federal agency's acceptable use policy.[36]

Agencies must report all information security incidents to the National Cybersecurity and Communications Integration Center (NCCIC). The federal IR center is also known as the US-CERT. Under FISMA, an incident is an event that

- "actually or imminently jeopardizes the integrity, confidentiality, or availability of information or an information system" or
- "constitutes a violation or imminent threat of violation of law, security policies, security procedures, or acceptable use policies."[37]

When an agency reports an incident, it must share as much information about the incident as possible. They must make reports to the NCCIC/US-CERT within 1 hour of discovering an incident that potentially compromises the confidentiality, integrity, or availability of a federal IT system.[38] An agency must share the following information about an incident when it makes a report:

- The impact the incident has had on the agency
- Whether any information has been lost, compromised, or corrupted
- The estimated amount of time and resources that are needed to recover from the incident
- When the incident was first detected
- The number of systems, records, and users impacted
- The network location of the incident
- Contact information if the NCCIC/US-CERT needs more information

The NCCIC/US-CERT coordinates IR across the U.S. government, shares information to help the government respond to threats, and also provides information security tips to the public. You can learn more at https://www.cisa.gov/securing-federal-networks.

### *National Security Systems*

FISMA requires federal agencies to secure NSSs using a risk-based approach. An NSS includes systems that are for:

- Intelligence activities
- Command and control of military forces
- Weapons or weapons-control equipment
- Use cryptography to protect national security
- Critical to military or intelligence missions
- Must be kept classified for national defense or foreign policy[39]

**FYI**

FISMA does not apply to classified information. Classified information, which is protected by presidential executive order, is information that is labeled Confidential, Secret, or Top Secret. Its label is based upon its national security importance. This data must be protected to meet national security goals.

The Committee on National Security Systems (CNSS) oversees FISMA activities for NSSs. The CNSS has 21 voting members. They include officials from the National Security Administration (NSA), Central Intelligence Agency (CIA), and Department of Defense (DoD). A DoD member leads the committee. The CNSS also includes several subcommittees and panels. You can learn about the CNSS at www.cnss.gov.

Federal agencies with NSSs must follow CNSS policies. Today, CNSS policies favor following NIST guidelines and processes whenever possible.[40] However, it was not always this way. Before 2012, the CNSS often had information security policies and procedures for NSSs that were either similar to NIST guidance or very different from NIST guidance. Many commentators thought that practice caused unnecessary complexity. Today, CNSS adopts NIST guidance whenever it makes sense to do so. It only issues separate guidance when NIST guidance does not meet the information security needs of NSSs.

FISMA permits the directors of the DoD and CIA to develop additional information security policies for NSSs within their own agencies. The OMB must report to Congress on FISMA compliance for NSSs. It also makes sure that agencies with an NSS are meeting FISMA's legal requirements. The OMB makes sure that agencies with an NSS create an information security program and test it each year.

## Oversight

The OMB and the DHS share responsibility for FISMA compliance. The OMB oversees FISMA-related budgetary issues. It can also withhold funding from agencies that fail to follow FISMA. In addition, the OMB must continue to issue a report to Congress each year on the government's FISMA compliance. This report details how federal agencies are complying with FISMA. It also identifies problem areas.

The DHS has had the power to ensure that agencies are meeting their FISMA obligations. It can also create rules and other guidance that these agencies must follow. These rules are called binding operational directives. The DHS also keeps track of how all federal agencies are complying with FISMA and annually reviews their cybersecurity programs. DHS also has responsibilities for governmental IR activities.

**FYI**

The FY2018 FISMA annual report noted that the U.S. federal government continues to have security deficiencies.[41] The top deficiencies were:

1. Lack of data protection
2. Lack of network segmentation
3. Inconsistent patch management practices
4. Lack of strong authentication
5. Lack of continuous monitoring, audit, and logging capacities.

## Protecting Privacy in Federal Information Systems

Data privacy is an important issue for the federal government. There are several federal laws designed to protect data privacy. The two major laws protecting the privacy of data that the government uses in the course of business are:

- The Privacy Act of 1974[42]
- The E-Government Act of 2002[43]

### The Privacy Act of 1974

Congress created the Privacy Act of 1974 to protect data collected by the government. Although it applies to records created and used by federal agencies in the executive branch, it does not apply to state or local governments.

Under the Privacy Act, a **record** is any information about a person that an agency maintains. It includes a person's educational, financial, medical, and criminal history information.[44] The act requires agencies to keep accurate and complete records. It also states that an agency should store only the data that it needs to conduct business. It should not store any extra or unnecessary data.

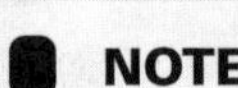
**NOTE**

The Privacy Act applies only to data collected about U.S. citizens and permanent residents.

The Privacy Act states the rules that an agency must follow to collect, use, and transfer PII. An agency cannot disclose a person's records without his or her written consent. There are 12 exceptions to this general rule.[45] If a situation falls within an exception, then the agency can disclose records without consent. An agency does not need written consent to disclose a record if the disclosure is:

- Made to a federal agency employee who needs the record to perform his or her job duties
- Required under the Freedom of Information Act
- Made for an agency's routine use
- Made to the U.S. Census Bureau to perform a survey
- Made for statistical research or reporting, and all personally identifiable data has been removed
- To the National Archives and Records Administration because the record has historical value
- Made in response to a written request from a law enforcement or regulatory agency for civil or criminal law purposes
- Made to protect a person's health or safety
- Made to Congress
- Made to the U.S. Comptroller General in the course of the performance of the duties of the U.S. Government Accountability Office
- Made in response to a court order
- Made to a consumer reporting agency for certain permitted purposes

Under the Privacy Act, a person may ask for a copy of any records that an agency has about that person.[46] The person can ask only for records that are retrievable by the person's name,

SSN, or some other type of unique identifier. A person also may ask an agency to amend any incorrect records. If an agency refuses to amend a person's record, then that person may sue the agency to have the record amended. A person also can sue the agency if it denies access to his or her records.

Federal agencies must protect the data that they collect. The Privacy Act requires them to implement administrative, technical, and physical safeguards to protect the records that they maintain. They must protect their records against any anticipated threats that could harm the people identified in the records. Under the act, harm includes embarrassment.[47]

The law requires agencies to give the public notice about their record-keeping systems. This notice is called a **system of records notice (SORN)**. An agency must publish a SORN for any system that holds records on an individual. It must publish SORNs only for systems that retrieve records either by a person's name or some other personal identifier. An agency must publish its SORNs in the Federal Register.[48]

**FYI**

Every agency is required to post its SORNs on its webpage. You can find the SORNs for the National Aeronautics and Space Administration (NASA) at https://www.nasa.gov/content/nasa-privacy-act-system-of-records-notices-sorns.



An agency that violates the Privacy Act can be subject to both civil and criminal penalties. A person can sue a federal agency for any Privacy Act violation. For example, people can sue if an agency denies them access to their records. They also can sue if an agency refuses to amend a record. If a court finds that an agency has intentionally or willfully violated the act, it can award a plaintiff the actual damages that he or she suffered because of the violation. Under the law, a person is entitled to recover at least $1,000.[49] A court also can order the agency to pay the plaintiff's attorney fees.

A federal agency employee can be criminally responsible for violating the Privacy Act.[50] If an employee improperly discloses information, he or she can be charged with a misdemeanor. The employee also could be fined up to $5,000. An agency employee who keeps records without filing a SORN can be fined up to $5,000.

The OMB oversees Privacy Act compliance. It can publish rules for federal agencies to follow to meet their Privacy Act responsibilities.

## The E-Government Act of 2002

The E-Government Act of 2002 has privacy provisions that complement the Privacy Act. Under the E-Government Act, federal agencies must:

- Review their IT systems for privacy risks
- Post privacy policies on their websites
- Post machine-readable privacy policies on their websites
- Report privacy activities to the OMB

**NOTE**

A PIA is not the same as a SORN. An agency must perform a PIA any time it collects PII. However, it must post a SORN whenever that data can be retrieved using a personal identifier.

A **privacy impact assessment (PIA)** is an agency's review of how its IT systems use personal information.[51] An agency conducts a PIA to make sure that it uses personal information in a way that follows the law. The PIA also helps an agency determine the risks of collecting personal information. It also examines the types of controls that an agency must put in place to reduce privacy risks.

An agency must conduct a PIA before it develops or buys any IT system that will collect personal information. It also must perform a PIA anytime its IT systems change in such a way that new privacy risks are introduced. This includes situations where an agency changes from paper to electronic systems. An agency must conduct a PIA if it chooses to outsource an IT system or function that uses personal data.[52]

An agency's PIA must include information about its data collection practices. This information is similar to fair information practice principles. The PIA must contain the following information:

- What data the agency will collect
- Why the agency is collecting the data
- How the agency will use the data
- How the agency will share the data
- Whether people have the opportunity to consent to specific uses of the data
- How the agency will secure the data
- Whether the data collected will be a system of records defined by the Privacy Act[53]

**FYI**

You can read PIAs from the Federal Trade Commission at https://www.ftc.gov/site-information/privacy-policy/privacy-impact-assessments.

An agency must submit its PIAs to the OMB. They also must make them available to the public. The only time an agency does not have to make a PIA available to the public is when doing so might compromise the security of an IT system.

The E-Government Act requires agencies to post privacy policies on their websites. The privacy policies must contain the same types of information that are in a PIA. They make the public aware of how the agency collects information. They also state how the agency uses that information.

Agencies must post a link to their privacy policies on their main website home page and write them in language that is easy to understand.

**NOTE**

The website for the U.S. Department of Justice is at www.justice.gov. Can you find the agency's privacy policy link on that page?

The E-Government Act also requires agencies to adopt machine-readable privacy policies. These technologies alert users about the agency's website privacy practices. A machine-readable privacy policy lets users know if the agency's privacy practices match the user's browser privacy preferences. The machine-readable privacy policy standard is called P3P. You can read about it at http://osec.doc.gov/webresources/policies/machine_readable_privcy_policy_statements.html.

## OMB Breach Notification Policy

Some states have laws, called breach notification laws or data breach laws, that require businesses and other entities to notify their customers if they suffer a security breach that discloses personal information. Some of these state laws apply to businesses operating within the state. Some also apply to state governments. These laws are discussed further in Chapter 9.

Some federal laws have breach notification provisions. For instance, the rules promulgated as part of the Health Insurance Portability and Accountability Act (HIPAA) include notification requirements. There is no government-wide federal breach notification law, although federal laws have been proposed from time to time. As of this writing, no act has yet passed Congress. A federal breach notification law would eliminate confusion over when data breaches must be reported to the public.

Over the years the OMB has released several memoranda describing breach notification requirements for federal agencies. The most recent memorandum was released in 2017.[54] It states that agencies must create a plan for notifying individuals who might be potentially affected by a breach impacting the agencies' IT systems.

The OMB defines a breach as the "loss of control, compromise, unauthorized disclosure, unauthorized acquisition, or similar occurrence" where unauthorized individuals access PII. It can also include instances where an authorized individual accesses PII for a reason that is not authorized or allowed. Under the current guidance, agencies must review the data disclosed in a breach, determine the number of individuals affected by the breach, consider the likelihood that the data is usable by unauthorized individuals, and assess the risk of harm to the people whose data is disclosed.

An agency has discretion about whether they will notify people about a breach of their PII. If an agency decides to notify individuals about a breach, they must consider:

- **Source of the notification**—The highest-ranking agency official should notify people who are affected by the breach.
- **Time for notification**—Agencies must notify the people affected by the breach without delay. An agency may delay notice only for law enforcement or national security reasons.
- **Contents of the notice**—The notice should include a description of the breach and the type of data disclosed. It should include information on how people can protect themselves from having their data used by unauthorized individuals. It also should describe what the agency is doing to mitigate the breach.
- **Means of providing the notice**—The agency must consider how to give notice to the people affected by the breach. Telephone, first-class mail, email, website postings, and release to national media outlets may all be appropriate ways to provide notice. The agency must consider the best method for a given situation. Agencies also must think about how they will give notice to individuals who are visually or hearing impaired.

The OMB memo is clear that agencies must report breaches of both paper and electronic information. You can read it at https://www.whitehouse.gov/sites/whitehouse.gov/files/omb/memoranda/2017/m-17-12_0.pdf.

## Import and Export Control Laws

This chapter has discussed the laws that federal agencies must follow to protect the security and privacy of information. This section talks briefly about other laws that are in place to protect the export of certain kinds of data. The United States has export control laws that limit the export of materials, data, and technical information to foreign countries. The export of some of these items is limited based on U.S. security interests. It is important to be aware that these types of laws exist. These laws are very complicated and are reviewed briefly here.

Export means the shipment of items or transmission of technology outside of the United States. It also means the transmission of technology to a non-U.S. citizen or nonpermanent resident who is located in the United States. Import and export laws are reciprocal. An export from the United States is an import to another country. A person who is bound by U.S. export control laws cannot import controlled items somewhere else. Much as the United States forbids certain products from being exported, some other countries forbid certain products from being imported.

There are three different types of export control regulations that restrict the export of certain items overseas. They also restrict the transmission of certain types of information to foreign nationals who are living in the United States. The three main regulations are:

- International Traffic in Arms Regulations (ITAR)
- Export Administration Regulations (EAR)
- Regulations from the Office of Foreign Asset Control (OFAC)

The U.S. Department of State issues the ITAR.[55] They apply to military or defense applications and technology that does not have civil (nonmilitary or defense) uses. They are covered under export control laws because of national security concerns. For instance, the United States may want to prevent terrorists from acquiring certain types of technologies that could be used to harm the country. Any export of applications and technology covered by ITAR requires an export license, which is issued by the Department of State.

**FYI**

The U.S. Department of State is serious about pursuing ITAR violations. In 2017, a man was sentenced to 15 years in prison and ordered to pay over $4 million in restitution for selling U.S. Army property, including munitions, on eBay.[56]

Items that are covered by ITAR are listed on the U.S. Munitions List,[57] which is published in the Code of Federal Regulations. The list has 21 categories of different items. If an item falls within one of these categories, then it is covered by ITAR. Among the categories are guns and armament, military electronics, spacecraft, and nuclear weapons.

The penalties for violating ITAR are severe, as civil fines over $1 million are possible. The Department of State determines civil penalties.[58] ITAR violators also can be subject to criminal penalties. A person who willfully violates ITAR can be fined up to $1 million per offense. He or she also can be sentenced to up to 20 years in jail. In addition, companies that violate ITAR can be barred from selling products to the federal government.[59]

The U.S. Department of Commerce handles the EAR.[60] This responsibility is delegated to the Bureau of Industry and Security (BIS). The EAR applies to dual-use technologies, which have both military and commercial use.

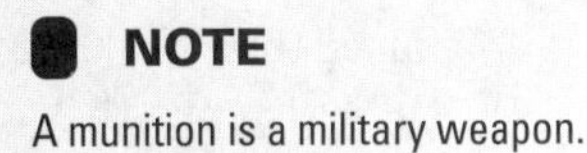


A munition is a military weapon.

Under the EAR, an exporter must have an export license for items and technologies that are on the Commerce Control List (CCL). In 2018, the BIS approved about 85 percent of these license applications.[61] The CCL has 10 broad categories. They include electronics, computers, telecommunications, and information security technologies. Some items are listed on the CCL when they are removed from the U.S. Munitions List.

Some items on the CCL cannot be exported even if a person tries to get a license to do so. Usually, this is because another law or regulation prevents it. For example, the United States has a comprehensive trade embargo against Cuba, which is the oldest U.S. embargo. An embargo is a ban against trade with another country. In this case, the government forbids almost all exports to Cuba.[62]

A person who violates the EAR can be subject to both criminal and civil penalties.[63] Violators can be fined either up to $300,000 or up to twice the value of the transaction. A person who willfully violates the EAR can be fined up to $1 million per offense. He or she also can be sentenced to up to 20 years in jail.[64]



**FYI**

The BIS prepares a report about export control violations. You can read the most recent report and learn more about BIS enforcement activities at https://www.bis.doc.gov/index.php/enforcement.

The Treasury Department also oversees some export laws. The Office of Foreign Assets Control (OFAC), which is part of the Treasury Department, enforces trade sanctions and embargoes. The OFAC administers trade sanctions and embargoes as part of U.S. foreign policy goals. It has the power to forbid some types of transactions based upon these goals. You can learn about the OFAC's sanctions programs at https://www.treasury.gov/resource-center/sanctions/Pages/default.aspx.

OFAC regulations may forbid people in the United States from engaging in any trade or financial transactions with other countries. People in the United States are prohibited from engaging in trade with certain people in other countries. For example, the government prohibits trade with known terrorists or drug traffickers.

The OFAC publishes a list of individuals and companies that people in the United States are generally forbidden from dealing with. The people on this list are called *specially designated nationals (SDN)*. You can view the OFAC's SDN list at https://www.treasury.gov/resource-center/sanctions/SDN-List/Pages/default.aspx.

Penalties for violating OFAC regulations are generally the same as for EAR violations.

## Case Studies and Examples

The OPM is the human resources department for the U.S. federal government. Among its many responsibilities, the OPM provides background check investigation services to other federal agencies.

In 2015, the OPM announced two separate information security incidents that compromised the PII of over 21.5 million people. The incidents were caused by hackers that infiltrated OPM systems. They also infiltrated the systems of contractors used by the OPM. They had access to data for more than 6 months. It appears that the two attacks were coordinated, and some government sources suspect that the attacks were coordinated by another country.

People impacted by the breach included anyone who underwent a federal background check investigation from 2000 to 2015. The pool of affected individuals included federal employees, federal contractors, and active duty service members and veterans. It also included immediate family members and references for anyone whose information was stolen. Some of the PII exposed in the incidents included:

- SSN
- Employment history
- Education history
- Medical history (including mental health history and information about drug or alcohol abuse)
- Criminal history
- Address and address history
- Foreign travel history
- Personal information of close family members (spouse, partner, parents, siblings)

The PII stolen also included almost 5.6 million records with fingerprint data. Because of the breaches and public outcry, the OPM director and CIO resigned.

A report from the U.S. House of Representatives Committee on Oversight and Government Reform noted that the breach happened because the OPM did not prioritize its information security activities. The report also noted that the OPM did not meet many FISMA requirements.[65]

The OPM maintains a web-based resource center for victims of the 2015 incidents. The resource center includes information on the incident, frequently asked questions, and guidance for how to sign up for identity theft coverage. The OPM is required to provide that coverage through 2026 for affected individuals. You can view the resource center at https://www.opm.gov/cybersecurity/.

## CHAPTER SUMMARY

This chapter reviews the laws that protect the security and privacy of data that the federal government uses. FISMA, the main law protecting the security of federal government IT systems, requires federal agencies to create information security programs. Agencies also must review their information security risks. The law requires them to implement controls to mitigate those risks.

The Privacy Act of 1974 and the E-Government Act of 2002 are the main laws protecting data privacy at the federal level. These laws govern how federal agencies use personally identifiable data. Under the E-Government Act, federal agencies must review their IT systems for any privacy impacts. Both laws require federal agencies to notify the public about their data collection practices.

## KEY CONCEPTS AND TERMS

Inspector general (IG)
National security systems (NSSs)
Privacy impact assessment (PIA)
Record
System of records notice (SORN)

## CHAPTER 8 ASSESSMENT

1. Which regulation controls the export of military or defense applications and technology?
   A. ITAR
   B. EAR
   C. OFAC
   D. FDIC
   E. None of these is correct.
2. What information must a federal agency include in a privacy impact assessment?
3. The information collected in a PIA and a SORN is based upon what principles?
   A. NIST standards
   B. OMB standards
   C. Fair information privacy practices
   D. ITAR regulations
   E. None of these is correct.
4. Which assessment must be completed any time a federal agency collects personal information that can be retrieved via a personal identifier?
   A. PIA
   B. SORN
   C. ACORN
   D. OFAC
   E. None of these is correct.
5. Which agency has primary oversight responsibilities under FISMA?
   A. DoD
   B. CIA
   C. NIST
   D. CNSS
   E. None of these is correct.
6. Federal agencies must report information security incidents to ______.
7. Federal agencies must test their information security controls every 6 months.
   A. True
   B. False
8. What are federal information security challenges?
   A. A culture of merely complying with reporting requirements
   B. Lack of an enterprise approach to information security
   C. Lack of coordination within the federal government
   D. All of these are correct.
   E. None of these is correct.
9. What is the name of the FISMA data-collection tool?
10. Which type of NIST guidance follows a formal creation process?
    A. Special Publications
    B. Federal Information Processing Standards
    C. Guidelines for Information Security
    D. Fair information practice principles
    E. None of these is correct.
11. How many steps are there in the NIST risk management framework?
    A. Six
    B. Five
    C. Four
    D. Three
    E. None of these is correct.
12. Which level of impact for a FIPS security category best describes significant damage to organizational assets?
    A. Low
    B. Moderate
    C. High
    D. Severe
    E. None of these is correct.

**13.** FedCIRC is the federal information security incident center.

A. True
B. False

**14.** How quickly must a federal agency report an unauthorized access incident?

A. Monthly
B. Weekly
C. Daily
D. Within 2 hours of discovery
E. Within 1 hour of discovery

**15.** How many categories of security controls are designated in FIPS 200?

A. 20
B. 19
C. 18
D. 17
E. None of these is correct.

## ENDNOTES


1. Remarks by the President, "On Securing Our Nation's Cyber Infrastructure," May 29, 2009. https://obamawhitehouse.archives.gov/the-press-office/remarks-president-securing-our-nations-cyber-infrastructure (accessed May 16, 2020).
2. Committee on Oversight and Government Reform, "Federal Information Security: Current Challenges and Future Policy Considerations," March 24, 2010. http://www.gpo.gov/fdsys/pkg/CHRG-111hhrg65549/html/CHRG-111hhrg65549.htm (accessed May 16, 2020).
3. U.S. Government Accountability Office, "Federal Information Security: Agencies and OMB Need to Strengthen Policies and Practices," July 2019. https://www.gao.gov/assets/710/700588.pdf (accessed May 16, 2020).
4. Computer Security Act of 1987, P.L. 100-235, 101 Stat. 1724.
5. Federal Information Security Modernization Act, Title III of the E-Government Act of 2002, P.L. 107-347, 116 Stat. 2899, 2946 (Dec. 17, 2002).
6. The Federal Information Security Modernization Act of 2014 (Pub. L. No. 113-283, Dec. 18, 2014) largely superseded the Federal Information Security Modernization Act of 2002 (FISMA 2002), enacted as Title III, E-Government Act of 2002, Pub. L. No. 107-347, 116 Stat. 2899, 2946 (Dec. 17, 2002).
7. Secretary of Defense Leon E. Panetta, "Remarks by Secretary Panetta on Cybersecurity to the Business Executives for National Security, New York City" (New York, NY: Oct. 11, 2012). Available at: http://www.gao.gov/assets/660/652170.pdf (accessed May 16, 2020).
8. Time, "Here's What We Know So Far About Russia's 2016 Meddling," April 18, 2019. https://time.com/5565991/russia-influence-2016-election/ (accessed May 16, 2020).
9. BBC News, "Ukraine Power Cut Was Cyber Attack," January 11, 2017. https://www.bbc.com/news/technology-38573074 (accessed May 16, 2020).
10. The New York Times, "The World Once Laughed at North Korean Cyberpower. No More," October 15, 2017. https://www.nytimes.com/2017/10/15/world/asia/north-korea-hacking-cyber-sony.html (accessed May 16, 2020).
11. U.S. Code Vol. 44, sec. 3551.
12. Statista, "Proposed Budget of the U.S. Government for Cyber Security in FY 2017 to 2021," February 2020. https://www.statista.com/statistics/675399/us-government-spending-cyber-security/ (accessed May 16, 2020).
13. U.S. Code Vol. 44, sec. 3552(b)(3).
14. U.S. Code Vol. 44, sec. 3544.
15. U.S. Code Vol. 44, sec. 3554(b)(5).
16. U.S. Code Vol. 15, sec. 278g-3.
17. U.S. Code Vol. 44, sec. 3554(a)(3).
18. U.S. Code Vol. 44, sec. 3554(c).

19. U.S. Code Vol. 44, sec. 3554(b)(3)(A)(ii).
20. Inspector General Act of 1978, U.S. Code Vol. 5 app, sec. 1.
21. Inspector General Act of 1978, U.S. Code Vol. 5 app, sec. 2.
22. U.S. Code Vol. 44, sec. 3554(c)(1)(B).
23. U.S. Office of Management and Budget, "OMB Circular A-130, Managing Information as a Strategic Resource, Section 5(f)," July 28, 2016. https://www.whitehouse.gov/sites/whitehouse.gov/files/omb/circulars/A130/a130revised.pdf (accessed May 16, 2020).
24. Committee on Oversight and Government Reform, "Federal Information Security: Current Challenges and Future Policy Considerations," March 24, 2010. http://www.gpo.gov/fdsys/pkg/CHRG-111hhrg65549/html/CHRG-111hhrg65549.htm (accessed May 16, 2020).
25. U.S. Code Vol. 44, sec. 3555.
26. National Institute of Standards and Technology, "Procedures for Developing FIPS (Federal Information Processing Standards) Publications," May 21, 2018. https://www.nist.gov/itl/procedures-developing-fips-federal-information-processing-standards-publications (accessed May 16, 2020).
27. U.S. Office of Management and Budget, "Federal Cloud Computing Strategy," Undated. https://cloud.cio.gov/strategy/ (accessed May 16, 2020).
28. Federal Risk and Authorization Management Program, "FedRAMP Security Assessment Framework," November 15, 2017. https://www.fedramp.gov/assets/resources/documents/FedRAMP_Security_Assessment_Framework.pdf (accessed May 16, 2020).
29. National Institute of Standards and Technology, "SP 800-37, Revision 1, Risk Management Framework for Information Systems and Organizations," December 2018. https://nvlpubs.nist.gov/nistpubs/SpecialPublications/NIST.SP.800-37r2.pdf (accessed May 16, 2020).
30. National Institute of Standards and Technology, "FIPS Pub 199, Standards for Security Categorization of Federal Information and Information Systems," February 2004. https://csrc.nist.gov/publications/detail/fips/199/final (accessed May 16, 2020).
31. National Institute of Standards and Technology, "FIPS Pub 200, Minimum Security Requirements for Federal Information and Information Systems," March 2006. https://csrc.nist.gov/publications/detail/fips/200/final (accessed May 16, 2020).
32. National Institute of Standards and Technology, "SP 800-53, Revision 4, Security and Privacy Controls for Federal Information Systems and Organizations," April 2013. https://csrc.nist.gov/publications/detail/sp/800-53/rev-4/final (accessed May 16, 2020).
33. National Institute of Standards and Technology, "SP 800-122, Guide to Protecting the Confidentiality of Personally Identifiable Information (PII)," April 2010. https://csrc.nist.gov/publications/detail/sp/800-122/final (accessed May 16, 2020).
34. National Institute of Standards and Technology, "SP 800-53A, Assessing Security and Privacy Controls in Federal Information Systems and Organizations: Building Effective Assessment Plans," December 2014. https://csrc.nist.gov/publications/detail/sp/800-53a/rev-4/final (accessed May 16, 2020).
35. U.S. Code Vol. 44, sec. 3556.
36. U.S. Government Accountability Office, "Federal Information Security: Agencies and OMB Need to Strengthen Policies and Practices," July 2019. https://www.gao.gov/assets/710/700588.pdf (accessed May 16, 2020).
37. U.S. Code Vol. 44, sec. 3552(b)(2).
38. U.S. Department of Homeland Security, Cybersecurity and Infrastructure Security Agency, "US-CERT Federal Incident Notification Guidelines," 2017. https://www.us-cert.gov/incident-notification-guidelines (accessed May 16, 2020).
39. U.S. Code Vol. 44, sec. 3552(b)(6)(A).
40. Committee of National Security Systems, "Policy No. 22, Cybersecurity Risk Management," August 2016. http://www.cnss.gov/cnss/issuances/Policies.cfm (accessed May 16, 2020).
41. Office of Management and Budget, "Fiscal Year (FY) 2018 Annual Report to Congress," August 2019. https://www.whitehouse.gov/wp-content/uploads/2019/08/FISMA-2018-Report-FINAL-to-post.pdf (accessed May 16, 2020).
42. Privacy Act of 1974, Pub. L. No. 93-579, 88 Stat. 1896, codified at U.S. Code Vol. 5, sec. 552a.
43. E-Government Act of 2002, Pub. L. No. 107-347, 116 Stat. 2899, codified in scattered sections throughout U.S. Code Vol. 44 (various sections) (2012).

44. U.S. Code Vol. 5, sec. 552a(a)(4).
45. U.S. Code Vol. 5, sec. 552a(b).
46. U.S. Code Vol. 5, sec. 552a(d).
47. U.S. Code Vol. 5, sec. 552a(e)(10).
48. U.S. Code Vol. 5, sec. 552a(e).
49. U.S. Code Vol. 5, sec. 552a(g)(4)(A).
50. U.S. Code Vol. 5, sec. 552a(i).
51. U.S. Office of Management and Budget, "Memo M-03-22: OMB Guidance for Implementing the Privacy Protections of the E-Government Act of 2002," September 26, 2003. https://obamawhitehouse.archives.gov/omb/memoranda_m03-22/ (accessed May 16, 2020).
52. E-Government Act of 2002, Pub. L. No. 107-347, 116 Stat. 2899, sec. 208.
53. E-Government Act of 2002, Pub. L. No. 107-347, 116 Stat. 2899, sec. 208.
54. U.S. Office of Management and Budget, "OMB Memorandum M-17-12, Preparing for and Responding to a Breach of Personally Identifiable Information," January 3, 2017. https://www.whitehouse.gov/sites/whitehouse.gov/files/omb/memoranda/2017/m-17-12_0.pdf (accessed May 16, 2020).
55. International Traffic in Arms Regulations, Code of Federal Regulations, Title 22, sec. 120-130.
56. U.S. Department of Justice, "Summary of Major U.S. Export Enforcement, Economic Espionage, and Sanctions Related to Criminal Cases," January 2018. https://www.pmddtc.state.gov/sys_attachment.do?sysparm_referring_url=tear_off&view=true&sys_id=6ae22ec1db2a9740c53a7d321f9619c4 (accessed May 16, 2020).
57. International Traffic in Arms Regulations, Code of Federal Regulations, Title 22, sec. 121.1.
58. International Traffic in Arms Regulations, Code of Federal Regulations, Title 22, sec. 128.
59. U.S. Code Vol. 22, sec. 2778(c).
60. Export Administration Regulations, Code of Federal Regulations, Title 15, sec. 730-774.
61. U.S. Department of Commerce, "Statistics of 2018 BIS License Authorization," April 3, 2019. https://www.bis.doc.gov/index.php/documents/technology-evaluation/ote-data-portal/licensing-analysis/2453-2018-statistical-analysis-of-bis-licensing-pdf-1/file (accessed May 16, 2020).
62. U.S. Code Vol. 22, sec. 2370.
63. Export Administration Regulations, Code of Federal Regulations, Title 15, sec. 730-774.
64. U.S. Code Vol. 50, sec. 4801-4852.
65. U.S. House of Representatives, Committee Oversight and Government Reform, "The OPM Data Breach: How the Government Jeopardized Our National Security for More Than a Generation," September 7, 2016. https://republicans-oversight.house.gov/wp-content/uploads/2016/09/The-OPM-Data-Breach-How-the-Government-Jeopardized-Our-National-Security-for-More-than-a-Generation.pdf (accessed May 16, 2020).

# State Laws Protecting Citizen Information and Breach Notification Laws

CHAPTER 9

IN THE UNITED STATES, there is currently no single comprehensive federal data privacy or security law. Instead, the United States has enacted industry-specific laws about security and privacy. These laws limit the use of personal information based on the nature of the data.

State governments also have entered this regulatory arena. States create data protection laws that are data specific. Many states have created laws to protect health and financial information. They also might try to protect data in certain types of records, such as motor vehicle records. In some ways, states are more aggressive in trying to protect personal information than the federal government. This chapter focuses on state data protection laws. It includes laws from different states to give you an overview of the types of laws being passed to protect data. As you encounter issues regarding the law, security, and privacy, you must consider the impact of state laws and rules.

## Chapter 9 Topics

This chapter covers the following topics and concepts:

- What the history is of state actions to protect personal information
- What state breach notification laws are
- What state data-specific security and privacy regulations are
- What encryption regulations are
- What data-disposal regulations are
- What some case studies and examples are

## Chapter 9 Goals

When you complete this chapter, you will be able to:

- Describe state approaches to protecting the security of personal information
- Describe laws that protect certain types of data

- Describe state breach notification laws
- Describe the differences between state breach notification laws

## History of State Actions to Protect Personal Information

States have created many laws to protect personal information. California, for example, has worked hard to make laws that protect the security and privacy of its residents' data. It was this state's breach notification laws and a breach at a large corporation that led to the growth of data protection laws in many states.

### ChoicePoint Data Breach

ChoicePoint was a data broker that merged public records, credit reports, and demographic data to create individual consumer profiles, which it then sold to the government and private companies. People used the profiles to conduct background checks. ChoicePoint also sold profiles to insurance companies. It collected many different types of personal information, such as names, addresses, and Social Security numbers (SSNs). Its databases also included credit history and DNA information.

In February 2005, ChoicePoint notified 35,000 California residents that their personal data had been exposed in a data breach. California was the only state at that time with a **breach notification law**, which applied to any business that stored the personal data of California residents. The law required them to notify state residents of any security breach involving their unencrypted personal information.

**NOTE**

At the time of the data breach, news media reported that ChoicePoint had collected over 9 billion public records on U.S. residents and had stored 250 terabytes of data.

ChoicePoint said that it discovered the breach in late 2004 after law enforcement officials contacted the company about an identity theft ring. ChoicePoint learned that the criminals pretended to be its customers. In order to become a ChoicePoint customer, applicants had to provide proof of a lawful reason for buying consumer data. At the time of the breach, ChoicePoint had over 50,000 customers, ranging from insurance companies to debt collectors.

ChoicePoint's validation processes did not find the fake customers, some of whom provided suspect documents to ChoicePoint. For example, multiple businesses submitted documents with the same information. This should have raised red flags for more review. ChoicePoint later found over 50 fake accounts that had access to ChoicePoint's databases.[1]

At first ChoicePoint notified only California residents affected by the breach, because it was the only state requiring such notification. However, 19 other states were outraged. The state attorneys general wrote a letter to ChoicePoint demanding that it alert all people affected by the breach. ChoicePoint later sent notification letters to over 160,000 people.[2]

In January 2006, the Federal Trade Commission (FTC) investigated ChoicePoint, alleging that ChoicePoint violated consumer privacy rights. It also charged the company with violating federal laws. ChoicePoint settled with the FTC in December of that year and paid $10 million in civil fines.[3]

ChoicePoint also agreed to pay $5 million to fund a consumer relief program that would pay people who were victims of identity theft because of the breach. The agreement with the FTC also required ChoicePoint to create an information security program. The company is required to get independent audits every year until 2026. At the time, the ChoicePoint settlement was the largest in the FTC's history.

In May 2007, ChoicePoint settled a multistate lawsuit over the breach. Forty-three states entered the settlement agreement. As part of that agreement, ChoicePoint promised to improve its process for verifying customers. It also agreed to strengthen how it protects the data that it collects. ChoicePoint also agreed to pay $500,000 to the states involved in the lawsuit.[4]

ChoicePoint was on the FTC's radar again in 2009, this time because of a 2008 security incident. ChoicePoint had changed some internal security controls, and the changed controls failed to alert it that someone had unauthorized access to its data. The wrongful access continued for about 30 days. During this time, the data of about 13,750 people—including SSNs—may have been disclosed.

The FTC alleged that the 2008 incident was a violation of the 2006 agreement. Therefore, ChoicePoint agreed to additional security requirements, such as strengthening its information security program again. It was also required to report to the FTC on its security efforts every 2 months until 2011.[5]

The ChoicePoint data breach is unique because it spurred the creation of data breach notification laws in many states. If it were not for the California breach notification law, ChoicePoint might not have notified any consumers at all about the data breach. Other states realized that their residents might not be able to protect themselves from identity theft in similar situations without these laws. Thirty-five states considered breach notification laws in 2005. The ChoicePoint case is widely seen as the reason why other states have these laws.

**NOTE**

ChoicePoint reported that it had many external audits after the 2005 breach. It was audited 80 times in the 24 months after the breach.

 **NOTE**

ChoicePoint was purchased by LexisNexis in 2008. To help protect consumer information, LexisNexis offered customers a copy of their consumer file. However, individuals were limited in only requesting their own file, and they needed to provide proof of identity to get a copy of the file. To learn more about this service, you can visit https://consumer.risk.lexisnexis.com/.

 **NOTE**

Illinois Governor Rod Blagojevich proposed the Personal Information Protection Act just days after the ChoicePoint breach went public. The ChoicePoint breach affected about 5,000 Illinois residents. The Act, which became Illinois's breach notification law, took effect January 1, 2006.



## Breach Notification Regulations

California was the first state to have a breach notification law. It required businesses to notify their customers if they suffered a data breach that disclosed personal data. Many states have modeled their own breach notification laws on the California law. This section discusses the California breach notification law, as well as the laws in other states.

## California Breach Notification Act

California's Database Security Breach Notification Act law went into effect on July 1, 2003, and has been updated several times. The California legislature created the law after a security breach at a state-operated data facility. The legislature recognized that identity theft was one of the fastest growing crimes in California. It stated that people must act quickly to limit the harm caused by identity theft. The purpose of the law was to give California residents timely information so that they can protect themselves.

The law applies to anyone who owns or uses computerized data that contains the unencrypted personal information of a California resident.[6] It applies to:

- State agencies
- Nonprofit organizations
- Private organizations
- Businesses

It also can apply to businesses that are not actually located in California. It actually covers any entity that stores the personal information of a California resident. Under the law, an entity must notify California residents of a breach of its computer systems and give notice if unauthorized individuals access and take the resident's unencrypted data.

**FYI**

Under California law, a security breach means unauthorized acquisition of computerized data. It must "compromise the security, confidentiality, or integrity of personal information" held by an entity.[7] This definition is confusing from an information security perspective because it refers to security and separately to confidentiality and integrity. Confidentiality and integrity are part of the standard definition of security. This type of imprecise definition is why information security professionals and lawmakers must work together to create laws that impact information security.

The law defines personal information very broadly as information that allows a person to be identified. *Personal information* is a person's first name (or first initial) and last name. The person's name is combined with any of the following:

- SSN
- Driver's license number or California Identification Card number
- Account number, or credit or debit card number, along with any security code, access code, or password that would allow access to a person's account
- Medical information
- Health insurance information
- Unique biometric information
- Information collected through the state's automated license plate recognition system

Under the law, personal information is unencrypted data. If any of the data is unencrypted, then all of the information is considered personal information. Information that is available to the public through government records is not personal information. The law also states that a username or email address, when combined with a password or answer to a security question, is personal information if those elements could be used to access an online account.

The law requires entities to notify California residents whenever a security breach occurs. They must also notify residents as quickly as possible if they reasonably believe that a breach has occurred. Under the law, there are two reasons to delay notification. The first is to figure out the scope of the security breach. An entity must do this so that it can notify the right people.

The second reason to delay notification is if law enforcement requires it. Law enforcement can allow entities to delay notification if they are conducting a criminal investigation. The entity must make the required notification as soon as possible after it is determined that it will not hurt the investigation.

The law requires entities to give written notice to California residents, and that the notice be written in plain language and clearly identify the entity making the notice. It must also contain the following headings:

- What Happened
- What Information Was Involved
- What We Are Doing
- What You Can Do
- For More Information

The law also contains a model security breach notification template that entities can use.

Sometimes providing notice to a large number of people can be very expensive. The California law allows entities to use a different type of notice if the entity can prove that:

- The cost of giving written notice is greater than $250,000.
- The number of people to be notified is greater than 500,000.
- It does not have sufficient contact information.

If an entity can prove one of these situations, it does not have to give individual written notices. Instead, it must do all of the following to provide "substitute notice" of the breach:

- Notify affected people by email if the entity has an email address for the person.
- Post notice of the security breach on its website (if it has one) for at least 30 days.
- Notify major statewide media outlets about the breach.

The California law provides a safe harbor for entities that encrypt personal information. A **safe harbor** is a legal concept that refers to specific actions someone can take to show a good-faith effort to stay within the law and avoid prosecution. Entities that properly encrypt the personal information that they own or maintain do not have to follow the notification requirements if they have a data breach.

**NOTE**

Under the California law, encrypted means rendering data "unusable, unreadable, or indecipherable to an unauthorized person through a security technology or methodology generally accepted in the field of information security." Think about whether this definition is sufficient to evaluate the effectiveness of the encryption method used.

**NOTE**

In the law, a plaintiff can generally recover only damages in the amount that he or she has actually lost because of harm or injury.

Finally, the law gives California residents a limited private cause of action against entities that do not follow the law. Residents who are harmed when an entity does not follow the law can sue for damages.[8]

## Other Breach Notification Laws

After the ChoicePoint breach, many other states created breach notification laws. Today, all 50 states, the District of Columbia, Guam, Puerto Rico, and the Virgin Islands have breach notification laws.[9] Many states based their laws on the California law, but there are some differences. They include:

- Activities that constitute a breach
- The time for notifying residents
- Requirements that a notification contain certain types of information
- Minimum requirements for encryption
- Civil or criminal penalties for failing to notify affected people

Additionally, unlike the California law, most other state laws typically do not allow a private cause of action for failure to give notification.

### *Activities That Constitute a Breach*

The California law applies to unauthorized acquisition of unencrypted personal information. If attackers access the data, that is enough to trigger the law's notification requirements. Some other states require a showing of harm before notification is required. This means that attackers must not only access the data, but do something with it. For instance, the attackers must steal, copy, or change the data before notification is required. In addition, some sort of harm therefore must be anticipated. Stealing data is an anticipated harm under these laws. You must review the definition of *breach* carefully in each law to see what triggers the notification requirements.

For example, Ohio law requires more than unauthorized acquisition to trigger notification. Under Ohio law, residents must be notified if the security breach reasonably causes a material risk of identity theft or other fraud to the resident.[10] The risk of harm can also be a future risk of harm. In this law, the material risk of identity theft is enough to require notification.

**NOTE**

Alabama was the last state to enact a breach notification law.

**NOTE**

Some other states that employ some sort of harm standard include Hawaii, Massachusetts, and Virginia. Guam also has such a provision. Look up the breach notification law for your state to study its breach definition.

### *Time for Notification*

Under the general California breach notification law, entities must give notice in the most expedient time possible without unreasonable delay. A majority of states follow the California approach. However, some states require that entities give notice within a certain period.

Ohio law, for example, requires that notification be given to state residents in the most expedient time possible. However, that law also states that entities must give this notice no later than

### Entities Excluded From Breach Notification Laws

Some states exclude some kinds of entities from their breach notification laws because these entities are already subject to other laws with specific data security requirements. Many of these other laws have security and privacy obligations that are stricter than the states' own laws. If the entities are following these other laws, then a security breach may be less likely. In some cases, state lawmakers determined that making entities follow both the state breach notification law and the other laws would be too hard. It might hurt businesses operating in the state.

Some states exempt financial institutions covered by the Gramm-Leach-Bliley Act (GLBA). GLBA requires these institutions to protect a customer's nonpublic financial information through security safeguards. They also must follow privacy rules. Breaches may be less likely if an institution follows GLBA. Many states exempt these entities from notification laws. They include Alaska, Connecticut, Indiana, and Minnesota.

Some states also exempt entities that are covered by the Health Insurance Portability and Accountability Act (HIPAA). HIPAA-covered entities must follow rules designed to protect personally identifiable health information, as well as the HIPAA Privacy and Security Rules. Recent amendments also impose breach notification rules on HIPAA-covered entities. These rules may be even stricter than some state notification laws. States that exempt HIPAA-covered entities from their laws include Arizona, Rhode Island, and Wisconsin.

45 days after the discovery of the breach.[11] Florida has a similar requirement and requires notification within 30 days.[12]

In Maine, an entity can only delay notification to help a criminal investigation. In that case, an entity must give notice once law enforcement determines that the notification will not hurt the investigation. At that point, the entity must provide notice within 7 days.[13]

**NOTE**

A business day is an official workday. Business days are the days of the week that include Monday through Friday. Saturday and Sunday are not business days. Public holidays also are not business days.

### *Contents of Notification*

Some states do not specify the types of information that should be included in a notice of a data breach. Alaska is one of these states. There is a growing trend, however, to specify the types of information that should be included in a notice. States do this to make sure that residents get enough information to protect themselves.

North Carolina law requires that notice be given in a "clear and conspicuous" form.[14] This means that it needs to be easily understandable. The notice also must:

- Describe the incident in general terms.
- Describe the type of personal information that was involved in the breach.
- Describe how the entity is going to protect the personal information from additional unauthorized access.
- Provide a telephone number for the entity, if one exists, that a person may call for more information.

**TIP**

Remember, the reason for notification is to let people protect themselves from identity theft. Any delay in notifying people should be as short as possible.

- Advise the person being notified to review his or her account statements and get a free credit report.
- Provide the toll-free telephone numbers and addresses for the major consumer reporting agencies.
- Provide the contact information for the FTC and the North Carolina attorney general's office, along with a statement that these sources have additional information about preventing identity theft.

North Carolina also allows entities to notify residents by telephone, but only if the entity makes direct contact with the people whose data was accessed in the breach. Colorado law allows notice to be given in written and electronic form.[15] It also allows notice by telephone.

### Encryption Requirements

The California law provides an encryption safe harbor. Entities do not need to give notice of a breach if the personal information in their computer system was encrypted. California law does not specify the lowest level of encryption needed to use the safe harbor. It also does not reference any industry standards.

**TIP**

Remember, a safe harbor is an action someone can take to show a good-faith effort to stay within the law.

**NOTE**

Algorithms are mathematical computations used to solve a problem and to encrypt data.

Many other states also provide an encryption safe harbor. However, most states do not specify a minimum level of encryption needed to take advantage of the safe harbor.

Some states, however, do specify the encryption standards required to take advantage of the safe harbor. For instance, Massachusetts defines encryption as the use of a 128-bit or higher algorithmic process to transform data.[16]

Indiana also provides an encryption safe harbor. Its law says that data is encrypted if it is changed by an algorithmic process. It must be changed into a form that is unreadable without the use of a confidential process or key.[17]

The Indiana law also addresses key management. For portable electronic devices, such as laptop computers, the data must be protected by encryption and the encryption key cannot be stored on the device. Indiana law also says that data is considered encrypted if it is secured by any other method that makes the data unreadable or unusable.

### Penalties for Failure to Notify

Some states can impose penalties for violations of their breach notification laws. In Texas, for example, the state can assess a fine against an entity that does not notify affected people.[18] The law states that an entity can be fined at least $2,000 for a violation. However, the fine cannot be larger than $50,000 for a single violation.

Other states have more complicated penalty structures. Under Florida law, an entity that does not provide notification within 30 days of a breach faces potentially large fines,[19] such as a $1,000-per-day fine for every day that the entity fails to give notice after the 30-day limit. This penalty is in effect for the first 30 days after the 30-day limit. After that, the fine increases to $50,000 for each additional 30-day period that the entity fails to give notice. This extends up to 180 days (about 6 months) after the 30-day mark for giving notice. If entities

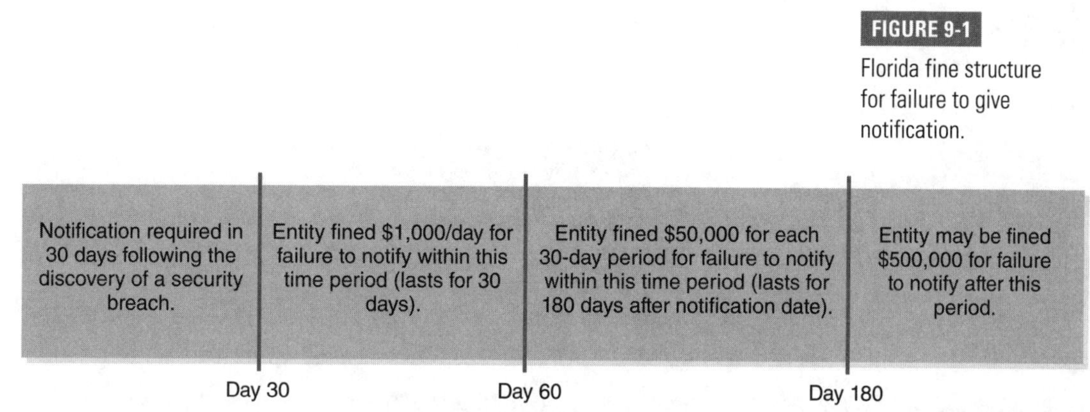


**FIGURE 9-1**
Florida fine structure for failure to give notification.

do not give notification within 180 days after a breach, the state may fine them up to $500,000. **FIGURE 9-1** illustrates the Florida fine structure.

> **NOTE**
>
> In Indiana, the failure to give notice is a deceptive act. The state attorney general's office has the power to prosecute deceptive acts. The fine for each act can be up to $150,000.[20]

### *Private Cause of Action*

California law does not assess any penalties against an entity that does not follow the notification law. However, it does allow a person a private cause of action against those entities. For example, people can sue the private entity for any damages they have because they did not receive notification in a timely manner. Some states, such as Alaska, Maryland, and South Carolina, allow a private cause of action; however, most states do not. The states that do not are generally seeking to protect the entity's business. They also do this to protect the court system, as it could be burdensome to the court system to process many individual cases. Instead, most of these states allow the state attorney general to pursue an action against the entity for failure to give notification. These states include Iowa, Michigan, and Oklahoma.

Every state now has a breach notification law to protect its residents. The laws have some similarities, and some laws also have unique requirements. These laws can be very confusing to businesses that operate in several states, because breaches at these entities are almost certainly going to affect people in many states. If this happens, an entity will have to review the laws of several states to properly notify people about the breach.

Breach notification is hard for entities because states have different laws about what constitutes a breach. An incident can be a breach in one state, but not another. It also can be hard if entities must give notice in a certain way or within a certain time. Differing penalties for noncompliance may also be a problem. Because the laws all have different nuances, it may not be enough for an entity to comply with the laws of its own state. **FIGURE 9-2** provides a general decision tree that entities can follow in reviewing a security breach to see if notice is required.

The lack of uniformity among states may place additional burdens on businesses that experience a security breach. People also may be confused if they get notices that do not look similar. Notices might look different depending upon the law that the entity followed

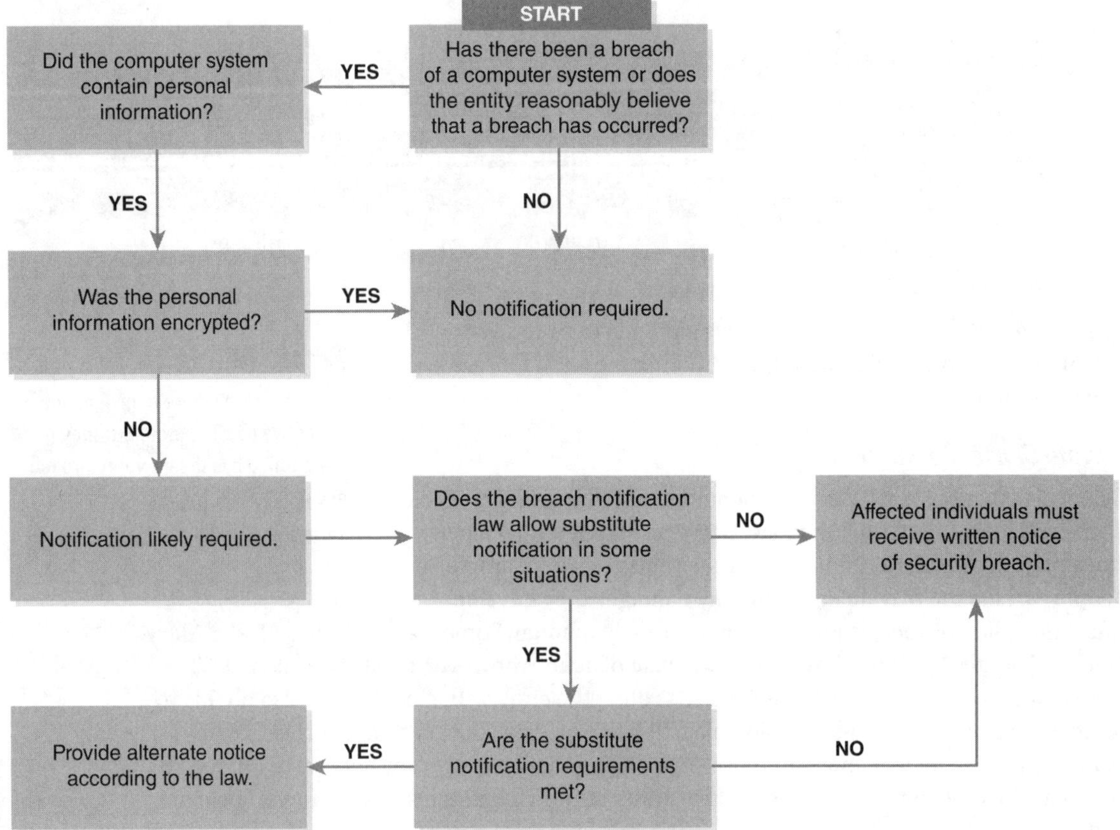


FIGURE 9-2
Breach notification decision tree.

in creating the notice. A federal breach notification law would help eliminate this confusion. Federal laws have been proposed from time to time. As of this writing, no such act has yet passed Congress.

## Data-Specific Security and Privacy Regulations

Many states have created laws to protect the use of certain types of information. Similar to the federal government, they create laws by data type. This section discusses some of the data-specific laws that states have created to protect personal information.

### Minnesota and Nevada: Requiring Businesses to Comply With Payment Card Industry Standards

Some states have started to create laws that require entities in the state to comply with industry security standards. For example, Minnesota and Nevada have created laws that

### When Is Federal Legislation Appropriate?

The federal government has limited lawmaking power. The U.S. Congress cannot make any laws outside of the scope granted to it in the U.S. Constitution. This means that Congress cannot usually interfere in state matters. It also cannot create a uniform federal law in areas legislated by the states unless there is a compelling reason to do so.

Congress can create laws in areas where the U.S. Constitution allows it. For instance, the Constitution grants the federal government the power to regulate commerce between the states. If an activity has the potential to affect the trade relations between the states, then Congress may address it under its Commerce Clause power.

Sometimes states enact laws that extend beyond their borders. If these laws affect trade between the states, then it is possible that they start to infringe upon an area where the federal government alone has the power to create laws. When this happens, the question arises whether that area has become "ripe" for federal legislation.

When deciding if an area is ripe for federal legislation, Congress looks at whether differing state laws affect activities that it traditionally regulates. It considers how many states have created laws addressing the specific topic and reviews whether there is state confusion or complexity on activities that might affect relationships between the states. Congress also looks at whether the differing state laws create an undue burden or economic cost on businesses operating in several states.

Congress may use its legislative power to enact federal laws if there is confusion among the states. It does this to eliminate confusion for businesses that operate in several states. If it creates a national law in an area where there are many different state laws, the federal law will preempt the state laws. The state laws will no longer be valid.

The Congressional Research Service has compiled reports on various federal laws that may create breach notification requirements. The report notes that breach notification laws are complicated and often confusing. You can read their 2019 report at https://crsreports.congress.gov/product/pdf/R/R45631.

require businesses operating in those states to comply with parts of the Payment Card Industry (PCI) Data Security Standard (DSS).

Minnesota's 2007 Plastic Card Security Act was the first state law that attempted to codify certain parts of the PCI DSS. It forbids businesses from storing cardholder information for more than 48 hours after the credit card transaction is approved.[21] Information that cannot be stored includes:

- Card verification number
- PIN number
- Contents of the card magnetic stripe

The PCI DSS also states that businesses may not retain this information. The Minnesota law has turned this part of the PCI DSS industry standard into a law.

The Minnesota law shifts the cost of a breach to a business that violates the law. If a business suffers a breach, and is found to have violated the storage requirements, then it can be held responsible for costs related to the breach. For instance, a bank or other financial institutions can sue the business to recover their costs in responding to the breach. These costs include issuing new cards or refunding unauthorized charges.[22]

**The Minnesota Plastic Card Security Act Supported by Financial Institutions**

One of the reasons the Minnesota Plastic Card Security Act was introduced was the 2007 TJX data breach. Financial institutions often paid the cost for notifying people that their credit and debit card information was disclosed in a breach. There were other costs as well. If another organization suffered a breach that included card data, financial institutions had to reissue the cards to their customers, which costs money. They had to refund unauthorized charges. They also suffered reputation damage when customers asked whether the financial institution was also involved in the breach.

 **NOTE**

Businesses that wish to accept credit cards for payment must follow the PCI DSS. The major credit card companies require it, although it is not a law. Credit card companies such as Visa and MasterCard enforce PCI DSS.

 **NOTE**

The Nevada law states that "personal information" is a person's name combined with SSN, financial account number, credit card number, health insurance number, and driver's license or other identification number.[25]

The Minnesota Credit Union Network, an association of more than 160 credit unions in Minnesota, was tired of paying for another organization's weak security practices. The Network engages in political advocacy, education, and awareness activities. It pushed for the creation of the Plastic Card Security Act to help reduce its costs for another organization's security breach.

In 2010, Nevada was the first state to make following the entire PCI DSS a state law requirement.[23] The Nevada law says that businesses will not be liable for damages for a data breach, such as paying for credit cards to be reissued, if they are following the law and did not engage in other intentional misconduct. Washington state also provided businesses with a safe harbor from data breach liability if the business can certify that it was PCI DSS compliant at the time of the data breach.[24] The Washington law, however, does not require businesses to follow PCI DSS.

The Nevada law is novel because it makes following the entire PCI DSS required by law. Some commentators thought that the Nevada law would encourage other states to adopt similar laws. However, widespread adoption has not really happened. This is because businesses that accept credit cards already have to comply with the PCI DSS under their contracts with credit card companies. If they violate the PCI DSS, they can be subject to large fines from those companies. Laws such as Nevada's do not protect businesses from fines from the credit card companies.

## Indiana: Limiting SSN Use and Disclosure

Some states have created laws protecting SSNs. These laws recognize that SSNs are highly sensitive pieces of information that can be very valuable to an identity thief. Thieves can use the number to easily establish new identities to commit identity theft crimes.

Indiana has laws designed to protect SSNs. For example, its laws forbid SSNs from appearing in public documents. It also has laws that forbid state agencies from disclosing a person's SSN to any other person or entity.

Since 2006, Indiana law has stated that county recorders' offices may not accept any document for recording that contains an SSN.[26] The only time that they can accept a

### The Importance of Legislative History

All laws have a **legislative history** that documents the number of times that a law is modified during the period from introduction to signing. It includes any materials generated in the course of creating legislation, committee reports and hearings, and transcripts of debate and reports issued by legislatures. The legislative history can be reviewed to help determine what a legislature intended when it created a law. The Nevada law requiring data collectors to follow PCI DSS went through many changes. You can read the law's legislative history at http://www.leg.state.nv.us/Session/75th2009/Reports/history.cfm?DocumentType=2&BillNo=227.

When Senate Bill 227 was first introduced, it contained no language requiring data collectors to follow PCI DSS. Instead, it required data collectors to use certain types of approved encryption technologies. After the bill was introduced, industry groups contacted the bill's author to express concerns about the bill. They opposed it because it was not technology neutral. You can read the letter submitted by industry groups at http://www.leg.state.nv.us/75th2009/Exhibits/Assembly/CMC/ACMC1140C.pdf.

After negotiation, the bill was amended to include the PCI language. Little information was included in the legislative history to indicate why the PCI language was added. A question that remains is whether the businesses that objected to the bill's original language are happy with the final law that requires PCI compliance.

document containing an SSN is when another law requires that the document contain an SSN. Some types of federal laws, such as releases of federal tax liens, require the use of an SSN.

**NOTE**

The Social Security Administration created the SSN in 1936 to track worker earnings. This was necessary to administer the Social Security program. The first person to receive Social Security benefits was Ernest Ackerman in January 1937. He received a one-time payout of 17 cents.

The state also was concerned that public records recorded before 2006 could contain SSNs and that identity thieves could use these documents to get SSNs. Since 2008, Indiana law states that county recorders cannot provide a recorded document to a member of the public unless they first search the document for SSNs. If they find a document with an SSN, they must redact it before allowing public inspection. It is a civil violation for a county recorder or any employee to disclose a recorded document containing an SSN without first searching the document for an SSN. The law does not cover disclosure of the last four digits of an SSN.



**FYI**

A county recorder's office keeps public records about certain types of transactions. These offices usually handle legal documents regarding real estate ownership. These documents are filed, or *recorded*, with a county recorder's office to give public notice of the transaction. Certain types of records also can be filed with a county recorder for future reference or safekeeping.

Indiana law also provides that a state agency may not disclose a person's SSN to anyone.[27] State agencies include an elected official's office and state educational institutions. However, there are limited exceptions to this law. A state agency is allowed to disclose an SSN if:

- A person gives explicit written consent for the disclosure of his or her SSN.
- The disclosure is required by state or federal law.
- The disclosure is required by a court order.

**NOTE**

One of the biggest differences between civil law and criminal law is punishment. In civil law, a defendant is not sent to jail as a punishment. Instead, civil law imposes fines. Civil law also requires a defendant to reimburse a plaintiff for damages. In criminal law, punishment usually involves fines or prison sentences, or both.

The law lists very specific penalties for an inappropriate disclosure of a person's SSN. The state agency is not responsible for these penalties. Instead, they are directed at the state agency employee who disclosed the SSN. For instance, a state agency employee who "knowingly, intentionally, or recklessly" discloses an SSN in violation of the law commits a Level 6 felony. This is a criminal sanction. In Indiana, a Level 6 felony can result in a prison term between 6 months and 2.5 years. In addition, a person can be fined up to $10,000.[28]

If a state agency employee negligently discloses an SSN, the person commits a Class A infraction. In Indiana, an infraction is a civil sanction that a person cannot be imprisoned for. However, he or she can receive a fine of up to $10,000.

Under the law, if a state agency impermissibly discloses an SSN, it must notify the affected person. It also must notify the state attorney general's office. Under the law, the state attorney general has the authority to investigate an improper disclosure of an SSN. The state attorney general also can make additional rules to carry out the nondisclosure law. Individuals do not have a private cause of action under the law. For example, they cannot sue a state agency for wrongfully disclosing an SSN.

Other states have laws designed to protect SSNs. Arizona law, for example, prohibits printing an SSN on government or private identification cards. This law also prohibits the transmission of a person's SSN over an unsecured internet connection.[29] California law forbids companies from requiring people to transmit an SSN over the internet unless the connection is secure or the SSN is encrypted.

## California: Protecting Consumer Privacy

California continues to be at the forefront of states that seek to protect the data of their citizens. In 2018, California enacted the California Consumer Privacy Act (CCPA).[30] The CCPA governs the protection of personal information that is collected by businesses, which must comply with the CCPA if they meet any of the following:

- Have gross annual revenues in excess of $25 million
- Buy, receive, or sell the personal information of 50,000 or more consumers, households, or devices
- Derive 50 percent or more of their annual revenues from selling consumers' personal information

If a business is covered by the CCPA, it must provide notice to consumers of their rights and how to exercise those rights before it collects data from the consumer. Consumers have the following rights under the CCPA:

- **The right to know**—A consumer has a right to know what personal information is collected, used, shared, and sold by the business.
- **The right to delete**—A consumer has the right to demand that a business delete the consumer's personal information.
- **The right to opt-out**—A consumer has the right to opt-out of the sale of his or her personal information or to tell the business to stop selling that information.
- **The right to nondiscrimination**—A consumer should not be subject to price or service discrimination when a consumer exercises a privacy right under CCPA.

**NOTE**

The individual rights included in the CCPA are similar to the individual rights guaranteed by the European Union General Data Protection Regulation (GDPR).

The California attorney general enforces the CCPA. The law allows for civil penalties of $2,500 for each violation or $7,500 for each intentional violation. Penalties can only be imposed after a business receives notice of the violation and has 30 days to correct the violation.

## Encryption Regulations

Some states require entities doing business within the state to follow basic information security practices to protect the security and privacy of data. Other states are more aggressive. They require entities to use specific security practices, such as encryption.

**FYI**

The Massachusetts Office of Consumer Affairs and Business Regulation held a public hearing on the data protection standards in January 2009. The hearing showed that businesses were worried about meeting the standards. You can read a transcript from the hearing and written comments at http://www.mass.gov/ocabr/docs/idtheft/201cmr17comments.pdf.

### Massachusetts: Protecting Personal Information

Massachusetts has created some of the nation's most rigorous data protection laws. For example, it created its breach notification law in 2007.[31] That law also required the state's consumer affairs department to issue standards for the protection of personal information. The law stated that the standards should:

- Protect the security and confidentiality of personal information consistent with industry standards.
- Protect against anticipated threats to the security or integrity of personal information.
- Protect against unauthorized access to or use of personal information that could harm a person.

The Massachusetts "Standards for the Protection of Personal Information of Residents of the Commonwealth" was released in September 2008 and went into effect in 2010. The law has very broad application.[32] Any person that uses and stores personal information about

Massachusetts residents as part of the sale of goods and services must comply with it. However, the law does not apply to state agencies.

Entities subject to the law must follow data protection standards to safeguard the personal information of Massachusetts residents. These entities must protect personal information in both electronic and paper form. The definition of personal information is similar to the definitions used in the breach notification laws discussed at the beginning of this chapter. Under the data protection standard, personal information is a person's first and last name, or first initial and last name, and any of the following:

- SSN
- Driver's license number or state identification card number
- Financial account number, or credit or debit card number, with or without password or PIN

**NOTE**

The GLBA is a law that requires entities engaged in certain kinds of financial transactions to follow privacy and information security rules. These rules are designed to protect customers' personal information.

The standard requires entities to create an information security program. It states that an entity's information security program must be a good fit for its size and scope. It also must fit the entity's type of business. It must describe the administrative, technical, and physical controls that protect the personal information used by the entity. The program requirements are similar to those stated in the GLBA Safeguards Rule.

The standard uses a risk-based approach to information security. It allows the entity to review its resources and data use. It also can review its needs for security and confidentiality. The entity can use the results of this review to determine the safeguards it should use. As part of its program, an entity must:

- Assign an employee to manage the program.
- Conduct a risk assessment to identify risks to the security, confidentiality, and integrity of information. Review current safeguards to make sure that they are effective.
- Develop policies for use of personal information off business premises.
- Develop disciplinary policies for failure to follow the information security program.
- Develop policies to keep terminated employees from accessing personal information.
- Select service providers and make sure that any contract includes terms to protect personal information.
- Develop policies to physically safeguard personal information.
- Monitor and review the program to make sure it is effective.
- Document actions taken in response to any security breach.[33]

The standard also includes computer system security requirements. This part of the standard directs entities to implement the security requirements. They must do this as long as the requirements are technically feasible. An entity does not have to apply requirements that are not technically feasible.[34]

The standard states that an information security program must include specific security requirements. They are:

- Secure user authentication
- Secure access control measures

- Encryption of all transmitted personal information that travels across public networks, and encryption of information to be transmitted wirelessly
- Reasonable monitoring of systems
- Encryption of all personal information stored on laptops or portable devices
- Up-to-date firewall protection and operating system security patches on computers containing personal information
- Virus and malware protection
- Security awareness and training activities

**NOTE**

Under the standard, "technically feasible" means that if there is a reasonable way to accomplish a required technology result, then an entity must do so.

**FYI**

Massachusetts has released a video about its data protection laws. You can view the video at https://www.youtube.com/watch?v=ETYwkTpeXHI.

The encryption requirements have received a lot of attention. They require businesses to encrypt the personal information of Massachusetts residents while it is stored on their systems. They also must encrypt it when it is transmitted. The standard does not define a preferred method of encryption. Instead, encryption is defined in a technology-neutral way. Under the standard, encryption is changing data into an unreadable form. The encrypted data cannot be read or understood without an encryption key, which is used to encrypt and decrypt data.

The Massachusetts attorney general has the authority to enforce the data protection standard. The law allows civil penalties of up to $5,000 for each violation. The attorney general can also make an entity pay for the costs of an investigation into any violations. Entities can also be charged attorneys' fees.[35]

The Massachusetts data protection standard is unique. It attempts to regulate businesses outside of Massachusetts by requiring businesses to encrypt the personal data of Massachusetts residents. This may be hard because businesses typically must follow only the laws of the state where they are located. Under the law, this is a jurisdiction issue. Only revisions to the standard, or a court case, will help clarify how widely the state may enforce this standard.

**NOTE**

Although the Massachusetts data protection standards do not define a preferred method of encryption, the Massachusetts breach notification law does. Under the state's breach notification law, encryption is defined as a transformation of data through the use of a 128-bit or higher algorithmic process. The process must change into a form that is unreadable without the use of a key.[37]

## Nevada Law: Standards-Based Encryption

Nevada law also has data encryption requirements. The Nevada law requires data collectors to use encryption if they are transmitting personal information outside of their business network. They must encrypt the data if it is sent externally via email or any other electronic transmission. This requirement helps protect data while it is being transferred from one entity to another. The Nevada law excludes facsimiles from the transmission encryption requirements.[36]

The law also requires data collectors to encrypt personal information on any data storage device that is moved beyond the technical or physical controls of their business. This means that they must encrypt any storage device that leaves the business location. They also must encrypt backup tapes containing personal information that they send to an off-site storage facility. This portion of the law helps protect data if the storage media is lost or stolen.

The encryption rule is novel because of its breadth. It covers data when it is stored and when it is transmitted. The law is also interesting because of how it defines encryption. This is one area where the Nevada law varies greatly from the Massachusetts encryption law. The Massachusetts law defines encryption in a technology-neutral way. It does not reference any industry standards. The Nevada law, however, references industry standards.

Under the Nevada law, data collectors must use encryption technologies adopted by a standards-setting body. The law references the Federal Information Processing Standards, which are issued by the National Institute of Standards and Technology (NIST). Under the law, the technology used must make the personal information unreadable.[38]

> **NOTE**
> Nevada law defines data storage devices as computers, cell phones, and external computer hard drives. It also includes backup storage media.

> **NOTE**
> You can read the Federal Information Processing Standards at http://csrc.nist.gov/publications/PubsFIPS.html.

The law also requires that data collectors use good cryptographic key management practices to protect encryption keys. Encryption keys encrypt and decrypt data. They must be carefully guarded. These keys protect the confidentiality of data. They also protect the integrity of the whole encryption process. The law requires data collectors to use key management practices created by a standards setting body. Again, the law specifically refers to NIST standards.[39]

A data collector that complies with the law is not liable for damages resulting from a security breach. This protection extends to a breach so long as the data collector's own gross negligence did not cause the breach.

## Data Disposal Regulations

As of January 2019, at least 35 states and Puerto Rico have created data disposal laws.[40] They have created these laws to make sure that personal information is properly disposed of. Personal data must be protected throughout its life cycle. This includes disposing of the information in an appropriate way.

### Washington: Everyone Has an Obligation

Washington State created its personal data disposal law in 2002.[41] In creating the law, the state legislature made comments about how important the law was. It said that:

- Careless disposal of personal information causes a significant risk of identity theft.
- Improper disposal threatens a person's privacy and financial security.
- Everyone in the state has a duty to dispose properly of personal information.[42]

The Washington disposal law applies to any person or entity in the state. It requires an entity to take reasonable steps to destroy records that contain health and financial data when it determines that it no longer needs those records.

**NOTE**

The only entity specifically excluded by the Washington law is the federal government. The law also states that entities that comply with the GLBA Safeguards Rule or HIPAA Security and Privacy Rules are considered compliant with the state law.

The law requires entities to properly destroy information held in their records. *Records* are defined as any material—paper or electronic—that holds information. Entities must make sure that they destroy any personal financial or health information in their records. Personal financial and health information is data that identifies a person and is commonly used for financial or healthcare reasons.

The law states that an entity must destroy information in records so that it is no longer readable or decipherable. The law also states that proper destruction includes shredding, erasing, or modifying records so that they are no longer readable.[43]

The Washington law allows a person harmed by a violation of the law to sue the entity that violated it. The law provides the plaintiff with several remedies that vary depending on the type of violation. If the entity's failure to comply with the law was because of negligence, a court may award a penalty of $200 or actual damages. The court must award a plaintiff whichever amount is greater.

If an entity's failure to comply with the law was intentional, then the court can award a penalty of $600 or actual damages. Again, the court must award whichever amount is greater. The law also allows the court to award "treble" (triple) damages, which are three times the amount of the actual damages incurred. The law states that treble damages may not be more than $10,000.[44]

**NOTE**

*Treble damages* are damages that punish a defendant for intentional conduct.

The law also allows the state attorney general to prosecute an entity that violates the law. In that instance, a court must award damages the same way that it awards damages to an individual plaintiff. The court may also grant injunctive relief. This means that it can order the entity to stop violating the law.



## New York: Any Physical Record

On the other side of the country, New York State also has a data disposal law.[45] Its law states that no person or business may dispose of a record containing "personal identifying information" without shredding, destroying, or modifying it so that the information is no longer readable. The law requires that any person or business destroying the records must take action that is consistent with commonly accepted industry practices. They must use these practices to make sure that no unauthorized person has access to information in the record.

Under the New York law, *records* are any information held in any physical form, either paper or electronic. They include reports, letters, and computer tapes. Any type of data storage medium is a record. Personal identifying information is information in a record that identifies a person by name and includes any of the following:

- SSN
- Driver's license number or identification card number
- Mother's maiden name, financial account numbers or code, or any other identification number

### Confidential Documents Used as Confetti

If you are a Yankees fan, 2009 was a very good year. It was their first World Series win since 2000. They celebrated their 27th World Series win with a ticker tape parade in New York City on November 4, 2009.

The term *ticker tape parade* originated in New York City. These parades are rare now, because real ticker tape has not been used since the 1960s. They are traditionally reserved for large celebrations, such as sports victories.

The 2009 parade for the Yankees was the first ticker tape parade in New York City since the Giants won the Super Bowl in 2008. Sports fans were very excited. When they ran out of confetti, they dumped any type of paper that they could find from skyscraper windows. This included documents containing personal information. News media reported that after the parade, law firm memos, banking records, and court files were recovered from the debris in the street.

One financial firm had to discipline an employee who threw documents marked for destruction instead of confetti. These documents contained financial information and SSNs.

**NOTE**

The New York law specifically excludes state agencies.

The law allows for penalties of up to $5,000 for improper disposal. The attorney general alone has the authority to pursue violations of the law. There is no private cause of action.

## Case Studies and Examples

**NOTE**

The U.S. Department of Veterans Affairs is also called the Veterans Administration (VA).

The following case highlights unclear federal policies about data breach notification. At the time of this incident, federal law did not require agencies to have breach notification policies. In fact, there is still no federal law that requires this. However, because of this incident, most federal agencies have implemented internal breach notification policies.

In 2006, an employee of the U.S. Department of Veterans Affairs (VA) took home a laptop computer and external hard drive. The hard drive held the personal information of every veteran discharged since 1975. It was not encrypted. On May 3, 2006, the employee's home was burglarized. Thieves stole the laptop and hard drive. The local police department investigated the burglary.

The employee immediately informed his supervisors about the theft, but they did not take the matter seriously. The secretary of the VA did not learn about it until almost 2 weeks later. The VA secretary then notified the Federal Bureau of Investigations (FBI) about the theft. The FBI began to investigate the theft with the local police department.

The VA issued a statement reporting the facts about the theft on May 22, 2006. It also said that the data stolen included names, SSNs, and dates of birth for 26.5 million veterans, as well as data on some of their spouses. At the time, the VA reported that the hard drive did not contain any health or financial information.

Congress was outraged that the VA waited so long to make a public statement. On May 25, 2006, the secretary of the VA appeared at hearings before the U.S. House and Senate to discuss the issue. In his Senate testimony, he stated that he was furious that he was not notified in a timely manner. He also stated that the VA was planning to notify all people affected by the theft. He said that it would take time to prepare the mailing because the VA had to verify addresses. He also said that 26 million envelopes "were not immediately available." The VA began mailing the notification letters on June 9, 2006.

As it carried out its investigation, the VA learned that the hard drive held some health information for 2.6 million people. It also learned that the hard drive contained the personal information of active-duty military personnel. On June 6, 2006, the VA reported that the hard drive held the data of 1.1 million active-duty troops. It also had information on 430,000 members of the National Guard and 645,000 members of the Reserves.

The police recovered the stolen laptop and hard drive in late June 2006. The FBI reported that a forensic review of the equipment showed that the database containing the personal information had not been accessed. In August 2006, the VA mailed a follow-up letter to people affected by the event.

The VA Inspector General investigated the incident and found that the VA employee was not permitted to take the laptop or hard drive home. The report faulted the employee for using poor judgment in taking the data home. It also faulted the employee for not properly protecting it. The report also criticized VA supervisors for not taking initial reports about the data loss seriously.

In January 2009, the VA agreed to pay $20 million to veterans whose information was potentially exposed in the incident. It paid this amount to settle lawsuits brought by five veterans groups. The money was used to create a compensation fund. Veterans who wished to make a claim against the fund needed to file claims by November 27, 2009.

Congress created the Veterans Affairs Information Security Act of 2006 in response to the breach. The law requires the VA to create a comprehensive information security program. It also requires it to create breach notification regulations. The VA issued those regulations in April 2008. They require the VA to notify people in the event of a security breach if there is a reasonable risk for the potential misuse of their personal information.[46]

**NOTE**

The U.S. Government Accountability Office released a report on lessons learned from the 2006 VA incident. You can read the report at http://www.gao.gov/new.items/d07657.pdf.

## CHAPTER SUMMARY

This chapter reviewed state laws that protect data. States have been very active in trying to protect the personal data of their residents. They have created many different laws to protect the security and privacy of this information because there is no one comprehensive federal data privacy or security law. When reviewing state laws that protect certain types of data, it is important for you to think about what other state or federal laws might also protect the data.

## KEY CONCEPTS AND TERMS

Breach notification law
Legislative history
Safe harbor

## CHAPTER 9 ASSESSMENT

1. The ChoicePoint data breach was the triggering event that caused many states to create data protection laws.
   A. True
   B. False

2. California's breach notification law went into effect in ______.

3. Most states define personal information as *name* plus which of the following elements?
   A. Date of birth
   B. Address
   C. Phone number
   D. Social Security number
   E. None of these is correct.

4. An encryption safe harbor is ______.

5. What is a state breach notification law?
   A. A law that requires that residents be notified if a dam breaks
   B. A law that requires that residents be notified if a business has a security breach that compromises their personal data
   C. A law that requires that residents be notified if a business has a security breach that compromises the business's confidential data
   D. A law that requires that businesses be notified if a government has a security breach that compromises the business's confidential data
   E. None of these is correct.

6. Which types of entities are sometimes excluded from breach notification laws?
   A. GLBA financial institutions
   B. HIPAA-covered entities
   C. Out-of-state businesses
   D. GLBA financial institutions and HIPAA-covered entities
   E. GLBA financial institutions, HIPAA-covered entities, and out-of-state businesses

7. What is *not* a business day?
   A. An official workday
   B. A day of the week that includes Monday through Friday
   C. Memorial Day
   D. Tuesday
   E. None of these is correct.

8. "Clear and conspicuous" notice means that ______.

9. Which states allow data breach notification to be given by telephone?
   A. California
   B. Colorado
   C. North Carolina
   D. California and Colorado
   E. Colorado and North Carolina

10. What technology standards are permitted under the Nevada encryption law?
    A. PCI DSS
    B. SO 1799
    C. NIST
    D. FTC
    E. HIPAA

11. Which states have required businesses to follow all, or part, of the PCI DSS?
    A. Minnesota
    B. Nevada
    C. California
    D. Minnesota and Nevada
    E. Minnesota and California

12. A private cause of action is ______.

13. If the U.S. Congress creates a federal breach notification law, what happens to state laws?
    A. They are no longer valid.
    B. They are still valid as long as they are stricter than federal law.
    C. They are still valid in their original form.
    D. They are still valid as long as they are weaker than federal law.
    E. None of these is correct.

14. What is the purpose of legislative history?
    A. To help determine which laws to abolish
    B. To help decide how to create new laws
    C. To help determine how old a law is
    D. To help determine what a legislature intended when it created a law
    E. None of these is correct.

15. What is one of the biggest differences between civil and criminal law?
    A. The amount of fines
    B. Whether a person can be sentenced to prison
    C. How long the offense stays on your criminal record
    D. The type of judge that hears the case
    E. The color of the prison jumpsuits

## ENDNOTES


1. CNET, "ChoicePoint Data Theft Widens to 145,000 People," February 18, 2005. https://www.cnet.com/news/choicepoint-data-theft-widens-to-145000-people/ (accessed April 27, 2020).
2. PC World, "ChoicePoint Details Data Breach Lessons," June 11, 2007. https://www.pcworld.com/article/132795/article.html (accessed April 27, 2020).
3. Federal Trade Commission, "ChoicePoint Settles Data Security Breach Charges; to Pay $10 Million in Civil Penalties, $5 Million for Consumer Redress," January 26, 2006. https://www.ftc.gov/news-events/press-releases/2006/01/choicepoint-settles-data-security-breach-charges-pay-10-million (accessed April 27, 2020).
4. InfoWorld, "States Settle With ChoicePoint Over 2004 Breach," May 31, 2007. https://www.infoworld.com/article/2662493/states-settle-with-choicepoint-over-2004-breach.html (accessed April 27, 2020).
5. Federal Trade Commission, "Consumer Data Broker ChoicePoint Failed to Protect Consumers' Personal Data, Left Key Electronic Monitoring Tool Turned Off for Four Months," October 19, 2009. https://www.ftc.gov/news-events/press-releases/2009/10/consumer-data-broker-choicepoint-failed-protect-consumers (accessed April 27, 2020).
6. California Civil Code, sec. 1798.29, and sec. 1798.82.
7. California Civil Code, sec. 1798.29, and sec. 1798.82.
8. California Civil Code, sec. 1798.84.
9. National Conference of State Legislatures, "Security Breach Notification Laws," March 8, 2020. https://www.ncsl.org/research/telecommunications-and-information-technology/security-breach-notification-laws.aspx (accessed April 27, 2020).
10. Ohio Revised Code, sec. 1347.12.
11. Ohio Revised Code, sec. 1347.12, and sec. 1349.19.
12. Florida Statutes, sec. 817.5681.
13. Maine Revised Statutes, Title 10, sec. 1348.
14. North Carolina General Statutes, sec. 75-65.
15. Colorado Revised Statutes, sec. 6-1-716.
16. Massachusetts Gen. Laws ch. 93H, sec. 1- 6.
17. Indiana Code, sec. 24-4.9-2-4.
18. Texas Business and Commercial Code Annotated, sec. 521.151.
19. Florida Statutes, sec. 817.5681.
20. Indiana Code, sec. 24-4.9-4-2.
21. Minnesota Statutes, sec. 325E.64.
22. Minnesota Statutes, sec. 325E.64.
23. Nevada Revised Statutes, sec. 603A.215.
24. Washington Revised Code, sec. 19.255.020.
25. Nevada Revised Statutes, sec. 603A.040.
26. Indiana Code, sec. 36-2-7.5-4.
27. Indiana Code, sec. 4-1-10-3(b).
28. Indiana Code, sec. 35-50-2-7.
29. Arizona Revised Statutes, sec. 44-1373.
30. California Civil Code Title 1.81.5, sec. 1798.100-1798.199.
31. Massachusetts General Law, chapter 93H, sec. 2.
32. Code of Massachusetts Regulations, Title 201, sec. 17.01-17.05.
33. Code of Massachusetts Regulations, Title 201, sec. 17.03.
34. Code of Massachusetts Regulations, Title 201, sec. 17.04.
35. Massachusetts General Law, chapter 93A, sec. 4.
36. Nevada Revised Statutes, sec. 603A.215.
37. Massachusetts General Law, chapter 93H, sec. 1.
38. Nevada Revised Statutes, sec. 603A.215.
39. Nevada Revised Statutes, sec. 603A.215.
40. National Conference of State Legislatures, "Data Disposal Laws," January 4, 2020. https://www.ncsl.org/research/telecommunications-and-information-technology/data-disposal-laws.aspx (accessed April 27, 2020).

41. Revised Code of Washington, Title 19, sec. 19.215.005 to 19.215.030.
42. Revised Code of Washington, Title 19, sec. 19.215.005.
43. Revised Code of Washington, Title 19, sec. 19.215.010.
44. Revised Code of Washington, Title 19, sec. 19.215.020.
45. New York's General Business Law, sec. 399-H.
46. Department of Veterans Affairs, Data Breach Fine Rule, Code of Federal Regulations, Title 38, sec. 75.117.

CHAPTER 10

# Intellectual Property Law

INTELLECTUAL PROPERTY (IP) is the area of law that protects a person's creative ideas, inventions, and innovations. It protects people's ownership rights in their creative ideas, gives them the right to control the use of their creative ideas, and protects their ability to profit from those ideas. It also prevents other people from exploiting a person's creative ideas.

IP protection in the United States has a long history. In fact, the U.S. Constitution recognizes the importance of protecting IP. This chapter reviews the major ways you can protect IP. It also reviews the role of information technology in IP issues.

## Chapter 10 Topics

This chapter covers the following topics and concepts:

- Why intellectual property law is important
- What the concept of legal ownership is
- What the basics of patent protection are
- What the basics of trademark protection are
- What the basics of copyright protection are
- What the basics of the Digital Millennium Copyright Act (DMCA) are
- What some case studies and examples are

## Chapter 10 Goals

When you complete this chapter, you will be able to:

- Describe the importance of intellectual property law
- Explain the basic concept of legal ownership
- Explain how patents are used and what they protect
- Explain how trademarks are used and what they protect

- Explain how copyrights are used and what they protect
- Describe intellectual property concerns with respect to internet use
- Describe the Digital Millennium Copyright Act (DMCA) and what it protects

## The Digital Wild West and the Importance of Intellectual Property Law

It is hard to know who coined the term *Digital Wild West*. It is clear, however, that the term is a good description for the state of the World Wide Web (WWW, or "web") today. Similar to the American "Wild West" in the latter half of the 19th century, the web still has a frontier. Its outer limits are unknown.

The web and our use of it are still changing and evolving. More people are accessing the internet and using the web than ever before. World internet usage grew over 1,167 percent between the years 2000 and 2020.[1] Many different devices can access the internet, which has led to a new term, the **Internet of Things (IoT)**. The IoT refers generally to the devices that collect and share data over the internet. Cell phones, smartphones, netbooks, and televisions all access the internet, as do healthcare devices, fitness trackers, home automation systems, and even appliances! People (and devices) can access the internet and web anytime, and from anywhere.

**NOTE**

The World Wide Web is a system of linked hypertext documents and other media that are connected through the internet. Even though we refer to them as one and the same, the internet and the World Wide Web are not the same. The internet is the infrastructure, whereas the web resides on the infrastructure.

We are still exploring how to use the web. Organizations are learning how to effectively and efficiently conduct business online, although some businesses already conduct all of their commerce online. People are joining social networking groups and taking many aspects of their lives "online." Many people share novel ideas and champion social causes online. Art and inventions are shared online as well.

One traditional area of law that is adapting to new issues raised through technology is intellectual property (IP) law. **Intellectual property (IP)** is the area of law that protects a person's creative ideas, inventions, and innovations once they are in a physical form. When materials are published on the web, they are in a physical form. Traditional legal concepts about IP ownership and how to protect it are applied to content on the World Wide Web.

## Legal Ownership and the Importance of Protecting Intellectual Property

A legal owner of property has the right to use it in any way he or she wants to, and the power to give those rights to another. This is a *property interest*. It means that the owner has certain rights to property, and a court will enforce those rights if necessary. There are several different types of property ownership:

- **Real property interest**—This type of property interest means that a person owns land or buildings.
- **Personal property interest**—This type of property interest means that a person owns physical possessions such as cars, books, and silverware.
- **IP interest**—This type of property interest means that a person owns some sort of creation. Creations include items such as art, designs, images, and inventions.

Corporations and businesses also can own property. So can governments. In the context of property law, a *person* is a real person or other legal entity. Legal entities include corporations, businesses, private organizations, and governments.

Owners of property can control how it is used. Ownership is an important concept for IP because an IP owner has certain exclusive rights. An owner, the person who created new works or inventions, is the only one who has these rights. Courts will enforce these rights, and can punish people who violate these rights.

The federal government determines many IP law rules in the United States. The U.S. Constitution specifically grants the power to do this. The Constitution grants Congress the power to "promote the progress of science and useful arts, by securing for limited times to authors and inventors the exclusive right to their respective writings and discoveries."[2] The drafters of the Constitution wanted to encourage innovation and discovery. To do this, they specifically said that authors and inventors must have the exclusive right to control their creations and inventions for a certain period.

The exclusive right to control how creations and inventions are used is the main purpose of IP law. Creators have a right to control how their creations are used for a certain period of time depending upon the underlying nature of the creation. Different laws protect inventions and literary works for different periods.

During the protected period, the creator or author of a work or invention is the only person who can use or reproduce it. This allows authors and inventors to profit from their creative efforts. People would not be encouraged to write new books or create new inventions if they did not have an opportunity to profit from their efforts. IP law protects these efforts. It also encourages them to continue to create. Ultimately, this helps the economy.

The federal law recognizes the following types of IP:

- **Patents**—Used to protect inventions such as machines, processes, designs, and specialized plants.
- **Trademarks**—Used to protect words, logos, symbols, or slogans that identify a product or service.
- **Copyrights**—Used to protect books, art, music, videos, computer programs, and other creative works.

Trademarks have the longest protection period. They are protected as long as an owner continues to use it in commerce.

Each type of IP right is demonstrated in a different way. Each applies to different types of creations and inventions. They give protection for different lengths of times. They also have different requirements for establishing and enforcing IP rights.

**NOTE**

The National Inventors Hall of Fame and Museum is located at the USPTO in Alexandria, Virginia.

## Patents

A **patent** is an IP right granted by the federal government. The U.S. Patent and Trademark Office (USPTO) grants patents. The USPTO is an agency located in the Department of Commerce.

**FYI**

Congress enacted the most recent version of U.S. patent law in the Patent Act of 1952.[3] Congress has amended this law several times. The most recent amendment to U.S. patent law was in 2011. In 2011, the America Invents Act (AIA)[4] introduced significant changes to U.S. patent law. Before March 2013, the United States followed a "first to invent" rule. This meant that the first person to invent something and show that it works could patent it. This rule had been in effect for more than 200 years.

The AIA drastically changed this rule. Starting in March 2013, the U.S. adopted a "first to file" system. This means that the first person to file for a patent has priority over all other people who have a similar idea. The change in the filing rules is meant to encourage inventors to patent their ideas sooner. It is intended to encourage innovation. It also aligns the United States with other countries, most of which follow "first to file" rules.

Patents are granted to encourage new and useful inventions. Patent owners have the right to keep others from making or using the patented invention. They also have the power to stop others from selling their invention. There are three basic types of patents:

**NOTE**

The USPTO granted 370,434 patents in 2019. Most of those patents were utility patents.[5]

- Utility patents
- Plant patents
- Design patents

**Utility patents**, which are issued for inventions and discoveries, are the most common type of patents. There are four main categories of utility patents:

- Machines
- Manufactured products
- Processes
- Compositions of matter

Improvements on any of the items in the previous list can also be patented. Utility patents are granted for a 20-year term that begins running on the date that the patent is granted.

Under patent law, a *machine* is an instrument or tool that completes a task by using moving parts. These parts interact with each other to accomplish a function. Machines are things such as lawnmowers, elevators, and automatic can openers. Devices that work because of an electrical process, such as computers, also fall into this category.

**NOTE**

A manufactured product is called *an article of manufacture* in patent law.

*Manufactured products* are products without moving parts. A milk carton is an example of a manufactured product. Although a manufactured product may have moving parts, the moving parts do not act together to accomplish a task. A folding table, even though it has moving parts, is a manufactured product. It is not a machine.

A *process*, also called a method, is a way of completing a task through a series of steps or actions. A process can be patented as a utility patent. A recipe might be patentable as a process, and some types of computer software may be patentable as processes as well.

A *composition of matter* is a chemical compound consisting of two or more substances combined to make something new. Manufacturers patent new drugs under this subcategory of utility patents. Naturally occurring chemical compounds are not patentable. For instance, the air is not patentable.

The second type of patent is plant patents. **Plant patents** are granted to an inventor who invents or discovers a new variety of plant. However, the inventor must prove that he or she can asexually reproduce the new plant. Asexual reproduction means that the plant is reproduced through cutting or grafting. Plants that grow from seeds do not reproduce asexually. Also, plants that are found in nature are not patentable. A plant patent can protect special kinds of hybridized plants or food crops. Plant patents, once granted, last for 20 years.

The last type of patent is design patents. **Design patents** are granted for new and original ornamental designs for manufactured objects. A design is apparent in appearance. They are used to protect the visual appearance of an object. For example, a design patent could protect the design for china or silverware. A design must be new and different from other designs to be patentable in this way. Design patents are granted for 14 years.

A design patent is different from a utility patent. Design patents protect only the appearance of an article, whereas a utility patent protects how the article works. Unless otherwise noted, this chapter discusses utility patents.

## Patent Basics

Inventions or discoveries must be *patentable* in order to be protected. To be patentable, they must meet certain requirements. An inventor must meet all of the requirements in a patent application.

### *Patent Requirements*

To be patentable, an invention or discovery must be:

- Novel
- Useful
- Non-obvious

To be patentable, an invention or discovery must be novel.[6] This means that it must be a new invention or discovery. The USPTO will not issue a patent for an item that is not new. To be considered new, an invention must be different from the **prior art**, or public knowledge about an invention that existed before the date upon which a patent application is filed. An invention or discovery must include elements that make it different from the prior art. An invention or discovery that merely contains prior art is not new and is not patentable.

The USPTO also looks at whether the invention was used in the United States or other countries before the date of the patent application. It also reviews whether the invention

**NOTE**

A different federal law governs plants that grow from seeds. The Plant Variety Protection Act of 1970 protects these types of plants.[7]

**NOTE**

In order to be patentable, the subject matter of an invention or discovery also must be patentable. The U.S. Supreme Court held in *Diamond v. Chakrabarty* (1980) that patentable subject matter is "anything under the sun that is made by man."[8] Some types of items are not patentable—including objects found in nature.

**NOTE**

Under the laws of many countries, if an inventor announces or sells an invention to the public before it is patented, it automatically becomes not patentable. The United States modifies this very strict rule with a limited 1-year grace period.

was patented or published in other countries. If people know about the invention or discovery in other places, then it is not new.

U.S. patent law does allow a limited exception to this general rule. It allows a 1-year grace period for inventions made available to the public,[9] which means that an inventor must file for a patent within 1 year of announcing the invention to the public. In some cases, an inventor may want to announce an invention or discovery before applying for a patent. Inventors do this to see if there is commercial interest in the invention. An invention or discovery is still patentable in the United States if the inventor files a patent application within 1 year of announcing it. The USPTO will not consider a patent application if it is submitted more than 1 year after the invention is announced.

Taking advantage of the 1-year grace period can be risky for an inventor because another person might see the invention and build upon it. If that person files for a patent before the first inventor, then the first inventor might lose the ability to patent his or her invention. This is because, in the United States, the first person to file for a patent has priority over all patents that claim a similar invention. In this example, the second inventor's patent application contains material that is considered prior art when the first inventor files his or her patent application later. The rules for determining priority in a patent application are very tricky, which is why many inventors hire attorneys to help them navigate the patent process.

The second patentability requirement is that an invention or discovery be useful.[10] This requirement is also called *utility*. An inventor can meet this requirement by showing that the invention or discovery is beneficial to society. The inventor also must show that the invention actually works. The USPTO may reject patent applications that do not show that an invention or discovery is useful. It also can reject patent applications where the claimed usefulness seems implausible.

The final patentability requirement is that the invention or discovery must be non-obvious.[11] This requirement is closely related to the "novelty" requirement. If an invention or discovery is not obvious, then it is patentable. Obvious inventions or discoveries are not patentable.

**FYI**

Judge Learned Hand was a U.S. federal court judge who served for the U.S. District Court for the Southern District of New York. He also served as a judge on the Second Circuit Court of Appeals. Courts and attorneys often quote his opinions on patent and copyright law. Judge Hand wrote very clearly on a complicated topic.

### How Do You Protect Inventions Internationally?

In the United States, inventors register their patents with the USPTO. However, the USPTO patent rights apply only to the United States. They do not protect patents in foreign countries. If a person or business wishes to protect an invention in other countries, a foreign patent is needed.

Different countries have very different patent laws. Because countries have different patent laws, they enter into international treaties to try to put all inventors on an even playing field for protecting their inventions internationally.

The Paris Convention for the Protection of Industrial Property (1883) was the first treaty to try to address patents on an international level. This treaty is important because it fixes the filing date of patent applications to the date that the inventor first files a patent application in his or her home country.

The Paris Convention says that someone who files for a patent in his or her home country can use that filing date with other member nations to establish his or her patent's priority in those nations. This protects an inventor's "place in line" in other countries. This priority right is available for only 12 months after the very first patent application. If an inventor wants to protect an invention in other countries, he or she must file patent applications in those countries within 12 months of first filing for a patent in the home country. Inventors who do not file within 12 months lose their place in line for determining patent ownership.

The United States joined the Paris Convention in 1887. The Paris Convention establishes only the priority filing date. It does not confer other benefits to member nations. Inventors still must follow all the other provisions of patent laws in other countries to protect their inventions internationally. It can be a very long and expensive process to file multiple patent applications within 1 year. The Patent Cooperation Treaty of 1970 (PCT) attempts to streamline the application process. The World Intellectual Property Organization (WIPO), which is part of the United Nations, administers the PCT.

The PCT was created to make international protection of patents easier by allowing an inventor to file for patent protection simultaneously in several member countries. The PCT allows inventors to file one international patent application. Inventors submit the international patent application to their national patent office or to the WIPO in some situations. This application then has the same effect as filing for a patent in member countries. The filing date for the international application is fixed in priority as soon as the application is submitted.

Under the PCT process, an international patent application is subject to an international search. Examiners review the published documents in all member countries to see if there is any information that might affect the patentability of the invention. The search is very comprehensive.

The PCT gives other benefits as well. Under the PCT, inventors have up to 18 months after they submit their international patent applications to decide whether they will pursue patents in other countries that are PCT members. If they do, the patent process is shortened because other countries will rely on the results of the international search in conducting their review of the patent application. In addition, the inventor is guaranteed patent protection as of the date of the original international application. This is important because many foreign countries grant patent protection only to the first inventor who files for a patent application.

The United States joined the PCT in 1978. More than 150 countries have signed the treaty. You can read more at https://www.wipo.int/pct/en/.

Sometimes this requirement is hard to understand. Many inventions or discoveries seem obvious once they are publicly announced or offered for sale. People often say, "Why did I not think of that?" when they see these types of products. Courts have recognized that an invention that seems obvious after it is created may meet the non-obvious requirement. That is the nature of some types of

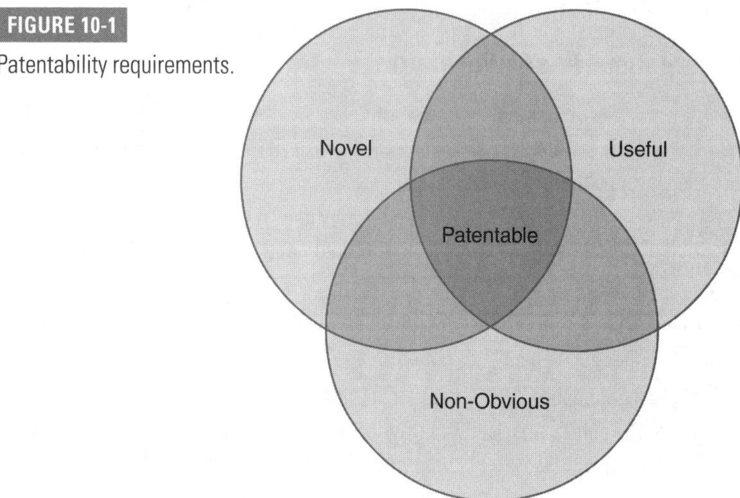


**FIGURE 10-1**
Patentability requirements.

inventions. Judge Learned Hand even said, "It certainly cannot be necessary to repeat the well-known principle that it is no indication of noninvention that the device should seem so obvious after it is discovered."[12]

The USPTO looks at prior art and how an invention is used to determine if it is non-obvious. An invention is non-obvious if a person with ordinary skill in the kind of technology used in the invention would not have discovered or invented it. The invention also must be sufficiently different from the prior art. It is important to remember that the USPTO reviews these elements based on the date of the inventor's patent application.

**FIGURE 10-1** shows how the three patentability requirements work together.

## The Patent Application Process

An inventor must submit a patent application to the USPTO to patent an invention or discovery. **Patent prosecution** refers to the actions the USPTO must complete in order to grant a patent. In March 2020, it took the USPTO almost 23 months to prosecute a patent application.[13] This is the period from submitting a patent application to receiving a decision on it.

A patent application contains the following basic parts:

- **Specification**—The written technical description of the invention. The specification also contains information about how to make and use the invention. The specification must include enough information that a person with ordinary skill in the relevant area could make the invention based on the specification.
- **Drawings**—The pictorial description of the invention. The drawings must completely describe the invention or discovery. They help the USPTO understand the invention or discovery.
- **Oath**—The inventor must sign an oath that he or she is the first inventor of the item described in the patent application.
- **Filing fees**—There are different filing fees based upon the type of patent. There are also additional fees for large patent applications, search fees, and examination fees.

A patent application specification must include at least one claim. A "claim" defines the part of the invention that is to be protected by the patent. A patent specification may have several different claims.

Once the USPTO receives a patent application, it reviews it to make sure that it meets the patentability requirements. Patent Office *examiners* conduct this review. An examiner is a USPTO employee with special skills. U.S. law requires patent examiners to have sufficient "legal knowledge and scientific ability" to conduct this review.[14] After review, an examiner either rejects the application or issues a patent.

An inventor must pay patent maintenance fees once the USPTO issues a patent. This keeps the patent in force. If an inventor does not maintain a patent, then other people can take advantage of it. Patent maintenance fees are due at 3.5, 7.5, and 11.5 years after the original patent issue date.

 **NOTE**

USPTO employees are not allowed to apply for patents of their own. See U.S. Code, Vol. 35, sec. 4.

 **NOTE**

The USPTO has a strong preference for patent applications to be electronically submitted. Applications that are submitted on paper require an additional processing fee.

## Infringement and Remedies

When an inventor receives a patent for an invention or discovery, he or she has the exclusive right to keep others from using that invention. The inventor is the only one who can make, sell, or use it. This protection begins when the patent is issued and lasts for as long as the patent is valid. The federal government does not enforce patents. Instead, inventors must enforce their own rights. They must sue people who violate their patent rights, as well as people who make, use, or sell the patented invention during the patent period. They also may sue a person who makes, uses, or sells a substantially similar product.

A person who violates the IP rights of another is called an *infringer*. It does not matter if the infringer intended to violate the inventor's patent. An inventor can hold an infringer liable for violating a patent even if the infringer acted unwittingly. This process, which is called **strict liability**, means that people can be held responsible for their actions even if they did not intend to cause harm.

 **NOTE**

A *patent troll* is a person who owns a patent but does not intend to make, use, or sell the invention. Instead, patent trolls enforce their patent rights and file lawsuits against alleged infringers. The term is not complimentary. It refers to a person who is overly aggressive and opportunistic.

If inventors want to sue for patent infringement, they must do so in federal court because patents are governed by federal law. Federal district courts have original jurisdiction for patent infringement cases.

Infringers have two basic defenses to an inventor's claim of patent infringement:

1. The patent is invalid.
2. The patent is valid, but the alleged infringer did not violate the patent.

The first defense is that the inventor's patent is invalid for some reason. For example, a patent is invalid if an invention was publicly announced or sold for more than 1 year before the patent application. The infringer would argue that the patent is not valid because the inventor violated the 1-year grace period rule. An infringer also could argue that a patent is invalid if the inventor violated certain federal laws. It could also be argued that a patent is not valid if the inventor misleads the USPTO during the patent application process.

Under patent law, an issued patent is presumed to be valid.[15] This means infringers cannot merely assert that a patent is invalid to defend themselves in a lawsuit. Instead, they must prove that the patent is invalid for some reason. This is called the burden of proof. The infringer has the burden of proving that an issued patent is invalid.

The second defense is that an alleged infringer can argue that even if an inventor's patent is valid, he or she did not violate it. The infringer can claim his or her products or inventions do not infringe upon the inventor's patent. These cases can become very technical. Courts and jurors must review the technical specifications of products and patents to decide whether infringement occurred.

Remedies in an infringement case include injunctive relief and damages. Inventors want the court to issue an injunction that orders the infringer to stop violating the inventor's patent. This type of order means that the infringer can no longer make, use, or sell a product that infringes on the inventor's patent.

Inventors also are entitled to money damages in an infringement case. Damages compensate the inventor for profits that he or she may have lost because of the infringer's actions. In some cases, an inventor may be entitled to treble damages if the infringer willfully violated the inventor's patent.[16] The inventor may also be entitled to recover his or her attorney's fees in some cases.[17]

**NOTE**

In the United States, the general rule is that each party in litigation will pay its own attorney's fees. In some cases, courts can order the losing party to pay the winning party's attorney's fees. Courts usually award attorney's fees as a penalty for bad behavior or frivolous lawsuits.

## What Is the Difference Between Patents and Trade Secrets?

Patents are IP rights that are granted under federal law. They grant exclusive rights to an inventor of an item for a certain period of time. A patent owner has the right to keep others from making or using the patented invention. He or she also has the power to stop others from selling their invention.

A **trade secret** is similar. Trade secrets protect the formulas, processes, methods, and information that give a business a competitive edge. Trade secrets must have value to a person or business. Otherwise, there is no reason to protect it. A trade secret is a common law concept that has been codified under federal law and by many states.[18] To establish a trade secret, the information that is to be protected must:

**FYI**

Trade secret law is considered a part of IP law. However, it sometimes does not receive as much attention as patent, trademark, or copyright issues. This is because patent, trademark, and copyright protection are based on federal registration and public disclosure. Trade secret protection is based on secrecy and confidentiality. The study of trade secrets is sometimes minimized because the process for protecting trade secrets is so different.

- **Have value**—The information must have economic value. This means that it is valuable to the business that protects it. It also means that it would be valuable to competitors of the business. This also considers the money, time, and resources that the business put into developing the information. The more valuable the information, the more likely that it is a trade secret.
- **Be unknown**—The information must not be known outside of the business. If other companies or people know about the information, then it is not a secret. Any public awareness of the information can end its protected status.
- **Be unascertainable**—The information must not be easy to duplicate or even reverse engineer. If little effort is needed to ascertain the information, then it is unlikely to be considered a trade secret.
- **Be protected**—The information must be protected. This means that the business must take steps to make sure that it does not become accessible or known to the public. To protect the information, a business should use confidentiality and nondisclosure contracts when they share the information with others. The more a business protects the information, the more likely it is a trade secret.

Unlike patents, trade secrets are not registered. A person or business does not have to meet any registration or procedural formalities to protect his or her trade secrets.

Because they are kept secret, trade secrets can be protected for an unlimited time. To enforce their trade secrets, a person or business must take actions that protect them and keep them secret. For example, an Alabama Court of Appeals case dealt with the protection of trade secrets. In that case, documents that contained trade secret information were left in an unmarked box on the back seat of a company vehicle. The keys to the vehicle were not safeguarded. Many company employees potentially had access to the vehicle. In determining that the company did not take proper steps to protect its trade secrets, the Alabama Court of Appeals said, "We aren't convinced that leaving allegedly confidential and sensitive documents in a cardboard box in a company vehicle for over one week . . . amounts to a reasonable step to ensure the secrecy of the information contained therein."[19]

If a trade secret is stolen, then a person can pursue remedies allowed under the law against the thief. A person who violates a trade secret can be held responsible under civil and criminal law.

## Trademarks

A **trademark** is an IP right used to protect words, logos, and symbols that identify a product or service. Businesses spend a lot of money developing their trademarks. A trademark is used to distinguish between different products. A mark used to identify services is called a **servicemark**.

The laws for trademarks and servicemarks are the same. Trademarks and servicemarks are collectively called *trademarks* in many texts, including this one. Even the USPTO uses the term *trademark* to describe both types of marks.

Trademarks represent a business's commercial identity. Some marks are well recognized by the public. For example,

The USPTO says the oldest U.S. trademark still in use was registered in 1884. The design is the word SAMSON with a picture of a man wrestling a lion. Samson Rope Technologies uses the trademark on its products. You can see the trademark at www.samsonrope.com.

### How Should an Invention or Process Be Protected?

A person or business has to weigh many factors when considering whether to protect an invention through a patent or as a trade secret. They include:

- Whether the invention currently protected by trade secret is patentable. If it is, the person must review whether a patent provides better IP protection.
- What processes and controls can be used to make sure that only a limited number of people know about the invention. A person must make sure that everyone knows that an invention protected as a trade secret must be kept extremely confidential.
- How long the person wishes to protect the invention and the type of protection required.

#### What Is the Invention?

Trade secrets can be used to protect almost everything. One of the best-known examples of a trade secret is the Coca-Cola secret formula. The Coca-Cola Company even has an exhibit in its company museum about how it protects its trade-secret formula. Trade secrets also can be used to protect special ways to manufacture products or a process for conducting business.

Patents are limited to protecting only certain types of inventions or discoveries. To be patentable, an invention or discovery must meet all patentability requirements. If an inventor fails to meet any one of the requirements, then the USPTO can deny the patent application.

*Advantage goes to*: Trade secrets. Trade secrets can protect more types of inventions and discoveries.

#### How Must the Invention Be Protected?

The owner of a patent has the exclusive right to use the invention or discovery that is patented. That means that the owner can stop anyone else from using it. It is a violation of a patent to reverse engineer a product and recreate it. Only the patent owner can make the patented product.

Under trade secret law, it is not a violation to reverse engineer a product. This means that a person can analyze products to try to determine their secrets. For instance, chemists have tried to figure out the Coca-Cola secret formula. So long as a person lawfully obtains the product, analyzing it to figure out its trade secrets is legal.

*Advantage goes to*: Patents. Patents give greater protection against use than trade secrets.

#### How Long Must the Invention Be Protected?

A patent's exclusive protection lasts only for the period of the patent. In most instances, this is 20 years. During this time, the inventor has the sole right to make, use, or sell the product. After the patented period is up, anyone may make the underlying product.

Trade secret protection can last forever, as long as the trade secret is kept confidential. For example, the Coca-Cola formula has been kept secret for over 134 years. Businesses implement many different types of policies to keep trade secrets confidential. For example, they use access-control mechanisms in computer systems. They limit physical access based on need-to-know principles. They may even use separation-of-duty principles to make sure that no one person knows an entire trade secret.

*Advantage goes to*: Trade secrets. Trade secrets can be protected longer.

If a company patents a process, invention, or method, it may lose trade secret rights in it. Patent applications are made available to the public 18 months after they are filed. The only exception to this rule is if the inventor states that he or she is not filing for a patent abroad. The USPTO makes patent information available when a patent is issued. Once information is made available to the public, it no longer can be protected as a trade secret.

the distinctive red bull's-eye design of the Target Corporation identifies a retail department store. The bull's-eye design is its registered trademark. The New York Times Company has used the trademarked slogan "All the news that's fit to print" since 1896. It registered the slogan in 1958. The slogan still appears on the front page of *The New York Times* today.

Trademarks encourage brand loyalty. They also make it easy for customers to recognize products made by a particular manufacturer. They represent goodwill. Goodwill is the image and reputation a business has with its customers. Entities protect their trademarks from misuse because they want to protect their business and reputation.

Both federal and state laws govern trademarks. Federal trademark protection is the most well-known. The federal government regulates trademark registration under the Commerce Clause powers granted by the U.S. Constitution. Congress enacted the first trademark law in the late 1800s. Today, the main federal law protecting trademarks is the Lanham Act (1946).[20] The Lanham Act allows for federal registration of trademarks. It also defines how trademarks can be protected. This chapter discusses federal trademark protection.

 **NOTE**

The Lanham Act also is known as the Trademark Act of 1946.

## Trademark Basics

Trademark protection rights belong to the first person who uses the trademark in commerce. This is different from patent and copyright laws, which award rights to the inventor or author. The first person or business to use the trademark in commerce will have certain common law rights to use the trademark. This is true under common law and state and federal trademark statutes. Entities that use trademarks in U.S. interstate commerce often register them with the USPTO. Entities that use trademarks only in one state may choose to register only in that particular state.

The rise in internet e-commerce may mean that more businesses will pursue federal registration for their trademarks. This is because business conducted over the internet cannot really be limited to customers of only one state. If an entity wants to conduct business over the internet, it may want to register its trademarks with the federal government. Over 640,000 trademark applications were filed with the USPTO in 2019.[21]

There are several benefits to federally registering a trademark. They are:

- **Notice of the date of first use**—The filing date of the registration application gives the public notice about the use of the trademark. It establishes a priority date for determining who was the first person or company to use a particular trademark. It establishes evidence of ownership of the trademark.
- **Right to sue in federal court**—A person or entity who registers a trademark with the USPTO has the right to sue infringers in federal court. They also have the right to recover damages and costs associated with an infringement lawsuit. In some cases, they may be able to recover attorney's fees.[22]
- **Limited ways to challenge the trademark**—After 5 years of registration, a trademark can be contested only in limited ways. There are very few exceptions to this rule.[23]
- **Right to use the federal registration symbol**—Only a federally registered trademark can use the federal registration symbol.[24] The symbol is an uppercase R in an enclosed circle or ®. A person violates federal law if he or she uses this symbol on a trademark that is not federally registered.

A person must meet two basic requirements to register a trademark with the USPTO. They are:

- Use of the trademark in interstate commerce
- Distinctiveness of the trademark

### Use in Commerce

First, the trademark must be used in interstate commerce.[25] A person uses a trademark in interstate commerce when it is placed on goods or services and sold to the public in several different states. The registration application must state when the trademark was first used in commerce.

A person may still register the trademark even if it is not used in interstate commerce at the time that the registration is filed. In this case, the person registering the trademark must show good faith intent to use the trademark in commerce in the future. "Good faith" means that a person honestly intends to use the trademark in interstate commerce.

Under the law, the person must begin using the trademark within 6 months after the USPTO approves it. The USPTO can extend this period up to 2.5 years.[26] A person must notify the USPTO once it begins to use the trademark. At this point, the USPTO will issue the trademark registration.

> **NOTE**
>
> Trademarks that are not federally registered often carry the raised "TM" symbol, or ™, to show that a person or business claims the underlying trademark as its own. Trademarks registered under state laws may use this notation.

> **NOTE**
>
> The federal government can regulate interstate commerce only under its Commerce Clause authority. That is why a trademark must be used in interstate commerce to be federally registered. A trademark that is used only in one state can be registered under the state's trademark law.

### Distinctive

The second basic requirement is that a trademark must be distinctive.[27] Almost anything used by a person to distinguish his or her goods and services from another person's goods and services can be a trademark. Words, numbers, logos, and pictures can all serve as trademarks.

The USPTO has two methods of registering trademarks. They are the "Principal Register" and the "Supplemental Register." Strong trademarks, which are registered right away on the "Principal Register," are inherently distinctive. This is a term of art in trademark law. Registration on the "Principal Register" is the main way of registering trademarks. It gives a trademark owner the greatest amount of rights under federal law.

Weaker trademarks can be registered on the "Supplemental Register." These trademarks meet all of the registration requirements except that they are not inherently distinctive. The only federal right granted by registering on the "Supplemental Register" is that the trademark owner may sue in federal court for trademark infringement. After 5 years of using the trademark, the owner may submit proof of trademark use and evidence that it has achieved secondary meaning. The USPTO will then move the trademark from the "Supplemental Register" to the "Principal Register."

> **NOTE**
>
> The trademark distinctiveness requirement is similar to the patent novelty requirement.

## Trademark Registration

An applicant must submit a trademark registration application to the USPTO to register a trademark. In July 2020, it was taking the USPTO about 10 months to review trademark applications.[28] The USPTO encourages trademark applications to be filed electronically as the USPTO processes electronic applications faster than paper applications. To encourage electronic applications, the USPTO makes paper application forms available only by special request over the telephone.

A trademark application must contain the following:

- Name and contact information for the owner of the trademark
- A drawing of the trademark
- A technical listing of the goods or services that the trademark represents
- Filing fee

**NOTE**

You can learn more about the USPTO's Trademark Electronic Application System (TEAS) at http://www.uspto.gov/trademarks/teas/index.jsp.

After the application is filed, it is forwarded to an examiner who reviews the application to determine whether it is complete. The examiner also reviews proof that the trademark is used in commerce. The examiner reviews the trademark to make sure that it is inherently distinctive. Finally, the examiner reviews other trademarks to search for conflicts.

An examiner can reject a trademark for several reasons.[29] They include:

- The proposed trademark is a generic name for goods or services.
- The proposed trademark is descriptive of the applicant's goods or services and there is no secondary meaning.
- The proposed trademark is similar to another trademark already registered, and use of it on the applicant's goods or services is likely to cause customer confusion.
- The proposed trademark contains immoral, deceptive, or scandalous matter.
- The proposed trademark may disparage or falsely suggest a connection with persons (living or dead), institutions, beliefs, or national symbols.

When the USPTO approves a trademark, it publishes the trademark in the *Official Gazette*, the USPTO's official publication. The *Official Gazette*, which is published every week, includes a listing for trademarks and a listing for patents.

**NOTE**

You can see entries in the *Official Gazette* online at https://www.uspto.gov/learning-and-resources/official-gazette.

The *Official Gazette* gives the public notice of new trademarks. Once the trademark is published, any party who has concerns about the trademark may contest it. These parties have 30 days from the date of publication in the *Official Gazette* to file an "opposition" to the registration.[30] An "opposition" is a proceeding before the Trademark Trial and Appeal Board that hears trademark disputes.

If no one opposes the trademark, the USPTO issues a Certificate of Registration for it, if it is already used in interstate commerce. If the person registering the trademark has not used it in commerce, he or she must begin using it within 6 months after the USPTO approves it. A person must notify the USPTO once he or she begins to use the trademark. The USPTO will then register the trademark.

## Strong Versus Weak Trademarks

The USPTO "Principal Register" is for trademarks that are "inherently distinctive." These are strong trademarks. Traditionally, trademarks are inherently distinctive if they do more than describe a good or service. Trademarks that are unrelated to a good or service and are fanciful, arbitrary, or suggestive are considered strong trademarks.

The USPTO's oldest registered trademark is a good example of a strong trademark. That trademark is the name SAMSON with a picture of a man wrestling a lion. It has nothing to do with the company's product, which is rope. However, it is a strong trademark because it is inherently distinctive. Customers who see the trademark will immediately associate it with the Samson Rope Corporation.

One of the best examples of an inherently distinctive trademark is the Apple Corporation's rainbow-colored apple, which is their registered trademark. The trademark is inherently distinctive because it has nothing at all to do with the company's product. When customers see the rainbow-colored apple with a bite taken out of it, they immediately think of Apple computers. This trademark would not have been inherently distinctive if an apple grower or a grocery store used it.

Weak trademarks are not inherently distinctive. The most common type of weak trademark is a descriptive trademark. A trademark is descriptive when it describes the underlying product that it represents.

Descriptive trademarks get protection when they achieve "secondary meaning," or when the public associates the trademark with a particular good or service. Once a person can show that a trademark has a secondary meaning, it is entitled to full trademark protection.

For example, the trademark Kellogg's Raisin Bran is a descriptive trademark that describes a kind of breakfast cereal. This registered trademark of the Kellogg Company has achieved secondary meaning as a particular type of cereal. The trademark Carpetland, USA for a flooring store is also descriptive. This registered trademark of the Carpetland, USA Corporation also has acquired secondary meaning as a particular type of flooring store.

If the USPTO determines that a trademark is descriptive and it has not yet achieved secondary meaning, that trademark is listed on the "Supplemental Register." The only federal right granted by registering on the "Supplemental Register" is that the trademark owner may sue in federal court for trademark infringement. After 5 years of using a trademark, the owner can submit paperwork to move the trademark from the "Supplemental Register" to the "Principal Register."

Some types of trademarks can never be registered. For example, generic trademarks cannot be registered. They are not eligible because they describe a class of products and are not unique. For example, the word *butter* cannot be trademarked because it describes a class of dairy products.

**NOTE**

An **affidavit** is a written statement a person signs, swearing that the content in the affidavit is true. The person signs the affidavit in front of a notary public or other official allowed by law to administer oaths and witness signatures.

The registration period for a trademark is 10 years for newly registered trademarks. Between the fifth and sixth year after a person first registers a trademark, he or she must submit an "Affidavit of Use."[31] This document shows that the person or business is still using the trademark. After that, the Affidavit of Use must be filed again right before the end of the 10-year registration period. The person or business also must pay a maintenance fee. A person or business must re-register the trademark every 10 years to maintain protection of the mark.[32]

## Infringement and Remedies

Trademark infringement is a violation of a person's trademark rights. A trademark owner has the right to use the trademark in commerce in association with certain goods and services. This protection begins as soon as the owner starts using the trademark in commerce. If a trademark is registered under either federal or state law, then the owner of the trademark has certain other rights as well. Federal and state governments do not enforce trademarks. Instead, owners must enforce their own rights and sue people who violate their trademarks.

**FYI**

Although this section discusses federal law, you should remember that many of these same types of trademark infringement actions also could be pursued in state court. Trademark owners may have additional types of tort actions that they can pursue in state court.

There are two main types of trademark infringement cases:

- Use of a similar trademark that is confusing or deceptive to the customer[33]
- Use of a similar trademark that dilutes the value of a famous trademark[34]

In the first type of case, a trademark owner can sue another person who uses a similar trademark in a way that is "likely to cause confusion, or to cause mistake, or to deceive."[35] The owner can bring this infringement action for innocent infringement and for willful infringement. The plaintiff, who is the trademark owner, has the burden of proof. The plaintiff must prove the following elements:

- The plaintiff owns a valid trademark.
- The defendant used a similar trademark in commerce.
- The defendant's use of a similar trademark is likely to confuse consumers.

 **NOTE**

Examples of famous trademarks include the Apple Computer, Coca-Cola, and Kleenex trademarks. They are all registered and used extensively across the United States. Most people recognize these trademarks and the associated brand of products.

If a trademark owner has registered his or her trademark with the USPTO, that registration is proof of ownership of the trademark. A plaintiff can use the defendant's own advertising materials to show that the defendant used the trademark in commerce. A plaintiff also can use these materials to show that the defendant's use of the trademark was confusing in some way. The confusion created could exploit the plaintiff's goodwill in his or her trademarks and products. That is, the defendant is using a similar trademark in the hopes of selling more products because of the plaintiff's good commercial reputation.

In reviewing whether a trademark is confusing, courts will compare the plaintiff's and defendants' trademarks. They will look at how similar the marks are. They will also look at the similarities between the goods and services that each trademark represents. They might also look at the defendant's intent in using a similar trademark. If the court finds the defendant's use of the trademark confusing, it can order the defendant to stop using the trademark.

The second type of trademark infringement case is for *trademark dilution*. This type of infringement case specifically applies to "famous" trademarks, or ones that are very well-known. Only holders of famous trademarks can file a lawsuit for trademark dilution.

In a dilution case, the trademark owner can sue for any use of a similar trademark that dilutes or tarnishes his or her trademark. Dilution occurs when a trademark is used to promote different goods. An example would be a Coca-Cola minivan or a Kleenex motorcycle. Customers would not be confused by the different use of the famous trademark. However, the value of the famous trademark is diluted when it is used with dissimilar products.

The trademark owner also has a dilution case if the use of a similar trademark tarnishes a famous trademark. A trademark is tarnished when it is used in an unflattering light. For example, in 1996 the children's toy store, Toys "R" Us, sued an adult website with the domain name "adultsrus." The court held that the defendant's use of "adultsrus" to sell adult products diluted the "family" image and goodwill that Toys "R" Us had built in its products. The court ordered the defendants to stop using the "adultsrus" name.[36]

Remedies in an infringement case include injunctive relief and damages. Trademark owners want the court to stop infringers from using their trademarks in a confusing or diluting way.[37] Trademark owners also may be able to get damages for the defendant's profits in using the trademark, their own damages, and costs of the litigation.[38]

**NOTE**

In some instances, treble damages can be awarded if a defendant intentionally used the plaintiff's trademark.[39]

## Relationship of Trademarks on Domain Names

The rise of e-commerce has created some interesting questions about trademark use. Today, people take it almost as a given that www.coca-cola.com will take you to the Coca-Cola Company's website. Their domain name serves as their internet business address. Many companies try to use their business name or trademark as their domain name.

A domain name includes a top-level domain, represented by the *.com*, *.net*, or *.gov* at the end of the domain name. The second level is the information that comes directly to the left of *.com*, *.net*, or *.gov*. This is usually the place where a business or entity might want to use its name or trademark. To do this, the entity must register its domain name.

**NOTE**

At the end of 2019, there were over 362 million top-level domain name registrations.[40]

A domain name is different from a uniform resource locator (URL). The domain name is only part of a URL. The complete URL is the actual internet address. A URL goes into much more detail than a domain name, providing much more information, including the specific page address, folder name, machine name, and protocol language, such as http://.

Companies register their domain names and create websites to advertise and sell their products. They want their domain name to be recognizable to their customers. The first company to register a domain name has the right to use that name. Domain name registrars do not review a domain name to make sure that it does not infringe on a trademark. If a domain name is available for use, then they will accept registration for that name.

In the mid to late 1990s, domain names were registered at a fast pace, and not all of these registrations were legitimate. *Cybersquatting* is the bad-faith registration of a domain name

### Registering a Domain Name

A domain name is the common name after *www* that people use to refer to their websites. People register these names to grow their businesses and help others find their businesses on the internet. Domain names are simply internet addresses.

Domain names must be registered with the Internet Corporation for Assigned Names and Numbers (ICANN), which coordinates the internet's naming system. You cannot directly register a domain name with ICANN. Instead, you must register it with a *domain name registrar*. ICANN authorizes these registrars to accept domain name registrations and creates policies for how these registrations should be handled.

ICANN and domain name registrars do not review whether a new domain name registration infringes upon a business or entity's trademark. Instead, they accept registrations for domain names on a first-come, first-served basis. Trademark laws and ICANN's Uniform Domain Name Dispute Resolution Policy (UDRP) are used to resolve domain name disputes regarding trademarks. You can view ICANN's dispute resolution materials at https://www.icann.org/resources/pages/help/dndr/udrp-en.

that is a registered trademark or trade name of another entity. A trade name is the business name of an organization. Cybersquatters tried to register these names before the legitimate owners of the trademark or trade name. They also registered domain names based on these famous trademarks or trade names but used a common misspelling of those names.

A cybersquatter registers trademarks or trade names to profit off of the other person's trademark or trade name. They also register them in the hopes of selling the domain name to the trademark owner for large amounts of money, or to attract customers who were looking for a specific product or business. The cybersquatter then redirects the customer to other websites.

**NOTE**

*Bad faith* means a malicious or harmful motive for taking a certain action.

Trademark owners have a legal right to protect their trademark, which includes protecting their trademarks from cybersquatters. Many people, businesses, and organizations were harmed by cybersquatters because they had to pay large amounts of money to get ownership of their trademarks. They sued cybersquatters to stop them from engaging in trademark infringement, which was a time-consuming and expensive process.

**NOTE**

The WIPO is an arbitrator under the UDRP. The WIPO reported a record number of domain name cases in 2019.[42]

Congress created the Anti-Cybersquatting Consumer Protection Act (ACPA) in 1999.[41] It was designed to stop people from registering domain names that were the trademarks of other entities and allows entities to sue others for cybersquatting. To prove their case, the plaintiff must show that the cybersquatter registered the trademark in bad faith with the intent to profit from the registration. Under the law, a plaintiff can recover damages and ask the court to issue an injunction that stops the cybersquatter from using the contested domain name. Courts also can award the contested domain name to the winning party.

Trademark owners also can pursue a domain name dispute under the ICANN UDRP. This process may be faster than pursuing an action under the ACPA. Under the UDRP, a contested domain name may be disconnected or transferred to a winning plaintiff.

# Copyright

**NOTE**

Federal law governs patent and copyright issues. State laws are preempted. This is because the Constitution granted the federal government the specific power to make laws to protect authors and inventors.

A **copyright** is an IP right. The U.S. Constitution establishes federal copyright protection. The first federal copyright law was established in 1790, and the most recent version of federal copyright law was the 1976 Copyright Act.[43] Copyright is protected under federal law; states are preempted from creating their own copyright laws.

The holder of a copyright has the exclusive right to do anything with the copyrighted work. The holder is the only one who can reproduce, perform, or sell the work. Copyright holders also have the power to keep others from using their copyrighted material.

Almost anything can be copyrighted. You need to remember that most materials posted to the internet are protected by copyright. In addition, most informational and advertising materials posted on websites by businesses and organizations are subject to copyright. Blog posts and personal websites also are protected. When reposting information that you find on the internet, you need to make sure that you do not violate the owner's copyright.

Sometimes copyrighted materials are marked with an uppercase "C" in an enclosed circle or ©. The law does not require this. Even if the material is not marked, it may be copyrighted.

## Copyright Basics

A copyright is used to protect almost any creative endeavor (called a "work"), such as books, art, music, videos, computer programs, and any other creative work. Works that can be copyrighted include:

- **Literary works**—This includes novels, newspapers, textbooks, and computer software.
- **Musical works**—This includes songs, scores for musicals, and jingles.
- **Dramatic works**—This includes plays, skits, monologues, and any music that might be included in the dramatic work.
- **Pantomimes and choreographic works**—This includes ballets or other expressions of dance. It also includes mime shows.
- **Pictorial, graphic, and sculptural works**—This includes photographs, sculptures, fine art, and cartoons.
- **Motion picture and audiovisual works**—This includes movies and television shows.
- **Sound recordings**—This includes recordings of music, sound, and words.
- **Architectural works**—This includes building designs, blueprints, and drawings.

**NOTE**

Copyright protection is not available for names. You can read more about it at https://www.copyright.gov/circs/circ33.pdf.

The categories are very broad. A work of authorship might be properly copyrighted in several different categories. For example, the advertising and information material that an organization posts on its website can be copyrighted as a literary work. Pictures on the website can be copyrighted as a pictorial or graphic work.

Federal law grants copyright protection to "an original work of authorship fixed in any tangible medium of expression."[44] To be eligible for copyright protection, a work must be both original and in a fixed form.

A work is original if it is not copied from another source. If a work is not original, it is not eligible for copyright. Works that are created completely from publicly known facts, with no other original material, are not copyrightable.

Unlike an invention or discovery that is patentable, copyrighted works do not have to be new or novel. They also do not have to be good or aesthetically pleasing. They simply have to be an author's original expression of an idea.

Copyright protection does not extend to mere ideas on their own. Instead, these ideas must be written down or put in a fixed format. This is why books are entitled to copyright protection, but ideas that are simply in the head of the author are not. Copyright also is not available for useful articles. Patents, however, may protect these types of articles, which can include clothing, furniture, machinery, and other items.

Works that are in the public domain also are not copyrightable. The **public domain** refers to the body of works that are free for public use. This includes works where the copyright has expired, as well as works of the U.S. government such as the United States Code. It is important for you to remember that information that is available on the internet is not necessarily in the public domain.

Copyright protection arises as soon as an original work is created in a fixed form. An author does not have to do anything to gain this protection. Instead, it arises as a matter of law. An author is not required to register a work to get copyright protection. Writers do not have to mark their work to get copyright protection.

The owner of a copyright has the exclusive right to do anything with the copyrighted work. Subject to only a few exceptions, only the copyright owner can reproduce, perform, or sell the work.[45] Copyright owners also have the power to allow others to use their copyrighted material by using a special kind of contract called a *license*. The law gives copyright holders the following broad rights:

- To reproduce the copyrighted work
- To prepare derivative works based upon the copyrighted work
- To distribute copies or phonorecords of the copyrighted work to the public
- To publicly perform the copyrighted work
- To publicly display the copyrighted work

 **NOTE**

A *derivative work* is a work derived from an original work. For example, a movie based on a best-selling novel is a derivative work.

 **NOTE**

A WFH situation is created via a contract.

Copyright owners also have the power to keep others from using their copyrighted material. It is important to understand who the owner of a copyright is. Often the owner of a copyright is the person who created the original work. This is not always the case, however. For example, when an employee creates work for his or her employer, the employer typically is the owner of the copyright. Copyright law calls this situation a "work made for hire" (WFH).

Other than in the employer/employee context, a WFH must be reflected in a written document. This document shows that a person has specifically commissioned a WFH. The document also reflects that the author agrees to work on a WFH and that copyright belongs to the person who commissioned the work. The following items are common works for hire:[46]

- A contribution to a collective work
- A part of a motion picture or other audiovisual work
- A translation
- A supplementary work
- A compilation
- An instructional text
- A test and answer material for a test
- An atlas

The length of copyright protection is determined through ownership. For original works created after January 1, 1978, a copyright lasts for the length of the author's life plus 70 years after the author's death. If two or more authors prepare a work, the 70-year period does not begin to run out until after the last author's death. For WFH, a copyright lasts for 95 years from the publication of the work. In limited cases protection also could extend for 120 years from the creation of the work. Whichever period is shorter is the proper term.[47]

## Copyright Registration

Copyright protection arises automatically as soon as an original work of authorship is fixed. An author is not required to register a work to get protection. However, there are many reasons why an author may choose to register for copyright protection. The main reason for a person to register a copyright is so that the copyright can be enforced. An author who created a work in the United States may not file a lawsuit for copyright infringement without first registering the copyright with the U.S. Copyright Office.[48]

The law creates several other reasons to register a copyright. Registration creates a public record of the copyright. In addition, if a copyright is registered within 5 years of publication, it creates a presumption of valid ownership.[49] This means a copyright is presumed to be valid, and the person challenging it must present proof that it is invalid.

**NOTE**

The U.S. Copyright Office is a unit of the Library of Congress.

An author must submit copyright registration to the U.S. Copyright Office, which accepts both paper and electronic registration applications. It reports that it takes on average 3 months to process electronic applications, whereas it takes 6 months on average to process paper-based applications.[50]

**NOTE**

The U.S. Copyright Office has prepared many documents to help people better understand copyright. You can see a list of those documents at https://www.copyright.gov/circs/.

A person registers a work by submitting an application and a copy of the work. The applicant also must pay a fee. The only way to register a copyright is with the U.S. Copyright Office. Some people believe that mailing a copy of their work to themselves via U.S. mail is copyright registration or proof of ownership in the work. This is sometimes called a *poor man's copyright*. However, this is not a valid way to register a copyright. To repeat: The only way to register a copyright in the United States is with the U.S. Copyright Office.[51]

### How Do You Protect Copyrights Internationally?

The Berne Convention for the Protection of Literary and Artistic Works (1886), administered by the WIPO, is the main treaty regarding international copyright protection. The Berne Convention also states that any party to the convention agrees to protect the copyrighted works of foreign citizens at least as much as it protects the copyrighted works of its own citizens.

More than 175 countries are members of the Berne Convention.[52] The United States became a member of the Berne Convention in 1989. It took a long time for the United States to join the Berne Convention because the convention requires member countries to provide a minimum level of copyright protection, and the United States had to rewrite its copyright laws to give these protections. The Berne Convention requires each member nation to recognize the following:

- A minimum term of copyright protection that is the life of the author plus 50 years
- Freedom from formalities such as notice or registration to recognize a copyright. Copyright protection arises automatically.
- Protection for certain moral rights of the author.

## Infringement and Remedies

Copyright holders have exclusive rights in the work that they create. These rights arise when the work is created and continue for the length of the copyright. The federal government does not enforce copyrights. Authors must enforce their own rights and can sue people who infringe on their copyright. Liability for infringement is based upon strict liability. A copyright owner can hold an infringer liable for violating a copyright even if the infringement was not intentional.

**NOTE**

*Piracy* refers to unauthorized copying and distribution of electronic, musical, and audiovisual works.

To pursue an action for copyright infringement, a plaintiff must prove ownership of the copyright. The plaintiff also must show that the defendant has infringed on that copyright. A plaintiff usually proves ownership of a copyright by showing a copyright registration as proof of the validity of the copyright.

Copyright infringement cases are very rarely simple cases of a defendant directly copying a plaintiff's work. To show that there has been an unauthorized reproduction, the plaintiff must show that the defendant had access to the copyrighted work. However, access to the copyrighted work alone is not enough to prove infringement. The plaintiff also must show that the plaintiff's and defendant's works are substantially similar.

One of the most common tests used to determine substantial similarity is "whether a lay observer would consider the works as a whole substantially similar to one another."[53] This is a fact-intensive inquiry. The court will look at all the ways in which the two works are similar. If the two works are substantially similar, then copyright infringement has occurred.

Remedies for copyright infringement are similar to remedies for infringements of other IP rights. A court can issue an injunction, which stops the infringer from violating the copyright holder's rights. A court also can order a defendant to pay damages for violating a plaintiff's copyright. A defendant also may be liable for statutory damages under copyright law. These damages are higher for willful copyright infringement.[54]

The most common way for a defendant to defend against a copyright infringement case is to argue that the plaintiff's work is not original. A defendant also can present facts that the works are not substantially similar. Another defense in a copyright infringement case is that the use of the copyrighted work is allowed under the fair use doctrine.

**NOTE**

Statutory damages are damage amounts that the law specifies. Lawmakers specify statutory damages in cases where it might be hard for a party to prove the amount of actual damages.

**FYI**

Posting a URL to another person's copyrighted materials on your own webpage is generally not considered copyright infringement. However, posting a copy of someone's content on your own webpage, even if you acknowledge their work, may be copyright infringement. This is because only the owner of the copyright has the right to reproduce and distribute his or her copyrighted materials.

### *Fair Use*

A copyright holder has a large number of rights in his or her original work. The scope of these rights is to encourage artistic expression. However, there are some limitations on a copyright holder's exclusive rights. These limitations are a defense to copyright infringement. **Fair use** is one of the most common limitations.

The law states that fair use of a copyrighted work is not copyright infringement.[55] The law lists several examples of fair use. Fair use is permitted in these situations to promote free speech. The examples include uses for:

**NOTE**

The U.S. Copyright Office Fair Use Index is a searchable database of court opinions about fair use. You can learn more and access the index at https://www.copyright.gov/fair-use/.

- Criticism
- Comment
- News reporting
- Teaching (including multiple copies for classroom use)
- Scholarship
- Research

If portions of a copyrighted work are used for these purposes, then a defendant might have a defense against an owner's claim of copyright infringement.

The law also lists several technology-neutral factors that should be considered in determining whether a use should be considered fair use. They can be used to analyze the use of any type of creative work. The factors are:[56]

- **The purpose and character of the use**—A use for nonprofit, educational, or comment purposes tends to favor fair use. A use that is for commercial or profit purposes tends to weigh against fair use.

- **The nature of the copyrighted work**—The more creative a work is, the more protection it will be afforded. Fair use tends to favor the use of facts and not the creative expression of an idea.
- **The amount and substantiality of the work used**—Use of a small amount of a copyrighted work tends to favor fair use. However, the use of a small part of a work that encompasses the substantial idea in that work weighs against fair use.
- **The effect of the use upon the potential market**—A use that has no effect on a potential market for a work tends to weigh in favor of fair use. A use of a work that has a major effect on the market is less likely to be considered fair use.

Courts weigh these factors against one another to determine whether the use of a copyrighted work is fair use. If fair use is indicated, it may be a defense to a copyright infringement claim. Fair use cases are very difficult to decide. Courts must engage in a very detailed analysis to determine fair use.

In 2009, the Second Circuit Court of Appeals reviewed a fair use case.[57] In that case, a book publisher created an illustrated biography about the history of the Grateful Dead rock band. As part of the book, it included pictures of concert posters. The plaintiff owned the copyrights to the posters and sued the book publisher for copyright infringement.

The defendant argued that its use of the posters was allowed under the fair use doctrine. In reviewing the case, the Second Circuit held that the use of the copyrighted posters was fair use. It said that the use did not exploit the copyrighted works, but was instead

### Fair Use for Educational Purposes

Some people believe that the use of any copyrighted work by an educator is always fair use. However, this is not true. The educator must still review the fair use factors.

For example, an education professor shares one short excerpt from a copyrighted academic journal article about teaching styles with students to illustrate a lesson. This activity is probably fair use. Analysis of the fair use factors shows:

- Use in an educational setting tends to favor fair use.
- The use of a scholarly journal article that contains facts tends to favor fair use.
- The use of a small amount of a copyrighted work tends to favor fair use.
- The use likely does not affect a potential market because it is being used in a restricted classroom setting.

The same education professor prepares a newsletter for a website. The professor includes a copyrighted cartoon about teaching students in the newsletter to illustrate a humorous point. This activity probably is not fair use. The cartoon's creator must give permission for the cartoon to be included in the newsletter. Analysis of the fair use factors shows:

- Use on a website for entertainment purposes tends to weigh against fair use.
- The use of creative works tends to weigh against fair use. A cartoon is a very creative work.
- The use of an entire work, such as a cartoon, tends to weigh against fair use.
- Use of the work could have a major effect on the cartoonist's ability to market his or her products, especially because it is made available through the internet. This weighs against fair use.

The rules for determining fair use can be very detailed. The U.S. Copyright Office has prepared fair use guidance for educators. You can read it at http://www.copyright.gov/circs/circ21.pdf.

transformative. This means that the purpose and character of the use were different from the original use of the copyrighted works. The posters were greatly reduced in size and used to commemorate events in the band's history in a biographical fashion. As such, the use was different from the original use of the posters and could properly be considered fair use.

# Protecting Copyrights Online—The Digital Millennium Copyright Act (DMCA)

In 1998, Congress passed the Digital Millennium Copyright Act (DMCA).[58] Congress created the DMCA to help protect copyrights in the digital world. It also contains provisions that help insulate internet service providers (ISPs) from the actions of their customers.

## DMCA Basics

The DMCA has five titles. They are:

- **Title I**—This title implements two WIPO treaties. It contains provisions about technological measures used to protect electronic copyrighted works.
- **Title II**—This title is called the Online Copyright Infringement Liability Limitation Act. It limits the liability of online service providers for copyright infringement by users.
- **Title III**—This title is called the Computer Maintenance Competition Assurance Act. It allows computer technicians to make a copy of a computer program for maintenance or repair.
- **Title IV**—This title contains miscellaneous provisions.
- **Title V**—This title is called the Vessel Hull Design Protection Act. It creates a new form of IP protection for the design of vessel hulls.

Titles I, II, and III are discussed in this section.

**NOTE**

Many college students are aware of the DMCA because of its Title II copyright infringement provisions.

### *Technology Protection Measures*

Title I of the DMCA implements two WIPO treaties: the WIPO Copyright Treaty and the WIPO Performances and Phonograms Treaty. The DMCA amended the Copyright Act (1976) to extend U.S. copyright law to creative works made by citizens in other countries. These changes were required as part of the WIPO treaties.

The WIPO treaties required two major changes. The first is that members of the treaties must prevent people from bypassing technological measures used to protect copyrighted works. Many digital products, such as DVDs, video games, electronic books, and websites, use access controls to protect certain types of content. For example, a website might password protect some sections so that only registered members can get to those sections.

The technology measures and tools that some businesses use to protect their content are referred to as *digital rights management (DRM)*. Many large businesses in the entertainment industry use DRM to protect their digital works.

The DMCA forbids people from accessing protected copyrighted content by bypassing these access controls. They may not tamper with content protected by technological access controls. This provision intends to protect content that is transmitted electronically from copyright infringement. In addition, a person is not allowed to make or sell devices that would allow other people unauthorized access to a copyrighted work that is protected by these types of access controls.[59]

Second, the DMCA also forbids the sale of devices that would allow other people to bypass technological controls to copy a copyrighted work. However, the DMCA does not prohibit people from actually bypassing technological controls on their own to copy a work. This is because copying might be necessary to use parts of a work under the fair use doctrine.

The provisions forbidding bypassing technological measures are called the "Circumvention of Technological Protection Measures." You also may hear these referred to as the DMCA anti-circumvention measures.

There are some exceptions to these anti-circumvention measures.[60] It may be possible for a person to bypass technological controls that prevent unauthorized access in these instances. Each of these exemptions has additional detailed terms that are described only briefly here. The exemptions include the following:

- Nonprofit libraries, archives, and educational institutions may bypass technology protection measures to make a good faith determination that they wish to obtain authorized access to the work.
- A person who has lawfully obtained a computer program may bypass technology protection measures to identify and analyze elements of the program in order to make sure it is compatible with other programs.
- A person may bypass technology protection measures and create tools to do so to research and identify weaknesses in encryption technologies.
- A person may bypass technology protection measures to protect children from certain material on the internet.
- A person may bypass technology protection measures when those measures are capable of collecting or sharing personally identifying information about a person's online activities.
- A person may bypass technology protection measures and create tools to do so for testing the security of a computer system or network. The owner of the system must specifically authorize the testing.

Title I criminalizes the act of bypassing technological measures. A person who willfully violates the technology protection measures for profit can be held criminally liable. Penalties include both prison time (up to 10 years is possible) and monetary fines (up to $1,000,000 is possible). The law makes nonprofit libraries, archives, and educational institutions entirely exempt from its criminal liability provisions.[61]

FYI

Title I also allows the Library of Congress to issue administrative exemptions. These exemptions are allowed when technology protection measures substantially limit the ability of people to make non-infringing uses of copyrighted materials. The Library of Congress must issue administrative exemptions every 3 years. You can read the administrative exemption rules at http://www.copyright.gov/1201/.

### Online Copyright Infringement

Title II of the DMCA is called the Online Copyright Infringement Liability Limitation Act. It limits the liability of an online service provider (OSP) for its customers' copyright infringement.[62] Online service providers lobbied hard for these provisions. They were concerned that they could be held liable for their users' actions under some secondary liability legal theories. In these theories, an OSP could be held liable for a user's actions if the OSP knew about them and contributed to them. This was worrisome to service providers whose entire function was to provide services to customers.

DMCA exempts OSPs from copyright infringement claims that result from the conduct of their customers if certain criteria are met. If they meet these criteria, they fall into a safe harbor. If an OSP qualifies for a safe harbor exemption, only the individual infringing customer is liable for monetary damages. The OSP's service or network, through which the customer engaged in the copyright infringement, is not liable. The DMCA provides safe harbors for common OSP activities.[64] They are:

> **NOTE**
>
> An *OSP*, as defined by the DMCA,[63] is a provider of online services or network access. An ISP is also an OSP.

- Transitory communications (providing network communications services)
- System caching
- Storage of information on systems or networks at the direction of users (hosting)
- Providing information location tools (search engines)

The safe harbors do not require an OSP to monitor the content posted or transmitted by the OSP's users for copyright infringement. To take advantage of any of the safe harbor provisions, the OSP must develop a policy of terminating the accounts of repeat copyright offenders. OSPs also must not interfere with any technological measures that copyright owners use to protect their copyrights. OSPs must also meet additional criteria for three of the safe harbors.

Under the transitory communications safe harbor section, an OSP is not liable for copyright infringement by its customers simply because the OSP provides digital transmissions, routing, or connections for the communicating content.[65] To use this safe harbor, an OSP must show the following:

- Someone other than the OSP initiated the transmission of content.
- The transmission was carried out through an automated process.
- The OSP does not select who receives the transmitted material except as an automatic response to the request of another person.
- No copy of the transmission is retained in a manner that makes it available to other recipients.
- OSPs transmit the material through its system without modification of its content.

This provision protects the OSP from user-initiated communications that the OSP automatically processes. In these situations where an OSP is merely transmitting material, it will not be liable for the alleged copyright infringement of system users.

> **NOTE**
>
> The transitory communications safe harbor is commonly called the *conduit* defense. This is because the OSP is merely providing a conduit for its users to communicate through. ISPs often rely on this safe harbor.

### DMCA Takedown Notices

Under the DMCA, if a copyright owner wishes to have allegedly infringing material removed from an OSP's network, the copyright owner must send a *notice and takedown letter* to the OSP's specified agent. DMCA requires each OSP to specify an agent who will receive these notices and respond to them.

The U.S. Copyright Office maintains a list of DMCA agents. You can find this list at https://www.copyright.gov/dmca-directory/.

A DMCA "notice and takedown" letter must be in writing and contain the following elements:[66]

- A physical or electronic signature of the copyright owner or representative
- Identification of the copyrighted work
- Identification of the infringing material that is to be removed, along with sufficient information to enable the ISP to locate it
- Contact information for the complaining party
- A statement that the complaining party has a good faith belief that the use of the copyrighted work is not authorized by the copyright owner or the law
- A statement that the information is accurate and that, under penalty of perjury, the complaining party is authorized to act for the copyright owner

After receipt of a valid notice, the OSP must notify the user and remove or disable access to the allegedly infringing material. If a user believes that the takedown is in error, the DMCA gives users an opportunity to require that the OSP reinstate the materials.

Under the information storage and information location tools safe harbor provisions, an OSP also must show that users control what material they post online. OSPs also must show that they do not have actual knowledge of users' infringing activities. OSPs must show that they do not profit from the user's infringing activities. OSPs further must show that they take down or block access to infringing material when they receive proper notice from a copyright owner.

### *Computer Maintenance*

Title III of the DMCA is called the Computer Maintenance Competition Assurance Act. It allows computer repair technicians to make temporary, limited copies of computer software while they are repairing a computer. The computer must already have a copy of the software program on it. These new copies cannot be used in any manner and technicians must delete them when the repair job is over. The DMCA allows a technician to make these copies to assist in repairing the computer.[67]

## DMCA Unintended Consequences

It has been over 20 years since the DMCA was enacted. Nonetheless, it still raises some concerns about unintended consequences. Most of the concerns are about the provisions of DMCA Title I and Title II. They include:

- Fears that Title 1 provisions will suppress legitimate activities such as research.
- Fears that the Title II provisions overburden OSPs.

#### Title 1 Concerns

There are many concerns about the anti-circumvention technology protection measures specified in Title I. Many scientists, educators, and industry groups are concerned that these provisions will stifle research. This is because of the criminal penalties that are attached to violating these provisions. There is already some indication that this concern is not unreasonable.

In 2001, the U.S. Federal Bureau of Investigation (FBI) arrested a security researcher from Russia for publishing software that bypassed access controls on e-books. This was allegedly a violation of DMCA's technology protection measures. The researcher was arrested after making a presentation about the security issues at the Def Con conference in Las Vegas. Both the researcher and the Russian company that he worked for were charged under the DMCA. The charges against the researcher were dropped. In 2002, a jury acquitted the Russian company of charges that it violated the DMCA.

Other complaints about these provisions center on the fact that the anti-circumvention provisions hinder fair use and, therefore, free speech. These complaints ask about what happens when DRM-protected materials enter the public domain. How can they be properly used in the public domain if there are no available tools to remove DRM protection?

> **NOTE**
>
> To acquit means to find a person *not guilty* of the crimes with which he or she was charged.

#### Title II Concerns

There are also concerns with Title II of the DMCA. Many people argue that it places too much of a burden on OSPs in responding to "notice and takedown" letters from copyright holders. Because the OSP must act on the notice to maintain its safe harbor protection, it might take down material inappropriately. Taking down material in such a broad manner could hamper free speech. Since the enactment of the DMCA, Google has received almost 5 billion requests to delete URLs that point to infringing content.[68]

> **NOTE**
>
> You can read Google's Transparency Report, https://transparencyreport.google.com, to learn more about the number of copyright claims that it receives.

## Case Studies and Examples

The following case studies show how the concepts discussed in this chapter are used. These case studies are real-world examples of how IP laws are applied.

### Trade Secrets

In 2008, the U.S. government charged a design engineer with stealing trade secrets from Intel about its newest microprocessor. The value of the trade secrets was estimated at $1 billion.

The engineer worked at Intel in Massachusetts. He resigned from his job at the end of May 2008 and told Intel that he would use his accrued vacation time for 2 weeks until his final day at work. His employment with Intel would officially end on June 11, 2008. The engineer did not tell Intel that he had a new job with an Intel competitor, which he started on June 2, 2008.

Intel heard rumors that the engineer had accepted employment with its competitor. The company began to review logs to see his network activities during his last 2 weeks with the company. It notified law enforcement once it discovered that the employee had accessed sensitive company documents.

**NOTE**

You can read the Department of Justice press release about the case at https://archives.fbi.gov/archives/boston/press-releases/2012/former-intel-employee-sentenced-to-prison-for-stealing-valuable-computer-chip-manufacturing-and-design-documents.

The U.S. FBI investigated the incident. Their investigation showed that the engineer remotely accessed the Intel system several times between June 8 and June 11, 2008. He downloaded highly sensitive Intel documents that contained data relating to the design of the new chip. However, the FBI found no evidence that he had disclosed or used the information that he downloaded from Intel.

In April 2012, the engineer pleaded guilty to charges of wire fraud for illegally accessing the Intel system and downloading documents. He was sentenced to 3 years in prison. The case highlights that even large companies must implement access control measures to protect their secrets.

## Service Provider Liability for Copyright Infringement

Napster was an online music file-sharing software program. For a brief period in time, it was the most popular peer-to-peer program in use. Napster freely distributed its software, which allowed computer users to share their music collections online with other computer users.

In 1999, several music companies filed a lawsuit against Napster for copyright infringement under the DMCA. They argued that Napster users were directly infringing on their copyrights and that Napster was responsible for copyright infringement on several secondary liability theories. They argued that Napster engaged in copyright infringement as well because it provided the services used by its customers to engage in copyright infringement. The case, *A&M Records, Inc. v. Napster*, was filed in the U.S. District Court for the Northern District of California.

Napster offered several defenses. It claimed that its activities fell within DMCA safe harbor provisions. These defenses were not successful after the district court determined that Napster failed to meet all the safe harbor requirements.

**NOTE**

The documentary *Downloaded* is about the quick rise and fall of Napster. How streaming services offer music today is influenced by the Napster story.

The district court held that at least some of Napster's users were engaging in activities that infringed upon the copyrights of others and that Napster knew about this activity. It also found that Napster provided services that its users used to engage in copyright infringement, as well as the fact that Napster profited financially from its users' activities. Napster lost the case in district court.

Napster appealed to the Ninth Circuit U.S. Court of Appeals, which upheld the district court's decision.[69] The court ordered Napster to monitor the activities of its network and to block access to infringing material when notified by copyright owners.

Napster shut down its service in July 2001 and declared bankruptcy in 2002. In 2003, it sold all of its assets. The Napster case is one of the most famous cases about service provider liability for copyright infringement under the DMCA.

## Digital Collections

In 2008, several U.S. college and university research libraries formed the HathiTrust. The HathiTrust digitizes and stores the printed collections of its partner libraries to preserve them. Several different organizations, such as Google and Microsoft, are partners in digitizing the collections. Since its creation, the HathiTrust has digitized over 17 million books and 6 billion pages.[70] You can see a list of participating institutions at http://www.hathitrust.org/community.

The HathiTrust also provides access to this digitized content when a copyright holder has allowed it. It also provides access to digital resources where allowed by law, as in providing materials to individuals with visual disabilities, as well as access to works in the public domain.

In September 2011, the Authors Guild sued the HathiTrust. The Authors Guild, which helps writers learn about copyright and how to protect it, alleged that the HathiTrust was violating the copyright of guild members by creating a digital archive of copyrighted materials. They argued that the HathiTrust and its partners copied and provided access to the materials without the owners' consent. The HathiTrust argued that the digitization of the materials was allowed under several different copyright law exceptions. It argued that its activities were fair use and fell under the preservation provision. In October 2012, a federal district court agreed with the HathiTrust and stated that the HathiTrust's activities did not violate copyright laws.

In November 2012, the Authors Guild appealed the case to the Second Circuit Court of Appeals, which heard oral arguments on October 30, 2013. In June 2014, the Second Circuit ruled in favor of HathiTrust.[71] It held the doctrine of fair use allowed HathiTrust to create a full-text searchable database of copyrighted works. It also held that HathiTrust could provide those copyrighted works in formats accessible to those with disabilities

## CHAPTER SUMMARY

IP protection is broad. It protects a person's ownership rights in their creative ideas and gives them the right to protect their ideas and profit from them. These rights are exclusive to the owners of IP, who can take action against people who violate their IP rights.

IP protection is particularly important to think about as more content becomes available on the internet. IP law protects ideas once they are in a physical form. When materials are published on the web, they are in a physical form. Traditional legal concepts about IP ownership are used to protect materials published on the internet.

## KEY CONCEPTS AND TERMS

Affidavit
Copyright
Design patents
Fair use
Intellectual property (IP)
Internet of Things
Patent
Patent prosecution
Plant patents
Prior art
Public domain
Servicemark
Strict liability
Trade secret
Trademark
Utility patents

## CHAPTER 10 ASSESSMENT

1. What intellectual property methods can be used to protect computer software?
   A. Patents
   B. Trademarks
   C. Copyrights
   D. Patents and trademarks
   E. Patents and copyrights
2. What is strict liability?
3. A design patent can be used to protect computer software.
   A. True
   B. False
4. A utility patent has a ______year term.
5. Which type of IP protection is mentioned in the U.S. Constitution?
   A. Patents
   B. Trademarks
   C. Copyrights
   D. Patents and trademarks
   E. Patents and copyrights
6. What is the main difference between patents and trade secrets?
   A. A trade secret is public, whereas a patent is confidential.
   B. A trade secret protects a process, whereas a patent protects a machine.
   C. A trade secret is confidential, whereas a patent is public.
   D. A trade secret protects a machine, whereas a patent protects a process.
   E. None of these is correct.
7. What are the two basic requirements to register a trademark with the USPTO?
8. The USPTO publishes the *Official Gazette* to give public notice about patents and trademarks.
   A. True
   B. False
9. What must an author do to protect his or her copyrighted works?
   A. Mark it with a ©.
   B. Register it with the U.S. Copyright Office.
   C. Nothing, copyright protection is automatic.
   D. Pay a fee to the Library of Congress.
   E. None of these is correct.
10. Which DMCA safe harbor is called the "conduit" exception?
    A. Transitory communications safe harbor
    B. System caching safe harbor
    C. Information storage safe harbor
    D. Information location tools safe harbor
    E. None of these is correct.
11. Which type of IP protection is governed by federal and state law?
    A. Patents
    B. Copyrights
    C. Trademarks
    D. Patents and copyrights
    E. None of these is correct.
12. What is the trademark registration period?
    A. 10 years
    B. 14 years
    C. 20 years
    D. 70 years
    E. None of these is correct.

13. Why is it important to know who is the owner of a copyrighted work?

14. What must a person show to prove trademark infringement?
    A. Ownership of a trademark
    B. That the defendant used a similar trademark in commerce
    C. That the defendant's use of a similar trademark is likely to confuse consumers
    D. Ownership of a trademark and that the defendant used a similar trademark in commerce
    E. Ownership of a trademark, that the defendant used a similar trademark in commerce, and that the defendant's use of a similar trademark is likely to confuse consumers

15. What is cybersquatting?
    A. When a person owns a patent but does not make, use, or sell his or her invention
    B. When a person registers a domain name that is a registered trademark or trade name of another entity
    C. When a person uses the copyrighted materials of another without appropriate acknowledgment
    D. When a person publicly advertises the sensitive confidential information of a business or other entity on the internet
    E. None of these is correct.

## ENDNOTES

1. Internet World Stats, "Internet Usage Statistics: World Internet Users and Population Stats," March 3, 2020. http://www.internetworldstats.com/stats.htm (accessed April 30, 2020).
2. U.S. Constitution, Art. 1, sec. 8, cl. 8.
3. U.S. Code, Vol. 35, sec. 1-376.
4. Leahy-Smith America Invents Act, Pub. L. No. 112-29, 125 Stat. 284 (2011).
5. United States Patent and Trademark Office, "FY 2019 Performance and Accountability Report," November 2019. https://www.uspto.gov/sites/default/files/documents/USPTOFY19PAR.pdf (accessed April 30, 2020).
6. U.S. Code, Vol. 35, sec. 102.
7. Plant Variety Protection Act (1970), U.S. Code Vol. 7, sec. 2421, 2422, 2541.
8. *Diamond v. Chakrabarty*, 447 U.S. 303 (1980).
9. U.S. Code, Vol. 35, sec. 102(b).
10. U.S. Code, Vol. 35, sec. 101.
11. U.S. Code, Vol. 35, sec. 103.
12. *Hartford v. Moore*, 181 F. 132 (S.D.N.Y. 1910).
13. United States Patent and Trademark Office, "Data Visualization Center, Traditional Total Pendency," April 2020. https://www.uspto.gov/corda/dashboards/patents/main.dashxml?CTNAVID=1004 (accessed April 30, 2020).
14. U.S. Code, Vol. 35, sec. 7.
15. U.S. Code, Vol. 35, sec. 282.
16. U.S. Code, Vol. 35, sec. 284.
17. U.S. Code, Vol. 35, sec. 285.
18. U.S. Code, Vol. 18, sec. 1831-1839.
19. *William L. Jones et al. v. Peggy Hamilton*, Alabama Court of Civil Appeals, Opinion, January 22, 2010. Available at: https://law.justia.com/cases/alabama/court-of-appeals-civil/2010/2081077.html (accessed April 30, 2020).
20. U.S. Code, Vol. 15, sec. 1051 *et seq.*
21. United States Patent and Trademark Office, "FY 2019 Performance and Accountability Report," November 2019. https://www.uspto.gov/sites/default/files/documents/USPTOFY19PAR.pdf (accessed April 30, 2020).
22. U.S. Code, Vol. 15, sec. 1114.
23. U.S. Code, Vol. 15, sec. 1065.
24. U.S. Code, Vol. 15, sec. 1111.
25. U.S. Code, Vol. 15, sec. 1051.
26. U.S. Code, Vol. 15, sec. 1051.
27. U.S. Code, Vol. 15, sec. 1052.
28. United States Patent and Trademark Office, "Data Visualization Center, Total Pendency," April 2020. https://www.uspto.gov/dashboards/trademarks/main.dashxml (accessed July 11, 2020).

29. U.S. Patent and Trademark Office, "Trademark Manual of Examining Procedure, Section 1200," October 2018. https://tmep.uspto.gov/RDMS/TMEP/current#/current/TMEP-1200d1e3042.html (accessed April 30, 2020).
30. U.S. Code, Vol. 15, sec. 1063.
31. U.S. Code, Vol. 15, sec. 1058.
32. U.S. Code, Vol. 15, sec. 1059.
33. U.S. Code, Vol. 15, sec. 1114.
34. U.S. Code, Vol. 15, sec. 1125.
35. U.S. Code, Vol. 15, sec. 1114.
36. *Toys "R" Us v. Akkaoui*, 40 U.S.P.Q.2d (BNA) 1836 (N.D. Cal. Oct. 29, 1996).
37. U.S. Code, Vol. 15, sec. 1116.
38. U.S. Code, Vol. 15, sec. 1117.
39. U.S. Code, Vol. 15, sec. 1117.
40. Verisign, "The Verisign Domain Name Industry Brief," March 2020. https://www.verisign.com/assets/domain-name-report-Q42019.pdf (accessed April 30, 2020).
41. U.S. Code, Vol. 15, sec. 1125(d).
42. World Intellectual Property Organization, "WIPO Arbitration and Mediation Center, 2019 Review," April 8, 2020. https://www.wipo.int/amc/en/new/2019review.html (accessed April 30, 2020).
43. Copyright Act (1976), U.S. Code, Vol. 17, sec. 101 *et seq*.
44. U.S. Code, Vol. 17, sec. 102(a).
45. U.S. Code, Vol. 17, sec. 106.
46. U.S. Code, Vol. 17, sec. 101.
47. U.S. Code, Vol. 17, sec. 302.
48. U.S. Code, Vol. 17, sec. 411.
49. U.S. Code, Vol. 17, sec. 410.
50. U.S. Copyright Office, "Registration Processing Times April 1-September 30, 2019," 2019. https://www.copyright.gov/registration/docs/processing-times-faqs.pdf (accessed April 30, 2020).
51. U.S. Copyright Office, "I've Heard About a 'Poor Man's Copyright.' What Is It?" Undated. https://www.copyright.gov/help/faq/faq-general.html#poorman (accessed April 30, 2020).
52. World Intellectual Property Organization, "Berne Convention for the Protection of Literary and Artistic Works," Undated. https://www.wipo.int/treaties/en/ip/berne/ (accessed April 30, 2020).
53. *Williams v. Crichton*, 84 F.3d 581, 590 (2d Cir. 1996).
54. U.S. Code, Vol. 17, sec. 504.
55. U.S. Code, Vol. 17, sec. 107.
56. U.S. Copyright Office, "More Information on Fair Use," April 2020. https://www.copyright.gov/fair-use/more-info.html (accessed April 29, 2020).
57. *Bill Graham Archives v. Dorling Kindersley Ltd.*, 448 F.3d 605 (2d Cir. 2006).
58. Digital Millennium Copyright Act, Pub. L. No. 105-304, 112 Stat. 2860 (1998), codified in scattered sections of U.S. Code Vol. 17.
59. U.S. Code, Vol. 17, sec. 1201.
60. U.S. Code, Vol. 17, sec. 1201.
61. U.S. Code, Vol. 17, sec. 1204.
62. U.S. Code, Vol. 17, sec. 512.
63. U.S. Code, Vol. 17, sec. 512(k)(1).
64. U.S. Code, Vol. 17, sec. 512.
65. U.S. Code, Vol. 17, sec. 512(a).
66. U.S. Code, Vol. 17, sec. 512(c)(3).
67. U.S. Code, Vol. 17, sec. 117.
68. Google,"Content Delistings Due to Copyright," Undated. https://transparencyreport.google.com/copyright/overview?hl=en (accessed April 30, 2020).
69. *A&M Records v. Napster, Inc.*, 239 F.3d 1004 (9th Cir. 2001).
70. HathiTrust, "Statistics Information," Updated daily. http://www.hathitrust.org/statistics_info (accessed April 30, 2020).
71. *Authors Guild, Inc. v. HathiTrust*, 755 F.3d 87 (2d Cir. 2014).

CHAPTER 11

# The Role of Contracts

CONTRACTS ARE USED to form relationships between parties for the sale of goods and services. People enter into contracts every day. Most of us never even think about the terms of everyday contracts or the rules governing those contracts. For example, you enter into a contract when you buy a cup of coffee at a local coffeehouse. Many people buy things online. The terms of those purchases are governed by a contract.

This chapter discusses contract law. It is important to understand the basics of traditional contract law so you can apply them to online contracts. This chapter also discusses special types of online contracts. Finally, this chapter introduces some emerging information security issues in contracting for services in cyberspace.

## Chapter 11 Topics

This chapter covers the following topics and concepts:

- What general contract law principles are
- How to contract online
- What special types of contracts in cyberspace are
- How these contracts regulate behavior
- What some emerging contract law issues are
- What some case studies and examples are

## Chapter 11 Goals

When you complete this chapter, you will be able to:

- Describe traditional contract law principles
- Describe the main differences between contracting on paper and contracting online
- Describe shrinkwrap, clickwrap, and browsewrap agreements
- Describe end user license agreements
- Discuss why it is important to include information security provisions in contracts

## General Contracting Principles

Contracts are used everywhere. A **contract** is a promise between people to sell goods or perform services. Some basic contractual principles apply to all contracts, no matter what the underlying transaction is. People use contracts to state the rules of their relationship. Contracts determine how parties will act with one another. They recite the promises that each party makes to the other. They also help describe what happens if the parties cannot complete their contract.

A mixture of common law and code law governs contract formation and performance. Many states have enacted statutes that govern certain types of contracts. One law that many states have in common is the law addressing the sale of goods. Laws governing the sale of goods are part of the Uniform Commercial Code (UCC), written by the National Conference of Commissioners on Uniform State Laws (NCCUSL). The NCCUSL works to develop uniform state laws and has been in existence since 1892.[1] Each state appoints commissioners to work on draft model laws. It took the NCCUSL 10 years to write the UCC.

The UCC is a model law that states can adopt. Every state has adopted all or parts of the UCC. However, states may amend portions of the UCC when they adopt it. For example, Article 2 of the UCC addresses the sale of goods. A "good" is a movable object such as a computer, desk, or chair. States have enacted similar laws governing the sale of goods so that commerce between the states can be predictable and uniform. This helps encourage even more commerce and business. The UCC does not cover every aspect of contract law, however. Many parts of contract law are left to each state's common law.[2]

**NOTE**

When reviewing contract laws in a particular state, it is important to study both the state's code law and its common law.

**NOTE**

The ALI and the NCCUSL worked together to create the UCC.

Common law contracting principles also are similar among the states. The Restatement (Second) of the Law of Contracts, a treatise on common law contract rules prepared by the American Law Institute (ALI),[3] summarizes the common law rules. The ALI is a group of highly distinguished judges, lawyers, and legal scholars who review cases on a certain type of law, then compile the principles stated in those cases into a series of rules. These rules are not binding authority on a court the way statutes or court rulings are. However, they do offer guidance on identifying the common law.

This chapter discusses the basic rules that are applicable to all contracts. It also discusses how those rules apply to online or electronic contracts. However, this chapter does not discuss the special rules that apply to certain types of contracts such as real estate or securities transactions.

The general contract law rules are derived from the common law. It is important to keep in mind that the common law traditionally applies to contracts for services, whereas the UCC applies to contracts for goods.

### Contract Form

A contract is a legally binding agreement that is enforceable in court. Contracts can be either oral or written. Oral contracts are contracts that parties do not write down, whereas written contracts are contracts that may have been negotiated verbally, but are then written down. An oral contract is just as enforceable as a contract that is written down. However, there are a few reasons why written contracts are best. They include:

> **NOTE**
>
> A lawyer's favorite line, "An oral contract is not worth the paper it is written on," is attributed to Samuel Goldwyn. Goldwyn was a Hollywood producer who rose to fame in the 1920s.

- **Proof**—It is easier for a person to prove the existence of a written contract.
- **Terms**—It is easier for a person to prove the terms of a written contract.
- **Precision**—A written contract requires the parties to be more precise in defining their relationship.
- **Clarity**—A written contract is more likely to have terms that clarify what happens if a contract relationship fails.

Some types of contracts must be written down and the contracting parties must sign them. Otherwise, the contemplated transaction cannot take place. These contracts must be written down to prevent fraud between the contracting parties, according to a rule called the **Statute of Frauds**. For example, contracts for the sale of land must be written down. Some contracts for goods that are valued over $500 also must be written down.[4] The law requires these contracts to be written down and signed to provide proof of their existence. The law does not specify how contracts must be written down. Even exchanged text messages can be sufficient to demonstrate proof of a contract.[5]

No matter what the form of a contract, all contracts must have certain elements in order to be enforceable. For example, contracts must be made between parties that have the legal ability to enter into them. Parties can contract only for transactions that are legal and that do not violate basic societal principles.

Finally, the parties to the contract must show that they intended to enter into a specific transaction with specific terms, which is called mutual assent. Mutual assent is shown through the "offer" and "acceptance" process.

## Capacity to Contract

The law assumes that almost anyone can enter into a contract. There are few exceptions to this rule. People who enter into contracts must be able to understand that they are negotiating for a relationship. They also must be able to understand that each party will have rights and obligations because of the parties' agreement.

A court will not find a contract enforceable if a person was not able to understand the consequences of entering into the contract at the time that it was formed. A person who is unable to understand the consequences of entering into a contract lacks **contractual capacity**.

> **NOTE**
>
> A person who lacks "contractual capacity" is not bound by his or her contracts. Courts will not enforce contracts against a person who lacks contractual capacity.

The law recognizes that the following classes of people may lack contractual capacity:

- Children under the age of 18
- People who are mentally incompetent
- People who are intoxicated by drugs or alcohol

In most cases, courts will not enforce contracts against people in these classes. However, there are special rules for contracts for necessary items such as medical care. People who lack contractual capacity can be held responsible for contracts that they enter into for necessary items. These rules are applied subjectively. Courts look at the facts and circumstances of each case. The legal representatives for both children and mentally incompetent people may approve certain types of contracts on behalf of the people that they represent.

The contractual capacity of an intoxicated person requires special review. To avoid a contract based on intoxication, a person must be so intoxicated that his or her mental capacity is limited. Courts will look at objective measures of intoxication and the actions of the party. An intoxicated person's deliberate actions, such as writing contract terms on a napkin, might be used to show that a valid contract existed.

**NOTE**

An intoxicated person can lack the capacity to contract through drug or alcohol use. A court can find contractual incapacity even if a person's drug or alcohol use was voluntary. It depends on the facts of the case.

A person who is trying to avoid a contract may claim that he or she lacked the capacity to enter into the contract. If a person raises this defense, then he or she bears the burden of proving the lack of contractual capacity.

## Contract Legality

**NOTE**

Courts will not enforce illegal contracts. An illegal contract is formed when parties try to enter into an agreement to commit a crime or other wrongdoing.

Some types of contracts simply are not enforceable because they are against public policy. Public policy refers to the principles that form the beliefs of a society. A contract that is contrary to those principles is not enforceable.

An example of an unenforceable contract is a contract for murder. It is against the law, and public policy, to murder another person. Therefore, a court will not enforce a contract where one party agreed to kill another party for a sum of money. This type of contract is called an illegal contract.

Contracts that are not enforceable because of public policy reasons include:

**NOTE**

Contracts that are unfairly burdensome are called *unconscionable*. Unconscionable contracts are not enforceable.

- Contracts that reduce commercial competition
- Contracts to commit a crime or other wrongdoing
- Contracts that are unfairly burdensome to one party
- Contracts that discriminate based on unchangeable characteristics such as race, color, religion, or disability

## Form of Offer

An **offer** is an invitation to enter into a relationship or transaction of some kind.[6] The person who makes an offer, called an **offeror**, must put enough detail into the offer so that the other party knows what he or she is agreeing to. The other party is called an **offeree**.

The offer must contain enough terms and detail to describe the underlying transaction. In a transaction for the sale of goods, an offer typically would include terms describing the goods, the quantity of goods available, and their price. That way, the offeree would know what and how much he or she gets for the contract price. These are material terms of the transaction. An offer has enough detail when the offeree knows what is part of the bargain.

To be valid, an offer must be communicated to the other person. For example, an offeror selling a couch must communicate the item to be sold, when the item is available, and the price for the item. He or she must communicate all of these terms in order to make a sufficient offer. An offer is valid as soon as the offeree receives it.

An offeree must take action once an offer is communicated. An offer remains open until it is accepted, rejected, or retracted. An offer also can expire if too much time passes before an offeree accepts it. Sometimes offers say that they are valid only for a certain period. When that period ends, the offer expires. If an offer does not include a time period, then it expires after a reasonable period of time.

If an offeree does not agree to the terms of the offer, then it is rejected. An offeree also rejects an offer if he or she proposes terms that are different from the original offer. This is called a counteroffer. In this situation, the original offer is rejected when the counteroffer is proposed. The original offeror then has to decide whether to accept or reject the counteroffer. The parties cannot go back to the original offer unless one of them proposes it again.[7]

An original offeror also can revoke an initial offer. This means that the offer is no longer available. If an offer is to be cancelled, this must be done before an offeree accepts it.

 **NOTE**

In contracts for the sale of goods, the offeror is called the seller. The offeree is the buyer.

 **NOTE**

Offers expire after a reasonable period of time. Courts determine what a reasonable period of time is by looking at the facts and circumstances surrounding a case.

 **NOTE**

Usually offers and counteroffers are made during the negotiation process. Verbal negotiations are very normal. Parties do not always write down the offers and counteroffers that they make during this process. Sometimes the only offers that are written down are the final, accepted offers. These end up becoming the contractual terms.

## Form of Acceptance

An offer is accepted when the offeree agrees to the terms of the offeror's bargain. Traditionally, an acceptance had to have exactly the same words and terms as the original offer. This was called the **mirror image rule**. The mirror image rule meant that even a small change in terms or language between the offer and an acceptance served as a rejection of the original offer. The new terms in the acceptance then became a counteroffer. Parties had to be very careful in their negotiations to use the same terminology all the time to avoid the rule.

Today there is less emphasis on the mirror image rule. An acceptance does not have to be identical to an offer to be enforceable. Under the more relaxed rule, an acceptance is viewed as a counteroffer only if the terms of the acceptance change a material term in the offer. If the acceptance does not alter material terms, then it is enforceable. The UCC follows the relaxed mirror image rule.[10]

The offeree must clearly communicate acceptance back to the offeror. This includes the use of words such as "Yes" or "I accept." Acceptance of an offer also can be communicated through actions. One action that clearly communicates acceptance is paying money.

The timing of the acceptance is an important consideration under the common law of contracts. When parties are in the presence of one another, acceptance is communicated

### What Communications Constitute an Offer?

Courts frequently encounter questions about the types of communications that constitute an offer. The general rule is that a communication is considered an offer if an objective, reasonable person would consider it an offer.

Courts have long held that an advertisement can constitute a valid offer. The *Carlill v. Carbolic Smoke Ball Company* (1892) case is one of the oldest and most cited cases in this respect.[8] It is an old English contract law case. The Carbolic Smoke Ball was a flu and illness remedy. The manufacturer advertised in newspapers that it would pay Smoke Ball users a "reward" if they caught the flu after using the product.

The plaintiff in the case used the product and caught the flu. She asked the manufacturer to pay the "reward." The manufacturer declined to pay the reward. Eventually the case went to court. The English Court of Appeal held that the advertisement did indeed constitute a valid offer. It said that the plaintiff's actions in using the Carbolic Smoke Ball were a valid acceptance of that offer. The court found that the plaintiff acted reasonably in relying on the terms in the advertisement. The manufacturer needed to pay the reward that had been advertised.

However, not all advertisements constitute a valid offer. In *Leonard v. Pepsico, Inc.* (S.D.N.Y. 1999), the plaintiff claimed that a Pepsi television advertisement showing that "Pepsi points" could be redeemed to claim a Harrier jet was a valid contractual offer.[9] The plaintiff claimed he accepted the offer when he submitted Pepsi points, cash, and a claim form for the jet to Pepsi. You can see the commercial at http://www.youtube.com/watch?v=ZdackF2H7Qc.

The court held that it was clear that Pepsi's "offer" of the Harrier jet was a joke. It said that an objective, reasonable person would not believe that the television advertisement constituted a real offer.

The best part about this case is the court's opinion. It is clear from the opinion that the judge had a sense of humor and dramatic flair. In discussing the commercial, the judge wrote, "Plaintiff's insistence that the commercial appears to be a serious offer requires the Court to explain why the commercial is funny. Explaining why a joke is funny is a daunting task. . . . " You can read the opinion at https://law.justia.com/cases/federal/district-courts/FSupp2/88/116/2579076/.

**NOTE**

A material term in a contract is one that is necessary to understanding the underlying transaction. Material terms include item, price, quantity, and time when the item is available for delivery.

**NOTE**

An offeree's silence is not acceptance of a contract. An offeree usually has no legal obligation to respond to an offer.

instantaneously. A contract is automatically formed when the offeror receives the acceptance; the parties are clear on the terms of the offer and of the acceptance because they are in each other's presence. There is no break in communication that might indicate that the offer has been revoked.[11]

The situation is different for delayed communications. For those communications, courts developed the **mailbox rule**. The mailbox rule means that an offer is deemed accepted for legal purposes as soon as an offeree puts a written acceptance into the mailbox. The mailbox rule developed because there was often a time lag in postal communications that could cause the parties to doubt whether a contract existed. The relationship between the parties is clear if a contract forms upon mailing the acceptance. Under the mailbox rule, an acceptance is valid as soon as it is dispatched or sent. The mailbox rule also applies to electronic communications such as email.

If an offeror specifies that an offer must be accepted in a certain way, then the mailbox rule will not apply. The mailbox rule also does not apply if an offeror states that a contract does not form until he or she receives the acceptance. Today, many offers specifically require receipt of the acceptance before a contract is formed to avoid the application of the mailbox rule.

**NOTE**

The mailbox rule says that an acceptance is valid as soon as an offeree sends it. It applies only to acceptances. It does not apply to situations where the offeror revokes his offer. A revocation of an offer is valid once the offeree actually receives it.

## Meeting of the Minds

It is a basic rule of contract law that the parties to a contract must agree to its terms. To determine whether the parties really did make a contract, courts look to see if there is mutual agreement. A court studies the parties' words and actions to look for evidence that both parties acted as if they had entered into a contract with one another.

The idea that contracts form when there is a meeting of the minds is a long-standing feature of American law. The United States Supreme Court held in *Baltimore & Ohio Railroad Co. v. United States* (1923) that a contract can be inferred from the conduct of the parties.[12] This is true even if no written contract exists.

Meeting of the minds is evidenced through words, such as saying "I accept" in response to an offer. It also can be shown through the actions of a party. If the parties behave in a way that suggests there is a contract, then courts likely will enforce some sort of agreement.

**NOTE**

Mutual agreement is a contract law principle that is used to describe how the parties intend to act with respect to a contract. It is also called *mutual assent* or *meeting of the minds*. The case study at the end of this chapter includes a mutual assent issue.

## Consideration

In forming a contract, the parties must bargain for something of value. This is called consideration. **Consideration** is an essential contract element that means the parties have negotiated for, and are exchanging, something of value. Every contract must be supported by consideration. If there is no consideration, the contract is not enforceable.

Consideration is reciprocal. It means that both parties are promising to do something. For example, the offeror offers to develop a web page for $50 and the offeree accepts the offer. The offeror's consideration is developing the web page, whereas the offeree's consideration is paying $50 for the developed web page.

In the United States, courts do not usually review the value of the consideration that the parties exchange. They leave it to the parties to determine the sufficiency of their own deals. As long as a party has the capacity to contract, he or she is free to bargain and enter into contracts. This is true even if the individual enters into contracts with terms that might seem unwise. Courts generally only review whether the consideration was truly bargained for and whether there was a mutual exchange of promises.

Some transactions do not have consideration. If there is no consideration, there can be no contract. For example, gifts do not

**NOTE**

Consideration is an exchange of money, goods, or a promise to perform a certain action.

involve consideration. In addition, there is no consideration when value is given for a service that a person has already performed. This is called *prior consideration*. Prior consideration cannot be used to form a new contract.

In addition, there is no consideration when a person is already required to do something because of a preexisting obligation. For instance, you cannot enter into a contract with a firefighter to save your burning home because the firefighter already has an obligation to fight the fire.

## Performance and Breach of Contract

A contract must be performed in order to be complete. This means that each party must fulfill his or her promises to one another. If the parties complete all of their promises to one another, then they are discharged from any further obligation. *Discharged* means that each party is freed from his or her contractual requirements.

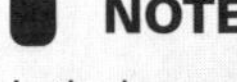

**NOTE**

In the law, a party is discharged when he or she no longer has any responsibilities or obligations toward the other party.

There are three general types of contractual performance:

- **Complete performance**—When a party performs all of his or her contract promises, this is called **complete performance**.
- **Substantial performance**—A party's performance of all material contract promises is known as **substantial performance**. Nonperformance of some terms results in a minor breach of contract.
- **Incomplete performance**—A party's failure to perform his or her contract promises constitutes **incomplete performance**. This kind of nonperformance results in a material breach of contract.

If one party does not fulfill all of his or her promises, then the other party may sue that party for breach of contract. The non-breaching party may sue for both a minor breach of contract and a material breach of contract. Once a lawsuit is filed, a court reviews the parties' contractual performance. It then determines what remedies are available to the non-breaching party.

**NOTE**

A **remedy** also is called *legal relief*. Courts grant remedies in order to enforce the rights of the parties that appear before it. A winning party is usually the party that receives a remedy.

In contract law, a court may order a variety of legal remedies. It awards remedies depending upon the facts of the case. The available legal remedies in a contract law case include money damages, specific performance, contract rescission, and contract reformation.

The most common type of remedy in a breach of contract dispute is an award of damages. *Damages* refers to money that the court awards to the party that did not breach the contract. For the most part, damages are used to make a non-breaching party whole. They try to compensate a party and put him or her in the same position as if the breach never occurred. Under the law, a non-breaching party has a duty to avoid or reduce the total damages caused by the other party's breach of contract.

There are four types of money damages that can be awarded in a contract case:

- **Compensatory damages**—A money award that compensates a non-breaching party for the other party's breach is called **compensatory damages.** These damages place the non-breaching party in the same position he or she would have been in had the contract been fully performed. This is the most common type of damages that courts award.
- **Consequential damages**—A money award that compensates the non-breaching party for foreseeable damages that arise from circumstances outside of the contract. The non-breaching party cannot mitigate these **consequential damages.**
- **Liquidated damages**—A contractual grant of money damages. The parties predetermine the amount of damages before entering into the contract. The contract specifically states the amount of damages that a non-breaching party is entitled to. Courts will approve **liquidated damages** as long as they are reasonable.
- **Nominal damages**—A money award to the non-breaching party even though he or she has not suffered any financial loss because of a breach of contract. An award of **nominal damages** recognizes that a breach occurred, but nothing more.

**NOTE**

A **duty to mitigate** is the non-breaching party's obligation not to aggravate the harm caused by a breach. A person may not allow the damages to rise if it is possible to keep the damages low. He or she must take reasonable actions to limit the amount of harm caused by the breaching party.

**NOTE**

Punitive damages are damages that punish a party for bad or wrongful behavior. Although punitive damages are usually available in tort law, they are generally not allowed in breach of contract cases.

**NOTE**

Specific performance is an equitable remedy. An equitable remedy forces a person to do (or not do) some act. Equitable remedies usually are awarded by courts only if legal remedies are inadequate. Legal remedies are requests for money damages.

Another remedy that courts can award is **specific performance.** Specific performance is a legal term that refers to situations where a court orders a party to complete his or her contractual duties. Courts do not usually award specific performance unless the underlying contractual transaction is unique. It is harder for courts to determine the damages amount when the underlying transaction is unique. If it is hard to determine damages, then it is more likely that a court will award specific performance.

Non-breaching parties usually do not ask for specific performance as a remedy. This is because if people are forced to perform their contractual duties, they sometimes perform those duties poorly. In addition, courts do not want to have to supervise performance to ensure that a party is performing properly. Courts award specific performance only when no other remedy will compensate the non-breaching party.

Courts also can rescind a contract. This remedy undoes the contract and puts the parties in the same position that they would have been in if there had been no contract at all. This remedy is often available if there has been a material breach of contract. In order to rescind a contract, the parties must return any consideration that they each received. For example, they must return the goods and money that they exchanged under the contract.

**FYI**

Sometimes a contracting party might sense that the other party has cold feet about a contract. This might lead the first party to worry about an eventual breach even if repudiation has not yet occurred. Under the UCC, a party concerned about repudiation can demand that the other party provide adequate assurance that he or she is not going to repudiate the contract.[13] If the other party fails to provide adequate assurance, then the first party can sue for breach of contract.

Finally, courts can reform a contract. In contract reformation, a court rewrites the contract to express the true intent of the parties to a contract. The parties are then expected to perform the contract as rewritten. Courts often use reformation to fix contracts that have obvious clerical errors. Contract reformation is an equitable remedy.

## Contract Repudiation

**Repudiation** is a refusal to perform a contract duty. It occurs when one party either denies the existence of a contract or refuses to perform his or her contractual obligations. Repudiation also is called anticipatory breach of contract. Repudiation occurs when one party clearly communicates that he or she will not perform his or her contractual duties.

Under the common law, a nonrepudiating party can react in three ways to repudiation:

- Immediately consider the contract terminated; that is, the party does not have to perform any of his or her own contractual obligations.
- Wait and see if the other party decides to perform his or her obligations after all.
- Immediately sue the repudiating party for breach of contract.

If one party repudiates a contract, the party who is relying on the contract bears the burden of proving that the contract is indeed valid and enforceable. Usually this is the person who files a breach of contract action. The filer must prove that there was a legitimate contract between the parties using the elements already discussed in this chapter.

Another aspect of repudiation has to do with how a contract is signed. This distinction becomes important later in this chapter. Under traditional legal principles, a party to a contract can always repudiate a contract on the basis that another person forged his or her signature on the contract.

If one party claims that the signature is not authentic, then the other party has the burden of proving that the signature is authentic. He or she has to present evidence that prevents the other party from repudiating the signature. The party presents this evidence because he or she wants a court to enforce the contract.

In traditional contract law, contracts are negotiated face-to-face. The parties know one another and would know if a signature was forged. Sometimes contracts are signed in front of witnesses. If witnesses watch the parties signing a contract, it is harder for one party to repudiate a signature. This is a way of assuring that a party cannot repudiate a signature in traditional, paper-based contracts.

**NOTE**

Nonrepudiation becomes an important issue in online contracts. Cryptography can be used to make sure that parties cannot repudiate the contracts that they enter into.

## Contracting Online

The rise of the internet and e-commerce has made online contracts very common. They are used every day. People enter into a contract when buying goods through online retailers, such as Amazon.com. They enter into auction contracts on eBay. A person agrees to terms-of-use contracts when using free wireless internet at a local coffee shop. In many instances, you might not even be aware that you are entering into valid, enforceable contracts.

**NOTE**

E-commerce sales in the United States are expected to exceed $740 billion by 2023.[14]

Online contracts are contracts that are entered into over the internet or through a technological medium. There is nothing particularly special about these contracts other than the medium used to form the contract. The underlying transactions are the same for online contracts and traditional contracts.

Although online contracts can make transacting business easier, they also present some unique challenges for the contracting parties and for the law. The law generally presumes that contracting parties at least know of one another before entering into a contract. That is not necessarily true for online contracts. When people contract over the internet (generally through a web-based service provider), it is unlikely that they are in the same state, geographical region, or even country. Parties that contract electronically give up certain rights when they contract online. They include:

**NOTE**

In this chapter, the term *traditional contracts* refers to written and oral contracts. *Online contracts* refers to contracts that are created through a technological communication process, such as via email, text message, or the internet.

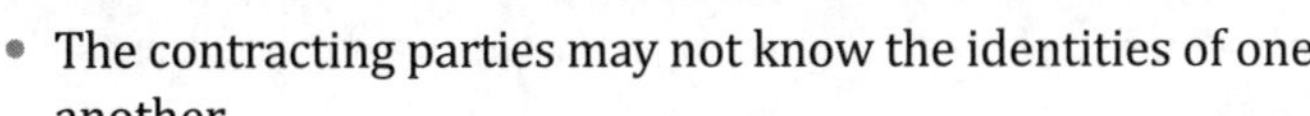

- The contracting parties may not know the identities of one another.

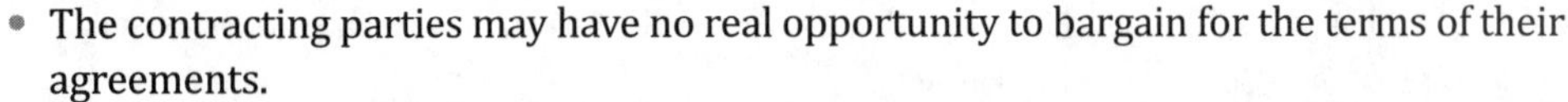

- The contracting parties may have no real opportunity to bargain for the terms of their agreements.
- It may be difficult to determine the material terms of the contract if the parties exchanged multiple electronic communications.

It is obvious today that people can indeed contract through online processes, but that was not always the case. The U.S. federal government has created legislation that states, for interstate commerce, that online or electronic contracts are just as valid as traditional, paper-based contracts.[15] States also have created their own laws. The Uniform Electronic Transactions Act (UETA) specifically states that its purpose is to "remove barriers to electronic commerce by validating" electronic contracts.[16] Forty-seven states have adopted the UETA,[17] whereas the states that have not adopted the UETA have adopted similar laws allowing electronic contracts.

**NOTE**

Jurisdiction is an important issue for online contracts. A complete discussion of jurisdiction is out of scope for this chapter. It is important to be aware that many online contracts contain clauses that require lawsuits about the contract to be litigated in certain places. This is an attempt by at least one party to control jurisdiction issues.

For the most part, the rise in the use of online contracts has not changed fundamental contract law principles. There still must be offer, acceptance, and consideration. The parties still must reach a meeting of the minds. The E-SIGN Act and UETA recognize that basic contracting principles apply to all contracts, even online ones.

Courts have acknowledged this in case law as well. The Second Circuit Court of Appeals has said, "[While] new commerce on the

## The Validity of Online Contracts: The UETA and E-SIGN Acts

The NCCUSL created the UETA in July 1999. The UETA covers business and commercial transactions. However, it does not cover transactions between private parties.

The NCCUSL created the UETA for several purposes. One of them was to legitimize electronic contracts. The UETA recognizes that parties contract electronically because of speed and other economic efficiencies. It also recognizes that some rules, such as the common law Statute of Frauds, can be a barrier to electronic contracts in some circumstances. The comments to the UETA make it clear that it does not create new rules for online contracting. Instead, it recognizes that general contract law rules and principles apply to transactions that are conducted electronically.

The main benefit of the UETA is that it specifically states that electronic contracts are enforceable. It also states that an "electronic record" satisfies any common law requirements that a contract be in writing. This helps to soften the application of a rule such as the Statute of Frauds for records that might exist only in electronic form in an information system. Under the UETA, an electronic record is any record that is stored in the memory of an information system.

The UETA also requires that courts and contracting parties give an electronic signature the same effect as a handwritten signature. Under the UETA, an electronic signature is "an electronic sound, symbol, or process attached to or logically associated with an electronic record and executed or adopted by a person with the intent to sign the electronic record."[18] Clicking on an "I agree" button on a web page is an electronic signature under the UETA definition. Typing your name at the bottom of an email also can be a valid, legal signature under the UETA as long as you intend it to serve as your electronic signature.

The UETA is not a digital signature statute. It does not define cryptographic or technology standards for digital signatures. It does acknowledge that electronic signatures that have certain security protections may provide additional reliability about the identities of contracting parties.

Forty-seven states have enacted the UETA and codified it within their own laws. The states that have not enacted it have created their laws regarding electronic contracts instead.

Congress enacted the Electronic Signatures in Global and National Commerce (E-SIGN) Act in June 2000. The E-SIGN Act validates the use of electronic records and signatures in interstate commerce. Similar to the UETA, it is designed to facilitate and promote e-commerce. It also does not affect fundamental contract law principles. The E-SIGN Act contains provisions that are very similar to the UETA. The E-SIGN Act allows contracting parties to use electronic records to satisfy any laws that require a contract be written.

Similar to the UETA, E-SIGN is technology neutral. In fact, it forbids any state or federal statute from requiring that a specific technology be used for electronic transactions in interstate commerce. E-SIGN specifically states that it does not preempt state laws based on the UETA. It also does not preempt state laws that are similar to the UETA. State laws that are significantly different from the UETA and E-SIGN are preempted by E-SIGN.

Internet has exposed courts to many new situations, it has not fundamentally changed the principles of contract."[19] Even though courts apply the same basic contracting principles to online contracts, they sometimes reach inconsistent results. This is particularly noticeable in early cases reviewing clickwrap contracts and current cases reviewing browsewrap contracts. How courts treat these types of cases is still evolving. They are discussed later in this chapter.

This section describes some of the ways in which online contracting is different from traditional contracting. It is important to remember that this area of law is continuing to develop.

## Legal Capacity Online

The rules for contractual capacity do not change in cyberspace. Unfortunately, in online contracting it can be very difficult for parties to determine whom they are doing business with. Courts do not enforce contracts against a person who lacks contractual capacity. Therefore, it is critical for organizations conducting business on the internet to know who their customers are.

Businesses must be concerned about children in particular. There are laws that protect children while they are on the internet. The Children's Online Privacy Protection Act (COPPA) requires websites to get parental consent before collecting personal information from children. A business would need to collect personal information in order to enter into a contract with a consumer. Therefore, COPPA can potentially apply to any business that does business on the internet. The Federal Trade Commission (FTC) oversees COPPA and can bring enforcement actions and impose civil penalties for COPPA violations.

There are several ways that website operators can identify children. If a business website can properly identify children, then it can make sure that it does not enter into potentially unenforceable contracts with them.

Another issue in online contracts is verifying the identity and authenticity of the contracting parties. This is a separate issue from contracting with parties that have legal capacity. Digital signatures can be used to verify the identity of contracting parties. They are discussed later in this chapter.

## Form of Offer and Acceptance

A person can enter into online contracts in several ways. Special types of contracts, such as clickwrap contracts, are discussed in a different section of this chapter. This section discusses contracts formed through direct electronic communications, including email, text messaging, and instant messaging.

In contract disputes, timing is everything. It is sometimes critical to know when a contract forms. This is usually because an offeror is arguing that he or she revoked an offer, whereas an offeree is arguing that he or she accepted the offer in a timely fashion. A court must determine which came first: revocation or acceptance. Electronic communications can complicate the analysis of these timing issues.

**NOTE**

Keep in mind that these discussions are academic. If all parties are performing their contractual duties without a problem, no one is concerned about when the contract was formed. Problems arise when a party claims that a contract did not exist or when the parties cannot agree on the terms of the contract. At that point, courts will analyze the entire contract formation process.

General contract law principles state that when parties are communicating instantaneously, a contract forms when the offeror receives an offeree's acceptance. Communications are instantaneous when there is no break in communications between offer and acceptance. The parties are, for the most part, clear on the terms of the contract. There is no doubt about the status of the offer and acceptance. Oral communications are clearly instantaneous communications. Courts also have held that fax and telephone communications also are instantaneous.

These same general contract law principles say that where there is a delay in communication, the parties must follow the mailbox rule to determine when an acceptance is valid. In these situations, unless otherwise specified in an offer, acceptance is valid once it is mailed. This is so that parties can be clear on the status of a contract when communications are not instantaneous. Communications that take place through U.S. mail are delayed communications. These communications must follow the mailbox rule.

**NOTE**

This section assumes that electronic communications between parties have not been forged or intercepted.

Both of these principles can be implicated in electronic communications. Electronic communications processes blur the line between sending and receiving communications. They can make it hard for the parties, and courts, to determine when offer and acceptance occurred.

### *Email Communications*

Email communications contain both instantaneous and delayed communication elements. Depending upon the nature of the email transmission, there may be a delay from when the message is sent to when it is received. There also may be a delay in the receiving party's actual receipt of the email if the party does not read the email at the moment when it is received.

**NOTE**

Email can be nearly instantaneous if the parties are reading and responding to emails as they are received.

A contracting party has the option of printing the emails and storing them. A chain of email messages, assuming that they are not altered, can be used to demonstrate that the contracting parties achieved a meeting of the minds. Parties also can use the email chain to help determine the material terms of an offer and an acceptance.

**NOTE**

Keep in mind that the rules of evidence govern how parties use records as proof in a lawsuit. A discussion of the rules of evidence is outside of the scope of this chapter.

Questions about email communications and timing arise if the status of the offer is called into question. Most commentators argue, and many cases have agreed, that the mailbox rule should apply to email communications. That is, an acceptance is valid as soon as an offeree clicks on the "Send" button to email their acceptance to the offeror. If an offeree receives the offeror's revocation after sending his or her acceptance, the revocation has no effect and the contract is formed.[20]

### *Text and Instant Messages*

Sometimes electronic communications do look more similar to face-to-face communications. For example, text messaging and instant messaging (IM) communications tend to occur in real-time. In this way, these communications parallel oral conversations, which are considered instantaneous. It can be argued that the common rules regarding instantaneous communications should apply here. That means that contracting parties can enter into enforceable contracts through text and instant messaging. The mailbox rule would not apply.

Contracts made through text and instant messages suffer the same problems as oral contracts. Similar to oral contracts, the parties might agree to terms too quickly and then have second thoughts. The parties can easily repudiate such contracts, especially if there is no log of the conversation. It can be hard for parties to prove the existence of these contracts and their terms later when the contract is disputed. Unless a contracting party saves these messages or prints them out, or asks his or her cellular or internet provider for records, it can be difficult for courts to determine the contractual terms.

**NOTE**

By their very name, instant messages are instantaneous communications.

### *Twitter and Other Social Networking Sites*

**NOTE**

Twitter limits updates to 280 characters. It calls these updates *Tweets*.

Consumer use of social networking sites is growing. Twitter reported 330 million monthly active users in 2019.[21] Facebook reported 2.45 billion global monthly active users during the same time.[22] Most social networking sites, including Facebook and Twitter, allow users to give periodic updates on what they are doing. The user's friends and followers can respond to the user's posts. These sites exist to facilitate online communication between parties.

**FYI**

It is clear that agreements can be violated via Facebook communications. In 2014, a Florida appellate court held that a court-approved confidentiality agreement was violated by a post on Facebook. In that case, two parties entered into a confidentiality agreement that protected the terms of a settlement agreement between the parties. The daughter of one of the parties posted a derogatory term about the other party immediately after the settlement was reached. The posting also included confidential information about the settlement agreement. The appellate court held that the posting violated the terms of the settlement agreement. It also held that the settlement agreement did not have to be honored.[23]

Because Facebook and Twitter both contain mechanisms for conversation exchange, it is entirely possible that parties can enter into a contract using these mechanisms. It will be interesting to see how courts review offer, acceptance, and mutual assent criteria using social network site postings. It might be easier to prove that a contract exists with Facebook, as Facebook pages can contain the contents of the parties' contract negotiations. This is especially true if parties are communicating through the Facebook Marketplace function to buy and sell goods. It might be more difficult to prove the existence of a contract, and the contract's material terms, when it is made through a service such as Twitter.

Courts sometimes skirt around the issue of the exact moment that a contract forms in electronic transactions. They routinely recognize that electronic communications do create valid contracts. To do this, they review the conduct of the parties to determine if the communications and the parties' actions show an offer, acceptance, or meeting of the minds.

To ensure that online contracts are enforceable, the best course of action is for contracting parties to state when acceptance takes place. Language such as "a contract is formed when I confirm that I have received your reply" can be added to email negotiations to make sure that parties understand when an enforceable contract is formed.

## Existence and Enforcement

As with traditional contracts, parties to an online contract must perform their obligations to be discharged. If a party does not fulfill his or her contractual obligations, that party is in breach of contract and can be sued by the non-breaching party.

In the online environment, it can be difficult for a party to prove the existence of a contract. This is because there is often no hard copy of the contract in existence, such as a contract agreed to via text or instant message. It also can be difficult to prove the terms of the contract because they may have changed over time, such as through a long-running email conversation. In some ways, online communications and contracts present some of the same proof problems as oral contracts.

Contracting parties must keep a paper or electronic record of the transactions that they enter into. These records are necessary to prove the existence of a contract. They also prove its material terms and conditions, such as the date the parties entered into the contract. It is important to save these records in case one party argues that the contract was improperly modified.

A party can save hard copies of contract terms by printing screen shots or email confirmations. They also can save an electronic record of the transaction. Under the UETA, information stored in information processing systems is an electronic record. It is a valid way to memorialize a contract.

Online contracts are enforced the same way as traditional contracts. If a court hears a case about a contract dispute, it must be able to determine if there has been a valid offer, acceptance, and mutual agreement. It will review the actions of the parties in order to make this determination.

**NOTE**

Sometimes the law comes down to common sense. Contracting parties should take steps to preserve the electronic communications that show a contract's material terms.

**NOTE**

The UETA specifically recognizes that agreements can be found through the actions of parties to a contract. This codifies the common law rule.

## Authenticity and Nonrepudiation

There is generally no real difference between traditional contracts and online ones other than the method of entering into the contracts. The traditional legal principles and methods that courts use to resolve contract disputes can be applied to online contracts in most instances with few modifications.

One area in which there is a notable difference, however, between traditional contracts and online ones are the issues of authenticity and nonrepudiation. *Authenticity* refers to the problem of attributing an electronic message to the person who allegedly sent it. *Nonrepudiation* ensures that a party cannot dispute the validity of the message. In the online environment, authenticity and nonrepudiation can be assured with technology processes.

It is important to distinguish between repudiation and nonrepudiation.

- Repudiation is a legal term. It refers to a party's ability to deny the existence of a contract.
- Nonrepudiation is a technical term. It refers to a process that is used to make sure that a party cannot repudiate, or deny the existence of, a contract.

Even though nonrepudiation is a technical term, it can be demonstrated in nontechnical ways. Assume that a traditional written contract is signed in front of witnesses. By signing the document in front of witnesses, the parties are taking steps to make sure that neither party can repudiate, or deny, his or her signatures. The use of witnesses is a nontechnical nonrepudiation process.

Nonrepudiation becomes an important issue in online contracts. Without a way to demonstrate nonrepudiation, parties that contract electronically might be able to deny that a valid contract exists. Cryptography can be used to make sure that parties cannot repudiate the contracts that they enter into. Contracting parties can use digital signature technology, which uses a cryptographic process to create and verify electronic communications, to provide assurance of their identities. Digital signature technology also can be used to verify that the contract exists and that it is unmodified.

> **NOTE**
>
> Digital signatures, digitized signatures, and electronic signatures are all different. A digital signature uses a cryptographic process to ensure authenticity and nonrepudiation. A digitized signature is a digital version of a handwritten signature. An electronic signature is any mark that a person uses with the intent to sign an electronic record.

The law recognizes that the use of digital signature technology adds a new element to contract law analysis. Under the UETA, digital signature technology is considered a security procedure.[24] A security procedure is a procedure or process used to:

- Verify that an electronic signature belongs to a specific person
- Detect changes or errors in the information in an electronic record

The use of a security procedure such as a digital signature strengthens reliance on an electronic communication. For information security purposes, use of a digital signature creates a presumption that the signature is valid. The party that wants to argue that the signature is invalid bears the burden of proving that it is invalid. This is different from the burden of proof for signature repudiation in traditional contracts.

In traditional contract law, the party that relies on a contract has the burden of proving that a handwritten signature is authentic. In the electronic realm, the party that wants out of a contract has the burden of proving that a digital signature is invalid. This shifting burden of proof illustrates one way in which traditional contract law principles must adjust for online contracts.

## Special Types of Contracts in Cyberspace

People encounter special types of online contracts every day. When you download software over the internet, you likely enter into a contract with the software developer regarding your use of that software. If you create a new online social networking profile, you enter into a contract with the social networking platform provider. It is fair to say that most people do not read the "terms of use" or "terms of service" documents before clicking on "I agree" in order to access an online product or service.

Such a contract is called a **contract of adhesion**. An offeror drafts these types of contracts for its own benefit. The offeree has little opportunity to negotiate the terms of the contract. In order to use the underlying product or service, the offeree must accept all the terms of the contract. It is a "take it or leave it" contract. In this type of contract, the offeror has all of the bargaining power. The underlying question in these types of contracts is whether there is agreement between the parties over the contract terms. Do the parties truly have a meeting of the minds?

**FYI**

Take a moment to look at the terms of service documents for common online services. You can read the Google Terms of Services document at http://www.google.com/policies/terms/. The Facebook terms of service document, called "Statement of Rights and Responsibilities," is available at https://www.facebook.com/legal/terms.

Contracts of adhesion sound bad, but they are sometimes necessary. This is especially true for e-commerce transactions. E-commerce could be substantially slowed if merchants had to negotiate the terms of every sale with a consumer. Thus, they create form contracts for multiple uses to expedite commerce.

Contracts of adhesion also are called "form" contracts or "boilerplate" contracts because they are presented as standard forms. They contain standard terms that are used regardless of where the transaction takes place. These terms typically favor the offeror. For instance, they might have terms that limit a person's rights if the offeror breaches the contract. They also may require any lawsuits about the contract to be filed in the offeror's home state.

In the online environment, end user license agreements are the most encountered contracts of adhesion. An **end user license agreement (EULA)** is a contract between the manufacturer or distributor of a piece of software or a service and the end user of the application. It states how the software or service can be used.

**NOTE**

In the law, *boilerplate language* is any standard language that a person or entity can reuse in multiple contracts with few edits.

EULAs are particularly important in the software context. This is because they help protect the software owner's copyright in his or her product. Computer software can be protected by copyright laws. Software owners traditionally license their products rather than selling them. This helps them protect their copy and distribution rights. In many instances, it even gives them more control over their products than copyright law allows because the EULA specifies how consumers use software and places limitations on that use.

**NOTE**

A license is a grant of permission to use a product or service in certain situations. It is not a sale of the underlying software.

Depending on the nature of the underlying transaction, a EULA also might be called a "terms of use" or a "terms of service" agreement. A EULA is traditionally used for products such as software that a user purchases or downloads. "Terms of service" is used for online services, such as search engine or social networking services. The phrase "terms of use" might be used for both products and services.

At the end of the day it really does not matter what these types of documents call themselves. It is important to understand that all of these documents try to create a contract between the software or service owner and the person who uses the software or service. This chapter uses the terms EULA and "terms of service agreement" somewhat interchangeably. However, there are several different specific terms for these types of contracts. They include:

- Shrinkwrap contracts
- Clickwrap contracts
- Browsewrap contracts

## Shrinkwrap Contracts

The term **shrinkwrap contract** almost exclusively refers to software license agreements, specifically those that are included within a box of physical-media software. This term does not refer to software that consumers purchase and download online. With the proliferation of online software download services, you may not see actual physical media with a shrinkwrap contract that often anymore.

These types of EULAs are called shrinkwrap contracts because software manufacturers put them in a software box, underneath the shrinkwrap cellophane and packaging. Consumers do not actually see the terms of the EULA until after they buy the software. They then become bound to the terms of the agreement when they break the shrinkwrap and open the packaging. The agreement usually creates a software license between the consumer and the software developer.

At first courts viewed these types of contracts with suspicion. They tended to interpret the terms of the contract against the software manufacturer. Courts did not rule on whether these contracts were valid; instead, they looked at the terms in the contract. They would hold that some provisions of the contracts were unenforceable.

> **NOTE**
>
> Shrinkwrap licenses grew in popularity in the 1980s. Software developers used them to protect their exclusive rights granted under copyright law. They also used them to state their software warranties and to limit their liability for software failures. This helped them avoid some UCC warranty provisions.

Today courts generally hold that shrinkwrap contracts are valid. There is an offer and acceptance, which is shown by the manufacturer offering the software for sale, and the purchaser buying and installing it. These contracts also are supported by consideration. The consideration is the exchange of a product for money, and a consumer's affirmative act of installing the software.

Courts tend to favor shrinkwrap contracts where the consumer receives the terms of the contract in multiple ways. A shrinkwrap contract is more likely to be enforceable when the agreement is printed on paper in the box and presented again to the consumer on the computer screen when the software is being installed. A shrinkwrap contract that allows a consumer to return the software without using it if he or she rejects its terms also is more likely to be enforceable. Meeting of the minds is shown through the actions of the consumer with respect to either installing the software or returning it.

## Clickwrap Contracts

A **clickwrap contract** is a variation of the shrinkwrap contract. A clickwrap contract is usually presented to a user when purchasing software via the internet. These agreements are not used just for software purchases. Vendors use them for any type of product or service purchase that is conducted over the internet or online.

> **NOTE**
>
> A distinction between shrinkwrap and clickwrap contracts is that a user has an opportunity to read a clickwrap contract before purchasing a product or using a service. A user also must affirmatively agree to the contract before getting access to a product or service.

These types of contracts usually appear on a user's computer or mobile device screen before installation of a product, application (mobile apps), or use of a service. They may be displayed in a separate pop-up dialogue box or on the main browser screen. A user has to click on an "I agree" or "I accept" button located on the same screen as the contract (or in the same pop-up window) before downloading and installing a product or using a service.

### Enforceability of Shrinkwrap Contracts: *ProCD Inc. v. Zeidenberg*

The most famous case involving shrinkwrap contracts is *ProCD Inc. v. Zeidenberg* (1996).[25] This was the first time that a federal court of appeal looked at a shrinkwrap case. The Seventh Circuit Court of Appeals, which covers Illinois, Indiana, and Wisconsin, decided this case.

ProCD sold a software product that was a searchable telephone directory database. It distributed its program and database on CD-ROM. ProCD spent more than $10 million to develop its product and to keep the database of telephone directory information current.

ProCD had both commercial-use and noncommercial-use versions of the product. The commercial-use product was more expensive than the noncommercial-use, or consumer, product. Businesses that bought the commercial version could use it to create mailing lists of potential customers and for other marketing purposes, although ProCD did not allow this in the consumer version of the product.

ProCD had to keep businesses from buying the consumer product and using it for commercial purposes. However, it did not do this through technological solutions. Instead, ProCD turned to contract law. People who bought the consumer version of the software were prohibited from using it for commercial purposes because of the license agreement that was included with the product.

The defendant, Matthew Zeidenberg, purchased the consumer version of the product. He then formed his own company and reposted the information on the internet, offering the information for sale at a price that was lower than ProCD's price for either its consumer or commercial product.

ProCD sued Zeidenberg, arguing that Zeidenberg breached the terms of the license agreement that was included in the ProCD software box. Zeidenberg argued that only the text written on the outside of the package containing the ProCD product was part of his contract with ProCD. He claimed that the license agreement that was inside the box was additional contract terms. He argued that they were not enforceable under various provisions of the UCC.

The district court agreed with Zeidenberg, and ProCD appealed the decision of the district court to the Seventh Circuit Court of Appeals.

The Seventh Circuit held that the license agreement inside the box was an enforceable contract. In reviewing the case, the court noted that ProCD offered a full refund to a purchaser who did not agree with the terms of the shrinkwrap contract and returned the product without using it.

One fact that also helped the court reach the decision that the shrinkwrap contract was enforceable was that Zeidenberg had multiple opportunities to read it before he installed the software. It was printed on paper inside the box, and it was displayed on the computer screen during the software installation process. Zeidenberg could not install the software without specifically clicking on an acceptance box that contained the terms of the contract. The court found that all these opportunities to read the contract put Zeidenberg on notice of it. Through his actions, he showed that he agreed with those terms. This included the term forbidding commercial use of the product.

The court's reasoning in *ProCD v. Zeidenberg* is used as the basis for validating other types of EULAs such as clickwrap agreements.

You can read the court's opinion at https://law.justia.com/cases/federal/district-courts/FSupp/908/640/1457490/.

Courts have generally held that clickwrap contracts are enforceable. These cases are highly dependent on how the clickwrap contract is presented to the consumer. In many cases, these types of contracts are enforceable if the actual agreement is prominently displayed. A consumer must have a reasonable opportunity to read and review the terms of the agreement. A consumer also must affirmatively agree to the contract before receiving a product or service. Clicking on the "I agree" or "I accept" buttons is evidence of the consumer's agreement.

## Browsewrap Contracts

**Browsewrap contracts** describe the situation where terms of use or service documents are listed on a web page. In these situations, a user does not have to make an affirmative action to accept the terms of the contract, such as clicking on a button. A browsewrap agreement assumes that a contract is entered into when a user merely visits a web page or downloads a product.

**NOTE**

A browsewrap contract is similar to a clickwrap agreement without the "click" requirement.

Terms of use and terms of service documents are browsewrap contracts when they do not require a user to affirmatively agree to the terms contained in the document. They are clickwrap contracts if a user must click on a button to show his or her agreement with the terms.

Many popular web pages use browsewrap contracts to display their terms of use or service provisions. For example, the CNN web page at www.cnn.com has a "terms of use" link listed in small type at the bottom of their home page. Users navigate to CNN's terms of use when they click on that link. That agreement sets forth the terms and conditions for use of the CNN web page. The agreement states that users who do not agree to the terms of service should not access or use CNN.com.

Courts often are slow to find that browsewrap contracts are enforceable. One reason for this is that consumers may not know about these contracts. Terms of use or service links on web pages are typically in very small type and located at the bottom of web pages. Consumers are not conditioned to look for these agreements or read them. If consumers do not know about the contract and have not read it, how can they agree to its terms?

Courts review the facts of browsewrap cases very closely. For instance, in *Specht v. Netscape Communications Corporation* (2002), the Second Circuit Court of Appeals did not enforce a browsewrap contract. In this case, the consumer downloaded software but did not have to click on any buttons to show agreement with a license before downloading the software. However, the consumer had to click on several embedded links to read the terms of the agreement. They were not eye-catching links. The website did not display the license agreement in a separate window and it did not "pop up" at the consumer. The court held there was not enough notice to the consumer about the terms of the contract; therefore, it held that the contract was not enforceable against the consumer.

**NOTE**

Websites that use browsewrap agreements will want to make sure that the embedded links to those agreements are noticeable to a consumer.

It is possible that courts will start enforcing browsewrap contracts as e-commerce and internet use continue to grow. This is particularly true if web pages do more to make a user aware of the browsewrap contract. For instance, a court might be more inclined to enforce a browsewrap agreement when its terms are specifically referenced during the course of a transaction.

A Missouri court upheld a browsewrap agreement requiring a user to click on a "Submit" button that had the following language written next to it: "By submitting you agree to the

Terms of Use."[26] The text included a link to the terms of use language. The court held that the user was on notice that the terms of use governed the transaction. It also found that the user had the opportunity to read those terms.

## How Do These Contracts Regulate Behavior?

EULAs, terms of use, and terms of service agreements attempt to regulate user behavior. They state how a consumer can and cannot use certain products or services. They tend to severely limit a consumer's rights and give the owner or vendor of the product or service many rights. If a consumer fails to follow the terms of these agreements, an owner can try to sue for breach of contract. If a consumer follows the terms of these contracts, then he or she is regulating his or her behavior in a manner that is most likely advantageous to the owner or vendor of the product or service.

Consumers need to take the time to read these types of agreements. They are not all created equal. It would be a mistake to think that these agreements simply govern the intellectual property rights of the owners of a product or service. Although many EULAs and terms of service do this, some also have unexpected terms. For example, some of these terms include language that would allow the vendor to install additional software onto a consumer's computer system. The additional software could be used to learn the consumer's internet habits in order to supply targeted advertisements. These types of contracts also can have terms about additional licensing fees or deeply buried upgrade, support, or maintenance fees. For applications used on mobile computing devices, such as smartphones, these types of contracts also might grant the application access to other types of personal user data stored on the device. Reading the EULA or terms of service agreement is the only way for a consumer to know what rights he or she is giving up.

**NOTE**

A 2010 study reported that more than half of the study's participants spent only 8 seconds reviewing EULAs.[27] A 2017 study found that 97 percent of people ages 18 to 34 agree to terms of service contracts without reading them at all.[28]

Consumers should look for some of the following terms when reading EULAs or terms of service contracts:

- **Use**—Does the contract give the vendor the right to change the service or product whenever it wants? Does the vendor have the unilateral right to stop providing certain important features? Does the vendor have the right to investigate how the user uses the product or service to determine if there has been a violation of the contract?
- **Fees**—Does the contract have any hidden licensing fees or any hidden upgrade, support, or maintenance fees?
- **Data use**—Specifically for apps downloaded onto mobile computing devices, does acceptance of the contract mean that the consumer is also granting the app owner access to other data on the consumer's device? Apps might grant access to content such as location data, pictures stored on the device, or the contacts that the consumer stores on his or her device. Does the contract allow the consumer the ability to limit how data is shared? Does it allow the consumer to prohibit the vendor from further sharing the consumer's data?

**NOTE**

A consumer should exercise caution if a contract says that products or services are provided "as is" or use is at the consumers' "own risk." This means that the seller is disclaiming several different consumer protection warranties.

- **Representations and warranties**—Does acceptance of the contract mean that the consumer bears all economic risk related to downloading and using the product or service? What is the consumer's recourse if the product or service includes viruses and errors, or causes data loss or hardware/software failure? Does the contract state that use of the product or service is at the consumer's own risk? Does it state that the products are provided "as is?"
- **Advertising**—Does the contract give the vendor the right to include embedded software or spyware with the desired product or service? Does acceptance of the contract mean that the consumer consents to receiving advertising content, from either the vendor or other third parties? Is the vendor allowed to collect usage data and other statistics related to the consumer's use of the service? How is this data used?
- **Criticism**—Does the contract specifically prohibit the consumer from publicly criticizing the product or service?
- **Updates—**Does the contract state that updates are covered by the original contract? Are updates covered by a new contract that the consumer must specifically agree to?
- **Termination and breach**—Does the contract allow a consumer to stop using the product or service at any time? Can the consumer stop using the product by uninstalling and destroying software and documentation? Must the vendor destroy any consumer personal data it has collected when the contract ends?
- **Boilerplate terms**—Does the contract state that it is subject to change without notice? Does it state that the consumer specifically consents to any modifications of the contract without notice? Does it include dispute resolution terms? Does it contain jurisdiction language? Does it require that consumers file lawsuits in a certain state and county within that state?

**NOTE**

Terms in a contract that state that consumers must file lawsuits in a certain state or county in that state are called forum selection clauses. Contracting parties use forum selection clauses to control questions about jurisdiction. They also use them so that they can litigate lawsuits in front of a familiar court. It is the legal equivalent of "home court advantage."

Consumers must think about what they are willing to agree to, or even give up, in order to use a particular product or online service. They must balance their need for the use of a product or service with other contract terms that might place them, or their data, at a disadvantage.

## Emerging Contract Law Issues

New developments in internet-based products and services are causing people and organizations to think more about information security. People and entities must take steps to protect and secure information at the same time as information is being shared more than ever before. Entities use contracts to make sure that their own data, and the personal information of their customers, is protected when it is shared.

Sometimes the law requires a contract. For example, both the Gramm-Leach-Bliley Act (GLBA) and the Health Insurance Portability and Accountability Act (HIPAA) require covered businesses to enter into contracts with their third-party service providers to

**NOTE**

A third-party agreement under HIPAA is called a business associate's agreement.

protect data. These contracts hold the third parties accountable for the minimum levels of data privacy and information security protection that those laws require for certain types of information.

Entities also enter into these contracts voluntarily when they use new services or buy new products. The importance of including data security terms in these contracts continues to grow. The newest development in internet-based products and services that highlights information security issues is cloud computing.

## Cloud Computing

The definition and limits of cloud computing are still evolving. **Cloud computing** is a type of computing where both applications and infrastructure capabilities can be provided to end users through the internet. Through cloud computing, entities no longer have to own their own computer hardware and infrastructure. They can purchase these services from cloud service providers. They only pay for the infrastructure and applications that they need. **FIGURE 11-1** is a basic cloud computing diagram.

> **NOTE**
>
> SaaS refers to the purchase of application services over the internet. Cloud computing refers to the purchase of application, infrastructure, and storage capabilities through the internet.

Cloud computing is not just for businesses. Individuals also use cloud computing services. For example, Yahoo! Mail is a cloud service. Google's G Suite of services are cloud services. So is Mozy's online computer backup service. Cloud computing has its beginnings in the **Software as a Service (SaaS)** model. In the SaaS model, a vendor hosts a web-based application and provides that application to its customers. The customers then purchase access to the hosted application. The entities access these services over the

**FIGURE 11-1**

Basic cloud computing diagram.

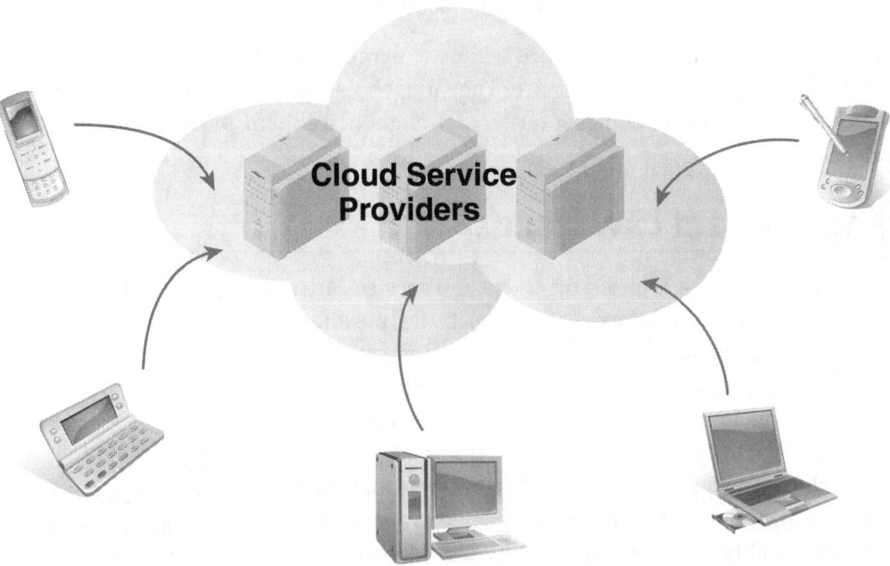

internet. The SaaS vendor hosts the applications and maintains the infrastructure necessary for running the application.

Cloud computing consumers can purchase infrastructure services such as data storage, backup facilities, and data processing. Cloud computing also includes the purchase of applications traditionally provided under the SaaS model such as email services. Cloud computing is attractive to many entities. Gartner, Inc., estimates that companies will spend $266 billion on cloud services in 2020.[29]

Many organizations believe that using cloud computing will help them save money on information technology (IT) costs. Cost savings include not spending money upfront on data centers, electricity, equipment, and physical security. It also might help save money on IT staff. Cloud computing is seen as scalable with the organization's own growth. An organization purchases only the services it needs at a fixed point in time. It can always buy more cloud services when it needs them. Buying cloud services can be faster than building the organization's own IT infrastructure.

> **NOTE**
>
> In 2007, Dell, Inc. tried to trademark the term "cloud computing." The U.S. Patent and Trademark Office rejected the trademark because it was too generic and described services offered by many companies.

Cloud computing leads to situations where an entity's data is not stored on its own physical computing infrastructure. This makes information security practitioners (and lawyers) nervous. The 2019 U.S. Federal Cloud Computing Strategy includes security as one of its three focus areas.[30] Information security concerns about cloud computing include:

- Loss of control of data, leading to a loss of security or lessened security
- Loss of privacy of data, potentially because of aggregation with data from other cloud consumers
- Dependency on a third party for critical infrastructure and data-handling processes
- Potential security and technological defects in the cloud provider's infrastructure
- No control over the third parties that a cloud vendor might contract with
- Loss of an entity's own competence in managing IT infrastructure security

There also are legal concerns about cloud computing. Contract law governs a cloud computing relationship. Disputes over the terms of the contract could be costly to resolve. They also could take too long to resolve. A lengthy dispute about critical services could harm a business and affect its ability to operate.

Another legal concern about cloud computing is where data and infrastructure are physically located. Local law might control how entities handle data. Questions of who owns the data also could be influenced by the law of the state where data is located, assuming that the data is actually stored in the United States. Location of the data could have an impact on how that data is provided in response to a public records request, subpoena, or court order. There also could be different rules for how that data must be secured. It also could affect how companies should respond to a breach of the systems used to store their data.

## Information Security Terms in Contracts

Entities entering into contracts for cloud computing services need to consider several items from a law and information security standpoint. A cloud computing consumer will want to make sure that a cloud computing provider physically protects the cloud computing infrastructure that holds the consumer's data. A cloud computing consumer also will want to make sure that the cloud computing provider follows good information security practices and protects the security of any data on that infrastructure.

> **NOTE**
> Because the cloud computing relationships include data, this is one time where an entity will want to make sure that it has a formal written contract with its vendors.

There are several information security issues to consider in any cloud computing contract. These same themes also can be considered in any contract where an entity's data might be stored, processed, transmitted, or handled by another party.

It is important for both contracting parties to understand the scope of data that they must protect in a contract. The parties must think about the following:

- How data is defined
- How data is used
- How data is protected
- How the parties meet their legal and regulatory requirements

### *Data Definition and Use*

Both parties to a contract must understand the type of data that they might transfer back and forth because of their relationship. A contract must have clear terms that define the data owned by each party. The parties also must clearly define data that must be protected.

It is also important for the parties to clearly specify in the contract how they can use any data that they share. An entity will want to make sure that its vendor, or cloud computing provider, does not use its data in a way that would violate its privacy policies. An entity also will want to make sure that there are limits on the vendor's own use of the data. For instance, a vendor should not be able to share the entity's data with other third parties without permission. Finally, the contract should specify what happens to the data when the contract ends.

> **NOTE**
> A contract should define the data elements used by the parties. For instance, if personal information is transmitted between the parties, then the contract should specify what data elements are considered personal information. This definition could change depending upon the type of data transmitted between the parties.

Data use terms also should specify what the parties cannot do with certain types of data. For example, if credit card information is transmitted as part of a cloud computing contract, that contract should require the vendor to comply with the Payment Card Industry Data Security Standards.

### *General Data Protection Terms*

An entity may want to specify particular data protection terms in a contract. These terms are more specific than data use terms. For instance, an entity may want to include terms that state the specific administrative, technical, and physical safeguards that a vendor must use. When an entity includes these types of terms, it is trying to guarantee a minimum level of confidentiality, integrity, and availability.

> **NOTE**
> A minimum level of acceptable information security is called a baseline.

An entity could include the following contract terms to ensure a minimum level of information security protection:

- Data transmission and encryption requirements
- Authentication and authorization mechanisms
- Intrusion detection and prevention mechanisms
- Security scan and audit requirements
- Security training and awareness requirements

Contracting parties can use resources developed by the National Institute of Standards and Technology (NIST) to make sure that a contract includes the appropriate controls. The International Organization for Standardization (ISO) and the International Electrotechnical Commission (IEC) also have prepared information security controls guidance.

### *Compliance With Legal and Regulatory Requirements*

Sometimes laws or regulatory controls will influence the relationship covered by a contract. This happens when the data or processes used between the parties falls within the scope of a particular law. GLBA and HIPAA were already mentioned as two federal laws that pull certain types of data and relationships into their scope.

**NOTE**

Contracts also have to include terms that help entities meet their breach notification duties in the event that a vendor's systems are compromised and the entity's data is disclosed.

State laws also could be implicated. For example, Massachusetts[31] and Nevada[32] have laws that require the personal information of state residents to be encrypted in certain instances. This requirement would need to be specified in a contract in order to ensure that a vendor meets it.

Additional terms that a contract should have to address regulatory requirements include:

- GLBA language if financial data is used or transmitted between the parties
- HIPAA language if health information is used or transmitted between the parties
- Family Educational Rights and Privacy Act (FERPA) of 1974 language if student information is used or transmitted between the parties
- Language addressing notification requirements if the vendor experiences any type of information security incident or event involving the contracting entity's data
- Language protecting the intellectual property rights of each party

An entity also will want to make sure that a contract contains terms that require the vendor to cooperate with security incident investigations. This is so the entity can meet its regulatory requirements. A contract also must have terms that require each party to assist the other with third-party litigation that occurs because of the contractual relationship. For example, a contract should state that the vendor will assist the entity with any litigation against the entity that arises because of a breach of the security of the vendor's systems.

As new technologies emerge and are developed, the rules for using that technology will become very important. One way that entities can establish rules is through contractual agreements.

## Case Studies and Examples

The following case study shows how the concepts discussed in this chapter are used. The case study that follows is a real-world example of contract law issues.

### Contract Formation via Email

Parties continue to argue about the enforceability of electronic contracts. California adopted its version of the UETA in 1999. This case began before California enacted its UETA law. Would the case have even reached a U.S. Court of Appeals if California's UETA law had been in existence when this transaction began?

Stewart Lamle invented a board game called Farook. He obtained two U.S. patents for his game. In May 1996, Lamle began negotiating with toy-giant Mattel to license his game. They signed a preliminary agreement for $25,000. Under this agreement, Lamle agreed not to license the game to anyone else until after June 15, 1997.

On June 11, 1997, the parties met and discussed the terms of a licensing agreement. They agreed to terms regarding the length of the license agreement. They also agreed to the geographic scope of the agreement, the percentage of royalties, and a schedule for payment of royalties. Mattel asked Lamle to draft a formal contract. It promised it would sign an agreement before January 1, 1998.

On June 26, 1997, a Mattel employee sent Lamle an email with the subject line "Farook Deal." The email repeated the terms agreed to at the earlier meeting. It also stated specifically that Mattel agreed in principle to the agreement and was waiting for the contract. The email concluded with a closing salutation and the employee's full name. Lamle faxed a draft licensing agreement to Mattel on August 19, 1997.

In August, Mattel displayed Farook at its Pre-Toy Fair. The purpose of the fair was to gauge potential interest in new toys. After the fair, Mattel decided that it was not interested in Farook. It notified Lamle in October.

Lamle sued for breach of contract in October 1999. He also made claims of patent infringement and intentional interference with economic relations.

The District Court for the Central District of California granted summary judgment in favor of Mattel. Summary judgment means that a court has decided that there is not a factual dispute between the parties. Lamle appealed the grant of summary judgment. The Federal Circuit Court of Appeals upheld his appeal and sent the case back to District Court.

The District Court again granted summary judgment for Mattel. The District Court rejected Lamle's breach of contract claim. It held that no reasonable juror would believe that there was a contract between the parties. It also held that even if there was a contract, it was not enforceable because it was not in writing as required by California's Statute of Frauds. Lamle appealed again.

The Federal Circuit Court of Appeals reviewed the conduct of the parties. It held that there was a genuine question whether the parties had reached mutual agreement on contractual terms at the June 11 meeting. It held that a trial was needed and evidence should be presented on the issue of mutual assent.

**NOTE**

One of the most interesting things about this case is that Lamle represented himself *pro se*. *Pro se* means that a person is not represented by a lawyer. Lamle represented himself throughout the whole case *pro se*, although he was not a lawyer.

**FYI**

States have statute of limitations rules. This means that people must bring a lawsuit for injuries that they have incurred within a certain period of time. In California, lawsuits for breach of oral contracts must be filed within 2 years of the date of the breach. The statute of limitations for written contracts is 4 years. Lamle sued Mattel exactly 2 years from the date that Mattel notified him that it was not interested in Farook. Why did Lamle sue at the 2-year mark?

The court also discussed California's Statute of Frauds. In reviewing the June 26 email from the Mattel employee, it held that the name of the Mattel employee at the end of the email was enough to overcome the signed writing requirements of the Statute of Frauds. It said that its ruling was consistent with other California laws that state that a typewritten name is considered a signature.

The Court also noted that if the email from the Mattel employee had been sent after January 1, 2000, there would be no question at all whether the email constituted a signed writing for Statute of Frauds purposes. California's version of the UETA went into effect at that time.

The Federal Circuit Court of Appeals ruling gave Lamle the right to have a jury trial on his breach of contract claim. Lamle and Mattel eventually settled their claims against one another.

You can read the court's opinion at http://scholar.google.com/scholar_case?case =5607112815760928119.

## CHAPTER SUMMARY

Contracts are used to form relationships between parties for the sale of goods and services. A mixture of common law and statutory law covers contracts. Contracts for the sale of services are usually covered by common law. Code law usually covers contracts for the sale of goods.

Electronic and online communications have created more efficient ways to enter into contracts. The traditional rules of contract law apply to contracts that are entered into online. Laws such as the Uniform Electronic Transactions Act help make sure that online contracts are enforceable in the same manner as traditional contracts.

## KEY CONCEPTS AND TERMS

Browsewrap contract
Clickwrap contract
Cloud computing
Compensatory damages
Complete performance
Consequential damages
Consideration
Contract
Contract of adhesion
Contractual capacity
Duty to mitigate
End user license agreement (EULA)
Incomplete performance
Liquidated damages

Mailbox rule
Mirror image rule
Nominal damages
Offer
Offeree
Offeror
Remedy
Repudiation
Shrinkwrap contract
Software as a Service (SaaS)
Specific performance
Statute of Frauds
Substantial performance

## CHAPTER 11 ASSESSMENT

1. Which common law rule requires an offer and acceptance to have substantially the same terms?
   A. The Statute of Frauds
   B. The mailbox rule
   C. The mirror image rule
   D. The silence rule
   E. The assurance rule

2. What is a clickwrap contract?

3. What types of damages usually are not awarded in a contracts case?
   A. Nominal damages
   B. Punitive damages
   C. Consequential damages
   D. Compensatory damages
   E. Liquidated damages

4. The law assumes that almost all people have contractual capacity.
   A. True
   B. False

5. Instantaneous communications must follow the mailbox rule.
   A. True
   B. False

6. How do courts determine if parties really did enter into a contract?
   A. They look for contractual capacity.
   B. They look for contract legality.
   C. They review the Statute of Frauds
   D. They look for a meeting of the minds.
   E. None of these is correct.

7. A remedy is ______.

8. Which type of online agreement are courts reluctant to enforce?
   A. Clickwrap contracts
   B. Shrinkwrap contracts
   C. Browsewrap contracts
   D. None of these is correct.

9. What was the precursor to cloud computing?
   A. SaaS
   B. EULA
   C. SO/IEC
   D. NIST
   E. None of these is correct.

10. What information security concerns surround cloud computing?

11. Which type of damages do the parties specifically agree to in a contract?
    A. Nominal damages
    B. Punitive damages
    C. Consequential damages
    D. Compensatory damages
    E. Liquidated damages

12. A contract to commit murder is enforceable.
    A. True
    B. False

13. What electronic signature law governs interstate commerce?
    A. UETA
    B. E-SIGN
    C. UATE
    D. COPPA
    E. GLBA

**14.** UETA states that electronic contracts are ______.

**15.** Which communications are instantaneous?

A. Oral communications
B. Text messages
C. Instant messages
D. All of these are correct.
E. None of these is correct.

## ENDNOTES


1. Uniform Law Commission, "About the ULC," undated. Available at http://www.uniformlaws.org/aboutulc/overview (accessed January 26, 2020).
2. White, James J., and Robert S. Summers. *Uniform Commercial Code*. 5th ed. St. Paul, MN: West Group, 2000, p. 7.
3. American Law Institute, "ALI Overview," undated. Available at https://www.ali.org/about-ali/ (accessed January 26, 2020).
4. American Law Institute and the National Conference of Commissioners on Uniform State Laws, Uniform Commercial Code, sec. 2-201 (2004). Available at http://www.law.cornell.edu/ucc/ (accessed January 26, 2020).
5. *St. John's Holdings, LLC. v. Two Electronics, LLC.*, 2016 WL 1460477 (2016).
6. American Law Institute, Restatement (Second) of Contracts, sec. 24 (1981).
7. American Law Institute, Restatement (Second) of Contracts, sec. 39 (1981).
8. *Carlill v. Carbolic Smoke Ball Company*, 1 QB 256; Court of Appeal (1892).
9. *Leonard v. Pepsico, Inc.*, 88 F.Supp.2d 116 (S.D.N.Y. 1999), aff'd 210 F.3d 88 (2d Cir. 2000).
10. Uniform Commercial Code, sec. 2-207.
11. Restatement (Second) of Contracts, sec. 64.
12. *Baltimore & Ohio Railroad Co. v. United States*, 261 U.S. 592 (1923).
13. Uniform Commercial Code, sec. 2-609.
14. Statista Digital Market Outlook, "Retail E-Commerce Sales in the United States From 2017 to 2023," February 2019. Available at https://www.statista.com/statistics/272391/us-retail-e-commerce-sales-forecast/ (accessed January 26, 2020).
15. Electronic Signatures in Global and National Commerce Act (2000), U.S. Code Vol. 15, sec. 7001 et seq. (2012).
16. Uniform Law Commission, Uniform Electronic Transactions Act (UETA), 1999. Available at https://www.uniformlaws.org/HigherLogic/System/DownloadDocumentFile.ashx?DocumentFileKey=4f718047-e765-b9d8-6875-f7a225d629a8&forceDialog=0 (accessed January 26, 2020).
17. Uniform Law Commission, Uniform Electronic Transactions Act (UETA) Fact Sheet, 1999. Available at https://www.uniformlaws.org/HigherLogic/System/DownloadDocumentFile.ashx?DocumentFileKey=c5976d91-07e2-b3f8-9b1e-4450fe809c21&forceDialog=0 (accessed January 26, 2020).
18. Uniform Law Commission, Uniform Electronic Transactions Act (UETA) Fact Sheet, 1999, sec. 2. Available at https://www.uniformlaws.org/HigherLogic/System/DownloadDocumentFile.ashx?DocumentFileKey=c5976d91-07e2-b3f8-9b1e-4450fe809c21&forceDialog=0 (accessed January 26, 2020).
19. *Register.com, Inc. v. Verio, Inc.*, 356 F.3d 393, 403 (2d Cir. 2004).
20. Watnick, Valerie, "The Electronic Formation of Contracts and the Common Law 'Mailbox Rule,'" *Baylor Law Review*, 56 (2004): 175.
21. Statista, "Twitter – Statistics & Facts," February 22, 2019. Available at https://www.statista.com/topics/737/twitter/ (accessed January 26, 2020).
22. Statista, "Facebook – Statistics & Facts," November 20, 2019. Available at https://www.statista.com/topics/751/facebook/ (accessed January 26, 2020).
23. CNN.com, "Girl Costs Father $80,000 With 'SUCK IT' Facebook Post," March 4, 2014. Available at http://www.cnn.com/2014/03/02/us/facebook-post-costs-father/ (accessed March 8, 2014).

24. Uniform Law Commission, Uniform Electronic Transactions Act (UETA) Fact Sheet, 1999, sec. 2. Available at https://www.uniformlaws.org/HigherLogic/System/DownloadDocumentFile.ashx?DocumentFileKey=c5976d91-07e2-b3f8-9b1e-4450fe809c21&forceDialog=0 (accessed January 26, 2020).
25. *ProCD Inc. v. Zeidenberg*, 86 F.3d 1447 (1996).
26. Missouri Court of Appeals, "Opinion: *Major v. McCallister*," No. CD29871, December 23, 2009. Available at https://www.courts.mo.gov/file.jsp?id=36294 (accessed January 26, 2020).
27. Böhme, Rainer, and Stefan Köpsell, "Trained to Accept? A Field Experiment on Consent Dialogues," CHI 2010, *Proceedings of the SIGCHI Conference on Human Factors in Computing Systems* (2010): 2403–2406.
28. Deloitte, "2017 Global Mobile Consumer Survey: US Edition," 2017. Available at https://www2.deloitte.com/content/dam/Deloitte/us/Documents/technology-media-telecommunications/us-tmt-2017-global-mobile-consumer-survey-executive-summary.pdf (accessed January 26, 2020).
29. Gartner, "Gartner Forecasts Worldwide Public Cloud Revenue to Grow 17% in 2020," November 13, 2019. Available at https://www.gartner.com/en/newsroom/press-releases/2019-11-13-gartner-forecasts-worldwide-public-cloud-revenue-to-grow-17-percent-in-2020 (accessed January 26, 2020).
30. U.S. Office of Management and Budget, "2019 Federal Cloud Computing Strategy," undated. Available at https://cloud.cio.gov/ (accessed January 26, 2020).
31. Code of Massachusetts Regulations, Title 201, sec. 17.04.
32. Nevada Revised Statutes, sec. 603A.215.

CHAPTER 12

# Criminal Law and Tort Law Issues in Cyberspace

CRIMINAL LAW REFERS to laws that the federal and state governments have created to define unacceptable behavior. People who violate society's acceptable levels of behavior commit crimes. Criminal law deals with crimes, whereas tort law refers to wrongful acts or harm for which an individual can sue the person who caused the harm. Tort law governs disputes between individuals.

This chapter focuses on criminal and tort law issues that are unique to cyberspace. In particular, it focuses on how people can use computers in cybercrime activities. It also reviews how people use computers to commit torts. Sometimes both criminal and tort law actions can be carried out against the same individual for the same actions.

## Chapter 12 Topics

This chapter covers the following topics and concepts:

- What general criminal law concepts are
- What common criminal law issues in cyberspace are
- What general tort law concepts are
- What common tort law issues in cyberspace are
- What some case studies and examples are

## Chapter 12 Goals

When you complete this chapter, you will be able to:

- Discuss common criminal law concepts
- Describe the common criminal laws used to prosecute cybercrimes
- Discuss common tort law concepts
- Describe common tort principles used in cyberspace
- Explain the difference between criminal and tort law

## General Criminal Law Concepts

Cybercrimes, sometimes called computer crimes, involve situations where people use the internet or computers as the medium for, or target of, criminal activity. Some crimes, such as computer trespass, are prosecuted by extending existing criminal laws to new situations that have arisen with new technology. Computer networks facilitate these crimes. Other laws define new crimes that did not exist before computers. The use of computers as a medium to commit crimes is growing. Criminals also target computers and the data that they contain. Consider the following:

- A federal judge sentences a computer hacker to almost 5 years in prison for violating the Computer Fraud and Abuse Act (CFAA). The hacker created botnets and sold access to them. Other attackers used the botnets to launch distributed denial of service (DDoS) attacks.
- A federal judge sentences a defendant to 2.5 years in prison for taking nude videos of a news reporter and posting them to the internet. The judge also orders the defendant to pay restitution to the victim.
- The federal government charges three members of a hacking group with hijacking the website of a telecommunications company. The company's users could not access the website for about 90 minutes.
- A man is charged with cyberextortion. He is alleged to have attempted to extort a life insurance company by threatening to send millions of computer spam messages. Authorities say he wanted to damage the reputation of the insurance company.

Crimes are instances of wrongdoing, or actions that harm society. They are deviations from behavior that society, through its government, has defined as unacceptable. Some crimes do not even need individual victims. Society is the "victim" of the crime.

In simple terms, a crime is a violation of society's code of conduct. Crime and the concept of criminal law are very old. The Sumerian and Babylonian civilizations included codes of conduct in their laws in 2100 B.C.E. Although these codes did not resemble modern criminal law, they did define conduct that society decided was not acceptable.

**NOTE**

Federal cases are titled "United States" versus the name of the defendant. This is because the government of the United States is prosecuting the defendant for a crime. State cases are titled with the name of the state versus the name of the defendant.

As discussed in other chapters in this book, the American legal system is based in large part on English common law. The U.S. Constitution is the main source of law for the United States. The Constitution presumes that U.S. citizens will behave lawfully. However, it includes provisions for how the government should handle crimes in Article III. The Constitution even defines a specific crime. Article III, section 3, states that treason against the United States is a crime.

The U.S. Congress has passed laws defining federal crimes since the formation of the government. Most states also have passed laws that have defined criminal offenses. Because crimes are wrongs against society, the government pursues the alleged wrongdoers. The federal government prosecutes violations of federal law, whereas state governments prosecute violations of state laws.

## Main Principles of Criminal Law

Criminal law is very different from civil law. Each system has different goals. Criminal law aims to deter wrongful behavior through a combination of punishment and rehabilitation of the offender. In contrast, civil law aims to right personal wrongs. It does this by allowing people to sue to recover monetary compensation for injuries.

This section focuses on substantive criminal law. Substantive law describes a person's rights and responsibilities. It defines how people should relate to one another and how they should relate to the government. Substantive law also is known as subject matter law. Criminal law is only one of many categories of substantive law. Contract law, business law, property law, and tort law are all different types of substantive law.

Substantive criminal law defines the conduct that constitutes a crime. It also establishes penalties. Governments can specify criminal penalties in the same statute that defines a crime. They also can list them in a separate penalty statute.

> **NOTE**
>
> Attorneys often specialize in different subject matter areas. This is because of legal ethics rules that require an attorney to be minimally competent. There are many areas of law. It is easier for attorneys to meet ethical competency rules by focusing their practices in certain areas.



### *Type of Wrongful Conduct*

Society recognizes two basic types of wrongful conduct. The first type is conduct or acts that society universally agrees are wrong, morally repugnant, or dangerous to other people. For example, almost all societies agree that murder and rape are wrong. ***Mala in se*** is a Latin term that defines these types of wrongful conduct. *Mala in se* means "evil in itself." It describes conduct that is inherently wrong. Crimes that are *mala in se* include murder, rape, kidnapping, robbery, theft, and arson.

Other types of conduct are *mala prohibita*. ***Mala prohibita*** is Latin for "wrong because it is prohibited." Society defines conduct that is *mala prohibita*. This conduct is not inherently evil, but society prohibits it nonetheless. Crimes that are *mala prohibita* include intellectual property violations (where prohibited by law, such as federal copyright offenses), traffic law violations, and tax evasion. Many types of cybercrimes are *mala prohibita*.

Crimes generally are classified into two groups, misdemeanors and felonies. The two types of crimes are usually distinguishable by the way society punishes the criminals who commit these crimes. **Misdemeanors** are less serious than felonies and bear a less severe penalty. A misdemeanor is generally punishable by no more than 1 year in prison. **Felonies** are more serious crimes. They are usually punishable by more than a year in prison.

The levels of felonies and misdemeanors may vary from state to state. Some states have different levels of misdemeanors and felonies. Language such as "first degree" or "second degree" differentiates between different levels of crime. A state can prosecute some types of crimes as either a misdemeanor or a felony depending on the circumstances surrounding the crime.

### *Elements of a Crime*

Criminal law is based on the principle that a guilty mind must accompany a criminal act. Another principle is that criminal conduct harms society. In short, the American system of law holds people responsible for their actions. A government must prove the following elements to show that a crime has been committed:

- *Mens rea*
- *Actus reus*
- Causation

To prove that a crime has been committed, a government must show that a person acted with criminal intent. It must show that a person knowingly, intentionally, or recklessly engaged in criminal conduct. The Latin term ***mens rea*** means "guilty mind." *Mens rea* describes a person's intent to commit a crime. Someone who lacks *mens rea* cannot be held responsible for a crime.

Most criminal laws have language that specifies the amount of *mens rea* that a person must have to be held responsible for a crime. For example, the Wisconsin first-degree murder statute states: "Whoever causes the death of another human being with intent to kill that person or another is guilty of a Class A felony."[1] The "intent to kill" portion of the statute describes the *mens rea* required to commit a crime.

**NOTE**

Some crimes do not require a particular mental state. For example, in most states, driving a car while under the influence of drugs or alcohol is a crime regardless of the mental state of the driver.

Acts that are purely accidental do not meet the required mental showing for criminal prosecution. However, that does not mean that the government prosecutes only intentional actions. The government also can prosecute a person who acts recklessly for criminal behavior.

A showing of recklessness means that a person acted in a manner that consciously disregarded whether or not harm could result from the actions. For example, the Wisconsin first-degree reckless homicide statute states: "Whoever recklessly causes the death of another human being under circumstances which show utter disregard for human life is guilty of a Class B felony."[2] The "which show utter disregard for human life" portion of the statute describes the *mens rea* required to commit this crime.

Criminal statutes do not require governments to prove damages to prosecute a defendant for a crime. However, governments can use the amount of harm that a defendant causes to increase the level of the crime.

The *actus reus* is the wrongful act that constitutes a crime. ***Actus reus*** is the Latin term for "guilty act." To be a crime, the action must be voluntary. The *actus reus* requires a physical act in furtherance of a crime. For example, the U.S. Supreme Court held that a California law that punished people for being addicted to illegal drugs violated the Constitution.[3] The California law made being "addicted" to drugs the offense, even if the person who was addicted to drugs never used or possessed drugs in the state. The law was challenged.

**NOTE**

In civil law, no showing of mental state, or *mens rea*, is required. Under civil law, wrongdoers are responsible for their actions even if they did not intend to cause harm to another person.

In *Robinson v. California* (1962), the U.S. Supreme Court said that there were many ways that the state could make certain acts related to drug use illegal. However, simply making the status of being an addict illegal was a violation of the Constitution. The case stands for the proposition that criminal activity requires a voluntary, physical act.

A wrongful act also can include the failure to act when there is a duty to do so. For example, parents have a duty to care for their children. A state may punish a parent who fails to take care of his or her children when that failure rises to a level of criminal conduct. For instance, in March 2010 the South Korean government arrested a couple for child neglect. The government alleged that the couple's video game addiction led them to neglect their daughter, who starved to death. Tragically, the video game that the couple was addicted to involved caring for a "virtual child" in an online game.[4]



### *Jurisdiction*

Courts can hear only *cases*, or disputes, that are within their jurisdiction. Jurisdiction describes the types of cases that a court has the authority to hear.

Jurisdiction can be described in several different ways. Jurisdiction can be used to describe the function of a court. For example, trial courts generally have original jurisdiction. This is the ability to conduct trials and to hear initial disputes between parties. Appellate courts such as the U.S. Supreme Court have appellate jurisdiction. They can only review decisions made by lower courts.

Jurisdiction also can describe the power of a court to hear a certain type of case and make a binding decision in that case. Courts must have the proper jurisdiction to make a valid judgment. To make a valid judgment, a court must have:

- Subject matter jurisdiction
- Personal jurisdiction

**Subject matter jurisdiction** is the power of a court to decide certain types of cases. A court cannot decide cases where it has no subject matter jurisdiction. For example, federal courts have jurisdiction only to decide cases about federal laws. This is federal question jurisdiction. They also can decide certain types of disputes between citizens of different states. This is diversity of citizenship jurisdiction. In contrast, state courts can decide only cases about state laws or actions that occurred within the geographic boundaries of the state.

**FYI**

In both state and federal courts, jurisdiction also looks at geographical and political boundaries. If a person violates a federal law in Massachusetts, federal district courts in Massachusetts most likely have subject matter jurisdiction to decide the case. If the person violated only state law, Massachusetts state courts would have jurisdiction to decide the case.

**Personal jurisdiction** refers to a court's ability to exercise power over a particular defendant. If a court does not have personal jurisdiction over a defendant, then it cannot impose a sentence on that person. Personal jurisdiction is important for both criminal and civil cases. Typically, state courts can exercise personal jurisdiction over people who commit acts within the state.

For criminal law, personal jurisdiction comes into play when criminal acts are committed in several different states. It is also implicated when crimes affect residents in many different states. The U.S. Supreme Court addressed this issue in 1911.[5] In *Strassheim v. Daily*, the Supreme Court used a "detrimental effects" test to determine if a state could exercise jurisdiction over a person who committed crimes outside of the state. The Court's test had three parts:

- Did the act occur outside the state?
- Did the act produce detrimental effects within the state?
- Were the acts the actual cause of detrimental effects within the state?

The test focuses on the defendant's intent. It also looks at the consequences of the defendant's actions in a particular state. Under the detrimental effects test, a state criminal court can exercise jurisdiction over a person who commits actions outside of the state if those actions cause harm within the state.

### Jurisdictional Issues for Cybercrime Cases

Jurisdiction is a particularly challenging issue concerning cybercrimes. Geographical boundaries do not limit computer networks. Cybercriminals can easily commit crimes that span across many states and countries. This makes it difficult for law enforcement to investigate these crimes. It is particularly difficult for law enforcement to identify criminals and collect evidence across the globe. It also makes it difficult for courts to hold cybercriminals responsible for their actions.

Nigerian scams highlight the jurisdiction issues in cybercrime cases. These types of scams also are called "419 scams" or "advance fee fraud" schemes. (The "4-1-9" refers to the section of the Nigerian criminal code that addresses fraud schemes.) This type of scam has been around since the early 1900s, when it was called the Spanish Prisoner Con. Today many organizations refer to these types of scams as *imposter scams*—where someone pretending to be someone else asks you to send money or share personal information.

Criminals originally conducted these scams via fax or mailed letters. They now conduct them with ease through email and even text messages. In these types of scams, a person receives an email from someone purporting to be an official of a foreign government or agency. The email writer usually offers large sums of money in return for helping someone in trouble. In some cases, the email claims that the government has made it difficult for the wealthy writer to cash a large check. (In the original scams the government referenced was the Nigerian government. This is how the modern-day version of the imposter scam got this name.) The writer asks the victim to advance the victim's own funds to cover the check, and to help cash it. The writer promises that the victim will get a hefty reward for his or her assistance.

A victim who advances funds soon learns that the check or underlying business transaction is fraudulent. The money advanced is lost. People operating outside the United States who send targeted emails to U.S. residents commit many of these types of crimes. In 2019, imposter scams featured prominently in the top international fraud reports to the econsumer.gov international partnership.[8]

These cases are extremely difficult to investigate and prosecute. How would a victim in Lafayette, Indiana, be able to use the resources of local law enforcement to investigate a crime committed by a person who lives in another country? Local police, prosecutors, and courts have limited power to investigate and prosecute these types of international cases. State subpoenas and court orders do not usually apply across international boundaries. These jurisdictional issues are becoming more common as internet crime grows.

The Supreme Court's detrimental effects test used in the *Strassheim* case is a common law rule. Many states have enacted legislation that codifies the detrimental effects test. For example, Alaska law states that state courts have jurisdiction over crimes that are "commenced outside the state but consummated inside."[6]

**NOTE**

The United States ratified the Convention on Cybercrime in August 2006.

Issues about jurisdiction are not just questions between the states. Personal jurisdiction also can be an international issue. It is one of the main obstacles in cybercrime cases because of the truly global nature of the internet. The Council of Europe Convention on Cybercrime, which went into force in 2004, increases cooperation in the investigation and prosecution of cybercrimes. Members of the convention must adopt legislation to criminalize certain types of cyber-related offenses and copyright infringement. They also agree to assist one another in criminal investigations. Sixty-five nations have ratified it.[7]



## Criminal Procedure

Criminal procedure is the body of rules that govern how governments prosecute people for crimes. These procedural rules make sure that criminal defendants receive due process. *Due process* means that a defendant in a criminal case is entitled to a fair and consistent process within the courts. The laws of criminal procedure make sure that the government safeguards the defendant's constitutional rights. They also provide the government with a method for fairly prosecuting defendants for their crimes.

**FYI**

A *prosecutor* is a government official who represents the government in criminal cases. Prosecutors decide whether to charge a person with a crime and put on the court case against that person. *U.S. attorneys* are federal prosecutors. States usually grant prosecutorial power to county governments. State prosecuting attorneys might be called district attorneys, county attorneys, state's attorneys, or simply county prosecutors.

Most criminal procedure principles stem from the U.S. Constitution. This means that many processes are similar among the states and the federal government. However, some procedural rules are unique to each jurisdiction. The description provided here is intentionally general and is meant to be a guide. The process also can be different depending upon whether the crime committed is a misdemeanor or felony.

A criminal case begins when a law enforcement agency begins an investigation. Law enforcement agencies have certain rules that they must follow as they conduct their investigation. When law enforcement officers complete their investigation, they send the case to the prosecutor. A prosecutor then reviews the case and decides whether to bring charges against the person that law enforcement identified as the perpetrator of the crime. Prosecutors have a lot of discretion in determining whether to charge a person with a crime.

If a prosecutor decides to charge a person with a crime, he or she must file a written document in court to start the criminal process. In some states, a prosecutor may file a document called an *information*. An information specifies the charges against the perpetrator of the crime. The prosecutor can exercise discretion when filing an information.

In other states, defendants have a right to a grand jury indictment. A *grand jury* is a panel of citizens who hear evidence presented by a prosecutor. The grand jury determines if there is enough evidence to bring a person to trial for a crime. The grand jury issues an *indictment* if it determines that the evidence is sufficient. An indictment is the formal written criminal charges issued by a grand jury.

**FYI**

The Fifth Amendment to the U.S. Constitution requires that a federal grand jury issue charges for some federal crimes. A defendant can waive the grand jury requirement. If a defendant waives the grand jury requirement, then the federal prosecutor files an information to start criminal proceedings. Federal grand juries contain between 16 and 23 people. The Federal Rules of Criminal Procedure set this number. Grand juries conduct their deliberations in secret. You can read the Handbook for Federal Grand Jurors at https://www.uscourts.gov/sites/default/files/grand-handbook.pdf.

A criminal prosecution begins once a grand jury returns an indictment or after a prosecutor files an information. At this point, the perpetrator of the crime becomes a *defendant*. In a criminal case, the defendant is the person accused of a crime.

The next step in the criminal process is the *initial hearing*. This is sometimes called an *arraignment*. The purpose of this hearing is to begin the formal court process. At this hearing, a court must:

- Inform the defendant about the charges.
- Advise the defendant about his or her legal and constitutional rights.

During the initial hearting the defendant must enter a response to the charges, called a *plea*. A defendant can enter a plea of guilty or not guilty. In some cases, she or he also can enter a plea of *nolo contendere*, which is Latin for "I do not wish to contend." It is also called a plea of no contest. A no-contest plea is not a guilty plea. However, it has the same effect as one. Most jurisdictions have limits on how and when defendants can use this type of plea.

If a defendant enters a guilty plea, the court will set a date to sentence the defendant. A 2018 study found that 90 percent of federal defendants plead guilty.[9] That same study found that only 2 percent of federal defendants have cases that go to trial.

If the defendant enters a not-guilty plea, the court sets the case for trial. The U.S. Constitution guarantees criminal defendants the right to a trial by jury. Article III of the Constitution guarantees this right, and the Sixth Amendment to the Constitution clarifies the scope of the right.

Under the Sixth Amendment, criminal defendants are entitled to a court-appointed attorney if they cannot afford one on their own. Courts usually grant this request only when a defendant faces a prison sentence. The Supreme Court case of *Gideon v. Wainwright* (1963) held that a court must appoint an attorney to an indigent defendant charged with a felony.[10] The defendant must prove that he or she is indigent and cannot afford an attorney. The Supreme Court in the *Gideon* case also held that a conviction is automatically reversed if a state denies a defendant the right to counsel.

After the arraignment, the prosecution and the defendant's attorneys will begin the discovery process. *Discovery* is the process where the government gives the defendant the evidence that it plans to use in the defendant's trial. U.S. Supreme Court cases have held that the government must disclose:

- Any deals that the prosecution made with a witness *(Giglio v. United States).*[11]
- Any evidence it has that might help prove the defendant's innocence *(Brady v. Maryland).*[12]

Courts strictly regulate the criminal discovery process. The rules for the process are clear. A court has a wide range of actions it can take against parties that fail to comply with discovery rules. A court can even dismiss the case if the prosecution fails to comply with the rules of the process. Failure to turn over evidence that might help prove the defendant's innocence can cause a conviction to be overturned.

**NOTE**

The defendant's right to an attorney arises when a criminal proceeding begins. A defendant may voluntarily waive the right to counsel and represent himself or herself. A court must decide that a person is mentally competent in order to do this. The court also must warn the person that there are dangers to self-representation.

If a criminal case goes to trial, the government bears the burden of proving that the defendant violated the law. In criminal cases, the government must prove the defendant's guilt beyond a reasonable doubt. This is the highest burden of proof that a prosecutor must meet. Reasonable doubt does not mean that a juror is 100 percent convinced of the defendant's guilt. It does mean, however, that a juror must be fully satisfied that the prosecution has eliminated any reasonable doubts about the defendant's guilt.

**NOTE**

The Sixth Amendment to the U.S. Constitution guarantees defendants a speedy trial. State criminal procedure rules include time limits for all the steps in the criminal process. In *Strunk v. United States* (1973), the U.S. Supreme Court held that a court must dismiss a criminal charge if a state violates the defendant's speedy trial rights.[13]

The government has a high burden of proof in criminal cases because criminal punishments infringe on a person's fundamental rights. These rights include the right to liberty, property, and life. Criminal penalties can include jail time, probation, financial penalties, or even a death sentence. A court may impose these penalties only if the government meets its high burden of proof.

A criminal case ends when a jury decides that a defendant is innocent or guilty. It also ends if the jury cannot reach a decision. A *hung jury* is a jury that is unable to reach a decision because the jurors disagree. A court will declare a *mistrial* if the jury cannot reach a decision. In this case, the government may decide to refile the charges and prosecute the defendant again.

A defendant who is convicted may appeal. Different rights allow a defendant to appeal a ruling or conviction to a higher court. These rules are beyond the scope of this discussion.

## Common Criminal Laws Used in Cyberspace

A computer, or any electronic device, can play one of four roles in crime:

- **To commit a crime**—Unauthorized access to data (hacking) and online fraud are two examples where a computer is used to commit a crime.
- **To facilitate a crime**— Cyberstalking, identity theft, phishing scams, and software piracy are examples of crimes facilitated, or aided, by computers.
- **As a target of crime**—Denial of service (DoS) and distributed denial of service (DDoS) attacks, computer viruses, and communications sabotage are examples of crimes where the computer itself is the target of the crime.
- **As a witness to crime**—Computerized record-keeping systems may provide evidence of an underlying crime or event.

Just because a computer or electronic device is involved in a crime does not make that crime a cybercrime. For example, a person simply using a computer and printer to create a forged document commits a criminal act. It is no different than if that same person used a printing press and ink to forge the document. The crime is still a forgery.

Cybercrimes are different. Cybercrimes, also called computer crimes, are crimes that use computers as a medium to commit a crime or where the computer itself is the target of the crime. Cyberstalking, identity theft, and phishing scams are examples of crimes facilitated by computers. DoS and DDoS attacks, computer viruses, and communications sabotage are examples of crimes where the computer itself is the target of the crime. The distinction between the types of crime is subtle but important.

Both the federal government and individual states have created several laws that address cybercrime. This chapter talks primarily about federal cybercrime laws. Federal laws will likely have the most impact on cybercrime. This is because geography or state and national borders do not matter to cybercriminals. The internet truly blurs these lines. A criminal can easily initiate a cybercrime in one state and harm a victim in another. Also, because cybercrime statutes vary widely between the states, federal laws may end up being more comprehensive.

**NOTE**

It is important to remember that many states criminalize the same behavior that federal cybercrime laws address.

**NOTE**

The Internet Crime Complaint Center (IC3) is a partnership between the U.S. Federal Bureau of Investigation (FBI) and the National White Collar Crime Center. Their 2019 Internet Crime Report showed that the total loss linked to online fraud was $3.5 billion.[15] You can read the report at https://pdf.ic3.gov/2019_IC3Report.pdf.

### The Computer Fraud and Abuse Act (1984)

Congress passed the Computer Fraud and Abuse Act (CFAA) in 1984.[14] It is the first piece of federal legislation that identified computer crimes as distinct offenses. The federal government used the CFAA in 1990 to prosecute the creator of the Morris worm. This was the first prosecution under the CFAA. The CFAA provides both criminal and civil penalties.

In enacting the CFAA, Congress chose to address a series of computer-related offenses in a single statute. The CFAA limits federal jurisdiction to situations where cybercrime is interstate in nature or when certain "protected computers" are the target of crime.

The CFAA criminalizes the act of causing certain types of damage to a protected computer without authorization or by exceeding authorized access. A protected computer is any of the following:

- A federal government computer
- A financial institution computer
- A computer used in interstate or foreign commerce[16]



**FYI**

The CFAA does not define what access "without authorization" means. However, it does define what "exceeding authorized access" means.[17] The failure to define the scope and limits of "without authorization" is one of the biggest criticisms of the CFAA. Many CFAA cases boil down to questions of access. There is a split among federal courts as to the meaning of authorized access under the CFAA. In April 2020, the U.S. Supreme Court agreed to hear a CFAA case in its upcoming term. As of this writing, no date for oral arguments has been set. The name of the case to watch is *Van Buren v. United States*. You can follow the court's docket at https://www.supremecourt.gov/docket/docketfiles/html/public/19-783.html.

The CFAA treats protected computers as the victim of a crime. It addresses the following types of criminal activity:

- Unauthorized access to a government computer
- Unauthorized access to information on a protected computer
- Unauthorized access to a protected computer that causes damage
- Unauthorized access to a protected computer with an intent to defraud
- Threatening to damage a protected computer
- Unauthorized trafficking of passwords or other computer access information that allows people to access other computers without authorization and with the intent to defraud
- Computer espionage

**NOTE**

Under the CFAA, essentially any computer that connects to the internet is a protected computer because the internet facilitates commerce between different states.

**NOTE**

Some sections of the CFAA require the government to show that the intruder caused damage. Under the CFAA, damage is "any impairment to the integrity or availability of data, a program, a system, or information."[19]

The CFAA does not just address intruders or outsider attacks on protected computers. It also considers that insiders may exceed the access that they have been granted in a protected computer system. Because these people already have access to these systems, their access is not unauthorized. However, in some cases, they commit a crime if they exceed their scope of authorized access. Under the CFAA, a person exceeds authorized access when he or she accesses a computer with authorization but uses that access to get or alter information that he or she is not allowed to use or alter.[18]

**TABLE 12-1** summarizes the CFAA provisions and potential penalties. In all instances, the penalties described are increased significantly if a defendant has a previous CFAA conviction.

**TABLE 12-1** Computer Fraud and Abuse Act Summary

| CRIMINAL ACTIVITY | ACTION | GENERAL PENALTY |
|---|---|---|
| Protected computer trespass | Unauthorized access | A defendant can receive a fine, or up to 1 year in prison, or both. |
| Obtaining information from a protected computer | Unauthorized access<br>Access in excess of authorized access | A defendant can receive a fine, or up to 1 year in prison, or both.<br>The defendant also can be sentenced for a felony and up to 5 years in prison if aggravating factors exist. Repeat offenders can receive a fine, or 10 years in prison, or both. |
| Access of a protected computer with intent to defraud | Unauthorized access<br>Access in excess of authorized access | A defendant can receive a fine, or up to 5 years in prison, or both. |
| Access to a protected computer that causes damage | Knowingly transmits a program, incorporation, or code that intentionally causes damage<br>Intentional access that recklessly causes damage<br>Intentional access that causes damage and loss | **Damage by Code Transmission:**<br>A defendant can receive a fine, or 10 years in prison, or both. The defendant also can receive 20 years in prison for subsequent convictions or causing damage leading to serious bodily injury.<br>A defendant can receive life imprisonment if the offense causes or attempts to cause death.<br>**Reckless Damage:**<br>A defendant can receive a fine, or 5 years in prison, or both. Repeat offenders can receive a fine, or 20 years in prison, or both.<br>**Damage and Loss:**<br>A defendant can receive a fine, or 10 years in prison, or both. |
| Threatening to damage a computer | Intent to extort | A defendant can receive a fine, or up to 5 years in prison, or both. |
| Trafficking in passwords | Knowing action, with intent to defraud | A defendant can receive a fine, or up to 1 year in prison, or both.<br>Repeat offenders can receive a fine, or 10 years in prison, or both. |
| Computer espionage | Knowing access and willful transmission of information that could be used to injure the U.S. or its interests | A defendant can receive a fine, or up to 10 years in prison, or both. |

## Computer Trespass or Intrusion

The CFAA is the main federal law addressing cybercrime. In addition to the CFAA, the federal government has some other laws that address computer trespass or intrusion. These laws generally address computers that the U.S. government owns or controls. Some laws, such as the CFAA, expand this definition to include computers used in interstate commerce.

### State Laws Against Computer Trespass

It is important to keep in mind that states also may have computer trespass statutes that prohibit unauthorized access to computer systems or networks. Depending on the jurisdiction, these crimes have a variety of names. In many states, the mere act of intentionally entering a computer system or network without permission is a crime. In most jurisdictions, first-time computer trespass is a misdemeanor. The penalties for computer trespass may escalate if a person is charged and convicted of more than one offense.

Most trespass statutes address only unauthorized access into a computer system. They stop short of addressing actual computer tampering, access to information, or the injection of computer viruses or worms. These types of crimes, which are malicious in nature, typically are addressed in other statutes.



Federal law addresses fraud and related activity in connection with access devices. It outlaws the production, use, or sale of counterfeit or unauthorized access devices.[20] Access devices include any item that can be used to obtain money, goods, or things of value. They include items such as card, plate, code, account number, electronic serial number, mobile identification number, personal identification number, or other telecommunications services. A person who violates this law commits a felony. He or she can be imprisoned for 10 to 20 years depending upon the nature of the violation.

## Theft of Information

Theft of information via computer networks is on the rise. Most of these crimes take the form of theft of personal identifying information or financial information. Financial gain is nearly always the motive for these crimes. The U.S. Federal Trade Commission (FTC) announced that fraud and identity theft were number one and two, respectively, on its list of top three consumer complaints for 2019.[21]

The federal Identity Theft and Assumption Deterrence Act (1998) makes identity theft a federal crime.[22] The law makes it illegal for anyone to knowingly transfer or use another person's identification with the intent to commit a crime. Under the law, an identification document is any document made or issued by the federal or a state government. Identifying information includes items you may be familiar with as *personally identifiable information*, such as name, Social Security number (SSN), and driver's license number. It also includes:

- Unique biometric data, such as fingerprint, voice print, retina or iris image, or other unique physical representation
- Unique electronic identification number, address, or routing code

- Electronic serial number or any other number or signal that identifies a specific telecommunications device or account
- Any other piece of information that may be used to identify a specific person

If a person violates the law, she or he is subject to fines and criminal penalties of up to 15 years in prison. This period increases to 30 years in special circumstances, such as where identity theft is used to facilitate terrorism. Violators also must give any personal property used to commit identity theft crimes to the government. The U.S. Secret Service, FBI, U.S. Postal Inspection Service, and Social Security Administration's Office of the Inspector General all have the power to investigate crimes committed under this law.

**NOTE**

The FTC's identity theft website provides useful information about preventing identity theft. You can read more at https://www.consumer.ftc.gov/topics/identity-theft.

## Interception of Communications Laws

Federal laws that address the illegal interception of communications forbid the use of eavesdropping technologies without a court order. Communications covered by the statutes include email, radio communications, electronic communications, data transmission, and telephone calls. The federal Wiretap Act (1968, amended) governs *real-time* interception of the contents of a communication.[23] It does not apply to transmission information. The Act forbids the real-time interception of any wire, oral, or electronic communication. Communications covered by the Act include email, radio communications, data transmissions, and telephone calls. A person who violates the Act can be fined or imprisoned for up to 5 years, or both.

**NOTE**

The Pen Register and Trap and Trace Statute governs access to the real-time interception of headers, logs, and other transmission information.[24]

The Electronic Communications Privacy Act (ECPA; 1986) governs access to *stored* electronic communications.[25] This includes access to the contents of the communication and the headers and other transmission information. The ECPA is an amendment to the original Wiretap Act.

The ECPA governs access to the contents of stored communications, as well as access to transmission data about the communications. Under the ECPA, no one may access the contents of these communications unless it is allowed somewhere else in the ECPA. A person who violates the Act can be fined or imprisoned for up to 5 years, or both. Repeat offenders can be imprisoned up to 10 years.

## Spam and Phishing Laws

Congress created the Controlling the Assault of Non-Solicited Pornography and Marketing (CAN-SPAM) Act in 2003.[26] The Act covers unsolicited commercial email messages known as spam. **Spam** is unsolicited electronic junk mail that a user may receive. Spam is a nuisance to the recipient. The CAN-SPAM Act has both civil and criminal provisions.

The CAN-SPAM Act requires commercial email senders to meet certain requirements. Commercial messages are messages with content that advertises or promotes a product or service. The Act also forbids sending sexually explicit email unless it has a label or marking that identifies it as explicit.[27]

Commercial email message senders must meet the following CAN-SPAM requirements:

- Do not use false or misleading header information.
- Do not use deceptive subject lines.
- Identify the email message as a commercial advertisement.
- Include a valid physical postal address.
- Inform message recipients how to opt-out of future email messages.
- Promptly process opt-out requests.
- Monitor the actions of third parties that advertise on the sender's behalf.[28]

**NOTE**

The FTC helps businesses understand the CAN-SPAM Act. You can view their business compliance guide at https://www.ftc.gov/tips-advice/business-center/guidance/can-spam-act-compliance-guide-business.



The FTC enforces the civil provisions of the CAN-SPAM Act. Violations of the Act are enforced by the FTC in the same way that it enforces unfair or deceptive trade practices.[29] The FTC also has promulgated rules for businesses to follow. The FTC completed its first review of the CAN-SPAM Act in 2019 and determined that it would make no changes to the rule because of its benefit to consumers.[30]

The CAN-SPAM Act also has criminal provisions. It includes penalties for:

- Accessing another person's computer without permission to send spam
- Using false information to register for multiple email accounts or domain names
- Relaying or retransmitting spam messages through a computer to mislead others about the origin of the email
- Harvesting email addresses or generating them through a dictionary attack
- Taking advantage of open relays or open proxies without permission to send spam[31]

The U.S. Department of Justice enforces the criminal provisions of the CAN-SPAM Act. Criminal penalties include fines or imprisonment of up to 5 years. The first conviction under the CAN-SPAM Act occurred in 2004. In that case, the defendant searched for unprotected wireless access hotspots and exploited them to send spam messages that advertised pornographic websites. Eventually, the court sentenced the defendant to 3 years' probation and 6 months of home detention. He also had to pay a $10,000 fine.[32]

**NOTE**

The criminal provisions of the CAN-SPAM Act allow the U.S. government to prosecute hackers who use email.[33]

**FYI**

Spam email messages also can be phishing attempts. There is no federal anti-phishing law. However, phishing attacks can be prosecuted under several different federal laws. This includes many of the laws already discussed in this section. For example, if the phishing attackers are attempting to steal personal information, they may be committing identity theft. In that case, the federal Identity Theft and Assumption Deterrence Act would apply. They also may be committing computer fraud or access-device fraud. Some phishing attacks also can be prosecuted under the CAN-SPAM Act.

If a phishing attack includes malicious activity, such as spreading computer viruses, then the CFAA would apply. Phishing scams also can violate state laws on fraud and identity theft.

## Cybersquatting

Cybersquatting is the bad-faith registration of a domain name that is a registered trademark or trade name of another entity. Congress created the Anti-Cybersquatting Consumer Protection Act (ACPA) in 1999.[34] It is designed to stop people from registering domain names that are trademarks that belong to other entities.

The ACPA allows entities to sue cybersquatters. To prove such a case, the plaintiff must show that the cybersquatter registered the trademark in bad faith with the intent to profit from the registration. The ACPA includes nine factors that help a court determine bad faith.[35] Those factors are:

- A person's intellectual property rights in the domain name
- Whether the domain name consists of the legal name of the person
- The person's prior use of the domain name in connection with the sale of goods or services
- The person's noncommercial or fair use of the domain name
- The person's intent to divert consumers from the mark owner's own website
- The person's offer to sell the domain name without having used the domain name for the sale of goods or services
- Whether the person gave false or misleading contact information when registering the domain name
- Whether the person registered multiple domain names that are identical or confusingly similar to marks owned by others
- Whether the mark incorporated in the domain name is famous and distinctive

Under the law, a plaintiff can recover damages and ask the court to issue an injunction that stops the cybersquatter from using the contested domain name. Courts also can award the contested domain name to the winning party.

## Malicious Acts

Common malicious information security acts include malware, worms, viruses, and Trojan horses. For the most part, the federal government can prosecute these types of activities under the CFAA.

Under the CFAA, the intentional transmission of malware, viruses, or worms that damage a protected computer is a felony. Remember that for the CFAA, almost any computer connected to the internet is a protected computer. The government can charge people who violate this provision of the CFAA with a felony that can be punished with up to 10 years in prison.

Cyberstalking, the use of the internet to stalk another person in a threatening way, is also a malicious act. Cyberstalkers could use email, instant messages, blogs, social networking platforms, and even entire websites to target their victims. Cyberstalking is sometimes also referred to as cyberharassment.

Many traditional state laws on stalking and harassment have been updated to include language about cyberstalking. Similar to many other cybercrimes, cyberstalking often crosses state borders. At the federal level, cyberstalking is prohibited under several different laws:

- **The Telephone Harassment Act**—Makes it illegal to use the internet to transmit any message to harass or threaten another person.[36]
- **The Interstate Stalking and Prevention Act**—Makes it illegal for anyone who travels across states to use any interactive computer service to cause substantial emotional distress.[37]
- **The Interstate Communications Act**—Makes it illegal to transmit in interstate commerce any threat to injure another person.[38]



Cyberbullying is closely related to cyberstalking. The distinction is that cyberbullying is harassment that takes place between school-aged children.[39] Depending on the situation, state cyberbullying or cyberstalking laws tend to apply most in these cyberharassment situations. Currently, no federal law directly addresses cyberbullying. The federal government has attempted to expand the use of the CFAA into the area of cyberbullying with little success.

In 2008, the Department of Justice indicted Lori Drew for violating the CFAA.[40] The government argued that her activities on a social networking service exceeded her authorization in the use of a protected computer. She exceeded her authorized access by using the site in excess of the use authorized by the site's terms of service agreement. A jury found her guilty of a misdemeanor CFAA violation. That conviction was set aside in August 2009. The judge found that there were several problems in applying the CFAA to the case.[41] The government did not appeal the judge's reversal. Many federal courts have since found that violating the terms of service agreement for a website is not a CFAA violation.

**NOTE**

Learn more about preventing cyberbullying at www.stopbullying.gov.

## Well-Known Cybercrimes

The list of well-known cybercrimes changes every day. The CFAA, the "go-to" act for federal prosecution of cybercrime, is very broad, and almost any type of internet-related crime involving computers will fall within its scope. Prosecutors often include CFAA charges with other federal criminal charges if a computer is involved in the commission of a crime.

Some cybercrimes are well known because they were "first." For example, the Morris worm was one of the first computer worms on the internet. At the time, it infected and overwhelmed many government systems. The creator of the worm was the first person charged with violating the CFAA.[42]

The CFAA also was used to prosecute the creator of the Melissa virus.[43] When it was released, the Melissa virus was one of the fastest-moving and most destructive viruses. David Smith created and distributed the Melissa virus in 1999. The virus caused more than $80 million in damage. He was sentenced to 20 months in federal prison in May 2002. He also was fined $5,000.

Other cybercrimes are well known because they are among the biggest or the perpetrators have received notable punishments. For instance, one of the hackers in the TJX Companies, Inc. case

**NOTE**

You can learn how the federal government is prosecuting cybercrime by visiting the Department of Justice Computer Crime and Intellectual Property web page. The "Press Releases" page lists recent cybercrime prosecutions. The web page is available at http://www.justice.gov/criminal/cybercrime/.

received the harshest-ever sentence for a hacking case in March 2010. The federal government had charged him with violating the CFAA, federal laws related to access device fraud, and the Identity Theft and Assumption Deterrence Act. The hacker, Albert Gonzalez, was sentenced to 20 years in prison. He was also fined $250,000.[44]

## General Tort Law Concepts

A *tort* is some sort of wrongful act or harm that injures a person. A person who is injured by a tort may sue the wrongdoer for damages. The word *tort* is from the Latin word *tortus*, which means wrong or twisted.

**NOTE**

A **tortfeasor** is a person who commits a tort. In this discussion, a person charged with committing a tort is called a defendant. A plaintiff is the person allegedly injured by the defendant's actions.

**NOTE**

*Tortious conduct* is wrongful conduct. It is conduct that is unreasonable given the situation.

In the United States, tort law has evolved from English common law. Many states give either common law or statutory recognition to most torts. When states enact tort laws, they typically are trying to expand or limit common law tort liability. Common law tort principles are similar among the states. The American Law Institute has prepared a review of tort law. The *Restatement (Second) of the Law of Torts* summarizes the common law tort rules.

Tort law is based on the premise that people should go about their daily business in a way that does not harm other people or their property. So long as people are acting reasonably, this is easy to accomplish. Tort law allows people a way to recover for their injuries if another person does not act reasonably.

Tort law uses the reasonable person standard to determine whether a person acts appropriately. Courts use this standard to determine if a person acts reasonably in response to a particular situation. This standard determines whether conduct is tortious.

There are three types of torts. They are:

- Strict liability torts
- Negligent torts
- Intentional torts

This section will briefly describe all three types of torts. However, you should keep in mind that most torts involving computers probably will fall under the intentional torts category.

### Strict Liability Torts

Strict liability is a legal concept that means that people can be held responsible for their actions even if they did not intend to cause harm to another person. Several areas of law apply this concept.

In tort law, a person is held liable for strict liability torts regardless of intent or negligence. Courts usually impose strict liability theories in unreasonably dangerous situations. These are situations where even a reasonable person cannot prevent risk. The main reason for imposing strict liability is to discourage unreasonably risky behavior.

The classic example of a strict liability tort is when a person keeps wild animals as pets. Wild animals are inherently dangerous. Even if the owner of the animal takes reasonable precautions, there is still a risk to the public if the animal escapes. If an animal were to escape and injure a person, courts would hold the owner liable for any damages that the animal caused. Courts hold the owner liable even if the owner takes every precaution available to ensure safety.

In a tort based on strict liability, the plaintiff must show that the defendant engaged in unreasonably dangerous activities. The plaintiff also must show that he or she was harmed. The defendant bears the burden of proving that the activities were not unreasonably dangerous.



## Negligence Torts

Negligence torts are based on the premise that a person is liable for any injuries or harm that are the foreseeable consequences of his or her actions. To prove a negligence-based tort, a plaintiff must show that:

- The defendant owed the plaintiff a duty of due care.
- The defendant breached his or her duty.
- The breach of duty caused the plaintiff's foreseeable injuries.
- The plaintiff was damaged.

Plaintiffs must prove that the defendant owed them a **duty of due care**. A duty of due care is a person's obligation to avoid acts or omissions that can harm others. The level of duty that one person owes to another is based on the reasonable person standard, a legal concept used to describe how an ordinary person would think and act. The plaintiff will present evidence on what a reasonable person in a similar circumstance would have done. This evidence shows the level of care that the defendant owes the plaintiff.

There are special duty of due care rules for people in learned occupations, professions where special training and skill are required. Under the law, people in these occupations are held to a higher standard of care that is reasonable for members of that profession. For example, a lawyer's duty of due care toward his or her clients is based on a reasonable lawyer standard. Doctors, architects, engineers, and airplane pilots are held to reasonableness standards based on their professions.

**NOTE**

The standard of care for professionals in learned occupations is important in professional malpractice cases.

The plaintiff also must show that the defendant breached a duty of due care. That is, the plaintiff must prove that the defendant's behavior fell below what a reasonable person would have done in the same situation. The plaintiff will compare the defendant's behavior against the evidence that was used to show that the defendant had a duty of due care. The plaintiff can show that the defendant breached his or her duty by showing that the defendant acted in a way that was unreasonable given the situation and the defendant's duty.

**NOTE**

A plaintiff also can prove a breach of the duty of due care by showing that the defendant failed to take a required action. This is called an omission.

For example, a plaintiff may be able to establish that people have a duty to keep their sidewalks free from ice in the wintertime. To prove that the defendant breached this duty, the plaintiff would present evidence that the defendant did not shovel his or her sidewalks. The plaintiff also would have to show that the defendant's failure to keep the sidewalks clear injured the plaintiff.

### The Reasonable Information Security Professional

Torts based on a professional's duty to provide competent services are among the oldest negligence torts. Is an information security professional a member of a learned occupation? Will information security professionals be held to a "reasonable security professional" standard when advising clients? There is some argument that this could be the case sometime in the future.

Information security as a career path continues to evolve. Many information security professionals are highly educated individuals who are experts in their fields. Most of them have certifications in various technical aspects of information security. Many computing vendors offer technology-specific security certifications for their products.

Several independent organizations offer security-related certifications as well. The International Information Systems Security Certification Consortium $(ISC)^2$ grants certifications to many information security professionals. This organization certifies that information security professionals have varying levels of experience and knowledge in the field. You can learn about $(ISC)^2$ at http://www.isc2.org/.

The Global Information Assurance Certification (GIAC) program also grants information security certifications. It offers special certifications in areas such as audit, intrusion detection, and operating system security. These certifications test technical skills. Many information security professionals hold GIAC certifications. You can learn about GIAC at http://www.giac.org/.

Both $(ISC)^2$ and GIAC require certificate holders to follow a code of ethics. Each group has a code that defines acceptable levels of behavior for certificate holders. Both codes require certificate holders to act responsibly when giving information security advice. These organizations also require certificate holders to engage in activities that keep their information security skills up to date.

As of this writing, no U.S. court has recognized a professional duty for information security professionals. Think about whether information security certifications and the ethical obligations that they sometimes require could be used to show that information security professionals are part of a learned profession. Could this change how information security professionals help their clients secure information systems?

The plaintiff also must show that the defendant's breach caused the plaintiff's foreseeable injuries. Often courts use the "but for" test to meet this requirement. Would the plaintiff's injuries have occurred "but for" the defendant's actions? Once it is established that the defendant caused the plaintiff's injuries, courts review whether those injuries are compensable.

The law recognizes that there are some instances where the defendant is no longer responsible for the plaintiff's injuries. This happens when the plaintiff's injuries are not foreseeable. The famous case that explored this concept is *Palsgraf v. Long Island Railroad* (1928).[45]

In the *Palsgraf* case, a passenger was running toward a moving train. Train employees tried to help the passenger board the train. As they helped him, they bumped a package from his arms that contained fireworks. The fireworks exploded on the train tracks and caused a scale on the train platform to topple over. When it fell, it injured Mrs. Palsgraf. She sued the railroad for her injuries.

The New York Court of Appeals decided the case. The court held that the plaintiff's injuries were not a foreseeable result of the actions of the railroad's employees. The court also held that the defendant had no duty to the plaintiff. The duty was owed to the passenger that the train employees were trying to help onto the train. Because there was no duty owed to the plaintiff, there could be no liability.

The *Palsgraf* case has come to stand for the rule that a defendant has no duty of due care to an unforeseen plaintiff for unforeseeable injuries. If there is no duty to an unforeseen plaintiff, then there is no negligence. This means that the relationship between the defendant's act or omissions and the plaintiff's injuries must have proximate or legal cause; that is, that the plaintiff's injuries must be the natural and foreseeable results of the defendant's negligence.

Once the plaintiff proves that the defendant committed a negligent act, the plaintiff must prove that he or she suffered an injury and is entitled to damages. A court awards damages in a tort case in an attempt to make a plaintiff whole. These are called compensatory damages. Compensatory damages try to place the plaintiff in the same position that he or she would have been in had no tortious act occurred. This is the primary goal of tort lawsuits.

A court does not usually award punitive damages in a negligent tort case. However, it may award punitive damages if the defendant's actions are grossly negligent. This does not happen often, though. Many states have placed limits on the amount of punitive damages that a court or jury can award in a tort lawsuit.

There are some defenses to negligence torts a defendant can use to help escape or limit liability. A defendant has the burden of proving her or his defenses. The three most common defenses are:

- **Assumption of risk**—The plaintiff had assumed the risk of the defendant's actions and any injuries resulting from those actions. If the defendant proves assumption of risk, he or she has no liability to the plaintiff.
- **Contributory negligence**—The plaintiff should recover nothing because his or her own actions also contributed to his or her own injuries. If the defendant proves contributory negligence, he or she has no liability to the plaintiff. Only a few jurisdictions follow this rule because it is very harsh.
- **Comparative negligence**—The plaintiff should recover only a *pro rata* share of damages because his or her own actions also contributed to his or her injuries. In most jurisdictions, a plaintiff less than 50 percent at fault can recover a *pro rata* share of damages based on the defendant's level of fault.

**NOTE**

In New York, the Court of Appeals is the state's highest court.

**NOTE**

In a tort case, damages can be economic or non-economic. Economic damages are damages that have monetary value. They include compensation for medical bills, lost wages, and damage to property. Non-economic damages are harder to prove. They include compensation for items such as pain and suffering, or loss of companionship.



## Intentional Torts

*Intentional torts* occur when the defendant intended to commit the tort. Intentional torts often share many common elements with a crime. It helps to remember that civil actions address torts and criminal actions address crimes. The same action can be both a wrong against society (a crime) and a wrong against an individual (a tort).

**NOTE**

Most of the torts associated with computers and cyberspace are intentional torts. These occur when the defendant uses a computer or takes some action involving a computer, intentionally, to harm the plaintiff.

The classic example of an intentional tort is battery. Battery is harmful or offensive contact with another person. The battery tort occurs when the defendant intentionally causes harmful contact with the plaintiff.

The most common defense to an intentional tort is that the plaintiff consented to the wrongful action. A defendant must prove that the plaintiff consented. A defendant can use the plaintiff's words or actions as evidence to prove consent.

## Civil Procedure

A plaintiff must sue a defendant in a civil lawsuit to recover for tort injuries. Civil procedure is the body of rules that govern how courts conduct civil cases. This section provides more detail on the civil trial process. One thing to keep in mind is that the laws of civil procedure vary from jurisdiction to jurisdiction. The federal and state governments all have different civil procedure rules. The description provided here is intentionally general.

**NOTE**

In civil procedure, the plaintiff is the party that brings the lawsuit. The defendant is the party that defends against the lawsuit. In some jurisdictions, and for some types of cases, the plaintiff could be called the petitioner. The defendant could be called the respondent.

A civil action begins when the plaintiff files a **complaint** with a court. A plaintiff uses a complaint to tell his or her story. The plaintiff states how he or she was injured and asks the court to make him or her whole. A complaint must contain "a short and plain statement of the claim showing that the pleader is entitled to relief."[46] It also must show that the court has jurisdiction to hear the case. The plaintiff also must specify the relief demanded. In a tort case, the plaintiff typically wishes to receive money damages. The damages compensate the plaintiff for any injuries.

The plaintiff must file a complaint within a certain period, called the **statute of limitations**, after the claimed injury. For example, in Indiana, the statute of limitations for most tort actions is 2 years.[47] The plaintiff must sue the defendant within 2 years of being injured by the defendant. Not all states have the same time limits, however. For example, in Montana, the statute of limitations for most tort actions based on negligent conduct is 3 years.[48]

*Service of process* refers to the procedure that delivers the complaint and a summons to the defendant. This process makes the defendant aware that the plaintiff has filed a lawsuit. Certain formalities must be followed to serve a complaint and summons on a defendant. For the most part, the complaint and summons are delivered physically to the defendant. This is to assure the court that the defendant received proper notice of the lawsuit.

The defendant must respond to the complaint after receiving it. That response is called an **answer**. All jurisdictions have time limits that a defendant must follow when answering the complaint. Under the Federal Rules of Civil Procedure, a defendant must file his or her answer within 20 days after receiving the complaint.[49] A court can allow a defendant more time to answer if necessary.

A defendant must respond to each claim in the plaintiff's complaint. He or she can admit to or deny the claims. The defendant must also state her or his defenses to each claim. The answer is the defendant's opportunity to tell her or his side of the story.

 **NOTE**

A defendant also can raise counterclaims in his or her answer. These are the defendant's claims against the plaintiff. The defendant also can raise cross-claims. These are the defendant's claims against another party to hold that third party responsible for the plaintiff's injuries.



A defendant also can raise defenses to the plaintiff's complaint. Some of these defenses are absolute. The court must dismiss the plaintiff's lawsuit if the defendant proves the defense. For example, the defendant can question the court's jurisdiction. If the court does not have jurisdiction over the matter, then it must dismiss the lawsuit. A defendant also can argue that the plaintiff does not have a legal basis for the claim. The court must dismiss the lawsuit if there is no legal basis for the plaintiff's claim.

After the complaint and answer, the plaintiff and defendant's attorneys will begin the discovery process. This is the period of the civil lawsuit where the parties share information with one another. Unlike the criminal discovery process, there are few affirmative disclosure rules in the civil discovery process. The parties must disclose their witnesses to one another. They also must provide each other with a list of documents that they have in their possession that are related to their claims and defenses. The documents that each party must disclose include a listing of documents stored in an electronic form.

After these general disclosures, it is up to each party to ask for information that is relevant to the case. The parties use various procedural rules to ask each other for information and documents. The process can get very complicated. It also can get very expensive. Sometimes the parties will ask the court to intervene in the discovery process. This happens when the parties dispute whether some types of information must be disclosed.

For example, a defendant may not want to disclose trade secret information through the discovery process, even if it is relevant to the case. This is because documents filed in a court case become public records. This includes documents exchanged during the discovery process and then used as evidence at trial. The defendant does not want to lose trade secret protection. The defendant could lose that protection if the information is available to the public or if it is shared with the other party's legal team. In this instance, the defendant could ask the court to issue a protective order. This type of order requires the parties to keep certain information secret. It helps protect the defendant's trade secrets.

After the discovery process ends, the parties either settle their lawsuits or proceed to trial. If a tort case goes to trial, the plaintiff must prove all the elements of his or her claim. He or she must prove the case through a preponderance of the evidence. This is a lower standard of proof than in criminal cases. A civil trial ends with the court or jury's decision on the case. Parties may appeal an adverse ruling at the trial court level. Either party may appeal a ruling to a higher court through several different procedural rules. These rules are outside of the scope of this chapter.

**NOTE**

Some civil cases, called *bench trials*, are tried in front of a judge alone. Bench trials are unusual in tort cases.

## Electronic Discovery

For the parties in a lawsuit, electronic data can be important evidence. This is especially true because many parties and witnesses store their data in an electronic format only. The introduction of electronic-format evidence and record-keeping systems caused some problems for the legal system. These problems were acute in the discovery phase of lawsuits, where parties would engage in expensive fights over the production of electronic information.

Electronic discovery deals with information stored in an electronic format. It is also known as E-discovery. Before 2006, courts decided E-discovery issues on a case-by-case basis under standard discovery rules. The most famous case for E-discovery issues is *Zubulake v. UBS Warburg, LLC.*[50] The U.S. District Court for the Southern District of New York decided this case.

There are actually several Zubulake decisions regarding electronic discovery. They stated the first real rules for parties to follow regarding electronic evidence. The rules related to the duty to preserve evidence, the duty to monitor compliance with preservation decisions, and the costs of providing electronic data.

In 2006, the U.S. Supreme Court amended the Federal Rules of Civil Procedure to clarify how parties should handle E-discovery. These revisions were largely because of the Zubulake case. Additional amendments to the Federal Rules of Civil Procedure regarding E-discovery were proposed in August 2013. The Judicial Conference Committee on Rules of Practice and Procedure received over 2,000 comments on the new rules.[51]

When a lawsuit begins, parties are obligated to preserve certain types of evidence. This includes evidence stored in an electronic format. The Federal Rules of Civil Procedure call this type of evidence "electronically stored information" (ESI). The definition is broad and is meant to include any type of information that can be stored electronically. The parties must address how discoverable ESI will be preserved. They also must address the format in which it will be shared with the other party. It can be shared in its native format, which may not be usable by the other party. It also can be shared in a reasonably useful form. If the parties do not specify how the ESI is to be shared, then a party providing ESI must notify the requesting party of the format.

In some instances, it can be hard to produce ESI for various reasons. A party does not have to produce ESI if it is not reasonably accessible because of undue burden or costs associated with retrieving the ESI. The party claiming that it cannot produce ESI for these reasons bears the burden of proving that production is overly costly or complex.

Usually, a court can sanction a party if it destroys evidence during a lawsuit. This is called the spoliation of evidence. It occurs when evidence in a lawsuit is inappropriately changed or destroyed. Spoliation sanctions can be severe. The Federal Rules of Civil Procedure recognize that sometimes ESI that is relevant to a case may be destroyed through the normal operations of information technology systems. The Rules provide a safe harbor to parties in these situations. The Rules state that a court may not impose sanctions on a party for failing to produce ESI that is destroyed because of the good-faith operation of information technology systems.

To fall into the safe harbor, the party must show that it took steps to preserve the ESI and acted in good faith. The duty to preserve ESI arises when a party is made aware of a legal claim or is put on notice that litigation is imminent or reasonably anticipated. Sometimes the attorney for a party might issue a preservation notice or litigation hold. These notices tell the party exactly what type of information must be preserved and for how long. Sometimes attorneys for opposing parties will send these types of notices to each other or witnesses to make sure that ESI is preserved.

## Common Tort Law Actions in Cyberspace

Torts are wrongful acts between individuals. Lawyers and commentators have started to use the term *cybertorts* to describe torts arising from internet communications.[52] (Terms are always trendier when *cyber* is added as a preface!) Courts are applying traditional tort law principles to areas where communications and personal interactions occur electronically. This section will briefly describe some of the ways that tort law concepts have been applied to online interactions.



### Defamation

Defamation is an intentional tort. Defamation occurs when one person speaks or publishes a false statement of fact about another person that injures that person's reputation. There are two types of defamation cases. They are:

- **Libel**—Written defamation
- **Slander**—Oral defamation

The distinction between **libel** and **slander** has diminished in recent years, with "defamation" being used generally to refer to both types of cases. Defamation cases in cyberspace involving written communications are considered libel cases. To prove defamation, a plaintiff must show all of the following:

- That the defendant made a false statement of fact
- That the defendant published the statement to third parties
- That the defendant knew or should have known that the statement was false

A defamatory statement must be more than mere opinion. For instance, in *Hammer v. Amazon.com* (2005), the plaintiff, a self-published author, sued Amazon.com for defamation. An online reviewer gave the plaintiff's book a negative review, which Amazon published. The plaintiff wanted Amazon to remove the review, which it refused to do. The court ruled that the reviewer's statements were opinion and could not support a defamation claim.[53]

The defamatory statement must be published to third parties. The publication requirement is easily satisfied when information is posted on the internet. In fact, because many people have access to the internet and materials posted on it, it may be easier for a plaintiff to show publication in an internet defamation case. Information posted on the internet may reach an audience more quickly. It also could lead to greater damage to the plaintiff.

**NOTE**

The term **flaming** refers to contentious debates between online posters, which often occur on online discussion boards. People might be able to use these types of statements to support a defamation case.

Finally, the plaintiff must show that the defendant knew, or should have known, that the statement was false. A plaintiff shows this by presenting evidence that the defendant did not check facts or the source of a statement.

Some types of statements are so scandalous that a court automatically presumes that defamation has occurred. These types of statements are called defamation *per se*. *Per se* is a Latin phrase that means "by itself." Types of statements considered defamation *per se* include:

- Statements that a person has a loathsome disease
- Statements that a person has committed a crime
- Statements about sexual misconduct or chastity
- Statements about professional impropriety

If a defamation case involves these types of statements, the plaintiffs do not have to prove all the defamation elements. They just must prove their damages.

Defamation is considered in context. A court must consider all the facts and circumstances around a case. In a traditional defamation case, the plaintiff can sue both the original maker of the defamatory statement and anyone who republishes the statement. These lines are blurred online. It makes it especially hard to determine where a defamatory statement first appears.

**NOTE**

Traditionally, loathsome diseases were diseases such as leprosy and venereal disease. They are diseases that have great social stigma.

Understanding what constitutes a defamatory statement online can be hard—especially in cases involving social media. In 2019, a unanimous jury held that Elon Musk did not

### Internet Service Provider Liability for Torts

Congress enacted the Communications Decency Act in 1996. However, the U.S. Supreme Court declared many portions of this Act unconstitutional because they infringed on free speech rights. One part of the Act that is still in effect is Section 230.[55]

Section 230 protects interactive computer service providers from liability for the actions of content providers. The Act recognizes that "[t]he rapidly developing array of internet and other interactive computer services available to individual Americans represent an extraordinary advance in the availability of educational and informational resources to our citizens."[56] It also recognized that Americans rely on interactive media for educational and entertainment information. In enacting the policy, Congress sought "to encourage the development of technologies which maximize user control over what information is received by individuals, families, and schools who use the Internet and other interactive computer services."[57]

Under the law, an interactive computer service is any electronic information service or system. It specifically includes a service or system that provides access to the internet. Courts interpret this definition as broadly as possible. The act states that an interactive computer service provider may not be treated as the "publisher" or "speaker" of content posted by service users. This is a safe harbor for interactive computer service providers. It protects them from legal liability for the actions of service users.

Courts have applied this provision quite broadly to many companies who offer services over the internet such as social networking or bulletin board posting services. For instance, courts have found that Facebook, Craigslist, YouTube, and Twitter are interactive service providers who fall under the section's protection.

ISPs rely on this law to insulate themselves from the actions of their customers. Section 230 specifically preempts state or local laws that would hold ISPs responsible for the acts of content providers.

defame another individual through statements that Musk made through three tweets over Twitter.[54]

The defendant can raise some defenses to a defamation allegation. Truth, for example, is an absolute defense to a defamation allegation. A court cannot hold a defendant responsible for defamatory statements if the statements were truthful. Another defense is that the defendant acted in good faith. Statements that a defendant makes in connection with judicial or legislative proceedings have immunity from a defamation action. These types of statements are called *privileged* statements.

One problem for online defamation cases is that it is sometimes difficult for a plaintiff to discover the identity of an online poster. This is particularly true if an anonymous poster makes defamatory statements in an online forum. Plaintiffs often have to go to court to get an ISP to turn over identifying information about an anonymous online poster.

A final item to remember is that online tort cases often involve jurisdictional issues as well. State courts can hold out-of-state defendants responsible for their actions only in limited circumstances. Most states have complicated tests, called "long-arm jurisdiction" tests, for when they can exercise jurisdiction over an out-of-state defendant. Lawyers and courts use this term because it describes situations where the "long arm of the law" can pull a defendant into a certain jurisdiction. This is the same type of problem that was discussed in the criminal law section of this chapter. These types of jurisdiction issues sometimes mean that a plaintiff must litigate a case in a state other than the state where she or he lives.



## Intentional Infliction of Emotional Distress

Intentional infliction of emotional distress (IIED) is known as the *tort of outrage*. This is because it is used to address conduct that is so offensive that a reasonable person would say "Outrageous!" To prove this tort, a plaintiff must show:

- That the defendant acted intentionally or recklessly
- That the defendant's conduct was extreme and outrageous
- That the defendant's conduct caused the plaintiff severe emotional distress

> **NOTE**
>
> Many states also recognize the tort of negligent infliction of emotional distress. This tort can be harder to prove because one of the elements is that the defendant owed the plaintiff a duty to act in a certain way. There is no duty requirement in IIED cases.

The *Restatement (Second) of the Law of Torts* notes that extreme and outrageous conduct is "beyond all possible bounds of decency and to be regarded as atrocious, and utterly intolerable in a civilized community."[58] Courts have recognized that people have the right to be free from this type of behavior. Even though courts recognize this cause of action, they have held that the defendant's conduct truly must be extreme and outrageous given the circumstances. Mere bad or boorish behavior is not enough under this tort.

The landmark case recognizing this tort happened in California.[59] In this case, the defendant won a contract for trash collection from a private entity. The contract was previously held by a member of the State Rubbish Collectors Association. The defendant was not a member of the association. The association intimidated the defendant into signing its membership agreement. Association members threatened to hurt the defendant and destroy his garbage truck.

The association then sued the defendant to collect dues as stated in the membership agreement. The defendant argued that the agreement was invalid because the association had threatened him and he signed the agreement under duress. He also argued that the plaintiff's actions caused him to become severely ill and miss work.

In ruling on the case, the court said that a person has the right to live his life without "serious, intentional, and unprivileged invasions of emotional and mental tranquility."[60] The court found that the defendant stated a claim for IIED and could recover damages based on his IIED claim.

IIED cases can arise through email, comments made on social networking sites, and instant messaging. Because IIED cases involve interactions between a plaintiff and defendant, evidence proving the contents of the electronic communications can be very important. Similar to defamation cases, in most instances ISPs are not liable for the actions of content providers that cause an IIED.

**FYI**

Often IIED cases involve situations where a person is using a work email account or internet access to commit the tortious activity. There are times when employers might be liable for the bad acts of employees. Employers can be liable for their employees' actions when those actions take place within the scope of the employee's job. An employer also must have knowledge of the employee's tortious acts. Courts have been reluctant to hold employers responsible for the cybertorts of employees unless the employer had knowledge of its employee's actions and did not take steps to stop them.

IIED claims also can involve claims of harassment. Some states recognize harassment as a tort, whereas most consider it criminal behavior. Some states also have included cyberstalking or online harassment in their criminal harassment laws. For example, Oklahoma and New York have anti-stalking laws that include online harassment as a prohibited activity.[61]

Harassment is similar to IIED in that the harasser intends to cause the plaintiff emotional distress. Harassment can include continuing to communicate with a person when she or he has asked that the harasser no longer talk to him or her. It also can include threats made against a person or that person's loved ones. Harassment also can include offensive sexual remarks and remarks based on characteristics such as race, national origin, religion, and gender.

Similar to IIED, harassment can very easily take place in the online environment. It can occur via email, postings on social networking web pages, and postings on other web pages.

## Trespass Torts

Common law recognizes trespass torts. In common law, there are two types of trespass cases: trespass on land and trespass to chattels. *Chattels* mean personal property. Trespass to chattels is intentionally interfering with a person's use or possession of personal property. The defendant's use of the plaintiff's personal property must cause an injury or damage. Often this happens when the defendant harms the personal property in some way.

Courts have extended trespass to chattels cases to online situations, such as spam email. The first court case holding spammers responsible for trespass to chattels was in 1997.[62] In that case, an ISP sued a defendant for bypassing the ISP's spam-blocking controls to send spam emails to the ISP's customers. The defendant had changed the header information on its spam emails so that the emails could could get past the ISP's spam filters. The ISP argued that the spam emails imposed a burden on its system. It also argued that the defendant's spam messages were an intrusion to the ISP's system because they bypassed filtering controls. The U.S. District Court for the Southern District of Ohio found that the defendant's spamming activities did indeed constitute a trespass of that system.[63]

**NOTE**

Remember, in tort cases, a plaintiff must show that he or she incurred damages from the defendant's bad conduct.



In a trespass to chattels case, the plaintiff must be able to prove that he or she was injured or harmed. This is the most difficult element to show in online cases. In 2003, the Intel Corporation sued an ex-employee for sending spam emails to over 30,000 Intel employees on multiple occasions. The California Supreme Court rejected Intel's trespass claim because it was unable to prove any damages. Intel was not able to show that the thousands of emails slowed its servers or caused some sort of adverse effect on its computer systems.[64]

## Privacy Violations

The four privacy torts are:

- Intrusion into seclusion
- Portrayal in a false light
- Appropriation of likeness or identity
- Public disclosure of private facts

Privacy torts were discussed earlier in this book. Courts are beginning to recognize that people have a right to privacy in their electronic equipment and electronic communications. The intrusion into seclusion privacy tort is used most often in this context. For example, a plaintiff may be able to sue a defendant for accessing the plaintiff's private electronic blog without permission. However, the rise of the internet as a communications and entertainment medium may mean that other privacy torts, such as portrayal in a false light, may grow as well.

A question that is yet to be resolved is whether people have a true right of privacy in their use of the internet, independent of any tortious or criminal activity. A person's privacy on the internet is somewhat limited by the logging mechanisms that ISPs and web pages employ to make sure that systems are operating correctly. Programs used by service providers to track activity for advertising purposes also are threats to privacy.

Tort cases are firmly rooted in state laws. There may be other tort actions that a plaintiff can use to seek redress for harmful activities in cyberspace. If a plaintiff is harmed by actions in cyberspace and has damages and injuries that he or she can prove, the plaintiff will need to review state laws and court cases for appropriate causes of action.

## Case Studies and Examples

The following case studies and examples show how the concepts discussed in this chapter are used. These case studies are real-world examples of criminal and tort law issues in cyberspace.

### CAN-SPAM Act

The U.S. government first brought criminal charges under the CAN-SPAM Act in April 2004. The U.S. Postal Inspection Service, U.S. Attorneys' office, and FTC were involved in investigating the case.

In this case, the federal government charged the defendants with sending spam messages to sell phony diet products. The defendants operated under the name Phoenix Avatar, LLC. The defendants hid their identities in spam messages by using corporate and government computer systems and spoofing third-party email addresses. They used computers belonging to Ford Motor Company, computers used by the U.S. court system, and the Unisys Corporation to hide their identities. Undeliverable spam bounced back to the innocent third-party email addresses. Phoenix Avatar sent millions of spam messages this way.

One of the defendants in the case, Daniel Lin, pleaded guilty to violations of the CAN-SPAM Act in January 2006. In June 2006, the court sentenced him to 3 years in federal prison.

The FTC filed a civil enforcement action against Phoenix Avatar. The FTC brought the action for violations of both the FTC Act and the CAN-SPAM Act. The FTC Act violations were related to the defendant's sale of the phony diet products.

In March 2005, the FTC settled civil charges against Phoenix Avatar. As part of the settlement, the defendants agreed to pay a $20,000 penalty. They also agreed not to violate the CAN-SPAM Act in the future.

**NOTE**

You can read the FTC enforcement action documents for the Phoenix Avatar case at https://www.ftc.gov/enforcement/cases-proceedings/042-3084/phoenix-avatar-llc-dba-avatar-nutrition-djl-llc-et-al.

### Defamation on College Campuses

The internet has many anonymous gossip websites. Juicy Campus, one of the first popular sites, started in 2007 and closed down in February 2009. It allowed college students to post anonymous gossip about events and people at their campuses. Juicy Campus had separate web pages for different colleges.

Juicy Campus billed itself as a way to promote free speech on college campuses. Among its features, anonymous users could post gossip about other students, read gossip posted by other users, and vote on the "juiciest" pieces of gossip. Students ridiculed or insulted on Juicy Campus had little recourse, as the postings were anonymous. As an ISP, Juicy Campus did not share the identities of its online posters without a court order.

Since Juicy Campus closed down, other online campus gossip websites have grown in popularity. One of the sites that opened when Juicy Campus shut down was College ACB. In a press release, the owner of the website wrote: "The College ACB or College Anonymous Confession Board seeks to give students a place to vent, rant, and talk to college peers in an environment free from social constraints and about subjects that might otherwise be taboo." College ACB closed down in 2011.[65]

AutoAdmit, a similar site, is an online law school discussion board. As on similar gossip websites, posts in that forum sometimes can be insulting and offensive. In 2007, two Yale Law School students sued anonymous AutoAdmit posters for defamation. The parties settled the case in 2009. The terms of the settlement were confidential. You can learn more about that case on the Citizen Media Law project web page at http://www.citmedialaw.org/threats/autoadmit#description.

Think about websites and apps that create experiences where you can hang out in chat rooms with nearby people. Some allow people to post anonymously. Some do not. How do they promote free speech? Are there occasions on these apps and websites where one person's right to free speech infringes upon another person's right to live peacefully?



## CHAPTER SUMMARY

This chapter discussed criminal and tort law issues in cyberspace. As part of the discussion, criminal and civil procedure rules were reviewed. Criminal and civil procedure refers to court processes used to conduct trials. Criminal procedure is the process governments use to hold criminals responsible for their actions. Civil procedure is the process individuals use to settle disputes with others.

The chapter also discussed substantive criminal and tort laws applicable to online activities. There are many federal laws that governments can use to help prevent and punish cybercrime. Individuals also can use traditional tort law concepts to seek redress for harm that they experience on the internet.

## KEY CONCEPTS AND TERMS

*Actus reus*
Answer
Complaint
Duty of due care
Felonies
Flaming
Libel
*Mala in se*
*Mala prohibita*
*Mens rea*
Misdemeanors
Personal jurisdiction
Slander
Spam
Statute of limitations
Subject matter jurisdiction
Tortfeasor

## CHAPTER 12 ASSESSMENT

1. Only the federal government prosecutes felonies.
   A. True
   B. False
2. Provide a brief definition of "crime."
3. What is *mala in se*?
   A. Conduct that a society declares is inherently wrong
   B. Conduct that society prohibits
   C. A person's criminal intent
   D. A criminal act
   E. None of these is correct.
4. What element(s) must a government prove to show a crime has been committed?
   A. *Mens rea*
   B. *Mala prohibita*
   C. *Actus reus*
   D. *Mens rea* and *mala prohibita*
   E. *Mens rea* and *actus reus*
5. What type of jurisdictional issue is a concern in a cybercrime case?
   A. Original jurisdiction
   B. Subject matter jurisdiction
   C. Personal jurisdiction
   D. Appellate jurisdiction
   E. None of these is correct.
6. The ______ guarantees a defendant the right to a speedy trial.
7. The Computer Fraud and Abuse Act applies to any unauthorized access to any kind of computer.
   A. True
   B. False
8. Which federal laws can be used to prosecute phishing scams?
   A. The Computer Fraud and Abuse Act
   B. The Patriot Act
   C. The CAN-SPAM Act
   D. All of these are correct.
   E. The Computer Fraud and Abuse Act and the CAN-SPAM Act
9. Cybertorts are most likely which type of tort?
   A. Intentional torts
   B. Negligent torts
   C. Strict liability torts
   D. Crimes
   E. None of these is correct.
10. To prove an intentional infliction of emotional distress tort, a plaintiff must show that the defendant's conduct is ______.
11. Internet service providers often have tort immunity for the actions of content providers.
    A. True
    B. False
12. What is the time period during which a plaintiff must begin a lawsuit?
    A. Statute of frauds
    B. Statute on liability
    C. Statute of limitations
    D. Pleadings statute
    E. None of these is correct.
13. What is a defense to a defamation case?
    A. Comparative negligence
    B. Contributory negligence
    C. Assumption of risk
    D. The truth
    E. None of these is correct.
14. The two types of defamation cases are ______.
15. What type of document must a plaintiff file to begin a civil lawsuit?
    A. Answer
    B. Discovery
    C. Motion for Summary Judgment
    D. Counter-claim
    E. Complaint

## ENDNOTES


1. Wisconsin Statutes, sec. 940.01.
2. Wisconsin Statutes, sec. 940.02.
3. *Robinson v. California*, 370 U.S. 660 (1962).
4. CNN.com, "Couple: Internet Gaming Addiction Led to Baby's Death," April 2, 2010. Available at https://www.cnn.com/2010/WORLD/asiapcf/04/01/korea.parents.starved.baby/ (accessed May 1, 2020).
5. *Strassheim v. Daily*, 221 U.S. 280 (1911).
6. Alaska Statutes, title 12, sec. 12.05.010.
7. Council of Europe, Treaty Office, "Convention of Cybercrime Signatories," undated. Available at https://www.coe.int/en/web/conventions/full-list/-/conventions/treaty/185 (accessed May 1, 2020).
8. U.S. Federal Trade Commission, "eConsumer Statistics," April 15, 2020. Available at https://public.tableau.com/profile/federal.trade.commission#!/vizhome/eConsumer/Infographic (accessed May 1, 2020).
9. Pew Research Center, "Only 2% of Federal Criminal Defendants Go to Trial, and Most Who Do Are Found Guilty," June 11, 2019. Available at https://www.pewresearch.org/fact-tank/2019/06/11/only-2-of-federal-criminal-defendants-go-to-trial-and-most-who-do-are-found-guilty/ (accessed May 1, 2020).
10. *Gideon v. Wainwright*, 372 U.S. 335 (1963).
11. *Giglio v. United States*, 405 U.S. 150 (1972).
12. *Brady v. Maryland*, 373 U.S. 83 (1963).
13. *Strunk v. United States*, 412 U.S. 434 (1973).
14. U.S. Code, Vol. 18, sec. 1030.
15. Internet Crime Complaint Center, "2019 Annual Internet Crime Report," 2019. Available at https://pdf.ic3.gov/2019_IC3Report.pdf (accessed May 1, 2020).
16. U.S. Code, Vol. 18, sec. 1030(e).
17. U.S. Code, Vol. 18, sec. 1030(e)(6).
18. U.S. Code, Vol. 18, sec. 1030(e)(6).
19. U.S. Code, Vol. 18, sec. 1030(e)(8).
20. U.S. Code, Vol. 18, sec. 1029.
21. U.S. Federal Trade Commission, "Consumer Sentinel Network Data Book 2019," January 2020. Available at https://www.ftc.gov/system/files/documents/reports/consumer-sentinel-network-data-book-2019/consumer_sentinel_network_data_book_2019.pdf (May 1, 2020).
22. U.S. Code, Vol. 18, sec. 1028.
23. U.S. Code, Vol. 18, sec. 2510.
24. U.S. Code, Vol. 18, sec. 3121.
25. U.S. Code, Vol. 18, sec. 2701.
26. U.S. Code, Vol. 15, sec. 7701; U.S. Code, Vol. 18, sec. 1037.
27. U.S. Code, Vol. 15, sec. 7704(d).
28. U.S. Code, Vol. 15, sec. 7704(a).
29. U.S. Code, Vol. 15, sec. 7706.
30. U.S. Federal Trade Commission, "FTC Completes Review of CAN-SPAM Rule," February 12, 2019. Available at https://www.ftc.gov/news-events/press-releases/2019/02/ftc-completes-review-can-spam-rule (accessed May 1, 2020).
31. U.S. Code, Vol. 18, sec. 1037.
32. Information Week, "War-Driving Pornographic Spammer Escapes Jail Time," August 1, 2007. Available at https://www.informationweek.com/war-driving-pornographic-spammer-escapes-jail-time/d/d-id/1057666 (accessed May 1, 2020).
33. U.S. Code, Vol. 18, sec. 1037.
34. U.S. Code, Vol. 15, sec. 1125(d).
35. U.S. Code, Vol. 15, sec. 1125(d)(1)(B).
36. U.S. Code, Title 47, sec. 223(a)(1)(c).
37. U.S. Code, Title 18, sec. 2261A.
38. U.S. Code, Title 18, sec. 875(c).
39. Stopbullying.gov, "What Is Cyberbullying?" May 30, 2019. Available at https://www.stopbullying.gov/cyberbullying/what-is-it (accessed May 1, 2020).
40. Department of Justice, "Missouri Woman Indicted on Charges of Using MySpace to Cyber Bully 13-Year-Old Who Later Committed Suicide," May 15, 2008. Available at https://www.justice.gov/archive/usao/cac/Pressroom/pr2008/063.html (accessed May 1, 2020).
41. *U.S. v. Drew*, 259 F.R.D. 449 (C.D. Cal. 2009).
42. U.S. Federal Bureau of Investigation, "Morris Worm," undated. Available at https://www.fbi.gov/history/famous-cases/morris-worm (accessed May 1, 2020).
43. U.S. Federal Bureau of Investigation, "Melissa Virus," undated. Available at https://www.fbi.gov/history/famous-cases/melissa-virus (accessed May 1, 2020).

44. The New York Times Magazine, "The Great Cyberheist," November 10, 2020. Available at https://www.nytimes.com/2010/11/14/magazine/14Hacker-t.html (accessed May 1, 2020).
45. *Palsgraf v. Long Island Railroad*, 162 N.E. 99 (N.Y. 1928).
46. Federal Rules of Civil Procedure, Rule 8.
47. Indiana Code, 34-11-2-4.
48. Montana Code Annotated, 27-2-204(3).
49. Federal Rules of Civil Procedure, Rule 12.
50. *Zubulake v. UBS Warburg, LLC*, 2004 WL1620866 (S.D.N.Y. July 20, 2004). This was the final E-discovery decision handed down in the Zubulake case.
51. Regulations.gov, "Proposed Amendments to the Federal Rules of Civil Procedure," undated. Available at http://www.regulations.gov/#!docketDetail;D=USC-RULES-CV-2013-0002 (accessed May 1, 2020).
52. Rustad, Michael L. *Internet Law*. St. Paul, MN: Thomson Reuters, 2009, p. 143.
53. *Hammer v. Amazon.com*, 392 F.Supp.2d 423 (E.D.N.Y. 2005).
54. Court Listener, "Docket for *Vernon Unsworth v. Elon Musk* (2:18-cv-08048)," March 11, 2020. Available at https://www.courtlistener.com/docket/7887513/vernon-unsworth-v-elon-musk/ (accessed May 1, 2020).
55. U.S. Code, Vol. 47, sec. 230.
56. U.S. Code, Vol. 47, sec. 230(a)(1).
57. U.S. Code, Vol. 47, sec. 230(b)(3).
58. Restatement (Second) of the Law of Torts, sec. 46, cmt. d.
59. *State Rubbish Collectors Association v. Siliznoff*, 240 P.2d 282 (Ca. 1952).
60. *State Rubbish Collectors Association v. Siliznoff*, 240 P.2d 282 (Ca. 1952).
61. New York Penal Code, Ch. 40, sec. 240.30; Oklahoma Statutes, Title 21, sec. 1173.
62. *CompuServe, Inc. v. Cyber Promotions, Inc.*, 962 F.Supp. 1015 (S.D. Ohio 1997).
63. *CompuServe, Inc. v. Cyber Promotions, Inc.*, 962 F.Supp. 1015 (S.D. Ohio 1997).
64. *Intel Corp v. Hamidi*, 71 P.3d 296 (Ca. 2003).
65. College ACB, "College ACB Press Release," February 5, 2009. Available at http://collegeacb.blogspot.com/2009/02/collegeacb-press-release.html (accessed May 1, 2020).

# PART III

# Security and Privacy in Organizations


CHAPTER 13 Information Security Governance 353

CHAPTER 14 Risk Analysis, Incident Response, and Contingency Planning 387

CHAPTER 15 Computer Forensics and Investigations 419

CHAPTER 13

# Information Security Governance

THIS CHAPTER DISCUSSES information security governance. It also discusses information security policies. An organization's governance structure is an important part of its information security program. Governance focuses on the structure used to protect resources and data. This structure must support business needs and provide security. Strong governance helps create strong security programs.

Organizations use policies, standards, guidelines, and procedures to create their security program. These documents help guide employee conduct and state the organization's rules for how information technology resources are secured. They also help protect an organization from legal liability.

## Chapter 13 Topics

This chapter covers the following topics and concepts:

- What information security governance is
- What information security governance documents are
- What recommended information security policies are
- What some case studies and examples are

## Chapter 13 Goals

When you complete this chapter, you will be able to:

- Describe the key concepts and terms associated with information security governance
- Describe the goals of different information security governance documents
- Describe the different types of policies that can be used to govern information security

## What Is Information Security Governance?

For almost any organization, data is a valuable asset. Yet, over 50 percent of large corporations report that they do not treat data as a business asset.[1] An organization must find ways to use its data to meet its business goals, such as providing services to consumers and making a profit. It also must protect its data. This balance is key to an organization's success. Failing to strike the right balance can harm the organization's goals. Consider the following:

- An organization cannot market its products without access to customer lists.
- Customers may complain about incorrect electronic data.
- If confidential data is disclosed, an organization faces embarrassment.

An organization's executive management team is responsible for governing the organization. This means it is also responsible for **information security governance (ISG)**, the executive management team's responsibility to protect an organization's information assets. ISG makes protecting information assets a business decision. To do this, an organization must align its information security goals to its business needs. ISG moves information security beyond technical decisions and makes security a strategic decision.

**NOTE**

The security goals of confidentiality, integrity, and availability are called the C-I-A triad or the A-I-C triad.

Organizations use ISG to enhance their business. ISG makes sure that information security concepts are applied in a way that helps meet business goals. ISG also makes sure that there is proper accountability and oversight for meeting these goals. The C-I-A triad appears in **FIGURE 13-1**.

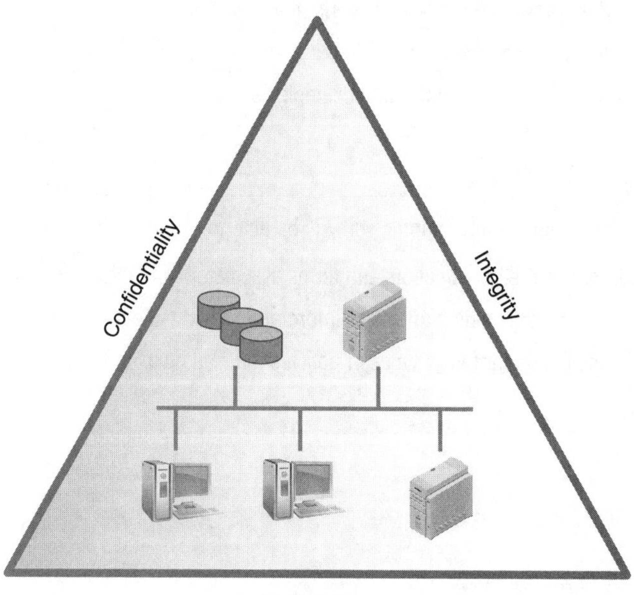


**FIGURE 13-1**
The C-I-A triad.

## Information Security Governance Planning

ISG refers to executive management's responsibility to provide strategic direction, oversight, and accountability for the security of its data and information technology (IT) resources. Their main duty is to make sure that the information security strategy supports its business goals.

A common business goal is to make a profit. The organization must consider many factors that affect this goal. Business drivers are the forces that influence the organization's business goals. They can be internal or external and include people, processes, and trends. Common business drivers may include the availability of raw materials and employees, the location of factories, and the costs of transporting products to market.

An organization must balance business drivers to meet its goals. They do this during the business planning process. There are three types of business planning. They are:

- **Strategic planning**—This is long-term planning. **Strategic planning** focuses on preparing new approaches and planning for new products, technologies, or processes. It lays the groundwork for new business directions.
- **Tactical planning**—This is short- to medium-term planning. **Tactical planning** allows organizations to be responsive to market conditions. It allows them to take advantage of short-term or unexpected opportunities. Tactical plans are usually 6 months or less in length.
- **Operational planning**—This is day-to-day planning. **Operational planning** focuses on the normal operations of an organization. It is responsive to daily issues.

**FIGURE 13-2** illustrates the different types of business planning.

The organization's executive management team carries out strategic planning. This is when it determines the business's goals. Once it determines its business goals, it must figure out how information security can help support these goals. It will use the same types of planning strategies to think about information security. This is ISG planning. When planning for information security, the organization must think about:

- **Information needs**—The organization must ask how it uses data to meet its business goals. It must then think about how information security can support this. For instance,



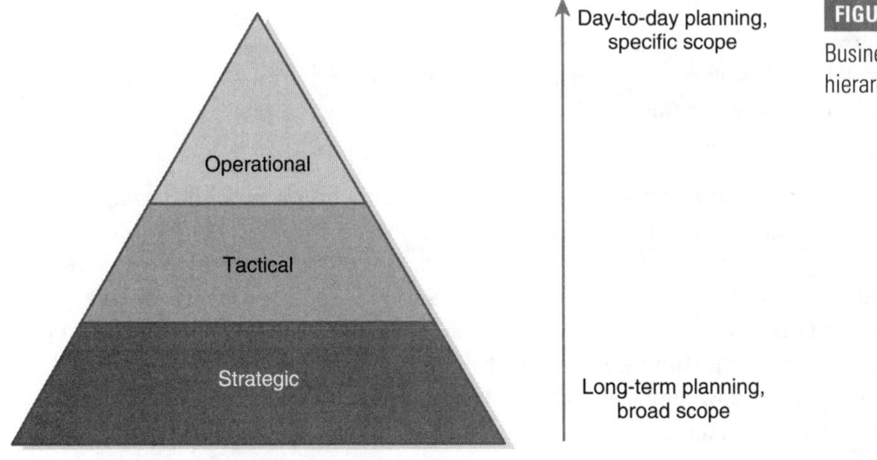


**FIGURE 13-2** Business planning hierarchy.

if an organization conducts most of its business on the internet, it may need to focus its attention on techniques to ensure availability and integrity. Its IT systems must hold accurate data and be ready to conduct business.

- **Regulatory requirements**—The organization must know its regulatory landscape. It must know the data protection laws that it must follow. Often these laws focus on protecting the confidentiality of certain types of data.
- **Risk management**—The organization must adopt a risk management approach. It must know the information security risks that it faces. It also must prioritize that risk and decide how it will respond to it.
- **Security failures**—The organization must think about information security failures and how those failures might harm the business. For instance, it must consider the impact of a security breach, malware-infected IT resources, or unavailable data. There are many negative impacts of an information security failure. These include lawsuits and breach notification costs. An organization will certainly lose customers after an information security incident. This affects its bottom line.

**NOTE**

A 2019 survey found the average organizational cost of a data breach in the United States is almost $4 million.[2]

An organization answers these questions to determine ISG strategic direction. It makes sure that its information security goals support its business objectives. This is the role of ISG.

## Common Information Security Governance Roles

It is important to know who makes information security decisions, whether they are strategic, tactical, or operational. Not every organization has the same structure. Organizations can have different legal forms, such as corporations, partnerships, or limited liability companies. These legal forms are governed by state law. This section reviews ISG roles. You will be more likely to find the roles described here in larger organizations, such as corporations. Smaller organizations may not fill all of these roles; rather, they may combine many duties within one role. Nonprofit and educational organizations may also have different roles for people. These organizations tend to have structures with many shared responsibilities.

Many different roles can make decisions about information security. The typical ISG roles are:

- Board of directors
- Chief information officer
- Chief information security officer
- Information security managers

The **board of directors (BOD)**, an organization's top governance group, runs the organization. A BOD is required by law to act with due care. It must make all of its decisions in the best interests of the organization. The BOD plans an organization's strategic direction and determines its business goals. It makes sure that an organization uses its resources effectively to meet these goals. Finally, it makes sure that an organization acts legally. If an organization does not have a BOD, then its top-ranking executive group performs these duties.

The BOD determines how information security will reduce risk and support business goals through strategic planning. The BOD issues high-level information security policies and delegates tactical and operational activities to other senior managers. The main duty of a BOD is governance for the organization and for information security.

The **chief information officer (CIO)** is the organization's senior IT official. The CIO focuses on strategic IT issues and defines the organization's IT mission. It is the CIO's job to keep the BOD advised about IT issues. CIOs are not usually involved in day-to-day IT operations. Their duties are strategic and tactical in nature. They often delegate responsibility for **information security management (ISM)** to a CISO.

A CIO is not the same as a **chief technology officer (CTO)**. A CIO is responsible for a company's internal IT systems and focuses on the systems used to run the organization's business. A CIO tends to be internally focused. In contrast, a CTO develops a company's technology products. These are the products that the company delivers to its customers. A CTO tends to be externally focused.

The **chief information security officer (CISO)** is the organization's senior information security official. The role of the CISO is relatively new and continues to evolve. Depending on an organization's structure, the CISO might report to the CIO. A CISO also could report to the organization's chief financial officer (CFO). CISOs are responsible for an organization's information security strategy. They also are very involved in tactical planning. However, they are not generally involved in daily IT operations.

The CISO makes sure that the CIO and BOD understand information security threats and how to respond to those threats. The CISO may make information security policy suggestions to the BOD. A CISO also helps determine information security safeguards, and usually delegates functional and operational tasks to other managers.

**NOTE**

In March 2009, U.S. President Barack Obama appointed the first federal CIO, who was responsible for government IT spending.

Information security managers are responsible for the functional management of an organization's information security program. They manage the operational activities and implement the controls specified by the CISO. These managers might also:

- Create information security standards, guidelines, and procedures
- Participate in risk assessments
- Manage the security infrastructure

These roles work together. The higher-level roles make governance decisions, whereas the lower-level roles are responsible for carrying out ISM and operational activities.

## Information Security Governance and Management

ISG and ISM are not the same thing. Although the terms are often used interchangeably, the distinction is subtle. You should keep in mind that sometimes the difference is not clear. Many organizations use one or both terms to refer to all ISG and ISM activities. Many activities have both ISG and ISM elements.

ISG, which is handled by the BOD, CIO, and CISO, makes sure that security is used to support business goals. It offers a process for oversight and accountability and makes sure that there is a structure in place to direct information security activities.

**TABLE 13-1** Comparison of Information Security Governance and Information Security Management

| INFORMATION SECURITY GOVERNANCE | INFORMATION SECURITY MANAGEMENT |
|---|---|
| Strategic and tactical | Tactical and operational |
| Creates policies and strategy | Implements policies and strategy |
| Ultimate compliance authority and oversight | Day-to-day management and authority |
| BOD, CIO, CISO | CISO and information security managers |

### Creating an Information Security Governance Program

There are many resources available to help organizations create an ISG program. The International Organization for Standardization (ISO) and International Electrotechnical Commission (IEC) have created a comprehensive standard to help guide this process.[3] The standard uses the term *ISM system* to refer to both ISG and ISM activities.

The standard helps organizations create an ISM system by using a risk-based approach. It reviews how to operate, monitor, review, maintain, and improve the ISM system. It walks through each step and outlines the processes that an organization must consider at each step.

Any organization can use this standard, as it is designed to be flexible to meet an organization's needs. It can be especially helpful to organizations that have never managed information security on a strategic level. It is also designed to work with the ISO/IEC security controls standard called "ISO/IEC 27002:2013, Information Technology—Security Techniques—Code of Practice for Information Security Controls."

Organizations must review their ISM systems regularly. They need to know if their ISM controls are improving security. To do this, they must measure their effectiveness. The ISO/IEC has guidance on this as well. That document is titled "ISO/IEC 27004:2016 Information Technology—Security Techniques—Information Security Management—Monitoring, Measurement, Analysis, and Evaluation."

This standard helps organizations review their ISM system. It helps organizations create control measurements and analyze the measurements. The process helps organizations decide if their policies or controls need to be changed.

ISM, the organization's day-to-day security operations, is the visible part of ISG activities. It makes sure that ISG policies are put into practice. ISM maintains the organization's overall security posture. ISG states what that posture must be. **TABLE 13-1** compares ISG and ISM.

## Information Security Governance in the Federal Government

Congress created the Federal Information Security Modernization Act (FISMA) to protect federal data and IT resources.[4] Federal agencies fall under the executive branch of the U.S. government and report to the president of the United States. U.S. federal agencies must comply with FISMA.

FISMA requires each federal agency to develop an information security program and name a CISO to lead the program. The program must assess the agency's information security risk, include plans to reduce that risk, and provide security awareness and training activities to employees. Agencies must report on their FISMA compliance progress each year. They send these reports to the Government Accountability Office (GAO).

**NOTE**

You can view the GAO high-risk website at https://www.gao.gov/highrisk/overview.

Information security is a high priority for the federal government. Since 1997, the GAO has included protecting the nation's information systems and cyber critical infrastructure on its "high risk list." Issues are high-risk if they are vulnerable to fraud, waste, abuse, or mismanagement. The GAO publishes the list every 2 years.[5]

## Information Security Governance Documents

An organization's ISG documents form the basis of its information security program. They document the organization's commitment to information security. They are used to address:

- The organization's information security goals
- How the organization protects its own data
- How the organization protects the data of others
- Compliance with legal and regulatory requirements
- Employee information security responsibilities
- Consequences for failing to meet responsibilities



Organizations use policies, standards, guidelines, and procedures to create their security program. These documents work together to support information security goals. A formal policy is the highest-level governance document. Standards are the next level. Then procedures. Guidelines provide security advice. The documents move from the general (policies) to the more specific (procedure). **FIGURE 13-3** shows how these documents work together.

For purposes of this discussion, these documents are collectively referred to as "ISG documents" or "policies." You should keep in mind that the term *policies* is often used in a very generic way. It is used to describe the entire suite of ISG documents. It will be clear from the text when the term is used in the generic way.

**NOTE**

ISG documents are administrative safeguards.

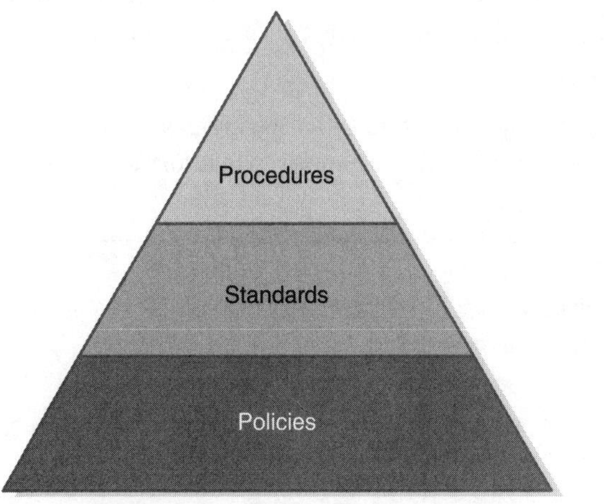


**FIGURE 13-3** Information security governance documents.

## Policies

A formal **policy** is executive management's high-level statement of information security direction and goals. They are the top level of governance documents and help minimize risk by laying out the organization's information security strategy. High-level policies are approved by an organization's BOD.

The BOD uses policies to set forth its information security goals. They also state compliance expectations. Not all organizations will have the same types of high-level policies. They are unique to each organization. Each organization develops policies by reviewing its regulatory landscape, taking into account the size and complexity of the organization and its IT systems. They also think about how information security can be used to help meet business goals.

Policies must be drafted with care. Policy elements vary among organizations. However, there are some common elements to all policies. They include:

- **Policy statement**—States the expected behavior, actions, or outcomes. It is a clear statement of permitted or forbidden actions.
- **Policy exclusions**—Lists situations or people who are not covered by the policy. For the most part, there should not be many exclusions in a high-level policy.
- **Policy rationale**—States the reason why the policy exists. This includes the legal or regulatory reasons for the policy. A policy might be drafted in response to information security threats.
- **Policy definitions**—Defines terms that have special meaning. Terms with common definitions do not need to be defined.
- **Who is affected by the policy**—States the people, units, or departments affected by the policy. In a high-level policy, this usually is all of the organization's employees.
- **Who must follow the policy**—Lists who must follow the policy as part of their job responsibilities, or if some people have special policy responsibilities because of their job duties.
- **Compliance language**—States how the organization will enforce the policy. It also states what happens to units and employees who fail to follow the policy.
- **Related documents**—Lists other documents that are related to the policy. Standards or procedures that support the policy should be listed in this section.
- **Policy contact**—Lists the person who is responsible for answering questions about the policy.
- **Policy history**—Lists historical data about the policy. This section should list revision and review dates.

High-level policies are concise and tightly worded so that they are easy to understand. A high-level information security policy states the organization's information security

**FYI**

The SANS Institute has a policy web page that gives drafting advice. It also has sample policies. You can view this resource at http://www.sans.org/security-resources/policies/.

expectations. They should be written in a way so that all employees can understand them. These high-level documents do not usually include explanations about how to meet those expectations. Supporting documents, such as standards, guidelines, and procedures, provide that detail.

Policy documents tend to go through a lengthy development and review process. The process can be very time consuming because policies are high-level governance documents from executive management. They have a broad scope and address the whole organization. Most policy development processes include multiple levels of review so that other leaders within the organization have a chance to comment on the policies while they are being developed. These leaders will tell executive management how the policy will affect their units or departments.

Policies are rarely changed because they contain language that sets forth general expectations. The broad goals stated in a policy should not need to be changed often. Standards and procedures are used to provide flexibility and are easier to change. An organization can easily update these documents in response to changing technology conditions.

## Standards

**Standards** support high-level policies and state the activities and actions needed to meet policy goals. They are just below policies in the ISG documents hierarchy. Standards are more specific than policies. Standards may require employees to take (or refrain from) certain actions and often state a minimum level of behavior or actions that must be met to comply with a policy. This is called a **baseline**.

Standards are technology neutral. They do not refer to specific technologies or products. Instead, they refer to the safeguards and controls an organization should use to protect data and IT resources.

Several different ISG levels can create standards. They are usually created at the CIO or CISO level. However, an organization's BOD is not usually involved in creating standards. An organization usually develops standards with input from information security managers because they have overall organizational responsibility for implementing information security. They are the subject matter experts in what it will take to implement the standard.

## Procedures

**Procedures** are the lowest level of ISG documents. They are step-by-step checklists that explain "how" to meet security goals or conduct security-related activities. Organizations often tailor their procedures to a certain type of technology. They also can be limited to the activities of specific departments or end users.

Procedures usually only address single tasks. They are designed to be flexible so they can change as technology changes. Information security managers usually create procedures, although a CIO or CISO may sometimes review procedures. For the most part, however, procedures are department- or technology-specific documents.

### Governance Documents Work Together

Policies, standards, and procedures work together to protect information security. Policies set forth the general expectation. Standards further define those expectations. Procedures tell end users how to comply with the expectations. An example might work as follows:

*Policy Statement:* All employees must use multifactor authentication to access organizational IT resources.

*Standard Statement:* Employees may use any of the multifactor authentication solutions provided by the information security department to access IT systems. Employees may use either the business-provided authenticator application on their mobile device or may use a physical token device.

*Procedural Statement:* To obtain the authentication application or a physical token device, employees must come to the technology center between 8:00 a.m. and 5:00 p.m. from Monday through Friday. Employees must bring their employee identification card and a state-issued identification card to receive access to the application or their token.

In this example, an employee knows what the expectation is ("multifactor authentication"), how the expectation is defined ("technology provided by the information security department"), and how to meet the expectation ("go to the technology center").

## Guidelines

**Guidelines** are the most flexible type of ISG document. Organizations can issue guidelines for several reasons. They issue guidelines to:

- Encourage employees to adopt good information security practices
- Educate employees about security threats and how to respond to them
- Encourage employees to take action in areas that the organization cannot

An organization can use guidelines to give information security advice. They can recommend actions that an employee can apply on his or her own. The guidelines help employees adopt behaviors that improve information security. Sometimes they address specific kinds of employee behavior. They also might address a specific security issue. For example, an organization might create a guideline to help employees learn how to avoid social engineering attacks.

Organizations might issue guidelines to address issues that they cannot control through technical measures or organizational authority. This is where the organization needs its employees to help it protect IT resources. They hope that they can encourage employees to read the guidelines and take individual action.

For example, an organization may allow its employees to access its IT systems from home because it increases productivity. It allows employees to work from home on days when they otherwise would not be working. (For example, if a parent stays home to care for a sick child or if an office is closed due to a global health pandemic.) Employees may use their home personal computing equipment to complete their work in these situations. However, the organization must safeguard its IT resources from security threats introduced by this activity, such as malware that might be on an employee's home computer that could be transmitted to the organization's IT resources.

The organization has no real way to make employees use good security practices at home. It has no real authority to require employees to protect their home computers. To encourage employees to secure their home computers, the organization can issue a guideline. The guideline outlines security safeguards that employees can use at home. Following the guideline benefits employees because it helps them secure their own personal data. It also helps protect the organization's IT resources if the employee follows the recommended practices. Both the employee's computer and the organization's IT resources are protected. It is a winning situation for everyone.

## Creating Information Security Policies

Each type of ISG document has a different role and focus. They might be directed at different audiences. They might address similar issues from different standpoints. However, they do share some similarities. These similarities include:

- They must be easy to understand.
- They must have a well-defined scope.
- They must be regularly reviewed.
- They must be communicated to all employees.

First, the documents must be easy to read. All employees must be able to understand them. Even if the subject matter deals with legal issues, the document itself should be free from legalese. The documents should not use technical jargon. The only time it is OK to use complex language is when it is needed to help employees know their responsibilities. Otherwise, these documents must be understandable so that employees can follow them.

Second, ISG documents must have a clear scope. They must clearly address a specific aspect of the organization's security program. Employees should not have to consult many high-level documents to determine the organization's stance on a single issue. Ensuring that policy scope is clearly outlined helps employees follow the policy.

Third, the organization must regularly review its ISG documents. Information security does not exist in a vacuum. Risks change. Laws change. Technology changes. An organization must respond to these changes in its security program. To do this, they must review their ISG documents on a regular basis to make sure that they are current.

Finally, an organization must communicate the ISG documents to its employees. Employees cannot follow policies that they do not know about. Good communication makes sure that employees view ISG documents as business enablers. Organizations can communicate ISG documents to employees in several ways. They can use newsletters, in-person and online training, or company-wide email messages. Many communication mechanisms should be used to make sure that employees know about the ISG documents.

### *Policy Development Process*

An organization should create a structured ISG document development process. It may even want to consider writing a "policy on policies" to specify the formal process. A formal process gives many units, departments, and stakeholders the opportunity to comment on a policy. This is very important for high-level policies that apply to the whole organization. A formal process also makes sure that final policies are communicated to employees. It also provides organizations with a way to make sure that policies are reviewed regularly.

### Legalese Versus Plain Language

*Legalese* is an unflattering term used to describe legal writing. Legalese is language that uses too many legal phrases and many Latin terms. It usually has long sentences with many commas that are dense and hard to read. Lawyers are needed to translate documents written in legalese.

There is a growing trend in the legal profession to write documents in *plain language*. This means that documents are written in the language that people use when they speak to help make documents more understandable. People can understand these documents faster. They also are less likely to misunderstand them.

The trend is to use plain language to write formal documents. However, legalese appears in high-level policies on a regular basis because these documents are formal governance documents. An organization's legal counsel often writes them.

Legalese can make it hard to understand some very simple concepts. This is frustrating for people who need to follow the policies. Some examples of legalese and plain language follow. Are there other ways that you can make these policy statements easier to read?

#### Example 1—Consent

*Legalese:* All users of the organization's information technology resources, as a condition to the use of such resources, specifically consent to the general rights of the organization as specified herein.

*Plain Language:* All users of the organization's IT resources agree to the terms of this policy.

#### Example 2—Least Privilege

*Legalese:* Any access permitted hereunder shall be the minimum access required in order to protect the organization's interests.

*Plain Language:* Access to IT resources is limited to the minimum amount needed.

#### Example 3—Warranties

*Legalese:* The organization makes no warranties of any kind with respect to the organization's information technology resources it provides. The organization will not be responsible for damages resulting from the use of the organization's information technology resources, including, but not limited to, loss of data resulting from delays, non-deliveries, missed deliveries, or service interruptions caused by the negligence of an organization employee, or by any user's error or omissions. The organization specifically denies any responsibility for the accuracy or quality of information obtained through the organization's information technology resources.

*Plain Language:* The organization provides IT resources "as is." The organization makes no promises about service level or data accuracy. The organization is not responsible for errors. Use of IT resources is at a user's own risk.

In general, a policy development process should include the following steps:

1. Development
2. Stakeholder review
3. Management approval
4. Communication to employees
5. Documentation of compliance or exceptions

6. Continued awareness activities
7. Maintenance and review

The need for a new ISG document is determined in the development phase. The BOD, CIO, or CISO might decide that there is a need for a high-level policy. An information security department might also notice situations that require a new high-level document to guide the organization. The idea for a new ISG document really can come from anywhere in an organization. This section focuses on how high-level policies are created. However, a similar development process is recommended for other ISG documents, such as standards and procedures, as well.

Once a policy need is identified, the BOD must determine the goals of the policy. To do this, it reviews several areas. It looks at its use of IT resources and reviews the data that it is legally required to protect. It considers its business objectives. An organization's CIO or CISO will give advice about information security issues. The BOD also might consider how other companies in the same industry approach a certain type of issue. After this review, the BOD establishes the policy goals.

An organization must take care when it drafts high-level policies. It must make sure that a new high-level policy does not conflict with any previously issued policy. Stakeholders must review the draft when it is finished.

**FYI**

In drafting an ISG document, it is important to be consistent. A writer should use consistent grammar, punctuation, and format. This makes the document more readable. It also makes it easier for employees to understand the document.



At the next step, stakeholders review the ISG draft documents. **Stakeholders** are interested parties. They are employees and departments that will be affected by the new policy. They also may be subject matter experts in the underlying policy subject matter. IT resource managers also will review the document at this point. They do this to make sure that they can implement technical controls to meet the policy.

This also is the step where legal counsel, risk management, and audit will review the document. These groups make sure that the document meets the organization's regulatory needs. Risk management and audit departments will want to make sure that they can measure policy compliance actions. Legal counsel makes sure that the document helps protect the organization from legal liability. The organization may revise the policy many times during this step.

The policy must be signed when it is in final form. The BOD must always review and sign high-level information security policies. Their support is crucial for a successful information security program. They do not always sign lower-level documents. The executive with authority over certain tasks may sign lower-level documents; for example, a CIO or CISO might sign standards or guidelines. Departmental managers and supervisors may sign procedures for their specific areas. Each organization will make its own rules about who needs to approve and sign each level of ISG document.

The next step, the communication step, is the most critical step in the development process. Communication is necessary to make sure that all employees know about the new policy. It helps employees know where to find resources to follow the policy. Organizations can communicate new policies in several different ways. Internal newsletters, memos, and company-wide emails can all be used to inform employees about a new policy.

As part of the overall development process, an organization must measure policy compliance. It must know how departments act to meet policy requirements. It also must note any exceptions to compliance. An organization can show compliance by documenting the following:

- When the ISG document was approved
- How and when it was communicated to employees
- Actions departments took to meet the responsibilities stated in the ISG document
- Deviations from the requirements in the ISG document

Sometimes departments might request an exception to a policy. They can request an exception for several reasons. For example, a policy might state a technical control that an IT system cannot meet for a very legitimate reason. Or it might require an action that a business unit cannot take because of some other regulatory requirement.

Organizations must have a formal way to review policy exception requests. For example, the BOD must review, approve, and document each high-level policy exception request. A BOD might assign this role to an upper management official with technology expertise such as a CIO or CISO. Exception requests from standards and procedures might be handled by the CIO or CISO as well.

An organization must carefully consider exception requests. This is because every policy exception weakens the organization's overall security posture. There are two main reasons to grant a policy exception request. The first is when following the policy negatively affects the organization's business objectives. This might happen when a policy control interferes with a critical business process.

**NOTE**

Compliance is an ongoing process that organizations must continuously monitor.

The second reason to approve an exception request is when the cost to comply with the policy is more than the cost of noncompliance. For example, an organization may grant an exception request if a particular IT resource is incapable of technically meeting a policy requirement. It might do this if buying new equipment is too expensive. In those cases, the organization still must implement controls to protect the IT resource. The policy exception request must document how an area will use compensating controls to meet the spirit of the policy.

The development process must continually educate employees about policy compliance. Ongoing security training and awareness are required to keep employees aware of their responsibilities. An organization must build regular policy awareness activities into its day-to-day routine. For example, they can be included in other training programs, such as workplace safety programs.

Finally, an organization must review its ISG documents on a regular schedule. They must make sure the documents continue to reflect business and information security goals. Sometimes internal or external factors change so much that an organization must change its policies. At this point, it can either update its policy or withdraw it and create a new one. A

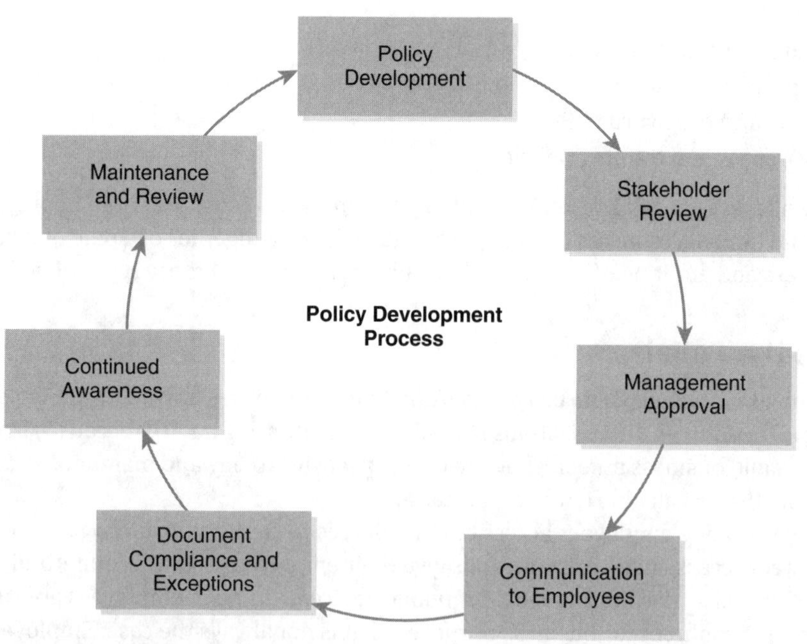


**FIGURE 13-4**
Policy development process.



BOD demonstrates due diligence and reasonable care when it regularly reviews its policies. **FIGURE 13-4** shows the policy development process.

An organization can adjust the development process if necessary. For example, it might need to create a new policy to respond to a new law. It can step that policy through the development process quickly, then go back and review the document once the urgent regulatory need has passed. In addition, the process can be shortened for some ISG documents. Standards and procedures that apply to one department only may go through an expedited review process. This is because there may not be as many people who need to comment on them.

An organization uses ISG documents to support its business objectives and information security goals. These policies form the basis of an information security program. They also set the tone for a culture of information security awareness.

## Recommended Information Security Policies

Information security policies will vary greatly across organizations because all organizations are different. They have different business goals. Their security needs are not the same. Their cultures are different.

The list of information security issues to address in a policy is endless. However, all organizations face some basic security issues. They should create policies to address these issues. The basic policies that organizations should consider include:

- Acceptable use policies
- Anti-harassment policies
- Workplace privacy and monitoring policies

- Data retention and destruction policies
- Intellectual property policies
- Authentication and password policies
- Security awareness and training policies

These policies address use of IT resources and the data in those resources. Often information security and human resources (HR) departments will work together on some of these policies. Business and auditing offices might help administer some of these types of policies.

## Acceptable Use Policies

An organization uses an **acceptable use policy (AUP)** to tell employees how to properly use organizational IT resources. Organizations should consider drafting an AUP because IT resources are valuable business assets. They are often expensive to buy and maintain. They also contain data that is valuable to the organization.

Organizations provide employees access to IT resources to support business goals. In addition to system access, many organizations give their employees email accounts and internet access. Some also give their executives mobile devices. Although employees are supposed to use these resources for business purposes, that is not always the case. Employees can use these resources in many non-business ways. Some of these uses include:

- Sending and receiving personal emails at a work email address
- Chain mail and hoax email messages sent around the office
- Non-business internet use (such as online shopping)
- Accessing social networking sites during work hours
- Downloading free software (or pirated software) for business or non-business use
- File sharing throughout a workplace or over the internet

Improper use of an organization's IT resources can be costly. It can result in information security compromises, introduce malware onto IT systems, or lead to unintentional data loss. An organization might be legally responsible for an employee's misuse of IT resources in some instances. Non-business use of IT resources can also distract employees and can lead to lost productivity.

An AUP can help prevent some of these issues. An AUP is a code of conduct that states permitted uses of IT resources. It also lists prohibited actions. Finally, it states the consequences for violating the acceptable use rules. An AUP is one of the most important information security policy documents. It can help prevent a wide range of activities that could harm the organization's IT resources.

An AUP can address several concerns including personnel, legal, and information security issues. HR departments like AUPs because they help promote workplace productivity. They also want to make sure that employees are not accessing or sharing objectionable electronic materials. Such behavior can cause severe disruptions in the workplace. In some instances, it also can subject the organization to liability for its employees' actions. For instance, an employer can be held responsible in some cases where an employee is using IT resources to harass other individuals. AUPs give HR departments a rules-based reason to terminate employees who use IT resources inappropriately.

### Would an AUP Help in This Situation?

The "I Love You" or "Love Bug" worm was discovered in May 2000. At the time, it was thought to be one of the largest and most destructive computer worms ever. It spread via email messages with "ILOVEYOU" in the subject line. The messages included an attachment disguised as a love letter. Once a user opened the attachment (and who would not open a love letter?), the worm infected the user's computer. It sent itself to everyone in the user's email address book and destroyed computer files. It also searched for sensitive information and sent it back to its creator. At one point, industry experts estimated that the worm affected computers at more than 80 percent of U.S. businesses. Could an information security policy have helped stop the spread of the worm? What if an AUP stated that employees could not open email attachments that they were not expecting? What if the consequence for opening that type of attachment included job termination? Would that have helped in this case?

**FYI**

Lost productivity is not a new issue for organizations. Coffee breaks and water-cooler chats have always been productivity concerns. The internet and ease of access to non-work-related information and entertainment is a relatively new nuisance.



Legal departments use AUPs to help an organization meet regulatory responsibilities. They also use them to help limit an organization's legal liability. For instance, an AUP can state that employees may not use unlicensed software on their computers. This helps protect the organization from copyright infringement claims. An organization protects itself in these cases by pointing to its AUP and showing that the employee violated it. If the AUP forbids the action, the legal department has evidence that the employee acted in violation of company rules. This helps create a legal defense.

Information security departments also are interested in making sure that an organization has a well-written AUP. Improper use of IT resources can have information security consequences. Employees surfing the internet, exchanging personal emails, or visiting social networking sites are consuming network bandwidth. They may be using valuable network storage space for non-business content such as music or pictures.

Their activities also could introduce malware onto the organization's IT systems. Malware could compromise data and have wide-ranging consequences. At a minimum, productivity is hampered while IT departments work to remove the malware. At its worst, the malware could transmit sensitive organizational information to external attackers. It also could expose personally identifiable information. The disclosure of that type of information could trigger state breach notification laws.

AUPs also address internal employee threats. For example, employees can potentially use their access to IT resources to snoop, spy on, or steal from the organization. They also could spy on other employees. Disgruntled employees could use their access to sabotage IT resources and data. An AUP specifically prohibits these actions. An organization can fire an employee for violating an AUP.

### AUP Terms

An organization protects against these concerns by having a written AUP. Some general terms that you see in AUPs include:

- IT resources are provided for business use only.
- Employees must use IT resources and data on them for business purposes only.
- Employees must not tamper with IT resources or data on those resources.
- Employees should not access any data they do not have a business reason to see.
- No personal use of organizational IT resources is allowed.
- Do not use IT resources to circumvent security measures.
- IT resources may be monitored to ensure employee compliance.
- Use of IT resources is evidence of the employee's consent to the terms of the AUP.

AUPs may also include terms about a particular type of IT resource, such as email or internet use. Some organizations include these terms in one broad AUP. Other organizations may create a separate AUP for each type of technology. Common email and internet AUP terms include:

1. Do not send email with sensitive organization information to external recipients.
2. Do not send email with sensitive organization information to internal recipients unless they have a business need to have that information.
3. Do not send email with offensive text, pictures, or links to offensive websites. Content is offensive if it is demeaning based on race, gender, national origin, disability, religion, or politics.
4. Do not open email attachments from unknown senders. Do not open email messages with unexpected attachments.
5. Do not click on embedded links in an email from unknown senders.
6. Do not download files from the internet without permission from a business supervisor and the information security department.
7. Do not use file-sharing applications or services without permission from a business supervisor and the information security department.
8. Do not use IT resources to access the internet to view offensive material.
9. Do not use IT resources to access the internet to visit social networking sites.
10. Do not use IT resources for online shopping or any other personal activity.
11. Do not use IT resources to engage in activity that violates the law.

Mobile devices such as cell phones, smartphones, and personal digital assistants (PDAs) pose special information security threats. They are small, pocket-sized computing devices. Use of mobile phones is rising. A 2019 Pew Research Center report found that 96 percent of U.S. adults have cell phones or smartphones. Thirty-eight percent of U.S. adults mostly use their smartphones to access the internet.[6]

Many people buy their own mobile devices and use them for work purposes, although organizations sometimes give their employees mobile devices. These devices pose security threats because they can access or store an organization's sensitive information. Employees can use these devices to browse the internet, send and receive email, and view documents.

The computing capacity of these devices continues to grow. They can store large amounts of data. Many of the same types of malware that infect larger IT resources also can harm these devices.

Mobile devices also are a vulnerability because of their portable nature. People can easily lose or misplace their mobile devices. They are also easy to steal. A lost or stolen mobile device can put an organization's data at risk.

An AUP places controls on the use of mobile devices for business purposes. In addition to terms about email and internet use, an AUP might have specific terms about mobile devices:

- Mobile devices that are used to access organizational resources or data must be password protected.
- Mobile devices (whether provided by the organization or purchased by an employee and used for business purposes) must not store sensitive organizational information.
- Employees must immediately report the loss of a mobile device used to access organizational resources.

Organizations typically make employees aware of their AUPs when the employees begin employment. They may print it in an employee handbook. Organizations may ask employees to read the AUP. They also might ask employees to sign an acknowledgment form that states the employee understands and agrees to follow the rules in the AUP. The acknowledgment also might state that an employee understands the consequences for failing to follow an AUP.

Organizations should require employees to review the AUP yearly. They also must require that employees review the AUP any time it is revised. They may ask employees to sign a new acknowledgment form at that time. This helps the organization make sure that employees are aware of their responsibilities.



### *Enforcement*

The 2007 Electronic Monitoring and Surveillance Survey found that 28 percent of employers have fired employees for email abuse. The same survey said that of those employees fired for email abuse, 64 percent were fired for violating company policy.[7] An AUP must specify the consequences for violating it. Consequences for violating an AUP can include:

- Suspension of access to IT resources
- Limited access to IT resources
- Employee reprimand
- Employment suspension
- Employment termination
- Referral to law enforcement

Modest AUP violations may result in a reprimand or retraining on the AUP terms. In some cases, an organization may choose to suspend an employee's access to IT resources for a period of time. Suspending access to IT resources can be a drastic response to a violation if an employee's job role requires IT access. An organization could fire an employee for a particularly harmful AUP violation. AUP violations that amount to criminal conduct should be reported to law enforcement. For example, an organization should notify the police if an employee uses its IT resources to launch a malware attack.

It can sometimes be hard for organizations to enforce their AUPs because many AUPs require employees to change their behaviors. AUPs are especially hard to enforce if an organization has no technical methods to monitor compliance. Most organizations depend on employees to police their own behavior. They may have a procedure for employees to report AUP violations.

## Anti-Harassment Policies

Workplace harassment is a serious issue. *Harassment* is unwanted verbal or physical conduct that demeans or threatens a person. Some examples include:

- Telling lewd, sexist, or racist jokes
- Making racially derogatory comments
- Making remarks about body shape, looks, or clothing
- Staring at people in a suggestive manner
- Making negative comments about a person's religious beliefs
- Threatening a person or his or her family with harm

Workplace harassment can violate federal law. This happens when the unwanted conduct is based on certain characteristics. The main law in this area is Title VII of the 1964 Civil Rights Act.[8] It forbids workplace discrimination based on race, sex, religion, disability, and ethnicity. These are called immutable characteristics. A person cannot change them.

Title VII applies to most public and private employers. Employers with 15 or more employees must follow it. The law states that employers have a duty to prevent workplace discrimination, and to stop it if they know about it. Workplace discrimination and harassment claims are often tied together.

Workplace harassment has always been a major issue for employers. The rise in internet and email communications in the work environment adds extra complications because they introduce a new way for harassers to communicate with victims. Emails shared among employees that have offensive, explicit, or violent content could lead to harassment claims. So could viewing offensive material from a work computer screen in a public area. Employee-downloaded screensavers on an organization's computers can be a problem if they are offensive.

These activities raise legal liability when other employees are offended or feel harassed. Employees also could make tort claims against an employer for intentional infliction of emotional distress.

Employers use anti-harassment policies to help limit liability for workplace harassment. Many organizations develop no-tolerance policies. They often use their AUPs to forbid offensive use of IT resources as well. Many organizations do this. However, the issue is serious enough that organizations should have a separate anti-harassment policy. Although an anti-harassment policy is not specifically an IT policy, the use of IT to harass another must be addressed in an anti-harassment policy. In addition to forbidding in-person harassment, the policy should state that an organization's IT resources cannot be used to harass others.

Anti-harassment policies should contain the following elements:

- **Definition of harassment**—It should define inappropriate conduct. This includes in-person and electronic interactions that are threatening, intimidating, or offensive in nature. Conduct is offensive if it is demeaning based on race, gender, national origin, disability, religion, or politics.

- **Reporting**—The organization must give employees a way to report harassment. The reporting method must include alternatives if the alleged harasser is a victim's direct supervisor.
- **Investigation**—An organization must investigate harassment complaints. They must stop harassment when they have reasonable evidence that it is occurring.
- **No retaliation**—The organization must make sure that it does not retaliate against employees who file harassment complaints. *Retaliation* is an adverse employment action made for a non-job-related reason. An organization may not take an adverse employment action against an employee who files a harassment complaint just because that employee filed a complaint.
- **Sanctions**—The policy should state the consequences for violating the policy.

Information security personnel may participate in a harassment investigation and investigate whether the organization's IT resources hold evidence related to the claim.

The law allows victims to recover damages from their harassers. They also might be able to recover damages from the harassers' employers if they failed to respond to harassment complaints. The law allows victims to receive compensatory damages. They also can receive punitive damages in some cases, which can be substantial.

**NOTE**

In 2000, Dow Chemical Co. fired 74 employees for sending emails with pornography and violent images. It also disciplined more than 400 additional employees for similar actions. Dow had policies that prohibited employees from sending such emails.



## Workplace Privacy and Monitoring Policies

Workplace privacy addresses an employee's privacy rights at work. It is a controversial issue, because employees do not want to have their activities monitored. It can create feelings of distrust in a workplace.

Workplace privacy and monitoring is an area of law that is changing rapidly. For the most part, however, U.S. employees have few privacy rights in their use of an organization's IT resources. An organization may monitor an employee's work email and internet use in many instances. Monitoring is usually allowed if there is a legitimate business reason for it. Legitimate reasons to monitor email and internet access include:

- Assessing employee productivity
- Monitoring operational use of IT resources
- Monitoring policy compliance
- Monitoring the use of the organization's intellectual property
- Investigating allegations of wrongdoing
- Managing risk and protecting against legal liability

The information security department is often involved in workplace monitoring activities. This department has the knowledge and ability to carry out an organization's desire to monitor IT resource use.

### Does Cyber Monday Pose a Productivity Problem?

*Black Friday*, the day after the U.S. Thanksgiving holiday, is the traditional start of the winter holiday shopping season. Stores and retailers often have sales on this day to encourage shoppers to visit stores and spend money.

*Cyber Monday*, the first Monday after the Thanksgiving holiday, is the cyber-equivalent to Black Friday. Many retailers noticed an increase in online sales on this day. They suggested that this was because employees used their employer's computers and high-speed connections to shop online when they returned to work after the holiday. The National Retail Foundation reported that 83.3 million shoppers shopped online on Cyber Monday in 2019.[9]

How should an organization deal with Cyber Monday? What are the problems that it poses for productivity? What are the problems that it poses for information security?

Employers usually win employee legal challenges against monitoring of business email and internet use. To win these challenges, organizations must show that they had a legitimate business reason for monitoring IT resources. They also must show that they conducted the monitoring in a proper way.

Workplace privacy and monitoring policies are often combined together. They inform employees that:

- Their use of IT resources is not private.
- Their use of IT resources is monitored.

Well-written policies give employees clear notice that they have no expectation of privacy in an organization's IT resources. They give an employee notice that their use of IT resources will be monitored. They also might state why an organization monitors its IT resources. Finally, they should state that an organization does not waive its right to monitor IT resources even if it chooses not to do so all the time.

## Data Retention and Destruction Policies

Data retention and destruction is a hot topic for many organizations. **Data retention policies** state how data is controlled throughout its life cycle. Laws and organizational policies help determine retention periods.

**Data destruction policies** state how data must be destroyed when it reaches the end of its life cycle. Organizations must destroy paper and electronic data when it is no longer needed. For electronic data, this means destroying it in primary and backup storage systems. For both types of data, it means destroying it in such a way that it cannot be recovered. Data destruction policies are influenced by federal and state laws.

These policies help organizations cope with the large amounts of data that they use and produce. Without these policies, records management can be difficult. An organization might not know what types of data it has. It might not be able to find data when it needs it for business reasons. It might use too many resources to store data for longer than it must. Storage space for both paper and electronic data is a valuable resource.

Even if an organization has information security controls in place, data is still a vulnerability. It is vulnerable to external threats such as natural disaster or hackers. It is also vulnerable to unintentional acts committed by employees. For instance, employees can easily delete emails that they should keep. They also can save email that should have been deleted because there was no business reason to retain it.

In order to create data retention and destruction policies for electronic data, an organization must know how its IT resources work. They must know what data is stored on its IT systems. They also must know how to retrieve that data from these systems. Finally, they must know how to remove data from these systems.

Employee awareness is critical for successful data retention and destruction policies. Employees need to be well educated on data retention requirements. They also need to know how to properly file and maintain data that the organization must retain. Finally, they need to understand proper destruction methods. This is very important to avoid accidental disclosures of either paper-based or electronic media.

### *Data Retention Policies*

Data retention policies define the types of data that an organization has. They also address where data is stored and how it is protected. They specify how long different types of data must be retained. These policies also are called document retention policies.

Different types of data have different retention periods. This period is usually driven by a combination of federal and state laws. It is also influenced by business needs. Externally, many federal and state laws govern what organizations can do with their data. These laws also state how long certain types of data must be kept. For example, organizations that are subject to the Health Insurance Portability and Accountability Act (HIPAA) have to retain certain types of data for 6 years.[10]

Laws are not the only factor affecting data retention. Organizations also have to think about data retention if they become involved in a lawsuit. Most federal and state courts have procedural rules that require organizations to maintain data if they are party to a lawsuit. This rule might apply even before an actual lawsuit. For example, an organization must retain paper and electronic data in situations where litigation against it is reasonably anticipated. If an organization does not maintain this data, it can be sanctioned by a court. Maintaining electronic data for this purpose can be very difficult. There are special rules to follow to maintain electronic evidence that might be used in a lawsuit. They are called E-discovery rules.

**NOTE**

State laws might require governmental agencies to retain financial or other types of data for different lengths of time. This is to meet state auditing requirements or comply with open records laws.

In addition to legal requirements, organizations keep data for business purposes. They keep it to conduct business, market products, or to recover from a disaster. Organizations also preserve some types of data indefinitely. This might be because it has legal, fiscal, research, or historical value.

Data retention policies help an organization manage these competing concerns. A cross-functional team helps review and determine data retention requirements. This team should include experts who understand the legal requirements. Experts who know how the organization creates data should be on the team as well. The team must include experts who know the organization's IT systems. This team must understand how the organization uses data and threats to that data.

Data retention policies need to include the following elements:

- Types of organizational data
- Where that data is stored
- How that data is protected
- Legal, business, historical, or other reason for keeping that data
- How long the data should be retained

A data retention policy must be matched with a data destruction policy. An organization must destroy data that it no longer must keep for business, archival, or historical purposes.

### *Data Destruction Policies*

An organization creates data destruction policies to make sure that it destroys data properly. An organization's data destruction process must work hand-in-hand with a data retention policy. The data destruction policy must include the following:

- Identify data ready for destruction.
- Specify proper destruction methods for different kinds of data or storage media.
- Provide validation procedures to make sure data is properly destroyed.
- Provide consequences for improper destruction.

Legal requirements can influence an organization's data destruction policy. For example, the Gramm-Leach-Bliley Act (GLBA) requires that paper documents holding customer information be destroyed.[11] It also states that data must be destroyed in such a way that it cannot be read or reconstructed. The law also requires that electronic data be destroyed or completely erased. State laws also may require organizations to destroy data in a certain way.

Data destruction policies must be consistently followed. This is important for normal maintenance reasons. It is easy to destroy data when it is done on a regular basis. Following a consistent process is critical if an organization is involved in a lawsuit. It helps protect an organization from claims that it intentionally destroyed evidence.

#### State Law Data Destruction Requirements

Some state laws require specific data destruction methods. The State of Indiana has this type of law. All business in the state must follow the law requiring that they properly dispose of the unredacted personal information of their customers. This information includes a customer's Social Security number (SSN) or certain types of financial account information. The law applies to both paper and electronic information.

The law requires that information be disposed of in a way that makes it unreadable or unusable. It says that proper disposal methods include shredding, incinerating, mutilating, and erasing.

The state can fine a business that does not comply with the law, imposing fines that range from $500 to $10,000 per violation. You can read Indiana's data disposal law at http://iga.in.gov/legislative/laws/2019/ic/titles/024#24-4-14.

## Intellectual Property Policies

Intellectual property laws protect people's or organizations' ownership rights in their creative ideas. It gives them the right to protect their ideas and profit from them. These rights are exclusive to the owners of intellectual property. They can act against people who violate these rights.

Intellectual property policies are very important for most organizations. There are two main reasons why an organization should consider an intellectual property policy. They are:

- To protect its own intellectual property
- To make sure that its employees respect the intellectual property rights of others

Organizations have large amounts of data that they use in carrying out their business. This may include information protected by patents, copyrights, and trademarks. It also can include information protected as a trade secret. Because it is important to the viability of the organization, an organization must protect it.

An organization uses a policy to specify the intellectual property that it owns. As in an AUP, so too in a policy governing the use of its intellectual property; an organization will want to state its expectations:

- That the organization's intellectual property may be used only for authorized business purposes
- That the organization's intellectual property may not be disclosed outside the organization
- Whether the intellectual property may be removed from the building, copied onto removable media, or stored in cloud computing infrastructure
- What the rules are for using the organization's name or trademarks in correspondence

There is an information security component to protecting the organization's intellectual property. For example, an organization's electronic proprietary and trade secret data must be secured against internal misuse. It also must be secured against external attack.

The second reason for an intellectual property policy is to make sure that an organization does not violate the rights of others. An organization can be held liable for the infringing activities of its employees. For example, an organization will want to make sure that its employees honor software licensing agreements. It will want to make sure that employees do not use software without a valid license to do so. It also must make sure that employees do not copy or distribute unauthorized copies of software. The organization also will want to make sure that employees do not share or download pirated software onto organizational computers.

## Authentication and Password Policies

Authentication controls are among the most basic types of information security controls that an organization can use to protect its IT resources. **Authentication** is the process whereby a user proves his or her identity to access an IT resource. Good authentication provides controlled access to an organization's IT resources.

The user does this by presenting credentials. **User credentials** are used to access IT resources. They usually include a username and one of the following:

- **Something a user knows**—This includes passwords, passphrases, and personal identification numbers (PINs).
- **Something a user has**—This includes tokens, smart cards, and digital certificates.
- **Something a user is**—This includes biometric data such as a fingerprint or retina scan.

Organizations can implement authentication methods in many ways. Some ways are more complicated and expensive than others. For example, biometric authentication can be very expensive. Organizations also can choose to implement **multifactor authentication**. This type of authentication requires employees to use two or more different types of credentials to access IT resources.

Many organizations choose to implement passwords. This is because they can easily implement them. They also are relatively inexpensive to use. Employees generally are familiar with using passwords. Employees may be unfamiliar with other types of authentication methods, such as using biometric data.

There are several problems with using passwords as the only authentication method. An organization's IT resources are vulnerable if a password is compromised. A password can be compromised if an employee shares his or her password. It also can be compromised through a phishing or dictionary attack.

**NOTE**

A dictionary attack tries to crack passwords by running through words or phrases listed in a dictionary. Strong passwords help combat dictionary attacks.

Organizations implement authentication and password policies in an attempt to reduce risk caused by password use. Sometimes these types of policies are stand-alone policies, but they also can be included as a policy statement in an organization's main information security policy if it has one. These types of policies state the user credential rules that employees must follow. Some policies state that an organization's IT department will never ask employees to share their passwords. These policies often include password creation rules. For example, they may state the number of characters that a password must have.

### Would You Share Your Password for Chocolate?

Researchers at the University of Luxembourg studied whether or not people would be willing to exchange their passwords for chocolate. In a fascinating social engineering study, they found that the timing of the gift (before or after the request to share the password) and gender of the recipient were important. Men were more likely to share their passwords if given chocolate right before being asked to share their passwords. About 30 percent of the participants in the study shared their passwords with the researchers.[12] The study did not verify whether people were sharing valid passwords. It is possible that the survey results could be influenced by chocolate lovers sharing fake passwords.

Other common password policy statements include:

- Passwords should not be written down. If they must be written down, that paper should be stored in a secured place.
- Passwords must never be shared with anyone, including trusted colleagues, friends, or family members.
- Passwords must not contain dictionary words.
- Passwords must not include a user's name or parts of his or her name.
- Employees must create strong passwords that meet the organization's character and complexity requirements.
- Passwords expire after a certain period and must be changed.
- New passwords must be different from the previous password or parts of the previous password.
- Passwords may not be reused for a specified period.
- Passwords must not be inserted into email messages or other forms of electronic communication.

Information security departments also can create their own policies for how passwords should be used within IT resources. For instance, they might specify that passwords should never be stored in IT resources as cleartext. These policies might require that system authentication take place via encrypted channels. These also might specify that a password cannot be displayed on screens as cleartext when an employee enters it. This would help prevent shoulder surfing attacks. Where possible, passwords should expire automatically, and employees should be prompted to create new ones.



## Security Awareness and Training

A 2016 survey asked about corporate information security policies. A total of 8,000 people participated in the survey. Of these, 88 percent of the employees surveyed did not know about their organization's information security policies. [13]

An important part of any information security program is the training and awareness component. This is because employees play a large role in meeting information security goals. Employees often view information security training as a waste of time. As one author writes, "Given a choice between dancing pigs and security, users will pick dancing pigs every time."[14]

Employee behavior can help protect data and IT resources. It also can be harmful. Employees who are not aware of their responsibilities pose a threat. They may engage in risky online activities that could harm the organization's IT resources. Their actions also could disclose data. They can subject an organization to liability. Training and awareness activities help reduce this threat.

A high-level awareness and training policy or policy statement lets employees know that the BOD supports information security educational activities. Similar to authentication policies, sometimes these types of policies are stand-alone policies, or they can be included as a policy statement in an organization's main information security policy if it has one.

**Creating an Information Security Awareness Program**

Many organizations struggle with information security training and awareness. This includes the U.S. federal government. FISMA requires federal agencies to implement security awareness training as part of their overall information security programs.

The National Institute of Standards and Technology (NIST) created guidance for training and awareness activities. NIST Special Publication 800-50, "Building an Information Technology Security Awareness and Training Program," was published in 2003. It steps organizations through how to design and implement a training and awareness program. It also discusses how to develop training material. Finally, it provides advice on how to review the program's effectiveness.

Any organization can use the NIST guidance to help create an information security awareness program.

An information security awareness and training policy or policy statement should include the following elements:

- Why security awareness and training are important
- Who has overall responsibility for the policy
- Who provides training and awareness activities
- Which employees must take part in training activities
- How often training must take place
- What the consequences are for not participating in required training

BOD support of training activities is vital. It makes sure that employees understand that training is important and makes them take it seriously.

A variety of training and awareness events are necessary to reach employees. Organizations can use multiple training tools to help their employees know about security policies.

## Case Studies and Examples

The following case study shows how the concepts discussed in this chapter are used.

### Acceptable Use Case Study

Autoliv is a seatbelt and airbag technology company. In 1998, Autoliv's employee handbook included several policies. It stated employee rules of conduct, including an anti-harassment policy. It also included a computer AUP. Autoliv gave this handbook to all of its employees.

Autoliv's general rules of conduct stated:

- "Each employee is required to be familiar with these rules and with additional rules which apply to particular jobs and operations. In addition, each employee is expected to maintain conduct consistent with job efficiency and accepted standards of behavior for a business environment. Deviation from those standards may be cause for disciplinary action."

- "Disciplinary action may be taken for violation of any single rule or combination of rules, or for other improper conduct or unsatisfactory performance, and may include any of the following actions: 1) Employee Discussion; 2) Notice of Caution; 3) Involuntary Suspension; 4) Termination."

Autoliv's anti-harassment policy stated that the company did not "tolerate or permit illegal harassment or retaliation of any nature within our workforce." Its computer AUP prohibited non-business uses of company email. It also prohibited "conduct that reflects unfavorably on the corporation."[15]

In 1998, Autoliv investigated employee use of its email system because of system performance issues. It found that email use was causing the performance issues and determined that the bulk of email use was not business related.

In June, Autoliv sent an email to all of its employees reminding them about company policy. It said: "E-mail is to be used for business only. We do not wish to 'police' the e-mail system, so your cooperation would be appreciated. Please refrain from sending/receiving these types of messages as it is interfering with legitimate business e-mail."

Autoliv sent another reminder email to its employees in September 1998. This email warned that an employee could be fired for AUP violations.

In January 1999, Autoliv sent another email to its employees. This email stated that it was a violation of the AUP to share chain letters, jokes and stories, and non-business-related announcements. It also instructed employees to delete those types of emails and not forward them.

A former employee complained to Autoliv that she had received harassing emails from two current employees. Autoliv investigated. It learned that one employee had sent 11 non-business email messages. These messages included jokes, photos, and short videos that were sexually explicit. It found that another employee had sent 25 non-business email messages with similar content. Autoliv immediately fired both employees.

**NOTE**

You can learn about the company at http://www.autoliv.com.

The fired employees filed for unemployment benefits. Autoliv contested this request. A state can deny unemployment benefits if an employee is fired for "just cause," which means that there is a legally sufficient reason for firing an employee. Autoliv said that it had just cause for firing the two employees.

At the unemployment hearing, the employees admitted that they had received Autoliv's handbook. They also stated that they knew about the anti-harassment policy. They said they probably had received the three emails about email abuse, but claimed they deleted these emails without reading them. They argued that their firing was not "just" because they did not know they could be fired for sending non-business emails.

The Utah Department of Workforce Services found that Autoliv did not have just cause to fire the employees because the employees said they did not know that they could be fired for their behavior. They were awarded benefits.

Autoliv appealed the agency's decision to the Workforce Appeals Board. It lost its appeal. Autoliv appealed the decision to the Utah Court of Appeals. Autoliv argued again that the employees had plenty of knowledge that they could be fired for their actions.

Think about the following:

- What do you think the Utah Court of Appeals decided?
- What facts support Autoliv's argument that the employees had knowledge that their conduct was unacceptable?
- What facts support the employees' argument that they did not have knowledge that their conduct was unacceptable?
- Do you think sending offensive emails is a "flagrant violation of a universal standard of behavior"?
- Could Autoliv make any changes to its general rules of conduct, anti-harassment policy, or computer AUP that would make employee email responsibilities clear?

The Utah Court of Appeals reversed the decision of the Workforce Appeals Board. It held that Autoliv did have just cause to fire the employees. In its opinion the court stated: "There are two ways to establish that a claimant had knowledge: 1) the employer must have provided a clear explanation of the expected behavior or a written policy regarding the same; or 2) the conduct involved is a flagrant violation of a universal standard of behavior."[16]

The court held that the employees' email activities had violated a universal standard of behavior. It wrote, "We conclude that in today's workplace, the email transmission of sexually explicit and offensive jokes, pictures, and videos constitutes a flagrant violation of a universal standard of behavior."[17]

You can read the court's opinion at http://caselaw.findlaw.com/ut-court-of-appeals/1369016.html.

## CHAPTER SUMMARY

ISG provides strategic direction for an information security program. Organizations must protect data in a way that supports their business goals. They use high-level policies to state their information security goals. These policies set forth employee responsibilities. An organization can address information security issues in many different policies.

Standards, guidelines, and procedures are used to support policies. They explain how employees meet policy goals. A training and awareness program is a key part of an information security program. It helps make sure that employees are aware of their duties.

## KEY CONCEPTS AND TERMS

Acceptable use policy (AUP)
Authentication
Baseline
Board of directors (BOD)
Chief information officer (CIO)
Chief information security officer (CISO)
Chief technology officer (CTO)
Data destruction policies
Data retention policies
Guidelines

Information security governance (ISG)
Information security management (ISM)
Multifactor authentication
Operational planning
Policy
Procedures
Stakeholders
Standards
Strategic planning
Tactical planning
User credentials

## CHAPTER 13 ASSESSMENT

1. What is a policy?
   A. An overall statement of information security scope and direction
   B. A minimum threshold of information security controls that must be implemented
   C. A checklist of steps that must be completed to ensure information security
   D. A technology-dependent statement of best practices
   E. Recommended actions and operational guides
2. What is information security governance?
3. What type of policy would an organization use to forbid its employees from using organizational email for personal use?
   A. Privacy policy
   B. Intellectual property policy
   C. Anti-harassment policy
   D. Acceptable use policy
   E. Monitoring policy
4. What is software piracy?
   A. Unauthorized copying of software
   B. Unauthorized distribution of software
   C. Unauthorized use of software properly purchased by an organization
   D. All of these are correct.
   E. None of these is correct.
5. What is information security management?
6. Employer monitoring of employee electronic communications can be a normal term of employment if advance notice is given.
   A. True
   B. False
7. What is a standard?
8. Which law states requirements for federal agency information security governance?
   A. FISMA
   B. FERPA
   C. HIPAA
   D. GLBA
   E. FIPPS
9. A guideline is a list of mandatory activities that must be completed to achieve an information security goal.
   A. True
   B. False
10. Which role is usually the most senior information technology official in an organization?
    A. CFO
    B. CISO
    C. CTO
    D. CIO
    E. None of these is correct.
11. What is a procedure?
12. Which management layer has overall responsibility for information security governance?
    A. CIO
    B. CISO
    C. Board of directors
    D. Employees
    E. Information security managers
13. What is the final step in the policy development process?
    A. Maintenance and review
    B. Management approval
    C. Continued awareness activities
    D. Communication to employees
    E. Stakeholder review

**14.** What factors drive data retention policies?

A. Legal requirements
B. Business need for information
C. Historical need for information
D. Storage space requirements
E. All of these are correct.

**15.** What is a valid reason for allowing an information security policy exception?

A. The cost of implementing security policy is too high.
B. The cost of compliance with the policy is more than the cost of noncompliance.
C. It is not technically feasible to implement the policy.
D. End users believe that the policy makes their work harder.
E. It is too difficult to implement the policy.

## ENDNOTES


1. New Vantage Partners, "Big Data and AI Executive Survey 2019," January 2019. Available at http://newvantage.com/wp-content/uploads/2018/12/Big-Data-Executive-Survey-2019-Findings-Updated-010219-1.pdf (accessed February 17, 2020).
2. Ponemon Institute, "2019 Cost of Data Breach Study: Global Analysis," undated. Available at https://www.ibm.com/security/data-breach (accessed February 17, 2020).
3. International Organization for Standardization, "ISO/IEC 27001:2013, Information Technology –Security Techniques–Information Security Management Systems–Requirements," 2013. Available at https://www.iso.org/standard/54534.html (accessed July 25, 2020).
4. Federal Information Security Management Act of 2002, Title III of the E-Government Act of 2002, U.S. Code Vol. 44, sec. 3541 et seq. (2012).
5. U.S. Government Accountability Office, "High Risk Series: Substantial Efforts Needed to Achieve Greater Progress on High Risk Areas," March 2019. Available at https://www.gao.gov/products/gao-19-157sp (accessed February 18, 2020).
6. Pew Research Center, "Mobile Technology and Home Broadband 2019," June 2019. Available at https://www.pewresearch.org/internet/2019/06/13/mobile-technology-and-home-broadband-2019/ (accessed February 18, 2020).
7. American Management Association, "The Latest on Workplace Monitoring and Surveillance," April 8, 2019. Available at https://www.amanet.org/articles/the-latest-on-workplace-monitoring-and-surveillance/ (accessed February 21, 2020).
8. Civil Rights Act of 1964, Pub. L. No. 88-352, 78 Stat. 241, codified as amended in scattered sections throughout U.S. Code Vols. 2, 28, and 42 (2012).
9. National Retail Federation, "Thanksgiving Weekend Draws Nearly 190 Million Shoppers, Spending Up 16 Percent," December 3, 2019. Available at https://nrf.com/media-center/press-releases/thanksgiving-draws-nearly-190-million-shoppers (accessed February 21, 2020).
10. Health Insurance Portability and Accountability Act of 1996 (HIPAA), Pub. L. No. 104-191, codified at U.S. Code Vol. 42, sec. 1320d (2012).
11. Gramm-Leach-Bliley Act (1999), Title V of the Financial Services Modernization Act of 1999, Pub. L. No. 106-102, 113 Stat. 1338, codified at U.S. Code Vol. 15, sec. 6801, et seq. (2012).
12. Happ, Christian, André Melzer, and Georges Steffgen, "Trick With Treat—Reciprocity Increases the Willingness to Communicate Personal Data," 2016. *Computers in Human Behavior*. Available at https://www.researchgate.net/publication/298187172_Trick_with_Treat_-_Reciprocity_Increases_the_Willingness_to_Communicate_Personal_Data (accessed February 20, 2020).
13. TechRepublic, "88% of Employees Have No Clue About Their Organization's IT Security Policies," January 11, 2018. Available at https://www.techrepublic.com

/article/88-of-employees-have-no-clue-about-their-organizations-it-security-policies/ (accessed February 20, 2020).

14. McGraw, Gary, and Ed Felten, *Securing Java.* New York, NY: John Wiley & Sons, Inc., 1999. Also available at http://www.securingjava.com/ (accessed February 20, 2020). View Chapter 1, part 7.
15. *Autoliv ASP, Inc. v. Department of Workforce Services*, 29 P.3d 7 (Utah Ct. Appeals, 2001). All quoted statements are from this case.
16. *Autoliv*, 29 P.3d at 11.
17. *Autoliv*, 29 P.3d at 12–13.

CHAPTER 14

# Risk Analysis, Incident Response, and Contingency Planning

RISK MANAGEMENT IS an important information security tool. The risk management process helps an organization understand the risks, vulnerabilities, and threats that it faces each day. It helps the organization understand its security posture. It also helps the organization know where to strengthen that posture. An organization cannot meet its information security goals if it does not understand its risks. It may not be able to properly protect its resources and data.

This chapter focuses on information technology (IT) risk management. It reviews fundamental risk concepts and how they are applied. It explains how organizations use risk management to help them create their other contingency plans.

## Chapter 14 Topics

This chapter covers the following topics and concepts:

- How to plan for contingencies
- What risk management is
- What three types of contingency planning are
- What incident response (IR) is
- What some special considerations are

## Chapter 14 Goals

When you complete this chapter, you will be able to:

- Describe the risk assessment (RA) process
- Describe how to create an incident response (IR) plan
- Describe the business continuity (BC) planning process
- Describe how to create a disaster recovery (DR) plan
- Explain the differences between RA, IR, BC planning, and DR

## Contingency Planning

Organizations must plan for many events. Contingency plans do not focus just on an organization's information technology (IT) assets. Instead, the field has grown to include all types of planning to make sure that an organization can continue to operate in the event of an interruption, emergency, or disaster. In recent years, the United States has seen several dramatic events that highlight the need for all types of contingency plans: the September 11 terrorist attacks of 2001, the northeastern U.S. power-grid failure in 2003, the H1N1 flu outbreak in 2009, Hurricane Sandy in 2012, and power blackouts caused by California wildfires in 2019.

When organizations talk about contingency plans, they are talking about holistic plans. These are plans that cover the whole organization and all of its processes. They identify operations that are critical to the business's survival and recovery. These plans must include IT resources and operations. Many organizations store their data and records electronically. Many of them have grown dependent on their IT resources and the automated processes those resources provide. Thus, focusing on how to protect and recover IT assets is an important contingency planning component. This is especially important for small organizations. For example, some studies indicate that 43 percent of cyberattacks target smaller businesses.[1]

This chapter discusses contingency planning processes as they relate to IT resources. The different planning processes discussed in this chapter are:

- Incident response (IR) planning
- Disaster recovery (DR) planning
- Business continuity (BC) planning

The scope of any kind of contingency planning is very broad. It can range from planning for life safety issues to how to conduct business without electricity. This chapter focuses on only one narrow piece: planning for the security of IT resources. Although all contingency plans have different goals, the foundation for these processes is the same. In order to prepare contingency plans, organizations must analyze and plan for the IT risks that they face. The risk analysis and foundation process helps an organization understand how it needs to protect its IT resources. An organization cannot make any contingency plans until it understands the risks to its IT resources.

**FYI**

This chapter talks about risk management, incident response, and contingency planning. Risk management and contingency planning are used to protect IT resources. Incident response is a type of contingency planning that an organization uses to react to attacks against its IT infrastructure. **Disaster recovery (DR)** and **business continuity (BC)** plans are contingency plans that help an organization continue business operations following a disaster.

It is important to remember that protecting IT resources is not the only goal of a contingency plan. It is not even the most important goal. Natural and man-made events disrupt thousands of lives each year. The most important goal of any type of contingency plan is to preserve human life. Continuing business operations and restoring data are secondary goals.

## Risk Management

The National Institute of Standards and Technology (NIST) says that risk management is "a complex, multifaceted activity that requires the involvement of the entire organization."[2] **Risk management (RM)** helps an organization identify the risks that it faces. It also makes sure that organizations respond to risk in a cost-effective manner. Organizations use RM to support their business goals.

One of the main goals of RM is to protect the organization's bottom line. When risk is realized, it negatively affects an organization's profits. RM helps an organization align its information security practices to its business goals. It makes sure that an organization spends its limited resources wisely and in ways that enhance business goals. An organization uses RM to plan and prioritize its information security activities.

For example, suppose an organization has a database that holds customer data. The database is critical to the organization's business. It uses the information in the database to develop products for its customers. The database also holds marketing information. The organization would be harmed if it did not have access to this resource. Its development and marketing activities would be negatively impacted. The organization must protect this database.

A risk analysis shows that the database is at risk because system administrators share a single administrator account with a weak password to access the database. This is a vulnerability. Therefore, the database is open to attack. If it is attacked, the confidentiality and availability of data on the resource are compromised. Attackers could steal this data. They also could harm the database so that the organization could not use it. The risk analysis shows that the vulnerability (a single administrator account with a weak password), together with the threat (attackers) is very critical given the organization's business.

As part of its RM function, the organization must review the potential impact of this risk. The cost of a data breach could be quite high given the type of data in the customer database. The organization might have to notify its customers about the breach. It also might have to report the breach to its regulatory authorities. Those agencies could fine the organization for failing to secure its data. Its customers could sue it as well. The organization could lose current and future customers. It also faces its own operational issues if that database is not available for a certain period.

Once the organization identifies the risk and potential impact, it can take steps to mitigate it. In this example, the organization must reduce the risk posed by a single shared account with a weak password. It can require its system administrators to use different accounts, with multifactor authentication, to access this critical resource. It also can configure its systems to enforce authentication requirements technically. Finally, it can make sure that it backs up its customer data properly. In this short example, the RM process identified a risk to a resource. It offered different options for addressing the risk. In addressing the risk the organization was able to secure an important resource. Therefore, it was able to protect its business operations and bottom line.



**FYI**

The RM process described in this chapter is very similar to the risk management framework used by the U.S. federal government. An organization could easily use that framework to protect its IT systems. The NIST has created guidelines that federal agencies use to implement this framework.

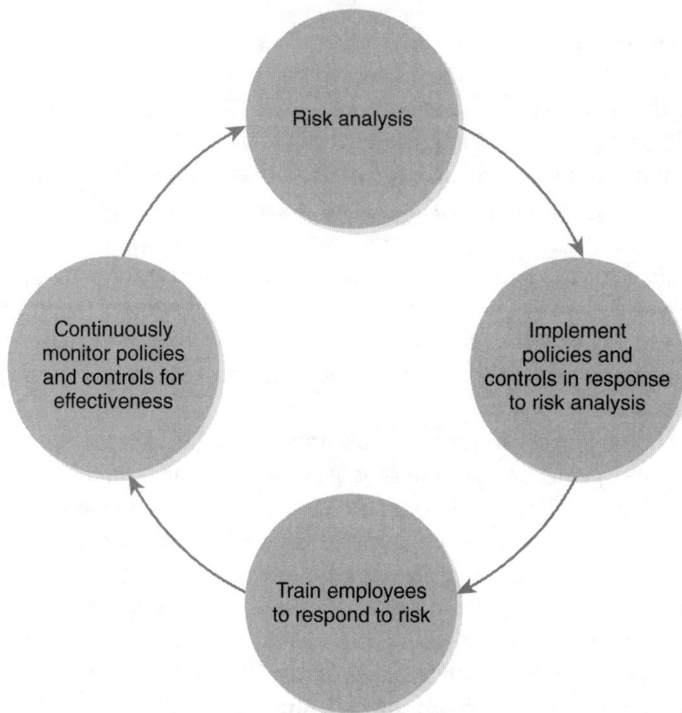


FIGURE 14-1
Risk management process.

Each step in the RM process supports an organization's business goals. The most basic RM process includes the following steps:

- **Risk assessment**—Identify the threats and vulnerabilities to the organization's IT resources. Determine the impact of those threats and vulnerabilities.
- **Risk response**—Use policies and controls to respond to risk. An organization responds to risk according to its business strategy.
- **Employee training**—Train employees on known threats and vulnerabilities. Training can help avoid risk.
- **Continuous monitoring**—Monitor the organization's policies and controls for continued effectiveness. Update policies and controls that are not effective.

FIGURE 14-1 shows this basic RM process.

The RM process and information learned during that process can form the basis for an organization's contingency plans. In a basic sense, contingency plans are an organization's response to very narrow risk assessments. For example, BC and DR plans are detailed contingency plans that respond to the risks of natural or man-made disasters. These risks are discovered during the RM process.

## Risk Assessment Process

A **risk assessment (RA)** identifies the threats and vulnerabilities to IT resources. It reviews the probability of those threats and vulnerabilities actually happening. This is called a

**realized risk**. Then the RA reviews the potential harm from a realized risk. Finally, the RA identifies policies and controls that could respond to the potential risk. Risk response is the action taken by an organization to reduce realized risk to an acceptable level. The amount of risk that is left over after realized risk is reduced is called **residual risk**.

The RA is a tool in the risk management process that provides executive management with the data that it needs to make smart decisions about information security controls. Without an RA, the executive management team has no way to know if the controls and policies that it implements are needed or cost effective. For example, an organization could spend a lot of money implementing a control to respond to a perceived threat. Without an RA, the organization does not know whether the cost of the control is reasonable given the probability and potential of the underlying risk. The organization may be making a poor decision if it spends more money to respond to a risk than the actual cost of the realized risk itself. An RA helps the organization know where to spend money to respond to and mitigate information security risk.

There are several different methods for conducting a risk assessment. Some of them will be discussed in this chapter. In general, all methodologies have similar basic steps. The basic steps in a RA are:

- Inventory the assets included in the assessment
- Identify threats and vulnerabilities to those assets
- Categorize likelihood of occurrence and potential loss
- Document where controls are needed

### Risk Assessment Team

An RA team must include people in several different roles throughout an organization. Even though the RA focuses on risks to IT systems, it is not sufficient to only include IT personnel on the team. IT personnel may not know about all of the organization's critical business processes. For the same reason, it is not enough to include only business personnel on an RA team. Business personnel may not appreciate the technology processes that support business operations. The RA team members should represent all areas involved in a business process workflow.



**FYI**

Many laws have RA components. The Federal Information Security Modernization Act (FISMA) and the Sarbanes-Oxley Act (SOX) are two of them. The risk assessments required in these types of laws are very narrowly tailored to the systems and processes that are covered by the law. The RA processes described in this chapter are more general.

RA team members should include:

- **Business personnel**—These people are responsible for business process operations. They know the steps that must be completed in each business process. They also can describe how they use IT systems to accomplish their job duties.

- **IT personnel**—These people run the organization's various IT systems. This group also might include the IT system owner. These personnel understand how their IT systems work and are responsible for maintaining those resources. They also would be responsible for implementing any changes to IT systems.
- **Information security managers**—These people run the organization's information security program. They have knowledge about information security threats and vulnerabilities. They also know how threats and vulnerabilities can be mitigated.
- **Human resources personnel**—These people understand how to deal with people issues. They can offer advice and input on how to address human-based threats and vulnerabilities. They also will be able to assist with awareness training after the RA is complete.
- **Executive management**—These people make sure that the RA team has the support and resources that it needs to complete the assessment. They can hold business units accountable for participating in the assessment. They also can make sure that the RA remains properly scoped to its original goal.

Members of the team must be objective. They must be willing to take a hard look at an organization's business objectives and processes for risk potential. They must do the same thing for IT resources. Members of the team must avoid **conflicts of interest**. In the RA context, a conflict of interest is a situation where a member's responsibilities as part of the RA team might conflict with his or her job responsibilities. A conflict of interest prevents the team member from meeting his or her RA responsibilities.

In many cases, team members are picked because they work in a certain area that is being reviewed as part of an assessment. These members are helpful in making sure that the whole RA team understands how these areas work. However, these members may not be as objective in assessing vulnerabilities, threats, and risks in their areas. These team members will have to work hard to be objective throughout the whole RA process. An organization must remove members from the RA team if they are unable to be objective.

 **NOTE**

In general, a conflict of interest is any situation where a person's private interests and professional obligations collide. In these situations, independent observers might question whether a person's private interests improperly influenced his or her professional decisions.

Some organizations hire consultants to help with an RA. Consultants are not employees of the organization. They help in a risk analysis by bringing objectivity to the team. They also help by bringing risk analysis expertise to the process. They can hurt the team if they do not quickly learn how an organization's business processes and IT systems work. They also can hurt the team if they are not respectful of an organization's culture.

An RA team is responsible for collecting information about assets and risks. It is also responsible for reporting the assessment results to an organization's executive management.

### *Identifying Assets, Vulnerabilities, and Threats*

An RA must be narrowly scoped. Otherwise, it can grow too large for the RA team to manage. If it is too large, the team will have a hard time determining the risks that the organization must address. A good practice is to conduct a focused RA. Rather than doing an assessment of the organization's whole IT infrastructure, the RA team should review one infrastructure component at a time. This way the team can better manage the RA and produce better overall results.

The scope of the RA must be clearly stated in an RA project plan. RA team members can refer back to the project plan anytime they are asked to consider a new system or process as part of the RA. If the new system or process is not within the scope of the project plan, then the team should not consider it. Executive management must approve the project plan before the RA team begins to work.

After the organization approves the scope of the RA, the RA team must identify all the assets that are within the scope of the assessment. This inventory must include the IT resources. The inventory also must include a listing of the personnel who run business processes that are in the scope of the RA. It also must contain the data included in those processes. For instance, an organization decides to conduct a RA of its email infrastructure. For this assessment, the RA team must consider not only the operation of the organization's email servers, but also whether employees are sending confidential data via email. Depending upon how the RA team defines the project, mobile devices that send and receive email could be outside of the scope of the assessment.

**NOTE**

Many RA projects have a project manager. This person is in charge of making sure that the RA moves forward in a timely manner. The project manager is not necessarily a participant on the RA team. Instead, this person helps the RA team meet their project goals and final deliverables.

The RA team should consider many assets for the inventory. Assets to be considered include:

- Personnel
- Data
- Hardware and software
- Physical facilities
- Business process workflows
- Current controls that help safeguard any assets

It is important to identify all assets that are associated with the RA project. The RA team must list assets that are critical to business functions because they also must identify threats and vulnerabilities to those assets. The RA team must identify vulnerabilities and threats in order to determine the risk to the organization's assets. For IT resources, the organization needs to know how vulnerabilities and threats might affect confidentiality, integrity, and availability.

A vulnerability is a weakness or flaw in an IT system. Information security is compromised when vulnerabilities are exploited. An exploit is a successful attack against a vulnerability. There are many different kinds of vulnerabilities, but they fall into four broad categories: people, process, facility, and technology vulnerabilities. Vulnerabilities can be design mistakes. They also can be configuration mistakes.

Threats are anything that can cause harm to an information system. They are successful exploits against vulnerabilities. A threat source carries out a threat or causes it to take place against a vulnerability. A threat source can be a person or a circumstance. Similar to vulnerabilities, threats also fall into four broad categories: human, natural, technology and operational, and physical and environmental. Threats can be deliberate or accidental.

**TABLE 14-1** Examples of Vulnerabilities and Threats

| VULNERABILITY | THREAT SOURCE | THREAT |
|---|---|---|
| Data center has few physical security controls to prevent unauthorized access to data center hardware | Unauthorized users (e.g., criminals, terminated employees, curious employees) | Theft of data center hardware<br>Theft of data<br>Damage or destruction of hardware or data |
| Failure to remove user accounts in a timely manner when an employee leaves the organization | Terminated employees | Access to IT resources and theft of sensitive company data<br>Destruction of data |
| No access controls for sensitive files stored on IT resources | Curious employees | Review of data without need to know<br>Review of proprietary data<br>Invasion of privacy of other employees and/or customers<br>Unauthorized modification of data<br>Theft of data |

Threat sources act upon vulnerabilities. **TABLE 14-1** shows examples of vulnerabilities and threats.

The RA team must put forth a good-faith effort to identify as many vulnerabilities and threats as possible. It can do this in several ways. For vulnerabilities that are internal to the organization, the team could interview employees in areas that are part of the assessment. The team also could send a questionnaire to a sampling of employees to ask questions that are relevant to the assessment. The RA team also should review the organization's policies and procedures. The team could use automated scanning tools to look for vulnerabilities in its IT systems.

The RA team also must learn about vulnerabilities and threats that are external to the organization. They can review industry guides and can use NIST guidance to learn more about information security issues and controls. The RA team can review information from the U.S. government and other industry experts. The SANS Institute has one of the largest collections of information security resources in the world. (See www.sans.org for more information.) The team also can review known system problems listed in the National Vulnerability Database (NVD). (See https://nvd.nist.gov/home.)

It is not possible for the RA team to identify every security vulnerability or threat. This is because technology changes so rapidly. For example, zero-day exploits are a type of exploit that is hard for an organization to prepare for. An organization can only prepare for zero-day exploits generally. It is hard to prepare for or assess specific zero-day exploits because they are exploited so quickly after they are discovered.

### *Likelihood and Potential Loss*

A risk is the likelihood that a threat will exploit a vulnerability and cause harm. The RA team is responsible for determining how likely it is that identified risks will occur. The team also must determine the potential loss or harm that the organization could have if the risk is realized. Likelihood and potential loss can be stated as either a qualitative measure or a quantitative measure. It depends on the risk methodology that the RA team uses.

**Quantitative Risk Analysis. Quantitative risk analysis** attempts to use real numbers to calculate risk and potential loss. The organization assigns real numbers to the value of its assets. It also assigns real values to the cost of countermeasures and controls. One of the greatest advantages of a quantitative RA is that it provides an objective and monetary-based assessment of cost. It helps an organization understand both the cost of risk and the cost of controls. This type of RA allows management to directly compare the cost and benefits with recommended controls. One of the greatest disadvantages of quantitative risk assessments is that they are very difficult to administer.

In a quantitative risk analysis, the RA team must assign a value amount to each of the organization's assets. Several factors shape the cost of an asset, such as the cost of developing it and then the ongoing cost of maintaining the asset each year. The asset might have value that is hard to measure. For example, it might be hard to value the intellectual property that goes into creating and developing an asset. It is also hard to place a value on an asset that provides an organization with its competitive edge. Although quantitative risk analysis does give an organization actual money amounts for its assets, there is a subjective element to these values that is hard to measure. This is particularly true if an asset has intangible value.

After the RA team determines the organization's vulnerabilities and threats, it must determine **exposure factor.** The exposure factor is the percentage of asset loss that is likely to be caused by an identified threat. For example, an RA team determines that an organization's data center is vulnerable to tornadoes. This is because the data center is located in the part of the midwestern United States known as "tornado alley."[3] The RA team estimates that if a tornado struck the data center, it would be destroyed and the data center's value would be reduced to zero. The exposure factor is 100 percent.

The RA team determines that the same data center is also subject to a threat of fire. The RA team determines that if a fire were to occur, only 50 percent of the data center would be destroyed. (This is because the data center has a fire suppression system.) In this scenario, the exposure factor is 50 percent. Exposure factor also is called *likelihood.*

Once the RA team determines the exposure factor, it must determine **single loss expectancy (SLE)**. The SLE is the amount of money that an organization will lose if a risk is realized. In other words, it is the loss that an organization will suffer every time that risk occurs. SLE is often expressed as an equation:

$$\text{SLE} = \text{Asset value} \times \text{Exposure factor}$$

In our data center example, suppose that the data center is relatively small and is worth \$2 million. The SLE for the data center being struck by a tornado is \$2 million, whereas the SLE for the data center experiencing a fire is \$1 million.

The RA team also must figure out how many times a specific risk might occur during a 1-year time frame. This is called the **annual rate of occurrence (ARO)**. An RA team can use historical data to determine this number, as well as perform research to understand the likelihood of risks within a certain area. For instance, police departments can provide information about crime statistics. Insurance companies can provide information about how often organizations are likely to experience a serious fire or other devastating incident. ARO is expressed as a number. It can range from zero (a threat will never take place) to any number greater than zero. A risk that will happen only once a year has an ARO of one.

In our example, the RA team estimates that a fire might strike its data center once every 20 years. The ARO for that event is 1/20, or .05. The RA team estimates that a tornado might strike its data center once every 15 years. The ARO for that event is 1/15 or .067.

ARO is used to calculate **annualized loss expectancy (ALE)**. The ALE is the amount of loss that an organization can expect to have each year because of a particular risk. In a quantitative risk analysis, the ALE is the end-result number. An organization can use this number to determine how much money it should invest each year in controls to mitigate a particular risk. As a matter of good business practice, an organization should not spend more than the ALE amount each year on particular risks. ALE is often expressed as an equation:

$$\text{ALE} = \text{SLE} \times \text{ARO}$$

In our example, the ALE for the tornado risk is $134,000 ($2 million × .067). The ALE tells the organization that it can afford to spend up to $134,000 per year to mitigate the potential loss caused by a tornado. The ALE for the fire risk is $50,000 ($1 million × .05). The organization can spend up to $50,000 per year to mitigate potential fire loss. Spending more on controls than the ALE amount might be unwise from a business standpoint because the cost of the controls is then more than the cost of the risk. It does not make sense to spend more money on controls than the cost of the risk.

Organizations also can use these formulas to determine the value of a control. The value of a safeguard to the organization can be determined by comparing the ALE before implementing a control to the ALE after implementing the control. This also can be expressed as an equation:

$$\text{Value of control} = (\text{ALE before safeguard}) - (\text{ALE after safeguard}) - \text{Cost of control}$$

These equations are used in quantitative risk analysis. Many vendors have created software products that can help RA teams perform these equations.

Organizations often choose to do a quantitative RA because it computes risk in terms of money value. Sometimes executive management finds this information very helpful. It gives them concrete values upon which to measure the costs of risks and the effectiveness of controls. A quantitative risk analysis speaks the language of business: money.

**Qualitative Risk Analysis. Qualitative risk analysis** uses scenarios and ratings systems to calculate risk and potential harm. Qualitative risk analysis does not assign money value to assets and risk. Instead, it uses descriptive categories to express asset criticality, risk exposure (likelihood), and risk impact.

One of the greatest advantages of this method is that it is relatively easy to use. It does not require RA team members to have specialized financial knowledge. It also does not require them to deduce the costs of assets, controls, and potential harm. One of the biggest disadvantages of qualitative risk assessments is that they are very subjective. The opinions of members of the RA team can highly influence the results of the RA.

Qualitative risk analysis is scenario-based. In this type of assessment, the RA team considers a specific vulnerability or threat. The team then considers a scenario based on it. As team members walk through the scenario, they think about how the scenario will affect business operations and resources. The team members will use their own experiences to determine threat likelihood. They can also use industry resources.

The RA team will create likelihood and impact categories to help them classify and compare different risks. These categories are usually based on either a numeric rating system (scale of 1 to 10) or a low-medium-high standard.

Risk exposure categories classify the likelihood of certain risks. An RA team might use the following categories to determine risk exposure:

- **Low**—Events that are unlikely to happen within a year
- **Medium**—Events that are somewhat likely to happen within a year
- **High**—Events that are likely to happen within a year

Risk impact is determined the same way. Impact categories classify the harm to an organization if a risk is realized. The RA team might use the following impact categories:

- **Low**—A realized risk will have little or no effect on the organization. The organization will experience light disruption to its business processes. It will incur only low costs related to lost productivity and data and will not experience reputational loss.
- **Medium**—A realized risk will have a moderate effect on the organization. The organization may experience moderate disruption to its business processes. It will incur moderate costs related to loss productivity and data and a moderate reputational loss.
- **High**—A realized risk will have a severe effect on the organization. The organization may experience severe disruption to its business processes. It will experience high costs related to loss productivity and data, and its reputational loss will be significant.

The RA team also will need a way to compare likelihood and impact levels to determine overall risk level. The RA team will use the overall risk level to determine where the organization should apply controls. An organization will not want to implement costly controls on a system that has low exposure and impact results. However, it will want to implement controls where there is a high likelihood rating and a high impact rating. It must create a method to analyze likelihood and impact rating levels. It uses this analysis to determine the priority of issues that the organization must address. **TABLE 14-2** shows a generic risk level matrix.



**TABLE 14-2** Risk Level Matrix

| | | LIKELIHOOD | | |
|---|---|---|---|---|
| | **RATING** | **LOW** | **MEDIUM** | **HIGH** |
| **IMPACT** | **Low** | Low | Low–Medium | Medium–High |
| | **Medium** | Low–Medium | Medium | Medium–High |
| | **High** | Medium–High | Medium–High | High |

**TABLE 14-3** Risk Level Outcomes

| VULNERABILITY | THREAT SOURCE | THREAT | THREAT LIKELIHOOD | THREAT IMPACT | RISK LEVEL |
|---|---|---|---|---|---|
| Data center has few physical security controls to prevent unauthorized access to data center hardware | Unauthorized users | Theft of data center hardware | Medium | High | Medium–high |
| Failure to remove user accounts in a timely manner when an employee leaves the organization | Disgruntled terminated employees | Theft of sensitive company data | High | High | High |
| No access controls for sensitive files stored on IT resources | Curious employees | Review of data without need to know | Medium | Low | Low–medium |

Organizations use their risk level matrix to determine the priority of the risks that they must address. **TABLE 14-3** shows how the results of a qualitative risk analysis might look. It uses the vulnerabilities and threats from Table 14-1. In this example, the RA team would first recommend that the organization implement controls to remove user accounts for terminated employees in a timely manner. This is because the risk level for that vulnerability is higher than the others listed in the table.

The problem with qualitative risk assessments is that the organization has no way to determine the amount of money to spend on controls. It also has no way of knowing if it is spending too much on a control relative to the actual loss that it could have because of a realized risk. For some organizations, this is a significant failure of a qualitative risk analysis. This is one reason why an organization might prefer to complete a quantitative risk analysis. **TABLE 14-4** compares the features of qualitative and quantitative risk assessments.

### *Document Needed Controls*

The final part of an RA is to document where security controls are needed. The RA team does this by reviewing the results of its assessment. In a quantitative risk analysis, the RA team has a list of risks that it can prioritize by ALE and ARO. The RA team should review risks with high ALEs and high AROs to recommend controls.

Through a qualitative risk analysis process, the RA team has a list of risks organized by potential harm. The risk level is based on the classifications that the RA team used for risk likelihood and impact. The RA team should look at high and medium risk levels to recommend controls.

An RA team needs to suggest controls to executive management. It must identify risks that are high priorities. It also should identify controls that can mitigate or eliminate those risks. If the RA team performed a quantitative analysis, it should include a cost-benefit

TABLE 14-4 Qualitative and Quantitative Risk Assessment Comparison

| | QUALITATIVE RISK ASSESSMENT | QUANTITATIVE RISK ASSESSMENT |
|---|---|---|
| Positive Aspects | Easy to administer<br>Does not require formal knowledge to administer<br>Calculations are simple<br>Scope of the assessment can be changed easily if necessary | Measures the money cost of a risk<br>Very objective, can be used to make cost-benefit decisions<br>Easy for executives and financial managers to understand |
| Negative Aspects | No measure of money cost of risk<br>Very subjective, cannot be used to make cost-benefit decisions | Hard to administer<br>Requires formal knowledge to administer<br>Calculations are complex<br>Must put effort into valuing assets (and that value may be hard to calculate)<br>Very difficult to change the scope of the RA |

## Risk Assessment Methods

There are several different RA processes to choose from. Some vendors offer software that organizations can use to complete RAs. This sidebar describes some of the RA methods you might hear about in the information security profession.

NIST "SP 800-30 (Rev. 1): Guide for Conducting Risk Assessments" is a qualitative RA method. Any type of organization can use it. It describes several tasks to be completed in the RA process. You can view this NIST guide at http://nvlpubs.nist.gov/nistpubs/Legacy/SP/nistspecialpublication800-30r1.pdf.

ISO 31010:2019, "Risk Management – Risk Assessment Techniques," offers guidance on how to assess risk in several different ways. You can learn more at https://www.iso.org/standard/72140.html.

Another framework developed in Britain is the M_o_R framework. This framework describes the processes that need to be put in place to implement risk management. You can read more at https://www.itgovernance.co.uk/m_o_r.

Carnegie Mellon University's Software Engineering Institute developed OCTAVE (Operationally Critical Threat, Asset, and Vulnerability Evaluation). OCTAVE is a qualitative RA process that is designed to be self-directed. It allows organizations to align security operations to business strategy. You can learn about OCTAVE at https://resources.sei.cmu.edu/library/asset-view.cfm?assetid=309051.

Thomas Peltier developed the Facilitated Risk Analysis and Assessment Process (FRAAP) in 1993. It is a three-step process based on ISO/IEC 27001 that helps organizations identify risks and threats.

The Microsoft Corporation describes a risk analysis process that contains both quantitative and qualitative elements in its "Security Risk Management Guide." It created this guide in 2006. You can learn about it at http://technet.microsoft.com/en-us/library/cc163143.aspx.

analysis for each of its suggested controls. If the team performed a qualitative analysis, it should show how the suggested control affects the overall risk level for a specific threat or vulnerability.

Executive management reviews the RA team's report as it makes business decisions. It will use the report as part of its information security governance (ISG) activities. The organization must make sure that its response to the risks identified in the RA team's report supports its business objectives. The executive management team shows due care and due diligence when it responds to issues that are raised in a risk assessment.

## Risk Response

**NOTE**

Controls reduce the harm posed by vulnerabilities or threats. They may eliminate or reduce risk of harm. They are also called safeguards or countermeasures.

Executive management must decide how an organization responds to risk. Risk response is the actions taken by executive management to reduce risk to an acceptable level. Executive management must apply the most appropriate controls to decrease its risk. The organization's risk response must be cost-effective. It also should have a limited impact on the organization's business.

Executive management must prioritize how it will respond to risks. It should respond quickly to the risks that have the greatest potential to harm business goals. Executive management must assess each risk individually, as an organization will not handle all risks in the same manner.

Executive management can use several approaches to respond to risk. They are:

- **Risk avoidance**—The organization applies controls or takes other action to completely avoid a particular risk. This strategy removes all risk caused by a particular vulnerability or threat. For example, executive management could decide that the risks posed by a function in an IT system outweigh the benefit of that function. It could instruct system owners to disable that function in order to avoid the risk. The risk caused by that function is completely eliminated.
- **Risk mitigation**—The organization applies controls or takes other action to reduce a particular risk. This strategy does not eliminate all harm that could be caused by that risk. Instead, it reduces the risk to an acceptable level. The risk that is left over is called residual risk. For example, executive management could decide that the risks posed by a function in an IT system could be lessened if access to that function was limited. The organization could use access controls to limit access to that function to only a few trusted employees. The risk caused by that function is reduced because fewer people have access to it.
- **Risk transfer**—The organization takes no action against a particular risk. Instead, it passes its risk to another entity that bears the risk of loss. Usually an organization transfers risk of loss to an insurance company. It can purchase a cyberliability insurance policy to insure against specific risks. For example, the organization could purchase insurance to cover losses because of unauthorized access to IT systems. These types of policies are called technology errors and omissions policies.
- **Risk acceptance**—The organization takes no action against the potential risk. It makes an intentional decision to do nothing. Executive management may choose this strategy if the cost of the risk is less than the cost to avoid, mitigate, or transfer the risk.

### Training Employees

The RM process includes educating employees about risk and how to avoid it. Often employees contribute to an organization's risk by engaging in behavior that puts the organization and its data at risk. Risk can be reduced if employees understand why certain behaviors are not allowed or acceptable. The organization can use policies to help direct employee behavior. Risk is reduced when employees behave according to company policy.

Security awareness training is an important part of any information security program. It is required to keep employees aware of their security responsibilities. An organization must include security education in its day-to-day routine.

### Continuous Monitoring

Organizations must always monitor their information security risk. They also must monitor the controls that they put in place to respond to that risk. This is an ongoing process. Because technology changes quickly, executive management must be diligent reviewing its risk and response to that risk.

Many laws require organizations to continually assess their risk. For example, the Gramm-Leach-Bliley Act (GLBA) Safeguards Rule requires covered financial institutions to conduct RAs to identify risks to customer information as part of their information security program. Covered financial institutions must apply controls to respond to identified risks. They also must assess their current controls to make sure that they are effective. Financial institutions also must review their information security programs on a regular basis.

The Health Insurance Portability and Accountability Act (HIPAA), FISMA, and SOX also require covered organizations to conduct regular risk assessments.

> **NOTE**
>
> Executive management can implement administrative, technical, or physical controls to avoid or mitigate risk.

> **NOTE**
>
> Many U.S. laws require federal agencies and other organizations to engage in regular RA and management activities.

## Three Types of Contingency Planning

One of the most important things about conducting an RA is that it forces an organization to think "What if?" An organization must plan for the risks that it accepts or cannot avoid, mitigate, or transfer. It creates contingency plans to limit the financial loss it might experience because of an adverse event. Contingency plans help to minimize the length of time that services and processes are interrupted. They also help minimize customer impact because of a serious event.

The three main types of contingency plans are:

- Incident response (IR) plans
- Disaster recovery (DR) plans
- Business continuity (BC) plans

An organization creates these plans to respond to events that might negatively affect IT resources and business processes. Keep in mind that this chapter discusses these types of contingency plans from an information security perspective. These plans can have a much larger scope than just IT.

It is also important to remember that the most important goal of any type of contingency plan is to preserve human life. Other goals are secondary.

## Incident Response Planning

An organization uses its **incident response (IR)** process to react to attacks against its IT infrastructure. Having an IR process is important because it helps make sure that an organization can recover from security incidents. Organizations that are able to recover quickly from incidents are more likely to be able to continue business operations. IR is also called incident handling.

> **NOTE**
>
> IR is a reactive term that describes how an organization responds to an incident. Incident handling is a proactive term that describes how an organization manages an incident. Organizations may use both terms interchangeably.

IR describes how an organization:

- Detects information security incidents
- Determines the cause of the incident
- Mitigates the damage caused by the incident
- Recovers from the incident

An **incident** is any event that involves the organization's equipment, data, or other resources. An incident must adversely affect the confidentiality, integrity, and/or availability of the organization's data and IT systems. The intent of the threat source does not matter. An incident includes malicious attacks, as well as the harmful acts of well-meaning employees. Incidents are usually violations of the organization's policies, accepted security practices, or the law.

Organizations encounter several information security threats each day. Each one of these can be an incident if it adversely affects the security of an organization's resources and data. You hear about these incidents in the media nearly every day. For example, in 2015 a student installed keystroke loggers on computers at his university to gather username and password information from university professors. The student then used that information to change his grades in the university's computer system. The university discovered the hack through logging and audit review security measures. In 2018 the student was sentenced to 4 months in prison, 2 years of supervised probation, and ordered to pay restitution to the university for unauthorized access and damage to its computer network.[4]

When the university discovered that records had been improperly modified, it would have declared an information security incident and formed a team to respond to the system intrusion. That team would have been responsible for determining the damage that the incident caused, finding the source of the incident, mitigating the damage caused by the incident, and recovering the computer systems affected by the incident.

The student hacker's conduct was most likely a violation of the university's acceptable use policy (AUP). Many organizations have these policies to define acceptable behaviors for the use of its IT resources. In this case, the student hackers violated policies and also broke the law.

Based upon what we know about this case from publicly available information, we know that the university involved did the following:

- **Detecting the incident**—The university used normal information security practices such as logging and audit review to discover that information in an IT system had been changed.

- **Determining the cause of the incident**—These same measures, and most likely computer forensic analysis, helped the university discover that the cause of the incident was student hackers who had installed a keystroke logger.
- **Mitigating the damage caused by the incident**—The university was able to restore the changed data because it made regular data backups.
- **Recovering from the incident**—The university restored data and, likely, hardened its systems to prevent this type of incident from happening again in the future.

One of the most important parts of IR is documentation. An organization must document every incident that it encounters. That way it can refer to its documentation if it encounters a similar incident in the future.

### *Incident Response Team*

The IR team is responsible for creating the organization's IR policy and plan. This team has a different focus from that of the operational information security employees who will follow the IR plan and respond to incidents. Often the IR team will include many information security team members. Similar to an RA team, the IR planning team must include advisors from several departments across the organization.

The IR team may help draft the initial IR policy and create the plans that define the organization's IR structure. Even though IR is often an information security responsibility, other departments may need to participate in an IR process. The information security team may have to interact with many of these departments when handling an incident.

For instance, the operational team will be involved if there is an incident involving a physical trespasser to the organization's data center. The operational team most likely will involve the organization's physical security personnel in handling the incident because the incident included actual trespass onto the organization's property. IT personnel will be involved to see if any equipment has been stolen, and internal audit and legal counsel will be involved if any equipment or data are stolen. Human resources (HR) personnel could become involved if it appears that the trespasser is a former employee. Marketing and communications personnel could become involved if the facts of the incident trigger the laws that require security breach notification.

The IR team is responsible for making sure that the procedures are in place to help all of these different departments work together. They must be able to respond quickly and efficiently in the event of an incident. The operational information security team needs to know whom they can contact in each department for help. The IR team's planning puts this structure in place.

The IR planning team should include information security and IT representatives. It also should have members from physical security, HR, and internal audit. Legal counsel should be included on the team to address any legal or regulatory issues.

The IR team will help the organization create its IR policy. These policies are very specific to an organization's structure and culture. Similar to all information security policies, the IR policy is a statement of executive management's commitment to the IR process. The policy should state the purpose and goals of IR. It also should define what an incident is. The policy must set forth, at a high level, the organization's operational IR structure. It should define the roles and responsibilities within this structure. The IR policy also can contain information about how to measure the effectiveness of the IR process.

### *IR Plan Process*

Once the organization approves its IR policy, the IR team can continue to define the IR plan. The IR policy contains the overall IR goals, whereas the IR plan contains the procedural elements that are necessary to meet those policy goals. Operational information security teams will follow the IR plan to fulfill their IR job duties. In this section, the term *incident handlers* will be used to refer to the operational teams that respond to an incident.

An IR plan is specific to a particular organization. However, most IR plans have five basic parts. They are:

- Incident triage
- Investigation
- Containment or mitigation
- Recovery
- Review

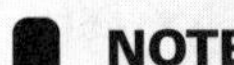 **NOTE**

The word *triage* is most commonly associated with the medical profession. It is the process of sorting and prioritizing patient care based on the severity of a patient's condition.

The triage phase is the first phase in the IR process. In this phase, a potential incident is initially assessed. It is at this point that the primary handler will verify whether an adverse event meets the definition of an incident. The primary handler is the person who is in charge of coordinating an organization's response to an information security incident. This person is often a member of the organization's information security team.

#### The Operational Incident Response Team

An organization often plans and coordinates IR at a high level within an organization. A cross-functional team, called the IR team, puts the IR plan into place. The responsibility for the daily operations of the IR plan often falls to an organization's information security team and other IT personnel.

There are several different roles involved in IR, which are reviewed briefly here. You may find these terms used in resources describing how to plan and implement an IR program:

- **Victim**—The person or resources that are targeted in an incident. The victim is often the organization and its IT resources and data.
- **Attacker**—The person or mechanism that caused the incident.
- **Incident reporter**—The first person or mechanism that reports an incident. The incident reporter does not have to be a person. An automated intrusion detection system (IDS) can be an incident reporter. A person who notices an unusual incident and reports it is also an incident reporter.
- **Primary handler**—The person who is in charge of coordinating the response to a particular incident. This person is responsible for making sure that the IR process is documented. Often this person is a member of the organization's information security department. If an organization does not have a dedicated information security department, this is the person with information security job duties.
- **Secondary handlers**—These are the personnel involved in investigating, responding to, and recovering from an incident. Secondary handlers include technicians, analysts, and operational staff who take part in handling the incident. Legal counsel and an organization's internal auditors also can be secondary handlers. The type of secondary handlers involved in IR depends on the nature of the incident.

Not all events are information security incidents. The event must have an adverse effect on the confidentiality, integrity, and/or availability of an organization's IT resources or data. For example, it might be an incident if an employee mistakenly deletes a critical file needed for processing the organization's weekly payroll because the employee has compromised the availability of needed data. It might not be an information security incident if the employee mistakenly deleted a non-critical file. (Although it certainly would be a business process issue.) The primary handler decides whether a reported event is actually an incident.

If an event is an incident, the primary handler must classify it, which can be done in several ways. They can be sorted based on threat source. An example would be whether the incident occurred because of an internal threat or an external threat. Incidents also can be sorted based upon the type of vulnerability or threat that is exploited.

Organizations may use any method for sorting incidents. For example, some organizations must use guidance prepared by NIST.[5] The U.S. Department of Homeland Security's National Cybersecurity and Communications Integration Center (NCCIC) uses IR categories that are based on NIST guidance. The NCCIC is the federal government's IR center and is sometimes referred to as the United States Computer Emergency Readiness Team (US-CERT). All federal agencies must report information security incidents to the NCCIC/US-CERT. The NCCIC/US-CERT's incident categories are:

- **Category 1:** Unauthorized Access—Unauthorized access is technical or physical access to an IT system without permission. An agency must report these incidents even if data is not compromised.
- **Category 2**: Denial of Service (DoS)—Any event that prevents the normal operation of IT resources such that use of those resources is harmed.
- **Category 3**: Malicious Code—Any event that involves the use of malicious code to successfully infect, breach, or compromise IT resources. These events include viruses, worms, and Trojan horses.
- **Category 4:** Improper Use—Any event that is a violation of the agency's AUP or other related policies.
- **Category 5**: Scans, Probes, and Attempted Access—Any event where an IT resource is scanned or probed in an attempt to access or identify the agency's IT systems.
- **Category 6**: Investigation—This category is for unusual events that do not fall into one of the other categories. These incidents require more review because they are odd or potentially harmful.

The classification of an incident may change as the incident is investigated because the organization learns more about the incident as the investigation progresses. Incidents also should be sorted based upon potential severity. Severity is assessed based upon the perceived level of impact to the confidentiality, integrity, and availability of an organization's IT resources or data. The severity of an incident also may change. Organizations often classify severity on a low-medium-high scale. An organization might classify severity as follows:

- **Low**—The adverse effect on the confidentiality, integrity, or availability of the organization's data or IT resources is limited. A low-impact event causes little or no damage.
- **Medium**—The adverse effect on the confidentiality, integrity, or availability of the organization's data or IT resources is moderate. A medium-impact event results in significant damage to assets.

- **High**—The adverse effect on the confidentiality, integrity, or availability of the organization's data or IT resources is severe. A high-impact event results in major damage to assets.

Classifying the nature and severity of an incident helps incident handlers know which incidents require priority handling. If the incident handlers must respond to multiple incidents, classification promotes efficiency. It also makes sure organizations respond to incidents according to the incident's potential to hurt the organization. Classification also helps incident handlers know which incidents to escalate to management.

Investigation is the second phase in the IR process. During this phase, the incident handlers learn about the incident and its source, as well as the impact that the incident is having on the organization. The incident handlers must find all the resources that are affected by the incident. They also must contact other areas as needed to fully understand the scope of the incident. The IR policy and plan let the incident handlers know who they must contact.

The incident handlers must keep management informed of their IR activities. It is important that management be informed in case there are any regulatory requirements that need to be considered as the organization responds to the incident. For example, if an incident involves the disclosure of the protected health information of more than 500 people, HIPAA requires that the organization notify the Department of Health and Human Services about the disclosure.[6] Executive management, in consultation with legal counsel, must make the final decisions about contacting third parties or the media.

It is also important during the investigation phase for the incident handlers to follow the organization's own internal policies. If handlers are investigating an incident that might be a crime, it is important that the team follow good evidentiary practices. If an incident appears to be a crime, the incident handlers must contact law enforcement according to the terms of the IR plan.

The organization must begin the containment phase almost as soon as an incident is reported. During this step, incident handlers must take steps to limit the damage caused by the incident. They will use different methods to contain an incident depending upon its nature. For example, if the incident is a self-propagating virus, incident handlers may remove an infected system from the organization's network. If the incident is a particularly authentic-looking phishing email, incident handlers might issue an alert or other notification to the organization's employees. The alert would tell the employees not to respond to a phishing email. Incident handlers might use several different tactics to mitigate an incident.

The organization repairs and recovers its IT resources and data during the recovery phase. The IT resources and data should be repaired in such a way that they are not vulnerable to the same type of incident again. This is called hardening. In addition to hardening damaged IT resources, the organization must harden resources that are similar to the damaged resources. This makes sure that similar resources are not harmed by similar incidents.

After an IT resource is repaired, it should be tested for any additional vulnerabilities or weaknesses before it is put back into production. The recovery and repair method will depend upon the nature of the incident.

All stages in the IR process must be fully documented. The primary incident handler is responsible for making sure that each step in the process has been fully documented. This is important because the IR planning team can review the notes from the incident handlers to determine whether the IR plan worked as intended. The IR planning team will want to know which part of the plan worked well, and which parts need to be improved for the future. During the review stage, both the incident handlers and the IR planning team can review the documentation to learn:

> **NOTE**
> As a general information security best practice, a repaired IT resource should not be tested by the same person that repairs or recovers it. This is a separation of duties best practice to make sure that vulnerabilities and weaknesses are not overlooked.

- Dollar amount spent in handling the incident
- Dollar amount spent to prevent similar incidents in the future
- Loss of staff time in handling the incident
- How the response to the current incident compares with similar incidents in the past
- Recommendations on policy and procedural changes because of lessons learned from the incident

The review phase is often overlooked because it is easy for an organization's employees to go back to their normal operational duties after an incident. The IR planning team must make sure that the review process is formally required by policy.

The IR process is shown in **FIGURE 14-2**. As described in this section, many of the stages overlap with one another. The lines between each stage can be indistinct at times.

## Disaster Recovery and Business Continuity Planning

DR and BC plans help an organization respond to a disaster. A **disaster** is a sudden, unplanned event. Disasters negatively affect the organization's critical business functions for an unknown period. The difference between a disaster and an incident is subtle. A disaster severely affects the organization's infrastructure and interrupts critical business functions. An incident tends to refer to service failures that affect the confidentiality, integrity, and/or availability of the organization's data and IT systems. An incident may become a disaster in some situations.

> **NOTE**
> It helps to think of an incident as an event that an organization can deal with during its normal operations. A disaster is an event that completely disrupts those normal operations.

Examples of disasters include natural threats and deliberate, human-made threats. Natural threats are uncontrollable events. They include earthquakes, fires, and flood. Human-made threats include sabotage and terrorist activities. Threats that can evolve into a disaster also include equipment, electrical, and communications infrastructure failure. Disasters are not predictable. Organizations cannot control these types of threats. All they can do is take measures to try to limit the damage caused by these events. Organizations also can make plans to respond to these types of events.



**FIGURE 14-2**
Incident response plan phases.

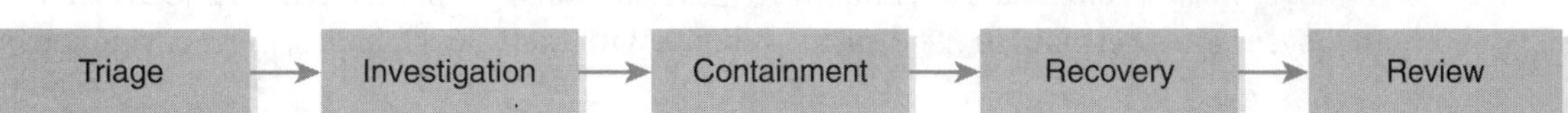

DR plans focus on how an organization recovers its IT systems after a disaster. These plans focus on IT systems only. They are the organization's immediate response to restoring critical IT resources after a devastating disaster or event. DR is largely a function of IT and is part of a larger BC plan.

BC plans focus on how the organization continues its business during and after a disaster. These plans tend to be more comprehensive. They cover all parts of a business, not just IT systems. These plans address the period between the disaster and a return to normal operations.

The formal distinction between DR and BC plans is eroding. This is because organizations rely on IT systems for many of their critical functions. Some organizations build their whole business model on their IT systems. Today, most organizations consider DR and BC to be the same thing. You may find the terms used interchangeably. Most references recognize that a DR plan must be part of a comprehensive BC plan.

In this chapter, DR and BC plans will be discussed together, unless it is necessary to differentiate between the two. If it is necessary to differentiate between the two types of plans, the distinction will be made clear in the text.

### *DR/BC Team*

The DR/BC team is responsible for creating an organization's DR/BC policy and plans. Similar to the RA and IR teams, this team must include members from many areas of the organization. The people who are going to be responsible for carrying out the plan in the event of a disaster also should be included on the team.

A DR/BC plan is an organization-wide plan; however, specific departments may have secondary DR/BC plans. These department-level plans must be consistent with the organization's DR/BC plan. An organization's overall DR/BC plan has several goals:

- Ensure that the organization's employees are safe.
- Minimize the organization's amount of loss.
- Recover critical business systems and infrastructure within a certain period.
- Resume critical business operations within a certain period.
- Repair or replace damaged facilities.
- Return to normal operations.

The DR/BC team will help the organization create its DR/BC policy. These policies are very specific to an organization's structure and culture.

A DR/BC team must include members from IT, HR, executive management, physical security, and legal counsel. It also must include the managers or owners of critical business processes. The team also should include the employees, and their backups, who will be in charge of directing the organization's activities in a real disaster. It is important that backup personnel be included in case the people with primary DR/BC responsibilities are not available in a disaster.

One thing to keep in mind for DR/BC plans is that disasters are not always limited to the organization. A disaster in a geographic region may mean that both the organization and its employees will be affected by it. Employees must personally respond to the same disaster. If employees must respond to the disaster at home with their own families, they may not be in a position to help the organization respond to the disaster as well. An organizational DR/BC plan must acknowledge this risk.

### *DR/BC Plan Development*

Many of the steps in the DR/BC planning process are similar to the RA and IR planning processes. Contingency planning is a part of risk management. The steps in the DR/BC planning process are:

- Develop the DR/BC policy.
- Conduct a business impact analysis.
- Identify threats and potential controls.
- Determine recovery strategy.
- Design and maintain the plan.

The DR/BC team must make sure that policies and plans are in place that help the organization complete these steps. The DR/BC policy is a statement of executive management's commitment to the BC planning that should state the purpose and goals of DR/BC. The policy should define DR/BC roles and responsibilities. The policy should include the organization's resource requirements for any DR/BC plan.

After a DR/BC policy is approved, the DR/BC team must conduct a **business impact analysis (BIA)**. A BIA identifies key business operations. It also identifies the resources that support those operations. The DR/BC team uses a BIA to estimate how long those critical operations and resources can be offline before the organization's entire business is negatively affected.

To complete a BIA, the DR/BC team must:

- Identify critical business processes—The BR/DR team must identify the organization's critical business processes. There is no master list of processes that are critical to all organizations. Each organization is different. Some critical processes might include payroll, attendance scheduling, and customer service activities.
- Identify IT resources that support critical business processes—The BR/DR team must identify the resources that support its critical business processes. Resources can include the organization's communications infrastructure. They also can include individual IT systems and components.
- Determine how long IT resources can be offline—The DR/BC team must identify the effect on business organizations if a resource is disrupted or damaged and a critical process cannot run.
- Determine recovery criticality—The DR/BC team must prioritize how the organization will handle IT resources and business processes following a disaster.

A BIA closely resembles a risk assessment. Many of the same tools and techniques used in an RA are used to complete a BIA. The team can interview employees throughout the organization to learn about its many business processes. The team also could send a questionnaire to a sampling of employees. The questionnaire could ask questions about business processes and resources.

Once the DR/BC team determines the organization's critical processes and resources, it must figure out how long those processes and resources can be offline before the organization experiences irreparable harm. This period is called **maximum tolerable downtime (MTD)**. Some processes and systems are so critical that they can be down only for a few minutes before an organization suffers irreparable damage. If these processes are offline longer than the MTD, the organization might fail. Processes and systems that are not essential to business operations may have an MTD of days or weeks.

The DR/BC team must determine the order in which IT resources will be reviewed and restored following the disaster. It uses the results of the BIA to make this determination. If an organization must resume a business process within a short period, it will need to make sure that it can put people and processes in place to recover the process within that period. The priority list of processes and resources helps executive management make recovery strategy decisions.

**NOTE**

Some resources use the term *maximum acceptable outage (MAO)* in place of MTD. The two terms mean the same thing.

After the BIA is complete, the DR/BC team must identify threats and potential controls. This step is very similar to a risk assessment. In fact, the organization may have completed this exercise as part of an RA. If so, the DR/BC team can use those results at this step. The DR/BC team must identify the threats to the organization that have disaster potential. It also must identify potential controls to respond to those threats. These controls try to reduce the possibility of the organization experiencing a disaster. If a disaster cannot be avoided, these controls may lessen the amount of damage to the organization.

For example, an organization's data center may be located in an area prone to tornadoes. If the organization cannot move its data center, it may try to fortify it. The organization might try to make the data center more resistant to wind-related damage to protect its business processes.

Some common preventative controls that an organization can implement include:

- Fire detection and suppression systems
- Installing backup generators or uninterruptible power supplies
- Offsite storage of system backup media
- Frequent backups of critical data
- Extra equipment inventories for critical IT resources

The DR/BC team also must determine a recovery strategy. It consults with executive management to do this. An organization's recovery strategy addresses the resources that it must recover after a disaster and the order in which those resources must be recovered. An organization will have to consider a wide variety of recovery strategies.

An organization must prepare recovery strategies for its:

- **Critical business processes**—The organization must plan for recovering its business processes. It must understand all the workflow steps needed to complete a business process. It must know the resources and supplies needed to support these processes.
- **Facilities and supplies**—The organization must make sure that it has a plan to restore its main facility. It also must restore the utilities needed to support that facility. Utilities include telecommunications and electrical infrastructure.

## Backup Site Options

It is rare when an organization experiences a disaster that forces it out of its main facility for a long time. However, the organization still must plan for this possibility. It must have a location to which it can move its operations, which is called a *backup site*. An organization has several planning options for a backup site. It is important for you to know the differences between them.

A **mirrored site**, a fully operational backup site, actively runs the organization's IT processes in parallel with the organization's main facility. In this way, a mirrored site is a redundant facility. An organization can immediately transfer all of its IT operations to the mirrored site, which is already staffed with the organization's employees. This is the most expensive type of backup site to maintain. This type of backup site is appropriate for organizations that have a low MTD for critical processes. This type of backup site supports high availability.

A **hot site** is an operational backup site that has all of the equipment and infrastructure that an organization needs to continue its business operations. The equipment in the hot site is fully compatible with the organization's main facility. A hot site can become operational within minutes to hours after a disaster. However, it is not staffed with people, and it does not process data in parallel with the main facility. If needed, the organization must bring data backups to the hot site facility. A hot site, although expensive to maintain, may be the best choice for an organization that can afford some, but not a lot, of downtime.

A **warm site** is a compromise between a hot site and a cold site. A warm site is space that contains some, but not all, of the equipment that an organization will need to continue operations in the event of a disaster. The warm site is partially prepared for operations, in that it has electricity and network connectivity. This type of site is more expensive than a cold site.

A **cold site** is a backup site that is little more than reserved space. It is the most inexpensive type of backup site, as it does not have any equipment or hardware set up. Although it will have electrical service, it most likely will not have network connectivity. It can take weeks for an organization to get a cold site ready for business operations. An organization will have to acquire equipment and infrastructure to make the site operational.



- **Employee environment**—The organization must have plans in place for supporting its employees during a disaster. This means making sure that it has ways to communicate with employees during a disaster. The organization also must have plans in place to manage employee responsibilities until the organization can return to normal operations.
- **IT operations**—The organization must have plans in place to resume its IT operations. This means making sure that infrastructure components are in place so that business can resume. The organization will want to have contracts with its vendors so that it can get replacement equipment quickly.
- **Data recovery**—The organization must have a way to recover its data and operational information, as well as retrieve data from offsite storage facilities. It also must have plans to retrieve paper-based information from its main facility.

A recovery strategy also must include the people that will implement it. A team with specialized skills and knowledge must head each recovery area. For example, the organization's storage administrators should serve on the team in charge of data recovery. Each team must have a leader.

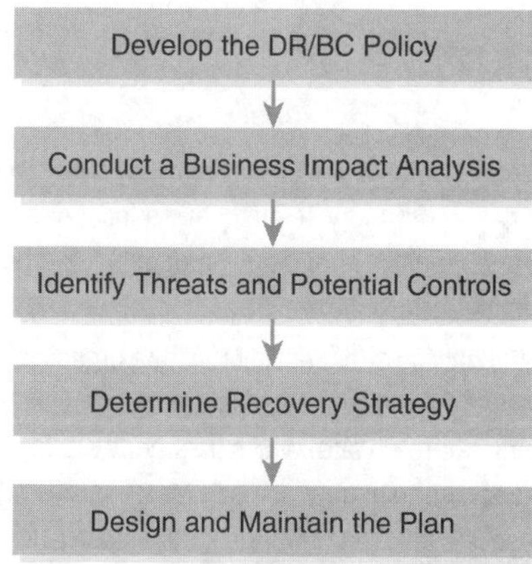


**FIGURE 14-3**
DR/BC planning process.

Once an organization develops its DR/BC plan, it must monitor and update it in response to changing conditions. An organization must update its plan anytime its business processes or technology change. It must update the plan any time key personnel change. Organizations put contingency plans in place so that they can respond to events that adversely affect them. It is not enough to create a plan and put it away on a shelf for use "just in case."

A DR/BC plan helps an organization respond to a disaster. These plans are an important part of an organization's risk management activities. The DR/BC planning process is shown in **FIGURE 14-3**.

## Testing the Plan

Organizations must test their contingency plans on a regular basis to make sure that the plan accounts for all critical business functions and processes. It also should test its contingency plans to make sure that the plans do not have any deficiencies. An organization must correct plan deficiencies.

Contingency plan testing has several objectives. They include:

- Help employees become familiar with and accept the DR/BC plan.
- Train employees how to respond during an emergency.
- Identify weaknesses or deficiencies within the plan.
- Make sure that all of the checklists and procedures needed to implement the plan are created and in place.
- Make sure that all the resources and supplies needed to implement the plan are in place and are operational.
- Make sure that all communications mechanisms work properly.
- Make sure that all DR/BC teams are able to work well together.

**NOTE**

In the DR/BC plan context, a single point of failure is a step in the plan or an assumption within the plan that is critical to the performance of the entire plan. If that step or the assumption fails, then a critical portion of the plan, or the entire plan, could fail. Identifying single points of failure is a critical part of testing contingency plans.

Through testing, an organization can learn that it is missing key business process areas. It also can identify single points of failure within the plan and take steps to correct them. Any changes that are made to the DR/BC plan as part of the test review must be fully documented. Changes to the plan also must be communicated to all members of the organization.

There are five ways to test DR/BC plans. These tests also could be used to test an organization's IR capability.

A **checklist test** is one of the most basic types of DR/BC tests. In this type of test, the DR/BC team makes sure that supplies and inventory items that are needed to execute the DR/BC plan are in place. This type of test makes sure that sufficient supplies are stored at backup facilities. It also makes sure that the organization has enough reference copies of the DR/BC plan and that all copies have current information.

A **walk-through test** is often used with a checklist test. In this type of test, the DR/BC team "walks through" the entire DR/BC plan. They study each area of the plan to make sure that all of the assumptions and tasks stated in it are correct. This type of test also helps the people who are responsible for executing the DR/BC plan become very familiar with it. This type of test is sometimes called a *tabletop walk-through test* or *tabletop test* because the members of the team will sit around a table as they study the plan.

A **simulation test** is a more realistic version of a walk-through test. In this type of test, the organization role-plays a disaster scenario. The scope of these types of tests has to be carefully defined so that they do not negatively affect normal business activities. This test is designed to measure the effectiveness of employee notification procedures. Depending upon the scope of the test, an organization might try to measure how fast it can set up its backup site. It also could measure how fast its vendors can provide additional equipment.

**FYI**

Organizations with critical business functions that affect many customers tend to be serious about DR/BC planning and testing. AT&T has a Network Disaster Recovery Team, whichis responsible for restoring voice and data network communications to an area that is affected by a disaster. The team conducts four DR exercises each year. It was deployed in 2017 to respond to wildfires in California. You can read about the team's efforts at https://www.business.att.com/solutions/family/network-services/network-disaster-recovery.html.



A **parallel test** is designed to test the organization's IT recovery processes. In this type of test, the organization tests its ability to recover its IT systems and its business data. The organization brings its backup sites online. It will then use historical business data to test how those systems operate. In this test, the organization tests both data processing and data recovery. During the test, the organization continues normal business operations at its main facility. The test is conducted using historical data.

A **full interruption test** is designed to test the organization's entire DR/BC plan. This test involves a scenario that destroys or severely damages the organization's main facility. The organization must transfer all business and IT functions to its backup site. In this type of test, all normal business operations stop. Operations are shut down at the main site. They must be transferred to the backup site using the processes stated in the DR/BC plan.

A full interruption test is the most expensive kind of contingency plan test. It can help the organization learn a lot about its DR/BC plan's effectiveness. However, it also has the potential to negatively affect the organization's business. If the organization cannot get business operations resumed at the backup site, then the test itself can create a disaster situation for the organization. Organizations undertake these types of tests with great care.

## Special Considerations

Risk management and contingency planning activities make good business sense. They help an organization prepare for threats and events that harm its ability to meet its business goals. Organizations that engage in these activities understand their information security posture and know where they have weaknesses. They also know the threats to the confidentiality, integrity, and availability of their IT resources and data.

### Addressing Compliance Requirements

For many organizations, RM and contingency planning are not just good business practices. Sometimes they are required by law. Many laws require the organizations they cover to complete risk assessments and create contingency plans. **TABLE 14-5** reviews some laws that have these requirements.

**TABLE 14-5** Laws With Risk Assessment and Contingency Plan Requirements

| NAME OF LAW | RISK ASSESSMENT REQUIRED? | DR/BC PLAN REQUIRED? |
|---|---|---|
| Gramm-Leach-Bliley Act<br>Consumer financial information | Yes | Yes |
| Payment Card Industry Standards*<br>Companies that accept credit cards for payment | Yes | Yes |
| Health Insurance Portability and Accountability Act<br>Protected health information | Yes | Yes |
| Sarbanes-Oxley Act<br>Corporate financial information | Yes | Implied if contingency plans are indicated as an internal control required to secure financial reporting processes and systems |
| Federal Information Systems Modernization Act<br>Federal information systems | Yes | Yes |

*The Payment Card Industry (PCI) Standards are not a law. Organizations that wish to accept credit cards for payment of goods and services must follow these standards. Banks that process credit card information enforce PCI compliance.

## When to Call the Police

Children learn the basics of "when to call 9-1-1" at a very early age. Children are taught to call the police or emergency responders when:

- Someone's life is in immediate danger
- When smoke or fire is present
- When emergency medical help is needed
- When a crime is being committed

These are good rules for an organization as well. Organizations should include rules for when to call law enforcement or emergency responders in their contingency plans.

### Must People Report Crime?

Under common law, in general, a person has no duty to report a crime that he or she witnesses. For purposes of the law, an organization is considered a "person." Thus, most organizations also have no obligation to report crimes they witness.

There are some instances where people are required by law to report crimes, however. For instance, in the United States most people are required to report crimes where children or vulnerable adults are in danger. These laws require people to report suspected abuse and neglect to law enforcement.

Some U.S. states have laws that require IT workers to report the discovery of child pornography on computers. They must report the discovery to law enforcement. The IT worker must have discovered the pornography within the scope of his or her employment. An IT worker is not required to search for this type of material. However, if it is discovered, he or she must report it. At the time that this was written, at least 12 states had such laws.[7]

Most organizations should report any criminal activity that involves their IT resources or data. It is important to contact law enforcement right away to start investigating the crime.

Sometimes it is hard to know if a crime is committed. If the organization experiences a data breach, it is likely that a crime upon the organization was committed. Possible crimes include trespass, theft of data, theft of resources, unauthorized access, and similar crimes.

One of the most important reasons to promptly report crimes involving IT resources is so that forensic evidence can be collected. This type of evidence can be used to investigate computer crimes. However, this type of evidence is very volatile and must be preserved properly.

One of the things that organizations must account for in their contingency plans is the fact that communications systems will likely be overloaded in a regional disaster or emergency. It may take time to contact first responders, as well as extra time to receive their assistance. In regional natural disaster situations, people are usually discouraged from calling emergency responders unless a person's life is in immediate danger. This is to keep emergency phone lines, such as 9-1-1 trunk telephone lines, from being overloaded with calls.



## Public Relations

An organization's contingency plans must consider its public relations strategy. **Public relations (PR)** is a marketing field that manages an organization's public image. It includes marketing the organization's products and services, as well as protecting the organization's reputation and image. PR includes responding to crises that threaten that image.

An organization's PR team develops communication strategies. These strategies are used to guide communications with employees, customers, and stakeholders. Coordinating an organization's public message is sometimes difficult under normal business operations. It is even more difficult in an emergency. A PR strategy for emergencies must consider:

- Who is authorized to make comments on the organization's behalf?
- Who is authorized to approve the contents of comments shared with the public?
- How often should information be shared with the public?
- How should information be shared with the public?
- How should information be shared if normal communications methods are unavailable in an emergency?

It is important that an organization have a PR strategy for emergencies. The organization must make sure that information is given to stakeholders in a reliable and organized manner. It also must make sure that reliable information is communicated to employees. An organization's reputation can suffer if it does not share enough information or shares it in a chaotic manner. Its reputation also can be harmed if the organization distributes conflicting information from different sources.

## CHAPTER SUMMARY

This chapter reviewed risk management and contingency planning concepts. The RM process helps an organization understand the risks that it faces each day. It also helps organizations strengthen their security posture in response to threats and vulnerabilities. Many laws require organizations to use RM concepts to create information security programs.

This chapter also reviewed different types of contingency plans. An organization uses contingency plans to limit financial loss because of an adverse event. Contingency plans help minimize the length of time that an organization's services and critical processes are interrupted after an emergency.

## KEY CONCEPTS AND TERMS

Annual rate of occurrence (ARO)
Annualized loss expectancy (ALE)
Business continuity (BC) plans
Business impact analysis (BIA)
Checklist test
Cold site
Conflicts of interest
Disaster
Disaster recovery (DR) plans
Exposure factor
Full interruption test
Hot site
Incident
Incident response (IR)
Maximum tolerable downtime (MTD)
Mirrored site
Parallel test

| | | |
|---|---|---|
| Public relations (PR) | Residual risk | Single loss expectancy (SLE) |
| Qualitative risk analysis | Risk assessment (RA) | Walk-through test |
| Quantitative risk analysis | Risk management (RM) | Warm site |
| Realized risk | Simulation test | |

## CHAPTER 14 ASSESSMENT

1. A parallel test uses current processing data to test IT system operation.

   A. True
   B. False

2. Which item is *not* part of the risk management process?

   A. Risk analysis
   B. Risk response
   C. Continuous monitoring
   D. Training employees
   E. All of these are parts of the risk management process.

3. What does a risk assessment do?

4. Which type of contingency plan test is the least expensive?

   A. Full interruption test
   B. Parallel test
   C. Simulation test
   D. Checklist test
   E. None of these is correct.

5. Which type of risk analysis uses real numbers to calculate risk?

   A. Quantitative
   B. Qualitative
   C. Quasi-quantitative
   D. Quasi-qualitative
   E. None of these is correct.

6. The ______ is the percentage of asset loss that is likely to be caused by an identified threat.

7. How is annualized loss expectancy calculated?

8. What is the main benefit of a qualitative risk assessment?

   A. Measures the money cost of a risk
   B. Scope of the assessment can be easily changed
   C. Easy to administer
   D. All of these are correct.
   E. None of these is correct.

9. Which of the following is a qualitative risk assessment methodology?

   A. OCTAVE
   B. ARO
   C. MTD
   D. BIA
   E. None of these is correct.

10. Which risk response eliminates all risk of harm posted by a threat or vulnerability?

    A. Risk transfer
    B. Risk mitigation
    C. Risk acceptance
    D. Risk avoidance
    E. None of these is correct.

11. Which type of contingency plan reacts to attacks against an organization's IT infrastructure?

    A. BC plan
    B. DR plan
    C. IR plan
    D. BC and DR plans
    E. None of these is correct.

12. A(n) ______ is an event that adversely affects the confidentiality, integrity, and/or availability of an organization's data and IT systems.

13. A(n) ______ is a sudden, unplanned event that negatively affects the organization's critical business functions for an unknown period.

**14.** Which backup site is a fully operational backup site?

A. Mirrored site
B. Hot site
C. Warm site
D. Cold site
E. None of these is correct.

**15.** A business impact analysis identifies key business operations and resources.

A. True
B. False

## ENDNOTES


1. Verizon, "2019 Data Breach Investigation Report," 2019. Available at https://enterprise.verizon.com/resources/reports/dbir/ (accessed February 23, 2020).
2. National Institute of Standards and Technology, "Special Publication 800-39: Managing Information Security Risk: Organization, Mission, and Information System View," March 2011. Available at http://nvlpubs.nist.gov/nistpubs/Legacy/SP/nistspecialpublication800-39.pdf (accessed February 23, 2020).
3. National Oceanic and Atmospheric Administration (NOAA), "Tornado Alley," undated. Available at https://www.ncdc.noaa.gov/climate-information/extreme-events/us-tornado-climatology/tornado-alley (accessed February 23, 2020).
4. U.S. Department of Justice, "Former Student Sentenced for Causing Damage to University of Iowa Computer Network," August 23, 2018. Available at https://www.justice.gov/usao-sdia/pr/former-student-sentenced-causing-damage-university-iowa-computer-network (accessed February 23, 2020).
5. National Institute of Standards and Technology, "Special Publication 800-61 (Rev. 2): Computer Security Incident Handling Guide," August 2012. Available at https://csrc.nist.gov/publications/detail/sp/800-61/rev-2/final (accessed February 23, 2020).
6. Code of Federal Regulations, Title 45, sec. 164.408 (2013).
7. Holt, Thomas J., Adam M. Bossler, and Kathryn C. Seigfried-Spellar, *Cybercrime and Digital Forensics: An Introduction.* New York, NY: Routledge, 2017.

CHAPTER 15

# Computer Forensics and Investigations

COMPUTER FORENSICS IS the scientific process of collecting and examining data stored on, received from, or transmitted by an electronic device. It is a demanding area of study. New technologies that store data are created every day. People who choose to work in this area must constantly study these new technologies. They must learn how to collect and examine data from devices that use the new technology. Computer forensics is also a rapidly expanding profession. The U.S. Department of Labor estimates higher-than-average job growth for people in this career.[1]

This chapter introduces basic concepts about computer forensics. It also discusses the role of the computer forensic examiner. Finally, it reviews legal issues surrounding how digital evidence is gathered and used.

## Chapter 15 Topics

This chapter covers the following topics and concepts:

- What computer forensics is
- What a computer forensic examiner does
- What the general rules for collecting, handling, and using digital evidence are
- What some legal issues regarding the seizure of digital evidence are

## Chapter 15 Goals

When you complete this chapter, you will be able to:

- Define computer forensics
- Explain the role of a computer forensic examiner
- Explain why digital evidence must be carefully handled
- Describe why chain of custody is important
- Explain the laws that affect the collection of digital evidence
- Describe concerns regarding the admissibility of digital evidence

## What Is Computer Forensics?

**Computer forensics** is the scientific process for examining data stored on, received from, or transmitted by electronic devices. The data is examined to find evidence about an event or crime. Law enforcement uses computer forensics to investigate almost any type of crime. Consider the following:

- Illinois state prosecutors used cell phone records and data gathered by computer forensic examiners to convict a defendant of murdering two people. The defendant had used his computer to search "hire a hit man." He had also searched for directions from his home to the victim's home. The case was unique because almost no physical evidence existed to link the defendant to the murders. A judge sentenced him to life in prison.
- A Hong Kong shipping company pleaded guilty to violating U.S. pollution laws and was fined $10 million. A ship operated by the company ran into the San Francisco Bay Bridge and spilled more than 50,000 gallons of fuel into the San Francisco Bay. Computer forensic examiners found that someone on the ship altered its computerized navigation charts after the crash.
- The U.S. Department of Justice charged nine foreign nationals with stealing more than 31 terabytes of data from U.S. colleges and universities, companies, and government agencies. Computer forensic examiners found that the hackers used several different tactics to gain access to the stolen data.

Computer forensics has many different names. It is also called system or digital forensics, computer forensic analysis, computer examination, data recovery, and sometimes inforensics (information forensics). These terms are used interchangeably. This chapter uses the term *computer forensics*.

**NOTE**

The word *forensics* is from the Latin word *forensis*, which means "belonging to the forum." It refers to the types of arguments used in a court or public forum to prove or disprove past theories or arguments.

Computer forensic examiners use specialized software and tools to collect and study data stored on electronic devices. The evidence collected is called **digital evidence** or just electronic evidence. Computer forensics includes all the steps through which this evidence is collected, preserved, analyzed, documented, and presented.[2] The goal of computer forensics is to find evidence that helps investigators analyze an event or incident.

Computer forensic examiners study and collect electronic data for many reasons. They do not just investigate crimes. Other computer forensics uses include:

- **Individuals**—People may hire computer forensic examiners to find evidence to support tort claims. They can find digital evidence about sexual harassment or discrimination. Examiners also can uncover evidence for any type of civil litigation. They also can find evidence to support a criminal defense case.
- **Military**—The military uses computer forensics to gather intelligence information to support its operations. It also uses computer forensics to prepare for and respond to cyberattacks.
- **Organizations**—Organizations use computer forensics the same ways that individuals use it. Computer forensic examiners also can investigate employee wrongdoing. They can

look for embezzlement or theft of intellectual property (IP). They also can look for unauthorized use of information technology (IT) resources and attempts to harm them. An organization's incident response (IR) program can include forensic activities.
- **Colleges and universities**—Many colleges and universities offer programs in computer forensics. Some may have forensic research programs. They also use computer forensics for the institution's own IR activities.
- **Data recovery firms**—Data recovery firms use computer forensics to rescue data for their clients. They also advise clients how to keep data safe from loss.

Most electronic devices hold some type of data. Computer forensics can study any of them. Potential sources of digital evidence include:

- **Computer systems**—This includes laptop and desktop computers, as well as servers. It also includes the hardware and software that the system uses. This category also includes peripheral devices that can be attached to computer systems. These devices enhance the user experience. They may include keyboards, microphones, web cameras, and memory card readers.
- **Storage devices**—This includes internal and external hard drives, as well as removable media such as floppy disks, Zip disks, compact discs (CDs), digital versatile discs (DVDs), thumb flash drives, and memory cards.
- **Mobile devices**—This includes cell phones and smartphones. It also includes tablets, personal digital assistants (PDAs), and pagers. Global positioning system (GPS) devices hold data as well. Digital and video cameras, and audio and video multimedia devices, also fall into this category.
- **Networking equipment**—This includes network hubs, routers, servers, switches, and power supplies. Networking equipment can be wired or wireless.
- **Other potential sources**—Any device with computer capabilities can potentially hold digital evidence. For example, many office devices have data storage ability. This includes copiers and fax machines, answering machines, printers, and scanners. Entertainment devices store data as well. They include digital video recorders (DVRs), digital audio recorders, and video game systems. Surveillance equipment is included in this category. This category includes any device not already mentioned that can store data. Any Internet of Things (IoT) device can also potentially hold digital evidence because these devices collect data via sensors and transmit it via the internet. Fitness trackers, medical devices, environmental sensors, and even industrial equipment all have data that can be used as digital evidence.

People's dependence on electronic devices to live their lives continues to grow. Therefore, computer forensics as a special area of study also grows. Computer forensic examiners are not always experts in collecting data from every possible type of electronic device. They often focus on certain types of devices. In addition, most computer forensic examiners focus their skills in specific areas. The three main areas of computer forensics are:

- Media analysis
- Code analysis
- Network analysis

**Media analysis** focuses on collecting and examining data stored on physical media. This includes computer systems and storage devices. It also includes mobile devices. When people think about computer forensics, they most often think about media analysis. This type of analysis discovers normal and deleted data. It also finds encrypted, hidden, and password-protected data. This chapter focuses mostly on media analysis concepts. These concepts apply to other types of computer forensic analysis as well.

**NOTE**

Most antivirus programs use signatures to help them detect malware on a computer system.

**Code analysis**, also called malware forensics, focuses on reviewing programming code. This area looks for malicious code or signatures from viruses, worms, and Trojans. It looks for the signature of anything that has modified a system without permission. A signature is the executable part of a malicious code. The need for code analysis continues to grow as malware types change. A 2019 report estimated a rise of almost 14 percent in different types of malware during that year.[3]

**Network analysis** focuses on collecting and examining network traffic. An examiner reviews transaction logs and uses real-time monitoring to find evidence. Organizations often use this type of analysis to investigate incidents.

Some computer forensic examiners also might have specialties within these three major categories. For example, some examiners might specialize in email forensics. Email forensics, which includes a combination of media and network analysis, is used to find the sender, recipient, date, time, location information, and contents of email messages. This is a hot area as almost 94 percent of all malware was delivered via email in 2019.[4] As technology advances, it is not unusual to find examiners with very specialized skills. **FIGURE 15-1** shows examples of different computer forensic categories.

**FIGURE 15-1**

Computer forensic categories.

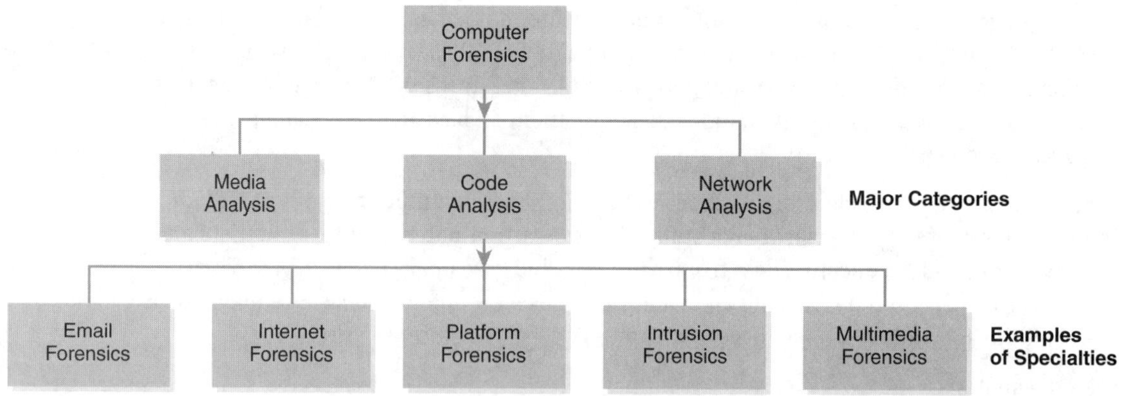

## What Is the Role of a Computer Forensic Examiner?

Computer forensics is a fairly new field. It is only a few decades old, but is growing quickly. In 1984, the U.S. Federal Bureau of Investigation (FBI) began creating software programs to collect computer evidence.[5] In 1990, the International Association of Computer Investigative Specialists (IACIS) was formed. The IACIS, the oldest computer forensic professional group, was the first group dedicated to *computer forensics*.[6]

The first international conference on computer forensics was held in 1993. In 1995, the International Organization on Computer Evidence (IOCE) was formed. Although the IOCE no longer exists, it created some of the earliest guiding principles for computer forensic examiners. In the United States, the Scientific Working Group on Digital Evidence (SWGDE) was created in 1998 to participate in IOCE efforts.[7]

> **NOTE**
> The scientific method is a way to answer questions in a repeatable and verifiable way. It is a formal method of investigation.

Computer forensic examiners find evidence on electronic devices and collect it for both civil and criminal cases. They must collect this evidence in a scientific manner, regardless of the underlying case. They also must have a full understanding of various technologies, hardware, and software. An examiner helps answer who, what, where, when, why, and how.

A computer forensic examiner must have the following traits:

- A sound knowledge of computing technologies
- Use of the scientific method to conduct repeatable and verifiable examinations
- Understanding of the laws of evidence and legal procedure
- Access to computer forensic tools and the skill to use them
- Outstanding record-keeping skills

No matter how careful they are, people always leave traces of their activities when they interact with other people and with their surroundings. This is a basic principle of forensic science known as **Locard's exchange principle**. It applies to both the digital world and the physical world. If people attempt to steal electronic information or delete incriminating files, they leave electronic traces of their activities. For example, log information can document these activities. A computer forensic examiner needs to know how to find this trace evidence material, which is used to help prove a person's actions in a computer system.

Computer forensic examiners do more than turn on a computer and search through files. They must perform complex data recovery procedures. In particular, they must:

- Protect the data on any electronic device.
- Avoid deleting, damaging, or altering data in any way on any electronic device.
- Make exact copies of electronic data without altering the original device.
- Discover normal, deleted, password-protected, hidden, and encrypted files.

> **NOTE**
> Dr. Edmond Locard was a forensics pioneer who lived from 1877 to 1966. He argued that scientific methods should be applied to criminal investigations. He believed that when people or objects interact, they transfer physical evidence to one another. Forensic scientists recover that evidence, then study and learn from it.

- Study data to create timelines of electronic activity.
- Identify files and data that may be relevant to a case.
- Fully document all evidence-collection activities.
- Provide expert testimony on the steps taken to recover digital evidence.

Computer forensic examiners must have special skills beyond those of the traditional information security professional. The law requires that computer forensic examiners be competent at what they do. Examiners can show that they are competent by earning advanced degrees. They also can become certified. Because the profession is still relatively new and evolving rapidly, there are many computer forensic certifications to choose from. Both independent organizations and vendors offer them.

States and courts struggle with how to make sure computer forensic examinations are done only by competent examiners. Courts rely on legal principles and trial rules to screen examiners before they testify. Sometimes states create laws that govern the activities of these examiners. Often, computer forensic examiners are governed under the broad terms of a state's private detective laws.

Many states regulate private detectives and investigators. They require a private detective to have a state-issued license before he or she can conduct investigations. These laws were created before computer forensics existed as a separate field. The broad language of these laws can pull computer forensic examiners within the scope of these regulated professions. This is not unusual.

### Computer Forensic Examiner Certifications

There are many independent and vendor-specific computer forensic credentials. An examiner must weigh which credential best suits his or her career path. The following are popular credentials:

- **Certified Computer Examiner (CCE)**—The International Society of Forensic Computer Examiners (ISFCE) offers the CCE. The ISFCE has offered the CCE, a vendor-neutral certification, since 2003. CCE holders have basic knowledge of forensic examination procedures. You can learn more at http://www.isfce.com/.
- **Certified Computer Forensics Examiner (CCFE)**—The Information Assurance Certification Review Board (IACRB) offers the CCFE, which is also vendor neutral. CCFE candidates must take a written exam and a practical application test. There are nine subject-matter areas in the CCFE exam. You can learn more at http://www.iacertification.org/index.htm.
- **Certified Forensic Computer Examiner (CFCE)**—The IACIS offers the CFCE. However, only law enforcement personnel may earn it. It is vendor neutral. CFCE candidates must pass an intensive practical exam. You can learn more at http://www.iacis.com/.
- **GIAC Certified Forensic Analyst (GCFA)**—The Global Information Assurance Certification (GIAC) program offers the GCFA. Similar to the CCE and CCFE, this certification also tests practical knowledge. It is vendor neutral. GIAC offers several certifications related to digital forensics. You can learn about GIAC at http://www.giac.org/.

Some forensic software vendors offer certifications for their products. For example, EnCase is a popular forensic tool sold by Guidance Software. It offers the EnCase Certified Examiner (EnCE) credential. The EnCE exam has a written section and a practical section. The practical section covers use of the EnCase forensics program. You can learn more at https://www.opentext.com/products-and-solutions/services/training-and-learning-services/encase-training/examiner-certification.

Another software vendor that offers a certification is AccessData. AccessData offers a product called the Forensic Toolkit, but is better known as FTK. AccessData offers the AccessData Certified Examiner (ACE) credential, which tests knowledge of the FTK tool. The ACE exam is a multiple-choice test. You can learn more at https://accessdata.com/training/computer-forensics-certification.

Some states require computer forensic examiners to have a private detective license. Examples include Illinois,[8] Michigan,[9] Oregon,[10] and Texas.[11] In Texas, the law is interpreted very broadly. It actually includes computer technicians and computer repair personnel within the scope of its law.

Some states do not include computer forensic examiners within their private detective licensing laws. North Carolina[12] and Virginia[13] are examples. North Carolina law states that any person who performs computer forensic services in order to collect evidence is not a private investigator. The North Carolina law also excludes examiners who provide expert testimony, as well as any person who engages in network or system vulnerability testing.

In 2008, the American Bar Association (ABA) issued a report and resolution on computer forensic examiners. The ABA asked states to stop requiring computer forensic examiners to get a private detective license. It said that the role of private detectives is different from that of computer forensic examiners. It also stated that courts have broad discretion to make sure that digital evidence used in trials is reliable. Because the courts have that discretion, the ABA argued that there is no need to license computer forensic examiners.[14]

## Collecting, Handling, and Using Digital Evidence

Computer forensic examiners find evidence on electronic devices and use this evidence to help reconstruct past events or activities. They use the evidence to gain a better understanding of a crime or event. It can be used to show possession and use of digital data. This section discusses how computer forensic examiners collect digital evidence. It focuses on how this evidence is collected in a criminal investigation. You need to keep in mind that almost the same process will be used in a civil investigation. An organization's IR process also will be similar.

A computer, or any electronic device, can play one of four roles in computer crime:

- **To commit a crime**—Unauthorized access to data (hacking) and online fraud are two examples where a computer is used to commit a crime.
- **To facilitate a crime**— Cyberstalking, identity theft, phishing scams, and software piracy are examples of crimes facilitated, or aided, by computers.
- **As a target of crime**—Denial of service (DoS) and distributed denial of service (DDoS) attacks, computer viruses, and communications sabotage are examples of crimes where the computer itself is the target of the crime.
- **As a witness to crime**—Computerized record-keeping systems may provide evidence of an underlying crime or event.

**NOTE**

Computer forensic examiners should always collect digital evidence in a reliable (forensically sound) manner. The nature of the underlying investigation does not matter. The examiner should always use a reliable and repeatable process.

If the computer forensic examiner knows how the computer was used, he or she will be able to tailor the examination to that use.

**FYI**

It is important that evidence used in a court case be admissible because a judge or jury can consider only admissible evidence when they decide cases. Evidence that is invalid for some reason is called inadmissible evidence and cannot be presented to a judge or jury. A judge or jury who accidentally hears about that evidence cannot consider it later in deliberations. Admissible evidence is good evidence, whereas inadmissible evidence is bad evidence.

The examiner must gather evidence in a way that makes it admissible in court. Evidence is useful only if it is admissible. To be admissible, evidence must be collected in a lawful way. It also must be collected in a scientific manner. For digital evidence, this means that a computer forensic examiner conducts a repeatable and verifiable examination of an electronic device. The examiner must use established practices and procedures. The examiner also must be able to explain the results of his or her work to a client, judge, or jury in a clear way.

## The Investigative Process

Different law enforcement agencies and organizations may use different investigative processes. The process used can depend on the type of case, as well as the urgency of the case. The process also can depend on the agency or organization that performs the investigation. In general, the investigative process has the following basic steps:

- Identification
- Preservation
- Collection
- Examination
- Presentation

This basic process is used by both law enforcement agencies and other organizations to identify, collect, and preserve digital evidence.

### *Identification*

During the identification step, the computer forensic examiner learns about the crime, event, or activity that is being investigated. He or she must identify the types of electronic devices that may be involved and prepare to conduct the investigation. The examiner must make sure that he or she has all the tools needed to conduct the investigation. A computer forensic examiner's approach to a case may depend heavily on its facts and circumstances.

### *Preservation*

During the preservation step, computer forensic examiners must secure the crime scene and any electronic devices. This means that they must make sure that no one tampers with the scene or electronic devices. This is to make sure that suspects and witnesses do not have a chance to access, destroy, or modify digital evidence. Examiners also must make sure that no one can access electronic devices remotely once they are seized. All of these actions make

### Chain of Custody

The **chain of custody** is an important evidentiary concept. Courts and attorneys use a chain of custody document to help prove that evidence is admissible. This document shows who obtained evidence, where and when it was obtained, who secured it, and who had control or possession of it. It is used to prove that evidence is reliable. Evidence is reliable when it is not destroyed, changed, or altered. It cannot be modified after it is originally collected. A court may find that evidence is not admissible in court if its chain of custody is poorly documented or incomplete. A chain of custody protects the integrity of evidence.

A chain of custody documents how evidence is collected, used, and handled throughout the lifetime of a particular case. It is a journal that records every interaction that a person or object has with the evidence.

sure that potential digital evidence cannot be altered. This step is very important because once digital evidence is altered, it is difficult, if not impossible, to reverse the results.

In some instances, the examiner may not be able to take electronic devices away from the crime scene. In these instances, they must collect data on-site, which requires additional expertise. This might happen in cases where evidence is located on an organization's business computers. It also might be the case if the computers belong to a witness and not to a criminal suspect. Sometimes the examiners may not be able to seize electronic devices if there is a concern that the devices are being used as part of a larger ongoing criminal activity that is being investigated.

Computer forensic examiners also should learn about the operation of the electronic devices they will be examining. They will want to gather information from people at the scene to learn how the devices are used. They should try to learn logon names and passwords for access to the devices. They also should try to discover the type of internet access used by each electronic device and programs used on each device. It is also important for examiners to know whether devices are encrypted, or whether they are equipped with software that could destroy evidence.

This step also includes documenting the crime scene. Examiners must record the location of all electronic devices. They also should note whether the device is on or off. They should record the condition of all devices. Examiners also should record the content of any display screens before electronic devices are moved. The crime scene can be documented using video, photos, and written notes. The documentation created at this step is important for creating a chain of custody.

### *Collection*

The collection step also is known as the "bag and tag" step. During this step, computer forensic examiners must collect the electronic devices. These devices require special

**FYI**

Slack space is the space between the end of a data file and the end of the disk space that is allocated to store it. Data does not always fill the whole space that is allocated to it. Residual information can be left over when a smaller file is written into space that used to be occupied by a larger file. This leftover data may be located in the slack space. Computer forensic examiners look at the slack space because it might contain meaningful data.

### Can a Person Be Compelled to Provide His or Her Encryption Key or Password?

Many information security professionals advise their clients to use passwords, passcodes, biometric features, or other "locks" on their electronic devices to help keep the client's personal information safe. Often times these passwords are used to encrypt and decrypt computing devices as well.

In cases where electronic devices are seized for evidence, these locks and encryption keys can be a problem for a computer forensic examiner. Can the government compel a data owner to provide a password, passcode, or encryption key for an electronic device? Does requiring a suspect to provide this information violate the person's Fifth Amendment self-incrimination protections?

The U.S. Supreme Court has held that the Fifth Amendment protects communications that are compelled, testimonial, and incriminating in nature.[15] For instance, a defendant can potentially incriminate himself or herself if compelled to disclose information—such as a password or passcode—needed to access an electronic device. Under this established case law, a defendant usually does not have to share the contents of his or her mind.

The heart of the issue is whether providing a password, passcode, biometric identifier, encryption key, or some other unlocking mechanism is testimonial. Case law in this area continues to develop rapidly and there is a lot of uncertainty among the courts. At the time that this text was written, general rules of thumb that can be gleaned from case law include:

- Passwords, passcodes, and other electronic device locking mechanisms that are stored in a person's mind are more likely to receive protection under the Fifth Amendment. Compelling a person to share this information is testimonial—it forces the person to share a fact that could be used against him or her.
- Passwords, passcodes, and other electronic device locking mechanisms that are based on biometric identifiers (e.g., biometric device locking mechanisms) are less likely to receive protection under the Fifth Amendment. Compelling the production of this type of information is not testimonial because the information is something that a person is. The Fifth Amendment does not protect a person against the collection of physical features or acts. A person can be compelled to provide a blood sample, stand in a line-up, or provide a handwriting sample because these actions are not testimonial. Many courts have held that compelling a person to open his or her electronic device protected with a biometric device locking mechanism (e.g., fingerprint or facial identification) is not unconstitutional.

These general rules highlight a tension between protections afforded by the law, protections afforded by technology, and user convenience. Although biometric device locking mechanisms provide tremendous convenience for the user, the data stored on devices protected in this way may not be afforded legal protection from government searches. Some smartphone manufacturers are trying to merge the best of both worlds by creating features to quickly disable biometric device locking mechanisms in situations where the device owner might be worried that a law enforcement officer will try to force the owner to unlock his or her device. Some people refer to these disabling features as "the cop button." When these features are used, all biometric device locking mechanism features are disabled and the smartphone reverts to requiring a password or passcode to unlock the device. Under current law, to best protect the contents of electronic devices from exposure in criminal legal proceedings, the devices should be protected by the longest password or passcode that the device allows.

This same analysis and the general rules shared in this section will likely be applied to passwords, passcodes, and biometric device locking mechanisms for internet-enhanced applications and services. Device users must weigh the risk of incriminating data exposure with convenience. Although it may be convenient to protect a password manager application on a smartphone with fingerprint or facial identification, such applications may contain hundreds of passwords. Where possible, those types of applications should always be protected with a strong password or passcode (that is different from the device password or passcode).

This particular topic of the law continues to evolve. You can expect judges to continue to define the scope of the Fifth Amendment in these situations. Because this is an area of federal constitutional law, the U.S. Supreme Court has the power to make a decision on the issue.

collection, packaging, and transportation in order to preserve potential evidence. Examiners will collect electronic devices in different ways depending upon the device and its power status. They will follow different rules for devices that are on and devices that are off.

For example, in most instances, a cell phone must be kept powered on in order to preserve data stored on the device. However, it must be protected from any incoming calls or text messages that could change the data on it. The cell phone must be packaged and transported in a special evidence bag once it is collected. These special evidence bags, called Faraday bags, keep a cell phone shielded from incoming calls or from connecting to wireless networks. This is so that data stored on it cannot be changed by an incoming call or wireless network connection. A computer forensic examiner also must make sure that the collected cell phone has an additional power supply to maintain evidence that could be lost if its battery runs out.

During this step, examiners must be aware of other kinds of evidence that could be on electronic devices. For example, a keyboard or mouse could contain fingerprints or other physical evidence related to the case. Computer forensic examiners must work with other forensic technicians to make sure that this type of physical evidence is not destroyed.

As a practical matter, examiners must document how all electronic devices are configured. The cables and peripheral devices that are hooked up to each computer will need to be tagged. Examiners also must collect any manuals or other materials about the electronic devices that are located near the crime scene.

### *Examination*

During the examination step, computer forensic examiners will want to make duplicate images of any electronic storage media. This is called *imaging*. One thing to remember is that a **forensic duplicate image** is not the same as a file copy or system backup copy. This type of image is an exact copy of the storage media. It includes deleted files, slack space, and areas of the storage media that a normal file copy would not include. A forensic duplicate image is a bit-by-bit copy of the original storage media.

Computer forensic examiners use special tools called *write blockers* to create forensic duplicate images. These tools keep examiners from altering the original storage media. Write blockers can be either hardware- or software-based. They work similar to a one-way flow valve in plumbing in that they only allow data to move in one direction. Most examiners will make two or more duplicate images of the original storage media. One copy is a working copy that they will use to look for evidence. The other is a control copy that can be used if something goes wrong with the first copy.

A forensic duplicate image must be verified against the original storage media. This makes sure that the duplicate image is identical to the original and that nothing has changed on the original media or the image. Examiners verify the images using a cryptographic equation called an *algorithm*. They will apply the algorithm to the original media to create a *hash*, the value that is the result of the cryptographic equation on the image. The examiner will apply the same algorithm to the duplicate image to create another hash.

The examiner can prove that the duplicate image accurately represents the original media if the hashes are the same. If the hashes are different, the images are not the same. Different hashes mean that the imaging process was faulty or some sort of change took place between the original media and the duplicate image. Hashes are used to measure the integrity of the original media and the forensic duplicate. If the hashes do not match, then the data has changed somehow.

**NOTE**

The output of a hashing algorithm is sometimes called a *checksum*.

Computer forensic examiners need to know how to collect two very different types of data. **Persistent data** is stored on a hard drive or other storage media and is preserved when an electronic device is turned off. **Volatile data**, in contrast, is stored in memory and exists in registries, the cache, and random access memory (RAM), as well as the connections that one electronic device might have with another while both devices are powered on. Volatile data is lost when an electronic device is turned off, so examiners must know when this data must be collected and how to do it.

Computer forensic examiners search for relevant information on the duplicate image. They have checklists of items that they review and look for. In general, they might look at:

- File access history (when were files created, edited, and last accessed)
- File download history
- Internet browsing history
- Attempts to delete or conceal files or other data
- Email communications
- Instant message or internet chat logs
- Image files
- Files containing address books or other contact information
- Documents containing financial or medical information

Examiners produce a report of files or data that might be relevant to the investigation. They must use examination procedures that are auditable. That means that an independent party can verify and repeat all of the same steps and receive the same results.

### *Presentation*

Computer forensic examiners must be able to report on their findings and describe how they gathered digital evidence. They often have to explain how they collected this evidence if a case goes to trial. Examiners are usually considered expert witnesses when they testify in a court case. Expert witness testimony is governed by the Federal Rules of Evidence.[16] Expert witnesses must show that their activities followed a scientific methodology. A court assesses this process to make sure that evidence offered at trial is reliable.

The test for measuring the reliability of a scientific methodology is called the Daubert test. It was first discussed in a U.S. Supreme Court case called *Daubert v. Merrell Dow*

**The American Academy of Forensic Sciences**

The American Academy of Forensic Sciences (AAFS) recognizes computer forensics as a scientific discipline. The AAFS, one of the most well-known professional organizations for forensic scientists, has members from many different forensic disciplines. Its goals are to promote integrity and advance cooperation in the forensic sciences.

The AAFS has different sections for different areas. For example, it created a digital and multimedia sciences section in February 2008. The digital and multimedia sciences section was the first new AAFS section in 28 years. Members must show active participation in computer forensic activities. All AAFS members have ethical rules that they must follow.

You can learn more about the AAFS at http://www.aafs.org.

*Pharmaceuticals.*[17] This test is important to computer forensics. It comes into play because of the tools that examiners use to collect digital evidence. An expert witness is a person; therefore, the software tools used by examiners cannot be expert witnesses. Thus, examiners must testify on behalf of the tools.

The use of a tool must satisfy the Daubert test to show that the digital evidence gathered by the tool is reliable. The Daubert test asks the following questions to determine reliability:

- Has the tool been tested?
- Is there a known error rate for the tool?
- Has the tool been peer reviewed?
- Is the tool accepted in the relevant scientific community?

The examiner will testify about how the tool works. The examiner also will testify about his or her qualifications as a computer forensic examiner. Finally, the examiner will testify about the process the examiner used to collect the digital evidence. The court will use the Daubert test to decide whether to admit the evidence collected by the examiner.

## Ethical Principles for Forensic Examination

Computer forensic examiners all follow some common principles. The IOCE created one of the first sets of ethical principles for computer forensics examiners in 1999. The IOCE principles included:

- Examiners should not change digital evidence after they seize it.
- If original digital evidence must be accessed, the person accessing it must be competent.
- All digital evidence handling must be fully documented and available for review.
- Each person who handles digital evidence is responsible for it while it is in his or her possession.
- Any agency that handles digital evidence must comply with these principles.[18]

These basic principles are followed in different forms by other organizations. For example, the CCE credential requires CCE holders to follow a code of ethics. That code of ethics has terms that are similar to the principles stated originally by the IOCE. You can read the code of ethics at https://www.isfce.com/ethics2.htm.

## Legal Issues Involving Digital Evidence

There are special rules for collecting and handling digital evidence. However, the process for obtaining the electronic devices and the evidence on them in the first place must follow established legal principles. The law asks two basic questions about evidence:

- Did the person or organization that collected the evidence have the legal authority to do so?
- Is the evidence admissible in court?

Legal principles and statutes are used to address the first question. These laws focus on the situations where a private entity or the government can collect information about a person.

Court rules and case law are used to address the second question. Both the federal government and state governments have trial court rules for civil and criminal proceedings. In addition to these rules, federal and state courts have evidentiary rules that govern how parties introduce evidence at trials. This chapter uses the Federal Rules of Evidence (FRE) to illustrate admissibility requirements. Many states have their own evidence rules that are based on the FRE.

One thing to keep in mind as you review this section is that there are differences between how law enforcement and private entities conduct investigations. Law enforcement agencies have very specific rules that they must follow when they collect evidence because a law enforcement agency is acting on behalf of a government. They are agents of either the federal or a state government. In the United States, a government cannot take some actions against its citizens without proper authority. This is part of our "checks and balances" system of government. For example, unless special circumstances exist, law enforcement must get permission from a court to monitor a person's telephone conversations.

The rules are different for private entities. Private entities are individuals and organizations that are not related to a governmental agency. As long as a private entity is acting within the rule of law, it may take certain actions to protect its own interests. This is why an employer may monitor an employee's telephone conversations when the employee is using the employer's telephone equipment. A private entity generally has the right under the law to monitor and collect data about its own IT resources in order to protect them.

### Authority to Collect Evidence

There are many laws that define and limit the government's ability to monitor and collect data about individuals. The basic protections afforded to U.S. citizens stem from the Constitution. The Fourth Amendment protects citizens from an intrusive government.

Other laws further define how the government can collect and monitor data. These laws affect the activities of computer forensic examiners. The Electronic Communications Privacy Act,[20] the Wiretap Act,[21] and the Pen Register and Trap and Trace Statute[22] are discussed in this section.

#### *The Fourth Amendment and Search Warrants*

The Fourth Amendment protects people from unreasonable government search and seizure. A *search* happens when a person's reasonable expectation of privacy in a place or thing is

### The Silver Platter Doctrine

The difference between the government's ability to collect evidence of a crime and a private entity's ability to collect evidence about that same activity is an interesting area of study. It is also a complicated area of study. The resolution of many court cases depends on these differences. Sometimes laws create special rules for law enforcement and private entities.

For example, the Electronic Communications Privacy Act (ECPA)[19] sets out the rules for access, use, disclosure, and interception of stored electronic communications. Electronic communications include telephone, cell phones, computers, email, faxes, and texting. Under the ECPA, no one may access the contents of these communications unless it is allowed somewhere else in the ECPA. The law has different rules for the government and for private entities.

The ECPA has strict rules for the government. For example, the government cannot access any stored electronic communications without a search warrant. To get a search warrant, the government must prove to a court that it has probable cause to believe that criminal activity is taking place. The stored communications must hold evidence of the criminal activity. If the government cannot prove probable cause, then it cannot access these communications.

The ECPA has different rules for private entities. Private entities may access stored communications within their ordinary course of business. To use this exception, the private entity must have a legitimate business interest for accessing these communications. They also must show that the access occurred on equipment provided by a communications service provider. The ECPA also allows private entities to access employee communications if the employee gives consent. The private entity must be able to prove that it provided notice of access to its employees and that the employees consented to it. Most courts interpret these exceptions very narrowly.

Sometimes private entities find evidence of criminal activity. The ECPA allows most types of private entities to lawfully disclose this evidence to law enforcement agencies. This evidence often is very useful to a criminal investigation. Sometimes a prosecutor will want to use this evidence at a criminal trial. The evidence rule known as the *silver platter doctrine* applies in these cases. This rule is called the silver platter doctrine because the private entity gives admissible evidence to law enforcement "on a silver platter." Law enforcement did not need a search warrant to access the evidence because it did not collect it or direct its collection.

The silver platter doctrine allows the admission of evidence lawfully collected by a private entity. However, the evidence collected by the private entity must be collected and documented properly. To take advantage of the silver platter doctrine, the government must show that the private entity is not affiliated with law enforcement or a government (state or federal). The private entity must not be collecting the evidence under the direction of law enforcement or a government. The private entity also cannot be an internet service provider (ISP). There are special rules under the ECPA for ISPs.

compromised. A *seizure* happens when the government interferes with a person's property. Interference includes taking the property or using it in such a way that the person who owns it cannot use it.

The Fourth Amendment states that the government may not search or seize areas and things in which a person has a reasonable expectation of privacy. If a person has a reasonable expectation of privacy in a place or item, then the government must get a search warrant before searching it or taking it. Under the Fourth Amendment, the "government" includes law enforcement. This section uses the terms *government* and *law enforcement* interchangeably.

Several court cases have held that people have a reasonable expectation of privacy in their personal computers and mobile devices. The U.S. Court of Appeals for the Ninth Circuit has found that a person has a reasonable expectation of privacy in a personal computer. That case is called *United States v. Heckenkamp.*[23] Other courts have held that people have a reasonable expectation of privacy in data stored on personal pagers.[24] The U.S. Supreme Court has held that a warrant is required before searching a cell phone, even when the cell phone is seized when its owner is arrested.[25] It has also held that a person has a reasonable expectation of privacy in the location information collected by his or her smartphone and stored by his or her cell phone service provider.[26] To search any of these devices, law enforcement must get a search warrant.

**NOTE**

A search warrant is a court order. A judge issues a search warrant after the government proves that it has probable cause to believe that criminal activity is taking place. Probable cause is a burden of proof.

**FYI**

The Fourth Amendment applies to federal government actions only. However, most state governments have state constitutional protections that are similar to the Fourth Amendment. The Fourth Amendment does not apply to private individuals or entities that conduct searches or seizures. The private individual or entity must act alone and without government direction. The Fourth Amendment may apply when a private individual or entity follows government directions in conducting a search.

To get a search warrant, law enforcement must clearly specify the criminal activity that is being investigated. It must describe where the search will take place and also list the items that will be searched. Finally, law enforcement must state the evidence that they expect to find. They also must state how that evidence relates to the criminal activity that is being investigated.

If law enforcement conducts a search without a valid warrant, then any evidence that it finds is not admissible in court. This means that a judge will not allow the government to use that evidence to prove its case. Although the rule is strict, there are some limited exceptions. Court-recognized exceptions to the Fourth Amendment's search warrant requirements include:

- **Consent**—Law enforcement can search places and items if the person in control of them freely consents to the search. For example, a person can allow law enforcement to search his or her home, car, or computer. A person's consent must be free and voluntary. If law enforcement finds evidence of criminal activity during a voluntary search, it is admissible in court. Cases reviewing this exception often focus on whether a person's consent really was free and voluntary.
- **Plain view doctrine**—Law enforcement does not need a warrant to search and seize evidence that is in an officer's "plain view." The officer must be able to see the evidence from a place where the officer has a right to be. This exception is often used to seize drugs or other contraband. For example, a police officer can seize drug paraphernalia that he or she sees in a car if the officer can plainly see the items in the car's back seat while standing on a public street.

- **Exigent circumstances**—Law enforcement is allowed to make a warrantless search and seizure in emergency circumstances. This exception applies if public safety would be harmed or evidence would be destroyed if law enforcement took the time to go to court to get a warrant. This exception also is called the "emergency" exception. Law enforcement often seizes drugs and weapons using this exception. Court cases reviewing this exception focus on whether a true emergency existed at the time the search or seizure took place.
- **Search incident to a lawful arrest**—Law enforcement does not need a warrant to search for weapons or contraband on the body of an arrested person. In some cases, law enforcement may make a brief visual inspection of the area where a person is arrested to make sure that no accomplices are hiding nearby. Law enforcement officers are allowed to make these warrantless searches in order to protect their own safety. They also can use this exception to make sure that critical evidence is not destroyed during the arrest process. Courts strictly construe this exception to make sure that it is not abused. This exception is also called the *protective sweep* exception.
- **Inventory search**—Law enforcement may conduct inventory searches without a warrant when they arrest a suspect. These searches are allowed when they are made for a non-investigative purpose. For example, if a suspect has a laptop computer when he or she is arrested, law enforcement may seize the computer for safekeeping while the suspect is in custody. This helps protect law enforcement from claims that they lost or stole a suspect's property. For the exception to apply, the law enforcement agency must have standard policies and procedures for conducting inventory searches. They also must document the search. Court cases reviewing this exception focus on whether law enforcement was following a documented policy for inventory searches. They review whether the inventory search was a ploy to hide a more thorough search for evidence.

One important thing to keep in mind is that the Fourth Amendment search warrant exceptions allow for the seizure of the media containing the digital evidence. Law enforcement can seize the physical media only. If they want to conduct a forensic examination of that media, they must get a warrant to do so. Therefore, the search warrant must authorize the forensic examination. Unless emergency circumstances exist, the secondary search warrant ensures that any digital evidence collected from the media will be admissible in court. Computer forensic examiners must make sure there is a valid search warrant for any electronic devices that they collect. They also must make sure that the warrant allows them to search the data on the device.

### *Federal Laws Regarding Electronic Data Collection*

Three main federal laws govern the collection of electronic communications data. These laws cover many different communications, including email, radio and electronic communications, data transmissions, and telephone calls. Computer forensic examiners often study these communications when they investigate cases or events. An examiner must make sure that his or her actions follow the law.

These laws forbid the use of eavesdropping technologies. This means that the government, individuals, and private entities cannot use certain technologies to snoop on electronic communications. The only time use of these technologies is allowed is when the law says it is allowed. Usually this is when the law allows an exception or if an entity has a court order. The three laws are:

- The Electronic Communications Privacy Act
- The Wiretap Act
- The Pen Register and Trap and Trace Statute

**NOTE**

Keep in mind that states also might have laws governing the collection of electronic communications evidence. You must always review both federal and state laws when considering a legal issue.

**The Electronic Communications Privacy Act.** The ECPA, first passed in 1986, governs the use, disclosure, and interception of stored electronic communications. Congress has amended it several times. The ECPA governs access to the contents of stored communications, as well as access to transmission data about the communications. Transmission data includes header and log data. The ECPA does not apply to real-time collection of electronic communications.

The ECPA is a complicated statute. Under the ECPA, no one may access the contents of these communications unless it is allowed somewhere else in the ECPA. There are different rules for the government and for private entities. For example, the government cannot access any stored electronic communications without a search warrant. If it accesses them without a warrant, any evidence that it discovers will not be admissible. There are several exceptions to the ECPA for private entities. Some of these exceptions were part of the Uniting and Strengthening America by Providing Appropriate Tools Required to Intercept and Obstruct Terrorism Act (U.S.A. PATRIOT Act).[27] Congress passed the PATRIOT Act, which modified parts of the ECPA, in 2001. Under the ECPA, a private entity may voluntarily disclose the contents of stored communications to law enforcement. Law enforcement does not need a search warrant if the private entity discloses the information voluntarily. (This is the application of the silver platter doctrine.) As long as the evidence was collected and documented properly, it will likely be admissible.

Private entity voluntary disclosure is permitted under the ECPA as long as the private entity is not an ISP. If it is an ISP, then additional conditions must be met. These conditions prevent ISPs from having to monitor all communications across their networks. They also prevent ISPs from snooping on their subscribers and help ISPs maintain their safe harbor protections under U.S. IP laws.

If an ISP wishes to disclose the contents of a communication to law enforcement, the disclosure must fall under a permitted ECPA exception. If the disclosure does not fall under one, then it may not be admissible in court. The permitted exceptions that allow disclosure are:

- The disclosure is made with the consent of the sender or receiver of the communication.
- The disclosure is related to the ISP's services or is made to protect the ISP's rights.
- The ISP inadvertently received the contents of the communication and the contents appear to be related to criminal activity.
- The ISP reasonably believes that disclosure is required to prevent an emergency involving immediate danger of death or serious bodily injury.
- U.S. child protection laws require the disclosure.
- The disclosure is made in response to a court order.[28]

**The Wiretap Act.** The ECPA applies to access to and disclosure of stored communications only. The federal Wiretap Act governs real-time interception of the contents of an electronic communication. The Act does not apply to transmission information, but does apply to anyone who intentionally intercepts or tries to intercept any wire, oral, or electronic communication. The Act forbids the real-time interception of these communications. Communications covered by the Act include email, radio communications, data transmissions, and telephone calls.

**NOTE**

The Wiretap Act also is known as "Title III." This is because it was first passed as Title III of the Omnibus Crime Control and Safe Streets Act of 1968.

Under the Wiretap Act, no one is allowed to install wiretaps on telephones to intercept telephonic communications. The Act also forbids using network sniffers to intercept internet traffic or other computer-based communications. There are exceptions to the Wiretap Act, however. For example, law enforcement can install telephone wiretaps or network sniffers if it has a court order (warrant) to do so.

There are three main exceptions to the federal Wiretap Act for private entities. Private entities can use these exceptions to monitor content on their own communications systems. These exceptions are:

- The Consent Exception
- The Provider Exception
- The Trespasser Exception

A private entity may monitor content on its own communications systems when one of the parties to the communication consents to the monitoring. This is the consent exception. One way that entities gather consent is by using network banners. A **network banner** is a warning banner that provides notice of legal rights to the users of computer networks. These banners are displayed when a computer user logs on to a network or visits an entity's home page.

These banners have many purposes. They are used to show consent to monitoring under the Wiretap Act or consent to access under the ECPA. They are also used to eliminate a user's Fourth Amendment reasonable expectation of privacy in a computer network. They also may be used to inform a user of the terms of use for the computer network. Typically, these banners inform the user that use of the network (after viewing the banner) is proof that the user consents to network monitoring and the terms of use.

A private entity can monitor its communications systems to protect its "rights or property." This is called the provider exception. Monitoring under this exception must be reasonable and done in the ordinary course of business. This exception belongs only to the private entity, who may disclose evidence of business-related wrongdoing on its systems to law enforcement. This exception is not a general exception. The law does not allow a private entity to gather evidence of crime unrelated to it and turn that evidence over to law enforcement.

Court cases about the provider exception have upheld it in several situations. For example, an entity's system administrators can use this exception to monitor a hacker's communications within its network. They may do this to prevent damage to the entity's

**NOTE**

Under the Wiretap Act, a computer trespasser is a person who uses a computer system without permission. A computer trespasser has no relationship at all with the private entity.

network.[29] The entity can give any evidence collected from the monitoring to law enforcement. This is because hacking into a computer network is illegal.

The trespasser exception was created in 2001 as part of the PATRIOT Act. This exception recognizes that there might be times when private entities do not have the expertise needed to track or monitor system intruders. Because they do not have the skills to track system intruders, the provider exception is not helpful to them. The trespasser exception allows the entity to ask the government to help in these situations. The government can assist the entity in intercepting the communications of a computer trespasser.

The following conditions must be met in order to use this exception:

- Law enforcement must get the consent of the private entity.
- The interception must be legal.
- The interception must be part of a legitimate investigation.
- The interception must not monitor the communications of anyone other than the trespasser.[30]

If these conditions are met, then law enforcement may help a private entity monitor a computer trespasser. Law enforcement does not need a court order to take advantage of this exception.

**The Pen Register and Trap and Trace Statute.** The Wiretap Act governs real-time interception of the contents of a communication. It does not apply to transmission information. The Pen Register and Trap and Trace Statute governs real-time monitoring of this type of data. Transmission information includes headers, logs, network routing, and other transmission data. This law does not apply to communications content.

 **NOTE**

**Pen register devices** monitor outgoing transmission data. They record dialing, routing, signaling, or address information. **Trap and trace devices** monitor the communications of incoming transmission data. They capture incoming electronic signals that identify the origin of a communication.

Under the Pen Register and Trap and Trace Statute, no one is allowed to use pen register or trap and trace devices to intercept electronic communications transmission data. Similar to the Wiretap Act, however, some exceptions allow the use of these devices. For example, the law allows law enforcement to install pen register or trap and trace devices if they have a court order to do so.

There are three exceptions to the Pen Register and Trap and Trace Statute for private entities. Private entities can use these exceptions to use pen register or trap and trace devices on their own communications systems. The exceptions are:

- A private entity may use pen register or trap and trace devices if necessary to operate, maintain, or test its communication services. It also may use these devices to protect its property rights. (This is similar to the provider exception under the Wiretap Act.)
- A private entity may use pen register or trap and trace devices to protect the entity from fraudulent, unlawful, or abusive use of service. It would use these devices to prove the existence of a fraudulent, unlawful, or abusive electronic communication.
- A private entity may use pen register or trap and trace devices when the user of the electronic communications service consents.

These three laws, in addition to the provisions of the Fourth Amendment, are the main federal laws that govern the collection of electronic communications evidence. Computer forensic examiners must make sure that their evidence collection activities comply with these laws. Computer forensic examiners must also follow any relevant state laws. The examiner's credibility is damaged if the examiner does not follow the law. In addition, if the examiner does not follow the law, any evidence that he or she gathered might not be admissible.

## Admissibility of Evidence

Even if evidence is lawfully collected, it still must be admissible. At the federal level, the main guidance regarding the submission of evidence at trial is the FRE. The FRE apply to use of evidence at federal trials. Many states also have rules of evidence. Often these rules are based on the federal rules. One thing to keep in mind whenever you are reviewing evidence is that you need to understand whether you must follow state rules or federal rules.

 **NOTE**

In criminal cases, defense attorneys want to present exculpatory evidence to rebut the prosecution's case. The prosecution is interested in presenting inculpatory evidence to support their case.

Under the FRE, relevant evidence is admissible unless some other rule or law says that it is not. Admissible evidence is evidence that the judge and jury can consider when they deliberate about a case. Evidence can be either inculpatory or exculpatory. Inculpatory evidence supports or confirms a given theory, whereas exculpatory evidence rebuts or contradicts a given theory.

Computer forensic examiners are hired to find digital evidence. There are two basic types of digital evidence:

- **Computer-generated records**—These records and logs are the output of computer programs. They are created automatically by a computer program or process, even if a person initiates that program or process.
- **Records created by people and stored electronically**—These records are created by people. They just happen to be in a digital form. This kind of evidence includes files, pictures, images, spreadsheets, and other documents created by a person. It also can include internet browsing history.

### The Fruit of the Poisonous Tree Doctrine

The fruit of the poisonous tree doctrine is a long-standing legal doctrine, whose name stems from a biblical passage.[31] The doctrine has been in place since 1920.[32] The U.S. Supreme Court first used the term "fruit of the poisonous tree" in 1939.[33] The doctrine prevents the government from using illegally gathered evidence at a criminal trial. It also prevents the government from using any legally gathered evidence that it obtained because of the illegally gathered evidence.

This doctrine is used to keep the government from violating people's constitutional rights. If the government were allowed to use illegally gathered evidence at trial, the protections granted by the Fourth Amendment would be meaningless.

Under the fruit of the poisonous tree doctrine, the poisonous tree is evidence that is seized illegally. The fruit of the poisonous tree is evidence that is later gathered because of knowledge gained through the first illegal act. Neither the tree, nor its fruit, can be used at a trial.

The rules of evidence apply to digital evidence in the same way that they apply to traditional types of evidence. This section focuses on issues that are important for digital evidence. In order to be admissible, digital evidence must be:

- Lawfully gathered
- Relevant
- Authentic and reliable

Evidence is lawfully gathered if it is collected in accordance with the law. The main laws that govern the collection of electronic evidence were discussed earlier in this section. Evidence that is not gathered lawfully is tainted with illegality. This means that it cannot be used in court. It also means that any subsequent evidence gathered because of the illegally obtained evidence also cannot be used in court. In the law, this is known as the **fruit of the poisonous tree doctrine**. This doctrine primarily applies to criminal cases.

Evidence is admissible only if it is relevant. Another name for relevant evidence is **probative evidence**. Probative evidence proves or disproves a legal element in a case. If evidence is not probative, then it can be excluded from a trial. The FRE say that evidence is relevant if it makes "the existence of any fact that is of consequence to the determination of the action more probable or less probable than it would be without the evidence."[34] Evidence can be inculpatory or exculpatory.

Relevance can occasionally be a problem for digital evidence. This is because it is sometimes hard for judges and juries to understand very technical information. They might not understand why the evidence is relevant. This is where a good computer forensic examiner can help. The examiner can help explain the technical information in everyday language and help show how the evidence is relevant to the case. The party that wants to introduce digital evidence must show how it is relevant.

Evidence is admissible if it is authentic.[35] This means that the party introducing the evidence must show that the evidence is what it says it is. For example, suppose a party wishes to produce a printout of an electronic document and use it to prove an element in the case. Before being able to use the document, the party must show that the document was stored in a computer system. The party also must show that the document has not been altered, manipulated, or damaged since it was created.

Reliability is closely related to authenticity. It is often questioned in digital evidence issues. The reliability of digital evidence can be suspect if the program used to find the evidence has significant flaws. If the output of a program can change because of these flaws, then it is not reliable. If it is not reliable, then the information that the output represents may not be authentic.

Sometimes reliability is implicated at the forensic examination level. If a computer forensic examiner uses a new tool or program to conduct a forensic examination, the reliability of that tool must be demonstrated. The Daubert test is used to satisfy the court that new forensic tools are reliable. If the tool is reliable, then the court is more likely to admit the digital evidence.

As technology evolves, so too do the questions regarding the use of digital evidence in court. For legal practitioners, the *Sedona Principles for Addressing Electronic Document Production* is the best-known resource for how to properly use electronic evidence in legal proceedings.[36] The 14 Sedona Principles are best practices for how to use digital evidence in legal proceedings.

### *The Hearsay Rule*

There are other rules that may apply when courts consider the admissibility of digital evidence. For example, the hearsay rule[37] is often implicated with respect to computer records and digital evidence. The hearsay rule is a very complicated evidentiary rule with numerous exceptions. Sometimes even the most experienced attorneys can be confused by the hearsay rule and its many exceptions.

**Hearsay** is any out-of-court statement that is made by a person that is offered to prove some issue in a case. Hearsay statements are statements made by people. They are not usually made under oath. Hearsay statements are sometimes offered by parties at trial when there are no direct witnesses available to testify. Gossip is a common example of hearsay. Statements that a news reporter makes when he or she reports on events from an anonymous source are also hearsay. Hearsay is not admissible unless a specific exception applies.

Records recovered from a computer can be hearsay, depending on how they were created originally. Many courts have held that computer-generated records, the logs and output of computer programs, are not hearsay. These records are created without human intervention. Some courts have said that computer-generated information is not a statement of a person and cannot be hearsay.[38] If the records are not hearsay, then they are admissible.

Computer records that might be hearsay contain assertions by people. These types of records include documents and files, bookkeeping records, and records of transactions that are entered by people (and not through an electronic process). For these types of documents, a party must show that the document is admissible because of a hearsay exception. The party also must show that the document is authentic.

Some courts allow computer records to be admitted over a hearsay objection if they are created in the ordinary course of business. Records created in the ordinary course of business are often admissible, even if the hearsay objection would otherwise apply.[39] The theory is that records created as part of a business process tend to be reliable. This is because the records are created repeatedly.

#### Trial Court Objections

Trial attorneys often make *hearsay objections*. That is, they object when opposing attorneys pose questions meant to elicit hearsay from witnesses. An **objection** is a formal protest made to a judge. An attorney usually makes an objection if the opposing party is asking questions that are inappropriate or violate a court rule.

If the judge agrees with the attorney who made the objection, the court will sustain the objection. This means that the objection is correct. In this case, the attorney who originally asked a question must not ask it or must rephrase it. If the judge does not agree with the attorney who made the objection, the court will overrule it. This means that the original objection was not correct. When a judge overrules an objection, he or she is allowing the original line of questioning to continue.

### *The Best Evidence Rule*

The FRE require that original documents be used at trial to make sure that evidence is reliable and authentic.[40] This is called the best evidence rule. This rule can create an interesting problem for digital evidence. In its original form, digital evidence is almost never in a format that a person can read and understand. The original form of digital evidence would be particularly unhelpful at a trial, as it would not be usable. However, any printout that represents digital evidence would not meet the best evidence rule.

The FRE have made an exception for this quirk of digital evidence since 1972. The rule states that an accurate printout of computerized data is an "original" for purposes of the best evidence rule.[41] The FRE acknowledge that it is practical to address computerized evidence in this way.[42] Any other result would not make sense.

## CHAPTER SUMMARY

Computer forensics is the scientific process of collecting and examining data stored on electronic devices to find evidence about an event or crime. Evidence found on electronic devices is called digital evidence. Similar to traditional forms of evidence, digital evidence is subject to rules that govern how it can be used later. If digital evidence is not properly collected, it cannot be used in court.

Computer forensic examiners collect digital evidence using special programs and tools. They must collect the evidence carefully to make sure that it is not changed. Examiners often have special skills. They must have a thorough knowledge of computing technologies. They also must understand the scientific method. Finally, examiners must be familiar with the law and evidence rules.

## KEY CONCEPTS AND TERMS

Chain of custody
Code analysis
Computer forensics
Digital evidence
Forensic duplicate image
Fruit of the poisonous tree doctrine
Hearsay
Locard's exchange principle
Media analysis
Network analysis
Network banner
Objection
Pen register devices
Persistent data
Probative evidence
Trap and trace devices
Volatile data

## CHAPTER 15 ASSESSMENT

1. A system backup copy is considered a forensic duplicate image.
   A. True
   B. False
2. What is an exception to the Fourth Amendment's search warrant requirement?
   A. Consent
   B. Plain view doctrine
   C. Inventory search
   D. All of these are correct.
   E. None of these is correct.
3. Which principle is a basic assumption of forensic science?
   A. The silver platter doctrine
   B. Exigent circumstances
   C. Locard's exchange principle
   D. The Daubert test
   E. None of these is correct.
4. What are the three main electronic communications eavesdropping laws?
5. What is another common term for computer forensics?
6. Which type of computer forensics focuses on examining programming code?
   A. Media analysis
   B. Malware forensics
   C. Internet forensics
   D. Network analysis
   E. None of these is correct.
7. Which forensic certification is only available to law enforcement personnel?
   A. CCE
   B. GCFA
   C. CCFE
   D. EnCE
   E. None of these is correct.
8. A computer can play one of ______ roles in a crime.
9. Which investigative step includes "bag and tag"?
   A. Identification
   B. Preservation
   C. Collection
   D. Examination
   E. None of these is correct.
10. Which investigative step includes interviewing persons of interest for information about electronic devices?
    A. Identification
    B. Preservation
    C. Collection
    D. Presentation
    E. None of these is correct.
11. Which organization created the most well-known guiding principles for computer forensic examiners?
    A. IOCE
    B. ISO/IEC
    C. ISFCE
    D. IACRB
    E. None of these is correct.
12. What is volatile data?
13. Which law governs the collection of real-time transmission data?
    A. The Electronic Communications Privacy Act
    B. The Wiretap Act
    C. The Pen Register and Trap and Trace Statute
    D. The Fourth Amendment
    E. None of these is correct.
14. A trap and trace device monitors incoming transmission data.
    A. True
    B. False
15. A forensic duplicate image is a ______.

## ENDNOTES


1. U.S. Department of Labor, Bureau of Labor Statistics, "Forensic Science Technicians," *Occupational Outlook Handbook*. Available at https://www.bls.gov/ooh/life-physical-and-social-science/forensic-science-technicians.htm (accessed March 15, 2020).
2. Easttom, C., *System Forensics, Investigation, and Response*. 2nd ed. Burlington, MA: Jones & Bartlett Learning, 2013, p. 3.
3. Kaspersky, "Kaspersky Security Bulletin 2019: Statistics," December 2019. Available at https://securelist.com/kaspersky-security-bulletin-2019-statistics/95475/ (accessed March 15, 2020).
4. Verizon, "2019 Data Breach Investigations Report," May 2019. Available at https://enterprise.verizon.com/resources/reports/2019-data-breach-investigations-report.pdf (accessed March 15, 2020).
5. Federal Bureau of Investigation, "A Brief History of the FBI," undated. Available at https://www.fbi.gov/history/brief-history (accessed March 15, 2020).
6. International Association of Computer Investigative Specialists, "About IACIS," undated. Available at https://www.iacis.com/about/ (accessed March 15, 2020); Mark Pollitt, "A History of Digital Forensics," 6th IFIP WG 11.9 International Conference on Digital Forensics, January 2010. Available at https://hal.inria.fr/hal-01060606 (accessed March 15, 2020).
7. Scientific Working Group on Digital Evidence, "About Us," undated. Available at https://www.swgde.org/home (accessed March 15, 2020).
8. Illinois Compiled Statutes, Chapter 225, sec. 447, art. 5-10.
9. Michigan Compiled Laws, Chapter 338.822.
10. Oregon Revised Statutes, Chapter 703.401, 703.405, 703.407, 703.411.
11. Texas Occupations Code Annotated, sec. 1702.104.
12. North Carolina General Statutes, Chapter 74C, sec. 3(b)(17).
13. Virginia Code, title 9.1, sec. 140.
14. American Bar Association, Section of Science & Technology Law, "ABA Adopts Resolution Against Private Investigator Licenses for Computer Forensics," September 25, 2008. Available at http://cdfs.org/files/Positions/ABA%20Press%20release%20compforensics.pdf (accessed March 15, 2020).
15. *Fisher v. United States*, 425 U.S. 391 (1976).
16. U.S. Supreme Court, Federal Rules of Evidence, Rules 701–706, undated. Available at https://www.uscourts.gov/sites/default/files/federal_rules_of_evidence_-_dec_1_2019_0.pdf (accessed March 15, 2020).
17. *Daubert v. Merrell Dow Pharmaceuticals, Inc.*, 509 U.S. 579 (1993).
18. Federal Bureau of Investigation, "Digital Evidence: Standards and Principles, Scientific Working Group on Digital Evidence (SWGDE) International Organization on Digital Evidence (IOCE), IOCE International Principles," *Forensic Science Communications*, April 2000, Vol. 2, No. 2. Available at https://archives.fbi.gov/archives/about-us/lab/forensic-science-communications/fsc/april2000/swgde.htm (accessed March 15, 2020).
19. Electronic Communications Privacy Act of 1986 (ECPA), Pub. L. No. 99-508, 100 Stat. 1848, codified at U.S. Code Vol. 18, sec. 2510 (2020).
20. Electronic Communications Privacy Act of 1986 (ECPA), Pub. L. No. 99-508, 100 Stat. 1848, codified at U.S. Code Vol. 18, secs. 2510–2523 (2020).
21. Wiretap statutes, U.S. Code Vol. 18, sec. 2510; U.S. Code Vol. 47, sec. 605 (2020).
22. Pen Register and Trap and Trace Statute, U.S. Code Vol. 18, sec. 3121 et seq. (2020).
23. *United States v. Heckenkamp*, 482 F.3d 1142, 1146 (9th Cir. 2007).
24. *United States v. Al-Marri*, 230 F. Supp.2d 535, 541 (S.D.N.Y. 2002).
25. *Riley v. California*, 573 U.S. 373 (2014).
26. *Carpenter v. United States*, 138 S. Ct. 2206 (2018).
27. Uniting and Strengthening America by Providing Appropriate Tools Required to Intercept and Obstruct Terrorism Act of 2001 (PATRIOT Act), Pub. L. No. 107-56, 115 Stat. 272 (Oct. 26, 2001), codified at various sections of the U.S. Code (2020).
28. U.S. Code Vol. 18, sec. 2702(b) (2020).
29. *United States v. Mullins*, 992 F.2d 1472 (9th Cir. 1993).

30. U.S. Code Vol. 18, sec. 2511(2)(i) (2020).
31. Matt. 7:17-20, *The Holy Bible*, King James Version. Cambridge Edition: 1769; King James Bible Online, 2014. Available at http://www.kingjamesbibleonline.org/ (accessed March 15, 2020).
32. *Silverthorne Lumber Co. v. United States*, 251 U.S. 385 (1920).
33. *Nardone v. United States*, 308 U.S. 338 (1939).
34. Federal Rules of Evidence, Rule 401.
35. Federal Rules of Evidence, Rule 901.
36. The Sedona Conference, "The Sedona Principles, Third Edition: Best Practices, Recommendations & Principles for Addressing Electronic Document Production," 19 SEDONA CONF. J. 1 (2018).
37. Federal Rules of Evidence, Rule 801.
38. See *United States v. Washington*, 498 F.3d 225, 230-31 (4th Cir. 2007) (holding that printed results from a computerized test were not the statement of a person and are not excluded as hearsay); *United States v. Hamilton*, 413 F.3d 1138, 1142-43 (10th Cir. 2005) (holding that computer-generated header information is not hearsay).
39. Federal Rules of Evidence, Rule 803(6).
40. Federal Rules of Evidence, Rule 1002.
41. Federal Rules of Evidence, Rule 1001(3).
42. Federal Rules of Evidence, Rule 1001(3), Advisory Committee Notes (1972).

APPENDIX A

# Answer Key

## CHAPTER 1 Information Security Overview

1. C 2. E 3. D 4. C 5. A 6. Logical control 7. C 8. D 9. A 10. E 11. D 12. B 13. C 14. E 15. A

## CHAPTER 2 Privacy Overview

1. A 2. E 3. C 4. A 5. D 6. D 7. 8 8. B 9. A 10. B 11. A 12. A legitimate business reason 13. D 14. B 15. C

## CHAPTER 3 The American Legal System

1. E 2. B 3. A 4. D 5. C 6. A 7. *Stare decisis* 8. D 9. E 10. A 11. Congress 12. D 13. 9 14. C 15. 94

## CHAPTER 4 Security and Privacy of Consumer Financial Information

1. D 2. B 3. A 4. B 5. C 6. Social engineering 7. A 8. E 9. National Bank Act of 1864 10. B 11. C 12. B 13. 12 14. B 15. C

## CHAPTER 5 Security and Privacy of Information Belonging to Children and in Educational Records

1. B 2. A 3. B 4. 13 5. D 6. B 7. CIPA 8. Technical protection measure (TPM) 9. C 10. A 11. C 12. A 13. B 14. B 15. A

## CHAPTER 6 Security and Privacy of Health Information

1. Reasonable and appropriate 2. D 3. 60 4. 12 5. D 6. An organization that performs a healthcare activity on behalf of a covered entity 7. C 8. B 9. 30 10. D 11. A 12. B 13. C 14. E 15. Unsecured

## CHAPTER 7 Corporate Information Security and Privacy Regulation

1. A 2. A 3. To protect shareholders and investors from financial fraud. SOX also was designed to restore investor faith in American stock markets. 4. C 5. E 6. Internal controls are the processes and procedures that a company uses to provide reasonable assurance that its financial reports are reliable. 7. D 8. B 9. B 10. C 11. B 12. D 13. Provides management with reasonable assurance that: (1) financial reports, records, and data are accurately maintained; (2) transactions are

prepared according to generally accepted accounting principles (GAAP) rules and are properly recorded; and (3) unauthorized acquisition or use of data or assets that could affect financial statements will be prevented or detected promptly. 14. C 15. B

## CHAPTER 8 Federal Government Information Security and Privacy Regulations

1. A 2. A government agency must state what information is to be collected; why the information is being collected; the intended use of the information; how the agency will share the information; whether people have the opportunity to consent to specific uses of the information; how the information will be secured; and whether the information collected will be a system of records as defined by the Privacy Act of 1974. 3. C 4. B 5. E 6. NCCIC/US-CERT 7. B 8. D 9. CyberScope 10. B 11. A 12. B 13. B 14. E 15. D

## CHAPTER 9 State Laws Protecting Citizen Information and Breach Notification Laws

1. A 2. 2003 3. D 4. A legal concept that protects an entity from liability if it follows the law 5. B 6. D 7. C 8. A person must be able to easily understand it 9. E 10. C 11. D 12. A legal concept that describes a person's right to sue another for harm that the latter caused 13. A 14. D 15. B

## CHAPTER 10 Intellectual Property Law

1. E 2. A legal concept that means that people can be held responsible for their actions even if they did not intend to cause harm to another person. 3. B 4. 20 5. E 6. C 7. A person or business must use the trademark in interstate commerce, and the trademark must be distinctive 8. A 9. C 10. A 11. C 12. A 13. It is important to know the ownership of a copyrighted work in order to determine the length of copyright protection. 14. E 15. B

## CHAPTER 11 The Role of Contracts

1. C 2. An agreement where the complete terms of the agreement are presented on a computer screen, usually in the form of a pop-up window. A user must take an affirmative action to accept the terms of the agreement. 3. B 4. A 5. B 6. D 7. Legal relief granted by a court 8. C 9. A 10. Loss of control of data, loss of privacy of data, third-party dependency for critical infrastructure, potential security and technology defects, lack of control over third parties, loss of an entity's own competence in IT infrastructure security. 11. E 12. B 13. B 14. Enforceable 15. D

## CHAPTER 12 Criminal Law and Tort Law Issues in Cyberspace

1. B 2. Crimes are wrongdoings against society. 3. A 4. E 5. C 6. The Sixth Amendment to the U.S. Constitution 7. B 8. E 9. A 10. Extreme and outrageous 11. A 12. C 13. D 14. Libel and slander 15. E

## CHAPTER 13 Information Security Governance

1. A 2. Executive management providing strategic direction, oversight, and accountability for an organization's data and information technology (IT) resources. 3. D 4. D 5. Middle management providing day-to-day guidance and oversight for an organization's information and information resources. 6. A 7. A list of mandatory activities that must be completed to achieve an information security goal 8. A 9. B 10. D 11. A checklist of actions that should be performed to achieve a certain goal 12. C 13. A 14. E 15. B

## CHAPTER 14 Risk Analysis, Incident Response, and Contingency Planning

1. B 2. E 3. A risk assessment identifies the threats and vulnerabilities to IT resources. 4. D 5. A 6. Exposure factor 7. The annualized loss expectancy (ALE) is the amount of loss that an organization can expect to have each year because of a particular risk. ALE is often expressed as the equation: ALE = SLE × ARO. SLE is single loss expectancy. ARO is annual rate of occurrence. 8. C 9. A 10. D 11. C 12. Incident 13. Disaster 14. A 15. A

## CHAPTER 15 Computer Forensics and Investigations

1. B 2. D 3. C 4. The Electronic Communications Privacy Act; the Wiretap Act; the Pen Register and Trap and Trace Statute. 5. Computer forensics also is known as system forensics, digital forensics, computer forensic analysis, computer examination, data recovery, and inforensics (information forensics). These terms are used interchangeably.
6. B 7. E 8. Four 9. C 10. B 11. A 12. Data stored in the memory of an electronic device. Volatile data is lost when the electronic device is turned off. 13. C 14. B 15. Bit-by-bit copy

APPENDIX B

# Standard Acronyms

**2FA** two-factor authentication
**ACD** automatic call distributor
**AES** Advanced Encryption Standard
**ALE** annual loss expectancy
**ANSI** American National Standards Institute
**AO** authorizing official
**AP** access point
**API** application programming interface
**APT** advanced persistent threat
**ARO** annual rate of occurrence
**ATM** asynchronous transfer mode
**AUP** acceptable use policy
**AV** antivirus
**B2B** business to business
**B2C** business to consumer
**BBB** Better Business Bureau
**BC** business continuity
**BCP** business continuity plan
**BGP4** Border Gateway Protocol 4 for IPv4
**BIA** business impact analysis
**BOD** board of directors
**BYOD** Bring Your Own Device
**C2C** consumer to consumer
**CA** certificate authority
**CAC** common access card
**CAN** computer network attack
**CAN-SPAM** Controlling the Assault of Non-Solicited Pornography and Marketing Act
**CAP** Certification and Accreditation Professional
**CAUCE** Coalition Against Unsolicited Commercial Email
**CBA** cost-benefit analysis
**CBF** critical business function
**CBK** common body of knowledge
**CCC** CERT Coordination Center
**CCNA** Cisco Certified Network Associate
**CDR** call-detail recording
**CERT** Computer Emergency Response Team
**CFE** Certified Fraud Examiner
**C-I-A** confidentiality, integrity, availability
**CIO** Chief Information Officer
**CIPA** Children's Internet Protection Act
**CIR** committed information rate
**CIRT** computer incident response teams
**CISA** Certified Information Systems Auditor
**CISM** Certified Information Security Manager
**CISO** Chief Information Security Officer
**CISSP** Certified Information System Security Professional
**CMIP** common management information protocol
**CMMI** capability maturity model integration
**CND** computer network defense
**CNE** computer network exploitation
**COPPA** Children's Online Privacy Protection Act
**COS** class of service
**CRC** cyclic redundancy check
**CSA** Cloud Security Alliance
**CSFs** critical success factors
**CSI** Computer Security Institute
**CSP** cloud service provider
**CTI** Computer Telephony Integration
**CTO** Chief Technology Officer
**CVE** common vulnerabilities and exposures

**DAC** discretionary access control
**DBMS** database management system
**DCS** distributed control system
**DDoS** distributed denial of service
**DEP** data execution prevention
**DES** Data Encryption Standard
**DHCPv6** Dynamic Host Configuration Protocol v6 for IPv6
**DHS** Department of Homeland Security
**DIA** Defense Intelligence Agency
**DISA** direct inward system access
**DMZ** demilitarized zone
**DNS** domain name service OR domain name system
**DOD** Department of Defense
**DoS** denial of service
**DPI** deep packet inspection
**DR** disaster recovery
**DRP** disaster recovery plan
**DSL** digital subscriber line
**DSS** Digital Signature Standard
**DSU** data service unit
**EDI** Electronic Data Interchange
**EIDE** Enhanced IDE
**ELINT** electronic intelligence
**EPHI** electronic protected health information
**EULA** End-User License Agreement
**FACTA** Fair and Accurate Credit Transactions Act
**FAR** false acceptance rate
**FCC** Federal Communications Commission
**FDIC** Federal Deposit Insurance Corporation
**FEP** front-end processor
**FERPA** Family Educational Rights and Privacy Act
**FIPPS** fair information practice principles
**FIPS** Federal Information Processing Standard
**FISMA** Federal Information Security Management Act
**FRCP** Federal Rules of Civil Procedure
**FRR** false rejection rate
**FTC** Federal Trade Commission
**FTP** file transfer protocol
**GAAP** generally accepted accounting principles
**GIAC** Global Information Assurance Certification
**GigE** Gigabit Ethernet LAN
**GLBA** Gramm-Leach-Bliley Act
**GPS** global positioning system
**HIDS** host-based intrusion detection system
**HIPAA** Health Insurance Portability and Accountability Act
**HIPS** host-based intrusion prevention system
**HTML** hypertext markup language
**HTTP** hypertext transfer protocol
**HTTPS** hypertext transport protocol secure
**HUMINT** human intelligence
**IaaS** Infrastructure as a Service
**IAB** Internet Activities Board
**ICMP** Internet Control Message Protocol
**IDEA** International Data Encryption Algorithm
**IDPS** intrusion detection and prevention
**IDS** intrusion detection system
**IEEE** Institute of Electrical and Electronics Engineers
**IETF** Internet Engineering Task Force
**IG** Inspector General
**IGP** interior gateway protocol
**IMINT** imagery intelligence
**InfoSec** information security
**IoT** Internet of Things
**IP** intellectual property OR Internet protocol
**IPS** intrusion prevention system
**IPSec** Internet Protocol Security
**IPv4** Internet Protocol version 4
**IPv6** Internet Protocol version 6
**IR** incident response
**IS-IS** intermediate system-to-intermediate system

**(ISC)²** International Information System Security Certification Consortium
**ISO** International Organization for Standardization
**ISP** Internet service provider
**ISS** Internet security systems
**ITL** information technology infrastructure library
**ITRC** Identity Theft Resource Center
**IVR** interactive voice response
**L2TP** Layer 2 Tunneling Protocol
**LAN** local area network
**MAC** mandatory access control
**MAN** metropolitan area network
**MAO** maximum acceptable outage
**MASINT** measurement and signals intelligence
**MD5** Message Digest 5
**MFA** multifactor authentication
**modem** modulator demodulator
**MP-BGP** Multiprotocol Border Gateway Protocol for IPv6
**MPLS** multiprotocol label switching
**MSTI** multiple spanning tree instance
**MSTP** Multiple Spanning Tree Protocol
**MTD** maximum tolerable downtime
**NAC** network access control
**NAT** network address translation
**NFC** Near Field Communications
**NFIC** National Fraud Information Center
**NIC** network interface card
**NIDS** network intrusion detection system
**NIPS** network intrusion prevention system
**NIST** National Institute of Standards and Technology
**NMS** network management system
**NOC** network operations center
**NPI** nonpublic personal information
**NSA** National Security Agency
**NVD** national vulnerability database
**OPSEC** operations security
**OS** operating system
**OSI** open system interconnection
**OSINT** open source intelligence
**OSPFv2** Open Shortest Path First v2 for IPv4
**OSPFv3** Open Shortest Path First v3 for IPv6
**PaaS** Platform as a Service
**PBX** private branch exchange
**PCI** Payment Card Industry
**PCI DSS** Payment Card Industry Data Security Standard
**PGP** Pretty Good Privacy
**PHI** protected health information
**PIA** privacy impact assessment
**PII** personally identifiable information
**PIN** personal identification number
**PKI** public key infrastructure
**PLC** programmable logic controller
**POAM** plan of action and milestones
**PoE** power over Ethernet
**POS** point-of-sale
**PPTP** Point-to-Point Tunneling Protocol
**PSYOPs** psychological operations
**RA** registration authority OR risk assessment
**RAID** redundant array of independent disks
**RAT** remote access Trojan OR remote access tool
**RFC** Request for Comments
**RFID** Radio Frequency Identification
**RIPng** Routing Information Protocol next generation for IPv6
**RIPv2** Routing Information Protocol v2 for IPv4
**RM** risk management
**ROI** return on investment
**RPO** recovery point objective
**RSA** Rivest, Shamir, and Adleman (algorithm)
**RSTP** Rapid Spanning Tree Protocol
**RTO** recovery time objective
**SA** security association
**SaaS** Software as a Service
**SAN** storage area network

**SANCP** Security Analyst Network Connection Profiler
**SANS** SysAdmin, Audit, Network, Security
**SAP** service access point
**SCADA** supervisory control and data acquisition
**SCSI** small computer system interface
**SDSL** symmetric digital subscriber line
**SET** secure electronic transaction
**SGC** server-gated cryptography
**SHA** secure hash algorithm
**S-HTTP** secure HTTP
**SIEM** Security Information and Event Management system
**SIGINT** signals intelligence
**SIP** Session Initiation Protocol
**SLA** service level agreement
**SLE** single loss expectancy
**SMFA** specific management functional area
**SNMP** simple network management protocol
**SORN** System of Records Notice
**SOX** Sarbanes-Oxley Act of 2002 (also Sarbox)
**SPOF** single point of failure
**SQL** structured query language
**SSA** Social Security Administration
**SSCP** Systems Security Certified Practitioner
**SSID** service set identifier (name assigned to a WiFi network)
**SSL** Secure Sockets Layer
**SSL-VPN** Secure Sockets Layer virtual private network
**SSO** single system sign-on
**STP** shielded twisted pair OR Spanning Tree Protocol
**TCP/IP** Transmission Control Protocol/Internet Protocol
**TCSEC** Trusted Computer System Evaluation Criteria
**TFA** two-factor authentication
**TFTP** Trivial File Transfer Protocol
**TGAR** trunk group access restriction
**TNI** Trusted Network Interpretation
**TPM** technology protection measure OR trusted platform module
**UC** unified communications
**UDP** User Datagram Protocol
**UPS** uninterruptible power supply
**USB** universal serial bus
**UTP** unshielded twisted pair
**VA** vulnerability assessment
**VBAC** view-based access control
**VLAN** virtual local area network
**VoIP** Voice over Internet Protocol
**VPN** virtual private network
**W3C** World Wide Web Consortium
**WAN** wide area network
**WAP** wireless access point
**WEP** wired equivalent privacy
**Wi-Fi** wireless fidelity
**WLAN** wireless local area network
**WNIC** wireless network interface card
**WPA** Wi-Fi Protected Access
**WPA2** Wi-Fi Protected Access 2
**XML** extensible markup language
**XSS** cross-site scripting

APPENDIX C

# Law and Case Citations

## U.S. Federal Laws

Administrative Procedure Act (1946), Pub. L. No. 79-404, codified as U.S. Code Vol. 5, sec. 500–596 (2012).

Affordable Care Act of 2010 (ACA), Pub. L. 111–148, 124 Stat. 119, codified as amended at scattered sections of the Internal Revenue Code and in U.S. Code Vol. 42 (2012.)

American Inventor's Protection Act (1999), Pub. L. No. 106-113, 113 Stat. 1501 (1999).

American Recovery and Reinvestment Act (2009), Pub. L. No. 111-5, 123 Stat. 115 (2009).

Anti-Cybersquatting Consumer Protection Act (1999), Pub. L. No. 106-113, codified as U.S. Code Vol. 15, sec. 1125(d) (2012).

Bank Holding Act (1956), Pub. L. No. 84-511, 70 Stat. 133, U.S. Code Vol. 12 sec. 1841 *et seq.* (2012).

Bank Secrecy Act (1970), Pub. L. No. 91-508, 84 Stat. 1114 to 1124, codified as amended in scattered sections throughout U.S. Code Vols. 12, 15, and 31 (2012).

Banking Act of 1933 (also called the Glass-Stegall Act), Pub. L. No. 73-66, 48 Stat. 162, codified as amended throughout U.S. Code Vol. 12 (2012).

Banking Act of 1935, Pub. L. No. 74-305, 49 Stat. 684, codified as amended throughout U.S. Code Vol. 12 (2012).

Cable Communications Policy Act of 1984 (CCPA), Pub. L. No. 98-549, codified at U.S. Code Vol. 47 sec. 551 (2012).

Census Confidentiality Rules, U.S. Code Vol. 13, sec. 9 (2012).

Children's Internet Protection Act (2000) Pub. L. No. 106-554, 114 Stat. 2763A-335, codified in scattered sections of U.S. Code (2012).

Children's Online Privacy Protection Act of 1998 (COPPA), U.S. Code Vol. 15, sec. 6501 (2012).

Civil Rights Act of 1964, Pub. L. No. 88-352, 78 Stat. 241, codified as amended in scattered sections throughout U.S. Code Vols. 2, 28, and 42 (2012).

Communications Decency Act of 1996, (CDA), Pub. L. No. 104-104 (Tit. V), 110 Stat. 133, codified at U.S. Code Vol. 47, sec. 223, 230 (2012).

Computer Fraud and Abuse Act (1986), Pub. L. No. 99-474, 100 Stat. 1213, codified at U.S. Code Vol. 18, sec. 1030 (2012).

Computer Security Act of 1987, Pub. L. No. 100-235, 101 Stat. 1724, codified at U.S. Code Vol. 40, sec. 1441 (2012).

Consolidated Omnibus Budget Reconciliation Act (1986), Pub. L. No. 99-272, 100 Stat. 82 (1986).

Controlling the Assault of Non-Solicited Pornography and Marketing Act (CAN-SPAM Act), Pub. L. No. 108-187, 117 Stat. 2699, codified at U.S. Code Vol. 15, sec. 7701 *et seq.*, U.S. Code Vol. 18, sec. 1037 (2012).

Copyright Act (1976), U.S. Code Vol. 17, sec. 101 *et seq.* (2012).

Digital Millennium Copyright Act (1998), Pub. L. No. 105-304, 112 Stat. 2860, codified in scattered sections of U.S. Code Vol. 17 (2012).

Dodd-Frank Wall Street Reform and Consumer Protection Act (2010), Pub. L. No. 111–203, 124 Stat. 1376–2223, codified as amended in scattered sections throughout U.S. Code Vols. 12 and 15.

Driver's Privacy Protection Act of 1994, U.S. Code Vol. 18, sec. 2721 (2012).

Drug Abuse Prevention, Treatment, and Rehabilitation Act (1980), U.S. Code Vol. 21, sec. 1175 (2012).

E-Government Act of 2002, Pub. L. No. 107-347, 116 Stat. 2899, codified in scattered sections throughout U.S. Code Vol. 44 (various sections) (2012).

Electronic Communications Privacy Act of 1986 (ECPA), Pub. L. No. 99-508, 100 Stat. 1848, codified at U.S. Code Vol. 18, sec. 2701 (2012).

Electronic Signatures in Global and National Commerce Act of 2000 (E-Sign), Pub. L. No. 106-229, codified at U.S. Code Vol. 15, sec. 7001 *et seq.* (2012).

Fair and Accurate Credit Transaction Act of 2003 (FACTA), Pub L. 108-159, 117 Stat. 1952, made amendments to the Fair Credit Reporting Act of 1970.

Fair Credit Reporting Act (1970), U.S. Code Vol. 15, sec. 1681 *et seq.* (2012).

Family Educational Rights and Privacy Act of 1974 (FERPA), U.S. Code Vol. 20, sec. 1232g (2012).

Federal Credit Union Act (1934), U.S. Code Vol. 12, sec. 1751 *et seq.* (2012).

Federal Information Security Management Act of 2002 (FISMA), Title III of the E-Government Act of 2002, U.S. Code Vol. 44, sec. 3541 *et seq.* (2012).

Federal Information Security Modernization Act of 2014 (FISMA), Pub. L. No 113-283, 128 Stat. 3073 (2014).

Federal Reserve Act (1913), Pub. L. No 63-43, 38 Stat. 251, codified as amended throughout U.S. Code Vol. 12 (2012).

Federal Trade Commission Act (1914), U.S. Code Vol. 15, sec. 41-58 (2012).

Financial Institutions Reform, Recovery, and Enforcement Act (1989), Pub. L. No. 101-73, 103 Stat. 183, codified as amended in scattered sections of U.S. Code (2012).

Financial Institutions Regulatory and Interest Rate Control Act (1978), Pub. L. No. 95-630, 92 Stat. 3641, codified as amended in scattered sections of U.S. Code (2012).

Financial Services Regulatory Relief Act (2006), Pub. L. No. 109-351, 120 Stat. 1966 (2012).

Freedom of Information Act, U.S. Code Vol. 5, sec. 552 (2012).

Genetic Information Nondiscrimination Act of 2008 (GINA), Pub. L. No. 110-233, 122 Stat. 881 (2008).

Gramm-Leach-Bliley Act (1999), Title V of the Financial Services Modernization Act of 1999, Pub. L. No. 106-102, 113 Stat. 1338, codified at U.S. Code Vol. 15, sec. 6801 *et seq.* (2012).

Health Information Technology for Economic and Clinical Health Act of 2009 (HITECH Act), Pub. L. No. 111-5, 123 Stat. 226, codified at U.S. Code Vol. 42, sec 300jj *et seq.*, and sec. 17901 *et seq.* (2012).

Health Insurance Portability and Accountability Act of 1996 (HIPAA), Pub. L. No. 104-191, codified at U.S. Code Vol. 42, sec. 1320d (2012).

Identity Theft and Assumption Deterrence Act (1998), U.S. Code Vol. 18, sec. 1028 (2012).

Inspector General Act of 1978, U.S. Code Vol. 5 app, sec. 1 (2012).

Lanham Act (1946), U.S. Code Vol. 15, sec. 1051 *et seq.* (2012).

Leahy-Smith America Invents Act (2011), Pub. L. No. 112-29, 125 Stat. 284 (2011).

Mail Privacy Statute, U.S. Code Vol. 39, sec. 3623 (2012).

National Bank Act (1864), 13 Stat. 99 (1864), current version at U.S. Code Vol. 12 sec. 21-216b (2012).

Patent Act (1952), U.S. Code Vol. 35, sec. 1-376 (2012).

Pen Register and Trap and Trace Statute, U.S. Code Vol. 18, sec. 3121 *et seq.* (2012).

Plant Variety Protection Act (1970), U.S. Code Vol. 7, sec. 2421, 2422, 2541 (2012).

Privacy Act of 1974, Pub. L. No. 93-579, 88 Stat. 1896, codified at U.S. Code Vol. 5, sec. 552a (2012).

Public Company Accounting Reform and Investor Protection Act (2002), also called Sarbanes-Oxley Act (2002), Pub. L. No. 107-204, 116 Stat. 745, codified as amended in scattered sections of U.S. Code Vol. 15 (2012).

Red Flag Program Clarification Act of 2010, 15 U.S.C. 1681m(e)(4), Pub. L. 111-319, 124 Stat. 3457 (Dec. 18, 2010).

Securities and Exchange Act of 1934, U.S. Code, Vol. 15, sec. 78a *et seq.* (2006).

Uniting and Strengthening America by Providing Appropriate Tools Required to Intercept and Obstruct Terrorism Act of 2001 (PATRIOT Act), Pub. L. No. 107-56, 115 Stat. 272 (Oct. 26, 2001), codified at various sections of the U.S. Code (2012).

Veterans Affairs Information Security Act, Title IX of the Veterans Benefits, Health Care, and Information Technology Act (2006), U.S. Code Vol. 38, sec. 5722 *et seq.* (2012).

Wiretap statutes, U.S. Code Vol. 18, sec. 2510; U.S. Code Vol. 47, sec. 605 (2012).

(U.S. regulations and state laws are cited in the text and endnotes of each chapter.)

## Court Rules

Indiana Supreme Court, *Indiana Rules of Trial Procedure*, http://www.in.gov/judiciary/rules/trial_proc/index.html (accessed November 13, 2013).

U.S. Supreme Court, *Federal Rules of Civil Procedure*, http://www.uscourts.gov/uscourts/rules/civil-procedure.pdf (accessed November 10, 2013).

U.S. Supreme Court, *Federal Rules of Criminal Procedure*, http://www.uscourts.gov/uscourts/rules/criminal-procedure.pdf (accessed November 10, 2013).

U.S. Supreme Court, *Federal Rules of Evidence*, https://www.rulesofevidence.org/ (accessed November 10, 2013).

## Court Cases

*Authors Guild, Inc. v. HathiTrust*, 755 F.3d 87 (2014).

The Second Circuit Court of Appeals held that the doctrine of fair use allowed HathiTrust to create a full-text searchable database of copyrighted works.

*Autoliv ASP, Inc. v. Department of Workforce Services*, 29 P.3d 7 (Utah Ct. Appeals, 2001).

Utah Court of Appeals held that the transmission of sexually explicit and offensive jokes, pictures, and videos constitutes a flagrant violation of a universal standard of behavior.

*Baltimore & Ohio Railroad Co. v. United States*, 261 U.S. 592 (1923).

The U.S. Supreme Court held that mutual assent can be determined from the conduct of the parties, even if there is no express, written contract.

*Bill Graham Archives v. Dorling Kindersley Ltd.*, 448 F.3d 605 (2d Cir. 2006).

The Second Circuit Court of Appeals held that reduced versions of copyrighted posters used in an illustrated book were fair use.

*Brady v. Maryland*, 373 U.S. 83 (1963).

The U.S. Supreme Court held that the prosecution has a duty to disclose any evidence that it has that might help prove the defendant's innocence.

*Brown v. Board of Education*, 347 U.S. 483 (1954).

The U.S. Supreme Court overruled *Plessy v. Ferguson*. It held that separate but equal practices are inherently unequal and violate the U.S. Constitution.

*Burnet v. Coronado Oil & Gas Co.*, 285 U.S. 393 (1932).

The U.S. Supreme Court recognizes the value of precedent in deciding cases.

*Carlill v. Carbolic Smoke Ball Company*, 1 QB 256; Court of Appeal (1892).

English court case that held that an advertisement could constitute a valid offer.

*Carpenter v. United States*, 138 S. Ct. 2206 (2018).

The U.S. Supreme Court held that a person has a reasonable expectation of privacy in the location information collected by his or her smartphone and stored by his or her cell phone service provider.

*City of Ontario v. Quon*, 130 S.Ct. 2619 (2010).

The U.S. Supreme Court held that reviewing a police officer's text messages did not violate federal law and the police officer's privacy rights because the review was not intrusive and was for a legitimate business purpose.

*Claridge v. RockYou, Inc.*, United States District Court Northern District of California, C 09 6032 BZ (2009).

An Indiana man sued RockYou. The lawsuit claims that RockYou stored personal data in an unencrypted database and failed to take reasonable steps to secure that personal information.

*CompuServe, Inc. v. Cyber Promotions, Inc.*, 962 F.Supp. 1015 (S.D. Ohio 1997).

The first court case holding that spammers could be liable for the tort of trespass to chattels.

*Daubert v. Merrell Dow Pharmaceuticals, Inc.*, 509 U.S. 579 (1993).

The U.S. Supreme Court case that set forth the test for admitting scientific expert witness testimony.

*Deal v. Spears*, 980 F.2d 1153 (8th Cir. 1992).

Eighth Circuit Court of Appeals found that a recorder purchased at a consumer electronics store and connected to an extension phone line did not qualify as ordinary telephone equipment.

*Diamond v. Chakrabarty*, 447 U.S. 303 (1980).

The U.S. Supreme Court held that patentable subject matter is "anything under the sun that is made by man."

*Fisher v. United States*, 425 U.S. 391 (1976).

The U.S. Supreme Court held that the Fifth Amendment protects communications that are compelled, testimonial, and incriminating in nature.

*Free Enterprise Fund and Beckstead and Watts v. Public Company Accounting Oversight Board*, 537 F.3d 667 (Fed. Cir 2008).

Court case challenging the constitutionality of the Public Company Accounting Oversight Board. The case was on appeal to the U.S. Supreme Court at the time this book was written.

*Gideon v. Wainwright*, 372 U.S. 335 (1963).

The U.S. Supreme Court held that a state must appoint counsel to an indigent defendant who has been charged with a felony. Denial of the Sixth Amendment right to counsel at trial results in an automatic reversal of any conviction.

*Giglio v. United States*, 405 U.S. 150 (1972).

The U.S. Supreme Court held that the prosecution has a duty to disclose to the defendant any deals that it makes with witnesses.

*Griswold v. Connecticut*, 381 U.S. 479 (1965).

First U.S. Supreme Court decision to articulate a Constitutional right to privacy.

*Hammer v. Amazon.com*, 392 F.Supp.2d 423 (E.D.N.Y 2005).

The District Court for the Eastern District of New York held that a defamatory statement is more than mere opinion.

*Hartford v. Moore*, 181 F. 132 (S.D.N.Y. 1910).

The District Court for the Southern District of New York recognized that an invention that seems obvious after it is created may actually meet the non-obvious requirement for patentability.

*In re Boucher*, 2009 WL 424718 (D. Vt., February 19, 2009).

The District Court for the District of Vermont held that it is not a violation of the Fifth Amendment to require a defendant to provide an unencrypted version of his hard drive.

*Intel Corp v. Hamidi*, 71 P.3d 296 (Cal. 2003).

The California Supreme Court held that the plaintiff did not sustain any damages in a trespass to chattels spam case. As such, the plaintiff could not recover damages.

*Jacobellis v. Ohio*, 378 U.S. 184 (1964).

The U.S. Supreme Court stated that the First Amendment does not protect pornography or obscenity. The famous line, "I know it when I see it," is from the majority decision in this case.

*Jones v. Hamilton*, Alabama Court of Civil Appeals, Opinion, January 22, 2010, available at https://caselaw.findlaw.com/al-court-of-civil-appeals/1521828.html (accessed August 7, 2020).

The Alabama Court of Appeals held that information left in the back seat of a vehicle that was accessible to many employees was not properly protected as a trade secret.

*Katz v. United States*, 389 U.S. 347 (1967).

The U.S. Supreme Court held that the Fourth Amendment of the U.S. Constitution protects a person's right to privacy.

*Lamle v. Mattel, Inc.*, 394 F.3d 1355 (Fed. Cir. 2005).

The Federal Circuit Court of Appeals held that an email outlining contract terms is a signed writing under the California Statute of Frauds.

*Leonard v. Pepsico, Inc.*, 88 F.Supp.2d 116 (S.D.N.Y. 1999), aff'd 210 F.3d 88 (2d Cir. 2000).

Second Circuit Court of Appeals case that held an advertisement was a valid contractual offer only if a reasonable person considered it to be an offer.

*Major v. McCallister*, Missouri Court of Appeals, No. CD29871 (December 23, 2009).

The Missouri Court of Appeals held that a browsewrap contract was enforceable where the user was put on notice in many ways that the terms of the contract applied to the service provided on a website.

*Miller v. California*, 413 U.S. 15 (1973).

The U.S. Supreme Court created a three-part test for identifying materials as obscene.

*Nardone v. United States*, 308 U.S. 338 (1939).

The U.S. Supreme Court first uses the term "fruit of the poisonous tree" to describe evidence that is inadmissible at court because it is collected illegally.

*NASA v. Nelson*, 131 S.Ct. 746 (2011).

The U.S. Supreme Court held that background checks on contract NASA employees do not violate any constitutional right to information privacy.

*Owasso Independent School District No. I-011 v. Falvo*, 534 U.S. 426 (2002).

The U.S. Supreme Court held that the practice of peer grading does not violate the Family Educational Rights and Privacy Act (FERPA).

*Palsgraf v. Long Island Railroad*, 162 N.E. 99 (N.Y. 1928).

The New York Court of Appeals held that there is no duty to an unforeseen plaintiff for unforeseeable injuries.

*Pavesich v. New England Life Ins. Co.*, 50 S.E. 68 (Ga. 1905).

First state case to specifically recognize a right to privacy in a state constitution.

*Pemberton v. Bethlehem Steel Corp.*, 502 A.2d 1101 (Md. App.), cert. denied, 508 A.2d 488 (Md.), cert. denied, 107 S.Ct. 571 (1986).

Maryland Court of Appeals held that the publication of a mug shot is not a privacy violation because the photograph is part of the public record.

*People v. Weaver*, 12 N.Y.3d 433 (N.Y. 2009).

New York's highest court held that police officers need a warrant in order to place a tracking device on a suspect's car.

*Plessy v. Ferguson*, 163 U.S. 537 (1896).

The U.S. Supreme Court legalized racial, separate but equal, segregation practices. The Court stated that these practices did not violate the U.S. Constitution.

*ProCD Inc. v. Zeidenberg*, 86 F.3d 1447 (1996).

The Seventh Circuit Court of Appeals upheld a shrinkwrap contract where users had the opportunity to return software for a full refund if they did not agree to the terms in the contract.

*Register.com, Inc. v. Verio, Inc.*, 356 F.3d 393 (2d Cir. 2004).

The Second Circuit Court of Appeals has recognized that e-commerce has not changed the fundamental principles of contract law.

*Reno v. American Civil Liberties Union*, 521 U.S. 844 (1997).

The U.S. Supreme Court said that the principle of freedom of speech applies to the internet.

*Riley v. California*, 573 U.S. 373 (2014).

The U.S. Supreme Court held that law enforcement officers must get a warrant before searching a cell phone, even when the cell phone is seized when its owner is arrested (search incident to lawful arrest).

*Robinson v. California*, 370 U.S. 660 (1962).

The U.S. Supreme Court said that a state statute could not criminalize the status of being an addict. Criminal behavior is evidenced by a specific action, not status.

*Schifano v. Greene County Greyhound Park, Inc.*, 624 So.2d 178 (Ala. 1993).

Alabama Supreme Court case held that people cannot state a claim for false light when they are in a public place.

*Silverthorne Lumber Co. v. United States*, 251 U.S. 385 (1920).

The U.S. Supreme Court first articulated a doctrine that says that evidence is inadmissible at court if it is illegally collected.

*Smith v. Maryland*, 422 U.S. 735 (1979).

The U.S. Supreme Court found that there is no right of privacy in the routing information of electronic communications.

*Specht v. Netscape Communications Corporation*, 306 F.3d 17 (2002).

The Second Circuit Court of Appeals did not enforce terms of a browsewrap contract whose terms were located on a submerged web page.

*State v. Smith*, Slip Opinion No. 2009-Ohio-6426 (Oh. 2009).

The Supreme Court of Ohio found that individuals have a reasonable expectation of privacy in their cell phones.

*State v. Sveum*, 769 N.W.2d 53 (Wis. Ct. App. 2009).

Wisconsin Court of Appeals held that police did not need a warrant to attach a tracking unit to a suspect's car.

*State Rubbish Collectors Association v. Siliznoff*, 240 P.2d 282 (Cal. 1952).

Landmark case that recognized a cause of action for intentional infliction of emotional distress.

*Strassheim v. Daily*, 221 U.S. 280 (1911).

The U.S. Supreme Court used the detrimental effects test to determine if a state could exercise criminal jurisdiction over a person that committed acts outside of the state.

*Strunk v. United States*, 412 U.S. 434 (1973).

The U.S. Supreme Court held that a criminal charge must be dismissed if the defendant's speedy trial rights are violated.

*Toys "R" Us v. Akkaoui*, 40 U.S.P.Q.2d (BNA) 1836 (N.D. Cal. Oct. 29, 1996).

The District Court for the Northern District of California ordered an adult website to stop using its domain name because it cast a famous trademark in an unflattering light.

*United States v. Al-Marri*, 230 F. Supp.2d 535, 541 (S.D.N.Y. 2002).

The District Court for the Southern District of New York held that people have a reasonable expectation of privacy in data stored on personal pagers.

*United States v. American Library Association*, 539 U.S. 194 (2003).

The U.S. Supreme Court upheld the constitutionality of the Children's Internet Protection Act (CIPA).

*United States v. Barrows*, 481 F.3d 1246 (10th Cir. 2007).

Tenth Circuit Court of Appeals held that an employee did not have a reasonable expectation of privacy in his personal computer when he took no steps to protect his computer.

*United States v. Drew*, 259 F.R.D. 449 (C.D. Cal. 2009).

The U.S. District Court for the Central District of California held that a cyberbullying conviction under the Computer Fraud and Abuse Act was not valid.

*United States v. Heckenkamp*, 482 F.3d 1142 (9th Cir. 2007).

The Ninth Circuit Court of Appeals held that a person has a reasonable expectation of privacy in a personal computer.

*United States v. Jones*, 132 S.Ct. 945 (2012).

The U.S. Supreme Court held that installing a GPS unit on a car is a search under the Fourth Amendment to the U.S. Constitution.

*United States v. Kirschner*, 2010 U.S. Dist. Lexis 30603 (E.D. Mich., March 30, 2010).

The District Court for the Eastern District of Michigan held that it is a violation of the Fifth Amendment to require a defendant to provide the password to his computer.

*United States v. Miami University; Ohio State University*, 294 F.3d 797 (6th Cir. 2002).

The Sixth Circuit Court of Appeals held that disciplinary records are records that are protected by the Family Educational Rights and Privacy Act (FERPA). A student's consent is required before releasing the records.

*United States v. Mullins*, 992 F.2d 1472 (9th Cir. 1993).

The Ninth Circuit Court of Appeals held that the Wiretap Act's provider exception can be used by system administrators to track a hacker throughout an entity's computer network in order to prevent damage to the network.

*United States v. White*, 401 U.S. 745 (1971).

The U.S. Supreme Court found there is no right of privacy in information that is voluntarily disclosed to another person.

*Whalen v. Roe*, 429 U.S. 589 (1977).

The U.S. Supreme Court specifically recognized a right of "informational privacy."

*Wheaten v. Peters*, 33 U.S. 591 (1834).

The U.S. Supreme Court first acknowledged that a person has an interest in being "let alone."

*White v. Samsung Electronics of America, Inc.*, 989 F.2d 1512 (9th Cir. 1992).

A Ninth Circuit Court of Appeals case where a game show host argued successfully that being a host on a popular game show was her identity, and that a business misappropriated her identity.

*Williams v. Crichton*, 84 F.3d 581 (2d Cir. 1996).

The Second Circuit Court of Appeals stated a test used for determining "substantial similarity" between copyrighted works.

*Zubulake v. UBS Warburg, LLC*, 2004 WL 1620866 (S.D.N.Y. July 20, 2004).

A series of decisions in the District Court for the Southern District of New York that helped define the limits of electronic discovery.

# The Constitution of the United States of America*

*We the People of the United States, in Order to form a more perfect Union, establish Justice, insure domestic Tranquility, provide for the common defence, promote the general Welfare, and secure the Blessings of Liberty to ourselves and our Posterity, do ordain and establish this Constitution for the United States of America.*

## Article. I.

### Section. 1.

All legislative Powers herein granted shall be vested in a Congress of the United States, which shall consist of a Senate and House of Representatives.

### Section. 2.

The House of Representatives shall be composed of Members chosen every second Year by the People of the several States, and the Electors in each State shall have the Qualifications requisite for Electors of the most numerous Branch of the State Legislature.

No Person shall be a Representative who shall not have attained to the Age of twenty five Years, and been seven Years a Citizen of the United States, and who shall not, when elected, be an Inhabitant of that State in which he shall be chosen.

Representatives and direct Taxes shall be apportioned among the several States which may be included within this Union, according to their respective Numbers, which shall be determined by adding to the whole Number of free Persons, including those bound to Service for a Term of Years, and excluding Indians not taxed, three fifths of all other Persons. The actual Enumeration shall be made within three Years after the first Meeting of the Congress of the United States, and within every subsequent Term of ten Years, in such Manner as they shall by Law direct. The Number of Representatives shall not exceed one for every thirty Thousand, but each State shall have at Least one Representative; and until such enumeration shall be made, the State of New Hampshire shall be entitled to chuse three, Massachusetts eight, Rhode-Island and Providence Plantations one, Connecticut five, New-York six, New Jersey four, Pennsylvania eight, Delaware one, Maryland six, Virginia ten, North Carolina five, South Carolina five, and Georgia three.

When vacancies happen in the Representation from any State, the Executive Authority thereof shall issue Writs of Election to fill such Vacancies.

The House of Representatives shall chuse their Speaker and other Officers; and shall have the sole Power of Impeachment.

---

*The text of the U.S. Constitution is in its original form. Spelling, punctuation, and capitalization are the same as in the original document.

### *Section. 3.*

The Senate of the United States shall be composed of two Senators from each State, chosen by the Legislature thereof for six Years; and each Senator shall have one Vote.

Immediately after they shall be assembled in Consequence of the first Election, they shall be divided as equally as may be into three Classes. The Seats of the Senators of the first Class shall be vacated at the Expiration of the second Year, of the second Class at the Expiration of the fourth Year, and of the third Class at the Expiration of the sixth Year, so that one third may be chosen every second Year; and if Vacancies happen by Resignation, or otherwise, during the Recess of the Legislature of any State, the Executive thereof may make temporary Appointments until the next Meeting of the Legislature, which shall then fill such Vacancies.

No Person shall be a Senator who shall not have attained to the Age of thirty Years, and been nine Years a Citizen of the United States, and who shall not, when elected, be an Inhabitant of that State for which he shall be chosen.

The Vice President of the United States shall be President of the Senate, but shall have no Vote, unless they be equally divided.

The Senate shall chuse their other Officers, and also a President pro tempore, in the Absence of the Vice President, or when he shall exercise the Office of President of the United States.

The Senate shall have the sole Power to try all Impeachments. When sitting for that Purpose, they shall be on Oath or Affirmation. When the President of the United States is tried, the Chief Justice shall preside: And no Person shall be convicted without the Concurrence of two thirds of the Members present.

Judgment in Cases of Impeachment shall not extend further than to removal from Office, and disqualification to hold and enjoy any Office of honor, Trust or Profit under the United States: but the Party convicted shall nevertheless be liable and subject to Indictment, Trial, Judgment and Punishment, according to Law.

### *Section. 4.*

The Times, Places and Manner of holding Elections for Senators and Representatives, shall be prescribed in each State by the Legislature thereof; but the Congress may at any time by Law make or alter such Regulations, except as to the Places of chusing Senators.

The Congress shall assemble at least once in every Year, and such Meeting shall be on the first Monday in December, unless they shall by Law appoint a different Day.

### *Section. 5.*

Each House shall be the Judge of the Elections, Returns and Qualifications of its own Members, and a Majority of each shall constitute a Quorum to do Business; but a smaller Number may adjourn from day to day, and may be authorized to compel the Attendance of absent Members, in such Manner, and under such Penalties as each House may provide.

Each House may determine the Rules of its Proceedings, punish its Members for disorderly Behaviour, and, with the Concurrence of two thirds, expel a Member.

Each House shall keep a Journal of its Proceedings, and from time to time publish the same, excepting such Parts as may in their Judgment require Secrecy; and the Yeas and Nays of the Members of either House on any question shall, at the Desire of one fifth of those Present, be entered on the Journal.

Neither House, during the Session of Congress, shall, without the Consent of the other, adjourn for more than three days, nor to any other Place than that in which the two Houses shall be sitting.

### *Section. 6.*

The Senators and Representatives shall receive a Compensation for their Services, to be ascertained by Law, and paid out of the Treasury of the United States. They shall in all Cases, except Treason, Felony and Breach of the Peace, be privileged from Arrest during their Attendance at the Session of their respective Houses, and in going to and returning from the same; and for any Speech or Debate in either House, they shall not be questioned in any other Place.

No Senator or Representative shall, during the Time for which he was elected, be appointed to any civil Office under the Authority of the United States, which shall have been created, or the Emoluments whereof shall have been encreased during such time; and no Person holding any Office under the United States, shall be a Member of either House during his Continuance in Office.

### *Section. 7.*

All Bills for raising Revenue shall originate in the House of Representatives; but the Senate may propose or concur with Amendments as on other Bills.

Every Bill which shall have passed the House of Representatives and the Senate, shall, before it become a Law, be presented to the President of the United States: If he approve he shall sign it, but if not he shall return it, with his Objections to that House in which it shall have originated, who shall enter the Objections at large on their Journal, and proceed to reconsider it. If after such Reconsideration two thirds of that House shall agree to pass the Bill, it shall be sent, together with the Objections, to the other House, by which it shall likewise be reconsidered, and if approved by two thirds of that House, it shall become a Law. But in all such Cases the Votes of both Houses shall be determined by yeas and Nays, and the Names of the Persons voting for and against the Bill shall be entered on the Journal of each House respectively. If any Bill shall not be returned by the President within ten Days (Sundays excepted) after it shall have been presented to him, the Same shall be a Law, in like Manner as if he had signed it, unless the Congress by their Adjournment prevent its Return, in which Case it shall not be a Law.

Every Order, Resolution, or Vote to which the Concurrence of the Senate and House of Representatives may be necessary (except on a question of Adjournment) shall be presented to the President of the United States; and before the Same shall take Effect, shall be approved by him, or being disapproved by him, shall be repassed by two thirds of the Senate and House of Representatives, according to the Rules and Limitations prescribed in the Case of a Bill.

### *Section. 8.*

The Congress shall have Power To lay and collect Taxes, Duties, Imposts and Excises, to pay the Debts and provide for the common Defence and general Welfare of the United States; but all Duties, Imposts and Excises shall be uniform throughout the United States;

To borrow Money on the credit of the United States;

To regulate Commerce with foreign Nations, and among the several States, and with the Indian Tribes;

To establish an uniform Rule of Naturalization, and uniform Laws on the subject of Bankruptcies throughout the United States;

To coin Money, regulate the Value thereof, and of foreign Coin, and fix the Standard of Weights and Measures;

To provide for the Punishment of counterfeiting the Securities and current Coin of the United States;

To establish Post Offices and post Roads;

To promote the Progress of Science and useful Arts, by securing for limited Times to Authors and Inventors the exclusive Right to their respective Writings and Discoveries;

To constitute Tribunals inferior to the supreme Court;

To define and punish Piracies and Felonies committed on the high Seas, and Offences against the Law of Nations;

To declare War, grant Letters of Marque and Reprisal, and make Rules concerning Captures on Land and Water;

To raise and support Armies, but no Appropriation of Money to that Use shall be for a longer Term than two Years;

To provide and maintain a Navy;

To make Rules for the Government and Regulation of the land and naval Forces;

To provide for calling forth the Militia to execute the Laws of the Union, suppress Insurrections and repel Invasions;

To provide for organizing, arming, and disciplining, the Militia, and for governing such Part of them as may be employed in the Service of the United States, reserving to the States respectively, the Appointment of the Officers, and the Authority of training the Militia according to the discipline prescribed by Congress;

To exercise exclusive Legislation in all Cases whatsoever, over such District (not exceeding ten Miles square) as may, by Cession of particular States, and the Acceptance of Congress, become the Seat of the Government of the United States, and to exercise like Authority over all Places purchased by the Consent of the Legislature of the State in which the Same shall be, for the Erection of Forts, Magazines, Arsenals, dock-Yards, and other needful Buildings;—And

To make all Laws which shall be necessary and proper for carrying into Execution the foregoing Powers, and all other Powers vested by this Constitution in the Government of the United States, or in any Department or Officer thereof.

### *Section. 9.*

The Migration or Importation of such Persons as any of the States now existing shall think proper to admit, shall not be prohibited by the Congress prior to the Year one thousand eight hundred and eight, but a Tax or duty may be imposed on such Importation, not exceeding ten dollars for each Person.

The Privilege of the Writ of Habeas Corpus shall not be suspended, unless when in Cases of Rebellion or Invasion the public Safety may require it.

No Bill of Attainder or ex post facto Law shall be passed.

No Capitation, or other direct, Tax shall be laid, unless in Proportion to the Census or enumeration herein before directed to be taken.

No Tax or Duty shall be laid on Articles exported from any State.

No Preference shall be given by any Regulation of Commerce or Revenue to the Ports of one State over those of another; nor shall Vessels bound to, or from, one State, be obliged to enter, clear, or pay Duties in another.

No Money shall be drawn from the Treasury, but in Consequence of Appropriations made by Law; and a regular Statement and Account of the Receipts and Expenditures of all public Money shall be published from time to time.

No Title of Nobility shall be granted by the United States: And no Person holding any Office of Profit or Trust under them, shall, without the Consent of the Congress, accept of any present, Emolument, Office, or Title, of any kind whatever, from any King, Prince, or foreign State.

### *Section. 10.*

No State shall enter into any Treaty, Alliance, or Confederation; grant Letters of Marque and Reprisal; coin Money; emit Bills of Credit; make any Thing but gold and silver Coin a Tender in Payment of Debts; pass any Bill of Attainder, ex post facto Law, or Law impairing the Obligation of Contracts, or grant any Title of Nobility.

No State shall, without the Consent of the Congress, lay any Imposts or Duties on Imports or Exports, except what may be absolutely necessary for executing it's inspection Laws: and the net Produce of all Duties and Imposts, laid by any State on Imports or Exports, shall be for the Use of the Treasury of the United States; and all such Laws shall be subject to the Revision and Controul of the Congress.

No State shall, without the Consent of Congress, lay any Duty of Tonnage, keep Troops, or Ships of War in time of Peace, enter into any Agreement or Compact with another State, or with a foreign Power, or engage in War, unless actually invaded, or in such imminent Danger as will not admit of delay.

## Article. II.

### *Section. 1.*

The executive Power shall be vested in a President of the United States of America. He shall hold his Office during the Term of four Years, and, together with the Vice President, chosen for the same Term, be elected, as follows:

Each State shall appoint, in such Manner as the Legislature thereof may direct, a Number of Electors, equal to the whole Number of Senators and Representatives to which the State may be entitled in the Congress: but no Senator or Representative, or Person holding an Office of Trust or Profit under the United States, shall be appointed an Elector.

The Electors shall meet in their respective States, and vote by Ballot for two Persons, of whom one at least shall not be an Inhabitant of the same State with themselves. And they shall make a List of all the Persons voted for, and of the Number of Votes for each; which List they shall sign and certify, and transmit sealed to the Seat of the Government of the United States, directed to the President of the Senate. The President of the Senate shall, in the Presence of the Senate and House of Representatives, open all the Certificates, and the Votes shall then be counted. The Person having the greatest Number of Votes shall be the President, if such Number be a Majority of the whole Number of Electors appointed; and if there be more than one who have such Majority, and have an equal Number of Votes, then the House of Representatives shall immediately chuse by Ballot one of them for President; and if no Person have a Majority, then from the five highest on the List the said House shall in like Manner chuse the President. But in chusing the President, the Votes shall be taken by States, the Representation from each State having one Vote; A quorum for this purpose shall consist of a Member or Members from two thirds of the States, and a Majority of all the States shall be necessary to a Choice. In every Case, after the Choice of the President, the Person having the greatest Number of Votes of the Electors shall be the Vice President. But if there should remain two or more who have equal Votes, the Senate shall chuse from them by Ballot the Vice President.

The Congress may determine the Time of chusing the Electors, and the Day on which they shall give their Votes; which Day shall be the same throughout the United States.

No Person except a natural born Citizen, or a Citizen of the United States, at the time of the Adoption of this Constitution, shall be eligible to the Office of President; neither shall any Person be eligible to that Office who shall not have attained to the Age of thirty five Years, and been fourteen Years a Resident within the United States.

In Case of the Removal of the President from Office, or of his Death, Resignation, or Inability to discharge the Powers and Duties of the said Office, the Same shall devolve on the Vice President, and the Congress may by Law provide for the Case of Removal, Death, Resignation or Inability, both of the President and Vice President, declaring what Officer shall then act as President, and such Officer shall act accordingly, until the Disability be removed, or a President shall be elected.

The President shall, at stated Times, receive for his Services, a Compensation, which shall neither be increased nor diminished during the Period for which he shall have been elected, and he shall not receive within that Period any other Emolument from the United States, or any of them.

Before he enter on the Execution of his Office, he shall take the following Oath or Affirmation:—"I do solemnly swear (or affirm) that I will faithfully execute the Office of President of the United States, and will to the best of my Ability, preserve, protect and defend the Constitution of the United States."

### *Section. 2.*

The President shall be Commander in Chief of the Army and Navy of the United States, and of the Militia of the several States, when called into the actual Service of the United States; he may require the Opinion, in writing, of the principal Officer in each of the executive Departments, upon any Subject relating to the Duties of their respective Offices, and he shall have

Power to grant Reprieves and Pardons for Offences against the United States, except in Cases of Impeachment.

He shall have Power, by and with the Advice and Consent of the Senate, to make Treaties, provided two thirds of the Senators present concur; and he shall nominate, and by and with the Advice and Consent of the Senate, shall appoint Ambassadors, other public Ministers and Consuls, Judges of the supreme Court, and all other Officers of the United States, whose Appointments are not herein otherwise provided for, and which shall be established by Law: but the Congress may by Law vest the Appointment of such inferior Officers, as they think proper, in the President alone, in the Courts of Law, or in the Heads of Departments.

The President shall have Power to fill up all Vacancies that may happen during the Recess of the Senate, by granting Commissions which shall expire at the End of their next Session.

### *Section. 3.*

He shall from time to time give to the Congress Information of the State of the Union, and recommend to their Consideration such Measures as he shall judge necessary and expedient; he may, on extraordinary Occasions, convene both Houses, or either of them, and in Case of Disagreement between them, with Respect to the Time of Adjournment, he may adjourn them to such Time as he shall think proper; he shall receive Ambassadors and other public Ministers; he shall take Care that the Laws be faithfully executed, and shall Commission all the Officers of the United States.

### *Section. 4.*

The President, Vice President and all civil Officers of the United States, shall be removed from Office on Impeachment for, and Conviction of, Treason, Bribery, or other high Crimes and Misdemeanors.

## Article III.

### *Section. 1.*

The judicial Power of the United States shall be vested in one supreme Court, and in such inferior Courts as the Congress may from time to time ordain and establish. The Judges, both of the supreme and inferior Courts, shall hold their Offices during good Behaviour, and shall, at stated Times, receive for their Services a Compensation, which shall not be diminished during their Continuance in Office.

### *Section. 2.*

The judicial Power shall extend to all Cases, in Law and Equity, arising under this Constitution, the Laws of the United States, and Treaties made, or which shall be made, under their Authority;—to all Cases affecting Ambassadors, other public Ministers and Consuls;—to all Cases of admiralty and maritime Jurisdiction;—to Controversies to which the United States shall be a Party;—to Controversies between two or more States;— between a State and Citizens of another State,—between Citizens of different States,—between Citizens of the same State claiming Lands under Grants of different States, and between a State, or the Citizens thereof, and foreign States, Citizens or Subjects.

In all Cases affecting Ambassadors, other public Ministers and Consuls, and those in which a State shall be Party, the supreme Court shall have original Jurisdiction. In all the other Cases before mentioned, the supreme Court shall have appellate Jurisdiction, both as to Law and Fact, with such Exceptions, and under such Regulations as the Congress shall make.

The Trial of all Crimes, except in Cases of Impeachment, shall be by Jury; and such Trial shall be held in the State where the said Crimes shall have been committed; but when not committed within any State, the Trial shall be at such Place or Places as the Congress may by Law have directed.

### *Section. 3.*

Treason against the United States, shall consist only in levying War against them, or in adhering to their Enemies, giving them Aid and Comfort. No Person shall be convicted of Treason unless on the Testimony of two Witnesses to the same overt Act, or on Confession in open Court.

The Congress shall have Power to declare the Punishment of Treason, but no Attainder of Treason shall work Corruption of Blood, or Forfeiture except during the Life of the Person attainted.

## Article. IV.

### *Section. 1.*

Full Faith and Credit shall be given in each State to the public Acts, Records, and judicial Proceedings of every other State. And the Congress may by general Laws prescribe the Manner in which such Acts, Records and Proceedings shall be proved, and the Effect thereof.

### *Section. 2.*

The Citizens of each State shall be entitled to all Privileges and Immunities of Citizens in the several States. A Person charged in any State with Treason, Felony, or other Crime, who shall flee from Justice, and be found in another State, shall on Demand of the executive Authority of the State from which he fled, be delivered up, to be removed to the State having Jurisdiction of the Crime. No Person held to Service or Labour in one State, under the Laws thereof, escaping into another, shall, in Consequence of any Law or Regulation therein, be discharged from such Service or Labour, but shall be delivered up on Claim of the Party to whom such Service or Labour may be due.

### *Section. 3.*

New States may be admitted by the Congress into this Union; but no new State shall be formed or erected within the Jurisdiction of any other State; nor any State be formed by the Junction of two or more States, or Parts of States, without the Consent of the Legislatures of the States concerned as well as of the Congress.

The Congress shall have Power to dispose of and make all needful Rules and Regulations respecting the Territory or other Property belonging to the United States; and nothing in this Constitution shall be so construed as to Prejudice any Claims of the United States, or of any particular State.

### *Section. 4.*

The United States shall guarantee to every State in this Union a Republican Form of Government, and shall protect each of them against Invasion; and on Application of the Legislature, or of the Executive (when the Legislature cannot be convened), against domestic Violence.

## Article. V.

The Congress, whenever two thirds of both Houses shall deem it necessary, shall propose Amendments to this Constitution, or, on the Application of the Legislatures of two thirds of the several States, shall call a Convention for proposing Amendments, which, in either Case, shall be valid to all Intents and Purposes, as Part of this Constitution, when ratified by the Legislatures of three fourths of the several States, or by Conventions in three fourths thereof, as the one or the other Mode of Ratification may be proposed by the Congress; Provided that no Amendment which may be made prior to the Year One thousand eight hundred and eight shall in any Manner affect the first and fourth Clauses in the Ninth Section of the first Article; and that no State, without its Consent, shall be deprived of its equal Suffrage in the Senate.

## Article. VI.

All Debts contracted and Engagements entered into, before the Adoption of this Constitution, shall be as valid against the United States under this Constitution, as under the Confederation. This Constitution, and the Laws of the United States which shall be made in Pursuance thereof; and all Treaties made, or which shall be made, under the Authority of the United States, shall be the supreme Law of the Land; and the Judges in every State shall be bound thereby, any Thing in the Constitution or Laws of any State to the Contrary notwithstanding.

The Senators and Representatives before mentioned, and the Members of the several State Legislatures, and all executive and judicial Officers, both of the United States and of the several States, shall be bound by Oath or Affirmation, to support this Constitution; but no religious Test shall ever be required as a Qualification to any Office or public Trust under the United States.

## Article. VII.

The Ratification of the Conventions of nine States, shall be sufficient for the Establishment of this Constitution between the States so ratifying the Same.

## Amendments to the Constitution of the United States of America.

## Amendment I (1791)

Congress shall make no law respecting an establishment of religion, or prohibiting the free exercise thereof; or abridging the freedom of speech, or of the press; or the right of the people peaceably to assemble, and to petition the Government for a redress of grievances.

## Amendment II (1791)

A well regulated Militia, being necessary to the security of a free State, the right of the people to keep and bear Arms, shall not be infringed.

## Amendment III (1791)

No Soldier shall, in time of peace be quartered in any house, without the consent of the Owner, nor in time of war, but in a manner to be prescribed by law.

## Amendment IV (1791)

The right of the people to be secure in their persons, houses, papers, and effects, against unreasonable searches and seizures, shall not be violated, and no Warrants shall issue, but upon probable cause, supported by Oath or affirmation, and particularly describing the place to be searched, and the persons or things to be seized.

## Amendment V (1791)

No person shall be held to answer for a capital, or otherwise infamous crime, unless on a presentment or indictment of a Grand Jury, except in cases arising in the land or naval forces, or in the Militia, when in actual service in time of War or public danger; nor shall any person be subject for the same offence to be twice put in jeopardy of life or limb; nor shall be compelled in any criminal case to be a witness against himself, nor be deprived of life, liberty, or property, without due process of law; nor shall private property be taken for public use, without just compensation.

## Amendment VI (1791)

In all criminal prosecutions, the accused shall enjoy the right to a speedy and public trial, by an impartial jury of the State and district wherein the crime shall have been committed, which district shall have been previously ascertained by law, and to be informed of the nature and cause of the accusation; to be confronted with the witnesses against him; to have compulsory process for obtaining witnesses in his favor, and to have the Assistance of Counsel for his defence.

## Amendment VII (1791)

In Suits at common law, where the value in controversy shall exceed twenty dollars, the right of trial by jury shall be preserved, and no fact tried by a jury, shall be otherwise re-examined in any Court of the United States, than according to the rules of the common law.

## Amendment VIII (1791)

Excessive bail shall not be required, nor excessive fines imposed, nor cruel and unusual punishments inflicted.

## Amendment IX (1791)

The enumeration in the Constitution, of certain rights, shall not be construed to deny or disparage others retained by the people.

## Amendment X (1791)

The powers not delegated to the United States by the Constitution, nor prohibited by it to the States, are reserved to the States respectively, or to the people.

## Amendment XI (1795)

The Judicial power of the United States shall not be construed to extend to any suit in law or equity, commenced or prosecuted against one of the United States by Citizens of another State, or by Citizens or Subjects of any Foreign State.
*Note: Article III, section 2, of the Constitution was modified by amendment 11.*

## Amendment XII (1804)

The Electors shall meet in their respective states and vote by ballot for President and Vice-President, one of whom, at least, shall not be an inhabitant of the same state with themselves; they shall name in their ballots the person voted for as President, and in distinct ballots the person voted for as Vice-President, and they shall make distinct lists of all persons voted for as President, and of all persons voted for as Vice-President, and of the number of votes for each, which lists they shall sign and certify, and transmit sealed to the seat of the government of the United States, directed to the President of the Senate; — the President of the Senate shall, in the presence of the Senate and House of Representatives, open all the certificates and the votes shall then be counted; — The person having the greatest number of votes for President, shall be the President, if such number be a majority of the whole number of Electors appointed; and if no person have such majority, then from the persons having the highest numbers not exceeding three on the list of those voted for as President, the House of Representatives shall choose immediately, by ballot, the President. But in choosing the President, the votes shall be taken by states, the representation from each state having one vote; a quorum for this purpose shall consist of a member or members from two-thirds of the states, and a majority of all the states shall be necessary to a choice. And if the House of Representatives shall not choose a President whenever the right of choice shall devolve upon them, before the fourth day of March next following, then the Vice-President shall act as President, as in case of the death or other constitutional disability of the President. The person having the greatest number of votes as Vice-President, shall be the Vice-President, if such number be a majority of the whole number of Electors appointed, and if no person have a majority, then from the two highest numbers on the list, the Senate shall choose the Vice-President; a quorum for the purpose shall consist of two-thirds of the whole number of Senators, and a majority of the whole number shall be necessary to a choice. But no person constitutionally ineligible to the office of President shall be eligible to that of Vice-President of the United States.
*Note: A portion of Article II, section 1 of the Constitution was superseded by the 12th amendment.*

## Amendment XIII (1865)

### *Section 1.*

Neither slavery nor involuntary servitude, except as a punishment for crime whereof the party shall have been duly convicted, shall exist within the United States, or any place subject to their jurisdiction.

### *Section 2.*

Congress shall have power to enforce this article by appropriate legislation.
*Note: A portion of Article IV, section 2, of the Constitution was superseded by the 13th amendment.*

## Amendment XIV (1868)

### *Section 1.*

All persons born or naturalized in the United States, and subject to the jurisdiction thereof, are citizens of the United States and of the State wherein they reside. No State shall make or enforce any law which shall abridge the privileges or immunities of citizens of the United States; nor shall any State deprive any person of life, liberty, or property, without due process of law; nor deny to any person within its jurisdiction the equal protection of the laws.

### *Section 2.*

Representatives shall be apportioned among the several States according to their respective numbers, counting the whole number of persons in each State, excluding Indians not taxed. But when the right to vote at any election for the choice of electors for President and Vice-President of the United States, Representatives in Congress, the Executive and Judicial officers of a State, or the members of the Legislature thereof, is denied to any of the male inhabitants of such State, being twenty-one years of age, and citizens of the United States, or in any way abridged, except for participation in rebellion, or other crime, the basis of representation therein shall be reduced in the proportion which the number of such male citizens shall bear to the whole number of male citizens twenty-one years of age in such State.

### *Section 3.*

No person shall be a Senator or Representative in Congress, or elector of President and Vice-President, or hold any office, civil or military, under the United States, or under any State, who, having previously taken an oath, as a member of Congress, or as an officer of the United States, or as a member of any State legislature, or as an executive or judicial officer of any State, to support the Constitution of the United States, shall have engaged in insurrection or rebellion against the same, or given aid or comfort to the enemies thereof. But Congress may by a vote of two-thirds of each House, remove such disability.

### *Section 4.*

The validity of the public debt of the United States, authorized by law, including debts incurred for payment of pensions and bounties for services in suppressing insurrection or rebellion, shall not be questioned. But neither the United States nor any State shall assume or pay any debt or obligation incurred in aid of insurrection or rebellion against the United States, or any claim for the loss or emancipation of any slave; but all such debts, obligations and claims shall be held illegal and void.

### *Section 5.*

The Congress shall have the power to enforce, by appropriate legislation, the provisions of this article.
*Note: Article I, section 2, of the Constitution was modified by section 2 of the 14th amendment.*

## Amendment XV (1870)

### *Section 1.*

The right of citizens of the United States to vote shall not be denied or abridged by the United States or by any State on account of race, color, or previous condition of servitude—

### *Section 2.*

The Congress shall have the power to enforce this article by appropriate legislation.

## Amendment XVI (1913)

The Congress shall have power to lay and collect taxes on incomes, from whatever source derived, without apportionment among the several States, and without regard to any census or enumeration.
*Note: Article I, section 9, of the Constitution was modified by amendment 16.*

## Amendment XVII (1913)

The Senate of the United States shall be composed of two Senators from each State, elected by the people thereof, for six years; and each Senator shall have one vote. The electors in each State shall have the qualifications requisite for electors of the most numerous branch of the State legislatures.

When vacancies happen in the representation of any State in the Senate, the executive authority of such State shall issue writs of election to fill such vacancies: Provided, That the legislature of any State may empower the executive thereof to make temporary appointments until the people fill the vacancies by election as the legislature may direct.

This amendment shall not be so construed as to affect the election or term of any Senator chosen before it becomes valid as part of the Constitution.
*Note: Article I, section 3, of the Constitution was modified by the 17th amendment.*

## Amendment XVIII (1919)

### *Section 1.*

After one year from the ratification of this article the manufacture, sale, or transportation of intoxicating liquors within, the importation thereof into, or the exportation thereof from the United States and all territory subject to the jurisdiction thereof for beverage purposes is hereby prohibited.

### *Section 2.*

The Congress and the several States shall have concurrent power to enforce this article by appropriate legislation.

### *Section 3.*

This article shall be inoperative unless it shall have been ratified as an amendment to the Constitution by the legislatures of the several States, as provided in the Constitution, within seven years from the date of the submission hereof to the States by the Congress.
*Note: This amendment was repealed by amendment 21.*

## Amendment XIX (1920)

The right of citizens of the United States to vote shall not be denied or abridged by the United States or by any State on account of sex.

Congress shall have power to enforce this article by appropriate legislation.

## Amendment XX (1933)

### *Section 1.*

The terms of the President and the Vice President shall end at noon on the 20th day of January, and the terms of Senators and Representatives at noon on the 3d day of January, of the years in which such terms would have ended if this article had not been ratified; and the terms of their successors shall then begin.

### *Section 2.*

The Congress shall assemble at least once in every year, and such meeting shall begin at noon on the 3d day of January, unless they shall by law appoint a different day.

### *Section 3.*

If, at the time fixed for the beginning of the term of the President, the President elect shall have died, the Vice President elect shall become President. If a President shall not have been chosen before the time fixed for the beginning of his term, or if the President elect shall have failed to qualify, then the Vice President elect shall act as President until a President shall have qualified; and the Congress may by law provide for the case wherein neither a President elect nor a Vice President shall have qualified, declaring who shall then act as President, or the manner in which one who is to act shall be selected, and such person shall act accordingly until a President or Vice President shall have qualified.

### *Section 4.*

The Congress may by law provide for the case of the death of any of the persons from whom the House of Representatives may choose a President whenever the right of choice shall have devolved upon them, and for the case of the death of any of the persons from whom the Senate may choose a Vice President whenever the right of choice shall have devolved upon them.

### *Section 5.*

Sections 1 and 2 shall take effect on the 15th day of October following the ratification of this article.

### *Section 6.*

This article shall be inoperative unless it shall have been ratified as an amendment to the Constitution by the legislatures of three-fourths of the several States within seven years from the date of its submission.
*Note: Article I, section 4, of the Constitution was modified by section 2 of this amendment. In addition, a portion of the 12th amendment was superseded by section 3.*

## Amendment XXI (1933)

### *Section 1.*

The eighteenth article of amendment to the Constitution of the United States is hereby repealed.

### *Section 2.*

The transportation or importation into any State, Territory, or Possession of the United States for delivery or use therein of intoxicating liquors, in violation of the laws thereof, is hereby prohibited.

### *Section 3.*

This article shall be inoperative unless it shall have been ratified as an amendment to the Constitution by conventions in the several States, as provided in the Constitution, within seven years from the date of the submission hereof to the States by the Congress.

## Amendment XXII (1951)

### *Section 1.*

No person shall be elected to the office of the President more than twice, and no person who has held the office of President, or acted as President, for more than two years of a term to which some other person was elected President shall be elected to the office of President more than once. But this Article shall not apply to any person holding the office of President when this Article was proposed by Congress, and shall not prevent any person who may be holding the office of President, or acting as President, during the term within which this Article becomes operative from holding the office of President or acting as President during the remainder of such term.

### *Section 2.*

This article shall be inoperative unless it shall have been ratified as an amendment to the Constitution by the legislatures of three-fourths of the several States within seven years from the date of its submission to the States by the Congress.

## Amendment XXIII (1961)

### *Section 1.*

The District constituting the seat of Government of the United States shall appoint in such manner as Congress may direct: A number of electors of President and Vice President equal to the whole number of Senators and Representatives in Congress to which the District would be entitled if it were a State, but in no event more than the least populous State; they shall be in addition to those appointed by the States, but they shall be considered, for the purposes of the election of President and Vice President, to be electors appointed by a State; and they shall meet in the District and perform such duties as provided by the twelfth article of amendment.

### *Section 2.*

The Congress shall have power to enforce this article by appropriate legislation.

## Amendment XXIV (1964)

### *Section 1.*

The right of citizens of the United States to vote in any primary or other election for President or Vice President, for electors for President or Vice President, or for Senator or Representative in Congress, shall not be denied or abridged by the United States or any State by reason of failure to pay poll tax or other tax.

### *Section 2.*

The Congress shall have power to enforce this article by appropriate legislation.

## Amendment XXV (1967)

### *Section 1.*

In case of the removal of the President from office or of his death or resignation, the Vice President shall become President.

### *Section 2.*

Whenever there is a vacancy in the office of the Vice President, the President shall nominate a Vice President who shall take office upon confirmation by a majority vote of both Houses of Congress.

### *Section 3.*

Whenever the President transmits to the President pro tempore of the Senate and the Speaker of the House of Representatives his written declaration that he is unable to discharge the powers and duties of his office, and until he transmits to them a written declaration to the contrary, such powers and duties shall be discharged by the Vice President as Acting President.

### *Section 4.*

Whenever the Vice President and a majority of either the principal officers of the executive departments or of such other body as Congress may by law provide, transmit to the President pro tempore of the Senate and the Speaker of the House of Representatives their written declaration that the President is unable to discharge the powers and duties of his office, the Vice President shall immediately assume the powers and duties of the office as Acting President.

Thereafter, when the President transmits to the President pro tempore of the Senate and the Speaker of the House of Representatives his written declaration that no inability exists, he shall resume the powers and duties of his office unless the Vice President and a majority of either the principal officers of the executive department or of such other body as Congress may by law provide, transmit within four days to the President pro tempore of the Senate and the Speaker of the House of Representatives their written declaration that the President is unable to discharge the powers and duties of his office. Thereupon Congress shall decide the issue, assembling within forty-eight hours for that purpose if not in session. If the Congress, within twenty-one days after receipt of the latter written declaration, or, if Congress is not in session, within twenty-one days after Congress is required to assemble, determines by two-thirds vote of both Houses that the President is unable to discharge the powers and duties of his office, the Vice President shall continue to discharge the same as Acting President; otherwise, the President shall resume the powers and duties of his office.
*Note: Article II, section 1, of the Constitution was affected by the 25th amendment.*

## Amendment XXVI (1971)

### *Section 1.*

The right of citizens of the United States, who are eighteen years of age or older, to vote shall not be denied or abridged by the United States or by any State on account of age.

### *Section 2.*

The Congress shall have power to enforce this article by appropriate legislation.
*Note: Amendment 14, section 2, of the Constitution was modified by section 1 of the 26th amendment.*

## Amendment XXVII (1992)

No law, varying the compensation for the services of the Senators and Representatives, shall take effect, until an election of representatives shall have intervened.

*Source:* http://www.archives.gov/exhibits/charters/constitution_transcript.html

# Glossary of Key Terms

## A

**Acceptable use policy (AUP)** | States the proper use of an organization's information technology resources.

***Actus reus*** | A Latin term used to describe a crime. It means "guilty act."

**Administrative procedure** | Sets forth the process under which administrative agencies make and enforce rules.

**Administrative safeguards** | Management and regulatory controls. These safeguards are usually policies, standards, guidelines, and procedures. They also can be the laws an organization must follow.

**Adware** | Software that displays advertising banners, redirects a user to websites, and conducts advertising on a user's computer. Adware also displays pop-up advertisements.

**Affidavit** | A sworn written statement.

**Annual rate of occurrence (ARO)** | How many times a threat might affect an organization during a 1-year time frame.

**Annualized loss expectancy (ALE)** | The amount of loss that an organization can expect to have each year because of a particular risk. ALE is often expressed as the equation: ALE = SLE × ARO. SLE is single loss expectancy. ARO is annual rate of occurrence.

**Answer** | A defendant's response to a plaintiff's complaint.

**Appellate jurisdiction** | The power of a court to review a decision made by a lower court.

**Audit** | An evaluation and verification that certain objectives are met.

**Authentication** | The process through which a user proves his or her identity to access an information technology resource.

**Authorization** | A written consent that allows protected health information (PHI) to be shared. Patients sign consents. These documents are required for many purposes. This term is defined by the Health Insurance Portability and Accountability Act.

**Availability** | The security goal of ensuring that you can access information systems and their data when you need them. They must be available in a dependable and timely manner.

## B

**Baseline** | A minimum level of behavior or action that must be met in order to comply with a governance document. Baselines are often specified in standards.

**Beyond a reasonable doubt** | The standard of proof in a criminal case.

**Biometric data** | Data about a person's physical or behavioral traits used to identify a particular person. Biometric data is unique because it cannot be changed.

**Blog** | A personal online journal. Also called a weblog.

**Bluetooth** | A wireless communication technology designed to replace the data cables connecting devices.

**Board of directors (BOD)** | An organization's governing body that plans an organization's strategic direction. A BOD is required by law to act with due care and in the best interests of the organization.

**Breach notification law** | A law that requires that state residents be notified if an entity experiences a security breach that compromises their personal data.

**Browsewrap contract** | An agreement where the complete terms of the agreement are presented on a webpage. A user does not have to take any affirmative action to accept the terms of the agreement other than to use the webpage.

**Business associates** | Organizations that perform a healthcare activity on behalf of a covered entity. This term is defined by the Health Insurance Portability and Accountability Act.

**Business continuity (BC) plans** | Plans that address the recovery of an organization's business processes and functions in the event of a disaster. Business continuity plans tend to be comprehensive business plans for returning an organization to normal operating conditions.

**Business impact analysis (BIA)** | A process that identifies key business operations and the resources used to support those processes. A business impact analysis also identifies maximum tolerable downtime for critical business functions.

## C

**Chain of custody** | Documentation that shows how evidence is collected, used, and handled throughout the lifetime of a case. A chain of custody document shows who obtained evidence, where and when it was obtained, who secured it, and who had control or possession of it.

**Checklist test** | A basic type of disaster recovery and business continuity test that checks to make sure that supplies and inventory items needed for an organization's business recovery are on hand.

**Chief information officer (CIO)** | An organization's senior information technology official. This role focuses on developing an organization's own IT resources.

**Chief information security officer (CISO)** | An organization's senior information security official.

**Chief technology officer (CTO)** | An organization's most senior technology official. This role focuses on developing an organization's technology products.

**Civil procedure** | Sets forth the procedures and processes that courts use to conduct civil trials.

**Clickstream** | The data trail that an internet user creates while browsing. A clickstream is a record of the pages that a computer user visits when navigating on a particular website.

**Clickwrap contract** | An agreement in which the complete terms of the agreement are presented on a computer screen, usually in the form of a pop-up window. A user must take an affirmative action to accept the terms of the agreement.

**Cloud computing** | A type of computing where both applications and infrastructure capabilities can be provided to end users through the internet.

**Code analysis** | A category of computer forensics that focuses on examining programming code for malicious code or signatures. Code analysis also is known as malware forensics.

**Code law** | Law that is enacted by legislatures.

**Cold site** | A backup site for disaster recovery and business continuity planning purposes that is little more than reserved space. A cold site does not have any hardware or equipment ready for business operations. It will have electrical service, but most likely will not have network connectivity. It can take weeks to months for an organization to ready a cold site for business operations.

**Common law** | A body of law that is developed because of legal tradition and court cases. The U.S. common law is a body of law that was inherited from England.

**Compensatory damages** | A money award that compensates a non-breaching party for the other party's breach. These damages place the non-breaching party in the same position he or she would have been in had the contract been fully performed.

**Competitive edge** | The designs, blueprints, or plans that make an organization's product or service unique.

**Complaint** | The first document filed in a civil case. A plaintiff files it and it states the plaintiff's cause of action against a defendant.

**Complete performance** | Contractual performance where a party to a contract satisfies all of his or her promises.

**Compliance** | The action of following applicable laws and rules and regulations.

**Computer forensics** | The scientific process of collecting and examining data that is stored on or received or transmitted by an electronic device. Computer forensics also is called system forensics, digital forensics, computer forensic analysis, computer examination, data recovery, or inforensics.

**Concurrent jurisdiction** | Jurisdiction that is shared by several different courts.

**Confidentiality** | The security goal of ensuring that only authorized persons can access information systems and their data.

**Conflict of interest** | Any situation where a person's private interests and professional obligations collide. Independent observers might question whether a person's private interests improperly influence his or her professional decisions.

**Consequential damages** | A money award that compensates the non-breaching party for foreseeable damages that arise from circumstances outside of the contract.

**Consideration** | The mutual exchange of value between contracting parties. Consideration can be expressed as an exchange of money, goods, or a promise to perform a certain action.

**Consumer goods** | Items that an individual purchases for personal, family, or household use.

**Consumer services** | Services that an individual purchases for personal, family, or household use.

**Contract** | A legally binding agreement that is enforceable in court.

**Contract of adhesion** | A contract where one party has very little bargaining power. A contract of adhesion is a "take it or leave it" contract.

**Contractual capacity** | A legal term that refers to the ability of a party to enter into a contract.

**Control** | Any protective action that reduces information security risks. These actions may eliminate or lessen vulnerabilities, control threats, or reduce risk. Safeguards is another term for controls.

**Cookie** | A small string of code that a website stores on a user's computer. Websites use cookies to remember specific information about visitors to the site.

**Copyrights** | Used to protect books, art, music, videos, computer programs, and other creative works.

**Covered entity** | A health plan, healthcare clearing house, or any other healthcare provider that transmits certain types of health information in electronic form. Such an entity must follow the HIPAA Security and Privacy Rules. This term is defined by the Health Insurance Portability and Accountability Act.

**Criminal procedure** | Sets forth the procedures and processes that courts follow in criminal law cases.

**Cryptography** | The science and practice of hiding information so that unauthorized persons cannot read it.

## D

**Data destruction policies** | State how data is to be destroyed when it reaches the end of its life cycle.

**Data retention policies** | State how data is to be controlled throughout its life cycle.

**Deceptive trade practices** | Any commercial practice that uses false or misleading claims to get customers to buy a product or service.

**Defamation** | A tort that involves maliciously saying false things about another person.

**Denial of service (DoS) attack** | Attack that disrupts information systems so that they are no longer available to users.

**Design patents** | Issued to protect new and original ornamental designs for manufactured objects.

**Digital evidence** | Evidence collected from an electronic device.

**Disaster** | A sudden, unplanned event that negatively affects the organization's critical business functions for an unknown period.

**Disaster recovery (DR) plans** | Plans that address the recovery of an organization's information technology systems in the event of a disaster.

**Disclosure** | Refers to how a covered entity shares protected health information with other organizations that may not be affiliated with it. This term is defined by the Health Insurance Portability and Accountability Act.

**Disclosure controls** | A term used in the Sarbanes-Oxley Act. It refers to processes and procedures that a company uses to make sure that it makes timely disclosures to the U.S. Securities and Exchange Commission.

**Discovery** | The legal process used to gather evidence in a lawsuit.

**Distributed denial of service (DDoS) attack** | An attack that uses multiple systems to disrupt other information systems so that they are no longer available to users.

**Diversity of citizenship jurisdiction** | Refers to the power of federal courts to hear disputes between citizens of different states only when they are above a certain dollar amount.

**Dividend** | Represents a shareholder's portion of the company's earnings.

**Docket** | The official schedule of a court and the events in the cases pending before a court. Many courts publish their dockets online.

**Due process** | The principle that all parties in a case are entitled to a fair and consistent process within the courts.

**Dumpster diving** | Looking through discarded trash for personal information.

**Duty of due care** | A person's obligation to avoid acts or omissions that can harm others.

**Duty to mitigate** | A non-breaching party's obligation not to aggravate the harm caused by a breach.

## E

**Electronic protected health information (EPHI)** | Patient health information that is computer based. It is PHI stored electronically. This term is defined by the Health Insurance Portability and Accountability Act.

**End user license agreement (EULA)** | A contract between the manufacturer or distributor of a piece of software or a service and the end user.

**Exploit** | A successful attack against a vulnerability.

**Exposure factor** | The percentage of asset loss that is likely to be caused by an identified threat or vulnerability.

**External attacker** | An attacker that has no current relationship with the organization it is attacking.

## F

**Fair information practice principles** | Guidelines used to help describe how personal information should be collected and used.

**Fair use** | A copyright law concept that states some use of copyrighted works in limited ways is not copyright infringement.

**Federal question jurisdiction** | Refers to the power of federal courts to hear only disputes about federal laws or constitutional issues.

**Felonies** | The greater of two types of crimes. Felonies are more serious than misdemeanors. They are generally punishable by more than 1 year in prison.

**Flaming** | A series of insulting communications between internet users. Flaming often occurs on online discussion boards.

**Forensic duplicate image** | An exact copy of an electronic media storage device. A bit-by-bit copy includes deleted files, slack space, and areas of the storage device that a normal file copy would not include.

**Form 8-K** | A report that a public company must file with the U.S. Securities and Exchange Commission. A company must file it within 4 days of experiencing a major event that affects shareholders and investors.

**Form 10-K** | A report that a public company must file with the U.S. Securities and Exchange Commission at the end of its fiscal year. It is a detailed and comprehensive report on the company's financial condition.

**Form 10-Q** | A report that a public company must file with the U.S. Securities and Exchange Commission at the end of each fiscal quarter. It is a report on the company's financial condition at the end of its first three quarters in a fiscal year.

**Fruit of the poisonous tree doctrine** | A legal doctrine that states that evidence that is not gathered lawfully is tainted with illegality. Illegally gathered evidence cannot be used in court. In addition, any subsequent evidence gathered because of the illegally obtained evidence cannot be used in court either.

**Full interruption test** | A disaster recovery and business continuity test where an organization stops all of its normal business operations and transfers those operations to its backup site. This is the most comprehensive form of disaster recovery and business continuity plan testing. It also is the most expensive.

## G

**Global positioning system (GPS)** | A navigation technology that uses satellites above the Earth to compute the location of a GPS receiver.

**Guidelines** | Recommended actions and operational guides to users, IT staff, operations staff, and others when a specific standard does not apply.

## H

**Hearsay** | Any out-of-court statement made by a person that is offered to prove some issue in a case. Gossip is a common example of hearsay.

**Hot site** | An operational backup site for disaster recovery and business continuity planning purposes. It has equipment and infrastructure that is fully compatible with an organization's main facility. It is not staffed with people. A hot site can become operational within minutes to hours after a disaster.

## I

**Identity theft** | A crime that takes place when a person's personally identifiable information is used without permission in order to commit other crimes.

**Incident** | An event that adversely affects the confidentiality, integrity, and/or availability of an organization's data and information technology systems.

**Incident response (IR)** | A contingency plan that helps an organization respond to attacks against an organization's information technology infrastructure.

**Incomplete performance** | Contractual performance in which a party to a contract does not perform his or her contractual promises.

**Information** | Intelligence, knowledge, and data. You can store information in paper or electronic form.

**Information security** | The study and practice of protecting information. The main goal of information security is to protect its confidentiality, integrity, and availability.

**Information security governance (ISG)** | Executive management's responsibility to provide strategic direction, oversight, and accountability for an organization's information and information systems resources.

**Information security management (ISM)** | How an organization manages its day-to-day security activities. It makes sure that the policies dictated by the executive management team as part of its governance function are properly implemented.

**Inspector general (IG)** | A federal government official who independently evaluates the performance of federal agencies. Inspectors general are independent officials.

**Integrity** | The security goal of ensuring that no changes are made to information systems and their data without permission.

**Intellectual property** | The area of law that protects a person's creative ideas, inventions, and innovations. It is protected by patents, trade secrets, trademarks, and copyright.

**Internal attacker** | An attacker that has a current relationship with the organization he or she is attacking. It can be an angry employee.

**Internal controls** | A term used in the Sarbanes-Oxley Act. It refers to the processes and procedures that a company uses to provide reasonable assurance that its financial reports are reliable.

**Internet of Things (IoT)** | This term is used broadly to refer to any device that collects and shares data over the internet.

## J

**Judicial review** | A court's review of any issue. For federal courts, this refers to the authority of a court to declare actions unconstitutional.

**Jurisdiction** | The power of a court to hear a particular type of case. It also refers to the power of a court to hear cases involving people in a geographical area. For instance, a state court has the power to decide cases raised by citizens of that state.

## L

**Least privilege** | A rule that systems should run with the lowest level of permissions needed to complete tasks. This means users should have the least amount of access needed to do their jobs.

**Legislative history** | The materials generated while creating laws. It includes committee reports and hearings. It also includes transcripts of debate and reports issued by legislatures. The legislative history is reviewed to help determine what a legislature intended when it created a law.

**Libel** | Written defamation.

**Liquidated damages** | A contractual grant of money damages that the parties determined before entering into a contract.

**Locard's exchange principle** | A basic assumption in forensic science that states that people always leave traces of their activities when they interact with other people or with other objects.

## M

**Mailbox rule** | A common law rule that states that an acceptance is valid as soon as an offeree places it in the mail.

***Mala in se*** | A Latin term used to describe conduct that is inherently wrong. It means "evil in itself."

***Mala prohibita*** | A Latin term used to describe conduct that society prohibits. It means "wrong because it is prohibited."

**Malware** | A term that refers to any software that performs harmful, unauthorized, or unknown activity. The word *malware* combines the words *malicious* and *software*.

**Mantrap** | A physical security safeguard that controls entry into a protected area. This entry method has two sets of doors on either end of a small room. When a person enters a mantrap through one set of doors, that first set must close before the second set can open. Often a person entering a facility via a mantrap must present different credentials at each set of doors to gain access.

**Maximum tolerable downtime (MTD)** | The amount of time that critical business processes and resources can be offline before an organization begins to experience irreparable business harm.

**Media analysis** | A category of computer forensics that focuses on collecting and examining data stored on physical media.

**Medical identity theft** | A specialized type of identity theft. A crime that takes place when a person's personally identifiable health information is used without permission in order to receive medical services or goods.

***Mens rea*** | A Latin term used to describe the state of mind of a criminal. It means "guilty mind."

**Minimum necessary rule** | A rule that covered entities may only disclose the amount of PHI absolutely necessary to carry out a particular function. This term is defined by the Health Insurance Portability and Accountability Act.

**Mirror image rule** | A common law rule that states that an offer and acceptance must contain identical terms.

**Mirrored site** | A fully operational backup site for disaster recovery and business continuity planning purposes. This site actively runs an organization's information technology functions in parallel with the organization's mail processing facility. It is fully staffed and has all necessary data and equipment to continue business operations.

**Misdemeanor** | The lesser of two types of crimes. Misdemeanors are less serious than felonies. They are generally punishable by no more than 1 year in prison.

**Multifactor authentication** | A method of authentication that requires users to prove their identity in two or more ways.

## N

**National security systems** | Information technology systems that hold military, defense, and intelligence information.

**Near Field Communication (NFC)** | A very short-range wireless communication technology.

**Need to know** | A rule that users should have access to only the information they need to do their jobs.

**Network analysis** | A category of computer forensics that focuses on capturing and examining network traffic. It includes reviewing transaction logs and using real-time monitoring to identify and locate evidence.

**Network banner** | A warning banner that provides notice of legal rights to users of computer networks. They are generally displayed as a computer user logs into a network or on an entity's home page.

**Nominal damages** | A money award to the non-breaching party even though he or she has not suffered any financial loss because of a breach of contract.

**Nonpublic personal information (NPI)** | Any personally identifiable financial information that a consumer provides to a financial institution. This term is defined by the Gramm-Leach-Bliley Act.

## O

**Objection** | A formal protest made by an attorney to a trial court judge. An attorney usually makes an objection if the opposing party is asking questions or submitting evidence that is inappropriate or violates a trial court rule.

**Offer** | An invitation made by an offeror to an offeree to enter into a contract.

**Offeree** | A person who receives an offer.

**Offeror** | A person who makes an offer.

**Online profiling** | The practice of tracking a user's actions on the internet in order to create a profile of that user. The profile can be used to direct targeted advertising toward a particular user.

**Operational planning** | Day-to-day business planning.

**Original jurisdiction** | The authority of a court to hear a dispute between parties in the first instance, rather than on appeal.

## P

**Parallel test** | A disaster recovery and business continuity test where an organization tests its ability to recover its information technology systems and its business data. In this type of test, the organization brings its backup recovery sites online. It will then use historical business data to test the operations of those systems.

**Parental controls** | Software that allows a parent to control a child's activity on a computer. Parental controls can be used to restrict access to certain content, such as violent games, or to specific websites. They also can restrict the times a child can use a computer.

**Patch** | A piece of software or code that fixes a program's security vulnerabilities. Patches are available for many types of software, including operating systems.

**Patent prosecution** | The actions that the U.S. Patent and Trademark Office must complete in order to reject a patent application or issue a patent.

**Patents** | Used to protect inventions such as machines, processes, designs, and specialized plants.

**Pen register devices** | Devices that monitor outgoing transmission data. They record dialing, routing, signaling, or address information.

**Persistent data** | Data that is stored on a hard drive or other storage media. It is preserved when an electronic device is turned off.

**Personal jurisdiction** | A court's ability to exercise power over a defendant.

**Personally identifiable information (PII)** | Information that can be used to identify a specific person. This can be something used alone, such as a person's name. Or it can be pieces of data that, when combined, can be used to identify someone. PII is often defined with reference to a particular law. It can include elements such as name, address, Zip code, gender, GPS location, telephone number, or account numbers.

**Physical safeguard** | Controls that keep unauthorized individuals out of a building or other controlled areas. You can also use them to keep unauthorized individuals from using an information system. Examples include keycard access to buildings, fences, and intrusion monitoring systems.

**Plant patents** | Issued to protect inventions or discoveries of new varieties of plants that are reproduced asexually.

**Pleadings** | Documents filed in a court case.

**Policy** | An organization's high-level statement of information security direction and goals. Policies are the highest level governance document.

**Pop-up advertisements** | Advertisements that open a new web browser window to display the advertisement.

**Precedent** | This doctrine means that courts will look at prior cases to determine the appropriate resolution for new cases.

**Preemption** | A legal concept that means that a higher-ranking law will exclude or preempt a lower-ranking law on the same subject.

**Preponderance of the evidence** | The standard of proof in a civil case. It means that it is more probable than not that an action (or wrong) took place.

**Pretexting** | Obtaining unauthorized access to a customer's sensitive financial information through false or misleading actions. Also called social engineering.

**Prior art** | Evidence of public knowledge about an invention that existed before a claimed invention or discovery date.

**Privacy** | A person's right to have control of his or her own personal data. The person has the right to specify how that data is collected, used, and shared.

**Privacy impact assessment (PIA)** | A review of how a federal agency's information technology systems process personal information. The E-Government Act of 2002 requires federal agencies to conduct these assessments.

**Private cause of action** | A legal concept that describes a person's right to sue another for harm that the latter caused.

**Privately held company** | A company held by a small group of private investors.

**Probative evidence** | Probative evidence is evidence that proves or disproves a legal element in a case. If evidence is not probative, then it can be excluded from a trial. Probative evidence also is known as relevant evidence.

**Procedural law** | Branches of law that deal with processes that courts use to decide cases.

**Procedures** | Detailed step-by-step tasks, or checklists, that should be performed to achieve a certain goal or task. Procedures are the lowest level governance document.

**Protected health information (PHI)** | Any individually identifiable information about the past, present, or future health of a person. It includes mental and physical health data. This term is defined by the Health Insurance Portability and Accountability Act.

**Proxy server** | A server that accepts internet requests and retrieves the data. The proxy server can filter content to ensure that users view only acceptable content. Libraries and schools use proxy servers to comply with the Children's Internet Protection Act (CIPA).

**Public company** | A publicly traded company owned by several different investors. Investors own a percentage of the company through stock purchases. The stock of a public company is traded on a stock exchange.

**Public domain** | Refers to the collection of works that are free for public use. It includes works where the copyright has expired. It also includes some government works.

**Public employees** | Employees that work for the federal or state government.

**Public records** | Records required by law to be made available to the public. These types of records are made or filed by a governmental entity.

**Public relations (PR)** | A marketing field that manages an organization's public image.

## Q

**Qualitative risk analysis** | A risk analysis method that uses scenarios and ratings systems to calculate risk and potential harm. Unlike quantitative risk analysis, qualitative risk analysis does not attempt to assign money value to assets and risk.

**Quantitative risk analysis** | A risk analysis method that uses real money costs and values to determine the potential monetary impact of threats and vulnerabilities.

## R

**Radio Frequency Identification (RFID)** | A wireless technology that uses radio waves to transmit data to a receiver.

**Ransomware** | A type of malware that encrypts data to make it inaccessible, or may lock information systems, until an organization pays the attacker to decrypt the data or unlock the system.

**Realized risk** | The loss that an organization has when a potential threat actually occurs.

**Reasonable person standard** | A legal concept used to describe an ordinary person. This fictitious ordinary person is used to represent how an average person would think and act.

**Record** | Any information about a person that a federal agency maintains. This term is defined in the Privacy Act of 1974.

**Red Flag** | Any pattern, practice, or activity that may indicate identity theft. This term is defined by the Fair and Accurate Credit Transaction Act of 2003.

**Remedy** | Legal relief that a court grants to an injured party.

**Repudiation** | A refusal to perform a contract duty.

**Residual risk** | The amount of risk left over after safeguards lessen a vulnerability or threat.

**Risk** | The chance, or probability, that a threat can exploit a vulnerability. The concept of risk includes an understanding that an exploited vulnerability has a negative business impact.

**Risk acceptance** | A business decision to accept an assessed risk and take no action against it.

**Risk assessment (RA)** | A process for identifying threats and vulnerabilities that an organization faces. Risk assessments can be quantitative, qualitative, or a combination of both.

**Risk avoidance** | A business decision to apply safeguards to avoid a negative impact.

**Risk management (RM)** | The process that an organization uses to identify risks, assess them, and reduce them to an acceptable level.

**Risk mitigation** | A business decision to apply safeguards to lessen a negative impact.

**Risk transfer** | A business decision to transfer risk to a third party to avoid that risk.

## S

**Safe harbor** | A legal concept that refers to an action someone can take to show a good-faith effort to stay within the law and avoid prosecution.

**Safeguard** | Any protective action that reduces information security risks. They may eliminate or lessen vulnerabilities, control threats, or reduce risk. Safeguards also are called controls.

**Seal program** | A program administered by a trusted organization that verifies that another organization meets recognized privacy practices.

**Search engine** | A program that retrieves files and data from a computer network. Search engines are used to search the internet for information.

**Securities** | The general term used to describe financial instruments that are traded on a stock exchange. Stocks and bonds are securities.

**Security breach** | Any compromise of a computer system that results in the loss of personally identifiable information.

**Separation of duties** | A rule that two or more employees must split critical task functions. Thus, no one employee knows all of the steps required to complete the critical task.

**Servicemark** | Used to protect words, logos, symbols, or slogans that identify a service.

**Shoulder surfing** | Looking over the shoulder of another person to obtain sensitive information. The attacker does not have permission to see it. This term usually describes an attack in which a person tries to learn sensitive information by viewing keystrokes on a monitor or keyboard.

**Shrinkwrap contract** | A software licensing agreement where the complete terms of the agreement are in a box containing the physical-media software.

**Simulation test** | A disaster recovery and business continuity test where an organization role-plays a specific disaster scenario. This type of test does not interrupt normal business operations and activities.

**Single loss expectancy (SLE)** | The amount of money that an organization stands to lose every time a specified risk is realized.

**Single point of failure** | In an information system, a piece of hardware or application critical to the entire system's functioning. If that single item fails, then a critical portion or the entire system could fail. For networks, single points of failure could be firewalls, routers, switches, or hubs.

**Slander** | Oral defamation.

**Social engineering** | An attack that relies on human interaction. They often involve tricking other people to break security rules so the attacker can gain information about computer systems. This type of attack is not technical.

**Social networking sites** | Website applications that allow users to post information about themselves.

**Software as a Service (SaaS)** | Commerce model where a vendor hosts a web-based application and provides that application to its customers through the internet.

**Spam** | Unsolicited email. Spam is usually advertising or promotional email.

**Specific performance** | A legal term that refers to situations where a court orders a party to complete his or her contractual duties.

**Stakeholders** | People that are affected by a policy, standard, guideline, or procedure. They are people who have an interest in a policy document.

**Standards** | Mandatory activities, actions, or rules. Standards must be met in order to achieve policy goals. Standards are usually technology neutral.

**Statute of frauds** | A common law rule that states that certain types of contracts must be in writing and signed by the contracting parties.

**Statute of limitations** | The time period stated by law during which a plaintiff must take legal action against a wrongdoer. A plaintiff who does not take legal action within the stated time is forever barred from bringing that action in the future.

**Strategic planning** | Long-term business planning.

**Strict liability** | A legal concept that means that people can be held responsible for their actions even if they did not intend to cause harm to another person.

**Subject matter jurisdiction** | The power of a court to decide certain types of cases.

**Substantial performance** | Contractual performance in which a party to a contract satisfies all of his or her material promises. Substantial performance does not meet all contract terms. Nonperformance of some terms may result in a minor breach of contract.

**Substantive law** | Branches of law that deal with particular legal subject matter, arranged by type. Property law, contract law, and tort law are all substantive areas of law.

**System of records notice (SORN)** | A federal agency's notice about agency record-keeping systems that can retrieve records through the use of a personal identifier. The Privacy Act of 1974 requires federal agencies to provide these notices.

## T

**Tactical planning** | Short- to medium-term business planning.

**Targeted advertising** | Advertising designed to appeal to a consumer's specific interests.

**Technical safeguard** | Controls implemented in an information system's hardware and software. Technical controls include passwords, access control mechanisms, and automated logging. They improve the system's security.

**Technology protection measure (TPM)** | Technology used to filter objectionable content. CIPA requires the use of a TPM to protect children from objectionable content.

**Threat** | Any danger that takes advantage of a vulnerability. Threats are unintentional or intentional.

**Tort** | A wrongful act or harm for which a civil action can be brought. Tort law governs disputes between individuals.

**Tortfeasor** | A person who commits a tort.

**Trade secrets** | Used to protect formulas, processes, and methods that give a business a competitive edge.

**Trademarks** | Used to protect words, logos, symbols, or slogans that identify a product or service.

**Trap and trace devices** | Devices that monitor incoming transmission data. They capture incoming electronic signals that identify the originating transmission data.

**Two-factor authentication** | A method of authentication that requires users to prove their identity in two ways.

## U

**Unfair trade practices** | Any commercial practices that a consumer cannot avoid and that cause injury.

**Use** | How a covered entity shares or handles protected health information within its organization. This term is defined by the Health Insurance Portability and Accountability Act.

**User credentials** | Pieces of information used to access information technology resources. User credentials include passwords, personal identification numbers (PINs), tokens, smart cards, and biometric data.

**Utility patents** | Issued to protect inventions and discoveries such as machines, manufactured products, processes, and compositions of matter. They are the most common type of patent.

## V

**Volatile data** | Data that is stored in the memory of an electronic device. It is lost when an electronic device is turned off.

**Vulnerability** | A weakness or flaw in an information system. Exploiting a vulnerability harms information security. You reduce them by applying security safeguards.

## W

**Walk-through test** | A basic type of disaster recovery and business continuity test that reviews a disaster recovery/business continuity plan to make sure that all of the assumptions and tasks stated in the plan are correct. This type of test is sometimes called a tabletop walk-through test or tabletop test.

**Warm site** | A partially equipped backup site for disaster recovery and business continuity planning purposes. A warm site is space that contains some, but not all, of the equipment and infrastructure that an organization needs to continue operations in the event of a disaster. It is partially prepared for operations and has electricity and network connectivity.

**Web beacon** | A small, invisible electronic file that is placed on a webpage or in an email message. Also called a "web bug."

**Window of vulnerability** | The period between discovering a vulnerability and reducing or eliminating it.

**Workplace privacy** | Privacy issues encountered in the workplace. Hiring and firing practices and daily performance practices all have potential privacy concerns.

## Z

**Zero-day vulnerability** | A vulnerability exploited shortly after it is discovered. The attacker exploits it before the vendor releases a patch.

# References

Albion Research Ltd., "Risky Thinking—On Risk Assessment, Risk Management, and Business Continuity," 2010. http://www.riskythinking.com/ (accessed May 4, 2010).

American Bankers Association, "Credit Card Monitor," February 2020. https://www.aba.com/-/media/documents/reports-and-surveys/2019-q3-credit-card-monitor.pdf?rev=9c1664304c9149a8a08e6d146791126f (accessed April 29, 2020).

American Bankers Association, "Digital Banking Infographic," November 12, 2019. https://www.aba.com/news-research/research-analysis/digital-banking (accessed April 29, 2020).

American Bar Association, "Report to the House of Delegates, Section of Science and Technology Law," July 16, 2008. http://www.abanet.org/leadership/2008/annual/recommendations/ThreeHundredOne.doc (accessed May 11, 2010).

American Bar Association, Section of Science & Technology Law, "ABA Adopts Resolution Against Private Investigator Licenses for Computer Forensics," September 25, 2008. http://cdfs.org/files/Positions/ABA%20Press%20release%20compforensics.pdf (accessed March 15, 2020).

American Civil Liberties Union, "Court Orders Missouri School District to Stop Censoring LGBT Websites," February 15, 2012. https://www.aclu.org/press-releases/court-orders-missouri-school-district-stop-censoring-lgbt-websites (accessed March 24, 2020).

American Institute of Certified Public Accountants, "System and Organization Controls: SOC Suite of Services," No date. https://www.aicpa.org/interestareas/frc/assuranceadvisoryservices/sorhome.html (accessed April 26, 2020).

American Law Institute, "ALI Overview," undated. https://www.ali.org/about-ali/ (accessed January 26, 2020).

American Law Institute and the National Conference of Commissioners on Uniform State Laws, Uniform Commercial Code, sec. 2-201 (2004). http://www.law.cornell.edu/ucc/ (accessed January 26, 2020).

American Management Association, "The Latest on Workplace Monitoring and Surveillance," April 8, 2019. https://www.amanet.org/articles/the-latest-on-workplace-monitoring-and-surveillance/ (accessed February 21, 2020).

Anderson, Ross. *Security Engineering: A Guide to Building Dependable Distributed Systems*. New York: John Wiley & Sons, Inc., 2001.

BBC News, "Ukraine Power Cut Was Cyber Attack," January 11, 2017. https://www.bbc.com/news/technology-38573074 (accessed May 16, 2020).

Board of Governors of the Federal Reserve System, "Structure of the Federal Reserve System," March 3, 2017. https://www.federalreserve.gov/aboutthefed/structure-federal-reserve-system.htm (accessed April 29, 2020).

Böhme, Rainer, and Stefan Köpsell, "Trained to Accept? A Field Experiment on Consent Dialogues," CHI 2010, *Proceedings of the SIGCHI Conference on Human Factors in Computing Systems* (2010): 2403–2406.

Bonfield, Lloyd. *American Law and the American Legal System*. St. Paul, MN: Thomson/West, 2006.

Brinson, J. Dianne, et al. *Analyzing E-Commerce and Internet Law*. Upper Saddle River, NJ: Prentice-Hall, Inc., 2001.

Calder, Alan, and Steve Watkins. *International IT Governance: An Executive Guide to ISO 17799/ISO 27001*. London: Kogan Page Ltd., 2006.

Cannon, J. C. *Privacy: What Developers and IT Professionals Should Know*. Boston, MA: Addison-Wesley, 2005.

Carter, Patricia I. *HIPAA Compliance Handbook, 2019*. Frederick, MD: Aspen Publishers, 2019.

CBS News, "Cancer Patient Catches ID Thief," November 6, 2004. https://www.cbsnews.com/news/cancer-patient-catches-id-thief/ (accessed March 1, 2020).

CERT Coordination Center. *Handbook for Computer Security Incident Response Teams (CSIRTs)*. 2nd ed. Pittsburgh, PA: Software Engineering Institute, April 2003. https://resources.sei.cmu.edu/library/asset-view.cfm?assetid=6305 (accessed August 8, 2010).

CFA Institute, "IFRS: International Financial Reporting Standards," Undated. https://www.cfainstitute.org/en/advocacy/issues/international-finance-reporting-stds (accessed April 18, 2020).

CNBC, "Consumer DNA Testing Has Hit a Lull—Here's How It Could Capture the Next Wave of Users," August 25, 2019. https://www.cnbc.com/2019/08/25/dna-tests-from-companies-like-23andme-ancestry-see-sales-slowdown.html (accessed March 1, 2020).

CNBC, "Ex-Coca-Cola Worker Sentenced to 8 Years in Trade Secrets Case," May 2007. https://www.cnbc.com/id/18824080 (accessed January 19, 2020).

CNET, "ChoicePoint Data Theft Widens to 145,000 People," February 18, 2005. https://www.cnet.com/news/choicepoint-data-theft-widens-to-145000-people/ (accessed April 27, 2020).

CNN, "401(k) Investors Sue Enron," November 26, 2001. http://money.cnn.com/2001/11/26/401k/q_retire_enron_re/ (accessed April 11, 2020).

CNN, "America's Economy Just Had Its Worst Quarter Since 2008," April 29, 2020. https://www.cnn.com/2020/04/29/economy/us-economy-downturn-coronavirus/index.html (accessed April 29, 2020).

CNN, "The Guiltiest Guys in the Room," July 5, 2006. http://money.cnn.com/2006/05/29/news/enron_guiltyest/index.htm (accessed April 11, 2020).

CNN.com, "Couple: Internet Gaming Addiction Led to Baby's Death," April 2, 2010. https://www.cnn.com/2010/WORLD/asiapcf/04/01/korea.parents.starved.baby/ (accessed May 1, 2020).

CNN.com, "Girl Costs Father $80,000 With 'SUCK IT' Facebook Post," March 4, 2014. http://www.cnn.com/2014/03/02/us/facebook-post-costs-father/ (accessed March 8, 2014).

Cohen, Cynthia F., and Murray E. Cohen, "On-Duty and Off-Duty: Employee Right to Privacy and Employer's Right to Control in the Private Sector," *Employer Responsibility and Rights Journal* 19 (2007): 235.

College ACB, "College ACB Press Release," February 5, 2009. http://collegeacb.blogspot.com/2009/02/collegeacb-press-release.html (accessed May 1, 2020).

Committee of National Security Systems, "Policy No. 22, Cybersecurity Risk Management," August 2016. http://www.cnss.gov/cnss/issuances/Policies.cfm (accessed May 16, 2020).

Committee of Sponsoring Organizations of the Treadway Commission, "Guidance on Internal Control," No date. http://www.coso.org/IC.htm (accessed on April 26, 2020).

Committee on Oversight and Government Reform, "Federal Information Security: Current Challenges and Future Policy Considerations," March 24, 2010. http://www.gpo.gov/fdsys/pkg/CHRG-111hhrg65549/html/CHRG-111hhrg65549.htm (accessed May 16, 2020).

Congressional Research Service, "Computer Security: A Summary of Selected Federal Laws, Executive Orders, and Presidential Directives," April 16, 2004. http://fas.org/irp/crs/RL32357.pdf (accessed April 24, 2010).

Congressional Research Service, "Enron: A Select Chronology of Congressional, Corporate, and Government Activities," March 2003. http://www.policyarchive.org/handle/10207/1392 (accessed April 11, 2020).

Consumer Financial Protection Bureau, "Creating the Consumer Bureau," Undated. https://www.consumerfinance.gov/about-us/the-bureau/creatingthebureau/ (accessed April 29, 2020).

Council of Europe, Treaty Office, "Convention of Cybercrime Signatories," undated. https://www.coe.int/en/web/conventions/full-list/-/conventions/treaty/185 (accessed May 1, 2020).

Court Listener, "Docket for *Vernon Unsworth v. Elon Musk* (2:18-cv-08048)," March 11, 2020. https://www.courtlistener.com/docket/7887513/vernon-unsworth-v-elon-musk/ (accessed May 1, 2020).

Deloitte, "2017 Global Mobile Consumer Survey: US Edition," 2017. https://www2.deloitte.com/content/dam/Deloitte/us/Documents/technology-media-telecommunications/us-tmt-2017-global-mobile-consumer-survey-executive-summary.pdf (accessed January 26, 2020).

Dlabay, L., and J. L. Burrow, *Business Finance.* 2007, Cengage Learning, p. 339.

Duranske, Benjamin Tyson. *Virtual Law: Navigating the Legal Landscape of Virtual Worlds.* Chicago: American Bar Association, 2008.

Easttom, C., *System Forensics, Investigation, and Response.* 2nd ed. Burlington, MA: Jones & Bartlett Learning, 2013, p 3.

European Union, "Regulation on the Protection of Natural Persons With Regard to the Processing of Personal Data and on the Free Movement of Such Data, and Repealing Directive 95/46/EC (Data Protection Directive), 2016/679." April 14, 2016.

Federal Bureau of Investigation, "Business E-Mail Compromise: The 12 Billion Dollar Scam," July 2018. https://www.ic3.gov/media/2018/180712.aspx (accessed January 20, 2020).

Federal Communications Commission, "Children's Internet Protection Act (CIPA)," undated. https://www.fcc.gov/consumers/guides/childrens-internet-protection-act (accessed August 8, 2020).

Federal Deposit Insurance Corporation, "Who Is the FDIC?" May 3, 2017. https://www.fdic.gov/about/learn/symbol/index.html (accessed April 29, 2020).

Federal Financial Institutions Examination Council, "Annual Report 2019," March 30, 2020. https://www.ffiec.gov/PDF/annrpt19.pdf (accessed April 29, 2020).

Federal Risk and Authorization Management Program, "FedRAMP Security Assessment Framework," November 15, 2017. https://www.fedramp.gov/assets/resources/documents/FedRAMP_Security_Assessment_Framework.pdf (accessed May 16, 2020).

Federal Trade Commission, "About the FTC," Undated. https://www.ftc.gov/about-ftc (accessed April 29, 2020).

Federal Trade Commission, "Children's Online Privacy Protection Act of 1998," undated. http://www.ftc.gov/ogc/coppa1.htm (accessed March 5, 2010).

Federal Trade Commission, "Children's Online Privacy Protection Rule: A Six-Step Compliance Plan for Your Business," June 2017. https://www.ftc.gov/tips-advice/business-center/guidance/childrens-online-privacy-protection-rule-six-step-compliance (accessed March 24, 2020).

Federal Trade Commission, "Children's Privacy," undated. https://www.ftc.gov/tips-advice/business-center/privacy-and-security/children%27s-privacy (accessed March 1, 2020).

Federal Trade Commission, "ChoicePoint Settles Data Security Breach Charges; to Pay $10 Million in Civil Penalties, $5 Million for Consumer Redress," January 26, 2006. https://www.ftc.gov/news-events/press-releases/2006/01/choicepoint-settles-data-security-breach-charges-pay-10-million (accessed April 27, 2020).

Federal Trade Commission, "Complying With COPPA: Frequently Asked Questions," March 2015. https://www.ftc.gov/tips-advice/business-center/guidance/complying-coppa-frequently-asked-questions (accessed February 1, 2020).

Federal Trade Commission, "Consumer Data Broker ChoicePoint Failed to Protect Consumers' Personal Data, Left Key Electronic Monitoring Tool Turned Off for Four Months," October 19, 2009. https://www.ftc.gov/news-events/press-releases/2009/10/consumer-data-broker-choicepoint-failed-protect-consumers (accessed April 27, 2020).

Federal Trade Commission, "Federal Trade Commission, Consumer Financial Protection Bureau Pledge to Work Together to Protect Consumers," January 23, 2012. https://www.ftc.gov/news-events/press-releases/2012/01/federal-trade-commission-consumer-financial-protection-bureau (accessed April 29, 2020).

Federal Trade Commission, "Fighting Identity Theft With the Red Flags Rule, A How-To Guide for Business," May 2013. https://www.ftc.gov/tips-advice/business-center/guidance/fighting-identity-theft-red-flags-rule-how-guide-business (accessed August 8, 2020).

Federal Trade Commission, "Google and YouTube Will Pay Record $170 Million for Alleged Violations of Children's Privacy Law," September 4, 2019. https://www.ftc.gov/news-events/press-releases/2019/09/google-youtube-will-pay-record-170-million-alleged-violations (accessed March 24, 2020).

Federal Trade Commission, "Privacy and Data Security Update 2019," February 25, 2020. https://www.ftc.gov/news-events/press-releases/2020/02/ftc-releases-2019-privacy-data-security-update (accessed May 1, 2020).

Federal Trade Commission, *Privacy of Consumer Financial Information* ("Financial Privacy Rule"), Code of Federal Regulations, Title 16, sec. 313, May 24, 2000.

Federal Trade Commission, *Standards for Insuring the Security, Confidentiality, Integrity and Protection of Customer Records and Information* ("Safeguards Rule"), Code of Federal Regulations, Title 16, sec. 314, May 23, 2002.

Federal Trade Commission, "Young Investor Website Settles FTC Charges," May 6, 1999. https://www.ftc.gov/news-events/press-releases/1999/05/young-investor-website-settles-ftc-charges (accessed August 8, 2020).

Feinman, Jay M. *Law 101: Everything You Need to Know About the American Legal System.* New York: Oxford University Press, 2006.

FERPA SHERPA, "State Student Privacy Laws," Last updated 2019. https://ferpasherpa.org/state-laws/ (accessed March 24, 2020).

Ferrara, Gerald R., et al. *Cyberlaw: Your Rights in Cyberspace.* Cincinnati, OH: Thomson Learning, 2001.

Forbes, "America's Largest Private Companies," December 2019. https://www.forbes.com/largest-private-companies/list/#tab:rank (accessed April 11, 2020).

Fortune, "The World's Most Admired Companies," October 2, 2000. http://money.cnn.com/magazines/fortune/fortunearchive/2000/10/02/288448/index.htm (accessed April 11, 2020).

Gallegos, Frederick, "Computer Forensics: An Overview," *Information Systems Control Journal* 6 (2005): 16–19.

Gartner, "Gartner Forecasts Worldwide Public Cloud Revenue to Grow 17% in 2020," November 13, 2019. https://www.gartner.com/en/newsroom/press-releases/2019-11-13-gartner-forecasts-worldwide-public-cloud-revenue-to-grow-17-percent-in-2020 (accessed January 26, 2020).

Gartner, "The Future of Employee Monitoring," May 3, 2019. https://www.gartner.com/smarterwithgartner/the-future-of-employee-monitoring/ (accessed April 28, 2020).

Google, "Content Delistings Due to Copyright," Undated. https://transparencyreport.google.com/copyright/overview?hl=en (accessed April 30, 2020).

Grama, Joanna, and Scott Ksander, "Recent Indiana Legislation Hopes to Stem Release of Personally Identifying Information," *Res Gestae* 4 (December 2006): 50; reprinted in *Indiana Civil Litigation Review*, Vol. III, No. 2, Fall–Winter (2006).

Happ, Christian, André Melzer, and Georges Steffgen, "Trick With Treat—Reciprocity Increases the Willingness to Communicate Personal Data," 2016. *Computers in Human Behavior.* https://www.researchgate.net/publication/298187172_Trick_with_Treat_-_Reciprocity_Increases_the_Willingness_to_Communicate_Personal_Data (accessed February 20, 2020).

Harshbarger, William G., Jr., information technology security engineer, Purdue University. Interview by author. West Lafayette, Indiana, April 14, 2010.

HathiTrust, "Statistics Information," Updated daily. http://www.hathitrust.org/statistics_info (accessed April 30, 2020).

Hazelwood, Steven D., and Sarah Koon-Magnin, "Cyber Stalking and Cyber Harassment Legislation in the United States: A Qualitative Analysis," *International Journal of Cyber Criminology*, July–December 2013, Vol 7 (2): 155–168.

Hirsch, Eric Donald, Joseph F. Kett, and James S. Trefil. *The New Dictionary of Cultural Literacy.* 3rd ed. New York: Houghton Mifflin Co., 2002.

Holt, Thomas J., Adam M. Bossler, and Kathryn C. Seigfried-Spellar, *Cybercrime and Digital Forensics: An Introduction.* 2017.

House of Representatives Committee on Oversight and Government Reform, "Federal Information Security: Current Challenges and Future Policy Considerations," March 24, 2010. http://oversight.house.gov/index.php?option=com_content&task=view&id=4855&Itemid=28 (accessed April 21, 2010).

Houston Business Journal, "Enron Delists Stock as Financial Woes Continue," January 18, 2002. http://www.bizjournals.com/houston/stories/2002/01/21/story3.html (accessed April 11, 2020).

Houston Chronicle, "Jury Hears Ex-Enron CEO Curse in Wall Street Call," February 2, 2006. https://www.chron.com/business/enron/article/Jury-hears-ex-Enron-CEO-curse-in-Wall-Street-call-1637608.php (accessed April 11, 2020).

Identity Theft Resource Center, "End of Year Data Breach Report," January 8, 2020. https://www.idtheftcenter.org/wp-content/uploads/2020/01/01.28.2020_ITRC_2019-End-of-Year-Data-Breach-Report_FINAL_Highres-Appendix.pdf (accessed August 8, 2020).

Information Week, "War-Driving Pornographic Spammer Escapes Jail Time," August 1, 2007. https://www.informationweek.com/war-driving-pornographic-spammer-escapes-jail-time/d/d-id/1057666? (accessed May 1, 2020).

InfoWorld, "States Settle With ChoicePoint Over 2004 Breach," May 31, 2007. https://www.infoworld.com/article/2662493/states-settle-with-choicepoint-over-2004-breach.html (accessed April 27, 2020).

International Association of Computer Investigative Specialists, "About IACIS," undated. https://www.iacis.com/about/ (accessed March 15, 2020).

International Organization for Standardization, "ISO/IEC 27001:2013—Information Technology—Security Techniques—Information Security Management Systems—Requirements," 2013. https://www.iso.org/standard/54534.html (accessed August 8, 2020).

International Organization for Standardization, "ISO/IEC 27002:2013, Information Technology—Security Techniques—Code of Practice for Information Security Management," 2013. https://www.iso.org/standard/54533.html (accessed August 8, 2020).

Internet Crime Complaint Center, "2019 Annual Internet Crime Report," 2019. https://pdf.ic3.gov/2019_IC3Report.pdf (accessed May 1, 2020).

Internet Free Expression Alliance, "TITLE XVII—Children's Internet Protection," undated. http:// ifea.net/cipa.pdf (accessed March 14, 2010).

Internet World Stats, "Internet Usage Statistics: World Internet Users and Population Stats," March 3, 2020. http://www.internetworldstats.com/stats.htm (accessed April 30, 2020)

ISACA, "COBIT 5: A Business Framework for the Governance and Management of Enterprise IT," 2012. http://www.isaca.org/COBIT/Pages/COBIT-5-Framework-product-page.aspx (accessed December 30, 2013).

ISACA, "COBIT 2019: Introduction and Methodology," 2018. https://www.isaca.org/resources.

ISACA, *Control Objectives for Sarbanes-Oxley: Using COBIT® 5 in the Design and Implementation of Internal Controls Over Financial Reporting*. 3rd ed. 2014. https://www.isaca.org/bookstore/cobit-5/psox3 (accessed August 8, 2020).

Javelin Strategy and Research, "2013 Identity Fraud Report: Data Breaches Becoming a Treasure Trove for Fraudsters," undated. https://www.javelinstrategy.com/brochure/276 (accessed November 24, 2013).

Kaspersky, "Kaspersky Security Bulletin 2019: Statistics," December 2019. https://securelist.com/kaspersky-security-bulletin-2019-statistics/95475/ (accessed March 15, 2020).

Kesan, Jay, and Carol M. Hayes. *Cybersecurity and Privacy Law in a Nutshell (Nutshells)*. St. Paul, MN: West Academic Publishing, 2019.

Kidd, Donnie L., and William H. Daughtrey, Jr., "Adapting Contract Law to Accommodate Electronic Contracts: Overview and Suggestions," *Rutgers Computer and Technology Law Journal* 26 (2000): 215.

Kraft, Betsy Harvey. *Sensational Trials of the 20th Century*. New York: Scholastic Press, 1998.

Kroger, John R. *Convictions: A Prosecutor's Battles Against Mafia Killers, Drug Kingpins, and Enron Thieves*. New York: Farrar, Straus, and Giroux, 2008.

Kroger, John R., "Enron, Fraud, and Securities Reform," Colorado Law Review, Vol. 76, Issue 1 (2005): 57.

Ksander, Scott L., chief information security officer, Purdue University. Interview by author. West Lafayette, Indiana, April 14, 2010.

LaFave, Wayne, and Jerold H. Israel. *Criminal Procedure*. 2nd ed. St. Paul, MN: West Publishing Co., 1992.

Landoll, Douglas J. *The Security Risk Assessment Handbook*. Boca Raton, FL: Auerbach Publications, 2006.

Lonardo, Thomas, Doug White, and Alan Rea, "To License or Not to License Revisited: An Examination of State Statutes Regarding Private Investigators and Digital Examiners," *The Journal of Digital Forensics, Security and Law* 4, no. 3 (2009): 35–56. Reprint. http://www.jdfsl.org/subscriptions/JDFSL-V4N3-Lonardo.pdf (accessed May 10, 2010).

Mastercard, "What Merchants Need to Know About Securing Transactions," Undated. https://www.mastercard.ca/en-ca/merchants/safety-security/security-recommendations/merchants-need-to-know.html (accessed April 29, 2020).

Matt. 7:17-20, *The Holy Bible*, King James Version. Cambridge Edition: 1769; King James Bible Online, 2014. http://www.kingjamesbibleonline.org/ (accessed March 15, 2020).

McCafferty, Anne, "Internet Contracting and E-Commerce Disputes: International and United States Personal Jurisdiction," *The Global Business Law Review* 2 (2011): 95.

McGraw, Gary, and Ed Felten, *Securing Java*. New York, NY: John Wiley & Sons, Inc., 1999. Also available at http://www.securingjava.com/ (accessed February 20, 2020). View Chapter 1, part 7.

Microsoft Corporation, "Security Risk Management Guide," March 16, 2006. http://technet.microsoft.com/en-us/library/cc163143.aspx (accessed May 1, 2010).

Miller, Arthur R., and Michael H. Davis. *Intellectual Property: Patents, Trademarks, and Copyright*. St. Paul, MN: West Publishing Co., 2018.

Missouri Court of Appeals, "Opinion: *Major v. McCallister*," No. CD29871, December 23, 2009. https://www.courts.mo.gov/file.jsp?id=36294 (accessed January 26, 2020).

Moeller, Robert R. *Sarbanes-Oxley Internal Controls*. Hoboken, NJ: John Wiley & Sons, Inc., 2008.

National Conference of State Legislatures, "Data Disposal Laws," January 4, 2020. https://www.ncsl.org/research/telecommunications-and-information-technology/data-disposal-laws.aspx (accessed April 27, 2020).

National Conference of State Legislatures, "Privacy Protections in State Constitutions," November 7, 2018. https://www.ncsl.org/research/telecommunications-and-information-technology/privacy-protections-in-state-constitutions.aspx (accessed April 28, 2020).

National Conference of State Legislatures, "Security Breach Notification Laws," March 8, 2020. https://www.ncsl.org/research/telecommunications-and-information-technology/security-breach-notification-laws.aspx (accessed April 27, 2020).

National Conference of State Legislatures, "State Social Media Privacy Laws," May 22, 2019. https://www.ncsl.org/research/telecommunications-and-information-technology/state-laws-prohibiting-access-to-social-media-usernames-and-passwords.aspx (accessed April 27, 2020).

National Conference of State Legislatures, "State Social Media Privacy Laws," October 30, 2018. https://www.ncsl.org/research/telecommunications-and-information-technology/state-spyware-laws.aspx (accessed April 27, 2020).

National Credit Union Association, "About NCUA," Undated. https://www.ncua.gov/about-ncua (accessed April 29, 2020).

National Institute of Standards and Technology, "FIPS Pub 199, Standards for Security Categorization of Federal Information and Information Systems," February 2004. https://csrc.nist.gov/publications/detail/fips/199/final (accessed May 16, 2020).

National Institute of Standards and Technology, "FIPS Pub 200, Minimum Security Requirements for Federal Information and Information Systems," March 2006. https://csrc.nist.gov/publications/detail/fips/200/final (accessed May 16, 2020).

National Institute of Standards and Technology, "FISMA Detailed Overview," April 13, 2010. http://csrc.nist.gov/groups/SMA/fisma/overview.html (accessed April 17, 2010).

National Institute of Standards and Technology, "Procedures for Developing FIPS (Federal Information Processing Standards) Publications," May 21, 2018. https://www.nist.gov/itl/procedures-developing-fips-federal-information-processing-standards-publications (accessed May 16, 2020).

National Institute of Standards and Technology, "SP 800-37, Revision 1, Risk Management Framework for Information Systems and Organizations," December 2018. https://nvlpubs.nist.gov/nistpubs/SpecialPublications/NIST.SP.800-37r2.pdf (accessed May 16, 2020).

National Institute of Standards and Technology, "SP 800-53, Revision 4, Security and Privacy Controls for Federal Information Systems and Organizations," April 2013. https://csrc.nist.gov/publications/detail/sp/800-53/rev-4/final (accessed May 16, 2020).

National Institute of Standards and Technology, "SP 800-53A, Assessing Security and Privacy Controls in Federal Information Systems and Organizations: Building Effective Assessment Plans," December 2014. https://csrc.nist.gov/publications/detail/sp/800-53a/rev-4/final (accessed May 16, 2020).

National Institute of Standards and Technology, "SP 800-122, Guide to Protecting the Confidentiality of Personally Identifiable Information (PII)," April 2010. https://csrc.nist.gov/publications/detail/sp/800-122/final (accessed May 16, 2020).

National Institute of Standards and Technology, "SP 800-30 (Rev. 1): Guide for Conducting Risk Assessments," September 2012. http://csrc.nist.gov/publications/nistpubs/800-30-rev1/sp800_30_r1.pdf (accessed March 31, 2014).

National Institute of Standards and Technology, "SP 800-34 (Rev. 1): Contingency Planning Guide for Federal Information Systems," May 2010. http://csrc.nist.gov/publications/nistpubs/800-34-rev1/sp800-34-rev1_errata-Nov11-2010.pdf (accessed March 31, 2014).

National Institute of Standards and Technology, "SP 800-39: Managing Information Security Risk: Organization, Mission, and Information System View," March 2011. http://csrc.nist.gov/publications/nistpubs/800-39/SP800-39-final.pdf (accessed March 31, 2014).

National Institute of Standards and Technology, "SP 800-53 (Rev. 4): Recommended Security Controls for Federal Information Systems and Organizations," April 2013. https://csrc.nist.gov/publications/detail/sp/800-53/rev-4/final (accessed August 8, 2020).

National Institute of Standards and Technology, "SP 800-61 (Rev. 2): Computer Security Incident Handling Guide," August 2012. https://csrc.nist.gov/publications/detail/sp/800-61/rev-2/final (accessed February 23, 2020).

National Library of Medicine, "Greek Medicine: The Hippocratic Oath," Translated by Michael North, 2002. http://www.nlm.nih.gov/hmd/greek/greek_oath.html (accessed March 1, 2020).

National Oceanic and Atmospheric Administration (NOAA), "Tornado Alley," undated. https://www.ncdc.noaa.gov/climate-information/extreme-events/us-tornado-climatology/tornado-alley (accessed February 23, 2020).

National Retail Federation, "Thanksgiving Weekend Draws Nearly 190 Million Shoppers, Spending Up 16 Percent," December 3, 2019. https://nrf.com/media-center/press-releases/thanksgiving-draws-nearly-190-million-shoppers (accessed February 21, 2020).

National Vulnerability Database, *NVD Dashboard*. https://nvd.nist.gov/general/nvd-dashboard (accessed January 19, 2020).

New Vantage Partners, "Big Data and AI Executive Survey 2019," January 2019. http://newvantage.com/wp-content/uploads/2018/12/Big-Data-Executive-Survey-2019-Findings-Updated-010219-1.pdf (accessed February 17, 2020).

New York Times, "An Implosion on Wall Street," November 29, 2001. http://www.nytimes.com/2001/11/29/opinion/an-implosion-on-wall-street.html (accessed April 11, 2020).

New York Times, "Bush Signs Bill Aimed at Fraud in Corporations," July 30, 2002. https://www.nytimes.com/2002/07/31/business/corporate-conduct-the-president-bush-signs-bill-aimed-at-fraud-in-corporations.html (accessed April 11, 2020).

New York Times, "Jeffrey Skilling, Former Enron Chief, Released After 12 Years in Prison," February 22, 2019. https://www.nytimes.com/2019/02/22/business/enron-ceo-skilling-scandal.html (accessed April 11, 2020).

New York Times, "The World Once Laughed at North Korean Cyberpower. No More," October 15, 2017. https://www.nytimes.com/2017/10/15/world/asia/north-korea-hacking-cyber-sony.html (accessed May 16, 2020).

New York Times Magazine, "The Great Cyberheist," November 10, 2020. https://www.nytimes.com/2010/11/14/magazine/14Hacker-t.html (accessed May 1, 2020).

Obama, Barack, "Remarks by the President on Securing Our Nation's Cyber Infrastructure," May 29, 2009. https://obamawhitehouse.archives.gov/the-press-office/remarks-president-securing-our-nations-cyber-infrastructure (accessed April 21, 2010).

Office of the Comptroller of the Currency, "Who We Are," Undated. https://www.occ.treas.gov/about/who-we-are/index-who-we-are.html (accessed April 29, 2020).

Organization for Economic Cooperation and Development, "OECD Guidelines on the Protection of Privacy and Transborder Flows of Personal Data," September 1980. http://www.oecd.org/ document/18/0,3343,en_2649_34255_1815186_1_1_1_1,00.html (accessed February 6, 2010).

Oxford English Dictionary, "New Words List June 2006," June 2006. https://public.oed.com/updates/new-words-list-june-2006/ (accessed April 28, 2020).

Panetta, Leon E. , "Remarks by Secretary Panetta on Cybersecurity to the Business Executives for National Security, New York City" (New York, NY: Oct. 11, 2012). http://www.gao.gov/assets/660/652170.pdf (accessed May 16, 2020).

Patrick, Walter F., "Creating an Information Systems Security Policy" (SANS Institute, 2001). http://www.sans.org/reading_room/whitepapers/policyissues/creating_an_information_systems_security_policy_534 (accessed January 21, 2010).

PC World, "ChoicePoint Details Data Breach Lessons," June 11, 2007. https://www.pcworld.com/article/132795/article.html (accessed April 27, 2020).

PCI Security Standards Council, "About Us," Undated. https://www.pcisecuritystandards.org/about_us/ (accessed April 29, 2020).

PCI Security Standards Council, "PCI Data Security Standard, v 3.2.1," May 2018. https://www.pcisecuritystandards.org/document_library (accessed April 29, 2020).

PCI Security Standards Council, Payment Card Industry (PCI) Data Security Standard: Requirements and Security Assessment Procedures, Version 3.2.1, May 2018 (accessed May 1, 2020). The complete list of PCI DSS requirements is : https://www.pcisecuritystandards.org/index.htm.

Peltier, Thomas R. *Information Security Risk Analysis*. Boca Raton, FL: Taylor & Francis Group, LLC, 2005.

Pew Research Center, "Mobile Technology and Home Broadband 2019," June 2019. https://www.pewresearch.org/internet/2019/06/13/mobile-technology-and-home-broadband-2019/ (accessed February 18, 2020).

Pew Research Center, "Only 2% of Federal Criminal Defendants Go to Trial, and Most Who Do Are Found Guilty," June 11, 2019. https://www.pewresearch.org/fact-tank/2019/06/11/only-2-of-federal-criminal-defendants-go-to-trial-and-most-who-do-are-found-guilty/ (accessed May 1, 2020).

Pollitt, M., "A History of Digital Forensics," 6th IFIP WG 11.9 International Conference on Digital Forensics, January 2010. https://hal.inria.fr/hal-01060606 (accessed March 15, 2020).

Ponemon Institute, "The Cost of Cybercrime," 2019. https://www.accenture.com/_acnmedia/pdf-96/accenture-2019-cost-of-cybercrime-study-final.pdf#zoom=50 (accessed April 29, 2020).

Ponemon Institute, "2019 Cost of Data Breach Study: Global Analysis," undated. https://www.ibm.com/security/data-breach (accessed February 17, 2020).

Powers, William C., "Special Investigative Committee of the Board of Directors of Enron Corp.," February 1, 2002. http://i.cnn.net/cnn/2002/LAW/02/02/enron.report/powers.report.pdf (accessed April 11, 2020).

Privacy Rights Clearinghouse, "Oversight Hearing on Financial Privacy and the Gramm-Leach-Bliley Financial Services Modernization Act: Testimony for U.S. Senate Committee on Banking, Housing and Urban Affairs," September 20, 2002. https://privacyrights.org/resources/oversight-hearing-financial-privacy-and-gramm-leach-bliley-financial-services (accessed April 29, 2020).

Prosser, William L., et al. *Prosser and Keeton on the Law of Torts*. 5th ed. St. Paul, MN: West Pub. Co., 1984.

Public Company Accounting Oversight Board, "AU Section 230: Due Professional Care in the Performance of Work," June 12, 2007 amendments. http://pcaobus.org/Standards/Auditing/Pages/AU230.aspx#ps-pcaob_8b4d2389-b14e-4358-a4b2-93e6360eb378 (accessed April 26, 2020).

Public Company Accounting Oversight Board, Staff Preview of 2018 Inspection Observations, May 6, 2019. https://pcaobus.org/Inspections/Documents/Staff-Preview-2018-Inspection-Observations.pdf (accessed April 18, 2020).

Public Company Accounting Oversight Board, "2019 PCAOB Annual Report," March 24, 2020. https://pcaobus.org/About/Administration/Documents/Annual%20Reports/2019-PCAOB-Annual-Report.pdf (accessed April 18, 2020).

Red Flag Program Clarification Act of 2010, 15 U.S.C. 1681m(e)(4), Pub. L. 111-319, 124 Stat. 3457 (Dec. 18, 2010).

Regulations.gov, "Proposed Amendments to the Federal Rules of Civil Procedure," undated. http://www.regulations.gov/#!docketDetail;D=USC-RULES-CV-2013-0002 (accessed May 1, 2020).

Rideout, Victoria, and Michael B. Robb. *The Common Sense Census: Media Use by Tweens and Teens, 2019*. San Francisco, CA: Common Sense Media, 2019.

Rosenzweig, Paul. *Cyber Warfare: How Conflicts in Cyberspace Are Challenging America and Changing the World*. Santa Barbara, CA: ABC-CLIO, LLC, 2013.

Rudolph, Katie. Personal communication and unpublished manuscript on computer forensics. West Lafayette, Indiana, May 10, 2010.

Rustad, Michael L. *Internet Law*. St. Paul, MN: Thomson Reuters, 2009, p 143.

Scheb, John M., and John M. Scheb II. *An Introduction to the American Legal System*. Albany. NY: Delmar, 2002.

Scientific Working Group on Digital Evidence, "About Us," undated. https://www.swgde.org/ (accessed March 15, 2020).

Secureworks, "A Famous Data Security Breach & PCI Case Study: Four Years Later," October 25, 2012. https://www.secureworks.com/blog/general-pci-compliance-data-security-case-study-heartland (accessed April 29, 2020).

The Sedona Conference, "The Sedona Principles, Third Edition: Best Practices, Recommendations & Principles for Addressing Electronic Document Production," 19 SEDONA CONF. J. 1 (2018).

Solove, Daniel J., and Paul M. Schwartz. *Privacy, Information, and Technology*. 3rd ed. New York, NY: CCH Incorporated, 2011.

Soma, John T., and Stephen D. Rynerson. *Privacy Law*. St. Paul, MN: Thomson/West, 2008.

Sprague, Robert, and Corey Ciocchetti. "Preserving Identities: Protecting Personal Identifying Information Through Enhanced Privacy Policies and Laws," *Albany Law Journal of Science and Technology* 19 (2009): 91.

Statista, "Facebook – Statistics & Facts," November 20, 2019. https://www.statista.com/topics/751/facebook/ (accessed January 26, 2020).

Statista, "Proposed Budget of the U.S. Government for Cyber Security in FY 2017 to 2021," February 2020. https://www.statista.com/statistics/675399/us-government-spending-cyber-security/ (accessed May 16, 2020).

Statista, "Twitter – Statistics & Facts," February 22, 2019. https://www.statista.com/topics/737/twitter/ (accessed January 26, 2020).

Statista Digital Market Outlook, "Retail E-Commerce Sales in the United States From 2017 to 2023," February 2019. https://www.statista.com/statistics/272391/us-retail-e-commerce-sales-forecast/ (accessed January 26, 2020).

Stim, Richard. *Intellectual Property: Patents, Trademarks, and Copyrights.* Albany, NY: Delmar, 2001.

Stopbullying.gov, "What Is Cyberbullying?" May 30, 2019. https://www.stopbullying.gov/cyberbullying/what-is-it (accessed May 1, 2020).

Swire, Peter P., and Sol Bermann. *Information Privacy, Official Reference for the Certified Information Privacy Professional (CIPP).* York, ME: International Association of Privacy Professionals, 2007.

Target Corporation, "Target Confirms Unauthorized Access to Payment Card Data in U.S. Stores," December 19, 2013. https://corporate.target.com/press/releases/2013/12/target-confirms-unauthorized-access-to-payment-car (accessed April 29, 2020).

Target Corporation, "Target Provides Update on Data Breach and Financial Performance," January 10, 2014.

Tasker, Ty, and Daryn Pakcyk, "Cyber-Surfing on the High Seas of Legalese: Law and Technology of Internet Agreements," *Albany Law Journal of Science and Technology* 18 (2008): 79.

Taylor, Laura. *FISMA: Certification & Accreditation Handbook.* Rockland, MA: Syngress Publishing, 2007.

Taylor, Laura P. *FISMA Compliance Handbook.* 2nd ed. Waltham, MA: Elsevier, 2013.

TechRepublic, "88% of Employees Have No Clue About Their Organization's IT Security Policies," January 11, 2018. https://www.techrepublic.com/article/88-of-employees-have-no-clue-about-their-organizations-it-security-policies/ (accessed February 20, 2020).

Thomas, Daphyne Saunders, and Karen A. Forcht, "Legal Methods of Using Computer Forensics Techniques for Computer Crime Analysis and Investigation," *Issues in Information Systems* V, No. 2 (2004): 692. http://www.iacis.org/iis/2004_iis/PDFfiles/ThomasForcht.pdf (accessed May 12, 2010).

Time, "Enron: Who's Accountable?" January 13, 2002. http://content.time.com/time/magazine/article/0,9171,1001636,00.html (accessed April 11, 2020).

Time, "Here's What We Know So Far About Russia's 2016 Meddling," April 18, 2019. https://time.com/5565991/russia-influence-2016-election/ (accessed May 16, 2020).

Tipton, Harold, and Micki Krause, eds. *Information Security Management Handbook.* 5th ed. Boca Raton, FL: Auerbach Publications, 2004.

Uniform Law Commission, "About the ULC," undated. http://www.uniformlaws.org/aboutulc/overview (accessed January 26, 2020).

Uniform Law Commission, Uniform Electronic Transactions Act (UETA), 1999. https://www.uniformlaws.org/HigherLogic/System/DownloadDocumentFile.ashx?DocumentFileKey=4f718047-e765-b9d8-6875-f7a225d629a8&forceDialog=0 (accessed January 26, 2020).

Uniform Law Commission, Uniform Electronic Transactions Act (UETA) Fact Sheet, 1999. https://www.uniformlaws.org/HigherLogic/System/DownloadDocumentFile.ashx?DocumentFileKey=c5976d91-07e2-b3f8-9b1e-4450fe809c21&forceDialog=0 (accessed January 26, 2020).

Uniform Law Commission, Uniform Electronic Transactions Act (UETA) Fact Sheet, 1999, sec. 2. https://www.uniformlaws.org/HigherLogic/System/DownloadDocumentFile.ashx?DocumentFileKey=c5976d91-07e2-b3f8-9b1e-4450fe809c21&forceDialog=0 (accessed January 26, 2020).

U.S. Census, "American Community Survey, Presence and Types of Internet Subscriptions in Household Table B28002," 2018. https://data.census.gov/cedsci/ (accessed April 28, 2020).

U.S. Copyright Office, "Copyright Basics," Circular 1, last revised December 2019. https://www.copyright.gov/circs/circ01.pdf (accessed August 8, 2020).

U.S. Copyright Office, "I've Heard About a 'Poor Man's Copyright.' What Is It?" Undated. https://www.copyright.gov/help/faq/faq-general.html#poorman (accessed April 30, 2020).

U.S. Copyright Office, "More Information on Fair Use," April 2020. https://www.copyright.gov/fair-use/more-info.html (accessed April 29, 2020).

U.S. Copyright Office, "Registration Processing Times April 1-September 30, 2019," 2019. https://www.copyright.gov/registration/docs/processing-times-faqs.pdf (accessed April 30, 2020).

U.S. Copyright Office, "Reproduction of Copyrighted Works by Educators and Librarians," Circular 21, last revised November 2009. http://www.copyright.gov/circs/circ21.pdf (accessed March 21, 2010).

U.S. Department of Commerce, "Statistics of 2018 BIS License Authorization," April 3, 2019. https://www.bis.doc.gov/index.php/documents/technology-evaluation/ote-data-portal/licensing-analysis/2453-2018-statistical-analysis-of-bis-licensing-pdf-1/file (accessed May 16, 2020).

U.S. Department of Commerce, National Telecommunications and Information Administration, Report to Congress, "Children's Internet Protection Act Study of Technology Protection Measures in Section 1703," August 2003. https://www.ntia.doc.gov/files/ntia/publications/cipareport08142003.pdf (accessed March 24, 2020).

U.S. Department of Education, "Dear Colleague Letter GEN -16-12," July 1, 2016. https://ifap.ed.gov/dear-colleague-letters/07-01-2016-gen-16-12-subject-protecting-student-information (accessed March 24, 2020).

U.S. Department of Education, "FERPA and the Coronavirus Disease 2019 (COVID-19)," March 2020. https://studentprivacy.ed.gov/resources/ferpa-and-coronavirus-disease-2019-covid-19 (accessed March 24, 2020).

U.S. Department of Education, "Legislative History of Major FERPA Provisions," February 11, 2004. http://www2.ed.gov/policy/gen/guid/fpco/ferpa/leg-history.html (accessed February 16, 2010).

U.S. Department of Health and Human Services, "Breach Notification Rule," 2013. https://www.hhs.gov/hipaa/for-professionals/breach-notification/index.html (accessed February 1, 2020).

U.S. Department of Health and Human Services, "Enforcement Results by Year," April 3, 2019. https://www.hhs.gov/hipaa/for-professionals/compliance-enforcement/data/enforcement-results-by-year/index.html (accessed March 1, 2020).

U.S. Department of Health and Human Services, "The HIPAA Privacy Rule," 2015. https://www.hhs.gov/hipaa/for-professionals/privacy/index.html (accessed February 1, 2020).

U.S. Department of Health and Human Services, "The Security Rule," 2017. https://www.hhs.gov/hipaa/for-professionals/security/index.html (accessed February 1, 2020).

U.S. Department of Health, Education, and Welfare, "Records, Computers and the Rights of Citizens: Report of the Secretary's Advisory Committee on Automated Personal Data Systems," July 1973. http://aspe.hhs.gov/datacncl/1973privacy/c3.htm (accessed February 6, 2010).

U.S. Department of Homeland Security, Cybersecurity and Infrastructure Security Agency, "US-CERT Federal Incident Notification Guidelines," 2017. https://www.us-cert.gov/incident-notification-guidelines (accessed May 16, 2020).

U.S. Department of Justice, "Former Student Sentenced for Causing Damage to University of Iowa Computer Network," August 23, 2018. https://www.justice.gov/usao-sdia/pr/former-student-sentenced-causing-damage-university-iowa-computer-network (accessed February 23, 2020).

U.S. Department of Justice, "Medical Clinic Worker Pleads Guilty to Aggravated Identity Theft and Wire Fraud," January 30, 2020. https://www.justice.gov/usao-mdfl/pr/medical-clinic-worker-pleads-guilty-aggravated-identity-theft-and-wire-fraud (accessed March 1, 2020).

U.S. Department of Justice, "Missouri Woman Indicted on Charges of Using MySpace to Cyber Bully 13-Year-Old Who Later Committed Suicide," May 15, 2008. https://www.justice.gov/archive/usao/cac/Pressroom/pr2008/063.html (accessed May 1, 2020).

U.S. Department of Justice, "Searching and Seizing Computers and Obtaining Electronic Evidence in Criminal Investigations," 3rd ed. September 2009. https://www.justice.gov/sites/default/files/criminal-ccips/legacy/2015/01/14/ssmanual2009.pdf (accessed August 8, 2020).

U.S. Department of Justice, "Summary of Major U.S. Export Enforcement, Economic Espionage, and Sanctions Related to Criminal Cases," January 2018. https://www.pmddtc.state.gov/sys_attachment.do?sysparm_referring_url=tear_off&view=true&sys_id=6ae22ec1db2a9740c53a7d321f9619c4 (accessed May 16, 2020).

U.S. Department of Justice, Computer Crime and Intellectual Property Section, "Prosecuting Computer Crimes," February 2007. https://www.justice.gov/sites/default/files/criminal-ccips/legacy/2015/01/14/ccmanual.pdf (accessed August 8, 2020).

U.S. Department of Justice, National Institute of Justice, "Electronic Crime Scene Investigation: A Guide for First Responders," 2nd ed., April 2008. https://www.ncjrs.gov/pdffiles1/nij/219941.pdf (accessed August 8, 2020).

U.S. Department of Justice, National Institute of Justice, "Forensic Examination of Digital Evidence: A Guide for Law Enforcement," April 2004. http://www.ncjrs.gov/pdffiles1/nij/199408.pdf (accessed May 10, 2010).

U.S. Department of Justice and Federal Bureau of Investigation, "Regional Computer Forensics Laboratory, RCFL Annual Report for Fiscal Year 2009," 2009. https://www.rcfl.gov/file-repository/rcfl_nat_annual09.pdf/view (accessed August 8, 2020).

U.S. Department of Labor, Bureau of Labor Statistics, "Forensic Science Technicians," *Occupational Outlook Handbook*. https://www.bls.gov/ooh/life-physical-and-social-science/forensic-science-technicians.htm (accessed March 15, 2020).

U.S. Executive Branch, "The National Strategy to Secure Cyberspace," February 2003. http://www.us-cert.gov/reading_room/cyberspace_strategy.pdf (accessed April 24, 2010).

U.S. Federal Bureau of Investigation, "A Brief History of the FBI," undated. https://www.fbi.gov/history/brief-history (accessed March 15, 2020).

U.S. Federal Bureau of Investigation, "Digital Evidence: Standards and Principles, Scientific Working Group on Digital Evidence (SWGDE) International Organization on Digital Evidence

(IOCE), IOCE International Principles," *Forensic Science Communications*, April 2000, Vol. 2, No. 2. https://archives.fbi.gov/archives/about-us/lab/forensic-science-communications/fsc/april2000/swgde.htm (accessed March 15, 2020).

U.S. Federal Bureau of Investigation, "Melissa Virus," undated. https://www.fbi.gov/history/famous-cases/melissa-virus (accessed May 1, 2020).

U.S. Federal Bureau of Investigation, "Morris Worm," undated. https://www.fbi.gov/history/famous-cases/morris-worm (accessed May 1, 2020).

U.S. Federal Trade Commission, "Consumer Sentinel Network Data Book 2019," January 2020. https://www.ftc.gov/system/files/documents/reports/consumer-sentinel-network-data-book-2019/consumer_sentinel_network_data_book_2019.pdf (May 1, 2020).

U.S. Federal Trade Commission, "eConsumer Statistics," April 15, 2020. https://public.tableau.com/profile/federal.trade.commission#!/vizhome/eConsumer/Infographic (accessed May 1, 2020).

U.S. Federal Trade Commission, "FTC Completes Review of CAN-SPAM Rule," February 12, 2019. https://www.ftc.gov/news-events/press-releases/2019/02/ftc-completes-review-can-spam-rule (accessed May 1, 2020).

U.S. Federal Trade Commission, "In the Matter of Facebook, Inc.," April 28, 2020. https://www.ftc.gov/enforcement/cases-proceedings/092-3184/facebook-inc (accessed April 28, 2020).

U.S. Government Accountability Office, "Cybersecurity: Progress Made but Challenges Remain in Defining and Coordinating the Comprehensive National Initiative," GAO-10-338, March 5, 2010. http://www.gao.gov/products/GAO-10-338 (accessed April 23, 2010).

U.S. Government Accountability Office, "Federal Information Security: Agencies and OMB Need to Strengthen Policies and Practices," July 2019. https://www.gao.gov/assets/710/700588.pdf (accessed May 16, 2020).

U.S. Government Accountability Office, "High Risk Series: Substantial Efforts Needed to Achieve Greater Progress on High Risk Areas," March 2019. https://www.gao.gov/products/gao-19-157sp (accessed February 18, 2020).

U.S. Government Accountability Office, "Information Security: Concerted Response Needed to Resolve Persistent Weaknesses," March 24, 2010. http://www.gao.gov/new.items/d10536t.pdf (accessed April 23, 2010).

U.S. House of Representatives, Committee Oversight and Government Reform, "The OPM Data Breach: How the Government Jeopardized Our National Security for More Than a Generation," September 7, 2016. https://republicans-oversight.house.gov/wp-content/uploads/2016/09/The-OPM-Data-Breach-How-the-Government-Jeopardized-Our-National-Security-for-More-than-a-Generation.pdf (accessed May 16, 2020).

U.S. Office of Management and Budget, "Federal Cloud Computing Strategy," Undated. https://cloud.cio.gov/strategy/ (accessed May 16, 2020).

U.S. Office of Management and Budget, "Fiscal Year 2009 Report to Congress on the Implementation of the Federal Information Security Management Act of 2002," March 2010. https://obamawhitehouse.archives.gov/sites/default/files/omb/assets/egov_docs/FY09_FISMA.pdf (accessed August 8, 2020).

U.S. Office of Management and Budget, "Fiscal Year (FY) 2018 Annual Report to Congress," August 2019. https://www.whitehouse.gov/wp-content/uploads/2019/08/FISMA-2018-Report-FINAL-to-post.pdf (accessed May 16, 2020).

U.S. Office of Management and Budget, "Memo M-03-22: OMB Guidance for Implementing the Privacy Protections of the E-Government Act of 2002," September 26, 2003. https://www.whitehouse.gov/wp-content/uploads/2017/11/203-M-03-22-OMB-Guidance-for-Implementing-the-Privacy-Provisions-of-the-E-Government-Act-of-2002-1.pdf (accessed August 8, 2020).

U.S. Office of Management and Budget, "Memo M-10-15: FY 2010 Reporting Instructions for the Federal Information Security Management Act and Agency Privacy Management," April 21, 2010. https://www.whitehouse.gov/sites/whitehouse.gov/files/omb/memoranda/2010/m10-15.pdf (accessed August 8, 2020).

U.S. Office of Management and Budget, "OMB Circular A-130, Managing Information as a Strategic Resource, Section 5(f)," July 28, 2016. https://www.whitehouse.gov/sites/whitehouse.gov/files/omb/circulars/A130/a130revised.pdf (accessed May 16, 2020).

U.S. Office of Management and Budget, "OMB Memorandum M-17-12, Preparing for and Responding to a Breach of Personally Identifiable Information," January 3, 2017. https://www.whitehouse.gov/sites/whitehouse.gov/files/omb/memoranda/2017/m-17-12_0.pdf (accessed May 16, 2020).

U.S. Office of Management and Budget, "2019 Federal Cloud Computing Strategy," undated. https://cloud.cio.gov/ (accessed January 26, 2020).

U.S. Patent and Trademark Office, "A Guide to Filing a Design Patent Application," undated. http://www.uspto.gov/patents/resources/types/index.jsp (accessed March 19, 2010).

U.S. Patent and Trademark Office, "Data Visualization Center, Traditional Total Pendency," April 2020. https://www.uspto.gov/corda/dashboards/patents/main.dashxml?CTNAVID=1004 (accessed April 30, 2020).

U.S. Patent and Trademark Office, "FY 2019 Performance and Accountability Report," November 2019. https://www.uspto.gov/sites/default/files/documents/USPTOFY19PAR.pdf (accessed April 30, 2020).

U.S. Patent and Trademark Office, "General Information About 35 U.S.C. 161 Plant Patents," undated. https://www.uspto.gov/patents-getting-started/patent-basics/types-patent-applications/general-information-about-35-usc-161 (accessed August 8, 2020).

U.S. Patent and Trademark Office, "Trademark Basics," undated. http://www.uspto.gov/trademarks/basics/index.jsp (accessed March 21, 2010).

U.S. Patent and Trademark Office, "Trademark Manual of Examining Procedure, Section 1200," October 2018. https://tmep.uspto.gov/RDMS/TMEP/current#/current/TMEP-1200d1e3042.html

U.S. Securities and Exchange Commission, "About the SEC," November 22, 2016. https://www.sec.gov/about.shtml (accessed April 26, 2020).

U.S. Securities and Exchange Commission, "CF Disclosure Guidance: Topic No. 2, Cybersecurity," October 13, 2011. https://www.sec.gov/divisions/corpfin/guidance/cfguidance-topic2.htm (accessed April 26, 2020).

U.S. Securities and Exchange Commission, "Commission Guidance Regarding Management's Report on Internal Controls Over Financial Reporting," Code of Federal Regulations, Title 17, sec. 241. https://www.sec.gov/rules/interp/2007/33-8810.pdf (accessed April 26, 2020).

U.S. Securities and Exchange Commission, "Commission Statement on Implementation of Internal Control Reporting Requirements," May 16, 2005. https://www.sec.gov/news/press/2005-74.htm (accessed August 8, 2020).

U.S. Securities and Exchange Commission, "Final Rule: Management's Report on Internal Control Over Financial Reporting and Certification of Disclosure in Exchange Act Periodic Reports," June 5, 2003. http://www.sec.gov/rules/final/33-8238.htm#iib3a (accessed April 26, 2020).

U.S. Securities and Exchange Commission, "Form 8-K." https://www.sec.gov/fast-answers/answersform8khtm.html (accessed April 11, 2020).

U.S. Securities and Exchange Commission, "Staff Statement on Management's Report on Internal Control Over Financial Reporting," May 16, 2005. http://www.sec.gov/info/accountants/stafficreporting.htm (accessed April 26, 2020).

U.S. Securities and Exchange Commission, "Work Plan for the Consideration of Incorporating International Financial Reporting Standards Into the Financial Reporting System for U.S. Issuers, Final Report," July 13, 2012. http://webapp01.ey.com.pl/EYP/WEB/eycom_download.nsf/resources/ZRG_Emerging_Trends_Survay.pdf/$FILE/ZRG_Emerging_Trends_Survey.pdf (accessed April 18, 2020).

U.S. Supreme Court, Federal Rules of Evidence, Rules 701-706, undated. https://www.uscourts.gov/sites/default/files/federal_rules_of_evidence_-_dec_1_2019_0.pdf (accessed March 15, 2020).

Verisign, "The Verisign Domain Name Industry Brief," March 2020. https://www.verisign.com/assets/domain-name-report-Q42019.pdf (accessed April 30, 2020).

Verizon, "2019 Data Breach Investigation Report," 2019. https://enterprise.verizon.com/resources/reports/dbir/ (accessed February 23, 2020).

Verizon Business, "2020 Data Breach Investigations Report," undated. https://enterprise.verizon.com/resources/reports/dbir/ (May 22, 2020).

VISA, "Information Security," Undated. https://cw.visa.com/run-your-business/small-business/information-security/compliance-validation.html (accessed April 29, 2020).

VISA, "PCI Compliance Helps Keep You and Your Customers Safe," Undated. https://usa.visa.com/support/small-business/security-compliance.html (accessed April 29, 2020).

VISA, "What to Do if Compromised," October 1, 2019. https://usa.visa.com/dam/VCOM/download/merchants/cisp-what-to-do-if-compromised.pdf (accessed April 29, 2020).

Warren, Samuel, and Louis Brandeis, "The Right to Privacy," *Harvard Law Review* 4 (1890): 193.

Warsinske, John, et al. *Official (ISC)$^2$ CISSP CBK Reference*. Hoboken, NJ: Wiley, 2019.

Watnick, Valerie, "The Electronic Formation of Contracts and the Common Law 'Mailbox Rule,'" *Baylor Law Review* 56 (2004): 175.

Welytok, Jill Gilbert. *Sarbanes-Oxley for Dummies*. Hoboken, NJ: Wiley Publishing, 2008.

Whitcomb, Carrie Morgan, "An Historical Perspective of Digital Evidence: A Forensic Scientist's Point of View," *International Journal of Digital Evidence* 1, Issue 1 (2002): Reprint. http://www.utica.edu/academic/institutes/ecii/publications/articles/9C4E695B-0B78-1059-3432402909E27BB4.pdf (accessed May 12, 2010).

White, James J., and Robert S. Summers. *Uniform Commercial Code*. 5th ed. St. Paul, MN: West Group, 2000.

Winter, Cory S., "The Rap on Clickwrap: How Procedural Unconscionability Is Threatening the E-Commerce Marketplace," *Widener Law Journal* 18 (2008): 249.

Wood, Charles Cresson. *Information Security Policies Made Easy*. 8th ed. Houston: Pentasafe Security Technologies, 2001.

World Intellectual Property Organization, "Berne Convention for the Protection of Literary and Artistic Works," Undated. https://www.wipo.int/treaties/en/ip/berne/ (accessed April 30, 2020).

World Intellectual Property Organization, "WIPO Arbitration and Mediation Center, 2019 Review," April 8, 2020. https://www.wipo.int/amc/en/new/2019review.html (accessed April 30, 2020).

Wu, Stephen S., ed. *A Guide to HIPAA Security and the Law*. Chicago: American Bar Association Publishing, 2007.

# Index

*Note*: Page numbers followed by *f*, or *t*, indicate materials in figures, or tables, respectively.


## A

AAFS. *See* American Academy of Forensic Sciences
ABA. *See* American Bar Association
abuse and neglect, 152
ACA. *See* Affordable Care Act of 2010
acceptable use case study, 380–382
acceptable use policy (AUP), 368–372, 402
acceptance, 287, 289–291, 297–298
access contingency plans, 164
access control standard, 166–167
access to education record, 130–131
AccessData Certified Examiner (ACE), 425
accidental threats, 12
accountability principle, 44
ACE. *See* AccessData Certified Examiner
ACPA. *See* Anti-Cybersquatting Consumer Protection Act
*Act of Congress*, defined, 67
active data collection, 57
acts of God, 12
*actus reus*, 320
administrative procedure, 77
Administrative Procedures Act (APA), 208
administrative safeguards, 15, 17*t*, 162–164, 165*t*
Administrative Simplification provisions, 145
admissible evidence, 426, 439–442
advertising for service contracts, 307
adware, 45
affidavit, 264
affiliated party, 99
Affordable Care Act of 2010 (ACA), 145
agency information security programs, 204–206
AICPA. *See* American Institute of Certified Public Accountants
Alabama Court of Appeals, 259
A-I-C triad, 354
ALE. *See* annualized loss expectancy
algorithms, 232, 430
ALI. *See* American Law Institute
*A&M Records, Inc. v. Napster*, 279
amendment of education records, 131
American Academy of Forensic Sciences (AAFS), 431
American Bar Association (ABA), 304, 425
American Institute of Certified Public Accountants (AICPA), 190
American Law Institute (ALI), 286
American legal system, 64–72, 74
Analyst Conflicts of Interest (Title V), 182
annual notification, 130
annual rate of occurrence (ARO), 398
annualized loss expectancy (ALE), 398
answer, 338
Anti-Cybersquatting Consumer Protection Act (ACPA), 267, 332
anti-harassment policies, 372–373, 380
antivirus programs, 422
APA. *See* Administrative Procedures Act
appeal, 70
appellate jurisdiction, 68, 69
appropriation of likeness or identity tort, 42
architectural works, 268
Arizona law, 238
ARO. *See* annual rate of occurrence
arraignment, 324
assets, 392–394
assigned security responsibility standard, 163
Assumption of Risk defense, 337
attackers, 8, 13, 404
attendance, 129
audit, 80–81
audit committee, 195
audit controls standard, 167
Auditor Independence (Title II), 182
AUP. *See* acceptable use policy
authentication, 377–379
authenticity, 300–301
authorization, 154–155
Authors Guild, 280
Autoliv, 380–382
availability, 5, 8–10

## B

backdoors, 22
backup site options, 411
bad faith, 266, 267
balance, 354
balance sheet, 180
bank examiner, 95
Bank Secrecy Act of 1970, 89
baseline, 310, 361

BC. *See* business continuity plans
behavioral notes, 130
bench trials, 339
Berne Convention, 271
best evidence rule, 442
beyond a reasonable doubt, 76
BIA. *See* business impact analysis
Bill of Rights, 65, 118
biometric data, 34
BIS. *See* Bureau of Industry and Security
blog, 33
board of directors (BOD), 356–357, 360, 365, 366
BOD. *See* board of directors
boilerplate terms, 307
breach activities, 230
breach notification, 232
breach notification laws, 217, 226, 230–234
breach notification policy, 217
breach notification provisions, 160–161
breach notification regulations, 227–234
breach of contract, 292–294
*Brown v. Board of Education* (1954), 78, 79
browsewrap contracts, 305–306
burden-of-proof hierarchy, 77*f*
burdens of proof, 76, 258
Bureau of Industry and Security (BIS), 219
business associate contracts standard, 164
business associates, 147
business associate's agreement, 307
business continuity (BC) plans, 205, 388, 407–412, 412*f*
business impact analysis (BIA), 409
business personnel, 391
business planning hierarchy, 355*f*

## C

Cable Communications Policy Act (1984), 40
California Breach Notification Act, 228–230
California Consumer Privacy Act (CCPA), 238
California law, 230, 232, 238–239
California Office of Privacy Protection, 41
Cambridge Analytica, 51
capacity online, legal, 297
cardholder data, 107
case law, 38, 73. *See also* common law
causation, 320
CCE. *See* Certified Computer Examiner
CCFE. *See* Certified Computer Forensics Examiner
CCL. *See* Commerce Control List
CCPA. *See* California Consumer Privacy Act
CCPA. *See* California Consumer Privacy Act
censorship, 118
Census Confidentiality law (1952), 39–40
central incident response center, 211–212
certification under SOX, 187–191
Certified Computer Examiner (CCE), 424
Certified Computer Forensics Examiner (CCFE), 424
Certified Forensic Computer Examiner (CFCE), 424
certified public accountants (CPAs), 184
CFAA. *See* Computer Fraud and Abuse Act (CFAA) in 1984
CFCE. *See* Certified Forensic Computer Examiner
CFPB. *See* Consumer Financial Protection Bureau
chain of custody, 427
chattels, 344–345
checklist test, 413
checksum, 430
C-I-A triad, 5, 5*f*, 354, 354*f*
chief information officer (CIO), 357
chief information security officer (CISO), 206, 357
chief technology officer (CTO), 357
Child Online Protection Act (COPA), 120
child privacy, 119
children on the Internet, 116–119
Children's Internet Protection Act (CIPA), 27*t*, 115, 124–128
Children's Online Privacy Protection Act (COPPA), 27*t*, 115, 119–124, 297
ChoicePoint data breach, 226–227
choreographic works, 268
CIO. *See* chief information officer
CIPA. *See* Children's Internet Protection Act
circuit court, 136
"Circumvention of Technological Protection Measures", 275
CISO. *See* chief information security officer
*City of Ontario v. Quon*, 56
civil law, 238
civil procedure, 75, 338–339
claim, 257
clickstream, 45–46
clickwrap contracts, 303–305
cloud computing, 308–309, 308*f*
CNSS. *See* Committee on National Security Systems
COBIT. *See* Control Objectives for Information and related Technology
COBRA. *See* Consolidated Omnibus Budget Reconciliation Act of 1986
code analysis, 422
code law, 74
Code of Federal Regulations, 218
cold site, 411
collection limitation principle, 43
collection step of investigation, 427–429
Colorado law, 232
Commerce Control List (CCL), 219
commerce, use of trademark in, 262
Commission Resources and Authority (Title VI), 182
Committee of Sponsoring Organizations (COSO), 188–190

Committee on National Security Systems (CNSS), 213
common law, 41–43, 73
communicable diseases, vital statistics and, 151–152
communication, information and, 189
communications constitute, 290
Communications Decency Act (1996), 342
communications laws, interception of, 330
comparative negligence defense, 337
compensatory damages, 293, 337
competitive edge, 25
complaint, 338
complete performance, 292
compliance, 80–81, 366, 414, 414*t*
compliance risks, 14
composition of matter, 253
computer crimes. *See* cyber crimes
computer forensic examiner, 423–425
computer forensics, 420–422, 422*f*
Computer Fraud and Abuse Act (CFAA) in 1984, 326–327, 328*t*
computer-generated records, 439
Computer Maintenance Competition Assurance Act, 274, 277
Computer Security Act (CSA), 194, 203
computer systems, 421
computer trespass, 318, 329
computer use monitoring, 54–55
computer worm, 21
concurrent jurisdiction, 68, 69
conduit defense, 276
conference committee, 66
confidential documents as confetti, 244
confidentiality, 5–7
conflicts of interest, 195, 392
congress, 65
Congressional Research Service, 235
consent, 433
consent exception, 437
consequential damages, 293
consideration, 291–292
Consolidated Omnibus Budget Reconciliation Act of 1986 (COBRA), 144
constitutional law, 36–38, 74
consumer, 98
consumer compliance task force, 95
consumer financial information, 87, 90
Consumer Financial Protection Bureau (CFPB), 96
consumer goods, 90
consumer services, 90
content filtering, 125–126
contingency planning, 164, 388, 401–414, 414*t*
continuity of operations, 205
continuous monitoring, 390, 401
contract form, 286–287
contract law issues, emerging, 307–311
contract legality, 288
contract of adhesion, 301
contract repudiation, 294
contract types in cyberspace, 301–306
contracting online, 295–297
contracting parties, 307
contracting principles, 286–294
contracts, 23–24, 286, 310, 311
contracts as regulators of behavior, 306–307
contracts, role of, 285–313
contractual capacity, 287
contractual performance, 292–294
contributory negligence defense, 337
control activities, 189
control documentation, 398–400
control environment, 189
Control Objectives for Information and related Technology (COBIT), 192
Controlling the Assault of Non-Solicited Pornography and Marketing (CAN-SPAM) Act, 330–331, 346
controls, 15
cookies, 45–60
COPA. *See* Child Online Protection Act
COPPA. *See* Children's Online Privacy Protection Act
COPPA Rule, 119–121, 123, 124
copyright, 251, 268–274
Corporate and Criminal Fraud Accountability (Title VIII), 182
Corporate Fraud and Accountability (Title XI), 182
corporate fraud at Enron, 176–179
corporate information privacy issues, 195–196
corporate responsibility (Title III), 182
Corporate Tax Returns (Title X), 182
corrective safeguards, 17
COSO. *See* Committee of Sponsoring Organizations
COSO Framework, 188–190
counteroffers, 289
county recorder's office, 236, 237
court of appeals, 69, 71
"court of last resort", 69
covered accounts, 103
covered entities, 145–146, 147
CPAs. *See* certified public accountants
credit unions, 93
creditor, 103–104
crime reporting, 415
crimes, 319–321
criminal history data, 34
criminal law, 238, 318–325
criminal laws in cyberspace, 326–334
criminal procedure, 76–77, 323–325
critical business processes, 409, 410
criticism for service contracts, 307
cryptographic key management practices, 242
cryptography, 5
CSA. *See* Computer Security Act
CTO. *See* chief technology officer
*customer*, distinct from *consumer*, 98

CVS pharmacies, 169
Cyber Monday, 374
cybercrimes, 318, 326, 333–334
CyberScope, 206
cyberspace, contracts types in, 301–306
cybersquatting, 266–267, 332
cyberwar, 203

D

damages, 292–293, 337
data breach law, 217
data centers, 23
data definition and use, 310
data destruction policies, 374–375
data disposal regulations, 242–244
data privacy, 214
data protection standard, 239–241
data protection terms, 310–311
data quality principle, 43
data recovery, 411
data recovery firms, 421
data retention policies, 375–376
Data Security Standard (DSS), 107–108, 109*t*, 234–236
data-specific security and privacy regulations, 234–239
data storage devices, 242
data use, 306
Daubert test, 430–431
DDoS. *See* distributed denial of service attack
*Deal v. Spears* (1992), 53
deceptive trade practices, 96
decision tree, breach notification, 234*f*
defamation, 42, 341–342, 346–347
defendant, 324, 337–339
deliberate threats, 13
denial of service (DoS) attack, 9, 22–23
denial of service (DoS) category, 405
Department of Health and Human Services (HHS), 147, 151, 167, 170
depositor, 92
derivative work, 269
descriptive trademarks, 264
design patents, 253
detective controls, 17
device and media controls standard, 166
dictionary attacks, 378
digital collections, 280
digital evidence, 421, 425–431
Digital Millennium Copyright Act (DMCA), 274–278
digital rights management (DRM), 274
digital signature, 301
Digital Wild West, 250
digitized signature, 301
dilution case, trademark, 266
directory information, 132
disaster, 407
disaster recovery (DR) plans, 388, 407–412, 412*f*
discharged, 292
disciplinary records, 135–136
disclosure, 132–133, 148, 154–155
disclosure controls, 187, 188*f*
disclosure of education records, 131–132
discovery, 152, 325
distinctive trademark, 261, 264
distributed denial of service (DDoS) attack, 22
district courts, 69
diversity of citizenship jurisdiction, 69
dividends, 177
DMCA. *See* Digital Millennium Copyright Act
docket, 35
doctrine of precedent, 78
document retention under SOX, 185–187
documentation of controls, 398–400
domain name registrars, 267
DoS. *See* denial of service attack
DoS. *See* denial of service category
Dow Chemical Co., 373
DR. *See* disaster recovery plans
dramatic works, 268
drawings for patent, 256
Driver's Privacy Protection Act (1994), 40
DRM. *See* digital rights management
DSS. *See* Data Security Standard
due process, 75, 323
dumpster diving, 49
duty of due care, 335
duty to mitigate, 293

E

ECPA. *See* Electronic Communications Privacy Act 1986
ED. *See* U.S. Department of Education
EDGAR. *See* Electronic Data Gathering and Retrieval database
education records, 129, 130–132
educational purposes, fair use for, 273
E-Government Act of 2002, 39, 215–217
EHR. *See* electronic health record
Electronic Communications Privacy Act 1986 (ECPA), 39, 330, 432, 436
electronic contracts, 295, 296
electronic data, 340
electronic data collection, 435–439
Electronic Data Gathering and Retrieval (EDGAR) database, 196–197
electronic discovery, 340
electronic health record (EHR), 156, 161
electronic protected health information (EPHI), 161
electronic record, 296
electronic signature, 301
Electronic Signatures in Global and National Commerce (E-SIGN) Act, 296
electronically stored information (ESI), 340
email communications, 298
email monitoring, 53–54
email via contract formation, 312–313

employee environment support, 411
employee privacy rights, 56–57
employee training, 390, 401
employee's personal computer, monitoring, 55
EnCase Certified Examiner (EnCE), 424
EnCE. *See* EnCase Certified Examiner
encryption, 6
encryption keys, 232, 241, 242, 428–429
encryption regulations (states), 239–242
encryption requirements, 232, 241
end user license agreement (EULA), 302
enforcement, 300
Enhanced Financial Disclosures (Title IV), 182
Enron, 176–179
Entertainment Software Rating Board (ESRB), 117
E-passport, 47
EPHI. *See* electronic protected health information
equitable remedy, 293
E-Rate program, 125
ESI. *See* electronically stored information
ESRB. *See* Entertainment Software Rating Board
E.U. *See* The European Union's
EULA. *See* end user license agreement
The European Union's (E.U.), 59
evaluation standard, 164
evidence collection, 432–439
evidence silver platter doctrine, 433
examination of a bank, 95
examination step of investigation, 429–430
examiner education task force, 95
exculpatory evidence, 439
executive branch, 67
executive management, 392, 398, 401
Executive Order, 212
exigent circumstances, 435
existence, 300
exploits, 11
export control laws, 218–219
export control regulations, types of, 218
exposure factor, 395
external attackers, 8

F

Facebook, 23, 299, 342
facilities recovery, 410
facility access controls standard, 164
FACTA. *See* Fair and Accurate Credit Transaction Act of 2003
failure to notify penalties, 232–233
Fair and Accurate Credit Transaction Act of 2003 (FACTA), 103
Fair Credit Reporting Act of 1970 (FCRA), 99
fair information practice principles, 43
fair use, 272–274
Family Educational Rights and Privacy Act (FERPA), 27*t*, 115, 128–134
Family Policy Compliance Office (FPCO), 133
FCC. *See* Federal Communications Commission
FCRA. *See* Fair Credit Reporting Act of 1970
FDIC. *See* Federal Deposit Insurance Corporation
federal agencies, 79, 80, 90
federal agency employee, 215
federal and state judicial systems, comparison of, 72*t*
federal banking regulatory agencies, 91*t*
federal breach notification law, 217, 234
federal circuit, 69
Federal Communications Commission (FCC), 48, 126, 128
Federal Deposit Insurance Corporation (FDIC), 91*t*, 92
Federal Financial Institutions Examination Council (FFIEC), 95
federal funding, 128–129
federal government, 64–70, 358–359
Federal incident response (IR) center, 212
Federal Information Processing Standards (FIPS), 207, 242
Federal Information Security Management Act (FISMA), 380
Federal Information Security Modernization Act (FISMA), 194, 204–213, 358, 391
federal information systems, 214–219
Federal Information Systems Management Act, 27*t*, 414*t*
federal information technology (IT) systems, 202
federal judiciary, 68–70
federal laws, 38–40, 234
federal legislation, 235
federal question jurisdiction, 69
federal registration symbol, 261
Federal Rules of Criminal Procedure, 76
Federal Rules of Evidence (FRE), 439
Federal Trade Commission (FTC), 51, 80, 96–97, 102, 109–110, 116, 119, 124, 135, 169–170, 227, 297, 329, 346
Federal Trade Commission Red Flags Rule, 103–106, 106*t*
federalism, 65
fees for service contracts, 306
felonies, 319
FERPA. *See* Family Educational Rights and Privacy Act
FFIEC. *See* Federal Financial Institutions Examination Council
Fifth Amendment (U.S. Constitution), 37
filing fees for patent, 256
financial information, 34
financial institutions, 88–97
financial reporting, 179–181

financial risks, 14
FIPS. *See* Federal Information Processing Standards
First Amendment (U.S. Constitution), 36, 118
first-party cookies, 45
"first to invent" rule, 252
FISMA. *See* Federal Information Security Management Act
FISMA. *See* Federal Information Security Modernization Act
flaming, 341
FOIA. *See* Freedom of Information Act 1966
forensic duplicate image, 429–430
forensic examination ethical principles, 431
Forensic Toolkit, 424
forensics, 421
Form 8-K, 180–181
Form 10-K, 180
Form 10-Q, 180
form contracts, 286–287
form of acceptance, 289–291
form of offer, 288–289, 297–299
Fourth Amendment (U.S. Constitution), 37, 432–435
FPCO. *See* Family Policy Compliance Office
FRE. *See* Federal Rules of Evidence
Free Enterprise Fund, 186
Freedom of Information Act 1966 (FOIA), 35, 38
fruit of the poisonous tree doctrine, 439
FTC. *See* Federal Trade Commission
full interruption test, 414
futures contract, 178

**G**

GAAP. *See* generally accepted accounting principles
GAIT. *See* "Guide to the Assessment of IT Risk"
GAO. *See* Government Accountability Office
GAO high-risk web site, 359
Gartner, Inc., 309
GCFA. *See* GIAC Certified Forensic Analyst
GDPR. *See* General Data Protection Regulation
GDPR. *See* General Data Protection Regulation
General Data Protection Regulation (GDPR), 59
generally accepted accounting principles (GAAP), 178, 185
Genetic Information Nondiscrimination Act of 2008, 145
genetic testing, 145
GIAC. *See* Global Information Assurance Certification
GIAC Certified Forensic Analyst (GCFA), 424
*Gideon v. Wainwright* (1963), 325
GIF. *See* Graphics Interchange Format
GLBA. *See* Gramm-Leach-Bliley Act
GLBA. *See* Gramm-Leach-Bliley Act Safeguards Rule
Global Information Assurance Certification (GIAC), 336
global positioning system (GPS) technology, 48–49
good faith, 262
Government Accountability Office (GAO), 359
GPS. *See* global positioning system technology
Gramm-Leach-Bliley Act (GLBA), 26, 27*t*, 97–103, 196, 231, 307, 376, 414*t*
Gramm-Leach-Bliley Act (GLBA) Safeguards Rule, 240, 243
grand jury, 324
Graphics Interchange Format (GIF), 46
*Griswold v. Connecticut* (1965), 37
group health plans, 143, 146
"Guide to the Assessment of IT Risk" (GAIT), 190, 192–193
guidelines, 362–363

**H**

*Hammer v. Amazon.com* (2005), 341
harassment, 344, 372–373
harmful content, 118
hash, 430
HathiTrust, 280
health information, 34, 141–143
Health Information Technology for Economic and Clinical Health Act (HITECH), 144, 147, 156
Health Insurance Portability and Accountability Act (HIPAA), 26, 27*t*, 143–170, 196, 217, 231, 307, 375, 414*t*
health plan, 146
healthcare, 140–141, 145, 147
healthcare operations, 149–150
healthcare provider, 146
hearsay rule, 441
HHS. *See* Department of Health and Human Services
high-impact system controls, 211*t*
high-level policies, 360
high security category, 210
HIPAA. *See* Health Insurance Portability and Accountability Act
Hippocratic Oath, 141
HITECH. *See* Health Information Technology for Economic and Clinical Health Act
hot site, 411
human resources personnel, 392
human threats, 12
*hung jury*, 325

**I**

IACIS. *See* International Association of Computer Investigative Specialists
ICANN. *See* Internet Corporation for Assigned Names and Numbers
ICFR. *See* internal controls over financial reporting
identification number, 34
identification of children, 117
identity theft, 49, 81, 87, 329
Identity Theft Prevention Program, 104
IEC. *See* International Electrotechnical Commission
IFRS. *See* International Financial Reporting Standards

IG. *See* inspector general
IIED. *See* intentional infliction of emotional distress
illegal contract, 288
"I Love You" worm, 369
IM. *See* instant messaging
implementation specifications, 162–168
import control laws, 218–219
improper use category, 405
inadmissible evidence, 426
inadvertent disclosures, 158
incident, 211–212, 402, 403
incident handlers, 404
incident reporter, 404
incident response (IR), 205, 388, 402–407, 407*f*
incidental disclosures, 158
incomplete performance, 292
inculpatory evidence, 439
independent directors, 195
Indiana law, 232
indictment, 324
individual participation principle, 44
individual rights under the Privacy Rule, 155–156
industry sector, 23
information, 5, 324
information access management standard, 163
information needs, 355–356
information security, 3–27, 35, 81–82
information security governance (ISG), 353–382, 358*t*
information security governance (ISG) documents, 359–367
information security management (ISM), 357, 358*t*
information security managers, 392
information security policies, 363–380
information security professionals, 183
information security program, 101, 240
information security terms, contracts, 309–311
information sharing, 50
information sharing task force, 95
information theft, 329–330
informed consent, 154
infringement of copyright, 271–272, 276–277
infringement of patent, 257–258
infringement of trademarks, 265–266
initial hearing, 324
injunction, 45
inspector general (IG), 206, 207
Inspector General Act of 1978, 207
instant messaging (IM), 298
integrity, 5, 7–8
integrity controls standard, 167
intellectual property (IP), 250–251, 377
intentional infliction of emotional distress (IIED), 343–344
intentional torts, 337–338
interception of communications laws, 330
internal attackers, 13
internal controls over financial reporting (ICFR), 188, 190
internal controls under SOX, 188–191, 188*f*, 190*t*
International Association of Computer Investigative Specialists (IACIS), 423
International Electrotechnical Commission (IEC), 18, 193–194, 358
International Financial Reporting Standards (IFRS), 185
International Information Systems Security Certification Consortium (ISC), 2, 336
International Organization for Standardization (ISO), 18, 193–194, 358
International Organization on Computer Evidence (IOCE), 423, 431
international patents, 255
international privacy laws, 59
International Traffic in Arms Regulation (ITAR), 218
Internet browsers, 46
Internet Corporation for Assigned Names and Numbers (ICANN), 267
Internet Crime Complaint Center (IC3), 326
Internet defamation, 341
Internet e-commerce, 261
Internet of Things (IoT), 250
Internet safety policy, 127
Internet Service Provider Liability for Torts, 342–343
Internet service providers (ISPs), 33, 126, 274, 276, 343, 436
Interstate Communications Act, 333
Interstate Stalking and Prevention Act, 333
intoxicated person, 288
intrusion, 329
inventions, 253–256, 260
inventory search, 435
investigation category, 405
investigative process, 426–431
IOCE. *See* International Organization on Computer Evidence
IoT. *See* Internet of Things
IP. *See* intellectual property
IP interest, 251
IR. *See* Federal incident response center
IR. *See* incident response
ISC. *See* International Information Systems Security Certification Consortium
ISG. *See* information security governance
ISG. *See* information security governance documents
ISM. *See* information security management
ISO. *See* International Organization for Standardization
ISPs. *See* Internet service providers
IT. *See* federal information technology systems
IT operations, 411
IT personnel, 392
ITAR. *See* International Traffic in Arms Regulation

job lock, 143
judicial branch, 67
judicial review, 70
jurisdiction, 67, 295, 321–323

K

*Katz v. United States* (1967), 37
keys, 242
keystroke loggers, 21, 45
Kundra, Vivek, 202

L

landmark court decision, 78
Lanham Act, 261
law enforcement, 229
laws, 23, 27*t*, 73–77, 414*t*
least privilege, 16
legal capacity online, 297
legal duties, 23
legal entities, 251
legal ownership, 250–251
legal requirements, contract, 311
legalese vs. plain language, 364
legislative branch, 65–67
legislative history, 237
libel, 341
Library of Congress, 275
license, 269, 302
likelihood, 394–398. *See also* exposure factor
limited data set, 153–154
limited jurisdiction, 68
liquidated damages, 293
literary works, 268
loathsome diseases, 342
Locard's exchange principle, 423
logic bombs, 21–22
logical safeguards. *See* technical safeguards
"long arm jurisdiction" tests, 343
"Love Bug" worm, 369
low-impact system controls, 211*t*
low security category, 210

M

machine, 252
machine-readable privacy policy, 216–217
Mail Privacy Statute (1971), 40
mailbox rule, 290
*Mala in se*, 319
*Mala prohibita*, 319
malicious code category, 405
malicious information security acts, 332–333
malware, 20–21, 369
mantrap, 16, 16*f*
manufactured products, 252–253
MAO. *See* maximum acceptable outage
Massachusetts data protection laws, 239–241
material change, 159
material term, 290
maximum acceptable outage (MAO), 410
maximum tolerable downtime (MTD), 410
media analysis, 422
medical identity theft, 140–141
meeting of the minds, 291
Melissa virus, 333
*mens rea*, 320
merchant, 107–108
methodology, 192–193
MIB Group, Inc., 142
military uses, 420
Miller test, 119
minimum necessary rule, 155
Minnesota Credit Union Network, 236
Minnesota law, 235
Minnesota Plastic Card Security Act, 236
minor child, 148
mirror image rule, 289
mirrored site, 411
misdemeanors, 319
mobile devices, 370, 422
Model Privacy Notice Form, 100–101*f*
moderate-impact controls, 211*t*
moderate security category, 210
monitoring, 189, 390
Morris worm, 20, 21, 326, 333
motion picture and audiovisual works, 268
MTD. *See* maximum tolerable downtime
musical works, 268
mutual agreement, 291
MyDoom computer worm, 22

N

*NASA v. Nelson* (2011), 38
National Conference of Commissioners on Uniform State Laws (NCCUSL), 286, 296
National Credit Union Administration (NCUA), 91*t*, 93–94
National Credit Union Share Insurance Fund (NCUSIF), 93
National Cybersecurity and Communications Integration Center (NCCIC), 212
National Institute of Standards and Technology (NIST), 18, 25, 194, 204, 207–211, 213, 242, 380
National Institutes of Health (NIH), 202
national security information, 25–26
national security systems (NSSs), 204, 212–213
National Vulnerability Database (NVD), 13
natural threats, 12
NCCIC. *See* National Cybersecurity and Communications Integration Center
NCCUSL. *See* National Conference of Commissioners on Uniform State Laws
NCUA. *See* National Credit Union Administration
NCUSIF. *See* National Credit Union Share Insurance Fund
Nebraska, 71
need to know, 15
negligence torts, 335–337
negotiation process, 289
network analysis, 422
network banner, 437
networking equipment, 421
Nevada law, 236, 237, 241–242
New York Court of Appeals, 71
New York law, 244

New York State data disposal law, 243–244
NIH. *See* National Institutes of Health
NIST. *See* National Institute of Standards and Technology
*nolo contendere*, 324
nominal damages, 293
non-breaching parties, 293
nonaffiliated party, 99
nonprofit organization, 195
nonpublic personal information (NPI), 97–98
nonrepudiation, 294, 300–301
"notice and takedown" letter, 277
Notice of Privacy Practices, 159
NPI. *See* nonpublic personal information
NSSs. *See* national security systems
NVD. *See* National Vulnerability Database

**O**

oath for patent, 256
Obama, Barack, 201
objection, 441
obscene material, 118
obscenity, 118–119
OCC. *See* Office of the Comptroller of the Currency
OCR. *See* Office for Civil Rights
OCTAVE. *See* Operationally Critical Threat, Asset, and Vulnerability Evaluation
OECD. *See* Organization for Economic Cooperation and Development
OFAC. *See* Office of Foreign Assets Control
off-duty computer monitoring, 55
offer, 288–289
offeree, 288–291
offeror, 288
Office for Civil Rights (OCR), 168, 169
Office of Foreign Assets Control (OFAC), 219
Office of Management and Budget (OMB), 204, 206, 210, 213
Office of Personnel Management (OPM), 219–220
Office of the Comptroller of the Currency (OCC), 91*t*, 94
Official Gazette, 263
Ohio law, 230
Ohio Public Records Act, 135
OMB. *See* Office of Management and Budget
omission, 335
online bank websites, 90
online contracts, 295–297
Online Copyright Infringement Liability Limitation Act, 274, 276–277
online data gathering, 51
online profiling, 46
online service provider (OSP), 276
openness principle, 44
operational incident response team, 404
operational planning, 355
operational risks, 14
Operationally Critical Threat, Asset, and Vulnerability Evaluation (OCTAVE), 399
operator contact information, 121
OPM. *See* Office of Personnel Management
opt-out, 99, 150
Organization for Economic Cooperation and Development (OECD), 43
organizational governance, 24
organizations uses, 420–421
original jurisdiction, 68
OSP. *See* online service provider
outsourcing, 23–24
oversight, 191–192
ownership, legal, 250–251

**P**

*Palsgraf v. Long Island Railroad* (1928), 336
pantomimes, 268
parallel test, 413
parental consent, 117, 122–123
parental controls, 117
parental rights, 122
Paris Convention for the Protection of Industrial Property (1883), 255
passive data collection, 58
passwords, 15, 377–379, 428–429
patch, 10
Patent Cooperation Treaty (PCT), 255
patent prosecution, 256
patent troll, 257
patentable, 253, 256*f*
patents, 252–259
patient information directory, 150
payment, 117, 149–150
Payment Card Industry (PCI), 234–236
Payment Card Industry (PCI) Standards, 27*t*, 106–109, 109*t*, 414*t*
payment in arrears, 104
*Payne v. Tennessee* (1991), 78
PCAOB. *See* Public Company Accounting Oversight Board
PCI. *See* Payment Card Industry
PCI. *See* Payment Card Industry Standards
PCT. *See* Patent Cooperation Treaty
Pen Register and Trap and Trace Statute, 330, 438–439
pen register devices, 438
people-based privacy concerns, 49–51
persistent data, 430
person, 251
personal health record (PHR), 161
personal identifying information, 243
personal information, 4, 227, 228–232
personal jurisdiction, 321–322
personal property interest, 251
personally identifiable information (PII), 39, 129, 131, 132, 133
person/entity authentication standard, 167
PHI. *See* protected health information
phishing, 20–21, 49, 330–331
PHR. *See* personal health record

physical and environmental threats, 12
physical safeguards, 16, 17*t*, 164–166, 166*t*
PIAs. *See* privacy impact assessments
pictorial, graphic, and sculptural works, 268
PII. *See* personally identifiable information
piracy, 271
plain language vs. legalese, 364
plain view doctrine, 434
plaintiff, 334, 335, 336, 337–338
plant patents, 253
Plant Variety Protection Act, 254
Plastic Card Security Act, 236
plea, 324
pleadings, 35
*Plessy v. Ferguson* (1896), 78
policies, 24, 360–361
policy development process, 363–367, 367*f*
poor man's copyright, 270
pop-up advertisements, 45
portrayal in false light privacy tort, 42
potential loss, 394–398
potential sources, 421
Powers Report, 179
PR. *See* public relations
precedent, 78–79
preemption, 66
preexisting condition, 143, 144, 145
preponderance of evidence, 76
presentation step of investigation, 430–431
preservation step of investigation, 426–427
Pretexting Rule, 102–103
preventive controls, safeguards, 17
primary handler, 404
"Principal Register", 262, 264
prior art, 254
prior consideration, 292
privacy, 32–35, 81–82
Privacy Act (1974), 39, 214–215
privacy concerns, 49–51
privacy impact assessments (PIAs), 39, 216–218
privacy law, 36–44
privacy notices, 157
privacy policies laws, 58
privacy policy, 119, 121
privacy protection, information systems, 57–59
Privacy Rule, 98–99, 100*f*, 101*f*, 147–161, 149, 150, 154–155
privacy torts, 42–43, 345
privacy violations, 345
private cause of action, 160, 233–234
private entities, 432
privately held company, 177
*pro se*, 312
probative evidence, 440
*ProCD Inc. v. Zeidenberg* (1996), 304
procedural law, 75
procedures, 361–362
process, 253, 260
productivity, 369, 374
profit and loss statement, 181
property interest, 250
prosecutor, 76, 324
prospectus, 182
protected health information (PHI), 147–149, 150, 153–154, 155–156, 161
protective sweep exception, 435
provider exception, 437–438
proxy servers, 125–127
P3P, 216–217
Public Company Accounting Oversight Board (PCAOB), 182, 183–185
public company vs. private company, 177
public disclosure of private facts privacy tort, 42–43
public domain, 269
public employees, 56
public health, 162
public records and privacy, 35
public relations (PR), 415–416
punitive damages, 293, 337
purpose specification principle, 43

## Q

qualitative risk analysis, 396, 399*t*
quantitative risk analysis, 398, 399*t*

## R

RA. *See* risk assessment
Radio Frequency Identification (RFID), 47
ransomware, 21
real property interest, 251
realized risk, 390–391
reasonable information security professional, 336
reasonable person standard, 42, 334
records, 185–187, 214, 243, 439
recovery criticality, 409
Red Flags Rule, 27*t*, 81, 103–106, 106*t*
regulatory authorities, 79–80
regulatory requirements, 311, 356
remedial actions, 205
remedies for copyright, 271–272
remedies for patent, 257–258
remedies for trademark, 265–266
remedy, 292
reports task force, 95
representations and warranties for service contracts, 307
repudiation, 294
reputational risks, 14
residual risk, 14
*Restatement (Second) of the Law of Torts*, 343
retaliation, 373
RFID. *See* Radio Frequency Identification
right to sue in federal court, 261
risk acceptance, 15, 400
risk analysis, 163
risk assessment (RA), 189, 205, 390–400, 414*t*
risk avoidance, 14, 400
risk level matrix, 397*t*
risk level outcomes, 398*t*
risk management (RM), 356, 387, 389–401, 390*f*
risk management framework (RMF), 208, 209*f*
risk mitigation, 14, 400
risk response, 390, 400
risk transfer, 15, 400
risks, 14–15
RM. *See* risk management

RMF. *See* risk management framework
*Robinson v. California* (1962), 320

S

SaaS. *See* Software as a Service model
safe harbor, 229
safeguards, 15–17, 17*t*, 162–168
Safeguards Rule, 99–102, 109–110
sanctions, 373
SANS Institute, 360
Sarbanes-Oxley Act (SOX), 27*t*, 181–192, 194–195, 391, 414*t*
scans, probes, and attempted access category, 405
SDN. *See* specially designated nationals
seal program, 44
search, 432
search engine, 33
search incident to lawful arrest, 435
search warrants, 432–435
SEC. *See* Securities and Exchange Commission
seclusion privacy tort, intrusion into, 41
*Second. See Restatement (Second) of the Law of Torts*
secondary handlers, 404
secondary meaning, 264
securities, 177
Securities and Exchange Commission (SEC), 98, 177, 191–192
security awareness and training standard, 163, 205, 379–380, 401
security breaches, 48–49
security category, 210
security controls, 205, 210
security failures, 356
security incident procedures standard, 163–164
security management process standard, 163
security of social networking sites, 50–51
security-related certification, 336
Security Rule, 159, 161–168
security safeguards principle, 43
seizure, 433
self-representation, 325
separation of duties principle, 10, 407
service contracts, 306
service of process, 338
service provider, 102
service provider liability, 279
servicemark, 259
settlement agreement, 110
shoulder surfing, 6, 18, 49
shrinkwrap contracts, 303
silver platter doctrine, 433
simulation test, 413
single loss expectancy (SLE), 395
single point of failure, 9
slack space, 427
slander, 341
SLE. *See* single loss expectancy
small public company, 182
*Smith v. Maryland* (1979), 38
social engineering, 6–7, 19, 49. *See also* pretexting
social networking sites, 50–51, 299
Social Security numbers (SSNs), 32, 34, 40, 49, 202, 206, 236–238
Software as a Service (SaaS) model, 308
SORN. *See* system of records notice
sound recordings, 268
SOX. *See* Sarbanes-Oxley Act
spam, 330–331
spear phishing, 20
special publications (SPs), 207
specially designated nationals (SDN), 219
specific performance, 293
specification for patent, 256
SPs. *See* special publications
spyware, 21, 44–45
SSNs. *See* Social Security numbers
stakeholders, 365
standard transaction, 147
standards, 361
*Stare decisis*, 78
state breach notification acts, 27*t*
state government, 70–72
state laws, 40–41, 169, 329, 375, 376
Statute of Frauds, 287
statute of limitations, 313, 338
statutory damages, 272
statutory law. *See* code law
storage devices, 421
stored communication exception, 53
*Strassheim v. Daily*, 322
strategic planning, 355
strategic risks, 14
strict liability, 257
strict liability torts, 334
strong trademarks, 264
*Strunk v. United States* (1973), 325
student, 129
student records, 133
students data, state laws protecting, 134
Studies and Reports (Title VII), 182
subject matter jurisdiction, 321
subject matter law. *See* substantive law
subordinate plans, 205
substantial performance, 292
substantive criminal law, 319
substantive law, 75
sunshine laws, 35
supervision task force, 95
"Supplemental Register", 262, 264
supplies recovery, 410
Supremacy Clause, 71
Supreme Court, 70
surveillance systems task force, 95
system of records notice (SORN), 215
system/service risks, 14

T

tabletop test, 413
tabletop walk-through test, 413
tactical planning, 355
target department store, 110–111
targeted advertising, 46
targeted phishing scams, 20
technical safeguards, 15–16, 17*t*, 166–167, 167*t*

technically feasible standard, 240
technological and operational threats, 12
technology-based privacy concerns, 44–48
technology protection measure (TPM), 125–126, 128, 274–275
telephone and voicemail monitoring, 52–53
Telephone Harassment Act, 333
telephone monitoring, 52–53
Tenth Amendment, 70
termination and breach of service contracts, 307
terms in contract, 307
terms of service agreement, 302
terms of use agreement, 302
testing and evaluation, agency's information security program, 205
text messaging, 298
theft of information, 329–330
Third Amendment (U.S. Constitution), 36
third-party, 122
third-party company, 126
third-party cookies, 45
thisisyourdigitallife, 51
threats, 12–14, 392–394, 394*t*
thrifts, 94
Title II. *See* Auditor Independence
Title III. *See* corporate responsibility
Title IV. *See* Enhanced Financial Disclosures
Title IX. *See* White-Collar Crime Penalty Enhancements
Title V. *See* Analyst Conflicts of Interest
Title VI. *See* Commission Resources and Authority
Title VII. *See* Studies and Reports
Title VIII. *See* Corporate and Criminal Fraud Accountability
Title X. *See* Corporate Tax Returns
Title XI. *See* Corporate Fraud and Accountability
TM symbol, 262
top-level domain, 266
tort, 41
tort law, 334–339
tort law actions in cyberspace, 341–345
tortfeasor, 334
tortious conduct, 334
tort of outrage. *See* intentional infliction of emotional distress
TPM. *See* technology protection measure
trade secret, 258–259, 278–279
trademark, 251, 259–266
trademark registration, 261, 263–264
traditional contracts, 295
training employees, 401
transitory communications safe harbor, 276
transmission security standard, 167
Transportation Security Administration (TSA), 7
trap and trace devices, 438
trap-door. *See* backdoors
treatment activities, 150
treble damages, 243
trespass torts, 344–345
trespasser exception, 438
triage, 404
trial court objections, 441
Trojan horse, 21
TSA. *See* Transportation Security Administration
Twitter, 299

## U

UCC. *See* Uniform Commercial Code
UDRP. *See* Uniform Domain Name Dispute Resolution Policy
UETA. *See* Uniform Electronic Transactions Act
unauthorized access category, 405
unconscionable contracts, 288
unfair trade practices, 96
unicameral legislature, 71
Uniform Commercial Code (UCC), 286, 294
Uniform Domain Name Dispute Resolution Policy (UDRP), 267
Uniform Electronic Transactions Act (UETA), 295, 296, 300
uniform resource locator (URL), 266
*United States v. Barrows* (2007), 55
*United States v. White* (1971), 38
unreasonable government search and seizure, 432
updates of service contracts, 307
URL. *See* uniform resource locator
U.S. Attorneys, 323
U.S. Census Bureau, 32, 39
U.S. Congress, 65–66
U.S. Constitution, 36–37, 65, 235, 318
U.S. Copyright Office, 272, 277
U.S. Courts of Appeals, 69
U.S. Department of Commerce, 219
U.S. Department of Education (ED), 128, 133, 135–136
U.S. Department of Justice, 216, 331, 333
U.S. Department of State, 218
U.S. Department of Veterans Affairs (VA), 244
U.S. federal court system, 70*f*
U.S. Federal Reserve System (the Fed), 91–92, 91*t*, 92*f*
U.S. National Security Information, 25–26
U.S. Patent and Trademark Office (USPTO), 252–265
U.S. state court system, 72*f*
U.S. Supreme Court, 37–38, 67, 68*t*, 78, 118, 119, 124, 135
*U.S. v. Jones* (2012), 48
U.S.A. PATRIOT Act (2001), 436
use, 148
use, as defined in service contracts, 306
use limitation principle, 43
user credentials, 378
user input, 117
USPTO. *See* U.S. Patent and Trademark Office
utility patents, 253–254

## V

VA. *See* U.S. Department of Veterans Affairs
Vessel Hull Design Protection Act, 274
Veterans Affairs Information Security Act of 2006, 245
victim, 404
video surveillance monitoring, 55–56
viruses, 20
Visa and Mastercard, 111
vital statistics and communicable diseases, 151–152
voice mail monitoring, 52–53
voicemail monitoring, 52–53
volatile data, 430
voluntary agreements, 43–44
voluntary organizations, 26
vulnerabilities, 10–12, 11*f*, 392–394, 394*t*

## W

walk-through test, 413
warm site, 411
Washington State personal data disposal law, 242–243
weak trademarks, 264
Web beacon, 45–46
Web bug, 46
WFH. *See* work made for hire
*Whalen v. Roe* (1977), 38
whaling, 20
*Wheaten v. Peters* (1834), 37
White-Collar Crime Penalty Enhancements (Title IX), 182
window of vulnerability, 11
WIPO. *See* World Intellectual Property Organization
wireless technology, 47
Wiretap Act (1968, amended), 39, 330, 437–438
work made for hire (WFH), 269
workforce security standard, 163
workplace harassment, 372
workplace monitoring, 52, 56–57
workplace privacy, 51–57, 373–374
workstation security standard, 165–166
workstation use standard, 165
World Intellectual Property Organization (WIPO), 255, 267, 274
World Wide Web (WWW), 250
*writ of certiorari*, 69
write blockers, 429
wrongful conduct, type of, 319
WWW. *See* World Wide Web

zero-day vulnerability, 12